BRITISH GENERALS

OF THE

SECOND WORLD WAR

BIOGRAPHICAL DICTIONARY

OF

BRITISH GENERALS

OF THE

SECOND WORLD WAR

by

NICK SMART

Pen & Sword
MILITARY

First published in Great Britain in 2005 by
Pen & Sword Military
an imprint of
Pen & Sword Books Ltd
47 Church Street
Barnsley
South Yorkshire
S70 2AS

ISBN 1 84415 049 6

Typeset in Times New Roman by
Phoenix Typesetting, Auldgirth, Dumfriesshire

Printed and bound in England by
CPI UK

Pen & Sword Books Ltd incorporates the Imprints of Pen & Sword Aviation,
Pen & Sword Maritime, Pen & Sword Military, Wharncliffe Local History,
Pen & Sword Select, Pen & Sword Military Classics and Leo Cooper.

For a complete list of Pen & Sword titles please contact
PEN & SWORD BOOKS LIMITED
47 Church Street, Barnsley, South Yorkshire, S70 2AS, England
E-mail: enquiries@pen-and-sword.co.uk
Website: www.pen-and-sword.co.uk

CONTENTS

ACKNOWLEDGEMENTS

Though close colleagues have been far too busy to help in the preparation of this book, there are still many people who are to be thanked for the assistance they have given. Librarians and archivists are, I now realize, wonderful people. Nameless many of them were to me, but their service was impeccable. I am indebted to them.

To the staffs of the Public Record Office (National Archive), the Liddell Hart Centre for Military Archives, the Joint Services Staff College, the Tank Museum, Bovingdon, and the libraries of Exeter, Bristol and Southampton universities I offer thanks for their patience and cheerful efficiency. Nearer to home I have leant heavily on the expertise of the staff of The University of Plymouth Library (Exmouth campus). They never failed me nor lost their good humour. No matter how bizarre or ill-timed my requests, they always turned up trumps.

When not in libraries I worked in the best possible of environments, at home. To Sara, Katie and Jake, who put up with 'me and my generals' for many a long month, and who grinned away with weary loyalty as I recounted yet another long-winded military anecdote I thought funny, I am deeply grateful.

Exmouth
August 2004

INTRODUCTION

Plenty of historians say they work in order to satisfy their intellectual curiosity. This one, while operating at a lower level of intensity, makes no claim to originality in echoing the sentiment. There is nothing artful about presenting this biographical dictionary and justifying its compilation on the grounds that no motive other than curiosity about British Second World War generals lies behind it.

Having read a good deal about British military leadership during the war against the Axis powers, and having formed the view through books and television documentaries that I knew a fair bit about the generals who, whether in London or in the field, directed operations, I was always conscious that the famous names – the Brookes, the Montgomerys and the Alexanders – dominated the scene, but only represented the tip of a much larger command iceberg. I wanted to know more about those who, though of comparable rank, achieved, at best, only cursory mention in memoirs and campaign histories. In a literature that is broad and well established, though by now rather set in its form and positively creaking with age, the great are still celebrated while the vast majority of British Second World War generals still languish in their neglected state. Curiosity about those less well-known figures, those who make their brief appearance and then lapse into obscurity, underpinned the idea of the biographical dictionary.

Public interest in the Second World War remains buoyant, and though, over recent years, attention has shifted away from the leaders towards the led, the available literature on generals and generalship still constitutes a sizeable edifice. Chester Wilmot's *The Struggle for Europe*, first published in 1952, was the kind of work that cast a shadow over a generation of historians. But at the centre of it all lies the surprisingly large number of memoirs written by the generals themselves or which were ghosted for them. De Guingand was early off the mark in 1947 with his *Operation Victory*. The most productive period was from the mid 1950s through to the early 1970s. Then the output was prodigious. Slim, Brooke (courtesy of Arthur Bryant) and Montgomery brought out their memoirs in quick succession. Correlli Barnett's controversial *Desert Generals* (1960) seemed to encourage a further spurt of activity (Ismay, Alexander and Morgan), and the pace only slackened when death started to take its toll. Even though 'Jimmy' Marshall-Cornwall could, while well into his nineties, publish his memoirs as late as 1984, control of the literature on British Second World War generals had, by this stage, passed largely to the biographer.

There are of course many things that could be said about quality and credibility. But the purpose of this brief sally into historiography is not to rank-order military commanders in terms of their literary ability, rather to observe how the plethora of war memoirs impacted on the manner in which British Second World War generals have been presented and perceived. It may well have been a demand-led phenomenon. Certainly readership was as wide as it was partisan. But the underlying question always seemed to be 'which of them was the best?'. Memoirs and biographies could not but confront the issue and, because so prominent and influential, pushed the study of British Second World War generals into a distinctive groove. It was one in which reputation counted for everything. There really was a 'battle of the memoirs'. Campaigns were resurrected and re-fought so as to attack or defend the great commanders' role in them. It was as though an implicit league table of the great and the good existed in the minds of historians and their readers. Attempts at rehabilitation drew polite exchanges, but iconoclastic revisionism was answered with fire.

Much entertainment and a certain amount of controversy was provided. The main principals offered their accounts, and loyal acolytes continued to carry the baton, sometimes years after the principals themselves had passed away. As a result a species of history emerged which, for all its enduring popularity, is both lop-sided and top-heavy. The lop-sided emphasis on individuals and their differences has tended to render operational history obscure. Descriptions of a campaign were filtered through the chosen hero so that, for example, an Auchinleck fan's account of the desert war would be couched in terms quite different from the manner chosen by an admirer of Montgomery. But lop-sidedness has also militated against analysis of British generals in terms of their common characteristics; those features that made them through background, training and shared values a self-conscious military élite. Crudely put, we have quite a lot on the psychology of individual generals but very little on their collective sociology. Top-heaviness results from paying a great deal of attention to the few while reducing the many to episodic appearances, walk-on parts or dark obscurity. A biographical dictionary cannot, on its own, pose as a study of élite formation, attitude and behaviour. However it might help identify some aspects or features that British generals had in common. What is more it reduces the impact of personality. It may seem paradoxical but it is nonetheless true that a dictionary about people provides the least personalized form of narrative. Not the smallest virtue attached to compilation is the levelling effect induced by employing the alphabet and not reputation as the organizing principle.

The habit of concentrating on the great, the famous and the successful means that, with one or two rare exceptions, failure is not well covered in the literature on British Second World War generals.* Neither memoirs, nor biographies nor campaign histories are much concerned with the impact of downward social mobility on so much of the nation's military élite during the Second World War. Rank matters in an army, and wartime, we would imagine, imposes the same brutal performance yardstick on the general as the stopwatch does to the track athlete. Yet if rank equates with success, the match is seldom as obvious or clear-cut as may first appear. Field marshals were as often created as a form of consolation prize than as a reward for battlefield success. And just as plenty of generals were sacked during the war years, very few were demoted. Retirement or transfer were the usual method of getting rid of those deemed 'duds', and only one general, so far as can be ascertained, was dismissed from the service during the course of the war.** While the spectre, and sometimes the actuality, of the 'bowler hat' became one area of interest while working on the entries, that which may as well be called luck emerged as another. The fates of those generals whose wartime careers flourished briefly and then fell by the wayside for no obvious performance-related reason became an area of intrigued fascination. Far from being the sole criteria of success or failure, performance and 'efficiency' emerged as rather slippery values. Judgement on an individual seemed, as often as not, to be founded more on the refracted light of opinion than the certainty of fact. An additional problem was the constant nagging awareness that the category of the obscure and unfamiliar was large, and, chip away at it as one might, would not get markedly smaller.

Command in the British army during the Second World War was, in the 'teeth arms' at least, a very unsettled affair. It was an unusual major-general who stayed in command of a division for more than a year. By contrast, a much gentler regime appeared to operate at corps level. Promotion and advancement in the Service and Ordnance Corps was much more obviously governed by seniority. The 'Buggins turn' principle of promotion, if such it was, appears also to have applied to the medics. These, incidentally, constituted a large category. Not only was the RAMC always well represented on the general officers list, but it was also overwhelmingly Scottish. Given the breadth of the field and the variety of wartime career trajectories, the advantages of a common format imposed by the discipline of a dictionary seemed obvious. Within its confines justice could be done to the famous while, at the same time, the unlucky, the obscure and the otherwise unfamiliar might be accorded a share of the limelight and rendered accessible.

The famous have, in a sense, been well looked after. They have been constructed as central characters in an unfolding drama. The features of this are so well known and are indeed so deeply engraved in the collective memory, that the standard narrative of British Second World War generalship is not difficult to rehearse. Essentially it consists of two parts; the first heavily influenced by

* A notable exception, and a fine biography, is Lavinia Greacan's *'Chink': A Biography* (Macmillan, 1989).
** See entry on Freeman-Attwood.

the Liddell Hart image of pre-war neglect of mechanization, applies to the first three years of war. The second part has a distinct 'turn of the tide' Brooke-Montgomery flavour to it.

The story is of a Britain going to war in 1939 with its army still stuck as the 'Cinderella service'; small, ill-equipped and, if not ill-led in terms of character and personality, hidebound in doctrine, technologically backward and scarcely prepared for war against first-class opponents. Comeuppance, so it is said, came quickly. Having been expelled from continental Europe, a string of illusory victories in North and East Africa against Italians made defeat at the hands of Germans in North Africa and Japanese in the Far East all the harder to bear. Heads rolled. There was no precise moment of turnaround, but, a generalization that is not unreasonable, Britain's military fortunes did change around the middle of 1942. Of course America's entry into the war and *Wehrmacht* embroilment deep in the Soviet Union were of major contributory significance. Of course too the 'stupendous industrial capacity' of Britain's allies was now coming into play. But it so happened that the turnaround coincided with a revolution at the top of Britain's military hierarchy. Ironside and Gort had long gone. So too, or so it was thought, had Wavell. Dill was in America, and O'Connor and Percival were prisoners of war. Hutton, who had conducted the early stages of the retreat from Burma, had disappeared from the scene, and the 'old desert hands' of the Eighth Army had either gone, were about to be cleared out or, like Gott, killed in plane crashes. The GOC-in-C Middle East, Auchinleck, would soon fall victim to the 'Cairo purge'. He was not relieved of his command because he was thought to be no good. Highly regarded for his personal qualities, he was dismissed, as the legend developed, because he was 'a poor picker of men'.

The new generation of British commanders was neither that young nor, in a sense, so new. It was made up of men who, like their predecessors, had all had fought and been decorated in the First War, and had been through the inter-war mill of the Camberley or Quetta Staff Colleges. Like their peers they had endured slow promotion in peacetime and the constant threat, and sometimes actuality, of periods on half-pay. Most, though not all, had served a kind of subordinate command apprenticeship with the BEF in France during the 'phoney war' and thus had seared into their minds the memory of Dunkirk. Some, most obviously Brooke, Alexander and Montgomery, seemed to draw strength from the experience. Others, like Franklyn and Holmes, perhaps should have done but never quite 'caught the eye' thereafter. Adam, the commander of III Corps at the time of the fall of France, went on to have what many judge to have been a very good war as Adjutant General. Conversely, Barker, commander of I Corps, sank quickly into the obscurity of retirement. The brief and disastrous campaign in France and Flanders resulted in a number of generals being quickly removed from the active list. Yet in a strange sort of way having served with the BEF was also the necessary career stepping-stone for Britain's most successful Second World War generals.

Against a background of failure, disappointment and a badgering Prime

Minister, the tempo of change at the top was rapid during the first three years of the war. Such is usually justified, or merely explained, in terms of the necessity of 'cutting out the dead wood', or some other awkward 'making bricks without straw' metaphor. Whether these were the unfortunate ones who, inadequately resourced, paid the price for previous military neglect, commanders certainly came and went with a rapidity that must have puzzled contemporaries as much as it bewilders the reader of history books. The practice of showering honours on generals like Beresford-Pierse, Cunningham and Creagh, who, having won victories against Italians, were then dismissed for under-performing against Germans, had become, or so it seems, all but institutionalized. By the summer of 1942, however, the tempo of change adopted a different rhythm. It slackened at the top, where tenure of command acquired a level of stability, though the rate of turnover lower down, most noticeably among divisional commanders, continued at its fast pace.

Whereas in the first phase the implicit descriptive ethos is of generals who were 'gentlemen', the term that has adhered to the second is 'ruthless professionalism'. Brooke, quite an old general by Second World War standards, was by mid-1942 established as CIGS and was apparently irreplaceable in that position. Whereas the gentlemanly Dill had become quite worn out by his tussles with Churchill, Brooke, in his thumping the table and glaring back mode, was, supposedly, the quintessential dour professional. Montgomery, Brooke's pupil and protégé, and no spring-chicken himself, had thus far had a relatively quiet war. But as the victor of Alamein, he became as established, as irreplaceable and, naturally, as professional as commander in the field. It goes almost without saying that Montgomery, for all the controversy that surrounds his name, was never, even to his most fervent admirers, a 'gentleman'. Conversely Alexander, who by every account was, has tended to suffer for the status ascribed to him ever since; his reputation as commander whittled down by two generations of military historians who liked him more but admired him less.

There are those who will say that El Alamein was not, in overall strategic terms, a decisive battle, that it was not especially necessary, and that it achieved little save instil a Churchillian fixation with the 'soft-underbelly' of Europe, later dignified by the expression 'Mediterranean strategy'. Yet for all that this may be true, Alamein did have a considerable impact on the British army. It did provide a bedrock of confidence, but, importantly, a bedrock that Brooke in London and Montgomery in North Africa and later in Italy and North-West Europe were to shape, manage and cultivate over the remainder of the war. Indeed they and their followers were to do so for the rest of their lives. Alamein also marked a turning point in a particularly intense and often quite nasty internecine battle between the British and Indian armies. Auchinleck's reputation as 'poor picker of men' was a coded way of saying that he preferred Indian Army officers on his staff. When he went, the Indian Army-oriented patronage system he had operated in North Africa was broken. A different network, drawn from those who had served with Home Forces over the previous two years, was put in its place. With the threat of invasion lifted, Home Forces could be deployed in North Africa. Auchinleck and his lieutenants were packed off back to India, and Montgomery, with Alexander as his notional superior, disposed of Lumsden, won their victories, got rid of Anderson and went on to win their laurels in the European theatre.

Montgomery, quite happy to leave Alexander in Italy, ran the British army show in North-West Europe during the last year of the war. His battles did not always go exactly to plan, his relations with his American peers and superiors was seldom good, and he was as dismissive of Canadian commanders as he was of those British 'duds' and 'misfits' who had been appointed to positions with SHAEF. But he ran the British Liberation Army with an iron fist. Horrocks and Dempsey, de Guingand and Simpson, Whistler and Macmillan all had good wars thanks to Montgomery's patronage. Even Ritchie, the general responsible for bringing Eighth Army to the brink of disintegration and defeat in May-June 1942, ended his war on a reasonable note. One of Brooke's favourites, he commanded a corps in North-West Europe. Those who fell from favour, the Bucknalls, the Bullen-Smiths, the Verneys and the Erskines, were effectively 'air-brushed' out of the story. They may have underperformed as commanders. They were most emphatically expelled from the Montgomery camp. Thereafter their *Who's Who* entries tended to be short and there were few subsequent honours, reunion dinners or public appearances for them to enjoy in retirement.

Except in one theatre, the British army's command set-up was, by war's end, what the Brooke-Montgomery axis had made it. It was they who decided who had had a good war and who had not. As winners they accordingly wrote the history or had it written for them. Doubtless they believed their appointments derived from the exercise of their professional judgements. That they did so is frequently asserted and, just as there have been plenty who have remarked on both as shrewd judges of men, neither had the appearance of a regimental snob. Nevertheless it has to be said that there was precious little scientific, or even noticeably systematic, about the clientele systems they operated. Brooke, as his recently published war diaries demonstrate,* had his favourites. With no greater semblance of logic he often took a violent dislike to people. By the same token, Montgomery's 'completely useless' verdicts were as frequent as they were usually damning to the individual concerned. Both had the power and the authority to make or break a brother-officer's career and, without inflicting any damage to their digestive systems or sleep patterns, each exercised their power to promote those they approved of with confident relish. Neither, it seems, had much time for the operational research techniques or psychological testing that was beginning to feature in officer selection lower down. They had what the great captains had always had, their appetites, their long memories and their little black books.

That Brooke and Montgomery operated in such time-honoured particular-istic ways should not be regarded as unusual. Like the schoolboy delinquent

---

* See Danchev, A. & Todman, D., *Field Marshal Lord Alanbrooke: War Diaries 1939–1945* (Weidenfeld & Nicolson, 2001).

who becomes a tyrant when made a prefect, they did not question the established system. Authority they accepted as their due. Patronage in the army had always relied on personal knowledge, and British generals, even in wartime, tended to know one another – as often as not by their nicknames. Their sense of place was, whether in Secunderabad or Salisbury Plain, anchored by their knowledge of who stood where on the *Army List*. As the army expanded in wartime, so the number of generals increased. But while the cadence of change was palpable, there was no breakdown of the *Gemeinschaft*. Dilution was minimal – some territorials attained general officer rank, a few 'technocrats' drawn from business or commerce got their red tabs and did important staff work, and there were many medics. But the wartime *Generalität* was overwhelmingly drawn from the regular army. The military élite swelled in size but replacement and reinforcement came from its subaltern ranks. As in the years of peace its composition was as closed as its thought world was confined. It bore many of the features that an anthropologist would recognize in a caste system and among those who mattered competition and mutual animosity were part and parcel of professional life. Perhaps this was always so. Perhaps it remains the case in all self-policing occupational élites. But if this is conceded, it becomes difficult to sustain the view that, in the man-management sense of placing people in the right positions, the Brooke-Montgomery patronage axis of 1942–1945 was any more 'professional' than its superseded predecessors.

There was one famous British Second World War general who, however, was relatively immune from the Brooke-Montgomery controlled view of men's worth. This was Slim. The reason for this immunity probably owed as much to distance from the centre as anything else, but the story of Slim carving out an identity as much for the Indian army as for himself during his 'defeat into victory' campaign in Burma offers an interesting, and actually far from forgotten, counter-narrative of Second World War generals and generalship. It is a story of a different theatre. But it is also a story so differently constructed as to be worthy of comment. Of lower middle class origins, and from a decidedly non-military family background, Slim's career ascent was slow and laden with setbacks. Nor was he wholly successful. Yet, it is precisely because he won his laurels the hard way that Slim carved out a special niche for himself. If any British general of the war years rose to the heights of fame on his own merits it was he.

Slim was also lucky. Fortunate to survive the efforts of one army commander, Irwin, to dismiss him, he went on to see off a much bigger fish, Leese, a protégé of Montgomery no less, in 1945. He was also the general accredited with the reconquest of Burma and of inflicting on the Japanese their greatest defeat on land of the war. Perhaps the strategic point of all this was limited. Maybe the campaign contributed little to the eventual Japanese surrender. But in resurrecting the careers and reputations of such western desert 'failures' as 'Briggo' Briggs, Rees and Messervy, and in cultivating a persona calculated to make himself appear as unlike Montgomery as possible, Slim restored the military reputation of the Indian Army and emerged in the post-war years as an alternative and no less authentic hero. His attractiveness extended beyond his well-written memoirs and the memories of those who had served with XIV Army. Modest and earthily unflamboyant, he appealed to those whose sympathies lay, as it were, with the Attlees rather than the Churchills of this world. He struck a chord among those drawn to the quiet as opposed to the noisy exponents of virtue. Brought out of retirement in 1948 and appointed CIGS against Montgomery's wishes and advice, he was the first Indian Army officer to hold that position. The Indian Army had by then, of course, ceased to exist.

Scope and sources

Completeness was from the start a primary aim of this dictionary. Whereas other 'Who's Who in World War Two' type publications are, necessarily, selective, the intention here was to compile an entry on every British Second World War general. Yet from this egalitarian premise it has to be accepted that, in terms of the information available, some generals remain more equal than others. For the famous there is no shortage of material to consult, and concision became the operative principle. Conversely, there were always the few who remained defiantly and maddeningly obscure. It is recognized, therefore, that the unequal length of the entries compromises the initial holistic objective. Nevertheless, with very few exceptions (discussed below) every general officer (major general and above) whose name featured on the *Army List* at any point in the Second World War has an entry against his name. This entails personal and career details of more than six hundred serving officers who, whether holding their rank in an acting, temporary or substantive capacity, were members of the military élite during the war years. Listing is in alphabetical order. The rank given is the highest the officer attained during his career (not necessarily the same as the rank accredited upon retirement), and inclusion has been determined by date. In this way any general on the active list at any time between September 1939 and August 1945 qualifies for admission

Exclusions are few and not difficult to justify. No place was found for members of the Royal Family accredited with honorary rank. Royal Marine general officers have also been left out, as have those of the Commonwealth forces, unless they commanded a British military formation. There are no entries for Mountbatten or Spears; the former being better know as an admiral and the latter more for being 'a poet laureate of the war' than a serving general officer. Field Marshals have also, generally, been excluded. By convention only death removed a field marshal's name from the *Army List*. Hence while, in official terms, they never fully retired, most had effectively done so long before 1939. Naturally those generals who attained the rank of field marshal during the war years are included.

At the outset the exercise seemed a large though relatively straightforward undertaking. The basic business of finding the names of general officers appeared unproblematic and, in the event, it was not too difficult to translate listings based on seniority on to a card-index system. It was at about that stage in the identification process, however, that the problem of sheer number emerged. Names I had never heard of came tumbling forth. In the beginning, based on a rough count of generals in service at war's beginning, and a consideration of those appearing in the *Army List* at the end, a simple calculation produced a figure of some three hundred generals who would merit attention. That number was constantly revised upwards until, like some public-work project spiralling out of financial control, 'completeness' entailed compiling entries against some six hundred names.

This underestimation is, in itself, interesting and worthy of comment. The rate of turnover in positions of field command during the war years has already been mentioned. However the sheer rate of turnover among the generals themselves, the demography of it all, came as something of a surprise. It was as though the increase in live-births (promotions) was matched by a higher mortality rate (retirements). With the institution of half-pay abolished just before the war, a general for whom no further employment could be found was placed on the retired list. Having, in effect, instituted a redundancy system, the army ushered out nearly as many senior officers as it welcomed, and the constituency of pensioner generals – many of them in their sprightly fifties – was large by war's end. Equally, the number of retirees who appeared to do no further war work was quite striking. A few performed Home Guard duties. Some wrote for the newspapers or were absorbed into the BBC. One became the general manager of a London department store. The majority, however, appeared to do nothing more productive than tend their gardens.

Probably the average age of serving generals dropped slightly during the course of the war, though just as it was rare for an employed general to have been born before 1880 at war's beginning, it was uncommon to find one among the newly-promoted who had been born after 1900. It was therefore a tightly packed generation. Service in the Great War was an almost universal common bond. A twenty-year-old in 1914 was fifty in 1944, and there were many, it seems, who had discovered a taste for soldiering during their First War service. Decorations for gallantry abounded. A general without the DSO or the MC attached to his name, and sometimes both, was unusual. Eight Second World War generals wore the ribbon of the Victoria Cross. One, 'Jock' Campbell, received the award in 1941 and was killed in a car crash soon after. Of the remainder all, Gort most conspicuously, went on to have wars that were curiously disappointing. No doubt something more than courage was considered necessary as a qualification for high command, but, and this is admittedly not much more than the whiff of an idea, holders of the VC seemed not to have been especially well-liked by their peers. Johnson and Roberts commanded divisions early on and were sacked and retired, and Hudson's war seemed to consist of being shunted from one backwater to another. Beak disappeared from view after being summarily dismissed by Montgomery during the Mareth battle, Smyth was more or less forced into retirement on health grounds during the retreat from Burma, and not even the legendary *beau sabreur* Carton de Wiart had much opportunity to lead troops in battle.

xvii

Not many generals died during the war. Five were killed in action (Barstow, Hopkinson, Mallaby,* Lumsden and Rennie). Four died in accidents while on active service (Campbell, Lloyd, Malden and Tilly), and a further six (Gott, Heywood, Pope, Warren, Willans and Wingate) were killed in plane crashes. The rather broad 'natural causes' category accounted for the deaths of a further 11 generals. These were Beckwith-Smith (who died in captivity), Clewer, de Fonblanque, Dill, Fairtlough, Finnis, Hawkesworth, Karslake, Squires, Tabuteau and Wallace. Out of a constituency of more than six hundred this was not a high casualty rate. A further 12 generals were, at some time, prisoners of war. Fortune, taken prisoner in France in June 1940, endured the longest period of captivity. Carton de Wiart, Gambier-Parry, Neame, O'Connor and Reid were taken prisoner in North Africa, incarcerated in Italian jails and, through various routes, were freed by the end of 1943 and available for further employment. Those taken prisoner by the Japanese enjoyed no such luxury. The emaciated Heath, Key, Macrae, Maltby, Percival, Sitwell and Simmons had to wait until August 1945 before their release and repatriation.

If the above offers the impression that, in the round, British generals tended towards comfortable living during the war years, there were many who paid a heavy if indirect price for their involvement The number of generals' sons – and sometimes more than one – who were killed in action or died while on active service during the war became a constant, and even rather depressing, at-the-elbow companion to entry compilation.

One mild surprise was the relative absence of aristocratic connection. Led on by Orwellian notions of a British army recruited from the slum-dwelling riff-raff and officered by the sons of the nobility, I had anticipated confronting a military caste which was title-heavy; as if to say that *Burke's Peerage* would be a much-needed, and therefore much-thumbed work of reference. Actually *Burke's Peerage* was quite heavily used, but more as a source for those generals knighted during or after the war than for those who already had, through birth, a foot on the aristocratic ladder. The titled, or the sons of baronets, were quite rare exceptions. The field is one in which the occupational label 'professional,' or just upper middle class, would be safer forms of categorization. In some cases generals seem consciously to have played down their aristocratic pedigrees as the war progressed. Pile, for example, is invariably rendered 'Tim' and not Sir Frederick. That Leese, or his biographer, should make more of him being knighted in the field than of his baronetcy offers an interesting sidelight on how the 'People's War' was internalized and made sense of among those with an accredited ancestral right to lead.

There were ties that bound, however. Most generals had been privately educated. They had been to public school and had been cadets either at Camberley or Woolwich. It was not rare but it was certainly out-of-the-ordinary for a general outside the specialist services not to have benefited from the army's higher educational course of instruction at either the Camberley or Quetta staff

* Actually murdered in Java by Indonesian 'patriots' in August 1945.

colleges. Many, not unexpectedly, were of military family. Not a few were the sons of Indian civil servants, though probably the second most frequently cited occupation of a general's father was clergyman. Two Second World War generals, incidentally, took holy orders after they retired from the army.

Most generals were probably quite normal in that they were of that 'sensible military type' which, as Kim Philby observed, 'neither barked nor advocated Yoga'.* Normality, also probably, extended to sexual preference. There were not many generals who were 'confirmed bachelors'. They tended to marry young and often around the time when they had established themselves in their chosen profession and secured a place at staff college. Many married more than once. The incidence of wives dying young was quite striking and, perhaps a product of the disruptions and separations inherent in service life, the occurrence of divorce was marked before, during and after the war. Another occupational hazard was sport. Generals had often been quite sporty in their youth, and amidst the sprinkling of rugby internationals, there was a good deal of representative boxing and playing cricket. It may seem something of a cliché, but an awful lot did hunt, fish and shoot well into old age. If there is a contradiction between shooting birds for sport one weekend, while spending hours in 'twitcher' garb in another, few generals seemed conscious of it. Just as sport often loomed large in the generals' *Who's Who* entries, not a few, and sometimes quite charmingly, devoted more space in their memoirs to their field sport experiences than to their recollections of war.

British Second World War generals usually retired young, before they reached the age of sixty. A few went on to have distinguished post-war army careers, but these tended to be the exception. There was quite a clear-out in the immediate post-war years, such that the majority of Second World War generals had retired by 1950. They were, on the whole, long-lived too. The laborious, but worthwhile, process of searching for newspaper obituary notices resulted in most use being made of *The Times* microfilm reels for the 1970s and 1980s.

It was always interesting to read about how the generals lived and what they did in their retirements. However, the variety of post-army trajectories was such that no obvious pattern of occupation or lifestyle emerged. There were those who seemed to fit comfortably into the country gentleman stereotype. They lived in the shire counties, in houses with names rather than numbers, were local JPs or councillors, and presiding over the county cadet association, wore their regimental or MCC ties on trips up to town. A surprisingly large number, though not necessarily of Anglo-Irish origin, lived out their retirements in Ireland. Equally, quite a few, most noticeably from the Indian Army, settled in South Africa or Kenya. Yet set against this image of slightly impoverished gentility, another picture emerged. For the number of those who entered the metropolitan world of business, made money and amassed impressive-looking portfolios of directorships was large. Those who, in various guises, became patrons of the arts also made up a surprisingly bulky category. Writing was

* Philby, K., *My Silent War* (St Albans, Granada, 1969), p. 42.

common. Memoirs aside, dogs, gardening and fly-fishing were the usual subjects. One general's *Practical Polo* became, apparently, the sport's standard coaching manual. Another churned out opera scores and libretti that were never performed, and another still, a one-time successful playwright, ended his own life.

There was a great deal of charity work. Aside from county and old school associations and the Boy Scouts, a connection with the St John Ambulance Association was, it appears, a particular favourite. Civil Defence duties also consumed much occupational space. Many generals sat as school governors and on the development boards of new town corporations. As many were members of hospital group management committees. A general's name would often dignify a regional or national 'quango's' list of directors.

There was a strong involvement in local government, but very few retired generals entered national politics. Of those who were candidates in the 1945 election only one, Mason-Macfarlane, was elected. What his *Dictionary of National Biography* (*DNB*) entry described, rather curiously, as his 'long-standing lack of sympathy for the ruling party', presumably worked in his favour among the electors of North Paddington. Smyth was a Conservative MP from 1950 for a number of years, and Alexander was, rather unhappily, Churchill's Minister of Defence in the 1950s. But these were the rare exceptions. Public life for most retired generals was usually much more parochial, muted, 'dignified' and low-key.

As the compilers of *Who's Who* had their copies of the *Army List*, they would routinely contact a newly promoted major general and ask him whether he would like to feature in their publication. Probably they would send a form which, divided into categories, covered education, awards, position, personal details, work and recreations. More often than not the general would comply. However, so permissive were the *Who's Who* criteria that some would write about themselves at considerable and detailed length, while others would compose only the briefest of replies. Quite a few were excessively modest, and as many could not be bothered or never got round to it. *Who's Who*, such an obvious and important source at one level, proved a rather unpredictable asset; not quite as universally valuable as had been initially anticipated.

Yet in being very accurate in establishing dates of death, *Who's Who* (or more usually the CD ROM *Who Was Who*) provided a lead for tracing obituaries in *The Times*. Access was invaluable. Searches, however, would have been impossible without a printed index. Obituaries were often as surprisingly full and informative as they were sometimes unduly fulsome, frustratingly brief or non-existent. As mentioned earlier, *Burke's Peerage* was a useful back-up source for those generals who were knighted, and while the *DNB* was all right in its way, entries have a stilted feel to them and are often on the ponderous side. It is to be hoped that the new *DNB* will be wider in scope, less hagiographic and livelier in its coverage.

Electronic sources tend to be less reliable and hit-and-miss. 'Google' has its enthusiasts, and there is any number of military-oriented sites on the internet.

But for all the cheerfully anarchic 'history-from-the-bottom-up' value of internet web pages, the medium does not serve British Second World War generals especially well. Of much greater use was 'The Times Digital Archive'. This internet accessed source was particularly useful in tracing the career details of those generals who said little about themselves or who scarcely featured in the standard works of reference. As, pre-war, *The Times* printed extracts from 'The London Gazette' and was often quite full on 'Military Appointments' at home and abroad, much useful information was garnered. Most generals who had been at staff college said as much in their *Who's Who* entry. However, as they were often imprecise as to dates of attendance, annual graduation lists were there in the digital archive to provide confirmation.

The papers of generals held within the War Office files at the Public Record Office (National Archive) proved rather disappointing. War Office records of the Second World War years have been notoriously ill-kept and subject to raids. Save for the odd nugget there was precious little to find in the accumulated rag-bag of records deposited. Conversely, the 'semi official' correspondence that passed between field commanders and their London superiors; between, say, Auchinleck and Dill (held in the Liddell Hart Centre for Military Archives at King's College) was like gold dust. This was the kind of material that came closest to what I was looking for all along; judgements that may have been snap but were usually telling, in short the gossip of the military élite.

As regards archive sources there was always, when all else failed, the *Army List* to fall back on. Most archive centres, including the PRO and LHCMA, have their copies. However, through age and constant use the collections are often dog-eared and seldom complete. I was fortunate in being granted permission to consult the superbly organized and beautifully preserved series held at the Joint Service Staff College. There the Half-Yearly Army Lists with their 'gradations' yielded the level of detail necessary to compile entries on the more obscure, not to say most reclusive, of Britain's Second World War generals.

Nothing is ever quite finished to the point of total satisfaction. No doubt there is more that could be said on sources, and, no doubt too, there is more archive material that could have been usefully consulted. But, bearing in mind the historian's faith in the diminshing return value of primary source material, it would be unjust and even a little ungracious not to pay tribute to those who, over the years, have provided a wealth of secondary literature. The hundreds of Second World War veterans, whose published memoirs, biographies and campaign histories make library shelves sag, have built a terrific resource. In pillaging their work in order to compile this dictionary, I am conscious that I owe these authors a great debt. They inspired the thing and made it possible. Whatever the difficulties and frustrations that came with the territory, reading a general's memoirs was usually informative and never tedious. Reference to published material occurs on just about every page of the dictionary. A modified Harvard-type system of referencing is employed. After a citation the work is identified in parentheses; thus (Bloggs, 1985, 127) refers to the author's name, the year of publication and the page number. A full bibliography at the end offers details on how the work may be traced.

Naturally I was not always in sympathy with the author's views, nor was I always in agreement with the way men and events were interpreted. I too, I confess, developed partisan sympathies and had my favourites. Nevertheless, engaging with the literature was the most interesting and enjoyable part of the project. Earlier the claim was made that the history of British Second World War generals and generalship is creaking with age and is, moreover, 'lop-sided' and 'top-heavy'. I adhere to these views. But I would be the first to agree that as history goes, it is not bad history for all that.

GLOSSARY

AA	Anti-Aircraft
AAF	Auxiliary Air Force
ABCA	Army Bureau of Current Affairs
ACG	Army Chaplain General
ADC	Aide de Camp
ADGB	Air Defence of Great Britain
AEAF	Allied Expeditionary Air Force
AEC	Army Education Corps
AFHQ	Allied Force Headquarters
AG	Adjutant General
AHQ	Army Headquarters (India)
ALFSEA	Allied Land Forces South East Asia
AMGOT	Allied Military Government of Occupied Territories
AMQ	Assistant Quartermaster General
ARA	Associate, Royal Academy
ARP	Air Raid Precautions
ATC	Air Training Corps
ATS	Auxiliary Territorial Service
BA	Bachelor of Arts
BAOR	British Army of the Rhine
BBC	British Broadcasting Corporation
Bde.	Brigade
BEF	British Expeditionary Force
BGS	Brigadier General Staff
BLA	British Liberation Army
BMJ	British Medical Journal
BMM	British Military Mission
Bn.	Battalion
BRA	Brigadier Royal Artillery
BRCS	British Red Cross Society
Bt.	Baronet

CAS	Chief of the Air Staff
CB	Companion of the Order of the Bath
CBE	Commander of the Order of the British Empire
CCC	County Cricket Club
CCRA	Commander, Corps of Royal Artillery
CCRE	Commander, Corps of Royal Engineers
CCRSigs	Commander, Corps of Royal Signals
CGS	Chief of the General Staff
CID	Committee of Imperial Defence
CIE	Companion of the Order of the Indian Empire
CIGS	Chief of the Imperial General Staff
C-in-C	Commander-in-Chief
CMF	Central Mediterranean Force
CMG	Companion of the Order of St Michael and St George
CMO	Chief Medical Officer
CO	Commanding Officer
Comr.	Commissioner
Comdr.	Commander
COS	Chief of Staff
COSSAC	Chief of Staff to Supreme Allied Commander
CRA	Commander, Royal Artillery
CRE	Commander, Royal Engineers
CSI	Companion of the Order of the Star of India
CSO	Chief Staff Officer
CVO	Commander of the Royal Victorian Order
DAAQMG	Deputy Assistant Adjutant and Quartermaster General
DAAG	Deputy Assistant Adjutant General
DAQMG	Deputy Adjutant and Quartermaster General
DADMS	Deputy Assistant Director of Medical Services
DADOS	Deputy Assistant Director of Ordnance Services
DADQ	Deputy Assistant Director of Quartering
DADST	Deputy Assistant Director of Supplies and Transport
DAG	Deputy Adjutant General
DAQMG	Deputy Assistant Quartermaster General
DCIGS	Deputy Chief of the Imperial General Staff
DCLI	Duke of Cornwall's Light Infantry
DDME	Deputy Director of Mechanical Engineering
DDMI	Deputy Director of Military Intelligence
DDMO	Deputy Director of Military Operations
DDMS	Deputy Director of Medical Services
DDMT	Deputy Director of Military Training
DDST	Deputy Director of Supplies and Transport
DFC	Distinguished Flying Cross
DL	Deputy Lieutenant

DME	Director of Military Engineering
DMI	Director of Military Intelligence
DMO	Director of Military Operations
DMS	Director of Medical Services
DMT	Director of Military Training
DQMG	Deputy Quartermaster General
DSM	Distinguished Service Medal
DSO	Companion of the Distinguished Service Order
DST	Director of Supplies and Transport
ENSA	Entertainment National Service Association
FCGP	Fellow, College of General Practitioners
FCPS	Fellow, College of Physicians and Surgeons
FDS	Fellow in Dental Surgery
FICE	Fellow, Institution of Civil Engineers
FIST	Fellow, Institute of Science and Technology
FRAM	Fellow, Royal Academy of Music
FRCGP	Fellow, Royal College of General Practitioners
FRCP	Fellow, Royal College of Physicians
FRCS	Fellow, Royal College of Surgeons
FRGS	Fellow, Royal Geographic al Society
FRNS	Fellow, Royal Numismatic Society
FRS	Fellow, Royal Society
FRSA	Fellow, Royal Society of Arts
GBE	Knight Grand Cross of the Order of the British Empire
GCB	Knight Grand Cross of the Order of the Bath
GCIE	Knight Grand Commander of the Order of the Indian Empire
GCVO	Knight Grand Cross of the Royal Victorian Order
GHQ	General Headquarters
GOC	General Officer Commanding
GOC-in-C	General Officer Commanding-in-Chief
GQG	Grand Quartier Général
GSO	General Staff Officer
HG	Home Guard
HMS	His (or Her) Majesty's Ship
HMSO	His (or Her) Majesty's Stationery Office
Hon.	Honourable/Honorary
IA	Indian Army
IAC	Indian Armoured Corps
IAMC	Indian Army Medical Corps

ICI	Imperial Chemical Industries
ICS	Indian Civil Service
IDC	Imperial Defence College
IEF	Indian Expeditionary Force
IMS	Indian Medical Service
IS	Internal Security
JP	Justice of the Peace
KAR	King's African Rifles
KBE	Knight Commander, Order of the British Empire
KCB	Knight Commander, Order of the Bath
KCIE	Knight Commander, Order of the Indian Empire
KCMG	Knight Commander, Order of St Michael and St George
KCSI	Knight Commander, Order of the Star of India
KCVO	Knight Commander, Royal Victorian Order
KG	Knight of Order of the Garter
KHP	Hon. Physician to the King
KHS	Hon. Surgeon to the King
KT	Knight of Order of the Thistle
Kt.	Knight
LCC	London County Council (later GLC)
LHCMA	Lidell Hart Centre for Military Archives
LLB	Bachelor of Law
LofC	Lines of Communication
LTB	London Transport Board
MA	Master of Arts / Military Attaché
MBE	Member, Order of the British Empire
MC	Military Cross
MCC	Marylebone Cricket Club
MEF	Middle East Force
MELF	Middle East Land Forces
MGA	Major General in charge of Administration
MGGS	Major General, General Staff
MGO	Master General of the Ordnance
NAAFI	Navy, Army and Air Force Institutes
NWFP	North-West Frontier Province
OBE	Order of the British Empire
OCTU	Officer Cadet Training Unit
O i/c	Officer in charge
OM	Order of Merit

PMA	Personal Military Assistant
POW	Prisoner of War
p.s.c.	Passed Staff College
QMG	Quartermaster General
RA	Royal Artillery
RAC	Royal Armoured Corps
RADC	Royal Army Dental Corps
RAF	Royal Air Force
RAMC	Royal Army Medical Corps
RAOC	Royal Army Ordnance Corps
RAPC	Royal Army Pay Corps
RARO	Regular Army Reserve of Officers
RASC	Royal Army Service Corps
REME	Royal Electrical and Mechanical Engineers
RFA	Royal Field Artillery
RGA	Royal Garrison Artillery
RGS	Royal Geographical Society
RFU	Rugby Football Union
RHA	Royal Horse Artillery
RMA	Royal Military Academy (Woolwich)
RMC	Royal Military College (Sandhurst)
RN	Royal Navy
SEAC	South East Asia Command
SEALF	South East Asia Land Forces
SHAEF	Supreme Headquarters, Allied Expeditionary Force
SHAPE	Supreme Headquarters, Allied Powers Europe
SME	School of Military Engineering
SRO	Supplementary Reserve of Officers
TA	Territorial Army
T&AFA	Territorial and Auxiliary Forces Association
UNRRA	United Nations Relief and Rehabilitation Administration
VC	Victoria Cross
VCIGS	Vice Chief of the Imperial General Staff
VHS	Hon. Surgeon to Viceroy of India
VQMG	Vice Quartermaster General
WO	War Office

BRITISH GENERALS
OF THE
SECOND WORLD WAR

A

ABRAHAM, Major General Sir William Ernest Victor
(1897–1980), Kt, CBE, FGS
Born in Enniskillen and educated in Belfast and the Royal College of Science, Dublin, Abraham worked as a geologist for the Burmah Oil Company in India and Burma throughout the inter-war years. He joined the Burma Auxiliary force as a trooper, rose to the rank of lieutenant colonel by 1933 and commanded an auxiliary battalion.

Resigning his commission in 1938, Abraham enrolled in the Army Officers' Volunteer Reserve later that year and was re-commissioned into the Royal Engineers in 1940. After attending Staff College he served briefly at the War Office before staff postings to Greece, the Middle East and Malaya. Awarded the CBE he served thereafter in Burma and India. Promoted major general in 1944 he was Controller General of Military Economy, India, in 1945.

Re-employed by Burmah Oil in 1945, Abraham was chairman of the company by the time he retired in 1955. A lay-member of the Restrictive Practices Court, 1961–1970, he was National Chairman of the Burma Star Association, 1962–1967. Knighted in 1977 he was the father of a son and two daughters from his first marriage. He and his second wife lived in Lechlade.

ADAIR, Major General Sir Allan Henry Shafto
6th Bt (1897–1988). GCVO, CB, DSO, MC and Bar
Only son of Sir Shafto Adair of Ballymena, Co. Antrim, and born in London, Adair was educated at Harrow. Volunteering for service in 1916 and commissioned in the Grenadier Guards, he was awarded the MC in 1918.

Married in 1919 and father of two sons (one died in infancy) and three daughters, Adair was a captain for most of the 1920s. Amidst ceremonial duties for Guards battalions at home, food convoys to be protected during the General Strike and a good deal of sport, he had a long posting in Egypt in the mid-1930s. Second-in-command of the 3rd Battalion Grenadier Guards in 1939, his service in Alexander's 1st Division with the BEF was briefly interrupted by his appointment as Chief Instructor at Sandhurst. However, he had scarcely returned to England when the German offensive in the west began. Rushing back to his unit, he arrived in Brussels in a taxi to assume command of his battalion. Admitted to the DSO for his part in the campaign in France and Flanders, he was promoted brigadier.

Under Home Forces Adair commanded 30th Guards Brigade in 1941 and 6th Guards Brigade in 1942. Promoted major general that September, he succeeded Leese as commander of the 'thoroughly well organised' Guards Armoured Division (Ryder, 1987, 91). Small of stature and well-liked by subordinates, his high-pitched voice was much imitated. No man, it is said, 'read the Scriptures better in church' (Fraser, 2002, 196). Though grieved at his son's death (killed at Monte Cassino in 1943), he remained 'brave, sensible, courteous and kind' (Carrington, 1988, 43), and, surviving Montgomery's efforts to remove him from his command before D-Day (Baynes, 1989, 186), led his division in much hard fighting before the breakout in Normandy. In September 1944 he led a 100-mile dash to Brussels which was completed in less than 24 hours. After more hard fighting in Holland and northern Germany, Adair was present at the cere-mony near Bremen in June 1945, when the Guards Armoured Division formally reverted to its infantry role. Appointed CB, Adair served in Greece as commander of 13 Division from December 1945, and 'with properties and responsibilities to look after' (Lindsay (ed.), 1986, 188), retired from the Army in 1947.

A Freemason for most of his adult life, Adair was a lieutenant in the Yeoman of the Guard, Colonel of the Grenadier Guards from 1961 to 1974, and for several years a governor of Harrow School. Succeeding his father in 1949, he was made GCVO in 1974 for his services as DL for Co. Antrim, when he and his wife sold their Ballymena estate and moved to their property in Norfolk. A Suffolk JP with no heir, he sadly concluded his memoir notes with the comment that 'the Baronetcy dies with me' (Lindsay (ed.), 1986, 181).

ADAM, General Sir Robert Forbes 2nd Bt. *(1885–1982), GCB, DSO, OBE*
Born in London, the first son of Sir Frank Forbes Adam, and educated at Eton and RMA Woolwich, 'Bill' Adam, was commissioned in the Royal Artillery in 1905. A keen sportsman, much of his early soldiering was in India where he formed a lifelong friendship with the future CIGS, Brooke. Married in 1915, his First World War service was in France and Italy. Mentioned in despatches, he was admitted to the DSO in 1918.

Awarded the OBE for service with British forces in North Russia in 1919, Adam attended the Staff College, Camberley, 1920–1921. A staff officer at the War Office 1927–1931, he was made Brevet Major in 1930, and was an instructor at Camberley from 1932 to 1935. Promotion thereafter was steady and, in career terms, nicely balanced between staff and field posts. Chief Staff Officer at the War Office 1935–1936 and Deputy Director of Military Oper-ations there for some months, he was CRA 1st Division 1936–1937, before becoming Commandant at the Staff College Camberley. From early 1938 until November 1939 he was, as lieutenant general, a busy Deputy Chief of the Imperial General Staff because, due to the deteriorating relationship between Gort, his chief, and the war secretary, Hore-Belisha, he took on most of the work (Bond, 1972, xv). No single man in the army, it is said, did more 'to prepare it for the call which he never for one moment doubted was sure to come' (Brownrigg, 1942, 131).

In command of III Corps in France in the early months of 1940, Adam played only a limited part in the build-up of the BEF, as units were frequently held back in England in readiness for Scandinavian operations. However, his role in securing the Dunkirk perimeter during the army's retreat was crucial. He was borne from the beach, so it is said, on a raft. Made GOC-in-C of Northern Command in the summer of 1940 he found himself, in early 1941, back at the War Office as Adjutant General.

Adam made his enemies. Paget, when C-in-C Home Forces, described him as a 'serious menace both to morale and discipline' (Crang, 2000, 140). To others he 'combined inefficiency with vanity, and strong Socialist principles' (Goode, 1993, 32). Churchill, apparently, wanted to move him from the War Office and make him Governor of Gibraltar (Danchev & Todman, 2001, 514). He did, however, enjoy the constant support of Brooke, usually lunching with him on a weekly basis. But despite, or perhaps because of, the criticism he suffered, it seems generally agreed that Adam was an outstanding success as wartime Adjutant General. Knowing the ways of Whitehall, he applied his 'alertly pragmatic mind' (Mackenzie, 1992, 156) to transforming a hidebound War Office into a more human and intelligent organization, and for his efforts to make officer selection more rational he deserves to be remembered as the architect of a citizens' army. An 'unconventional soldier . . . deadly keen on the educational side' (Smart (ed.), 2003, 103) his organizational ability and reputation as a progressive made him much sought after by various civilian organizations after the war.

Retired in 1946 and made President of the MCC for a year, Adam was President of the British Council from 1946 to 1952 as well as being Colonel Commandant of the Royal Army Dental Corps. He chaired numerous committees concerned with workers' health and welfare. Unusually for a titled retired regular soldier, he took the United Nations seriously and, as well as receiving numerous honorary degrees and fellowships, was, for a number of years, President of the National Institute for Adult Education.

AIREY, Lieutenant General Sir Terence Sydney
(1900–1983), KCMG, CB, CBE
Born in Suffolk and educated at Gresham's School and RMC, Sandhurst, Airey was commissioned in the Durham Light Infantry in 1919. He saw service in the Eastern Arab Corps and was a staff officer at HQ Sudan Defence Corps, 1929–1935. After attending the Staff College, Camberley, 1935–1936, he was at war's outbreak in 1939 a lieutenant colonel.

Airey's record of service as a staff officer stood him in good stead. Attached to Platt's staff in the Sudan and in Abyssinia, he later served at GHQ Cairo, first on Special Operations and, from August 1942, as Director of Military Intelligence. With his 'lively and unconventional cast of mind' (Lewin, 1978,

181), he remained at Alexander's side for the rest of the war. As brigadier he was attached to the staff of 18 Army Group in 1943 and, made temporary major general in 1944, was Assistant CGS to Alexander in Italy. Playing his part in securing the surrender of German forces in April 1945, he was made Acting Deputy Supreme Allied Commander, Italy in 1945.

His distinguished post-war record consisted of service as Acting Deputy C-in-C Allied Forces in Italy in 1946, as Military Governor of Trieste 1947–1951, as Assistant Chief of Staff SHAPE, and as Commander British Forces, Hong Kong, 1952–1954. He retired from the army in 1954, when he was already Colonel of the Durham Light Infantry.

AIZLEWOOD, Major General John Aldam *(1895–1990), MC*

Commissioned in the 4th Dragoon Guards in 1914, Aizlewood's First War service was in France, latterly with the Machine Gun Corps. He was awarded the MC.

A great horseman and polo player, Aizlewood was a brigade major in India 1927–1931, and attended the Staff College, Quetta, 1932–1933. He commanded the 4th/7th Dragoon Guards 1936–1939, the 3rd (Meerut) Indian Cavalry Brigade, 1939–1940, and the 2nd Indian Brigade 1940–1941. Commander of the 252nd Indian Army Brigade Group 1941–1942, he commanded 30th Armoured Brigade in 1942.

Made GOC 42nd Armoured Division under Home Forces in December 1942, Aizlewood was made Commander of the Essex and Suffolk District after his division was disbanded in October 1943. Acting GOC and C-in-C Eastern Command 1943–1944, he retired in 1945. He was sometime Colonel of the 4th/7th Dragoon Guards.

AKERMAN, Major General William Philip Jopp *(1888–1971), CB, DSO, MC*

Educated at Oundle and RMA, Woolwich, Akerman was commissioned in the Royal Artillery in 1908 and saw service, for the next six years, in India. First War service was in Mesopotamia (1914–1916), where he was awarded the MC, and in France. Appointed to the DSO in 1918, a bar was added before the end of hostilities.

Married in 1920, but widowed in 1922, Akerman continued attending the Staff College, Camberley, from where he graduated in 1923. With a daughter to bring up, the unusual aspect to his second marriage in 1925 was that, as for the first, he married a general's daughter. He attended the Imperial Defence College in 1933. Assistant Director of Artillery at the War Office 1934–1936, he was Assistant Master General of the Ordnance 1936–1938, when he was promoted major general but reverted to half-pay.

In 1939 Akerman was appointed Major General Royal Artillery, Army HQ, India. He held that post until he retired from the army in 1942, when he and his wife settled in Surrey.

ALANBROOKE, *see BROOKE*

4

ALBAN, Major General Clifton Edward Rawdon Grant *(b. 1889), DSO*
Very few of this officer's personal details are known. Commissioned in the King's (Liverpool) Regiment in 1914, his First War service was in France where he was wounded, mentioned in despatches and admitted to the DSO, and latterly on the North-West Frontier, where he commanded a battalion of the Lancashire Fusiliers.

Reverting to the King's Regiment, Alban attended the Staff College, Camberley, 1921–1922. He served on the staff of Aldershot Command 1924–1925, with Eastern Command 1925–1929, and was a Deputy Assistant Adjutant General at the War Office 1932–1936. Commander of the 1st Battalion of the King's Regiment 1936–1939, he retired from the army with the rank of brigadier in 1939.

Recalled at war's outset, Alban was made Assistant Adjutant General for Personnel at the War Office. ADC to the King in 1941, he finally retired in 1944.

ALEXANDER, Field Marshal, the Hon. Sir Harold Leofric George, Earl Alexander of Tunis *(1891–1969), KG, GCB, OM, CGMG, CSI, DSO, MC*
Born in London, the third son of the 4th Earl of Caledon (Irish peerage), and educated at Harrow, Alexander entered RMC, Sandhurst, in 1910. There his school nickname 'Fat Boy' gave way to the less disagreeable and more enduring 'Alex'.

Commissioned in the Irish Guards in 1910, his initial commitment to soldiering was, by his own admission, not great. But the outbreak of the First World War put paid to ambitions to become a professional artist. Wounded in the first battle of Ypres, he was awarded the MC in 1915 and admitted to the DSO the following year. Thereafter, though wounded once again, he rose from acting commander of his battalion to acting commander of the 4th Guards Brigade.

Having 'acquired a taste for war' (Nicolson, 1976, 68) 'Alex' volunteered for service in the Allied Relief Commission in Poland in 1919. Finding himself in Latvia, in a tense political atmosphere and confused military situation, he assumed command of the Baltic Landwehr brigade (made up of ethnic Germans). which, the next year, played its part in driving Soviet forces out of the country and securing national independence.

Made second-in-command of his regiment in 1920, he attended the Staff College, Camberley, 1927–28, following postings to Constantinople and Gibraltar. After commanding the regiment and regimental district of the Irish Guards (1928–30), he attended the Imperial Defence College, served on the staff at the War Office and at HQ Northern Command. In between times he married Lady Margaret Bingham, younger daughter of the 5th Earl of Lucan. There were two sons and a daughter from the marriage. A daughter was adopted.

A brigadier in 1935, Alexander was appointed to command the Nowshera Brigade on the North-West Frontier where, though ill for a time, he was engaged for the next two years in punitive expeditions against Mohmand tribesmen. He learned Urdu, it is said, with the same ease he had shown in previously mastering

German and Russian, and gained a reputation for leading his men from the front.

Promoted major general on his return to England in 1937 (and therefore at forty-six the youngest general then serving in the British Army) he was GOC-in-C Aldershot Command until the outbreak of war. Incorporated in Sir John Dill's I Corps his division formed part of the BEF sent to France in October 1939. There, handsome, stylish and with the detached air of a man 'listening to something outside the room'(Ranfurly, 1998, 148), he was not an over-zealous trainer of his troops but distinguished himself during the retreat to and evacuation from Dunkirk. Made Corps Commander, he did his best to ensure all British troops were evacuated and was the last British general to leave the port. With a modesty that was as famous as it was engaging he told Anthony Eden, the war secretary, 'We were not pushed you know' (Avon, 1965, 113).

Continuing briefly as commander of I Corps, Alexander was promoted lieutenant general in December 1940 and succeeded Auchinleck as GOC-in-C Southern Command. Remaining in that post throughout 1941, he introduced basic battle drills into the troops' training régime and was commander-designate of 110 Force – a kind of rapid-response force available for offensive operations should opportunity arise – which was a product of Churchill's active imagination. Highly regarded by the Prime Minister, 'Alex' was promoted general and knighted in January 1942. The next month he was appointed to command British land forces in Burma.

Though expressing himself 'delighted to go' (Churchill, 1951, 146) and attempt to stem the Japanese advance in Burma, there was little Alexander could do in that theatre save shepherd British forces in their long retreat towards India. Narrowly escaping capture himself, he handed over command of land forces to Slim in late March to become C-in-C of all Allied forces in Burma. The conduct of a retreat is, perhaps, the severest test of generalship, and though Slim was characteristically gracious about Alexander's leadership in his memoirs (Slim, 1999, 55–6) the American Stilwell was, equally characteristically, not (White (ed.), 1948, 78). But, with reputation untarnished, he was recalled to England in July 1942 and made commander-designate of the British First Army, then assembling in preparation for the invasion of French North Africa in the Autumn of 1942.

Arrival in Africa came earlier than expected and in a different theatre. As a result of the Churchill-Brooke shake-up in Egypt in August 1942 'Alex' found himself C-in-C Middle East, with the older and more senior Montgomery appointed under him as 8th Army commander. As this was the combination that won victory at Alamein and succeeded in clearing Axis forces from North Africa, Alexander is usually credited with all the quiet qualities necessary in making the relationship work successfully. Never interfering, he did his best to supply his army commander with everything he asked for. His charm, tact and modesty certainly made him a very different character to Montgomery, though whether he was the only superior temperamentally able to get the best out of such an idiosyncratic and egotistical subordinate is an open question.

6

In February 1943 'Alex' assumed command of 18 Army Group (Anderson's First Army and Montgomery's 8th) and also became deputy to Eisenhower, the supreme commander. With the North African campaign concluded, he commanded Allied land forces during the invasions of Sicily in July and southern Italy from September 1943.

The going in Italy was not easy. The terrain, dreadful winter weather and stubborn German resistance made the climb up the Italian peninsula difficult and slow. In part Alexander was hampered by the downgrading of Italian operations and the removal of troops and commanders in preparation for OVERLORD, the 'main show' in North-West Europe. Yet he probably did not make the best use of the resources available to him; those very qualities that had made his relationship with Montgomery so successful in North Africa and Sicily telling against him over the last eighteen months of the war. His amiability and desire to be agreeable were perhaps necessary in an army made up of numerous and fractious allies, but opened him to the charge of lacking 'grip' and being unable to control headstrong commanders in the field.

Though honours and promotions followed – made Mediterranean supreme commander in November 1944 and promoted Field Marshal (back-dated to June) – Alexander's war ended on an anticlimactic note. He accepted the surrender of German forces in Italy in April 1945, but by then Brooke, the CIGS, had written him off for 'his deficiency of brain allow[ing] him to be dominated by others' (Danchev & Todman, 2001, 646).

Handing over command in October 1945, raised to the peerage as Viscount Alexander of Tunis, 'Alex' was appointed Governor-General of Canada in April 1946. He proved a popular uncontroversial figure in this dignified role, and Canadians, like most Americans, took to this dapper, stereotypically aristocratic Englishman. Rewarded with the customary advancement of one rank in the peerage in 1952, Earl Alexander dutifully accepted Churchill's invitation to become his Minister of Defence and was sworn into the Privy Council.

Happy enough in the House of Lords, though out of his depth as politician, 'Alex' left important defence matters to Churchill and spent much of his ministerial time on foreign tours. The novelist C.P. Snow captured something of his Whitehall isolation in *The Corridors of Power*, and, retiring at his own request in October 1954, 'Alex' painted, performed numerous colonel-in-chief duties and supplemented his half-pay with a several directorships until his death in 1969.

Alexander was the most honoured British soldier of the Second World War and, while he lived, contended in reputation to be commemorated as the finest of the country's wartime commanders. For all that he had a fabulous career, a less positive image has emerged in recent years, his legendary panache being presented less as a product of natural diffidence and charm than as disguise for dimness, even stupidity. As his biographer put it, he came to 'like him more, but admire him less' (Nicolson, 1997, 114). That the man who in life was famous for his role in the 1910 'Fowler's match' (the Eton-Harrow cricket fixture), the memory of which 'turn[ed] old men into boys' (Nicolson, 1976, 37), should in death be laid to rest in South Mimms churchyard – less than a mile from where the M25 London-orbital motorway services are now situated – provides its own comment on late twentieth-century notions of service and social change.

ALFIERI, Major General Frederick John *(1892–1961)*, *CB, CIE*
Born of a non-military family, Alfieri was educated privately and was gazetted into the 34th Royal Sikh Pioneers in 1914. He married in 1919. An engineer, his career combined a variety of regimental and staff appointments in the Indian Army, through the Royal Indian Army Service Corps. A brevet major in 1935, he was a brevet lieutenant colonel in 1937.

Assistant Director of Supplies and Transport, India, in 1938, Alfieri was Assistant Quartermaster General in 1939 and Assistant Adjutant General at the War Office in 1940. He was made Major General i/c Administration, India, in 1941. From 1943 to 1945 he was Deputy Quartermaster General, India, and 1945–1946 Director of Supplies and Transport, India.

Appointed CB and retired in 1947, Alfieri returned to England the live out the rest of his life at his home in Sussex.

ALLEN, Major General Robert Hall *(1886–1981)* *CB, MC*
The son of a barrister, Allen was educated at Charterhouse and RMA Woolwich. Commissioned in the Royal Artillery in 1905, his war service was in Gallipoli, where he was awarded the MC and twice mentioned in despatches, and in Egypt. In 1916 he married the daughter of a major general.

A graduate of the Staff College, Camberley, in 1920 and Assistant Adjutant and Quartermaster General in Aldershot Command 1937–1938, Allen specialized thereafter in anti-aircraft defence, and in particular training and commanding Territorial Army units in that role. Promoted major general in 1939, he commanded 5th AA Division for two years and in 1941 took command of 8th AA Division. Retired in 1942, he was appointed CB.

Living quietly in a long retirement in Wiltshire, Allen listed his recreation as 'solving simple chess problems'.

ALLFREY, Lieutenant General Sir Charles Walter
(1895–1964), *KBE, CB, DSO, MC*
Born in Warwickshire of military family, Allfrey was educated at the Royal Naval College, Dartmouth, though at the declaration of war in 1914 was commissioned in the Royal Artillery. A Captain in 1917, he was twice wounded and awarded the MC (with bar in 1918).

Regimental duties between the wars was as varied as promotion was slow. He spent three years at the Equitation School at Weedon, and after service in Kurdistan was admitted to the DSO in 1933 and promoted major. Married in 1935, he fathered a son and a daughter. Though he had no p.s.c against his name, he instructed at the Staff College, Camberley, between 1936 and 1938. A colonel in 1939, he served briefly in France with the BEF at HQ 2nd Division and, having come to Brooke's notice, was CRA IV Corps after Dunkirk, and commanded first a brigade, then the Devon and Cornwall County Division, during the invasion scare of 1940–1941.

In February 1941 Allfrey was appointed to command 43rd (Wessex) division and spent the next 20 months in Southern Command training troops. However, in March 1942, as acting lieutenant general, he was placed in command of V Corps, which, that November, as part of Anderson's 1st army took part in the TORCH landings in French North Africa. Allfrey's Corps was heavily involved in the gruelling Tunisian campaign, particularly in the bitter fighting for Longstop Hill. His troops, in tandem with units from Horrocks's X Corps, were the first to enter Tunis in May 1943 and it was he who first accepted General von Arnim's surrender.

Allfrey remained as commander of V Corps during the invasions of Sicily and mainland Italy. A 'lanky artilleryman' of 'considerable charm and cheerful disposition' (Blaxland, 1977,137), and said to be 'one of the most popular officers in the British army (Horrocks, 1960, 169), he nevertheless suffered from the prejudices 8th Army men harboured towards 1st Army 'amateurs'. While Montgomery regarded him as 'very slow, and . . . inclined to bellyache', but at least 'teachable' (Hamilton, 1983, 444), Leese, Montgomery's successor as 8th Army commander, took steps to sack him (Ryder, 1987,164). In March 1944 V Corps was temporarily broken up and in August Allfrey was despatched to Egypt to command British troops there. Knighted in 1946, he remained in Egypt until 1948 when, as lieutenant general, he retired from the army.

A determined horseman, good shot and dedicated fisherman, Allfrey, in retirement, sat on the board of a brewing concern, and combined honorary regimental duties (RE and RHA) with work on the Bristol bench. He was, till his death in November 1964, DL for Gloucestershire.

ANDERSON, Major General Alexander Vass (1895–1963) CB, CMG, MBE
Born in Scotland of a military family, Anderson volunteered for service in 1914 and was commissioned in the Royal Engineers. Serving in France, he rose to the rank of captain and was mentioned in despatches.

Most of Anderson's inter-war service was in India. Awarded the MBE for his part in the Malabar campaign, 1921–1922, he was Deputy Assistant Adjutant General, India, 1934–1937. A colonel in 1940, he served as Assistant QMG, Home Forces, for the early years of the war, and had a posting in Washington as QMG with the British Joint Staff Mission before returning to England in 1943. As major general he was Chief Administrator, Western Command, in 1944, and performed War Office duties as Director of Civil Affairs until his retirement in 1946.

Anderson and his wife lived out their retirement in the Channel Islands.

ANDERSON, Lieutenant General Sir Desmond Francis
(1885–1967) KBE, CB, CMG, DSO
Born in Sussex and educated at Rugby and RMC, Sandhurst, Anderson was commissioned in the Devon Regiment in 1905. Serving as Adjutant in the East

Yorkshire Regiment at the outbreak of the First World War he was wounded, admitted to the DSO, taken on to the General Staff and married all in the same year, 1915. A brevet major by war's end, Anderson, like so many junior British officers, volunteered for service with the Allied Military Mission in North Russia in 1919.

A brevet lieutenant colonel in 1921, Anderson graduated from the Staff College, Camberley, the same year. Commander of the 1st Battalion East Yorkshire Regiment, 1927–1931, he was Assistant Quartermaster General Aldershot Command 1932–1933 and served on the staff of 5th Division 1933–34. For the next four years Anderson worked in the War Office, first as Deputy Director of Military Operations and then as Deputy Director of Military Intelligence. In 1938 he was Major General i/c Administration, Eastern Command, and at war's outbreak was made Major General General Staff, Home Forces.

Unable to impress his superiors with his fitness to command troops in the field and, apparently, unwanted at the War Office, Anderson's war years were spent training troops. Made GOC 45th Division in February 1940, he switched to the newly-formed 46th Division in Scottish Command that June. Brooke, a month later, observed it as being 'in a lamentably backward state of training' (Danchev & Todman, 2001, 95). Perhaps the situation improved as, later that year, Anderson was promoted lieutenant general and posted to command III Corps. Made commander of II Corps in late 1943, he was, in common with a number of officers, made victim of the Montgomery-induced new broom that swept through 21 Army Group in preparation for OVERLORD. He retired from the army in 1944 and was, for the next ten years, a Trustee of the Imperial War Museum.

ANDERSON, General Sir Kenneth Arthur Noel *(1891–1959) KCB, MC*
Born in India on Christmas Day 1891, Anderson was educated at Charterhouse and RMC, Sandhurst, from which he was commissioned in the Seaforth Highlanders in 1911. He served in France in the Great War, was seriously wounded during the Somme offensive and was awarded the MC. In 1918, the year he married, he served with Allenby in Palestine.

Anderson graduated from the Staff College Camberley in 1928, He served on the staff at the War Office 1929–1930 and commanded the 2nd Battalion of the Seaforths on the North-West Frontier and saw more service in Palestine as a brigadier. A staff officer at AHQ, India, 1936–1937, he was appointed to command 11th Brigade in 1938 and, as such, served with the BEF in France with Montgomery's 3rd Division. When, during the withdrawal to Dunkirk in May 1940, Montgomery was elevated to command II Corps, Anderson stepped into his place to temporarily command the Division. Mentioned in despatches and appointed CB, he was promoted major general and for the next year, with first Thorne and then Montgomery as Corps commanders, led 1st Division in its anti-invasion role. Apparently locked into Home Forces, his promotion trail was gradual but steady. As lieutenant general he commanded first VI Corps from mid-1941, II Corps from early 1942 and that summer was made GOC-in-C Eastern Command.

His appointment as GOC-in-C 1st Army, assembling for the invasion of French North Africa in November 1942, was fortuitous. Alexander, the first choice, was appointed elsewhere and Schreiber was forced to cry off through ill health. Thus it fell to Anderson to head the eastern task force in the TORCH landings. Considering his 1st Army consisted of four British brigades, the inexperienced American II Corps and assorted ill-equipped former Vichy French troops, his task, to rush 500 miles eastwards and capture Tunis, was never going to be easy. Indeed it proved very difficult. Although forward units advanced to within 12 miles of Tunis before the end of November, lack of air cover and German counter-attacks so threatened 1st Army's loose front and supply lines that Eisenhower, the supreme commander, decided to consolidate and build up the army's strength before re-launching the offensive in Tunisia in early 1943.

A series of German spoiling attacks in January and February caused such concern, even momentary panic at Kasserine, that a whispering campaign against Anderson began. Considered 'earnest but dumb' by Patton (Rolf, 2001, 33), he was, it was said, 'unable to impose his personality or a master plan on his subordinates' (Jackson, 1975, 335). Alexander, by now commander of 18th Army Group, 'disagreed [so] entirely' with Anderson's operational plans (North (ed.), 1962, 38), that he persuaded Brooke he was 'not much good' (Danchev & Todman, 2001, 384) and asked Montgomery if he could spare Horrocks to assume command of 1st Army.

In the short term nothing came of these machinations. Anderson remained as 1st Army commander until the North African campaign was brought to its victorious end in May 1943. Montgomery's 8th Army might have stolen most of the headlines, but Anderson (a 'good plain cook' as Montgomery patronizingly dubbed him) played his part in making 1st Army the stationary anvil against which German resistance was crushed. The 'relentless forward move of the Eighth Army' no more saved 'First Army from serious disaster' (Montgomery, 1958, 138) than Patton's breakout in Normandy in 1944 saved Montgomery before Caen. A big abrasive Scot averse to exhibitionism Anderson may have been, but for all his easily arrived at 'dour, fretful and humourless' reputation (Richardson, 1987, 62), Eisenhower's tribute to his 'boldness courage and stamina' stands as an interesting corrective (Eisenhower, 1948, 93). The tenacity of his pessimism may have earned him the nickname 'Sunshine' (Allfrey Diary, LHCMA), but he did as much as could realistically have been expected of him in North Africa. Knighted for his services there, he might reasonably have expected plum postings to come his way thereafter.

Returned to Britain in June 1943 and made commander-designate of 2nd Army, in preparation for the invasion of North-West Europe, Anderson was disappointed to be told that Dempsey, not he, would command the liberation army. As Montgomery favoured subordinates with whom he was familiar against those who had held command independent of his influence, Anderson was duly judged a 'dud' and passed-over (Hamilton, 1983, 527). Considered unfit to command an army, he was shunted, humiliatingly, to Southern Command in January 1944. In June he made a surreptitious visit to the Normandy bridgehead and returned 'just before effect could be given to Montgomery's order that he should be placed under arrest' (Blaxland, 1977, 267).

Made GOC-in-C East African Command in 1945, Anderson was appointed Governor and C-in-C Gibraltar in 1947. Promoted general in 1949, the same year that his only son was killed on active service in Malaya, that personal tragedy was compounded, in 1952, by the death of his daughter. Retired to the south of France and in ill-health he died in Gibraltar in 1959. As his DNB entry concludes, 'A drawing by S. Morse Brown is in the Imperial War Museum'.

APPLEYARD, Major General Kenelm Charles *(1894–1967)* CBE
Born in London and educated at St. Paul's School, Appleyard made his career and reputation as a talented engineer in the north-east of England. He worked for Parsons, at the Armstrong Whitworth armament works and was managing director at Birtley Co, Ltd. 1919–1947.

Active in the Territorial Army, Appleyard, as lieutenant-colonel, was CRE 50th (Northumbrian) Division 1931–36 and was promoted brigadier in 1939. A local major general in 1940, he was Chief Engineer to the RAF component of the BEF in France.

For the remainder of the war Appleyard was assigned to special duties within the Ministries of Labour and Works. He was, 1940–41, Director of Labour Supply and, 1941–42, with the Ministry of Works, was made Director of Emergency Works, charged with repairing and bringing back into production bomb-damaged factories. From 1942 till war's end he was Director of Opencast Coal Production and, post-war, was an adviser on regional organization.

Married in 1920, and the father of one son, Appleyard was a JP in Chester-le-Street and, from 1953 till his death in 1967 DL for the County of Durham.

ARBUTHNOTT, Viscount of, Major General Robert Keith
(1897–1966) CB, CBE, DSO, MC
Born in Inverbervie, Kincardineshire, and educated at Fettes and RMC, Sandhurst, Arbuthnott was commissioned in the Black Watch in 1915. Serving in France from 1916 he was wounded, awarded the MC and mentioned in despatches. A captain in 1924, the year he married, he attended the Staff College, Camberley, 1931–1932, and, promoted major in 1938, assumed temporary command of the 6th Battalion Black Watch in Palestine. For service there he was admitted to the DSO.

Arbuthnott spent the first four years of the Second World War with Scottish Command training troops, and it was not until September 1943 that he saw active service overseas. This was in Italy. There he commanded 198th and 11th Brigades attached to the American General Mark Clark's V Army, and in October 1944 he was made acting commander of the battle-scarred 78th Division. In that role his 'humane [and] quietly humorous leadership' (Blaxland, 1979, 223) had such a positive effect on morale that the desertion rate –

previously alarmingly high – dropped to normal proportions. As part of Keightley's XIII Corps his Division penetrated the Argenta Gap in early 1945, thus allowing V Army to break out of the mountains and enter the Lombardy Plain. He was present at the German surrender in Italy in April 1945.

Made substantive major general and appointed CB and CBE in 1945, Arbuthnott was Chief of the British Military Mission to Egypt 1946–1947. He was CGS Scottish Command, 1948–1949 and commanded the 51st Highland Division and Highland District from 1949 until his retirement in 1952.

A local JP and created DL for Kincardineshire in 1959, Arbuthnott inherited the viscountcy from his cousin in 1960. He was Colonel of the Black Watch from 1960 to 1964.

ARCEDECKNE-BUTLER, Major General St John Desmond
(1896–1959), CBE, FRSA
Born in Hampshire and educated in the United States, Switzerland, RMC, Sandhurst, and École Supérieure d'Électricité, Arcedeckne-Butler was commissioned in the Royal Munster Fusiliers in 1915 and served in France and Belgium. Transferring to the Royal Sussex Regiment in 1922, he transferred again the next year to the Royal Signals, completing his military higher education in Paris. He married in 1929 and fathered two sons and a daughter.

Superintendent of the Signals Experimental Establishment 1934–1939, Arcedeckne-Butler was promoted colonel and served on the staff at GHQ in France with the BEF. Thereafter he was bound by staff work at the War Office. Promoted major general, he sat on the war cabinet's Radio Board and was Deputy Director Ministry of Supply 1941–1946, when, made CBE, he retired from the army

Resident on the family estate in County Wexford and a member of the Irish Broadcasting Advisory Committee, Arcedeckne-Butler died in a Dublin nursing home in 1959.

ARCHIBALD, Major General Sidney Charles Manley
(1890–1973), MC
Commissioned in the Royal Artillery in 1910, Archibald's First War service was in France, where he was awarded the MC.

Married in 1925 and a captain in 1926, Archibald attended the Staff College, Camberley, 1926–1927, and served on the staff of Northern Command, India, 1929–1930. He attended the Imperial Defence College in 1933 and served on the staff at the War Office 1934–1937. A colonel in 1937, he was an Assistant QMG in Anti-Aircraft Command in 1938 before commanding 34th AA Group (TA) in 1939.

Promoted major general in 1940, Archibald served with Home Forces. GOC 11th Anti-Aircraft Division, 1941–1943, he was Adviser to Canada on Anti-Aircraft Defences from 1943 until his retirement from the army in 1944.

Archibald, one of those officers of whom very few personal details are known, was Colonel Commandant Royal Artillery from 1952 to 1958.

ARMITAGE, General Sir Charles Clement *(1885–1973), KCB, CMG, DSO*
Born in York and educated at Marlborough and RMA, Woolwich, Armitage was commissioned in the Royal Artillery in 1902 and served briefly in the South African War. As a captain and graduate of the Staff College, Camberley, in 1914, he saw war service in France and Belgium, was admitted to the DSO in 1916 and mentioned in despatches seven times. Married in 1915, he fathered two sons and one daughter.

Numerous staff and regimental postings led to his appointment as Commandant School of Artillery, Larkhill, 1927–29, and command of 7th Infantry Brigade 1929–32. His first wife, having died in 1931, he married again in 1933. Promoted major general in 1934, and Commandant of the Staff College, Camberley, for the next two years, he was GOC 1st Division 1936–1938 and was knighted that year. Something of a victim of the Hore-Belisha campaign to promote younger and, supposedly, more radical-minded men, he was posted to India. He remained there, until his retirement in 1942, as Master General of the Ordnance.

Retired to Lechlade, Armitage was made DL for Gloucestershire in 1950.

ARNOLD, Major General Allan Cholmondeley *(1893–1962), CIE, CBE, MC*
The son of an Indian Army officer, Arnold was educated at Wellington and RMC, Sandhurst. Commissioned in the Middlesex Regiment in 1912, he saw war service in France, was awarded the MC in 1917 and was mentioned thrice in despatches. Volunteering for service in North Russia in 1919, he was awarded the OBE and mentioned in despatches.

After attending the Staff College, Camberley, 1920–1921, Arnold spent much of his subsequent career in India. He took part in operations on the North-West Frontier 1921–1922 and, though Deputy Assistant Adjutant General, Scottish Command, 1927–1930, he returned to India to command the 1st Battalion of the Royal Fusiliers engaged in punitive expeditions into Waziristan. A colonel in 1938, he was Military Attaché at the British Embassy in Ankara from 1940–1942, from where he was posted back to India. Awarded the CBE in 1941 and promoted major general in 1943, he played an important part in providing relief for the Bengal famine. He joined the government of India Food Department in 1946.

Retired from the army in 1947, Arnold worked for the Ministry of Food between 1949 and 1954. Subsequently he and his wife lived in Somerset.

AUCHINLECK, Field Marshal Sir Claude John Eyre
(1884–1981) GCB, GCIE, CSI, DSO, OBE
Born in Aldershot and raised by his widowed mother in straitened circumstances, Auchinleck was educated at Wellington, where as a scholarship boy 'he acquired an indifference to personal comfort that remained with him for the rest of his life' (Heathcote, 1999, 29). He attended RMC, Sandhurst, and, after some months on the unattached list, was commissioned in the 62nd Punjabi Regiment in 1904.

A captain in 1914, Auchinleck saw war service in Egypt, Aden and, from 1916, Mesopotamia. Appointed to the DSO in 1917, thrice mentioned in despatches and awarded the OBE in 1919 for service in Kurdistan, Auchinleck returned to India as a brevet lieutenant colonel. There he married in 1921, graduated from the Staff College, Quetta, and attended the Imperial Defence College in 1927. From 1930 to 1932 he was an instructor at Quetta and the following year assumed command of the Peshawar Brigade stationed on the North-West Frontier. Having acquired a solid military reputation and promoted major general in 1936, Auchinleck was made Deputy Chief of the General Staff in India. Intent on modernization, he pursued a policy of mechanization with vigour. Free from snobbery, able to listen and a keen talent-spotter, he impressed the visiting Chatfield committee with his proposals to phase out British officers by suitable Indian replacements

Tall and athletic, indeed 'handsome and charming' (Ranfurly, 1998, 168), 'The Auk' looked the part. Moreover, in an India 'where everybody watched everyone else' (Greacan, 1989, 140) he was as popular as he was highly regarded. Recalled to London in late 1939 and made commander of IV Corps, then assembling before being sent to join the BEF in France, he was posted instead to Norway in May 1940. There, as an expert in mountain warfare, he replaced Mackesy as C-in-C land forces and directed the assault on Narvik, the success of which was futile as the port was evacuated within a week of its capture. His subsequent description of the British troops he had commanded as 'callow' and effeminate', unlike the French, who were 'real soldiers' (Warner, 1982, 72), did not please Churchill.

Created commander of V Corps in June 1940 and succeeding Brooke as GOC Southern Command the next month, it fell to Auchinleck to prepare defences at points considered most vulnerable to German invasion. Montgomery, then a subordinate, was, typically, unable to recall agreeing with his GOC on anything at this time (Montgomery, 1958, 62), but, promoted general in November and sent back to India as C-in-C, we may infer that Auchinleck had impressed his seniors. Indian formations were already playing a major role in operations in East Africa and the western desert, and, with Home Forces heavily committed to an anti-invasion role, Auchinleck's brief was to enlarge the Indian Army both for internal security purposes and deployment elsewhere.

In this sense the pro-Nazi Raschid Ali rebellion in Iraq in early 1941 provided opportunity. Whereas Wavell, the C-in-C Middle East, considered intervention in Iraq to be politically undesirable and too large an undertaking for the forces at his disposal, Auchinleck's readiness to act quickly and send troops from India to southern Iraq helped crush the rebellion. When in June the Western Desert Force failed in its attempt to relieve Tobruk (BATTLEAXE), Churchill decided to sack Wavell and replace him with Auchinleck, a man 'of a fresh mind and a hitherto untaxed personal energy' (Churchill, 1950, 237).

The Middle East was a vast command, though in the public imagination the only area that mattered was the western desert. What had begun in 1940 almost as a colonial war, when Italian forces invaded Egypt, had become by mid-1941 the major theatre of Britain's war effort. Auchinleck's responsibility was great. No less heavy was the weight of Churchill's expectations. His 'splendid talents' were widely recognized. But so too was his supposed inability to 'understand Winston' (Moran, 1968,70).

That Auchinleck's tenure of Middle East Command lasted little over a year, with his dismissal in August 1942 coming at a time when Axis forces stood a mere 60 miles from Alexandria, suggests not merely that he disappointed Churchill but that he had failed in his command. Declining the offer of the new Iraq-Persia Command he returned to India where, languishing unemployed for nearly a year, he succeeded Wavell as C-in-C. Never again to command troops in battle, his fate from mid-1943 was to preside over the expansion of the Indian Army for the rest of the war, then witness its slide into impotence and disintegration upon independence and partition. Having divorced his wife in 1946 on the grounds of her adultery, his wish to stay on as supreme commander of Indian and Pakistan land forces was frustrated by Mountbatten, the Viceroy, who asked him to resign in September 1947.

Expressed in these bald terms Auchinleck's career trajectory, with its sudden rise and just as sudden fall, invites brief and no more than polite summary. Yet while failed generals, they say, should not be pitied, the verdict that Auchinleck, having had every opportunity to succeed, proved not quite up to the mark, is, in some quarters, stubbornly resisted. An extraordinary feature of the post-war 'battle of the memoirs' is the manner in which an alternative narrative of 'The Auk' has developed. In this version he is remembered not merely as 'one of the most underestimated soldiers of the war' (Boatner, 1996, 18), but also as a 'flaw[ed] . . . great man' (Barnett, 1983, 135), the nearest British equivalent to a Second World War tragic hero.

Promotion to Field Marshal was, in wartime, used by Churchill as a form of consolation for disappointment. That it was the Attlee government, not Churchill's, which bestowed the honour on Auchinleck in 1946 was significant in itself and registered officialdom's guilty conscience over the way 'The Auk' had been treated. Accepting an enhanced knighthood but declining the offer of a peerage, he characteristically wrote no memoirs. Such reticence has tended to increase and not diminish his reputation.

Auchinleck's 'failure' in North Africa remains hotly debated. This stems in part from a peculiarly Anglo-centric preoccupation with the desert war, but reflects too a tendency to dramatize events in terms of personality. Depending on what is read and the reader's temperament, Auchinleck can be dismissed as the commander who woefully mis-read Ultra intelligence and who, through interfering with his field commanders' dispositions, reduced 8th Army to a state of bewildered near defeat. Alternatively he can be elevated as the real victor of Alamein. The history of the desert war as siphoned through the Montgomery filter adheres to the former viewpoint, whereas those repelled by Montgomery's relentless egomania hold to the latter position. To them Auchinleck of the jutting jaw and piercing blue eyes remains the quintessential soldier's soldier, a man 'impossible not to like and admire' (Kennedy, 1957, 159). In the crisis month of July 1942, after 8th Army's defeat at Gazala and the loss of Tobruk, he assumed command in the field and kept his head sufficiently to save Egypt and leave Rommel 'outwitted as well as outfought' before Alamein (Barnett in Carver (ed.), 1976, 264). Hence, Auchinleck's supporters maintain, he laid the basis for eventual victory in North Africa.

Much attention has been paid to Auchinleck's relations with Churchill, though much less to the equally significant culture clash that developed within Middle East Command during his months as C-in-C. For the command Auchinleck left was very different in size and composition from that which he had inherited. With formations drawn from Home Forces beginning to predominate over 'old desert hands' drawn from all parts of the Commonwealth, British officers came to resent a command set-up so heavily biased towards the Indian Army. Hence Auchinleck's inability to select the right subordinates became a 'fact'; the fault lying less with those field commanders he dismissed than with those Indian Army officers he retained. One such was 'Chink' Dorman-Smith, who, allegedly, so 'mesmerized' the C-in-C with his 'fertile imagination' (Carver, 1989, 127), that, if Brooke's diary recollections are to be believed, Auchinleck's allowing himself to 'fall too deeply under Chink's influence . . . became . . . the major cause of his downfall' (Danchev & Todman, 2001, 224). The Middle East Command clear-out of August 1942, the so-called 'Cairo purge', represented many things, not least the triumph of Home Forces over the Indian Army. Within five years, of course, the Indian Army to which Auchinleck had devoted 44 years of his life had ceased to exist.

Any attempt at assessing Auchinleck's record as a wartime commander is made difficult in that the post-war 'battle of the memoirs' (from which he held himself aloof) has rendered him less a creature of flesh and blood than an item of historiography. Whatever his qualities and defects, he has been constructed as the personification of historical revisionism. Those who prefer their victors straight celebrate the achievements of Churchill, Brooke and Montgomery. Conversely Auchinleck remains an enduringly attractive figure among those for whom heroism is compounded of quieter, more subtle qualities.

Outliving most of his contemporaries and finding himself something of a legend by the end of his long life, Auchinleck received many honorary degrees, deposited his papers with Manchester University and, in 1968, left England for Marrakesh. There, attended by a batman-servant, he lived unpretentiously until his death.

AUSTIN, Major General Arthur Bramston (1893–1967), CB, FDSRCS

Born in Essex and educated at Bishop Stortford and London University, Austin was House Surgeon at the Royal Dental Hospital in 1915 and commissioned in the Army Dental Corps that year. War service took him to France and Macedonia. Married in 1918, there were two daughters from the marriage.

A captain in 1919, a steady climb up the promotion ladder saw Austin a colonel in 1940, where he was Deputy-Director of Dental Service with the BEF in France. Assistant-Director Dental Services, Aldershot Command, 1940–41 and South-Eastern Command 1941–42; he was promoted major general in 1942 and served as Director Army Dental Service at the War Office until his retirement in 1948. Appointed CB in 1946, he was honorary Dental Surgeon to the King and Colonel Commandant Army Dental Corps 1951–1958.

Retired in Wiltshire, Austin was a Salisbury City Councillor until his death.

B

BAILLON, Major General Joseph Aloysius *(1895–1951), CB, CBE, MC*
Educated at King Edward VI School Birmingham, Baillon volunteered in 1914 and was commissioned in the South Staffordshire Regiment in 1915. Serving in France he was awarded the MC in 1918.

Regimental duties between the wars were as various as promotion was slow. Baillon married in 1925 and from 1931 to 1932 attended the Staff College, Camberley. A lieutenant colonel in 1939, he was a staff officer with the Sudan Defence Force 1940–1941. Promoted brigadier in 1942 and Deputy Director of Military Training, Middle East Command, he was regarded by Auchinleck as 'full of energy and ideas' (Dill, 2nd Acc., 4, LHCMA). He was appointed CGS in the newly-created Persia and Iraq Command where he served under 'Jumbo' Wilson. Promoted major general in 1943, he was CGS Middle East Command, again under Wilson, until the end of the war.

Made Director of Organization at the War Office in 1946, Baillon commanded Aldershot District from 1947 until his retirement from the army in 1949. Thereafter he lived in Ireland and was a director of a Cork-based brewing concern.

BAIRD, General Sir Harry Beauchamp Douglas
(1877–1963), KCB, CMG, CIE, DSO
Educated at Clifton and RMC, Sandhurst, Baird entered the Indian Army in 1897 and was gazetted into Probyn's Horse (the Bengal Lancers) in 1899. A major in 1915 and married the same year, his First War service was in France, Mesopotamia and Palestine. Admitted to the DSO in 1915, he commanded a brigade 1916–1918 and was mentioned in despatches six times.

Having campaigned in the third Afghan War in 1919, Baird, a lieutenant colonel in 1920, commanded the 28th Punjabi Regiment that year and was Colonel Commandant Zhob Brigade Area 1920–1923. Commandant of the Senior Officers' School, Belgaum, 1920–1924, he was, as major general, Deputy Assistant QMG, Northern Command, India, 1929–1930. He held District commands in Kohat and the Deccan over the next four years; his wife died in 1935 and he was knighted the same year. He was appointed GOC-in-C Eastern Command, India, in 1936.

Retired in 1940, as one of the longest serving officers in the Indian Army, Baird returned to his native Scotland. Commander of the Morayshire Home Guard 1940–1942, he was also Colonel of the South Lancashire Regiment 1940–1947.

BAKER, Lieutenant General Sir William Henry Goldney
(1888–1964), KCIE, CB, DSO, OBE
The son of a Devon clergyman, Baker was educated in New Zealand, Bedford School and RMC Sandhurst. Gazetted into the 13th Duke of Connaught's Lancers (Indian Army) in 1910, he served in France 1914–1918, attached to the Connaught Rangers. He was mentioned in despatches and admitted to the DSO.

Except for spells in England attending the Staff College, Camberley, 1921–1922, and the Imperial Defence College in 1933, Barker spent most of his military career in India. Promotion was steady with numerous brevetcies. Married in 1924, a major in 1925, he transferred to Probyn's Horse (the Bengal Lancers) in 1934 and was a lieutenant colonel in 1935. He was mentioned in despatches in the Afghan War (1919) and again after the Waziristan campaign of 1937, when he was made OBE. Commander of Delhi Brigade Area from 1939–1940, he was promoted major general in 1940 and the next year was appointed Adjutant General in India.

Knighted upon his retirement in 1944, Baker and his wife returned to England where they settled in his native Devon.

BANNATYNE, Major General Neil Charles *(1880–1970), CB, CIE*
Born in Scotland and educated at Cheltenham and RMC, Sandhurst, Bannatyne was commissioned in 1899 and gazetted into the 128th Pioneers (Indian Army) in 1900. Married in 1917, he was Deputy Adjutant and QMG, Western Command, India, 1928–1931, and commanded the Abbottadbad Brigade, 1931–1933. Promoted major general, he was Military Secretary Army Headquarters India, from 1936 until he retired from the army in 1940.

Staying on in India for the remainder of the war, Bannatyne was Chief Censor, 1940–1942, and Deputy Chief Commissioner for the Indian Red Cross, 1942–46. He lived out a very long retirement in an Eastbourne hotel.

BARBER, Lieutenant General Sir Colin Muir
(1897–1964) KBE, CB, DSO, DL
Born of Scottish parents on the Wirral and educated at Uppingham, Barber's First War service was in France with the Liverpool Scottish and later the 1st Battalion of the Cameron Highlanders. In India for most of the 1920s, he married and attended the Staff College, Quetta, 1929–1930.

From 1931–1936 he held a succession of staff appointments in Scottish and Southern Commands, and served in Palestine before the outbreak of war. Then, as part of the 51st (Highland) Division, 'Tiny' Barber (at six foot nine inches he was one of the tallest officers in the British army) commanded the 4th Battalion Cameron Highlanders in France with the BEF. Awarded the DSO for his part in the division's retreat across France south of the Somme, the brigade to which he was attached was the only part of the Division not to be captured at St Valéry in June 1940.

Made commander of 46th Brigade in 1941, Barber was GOC 54th Division 1941–1943, and commanded a brigade in the 15th Division which landed in France in June 1944. After hard fighting in Normandy he had, in August 1944, the satisfaction of being promoted to command 'the most effective and best led infantry division in 21st Army Group' (D'Este, 1994, 239), when the GOC, Macmillan, was wounded. He held this command until war's end, having taken his division through France and Belgium and across the Rhine into North Germany.

In June 1945 Barber was appointed to command the Highland District (Scottish Command), and, 1949–1952, he was, as lieutenant general, Director of Infantry and Military Training at the War Office. He was also GOC-in-C Scottish Command and Governor of Edinburgh Castle from 1952 until his retirement in 1955.

Retiring to Yorkshre with his second wife, Barber, a keen golfer and first-class shot, was DL for York in 1959.

BARKER, General Sir Evelyn Hugh *(1894–1983), KCB, KBE, DSO, MC*

The youngest son of a major general, Barker was educated at Wellington and RMC, Sandhurst. Commissioned in the King's Royal Rifle Corps in 1913, his First War service was in France, Salonika and various Balkan countries. A captain in 1916, he was wounded, awarded the MC in 1917, admitted to the DSO in 1918 and was twice mentioned in despatches. Dropping rank at war's end, he served on the staff of the Allied Military Mission in South Russia.

Brief staff assignments at the War Office and with Southern Command were followed by attendance at Staff College, Camberley, 1927–1928. Thereafter 'Bubbles' Barker filled various regimental posts. A brigade major in the early 1930s, he commanded the 2nd Battalion KRRC from 1936–1938, first in Palestine and then at home with the Mobile Division. Over the next two years he commanded 10th Infantry Brigade which, as part of 4th Division with the BEF, was sent to France in 1939. Ever 'cheerful and brimming over with energy' (Horrocks, 1960, 76), he was awarded the CBE in 1940 and spent the next two years as GOC 54th Division with Home Forces.

Made commander of the 49th (West Riding) Division in 1943, Barker re-designed the divisional symbol and led his formation in the campaign in Normandy. Promoted lieutenant general in November 1944, he commanded VIII Corps of the British Liberation Army during the Rhine crossing and took the surrender of Dönitz's skeleton government in Flensburg in May 1945.

Knighted that year, in which he served as military governor of Schleswig-Holstein, he was GOC-in-C British Forces in Palestine and Transjordan in 1946. Controversially he forbade his officers 'fraternizing with Jews' in the wake of the King David Hotel terrorist outrage. GOC-in-C Eastern Command 1947–1949, he retired from the army in 1950.

Holding numerous honorary posts in his retirement, 'Bubbles' Barker was DL for Bedfordshire from 1952–1967.

BARKER, Lieutenant General Michael George Henry
(1884–1960), CB, DSO

The son of a clergyman, educated at Malvern and commissioned in the Lincolnshire regiment in 1903, after brief service in the South African War with the militia, Barker was a captain in 1914, the year he married. His First War service was in France. Admitted to the DSO in 1917 (bar 1918), he was a brevet lieutenant colonel in 1919 and was one of the first post-war batch of officers to attend the Staff College, Camberley.

Barker seemed destined for great things. A nice combination of staff and regimental duties saw him rise from commanding a battalion to brigadier's rank by 1930. An instructor at the Senior Officers' School, Belgaum, in the early 1930s, he was brought home and promoted major-general in 1935. From 1936–1938 he was Director of Resources and Recruiting at the War Office, and GOC-in-C British forces in Palestine and Transjordan 1938–1939. He was promoted lieutenant general and assigned to Aldershot Command in early 1940.

When Dill was recalled to London to serve as Vice CIGS in April 1940, Barker assumed command of the BEF's I Corps in France. With less than a month to familiarize himself with his surroundings before the German invasion of France and the Low Countries began, Barker had neither the time nor, perhaps, the fitness to adapt himself to the role. Said to be 'neither liked nor respected by the officers who served under him' (Colville, 1972, 180), he 'cracked under the strain of battle' (Hamilton, 1982, 355), became 'very tired . . . [and] rattled much too easily' (Bond (ed.), 1972, 322), and was, by the end of May, 'completely useless'. Regarded as expendable and designated by Gort as the senior officer who would surrender British forces trapped in the Dunkirk perimeter, a change of mind saw Barker bundled on to a destroyer and sent home.

Barker's military career was finished. Though still an impressive-looking soldier, War Office opinion seemed at one with Montgomery's insubordinate post-Dunkirk pronouncement that 'only a madman would give a Corps to Barker' (Hamilton, 2001, 806). After briefly holding the appointment of GOC-in-C Aldershot Command, Barker was retired from the army on health grounds in 1941. That same year he served as a Deputy Regional Commissioner for Civil Defence in the London District, but ill-health forced him to leave that post before the end of the year.

Retired to Essex, Barker sat out the rest of the war performing no higher duty than honorary colonel of the York and Lancaster Regiment. He was DL for the county in 1946 and his death in 1960 received only cursory acknowledgment.

BARKER, Major General Richard Ernest *(1888–1962), CBE*
A New Zealander, Barker was born in Christchurch and educated at Wanganui School and Sherborne (Dorset). After joining the New Zealand Mounted Rifles in 1907, he was commissioned in the South Lancashire Regiment in 1911. First War service was with the Indian Signal Corps in Mesopotamia 1915–1918.

Barker was Political Officer in Mesopotamia, Kurdistan and Persia 1918–1920 and then saw service in Ireland 1920–1922. Married in 1920 and transferring to the Royal Signals in 1921, he was a colonel in 1936. Chief Signal Officer in Palestine 1936–1937, he was promoted major general in 1940 and appointed Signal Officer-in-Chief Middle East.

It was in North Africa that Auchinleck, for all his alleged inability to select the right subordinates or root out inefficiency, became dissatisfied with Barker's performance. He was, Auchinleck wrote to Dill, 'simply not up to it' (Dill, 2nd ac., 11, LHCMA). Made CSO Scottish Command in 1942, he was appointed CSO Home Forces in 1944 prior to his retirement from the army that year.

Returning to New Zealand after the war, Barker took up farming in his native South Island.

BARNSLEY, Major General Robert Eric *(1886–1968), CB, MC, MB, BCh.*
Born in Birmingham and educated at Rydal, Cambridge University and St Bartholomew's Hospital, Barnsely's medical training led to his call-up into the forces in 1916. He served in France, Salonika and, 1919–1921, with the Army of the Black Sea. Mentioned in despatches and awarded the MC in that campaign, he spent most of the 1920s at the Royal Army Medical College.

Deputy Director of Army Medical Services in Egypt 1934–1937 and Assistant Director Medical Services, Northern Command, in 1937, Barnsley's early war service was in East Africa. Made Deputy Director Medical Services, Southern Command, in 1941, he retired from the army in 1946.

An honorary colonel of the Territorial Army, Barnsley was also Colonel Commandant of the Royal Army Medical Corps 1948–1951.

BARSTOW, Major General Arthur Edward *(1888–1942) CIE, MC*
Born of military family and educated at Bradfield and RMC, Sandhurst, Barstow was gazetted into the 11th Sikh Regiment, Indian Army, in 1909. A captain in 1915, his First War service was mainly in France where he was wounded, mentioned in despatches and awarded the MC in 1917.

Inter-war 'real soldiering' was, for Barstow, real enough. He served in operations in Afghanistan in 1919, Kurdistan in 1923 and on the North-West Frontier in 1930. He was mentioned in despatches in all three campaigns, and in the meantime attended the Staff College, Camberley, 1924–1925. He attended the Imperial Defence College in 1934 and commanded the 2nd Battalion 11th Sikh Regiment 1933–1935. A colonel in 1938 (he married in 1927), he was again mentioned in despatches and, in 1941, made CIE for his part in military operations chasing Haji Mizra Ali Khan, better known as the Fakir of Ipi, in Waziristan.

By this time war had broken out in the Far East. Promoted major general and placed in command of 9th Indian Division, Barstow fought the Japanese in Malaya. In the demoralizing conditions of the retreat, he had his share of ambiguous orders to cope with, and while a series of misunderstandings resulted in one of his brigades being badly mauled in the defence of the Kuantan airfield, another was surrounded and cut off at Layang Layang in Johore. It was there that he was killed in a Japanese ambush in January 1942 while trying to contact one of his brigade HQs. Regarded by Percival as an able commander and one of the few senior officers capable of dealing with the Australian general, Gordon Bennett, the division he had commanded nevertheless suffered a 'bad defeat' (Warren, 2002, 291), which the circumstances of his death – he was one of the few British generals killed in action in the Second World War – tended to obscure.

BARTHOLOMEW, General Sir William Henry
(1877- 1962), GCB, CMG, DSO
Born in Wiltshire and educated at Newton College and RMA, Woolwich, Bartholomew was commissioned in the Royal Artillery in 1897. A graduate of the Staff College, Quetta, in 1910, he married in 1912 and saw First War service as a staff officer in France and Palestine where, with XX Corps, he was BGGS to the Egyptian Expeditionary Force.

Admitted to the DSO in 1917, Bartholomew commanded the 6th Infantry Brigade 1923–1926 and was Director of Recruiting at the War Office 1927–1928. Promoted major-general, he was Commandant of the Imperial Defence College 1929–31, Director of Military Operations at the War Office 1931–1933 and Inspector of Artillery 1933–1934. He then moved on to what should have been the culmination of the career of 'one of the best minds on the General Staff in the inter-war period' (Bond, 1977, 55), Chief of the General Staff in India 1934–1937.

Promoted general in 1937, 'Barty' Bartholomew returned to Britain and, amidst rumours that he was to be made Adjutant General, took up instead the kind of appointment designed to ease him towards retirement, GOC-in-C Northern Command. He held that post until 1940 when, in order to make way for younger generals, he returned from France, accepted a step-up in the knighthood and retired. He did, however, chair a War Office committee convened to prepare an analysis of the BEF's fighting record in France. Several tactical recommendations were made, though the report was 'not fundamentally radical' (French, 200, 189), and possibly over-estimated operational mobility at the expense of fire-power.

North-East Regional Commissioner for Civil Defence for the rest of the war, Bartholomew finally retired to his home at Amesbury in Wiltshire in 1945.

BASSET, Major General Richard Augustin Marriott
(1891–1954), CB, CBE, MC
The son of a clergymen and educated at Marlborough, Basset was commissioned in the Queen's (West Surrey) Regiment in 1911. Married in 1914 and a captain in 1915, he was Adjutant to his regiment's 6th Battalion in France,

served on the divisional staff, was twice mentioned in despatches and was awarded the MC in 1917.

After attending the Staff College, Camberley, in 1920, Basset was promoted major in 1925 and lieutenant colonel in 1933 after three years' service as a Deputy Assistant Adjutant General at the War Office. He commanded the 1st Battalion of the Queen's in Gibraltar, was QMG for the 5th Division at Catterick in 1937 and served as Deputy Adjutant and QMG, Northern Command, 1937–1940. DA and QMG at GHQ in France with the BEF, he was mentioned in despatches and awarded the CBE after the campaign. He later served as DA and QMG Home Forces, and with Middle East Command.

Retired from the army in 1946, with the requisite CB to his name, Basset died at his home in Surrey after a long illness.

BASTYAN, Lieutenant General Sir Edric Montague
(1903–1980), KCMG, KCVO, KBE, CB
Of military family and educated at West Buckland and RMC, Sandhurst, Bastyan was commissioned in the Sherwood Foresters in 1923. A captain in the West Yorkshire Regiment in 1935, he attended the Staff College, Camberley, 1936–1937, and, with the Royal Irish Fusiliers, served in Palestine 1938–1939, where he was mentioned in despatches.

A major in 1940, Bastyan spent the first four years of the war in North Africa and Italy where, in January 1944, he came to the attention of 8th Army Commander, Leese, who appointed him to his staff as editor of Eighth Army News. Highly regarded by Leese as 'intelligent and experienced' (Ryder, 1987, 149), 'Dricky' Bastyan became a fixture on Leese's staff, becoming Chief Administrative Officer for Eighth Army.

Mentioned in despatches and with an OBE under his belt, the newly-married Bastyan was one of the large cluster of staff officers Leese took with him to South-East Asia at the end of 1944. There he was Major General i/c Administration for Allied Land Forces, and, outlasting Leese in that theatre, he played an 'outstanding' role in 14th Army's victory in Burma (Slim, 1986, 385).

Returning to England in 1946, Bastyan had a long and successful post-war career. He was an instructor at the Imperial Defence College in 1946, was Major General i/c Administration BAOR 1946–1948, and was Director of Staff Duties at the War Office 1950–1952. He commanded 53rd Welsh Infantry Division for the next three years, and from 1955 to 1957 was Vice Adjutant General at the War Office. Knighted and promoted lieutenant general in 1957, he commanded British forces in Hong Kong until his retirement in 1960.

A keen amateur artist Bastyan, having married an Australian, settled in that country. He was Governor of South Australia 1961–1968 and Tasmania 1968–1974.

BATEMAN, Major General Donald Roland Edwin Rowan
(1901–1969), CIE, DSO, OBE
Educated at Dulwich College and RMC, Sandhurst, Bateman entered the

Indian Army in 1920 and was gazetted into the 10th Baluch Regiment. With his fair share of operational experience in punitive expeditions along the North-West Frontier, he married in 1930, attended the Staff College, Quetta, 1933–1934 and was a battalion commander at war's beginning in 1939.

Commanding 9th Indian Infantry Brigade in the 4th Indian Division in the Middle East and Abyssinia, Bateman was admitted to the DSO in 1940 and, in 1942, was Senior Staff Officer with 4th Indian Division. Commander of 5th Indian Infantry Brigade, 1942–1943, he campaigned in Tunisia and Italy and had a bar added to his DSO. Promoted major general in 1944, he returned to India, where, in 1945, he was Director of Military Training, GHQ India. One of the last British soldiers to leave the sub-continent, he commanded Bombay Area until his retirement from the army in 1948.

BEAK, Major General Daniel Marcus William *(1891–1967)* VC, DSO, MC

A 'legendary figure' about whom surprisingly little is known, Beak served for most of the First World War with the Royal Naval Division. Awarded the MC and VC in France, he transferred to the Royal Scots Fusiliers in 1918 and was admitted to the DSO in 1918.

Transferring to the King's (Liverpool) Regiment in 1932, Beak commanded the 1st Battalion South Lancashire Regiment 1939–40. He was made commander of 12th Brigade in 1940. Ironside thought him 'the most extraordinary man [giving] a feeling of great energy and fire' (Macleod and Kelly, 1962, 375). After promotion to acting major general and brief service as GOC Malta in 1942, Beak dropped rank to brigadier in order to command 151st Brigade in Nichols's 50th Division which, as part of 8th Army, was set to invade Tunisia from Libya.

In the assault on the Mareth Line in March 1943, Beak's brigade was involved in the attack in the centre where the small bridgehead, having been gained at heavy cost, was pinched out by fierce German counter-attacks. The fault probably lay higher up the chain of command, but, for all that Montgomery could claim 'we recovered quickly and knocked the enemy out with a "left hook"' (Montgomery, 1958, 150), he made sure scapegoats were found for the initial reverse. Both Beak and 'Crasher' Nichols were relieved of their commands.

How Beak lived out the rest of the war, or indeed the rest of his life, after retirement from the army in 1945, is not known.

BEANLAND, Major General Douglas *(1893–1963)* CIE, OBE

Born in Yorkshire and educated at Marlborough and RMC, Sandhurst, Beanland was commissioned on the unattached list and was gazetted into the 22nd Punjab Regiment, Indian Army, in 1913. Adjutant at the Cadet College, Quetta, 1918–1919, he served as an instructor at Quetta 1919–1924, before becoming a student there 1927–1928. His first wife died in 1919 and he married again in 1922.

Deputy Assistant Adjutant and QMG Burma District 1931–1933, Beanland commanded the 10th Battalion of the 14th Punjab Regiment 1938–1940 and, as brigadier, commanded line of communication troops in the Eastern Army. In 1945 he was made Major General i/c Administration, North-Western Army, and from 1945 until his retirement in 1947 he was Deputy QMG in India.

Retired to Buckinghamshire, Beanland's second marriage was dissolved in 1953 and he married again that year.

BEARD, Major General Edmund Charles (1894–1974), CB, CBE, MC

Educated at Marlborough and Oxford University, 'Paddy' Beard was commissioned in the Royal Irish Regiment in 1914. His First War service was at Gallipoli and Salonika, in Palestine and in France. Mentioned in despatches and wounded, he was awarded the MC in 1917.

Transferred to the Prince of Wales's Volunteers in 1922, the year he married, Beard was a staff captain in India for the next four years and attended the Staff College, Camberley 1927–1928. After a period on the staff of Southern Command, he was Brigade Major 9th Infantry Brigade 1930–1933 and for the next five years served on the staff at the War Office. Transferring to the Duke of Wellington's Regiment in 1937, he commanded the 1st Battalion in 1939.

Assistant Adjutant and QMG with the 44th Division in France with the BEF, Beard commanded 133rd Infantry Brigade in England 1940–1942 and was BGS Home Forces 1942–1943. Promoted major general that year, he held area command in India until 1946 when he retired from the army

A keen sportsman who excelled at golf, Beard was Colonel of the South Lancashire Regiment 1948–1957. His eldest son was killed in Malaya in 1952.

BEAUMONT-NESBITT, Major General Frederick George
(1893–1971), CVO, CBE, MC

Of Anglo-Irish parentage, Beaumont-Nesbitt was educated at Eton and RMC, Sandhurst. Commissioned in the Grenadier Guards in 1912, his First War service was in France where he held a number of staff posts and was awarded the MC in 1917. A Francophile, he was seconded to teach English in a French military school 1920–1921, was later Adjutant to the Grenadier Guards and served as a staff officer at the War Office during which time he married for the second time. Returning to his regiment, he commanded the 2nd Battalion Grenadier Guards 1932–1935, and was from 1936–1938 Military Attaché at the British Embassy in Paris.

As someone who knew the French army as well as anyone, 'Paddy' Beaumont-Nesbitt became a key figure in preparing the British army for its impending continental commitment. Deputy Director Military Intelligence at the War Office 1938–1939, he was Director of Military Intelligence 1939–1940. Described as 'tall and polite', with 'his crisp moustache brushed up' (Cloake, 1985, 67), he was credited with being very bright. After a brief period as Military Attaché in Washington, he was promoted major general and, from 1941 to 1945, served on the General Staff in the Middle East, North Africa and Italy.

Retired from the Army in 1945, Beaumont-Nesbitt was, for a while, liaison officer on Field Marshal Alexander's staff, and Gentleman Usher to the Queen 1959–1967.

BECK, Major General Edward Archibald *(1880–1974). CB, DSO*
The son of a colonel and educated at Wellington and RMC, Sandhurst, Beck was commissioned in the Royal Scots Fusiliers in 1900. He served in the South African War and in the Egyptian Army from 1909 to 1912. A captain in 1914 he married in 1915 and commanded a battalion by war's end, having been mentioned in despatches six times and admitted to the DSO in 1916.

A graduate of the Staff College, Camberley, in 1919, and a colonel in 1923, Beck was Commandant of the Small Arms School, Hythe, for four years from 1925. A battalion commander (KOYLI) from 1929, he was engaged in operations on the North-West Frontier 1930–1931 and was an instructor at the Senior Officers' School, Sheerness, from 1932 to 1933. He served on the staff of Scottish Command 1933–1934 and commanded 3rd Infantry Brigade, Aldershot, 1935–1936. Promoted major general in 1936, he was Director of Personnel Services at the War Office 1938–1940, and for a three-month spell in 1940 commanded 9th Division which, that August, was re-designated 51st (Highland) Division.

Retired in June 1940, Beck commanded the Perthshire Home Guard for the rest of the war. He was County Commandant Perthshire Cadets 1943–1950 and Honorary Colonel of the 4/5th Battalion Royal Scots Fusiliers 1942–49. He lived to the age of 96.

BECKETT, Major General Clifford Thomason *(1891–1972), CB, CBE, MC*
Of military family and educated at Tonbridge and RMA, Woolwich, Beckett was commissioned in the Royal Artillery in 1911. His First War service was in Gallipoli, France, Salonika and Palestine, where he was wounded and awarded the MC.

Stationed in Iraq, Persia, Egypt and Turkey in the early 1920s, Beckett was a staff officer at the War Office 1926–1930. He was employed on the Strategic Reconnaissance of Western Europe 1929–1931 and in the mid 1930s served in Lahore area, India. A frequent visitor to French and German army manoeuvres in the later 1930s, he was, as lieutenant colonel, commander of the 12th Field Regiment, RA, 1938–1939.

Made commander of the 1st Survey Regiment, RA, in 1939, 'Joe' Beckett served with the BEF. Mentioned in despatches and promoted colonel, he was CRA 15th Division, 1940–1941 and for the next three years commanded the artillery on Malta.

With Malta to all intents and purposes under siege, Beckett rose to the occasion. He kept the guns going, visited the batteries regularly and helped organize 'Victory Kitchens' whereby bombed-out islanders could obtain hot meals. Acting GOC Malta for two months in 1942, Beckett was promoted major general and recalled to England where, for the rest of the war, he commanded 4th and 5th AA groups. He retired from the army in 1946.

27

A keen sportsman, Beckett had an active retirement. In demand as a judge for equitation competitions, he contributed to military journals, was president of the London Huguenot Society and was DL for Somerset 1952–1967 .

BECKWITH-SMITH, Major General Merton *(1890–1942), DSO, MC*
Born in Scotland and educated at Eton and Oxford University, Beckwith-Smith was commissioned in the Coldstream Guards in 1910. Admitted to the DSO in 1914, he had an outstanding record of service in the First War, being awarded the MC and mentioned four times in despatches, ending the war on the staff with GHQ.

Commandant of the Oxford University OTC for some years after 1918, Beckwith-Smith attended the Staff College, Camberley, 1921–1922 and transferred to the Welsh Guards in 1930. He commanded the 1st Battalion and Regimental District 1932–1937 and, promoted brigadier, was posted to India to command the Lahore Brigade Area 1938–1939. He was recalled to England and made commander of the 1st Guards Brigade just before the outbreak of war. Serving with Alexander's 1st Division in the BEF, 'Becky' Beckwith-Smith assumed command of the division when Alexander was appointed to supervise the last phases of the evacuation from Dunkirk.

Promoted major-general in July 1940, Beckwith-Smith was made GOC of the newly-formed 18th Division and spent the next year as a trainer of troops. In October 1941 the Division was posted to India, but had scarcely disembarked when the order came to move on to assist in the defence of Malaya. Arriving in Singapore in mid-January 1942, and with 'morale impossible to maintain' (Fraser, 1983, 195) in the rapidly deteriorating military situation, there was nothing the 'brave, intelligent and popular' (Connell, 1969, 129) Beckwith-Smith could do save obey his superiors and surrender himself and his troops to the Japanese.

Imprisoned in Changi jail on the eastern edge of the island, Beckwith-Smith's health declined rapidly. Having enjoyed, as his obituarist put it, 'a career of unbroken success', he died of a heart attack while suffering from acute diphtheria in November 1942.

BEITH, Major General John Hay *(1876–1952), MC, CBE*
Born in Manchester of Scottish parents and educated at Fettes and Cambridge University, it was as a novelist and playwright that John Beith, alias 'Ian Hay', became known. With his first novel *Pip* published in 1907, his reputation for light-hearted good humour was established well before the First World War.

Volunteering in August 1914, Beith served in France with the Argyll and Sutherland Highlanders, was mentioned in despatches and awarded the MC. His best-known literary contribution to the war effort was *The First Hundred Thousand* (1915).

A member of the British War Mission in the United States from September 1916, Beith worked as propagandist until war's end. For the next twenty years he concentrated on writing. His output was considerable and, it is said, he had a genius for adapting plays into novels and novels into plays. When, in May 1938, the War Secretary, Leslie Hore-Belisha, invited him to fill the vacant post of Director of Public Relations at the War Office, Beith, as 'Ian Hay', jumped at the chance.

Doing his bit in 'democratizing' the army, Beith, under wartime conditions, came quickly to be regarded as 'charming . . . though out of his depth' (de Guingand, 1947, 32). Retired in 1942, his literary output scarcely slackened (*Malta: The Unconquered Isle*, etc.), though the reception was muted. He died in a Hampshire nursing home.

BENOY, Major General John Meredith *(1896–1977), CBE*

The son of a clergyman and educated at Felsted and RMC, Sandhurst, Benoy was commissioned in the South Staffordshire Regiment in 1914. His First War service was in France, where he was twice wounded. He was a staff officer with the Supreme War Council at the Paris Peace Conference 1919.

Transferring to the Royal Warwickshire Regiment, Benoy married in 1920, served on internal security duties in Ireland in the early 1920s and later in Palestine. He was made OBE in 1931, attended the Staff College, Camberley, 1932–1933, and was a staff officer at the War Office 1934–1936. A brigade major at Aldershot, he had another spell of duty in Palestine 1938–1939.

In France with the BEF as Assistant Adjutant at GHQ 1939–40, Benoy served in the War Office until 1942. As a colonel he was Deputy Adjutant and QMG with 1st Army in North Africa and from 1943–1944 was Deputy Adjutant and QMG for 2nd Army pending the opening of the 'second front'. As with so many officers with 1st Army experience, he did not find favour with Montgomery who pronounced him 'quite unfit to be head of 'Q'' (Alanbrooke, 6/2/22, LHCMA). Somewhat sidelined, Benoy was made major-general i/c Administration AA Command, the position he held at war's end.

Chief Administrator in Eritrea 1945–1946, Benoy retired from the army in 1947. Active for some years as a member of the Council of Industrial Design, he worked occasionally as a consultant until well into his 70s.

BERESFORD, Major General Sir George de la Poer
(1885–1964), KCIE, CB, MC

Born and educated in Australia before attending RMC Sandhurst, Beresford joined the Indian Army in 1907 and was gazetted into Hodson's Horse. With them he saw First War service in France and Palestine, where he was awarded the MC.

Beresford attended the Staff College, Camberley, 1922–1923, after serving with his regiment in Kurdistan and on the North-West Frontier. Indeed he was with Hodson's Horse until 1933, when, after a brief spell of staff duties at AHQ, India, he commanded the (Prince Albert Victor's Own) Frontier Force Cavalry 1933–34. By now a brigadier, he commanded the 4th Cavalry Brigade 1934–1938. Awarded the CB and promoted major general in 1938, he was

29

Deputy Adjutant and QMG, Northern Command India, until the outbreak of war.

A District Commander in 1940, Beresford set up a skeletal divisional command in Basra in 1941 after the crushing of the Raschid Ali rebellion in Iraq. Retired in 1942, he was re-employed in the newly-formed Persia and Iraq Command later that year, charged with keeping open the Persian Gulf supply route to southern USSR.

Knighted in 1947, the year he finally retired, Beresford lived the rest of his life in Australia, outliving his wife by a year.

BERESFORD-PIERSE, Lieutenant General Sir Noel Monson de la Poer (1887–1953), KBE, CB, DSO

The son of an Indian Army colonel, Beresford-Pierse was educated at Wellington and RMC, Sandhurst. Commissioned in the Royal Artillery in 1907, his First War service was with the Royal Field Artillery in Egypt and Mesopotamia, and later in France where he was admitted to the DSO.

Aside from attendance at the Staff College, Camberley, from 1924 to 1925, Beresford-Pierse's inter-war soldiering was exclusively in India. Divorcing his wife in 1924, he was an instructor at the Senior Officers' School, Belgaum, 1936–1938, commanded the artillery in 4th Indian Division from 1938 and went with the division to Egypt in early 1940. After a brief spell with GHQ in Cairo, he commanded 4th Indian Division when, as part a Wavell-inspired 'training exercise', Italian encampments in Egypt were attacked and routed by O'Connor's Western Desert Force in spectacular fashion.

This heart-warming series of victories, particularly the 4th Indian Division's assault on Nibeiwa camp with all its booty, established Beresford-Pierse's reputation as a dashing commander. Transfer to Ethiopia. where, leading 4th Indian Division, he took part in the Battle of Keren, enhanced it. The 'solid, red-faced, cheroot-smoking artilleryman' (Barnett, 1983, 38) had captured the public imagination and among his peers he was regarded as 'no Napoleon, but a genuine personality' (Greacan, 1989, 162). Returned to the desert in April 1941, he was knighted and, promoted lieutenant general, made commander of the Western Desert Force.

His task was simple – to restore the strategic initiative, relieve the besieged Tobruk garrison and drive back Axis forces deep into Cyrenaica. With his armour reinforced, he hoped to achieve all this in his June 1941 offensive (BATTLEAXE). The offensive failed. Too many British tanks fell victim to breakdown and German anti-tank guns, and amidst the disappointment there was much bitter acrimony. Wavell was dismissed from Middle East Command and within three months Beresford Pierse, whose 'prestige ha[d] suffered' (Dill, 2nd Acc., LHCMA), was removed from the western desert theatre and made GOC-in-C Sudan.

The dashing commander was turned into a trainer of troops. Returned to India in April 1942, Beresford-Pierse was, for the rest of the war, GOC-in-C Southern Command India. From 1945 until his retirement in 1947 he was

Welfare General in India, whereby he oversaw welfare provision for all British forces in the sub-continent in the lead-up to independence and partition.

Retired to Wiltshire, the thrice-married but childless Beresford-Pierse died at his home near Salisbury.

BERNARD, Lieutenant General Sir Denis Kirwan
(1882–1956), KCB, CMG, DSO
Born in Co. Galway and educated at Eton and RMC, Sandhurst, Bernard was commissioned in the Rifle Brigade in 1902. A captain in 1912, his First War service was first in France and Gallipoli, then as a staff officer in Salonika and Egypt. It was there that he was admitted to the DSO in 1917.

A lieutenant colonel in 1927, Bernard commanded the 1st Battalion Ulster Rifles for the next three years. A brigadier on the General Staff in India from 1930–1934, he was Director of Recruiting and Organization at the War Office 1934–1936 and commanded 3rd Division 1936–1939. A colourful character bearing the nickname 'Podge', he 'still wore spurs and liked to see his men drilling in . . . fours' (Hamilton, 1982, 265). Promoted lieutenant general and knighted in 1939, he was made Governor and C-in-C Bermuda, the position he held until he retired to his castle in Galway in 1941.

BERNEY-FICKLIN, Major General Horatio Pettus Mackintosh
(1892–1961), CB, MC
Born in Norfolk and educated at Rugby and Cambridge University, Berney-Ficklin was gazetted into the Special Reserve in 1912 and commissioned in the Norfolk Regiment in 1914. Commanding the 8th Battalion in France in 1916, he was twice wounded, mentioned in despatches and awarded the MC in 1917. A brigade major in 1918, he was taken prisoner.

In 1919 Berney-Ficklin served as liaison officer in Ironside's GHQ at Archangel and was Adjutant to the Bristol University OTC 1923–1925. Resigning his commission in 1926, he re-joined the army ten years later after divorcing his wife. After brief service on the North-West Frontier, he commanded the 2nd Battalion Highland Light Infantry in Palestine from 1936–1939.

A brigadier in 1939, Berney-Ficklin was made commander of 15th Brigade which, forming in England, was designated part of HAMMERFORCE in April 1940 and held in readiness for an assault on Trondheim in central Norway. Made force commander when Hotblack, the original appointee, suffered a stroke, he was himself incapacitated when the aircraft carrying him and his staff to the Orkneys crashed on landing.

Promoted major general in June 1940 and made GOC 5th Division, Berney-Ficklin spent the next two years with Home Forces. Though the Division was posted to India in mid-1942, the detachment of two brigades for the invasion of Madagascar made the command untidy. Able, eventually, to re-form in Egypt in early 1943, the Division took part in the invasion of Sicily.

In command of 5th Division at the start of HUSKY, Berney-Ficklin, unable to inspire his 'slow, tired and unsure of themselves' troops' (Pond, 1962, 129), so displeased his superiors that he was posted home to serve with Home Forces before the five-week-long Sicilian campaign ended. Made commander of 48th Division in September 1943 and moved to command 55th Division in March 1944, he was President of the Court at the Belsen trial in 1945.

Retired from the army in 1946, Berney-Ficklin and his second wife (the daughter of a Russian general) went to live in South Africa. He died in Cape Town.

BIGGAM, Major General Sir Alexander Gordon *(1888–1963), KBE, CB*
Born in Stranraer and educated at George Watson's College and Edinburgh University, Biggam entered the Royal Army Medical Corps by university commission in 1912. He served in France with the BEF in 1914, but, promoted captain in 1915 and posted to the Middle East and later to India, he made his mark as a world authority in tropical medicine.

Service in the field in the early 1920s (Afghanistan, Waziristan) soon gave way to base hospital work. Director of the Medical Unit of Kasr-el-Aini Hospital, Cairo, Biggam was also Professor of Clinical Medicine at the Egyptian University 1926–1933. Married in 1933, he was, as major general, Director of Medical Services, Burma, 1940–1941, and Consulting Physician to the army from 1943 until his retirement in 1947.

Knighted in 1946, Biggam returned to Edinburgh. Made a Fellow of the Royal Society in 1950, he was, for a number of years, Director of Study for the Edinburgh Post-Graduate Board for Medicine.

BIRD, Lieutenant General Sir Clarence August
(1885–1986), KCIE, CB, DSO
Educated at Cheltenham and commissioned in the Royal Engineers in 1904, Bird served in India before the First War. In France with the Indian Expeditionary Force from 1914, he transferred to the British Army, rose to the rank of Major and was admitted to the DSO in 1917 after his successful mining work on the German position on Messines Ridge.

In India again before war's end, Bird married in 1919 and attended the Staff College, Camberley, 1920–1921. He served at AHQ, India, 1922–1925, and was Chief Instructor in Fortifications at the School of Military Engineering, Chatham, 1926–1929. Commandant of the Bengal Sappers and Miners 1930–1933, he was Assistant QMG at Aldershot 1933–1935 and, from 1935 to 1939 Chief Engineer, Aldershot Command.

A major general at war's beginning, Bird was Engineer-in-Chief, AHQ, India, 1939–1942. Promoted lieutenant general in 1941, he was Master General of Ordnance, India, from 1942 until his retirement from the army in 1944.

Knighted in 1943, the year his elder son was killed on active service, Bird was Colonel Commandant of the Royal Engineers 1942–1952, and Colonel Commandant of the Indian Electrical and Mechanical Engineers 1944–1948. He worked with the government of India's Department of Food before independence and, returned to Britain, was Food Officer for the North Midland Division, 1947–1948.

Possessing 'mental equipment of the highest order [which] continued to function lucidly into extreme old age', Bird was Chairman of Rhodesia Railways from 1948 till 1953.

BIRKS, Major General Horace Leslie *(1897–1985), CB, DSO*

Born in London and educated at University College School, Birks enlisted in the London Rifle Brigade in 1915 and served in France. Commissioned in the Machine Gun Corps in 1917, he was wounded, transferred to the Royal Tank Corps and was wounded again at Cambrai.

With a regular commission in 1918, with the Worcester Regiment, Birks transferred again to the RTC and was an instructor at the Tank Driving and Maintenance School 1919–1924. He spent the next five years in India. After attending the Staff College, Quetta, in 1928, he served on the staff at Western Command 1930–1934 and at the War Office from 1934 to 1937. From 1937 to 1939 he was back at Quetta, though this time as lieutenant colonel and instructor.

Birks served on the staff of the Mobile (7th Armoured) Division, then forming in Egypt under Hobart's command from 1939. Made 2nd-in-command of 4th Armoured Brigade in 1940, he was admitted to the DSO for his part in the assault on Bardia, while, next year, his brigade provided the armour for the garrison besieged at Tobruk. Said to have 'a lightness of heart and touch' (Roberts, 1987, 26), he was brought back to England in late 1941, probably at Hobart's instigation, to command 11th Armoured Brigade in the newly-formed 42nd Armoured Division. Promoted major general in 1943, he was sent out again to Egypt to assume command of 10th Armoured Division.

Although 10th Armoured Division had fought at Alamein, it remained on a reduced establishment for the rest of the war. As 8th Army drove westwards towards Tunisia, Birks took his tanks northwards to Palestine and, when the division was disbanded in late 1944, his consolation prize was the CB and a tour of duty in Italy advising on armoured warfare. Badly injured in a plane crash in 1945, he performed various War Office duties until his retirement from the army in 1946.

Secretary of University College Hospital Medical School 1946–1963, Birks continued to live in London until his death when well into his eighties.

BISHOP, Major General Sir William Henry Alexander
(1897–1984), KCMG, CB, CVO, OBE

Born in Plymouth and educated at Plymouth College and RMC, Sandhurst, 'Alec' Bishop was commissioned in the Dorset Regiment in 1915 and saw war service in Mesopotamia and Palestine.

In India with his regiment for most of the 1920s, Bishop attended the Staff College, Camberley, 1927–1928, married and, after staff duties in Southern Command, served on the staff at the War Office from 1933–1935. A brevet lieutenant colonel in 1938, he was seconded to the Colonial Office and worked briefly with the War Cabinet Secretariat. Chief Staff Officer East African Forces in 1939, he served in West and North Africa for the first three years of the war and, as brigadier, was on the planning staff for Operation HUSKY in 1943. Chief Commentator for the Ministry of Information in 1944, he was promoted major general and appointed Director of Quartering at the War Office 1944–1945. Said to be 'a very small but nice man who immerse[d] himself in endless detail' (Young (ed.), 1973, 448), he was, by war's end, Deputy Director General, Political Warfare Executive, at the Ministry of Information.

Post-war, Bishop was Chief of Information Services and Public Relations for the Control Commission in Germany (CCG) and, 1946–1948, Deputy Chief of Staff to the CCG. Regional Commissioner for North Rhine/Westphalia 1948–1950, he returned to the Colonial Office as Principal Staff Secretary to the Secretary of State for Commonwealth Relations. Numerous appointments followed in succeeding years, culminating in him being made British High Commissioner in Cyprus in 1964.

BLAKE, Major General Gilbert Alan *(1887–1971)*, CB, MB

Educated at Eastbourne College and Guy's Hospital, Blake joined the Royal Army Medical Corps in 1912. His First War service was in France. Thereafter his postings followed the standard pattern of British serving officers between the wars. Married in 1925, he served on the North-West Frontier, Afghanistan, East Persia (Iran), Egypt, Sudan and India, returning to England in 1938.

As a brigadier, Blake served as Chief Medical Officer for AVONFORCE in the Norway campaign in 1940 and, promoted major-general in 1942, he was, for the rest of the war, Deputy Director Medical Services, Western Command. Appointed CB in 1944, he retired from the army in 1946.

BLAKISTON-HOUSTON, Major General John *(1881–1959)*, CB, DSO

The fifth son of a very large family, Blakiston-Houston was educated at Cheltenham and, commissioned in the 11th Hussars, served in South Africa 1901–1902. Regimental duties took him to West Africa 1905–1908, and from 1910 to 1915 he was Adjutant to the Sussex Yeomanry.

First War service was in France, where he was wounded, mentioned in despatches and admitted to the DSO in 1916. For the remaining two years of the war he commanded the 3rd Battalion Royal Irish Rifles.

Reverting to the cavalry in peacetime, Blakiston-Houston graduated from the Staff College, Camberley, in 1919 and was Brigade Major, 1st Cavalry Brigade, 1920–1923. He commanded the 12th Lancers 1923–1927 and the 2nd Cavalry Brigade 1927–1931. For the next three years he was Brigadier i/c Administration, Northern Command, and, promoted major general in 1934, was Commandant of the Equitation School, Weedon, and Inspector of Cavalry until his retirement from the army in 1938. The year before, he had been considered for command of the Mobile Division, but, apparently, Hore-Belisha vetoed the appointment on the grounds that all Blakiston-Houston could do was 'slap his thigh and shout' (Macleod and Kelly, 1962, 34).

Cavalry-minded 'Mike' Blakiston-Houston may have been, but, like many recently retired senior officers, he was brought back to service in 1939. Appointed commander of the newly-formed 59th (Staffordshire) Division in September, he vacated the post in December to assume command of the Midland Area.

Reverting to retired pay in 1941, Blakiston-Houston and his French-born wife lived out their final years in their home of Weedon days near Banbury.

BLAXLAND, Major General Alan Bruce *(1892–1963)*, CB, OBE

The son of a clergyman and educated at Shrewsbury and Oxford University, Blaxland was gazetted into the 7th Rajput Regiment (Indian Army) in 1913. First War service was in France, where he was wounded and mentioned in despatches, and in the Persian Gulf. He married in 1919.

After service in Waziristan and the North-West Frontier 1921–1922, Blaxland was an instructor at the Small Arms School, India, 1922–1925, and was Military Adviser to the Central Indian States 1929–33. Commanding a battalion of Rajputs in the 1933 Mohmand Expedition, he was mentioned in despatches.

Second War service began in North Africa. Still a lieutenant colonel commanding a battalion of Rajputs, Blaxland was 2nd-in-command of the Mersa Matruh Fortress in 1940, and commanded 27th Infantry Brigade in Iraq and Persia 1941–1942. GOC of 10th Indian Division in North Africa and Cyprus 1942–43, he was briefly a corps commander before being invalided back to India that year.

Appointed GOC Lahore District in 1943, Blaxland retired from the army in 1946 and settled in Kent.

BODY, Major General Kenneth Marten *(1883–1973)* CMG, OBE, CB

Born in Devon and educated at Blundell's and RMA, Woolwich, Body was commissioned in the Royal Field Artillery in 1900. After brief service in South Africa, his military career competed with his sporting interests. A keen rugby and hockey player, he married in 1907.

A captain in 1913, Body's First War service was in France, where he rose to the rank of brevet lieutenant colonel. Assistant Director of Ordnance at the War Office 1921–1924, he transferred to the Royal Army Ordnance Corps in 1928 and was an instructor at the RAOC School of Instruction 1931–1934. Inspector of Army Ordnance Services in 1938 and promoted major general in 1939, he was Director of Army Ordnance Services at the War Office until his retirement in 1942.

Awarded the CB and Colonel Commandant of the RAOC between 1942 and 1949, Body and his wife lived in Bath, where he, widowed for the last two years of his life, lived to the age of 90.

BOLS, Major General Eric Louis *(1904–1985) CB, DSO*

The son of a general, Bols was educated at Wellington and RMC, Sandhurst. Commissioned in the Devonshire Regiment in 1924, he attended the Staff College, Camberley, 1935–36 and was a captain with the King's (Liverpool) Regiment in 1940. His war began with him an infantry officer in Ceylon (Sri Lanka) and ended with him commanding 6th Airborne Division in North-West Europe.

Between times Bols had worked as a COSSAC planner in the War Office prior to OVERLORD, and in June 1944 he commanded 185th Brigade in the 3rd Infantry Division in Normandy. As his leadership stood out when contrasted with the rather 'sticky' handling of the Division as a whole that summer, Bols found himself the beneficiary of a complicated command shake-up in the command of the Airborne Corps that came in the wake of the failed Operation MARKET GARDEN. With Gale, formerly commander of 6th Airborne Division, promoted to command the Corps, Bols – for all his lack of experience in airborne operations – assumed the divisional command in his place.

His baptism of fire came at Christmas 1944 when 6th Airborne Division was rushed from England to counter-attack the German forces in the Ardennes (the Battle of the Bulge). From there Bols led his division in the Rhine crossings in March 1945 and, less than two months later, units from 6th Airborne reached Wismar and were the first British troops to meet up with Soviet forces in Germany.

Having shot to fame, Bols sank into obscurity. He retired from the army in 1948 and died on his eighty-first birthday.

BOND, Lieutenant General Sir Lionel Vivian *(1884–1961), KBE, CB*

Born the son of a sapper major general, Bond, after education at Cheltenham and RMA, Woolwich, was commissioned in the Royal Engineers in 1903. Engaged in railway construction on the North-West Frontier 1903–1908, he was mentioned in despatches for his part in operations against 'those inveterate troublemakers' (Elliot, 1968, 175), the Zakha Khel Afridis.

Bond's First War Service was in France and Mesopotamia where, as brevet lieutenant colonel, he was again mentioned in despatches. A graduate of the Staff College, Camberley, in 1919, he married in 1925, was an instructor at the Senior Officers' School, Belgaum, India, and then served on the staff at the War Office 1931–1934. Appointed Chief Engineer, Aldershot Command 1934, he was promoted major general in 1935 and made GOC Chatham Area before becoming, in 1938, Commandant of the School of Military Engineering and Inspector of the Royal Engineers. He held these posts until the beginning of the war.

Sent out to Malaya as GOC land forces in 1939, Bond's brief as to improve the peninsula's defences from land and seaborne attack. Frustrated by lack of resources and enduring a deteriorating relationship with the C-in-C, Air Chief Marshal Brooke-Popham, he was replaced by Percival in mid-1941.

Retired from the army upon his return to Britain, Bond was knighted the following year and, Commandant of the Royal Engineers from 1940–1950, was for a number of years after a member of the House of Laity of the Church Assembly.

BOND, Major General Richard Lawrence *(1890–1979), CB, CBE, DSO, MC*
The son of a major general, Bond was educated at Wellington and RMA, Woolwich. Commissioned in the Royal Engineers in 1910, his First War service was in France. Admitted to the DSO in 1915, he was awarded the MC in 1918.

A major in 1926, Bond married, attended the Staff College, Camberley, 1926–1927, and served on the staff at the War Office 1930–1931. After attending the Imperial Defence College, he was Commander, Royal Engineers, India, 1934–37, during which time he was awarded the CBE for his part in the Waziristan expedition. Assistant Adjutant at the War Office 1937–1939, he was Chief Engineer, Aldershot Command, when was broke out in 1939.

Sent to France with the BEF, Bond was Chief Engineer to I Corps 1939–40. Promoted that summer, he was major-general i/c Administration at the War Office, before returning to India as Deputy QMG. Engineer-in-Chief in India 1942–1943, he was awarded the CB and 'kicked upstairs' as Commander Royal Engineers and retired from the army in 1946.

With his son killed in action in 1941, and his wife dying in 1943, Bond's war was touched by personal tragedy. However, he re-married in 1949 to live out his remaining years in Guildford.

BRADFIELD, Lieutenant General Sir Ernest William Charles
(1880–1963), KCIE, OBE
Educated at King Edward VI School, Birmingham, and London University, Bradfield joined the Indian Medical Service in 1903 and specialized in surgery. He saw service on the North-West Frontier, in France 1914–1917, and in Mesopotamia where he was mentioned in despatches and made OBE in 1918.

Superintendent of the Government General Hospital, Madras, for much of the 1920s, Bradfield, by now a professor of medical surgery, was mentioned in despatches for his part in the 1933 campaign against the Upper Mohmands and was Assistant Director of Medical Services, India, 1932–1935. For the next two years he was Surgeon General, Bombay, and, from 1937 to 1939 Director General of the Indian Medical Service. He was also Chairman of the Indian Red Cross Society 1938–1939.

Though officially retired in 1939, Bradfield was an adviser to the India Office throughout the war years. Knighted in 1941, he was also Indian Red Cross Commissioner in England 1940–1946. He was elected a Fellow of the Royal College of Surgeons a year before his death.

BRADSHAW, Major General William Pat Arthur *(1897–1966), CB, DSO*
Educated at Eton and RMC, Sandhurst, Bradshaw was commissioned in the Scots Guards in 1914 and served with his regiment in France where he was mentioned in despatches and admitted to the DSO in 1917.

A well-connected young man, 'Pat' Bradshaw served on the staff of the War Office and 1928–1929 was ADC to the Viceroy of India, Lord Irwin (later Halifax). A lieutenant colonel in 1935, he commanded the 2nd Battalion Scots Guards 1935–1938 and was Officer Commanding the Scots Guards Regiment and Regimental District 1938–1939. In 1938 he married a daughter of Lord Cadman.

Commanding 4th Infantry Brigade in France with the BEF, 1939–1940, Bradshaw commanded 104th Brigade, 1940–1941, and 24th Guards Brigade, 1941–1942. He was promoted major general in 1942 and appointed to command the 59th Infantry Division, which spent the next two years in Northeren Ireland. Removed from that command in 1944, he succeeded Berney-Ficklin as GOC of the lower establishment 48th Division. He retired from the army in 1946.

BRANDER, Major General Maxwell Spieker
(1884–1972), CB, OBE, MIMechE
Of military family and educated at Bedford School and RMC, Sandhurst, Brander was commissioned in the Army Service Corps in 1906. A captain in 1914, his First War service was in France and Palestine.

A brevet lieutenant colonel in 1918, it took fifteen years of peacetime soldiering for the now married Brander to achieve equivalent substantive rank. Thereafter promotion came faster. Promoted major general in 1936, he was Inspector Royal Army Service Corps for a year and from 1937–1940 Director of Supplies and Transport at the War Office. Awarded the CB and made Major General i/c Administration, Eastern Command, 1940–1941, he was Deputy Director General of Mechanization at the Ministry of Supply from 1941 until his retirement from the army in 1947.

Colonel Commandant of the RASC 1942–1949, Brander and his wife lived out a long retirement in Devon.

BRIDGEMAN, 2nd Viscount, Robert Clive *(1896–1982), KBE, CB, DSO, MC*
The eldest son of the 1st Viscount (created 1929) and educated at Eton, Bridgeman was commissioned in the Rifle Brigade in 1914. His First War service was in France. Admitted to the DSO he was, while convalescing from wounds, private secretary to his father when Minister of Labour in 1918.

A captain in 1921, Bridgeman attended the Staff College, Camberley, 1927–1928, and married in 1930. He was Brigade Major to 7th Infantry Brigade 1932–1934 and was a staff officer at the War Office 1934–1936. Having succeeded his father in 1935 he retired from the army in 1937, only to be re-commissioned in 1939 as a lieutenant colonel.

Serving first under Adam on the staff of III Corps with the BEF, then with GHQ, Bridgeman was admitted to the DSO for his part in the evacuation from Dunkirk. Made Deputy Director of the Home Guard in 1941, and ever 'helpful, reasonable and anxious to co-operate' (Mackenzie, 1995, 178), he was promoted major general and appointed Director General of the Home Guard and Territorial Army the same year. Holding this post until 1944, indeed until the Home Guard was stood down, was, perhaps, something of an achievement. For the remaining six months of the war Bridgeman was Deputy Adjutant General.

A member of the British War Crimes Executive, Bridgeman was a Shropshire JP, County Council Alderman and Lord Lieutenant 1951–1969. With numerous banking and commercial interests, he was President of the West Midlands Territorial Army and Volunteer Reserve Association 1968–1969, as well as being, for a number of years, President of the Army Cadet Force Association. The father of three daughters but no son, the Viscountcy passed to his nephew.

BRIGGS, Lieutenant General Sir Harold Rawdon
(1894–1952), KCIE, KBE, CB, DSO
Educated at Bedford School and RMC, Sandhurst, Briggs was gazetted into the Indian Army in 1914. Attached to the 4th Battalion King's (Liverpool) Regiment in France, he joined the 31st Punjab Regiment in 1915 and served the rest of the war in Mesopotamia and Palestine.

Briggs's inter-war career followed a pattern typical of Indian Army officers of the day. Transferring to the Baluch Regiment in 1923, he attended the Staff College, Quetta, 1927–1928, campaigned in Waziristan in 1930 and commanded the 2nd Battalion Baluch Regiment 1937–1940.

That year 'Briggo' Briggs re-married, was promoted brigadier and commanded 7th Indian Brigade first in Eritrea, and later, as part of 4th Indian Division, in North Africa. Admitted to the DSO for safely extricating his brigade from Benghazi in April 1941, he was promoted major general in early 1942 and appointed GOC 5th Indian Division. Playing his part in the 'leadership by committee' that brought on the defeat of 8th Army in the Gazala battle, Briggs and his Division were pulled out of the line in July and sent to Iraq for three months, then back to India.

Judged a failure in North Africa, Briggs had his second chance in Burma. Still commanding 5th Indian Division, his part in the successful Arakan campaign of 1944–45 earned him a second bar to his DSO. His handling of his Division in the relief of the Kohima garrison earned him a CBE and the unstinting praise of Slim, the XIV Army GOC-in-C, who wrote of him that he knew of no commander who 'made so few mistakes' (Slim, 1972, 145).

Promoted lieutenant general and, for a while, GOC-in-C Eastern Command, India, Briggs was GOC-in-C Burma from 1946 to 1948. That year he retired from the army and settled in Cyprus, though, as an authority in counterterrorist operations, he was re-employed as Director of Operations in Malaya 1950–1951. He died in Cyprus after a sudden illness the following year.

BRIGGS, Major General Raymond *(1895–1985) CB, DSO*
Volunteering for service with the Liverpool Scottish Regiment in 1914, Briggs was commissioned the following year. Serving in France, he was twice wounded and transferred to the Machine Gun Corps in 1917.

In 1920 Briggs transferred again; this time to the Royal Tank Corps. Adjutant to the Armoured Car Company in Egypt 1922–1933, he attended the Staff College, Camberley, 1925–1926, and married the following year. With promotion painfully slow, especially perhaps for officers who had a natural affinity for 'the armoured idea' (Lewin, 1976, 54), he was a brevet lieutenant colonel in 1938 and, at war's beginning in 1939, was attached to GHQ, BEF 'to advise on the handling of Armoured Fighting Vehicles' (Marshall-Cornwall, 1984, 144). Marooned in France during the BEF's retreat, he was absorbed into 'Jimmy' Marshall-Cornwall's staff in Normandy and helped with the evacuation of British service personnel from the western French ports.

Promoted brigadier, Briggs was appointed to command 2nd Armoured Brigade in 1941 which, as part of 1st Armoured Division, was sent out to North Africa at the end of that year. Wounded and admitted to the DSO for the manner in which he led the brigade's withdrawal from Cyrenaica, he assumed command of the division in August 1942, when Lumsden was elevated to command X Corps. His participation in the second battle of Alamein was not entirely happy. Montgomery, dissatisfied with the performance of his armour, and irritated by Briggs's 'wildly optimistic reports' (Hamilton, 1982, 801), threatened to remove him from his command.

The removal came in May 1943. Briggs, having led his division from Egypt to Tunisia, was wounded again during the approach to Tunis. Unable to 'establish the same kind of close rapport with Horrocks that he had enjoyed with Lumsden' (French, 1996, 1198), he was sent home and appointed Director of the Royal Armoured Corps at the War Office. He held this post until his retirement from the army in 1947.

President, for many years, of the Metropolitan area, Royal British Legion, as well as being Secretary to the London and South East Region of the Federation of British Industries, Briggs died in London, a widower for the last year of a long married life.

BRIND, General Sir John Edward Spencer
(1878–1954), KCB, KBE, CMG, DSO
Of military family and educated at Wellington and RMA, Woolwich, Brind entered the army in 1897 and as an artillery officer served in the South African War. Married in 1907 and a captain in 1914, he was attending the Staff College, Camberley, when war broke out and his war service consisted of an escalating series of staff duties in France and Italy. Admitted to the DSO in 1915, he was a brigadier general on the General Staff 1917–1918.

An artilleryman, 'James' Brind was Colonel Commandant RA, Aldershot Command, 1922–1927, and in the early 1930s served in India, latterly as Deputy Chief of the General Staff. Appointed GOC 4th Division in 1933, his duties included commanding the International Force in the Saar prior to the 1935 plebiscite. Knighted and tipped as a likely future CIGS (Brownrigg, 1942, 101), he returned to India in 1936, where he was Adjutant General 1936–1937 and when on shooting trips 'visit[ed] any of our troops near to hand' (Morgan, 1961,

98). He was GOC-in-C Southern Command, India, from 1937 until his retirement from the army in 1941.

Brind, a widower since 1924, returned to England and served as Deputy Regional Commissioner for the North-East Region until war's end.

BROAD, Lieutenant General Sir Charles (Noel Frank)
(1882–1976), KCB, DSO
Born in Lahore, India, the son of an army major, Broad was educated at Wellington and Cambridge University, and saw war service in South Africa. Commissioned in the Royal Artillery in 1905, he attended the Staff College, Camberley, 1913–1914, and began his First War service as a captain. Transferring to the newly-formed Tank Corps, he was admitted to the DSO in 1917 and ended the war as a breveted lieutenant colonel.

After instructing at the Staff College, Camberley, in 1919, Broad was Commandant of the Tank Gunnery School at Lulworth 1924–1927. An early armoured theorist, known to his peers as 'The Brain' (Harris, 1995, 199), he wrote the 'purple primer', the official manual Mechanized and Armoured Formations in 1929. A brigadier on the General Staff, Aldershot Command, 1931–1934, he commanded 5th Indian Brigade at Quetta for the next two years. Though tipped as the next Director of Staff Studies at the War Office, a certain 'want of tact' led to an argument with the soon-to-be appointed CIGS, Gort, in 1937, which resulted in him being appointed major general i/c Administration, Aldershot Command 1937–1939. In that post, it is said, instead of devoting his energies to mechanization, he was 'tasked with organizing the annual tattoo' (DNB). He was GOC-in-C Aldershot Command 1939–1940, before being appointed GOC-in-C Eastern Army, India. He held that post until he retired from the army in 1942, the same year as the death of his wife.

Colonel Commandant of the Royal Tank Regiment 1939–1947, Broad married again in 1944. He and his wife lived in Dorset near to the Tank School at Bovington he had helped nurture.

BROOKE, Field Marshal Viscount Alanbrooke, Alan Francis
(1883–1963), KG, GCB, OM, GCVO, DSO
Though his roots 'lay deep in the Irish Protestant ascendancy', Brooke was born in France and, allegedly, spoke French and German before he spoke English. An RMA, Woolwich, education was superimposed on what had been an unconventional schooling and in 1902 he was commissioned in the Royal Artillery.

As 'the youngest of one of the great landowning dynasties of Ulster (Fraser in Keegan, 1991, 90), it was appropriate that the first four years of Brooke's army life were spent in Ireland. Posted to India in 1906, he rode, hunted big game and took his regimental duties so seriously that, standing too near to his guns, he damaged his hearing. Studying unsuccessfully for entry to the Staff College Camberley in 1914, he married, was posted back to India on the outbreak of war but, assuming command of his regiment's ammunition column en route, led it back to France. A lieutenant in 1914, he was a lieutenant colonel in

1918. In between times he was admitted to the DSO in 1917, mentioned in despatches six times and, it is said, introduced the 'creeping barrage' into the British and Canadian artillery's fire-plans.

An 'outstanding student' (DNB) in first post-war entry at the Staff College, Camberley, in 1919, Brooke's three-year stint on the staff of the 50th (Northumbrian) Territorial Army Division, 1920–1923, is represented as a brief interlude before being, inevitably, recalled to Camberley as an instructor. While there, and tragically, Brooke's wife was killed when the car he had been driving was involved in an accident. With two young children to bring up, he attended the Imperial Defence College in 1927 and, by now a brigadier, commanded the School of Artillery at Larkhill from 1929 (the year in which he married again) to 1932. For the next two years Brooke was an instructor at the Imperial Defence College, and from 1934–1935 he commanded the 8th Infantry Brigade based at Plymouth. Promoted major general and appointed Inspector of Artillery at the end of 1935, he was, within a year, Director of Military Training at the War Office. It was from that post that he was selected to command the Mobile Division in 1937.

Not noted as a tank enthusiast and regarded in some quarters as 'an unimaginative Horse Artilleryman averse to mechanization' (Greacan, 1989, 117), Brooke's time with the Mobile Division was brief. In June 1938 he was promoted lieutenant general and appointed GOC of the Anti-Aircraft Corps, which then consisted of five Territorial anti-aircraft divisions. Considering how Britain's vulnerability to air attack preoccupied the public – and military – imagination at this time, this was a plum posting. With the Anti-Aircraft Corps transformed into a Command in March 1939, Brooke, as GOC-in-C, had to liaise closely with the RAF and cope as best he could with the command's rapid expansion. Made Colonel Commandant of the Royal Artillery in May 1939, he was knighted the next month and was appointed GOC-in-C Southern Command two months before the outbreak of war.

It was thus, with a career trajectory made up of a nice balance of staff, instructing and field posts, that Brooke became commander of II Corps with the BEF in France. Montgomery, as is well known, was one of his divisional commanders, though at this stage in the 'phoney war' Brooke found Franklyn 'a more attractive type of individual' (Danchev & Todman, 2001, 29). Critical of Gort's lack of strategic vision to the point of disloyalty, Gort, for his part, regarded Brooke as so pessimistic that he was 'inclined to replace him' (Liddell Hart, 1965, 262). No soothsayer, Brooke had no more idea of the disaster about to befall the Anglo-French forces than any of his contemporaries. His oft-quoted comments on the low morale of French troops were written in 1950, not 1940 and, just as he commended the Maginot line as 'a stroke of genius', he had no reservations about advancing deep into Belgium in the event of a German attack. The enactment of Gamelin's plan D had catastrophic consequences. Nevertheless, beforehand Brooke had thought it 'without doubt the right strategy' (Danchev & Todman, 2001, 18).

In the brief campaign of 1940 Brooke did gain credit for his cool and efficient conduct during the BEF's retreat to Dunkirk. Handing over command of his corps to Montgomery, he was recalled to London and sent, almost immediately, back to France with orders to organize a new BEF and construct a redoubt in Brittany. Realizing the hopelessness of the situation and, incidentally, having his first personal contact with Churchill (albeit over a bad telephone line) he helped in the evacuation of thousands of line of communication troops from western French ports. Returning to England by trawler, and enjoying an unbroken 36 hours sleep at his home in Hampshire, Brooke took a step up in the knighthood and re-assumed his role of GOC-in-C Southern Command.

A remarkable feature of Brooke's war thereafter was the amount of time he was able to spend at home, where, among other diversions, he could indulge his passion for bird photography. On weekdays he was, from July 1940 to December 1941, C-in-C Home Forces. Said to be 'untiring in his visits and unsparing in his scrutiny of every part of the expanding army' (DNB), he was not necessarily the obvious man to succeed Dill as CIGS at the end of 1941. Being but two years away from retirement age, a younger general might have been preferred. But, as 'the one person [Dill] wanted to hand over to was me' (Danchev & Todman, 2001, 198), Brooke got the job. Made chairman of the Chiefs of Staff Committee soon after, he was thus a central figure in the higher direction of the war during its middle and later stages.

As CIGS Brooke attended all the major Allied conferences. He was successful in obtaining American agreement to pursue a Mediterranean strategy in 1943, but in his 'tepidity of enthusiasm' for cross-channel operations (Keegan, 1983, 47), he was less successful in his dealings with American counterparts thereafter. Though he turned down Churchill's offer of command in the Middle East in August 1942, he was disappointed not to be made supreme commander of allied forces preparing for the invasion of North-West Europe. Being promoted field marshal was a compensation of sorts.

Had Brooke not had his ghost-written diaries published (*The Turn of the Tide* and *Triumph in the West*) in the later 1950s, it is unlikely that he would be remembered as anything other than a rather colourless back-room figure of the war years, a man whose experience in the field was slight and whose staff work was dutifully anonymous. Appropriate honours were heaped on him upon his retirement in 1946, but it was his diaries – however badly edited and sloppily annotated – that made him famous. In these Churchill was depicted as ungracious, exasperating, obsessive, deluded and, more often than not, wrong in his ideas on strategy; the marvel being, as Lord Moran put it, that this 'queer relationship between Alanbrooke and Churchill was not allowed to affect the conduct of the war' (Moran, 1966, 753).

The relationship between Brooke (the dour, humourless Roundhead) and Churchill (the impulsive, expansive Cavalier) has been discussed to the point of exhaustion, though over the years attention has shifted from the issue of who framed British wartime strategy to questions about overall effectiveness. But while it is undeniable that neither man, whether singly or in tandem, was able to arrest the decline of British influence on more powerful allies as the war drew to its close, an aspect of Brooke's career as CIGS that has received relatively little attention is the extent to which this 'narrow-shouldered, eagle-eyed Ulsterman' imposed his will, and his preferences, on the command set-up of Britain's wartime army.

A self-conscious, not to say self-advertising, professional, Brooke would not have admitted to having favourites. All the same, tough and impatient as he was, he used those powers of patronage available to him as CIGS to the full. Having seen Gort in action, he blocked any suggestion that he should be given another field command. That Auchinleck, Corbett and Dorman-Smith fell to his sword implies a career-long aversion to the Indian Army. But to those who had served under him, or who had been instructed by him at the Staff College, he was much more selectively generous. His promotion and protection of Montgomery and his rescue from oblivion of Ritchie were but two examples of his talent-spotting. No fewer than 22 of his former Staff College students rose to command divisions during the war, while of those who had served with him in the Mobile Division, 1937–1938, there was one future army commander, four future corps commanders and a further two divisional commanders to make up the number (French, 1996, 1193–4). It is a reasonable generalization to say that those British generals who, by 1945, had had a 'good war' tended to be those senior, and not so senior, officers who had served under Brooke in II Corps with the BEF. He may have had a 'highly geared personality' and been a shrewd judge of men (Lewin, 1976, 96), but in the vast organization that the British army became in the Second World War, his vision appears to have been on the blinkered side.

It was Sir Arthur Bryant's ghost-written diaries that made Brooke's post-war reputation. It is doubtful, however, whether the more recent 'complete and unexpurgated' Danchev and Todman edited version (2001) – a vastly better work of scholarship – will enhance it. For all that it highlights Brooke's sense of frustration, depression, betrayal and doubt in his dealings with Churchill, it nevertheless does nothing to diminish the impression fostered by the Bryant editions, which Ismay considered erroneous, of him as a 'self-satisfied, self-pitying, ungenerous and disloyal' man (Ismay, 1960, 318).

BROOKE, Lieutenant General Sir Bertram Norman Sergison
(1880–1967), KCB, KCVO, CMG, DSO
Educated at Eton and RMC, Sandhurst, Brooke was commissioned in the Grenadier Guards in 1899. A subaltern in the South African War, his First War Service began with him as a major. Wounded, mentioned in despatches seven times and admitted to the DSO, Brooke (who had changed his name on marriage in 1915 to Sergison-Brooke) ended the war a brevet lieutenant colonel.

Commanding a brigade in the Shanghai Defence Force in 1928, Brooke (who re-married in 1923) commanded the 1st (Guards) Brigade, Aldershot Command, 1928–1931, and was BGS Eastern Command, India, 1931–1934. GOC London District 1934–1938, he was Chairman of the Royal Tournament 1934–1938. Though retired in 1939, he was re-employed in September 1939 as

GOC London District. He held this post until 1942 when his cousin, the CIGS, General Sir Alan Brooke, had his knighthood enhanced and ordered him to retire on age grounds.

Remembered as 'one of the best soldiers who ever put on a Sam Browne belt' (Chandos, 1962, 52), 'Bertie' Brooke's chief wartime function seems to have been providing shooting facilities and company for his ornithologically-minded cousin. Serving as British Red Cross Commissioner with Allied Liberation Armies, 1943–1945, he still organized shoots for the hard-pressed CIGS. He did, however, outlive his illustrious relative.

BROWN, Lieutenant General Sir John
(1880–1958), KCB, CBE, DSO, TD, JP, DL
Born in Northampton and educated at Magdalen College School, Brackley, Brown enlisted with the Northamptonshire Regiment in 1901, married a local girl in 1904 and, as a territorial officer, saw First War service in Gallipoli and in Palestine. He was admitted to the DSO in 1918.

Senior partner in a firm of architects and Commander of 162nd (East Midland) Infantry Brigade from 1924–1928, Brown was Chairman of the British Legion 1930–1934. Knighted that year and made a Freeman of Northampton, he served as Deputy Director of the Territorial Army from 1937–1939, at a time when the force of volunteer 'weekend soldiers' was doubling in size. Adjutant General at the War Office 1939–40, Brown, for all that he was 'h'-less, self educated and somewhat proud of it' (Smart (ed.), 2001, 184) went on to become Inspector General of Welfare and Education until his retirement in 1941.

Twice Master of the Worshipful Company of Patternmakers, Brown was a Northampton JP in his retirement. He was also DL for Northamptonshire.

BROWNING, Lieutenant General Sir Frederick Arthur Montague
(1896–1965), GCVO, KBE, CB, DSO
The son of a colonel and educated at Eton and RMC, Sandhurst, Browning was commissioned in the Grenadier Guards in 1915. His First War service was in France. A specialist in trench raids he was admitted to the DSO in 1917 and ended the war as an acting captain.

His youthful appearance led to the nickname 'Boy' and, with regimental duties fairly light in the early 1920s, he won the AAA high hurdles championship three years running and was a member of the British team at the 1924 Paris Olympics. He also bobsleighed for England. From 1924 to 1928 Browning was Adjutant at Sandhurst where he was known as the 'best turned out officer in the army' (DNB). In 1932 he married Daphne du Maurier, the novelist, and from 1935–1939 commanded the 2nd Battalion of the Grenadier Guards.

At war's beginning Browning was promoted brigadier and made Commandant of the Small Arms School at Hythe before being appointed to various brigade training duties. However, in the reoganization of much of the army after Dunkirk, he was placed in command of an experimental airborne brigade which, the next year, became 1st Airborne Division. The operational significance of parachute and glider-borne troops was seldom as effective as the various pundits predicted in the latter years of the Second World War, but Browning did at least have the wit to instil a sense of pride among those under his command. Just as the 'Red Devils' tag was inspired by his suggestion, his leadership extended to getting himself injured in a glider crash in March 1943.

Despite the dreadful casualties incurred during the invasion of Sicily, the Airborne Division was transformed into a Corps in January 1944, and Browning, duly promoted lieutenant general, was appointed commander. Ever 'elegant and debonair' (Richardson, 1985, 184) he supervised the landings on the left flank of the Normandy invasion in June 1944, and, while Deputy Commander of the Allied Airborne Army, took a leading part in planning the ill-fated Operation MARKET GARDEN that September. Having told Montgomery that he thought the bridge at Arnhem was 'a bridge too far' for his airborne troops to reach and hold, he was made scapegoat for failure.

Transferred to the Far East in November 1944, the 'rather nervy and highly strung' (Bond (ed.), 1974, 193)) Browning served as Chief of Staff to Mountbatten, the Supreme Commander. Judged as being 'as wild and disorganized as Mountbatten himself' (Young (ed., 1973, 527), the two men found they liked one another. After spending nearly a year in Singapore, Browning was recalled to London and, knighted, was appointed Military Secretary at the War Office. Resigning from the army in 1948 to take up a post in the Royal Household, he served on the Duke of Edinburgh's staff from 1953. Ill-health brought on his retirement in 1959.

A member of the British Olympic Committee and President of the National Playing Fields Association, one of his daughters married Montgomery's son. Made DL for Cornwall in 1960, Browning's deteriorating heart condition led to his death in 1965.

BROWNING, Major General Langley *(1891–1974), CB, OBE, MC*

Born in Co. Cork, Browning was educated at Tonbridge School and RMA, Woolwich. Commissioned in the Royal Artillery in 1911, his First War service was in France, where he was awarded the MC in 1915, and later in Italy, where he was mentioned in despatches.

A captain in 1920, Browning attended the Staff College, Camberley, 1925–1926. After some years in India he was an instructor at the Staff College, Quetta, 1933–1935, and served on the directing staff of the Senior Officers' School, Sheerness, 1938–1939. Inspector of the Royal Artillery for the first few months of the war, he was promoted major general in 1941 and appointed to command the 10th Anti-Aircraft Division. In 1942 he became GOC Royal Artillery Training Establishments, a post he held until 1944 when he was appointed GOC of the military mission to the Italian Army.

Retiring from the army in 1946, Browning amassed a peculiar array of honours (Citizen of the State of Texas, Knight Grand Cross of the Crown of Italy, etc.). Fond of field sports he lived, until his death, in Ireland.

BROWNJOHN, General Sir Nevil Charles Dowell
(1897–1973), GBE, KCB, CMG, MC
Educated at Malvern and RMA, Woolwich, Brownjohn was commissioned in the Royal Engineers in 1915. His First War Service was in France and Palestine, where he was admitted to the DSO in 1917.

Married in 1929, Brownjohn attended the Staff College, Camberley, 1931–1932. A major general in 1942, he worked in the COSSAC planning staff in preparation for OVERLORD and was a Deputy Chief of Staff on SHAEF 1943–1944. Deputy QMG Middle East Command 1945–1946, 'BJ', as he was invariably known, was a Deputy Military Governor in the Control Commission for Germany 1947–1948.

Vice QMG at the War Office 1949–1950, Brownjohn was knighted in 1951, was Vice CIGS 1950–1952 and Chief Staff Officer at the Ministry of Defence 1952–1955. Made QMG at the War Office in 1956, he was advanced in the knighthood and retired from the army in 1958.

Active in retirement, Brownjohn was Colonel Commandant of the Royal Engineers 1955–1962, Chairman of Crawley Development Corporation 1960–1962 and President of the Malvernian Society 1964–1967. He was also Chairman of the Housing Association for Officers' Families.

BROWNRIGG, Lieutenant General Sir Douglas *(1886–1946), KCB, DSO*
The son of a Guards general and educated at Mulgrave Castle and RMC, Sandhurst, Brownrigg was commissioned in the Sherwood Foresters in 1905. His First War service was at Gallipoli and in Mesopotamia. Admitted to the DSO in 1916, he was mentioned in despatches six times and ended the war as a brevet lieutenant colonel.

Deputy Assistant Adjutant General at the War Office in 1919, the year he married, Brownrigg attended the Staff College, Camberley, 1920–1921, and was an instructor at Sandhurst the following year. Returning to the War Office, he performed staff duties there for the next four years. From 1928–1931 he was Assistant Adjutant and QMG in North China with the Shanghai Defence Force. After a concentration of staff posts in the 1920s Brownrigg in mid-career was given a succession of command appointments. He commanded the 159th (Welsh Border) Infantry Brigade 1931–1933, the 11th Infantry Brigade 1933–1934 and, 'the happiest [years] of my life' (Brownrigg, 1942, 120), the 51st (Highland) Division 1935–1938.

Made Military Secretary to the Secretary of State for War, Hore-Belisha, in 1938, 'Brownie' Brownrigg was knighted and became Director General of the Territorial Army the following year. Upon the declaration of war in 1939 he was appointed Adjutant General of the BEF in France. His name scarcely features in accounts of the campaign in France and Flanders. Sent home early, sup- posedly to co-ordinate the defences of Boulogne and Calais from Dover Castle, he was told that he 'would receive no further employment on the Army List' (Brownrigg, 1942, 155).

Retired in 1940, Brownrigg wrote his memoirs (*Unexpected*, 1942) and was a Sector Commander with the Home Guard from 1941. In addition to providing commentaries for Ministry of Information films, he was devoted to his dogs and contributed regularly to the Christian Science Monitor before his death, after a short illness, in 1946.

BRUCE, Major General George McIllrea Stanton *(1896–1966), OBE, MC*
Few of this officer's personal details are known. Commissioned in the Lincolnshire Regiment in 1915, Bruce's First War service was in France. Twice wounded, he was awarded the MC in 1917.

A captain in 1921 and a major in 1935, Bruce was employed under the Colonial Office as Officer Commanding the Malay Regiment 1933–1938. Married in 1934 and awarded the OBE, he was promoted colonel in 1938.

Commander of 204th Independent Brigade, Home Forces, 1940–1942, and acting GOC 79th Armoured Division in 1942, Bruce was promoted major general in 1943 and, after a brief spell as GOC Nigeria, was appointed to command 82nd West African Division in Burma. There, under Christison in XV Corps, certain odd behavioural habits were noted (appearing drunk, sporting pearl-handled revolvers, etc.). Driving Christison and a visiting American general straight into a Japanese ambush, the party had to withdraw under fire bearing the American general who, suffering a heart attack, subsequently died. Bruce, removed from his post and hospitalized, responded to the report brought to him by a staff officer by drawing his revolver from under the bed-clothes, saying 'Tear it up or you're a dead man' (Hickey, 1998, 213). Apparently he remained on the active list until 1949.

BRUCE, Major General John Geoffrey *(1896–1972), CB, DSO, MC*
The son of a colonel and educated at Rugby, Bruce was commissioned in the Glamorgan Yeomanry in 1914. With First War service in Egypt and Palestine, he transferred to the 6th Gurkha Rifles in 1919. He campaigned in Afghanistan and on the North-West Frontier, being admitted to the DSO in 1923. Having been a member of the 1922 Everest expedition, he joined another in 1924. After attending the Staff College Quetta 1927–1928, he attended the RAF Staff College, Andover, in 1932. An instructor at Quetta 1933–1936, he commanded the 2nd Battalion 6th Gurkha Rifles, 1937–1938.

Attending the Imperial Defence College, at war's beginning Bruce was first attached to the staff at GHQ, BEF; then, a supposed expert in mountain warfare, he served briefly in Norway. In command of an infantry brigade in India 1940–1941, he was Deputy Director of Military Operations, India, 1941–1942. Appointed Major General i/c British Military Mission to China in 1942, he was Deputy CGS, Indian Army, 1944–1946. GOC Lahore District, 1946–1947, he retired from the army in 1948 and, with his wife and two daughters settled in Devon.

BRUNSKILL, Major General Gerald *(1897–1964), CB, MC*
Born in Dublin, the son of a barrister, and educated at Shrewsbury and Trinity College, Dublin, Brunskill was commissioned in the Royal Sussex Regiment in 1914. First War service was in France where he was mentioned in despatches and awarded the MC.

Leaving the army, Brunskill worked in business in London, but was re-commissioned into the Royal Ulster Rifles in 1921. A captain for most of the 1920s, he attended the Staff College, Camberley, 1924–1925, was Brigade Major, North Midland Area, 1933–1936, and served in Palestine 1938–1939. At war's outbreak he was commanding the 1st Battalion Royal Ulster Rifles on the North-West Frontier.

A brigade commander 1940–1942, Brunskill, 'a dark, square-faced man [with] a black patch over one eye' (Ranfurly, 1994, 47), was appointed Director of Special Weapons and Vehicles at the War Office in 1943. Serving in that post till war's end, he was promoted major general in 1944. GOC British troops in Thailand, 1946, he was Deputy Master General of the Ordnance in India in 1947 and Deputy Chief of the General Staff, India, until his retirement from the army in 1948.

Employed for eight years by the Medical Research Council in London, Brunskill was a Commander of the Kent St John Ambulance Brigade and DL for that county in 1962.

BUCHER, Major General Sir (Francis Robert) Roy
(1895–1980), KBE, CB, MC
Educated at Edinburgh Academy and RMC, Sandhurst, Bucher was commissioned in the 1st Battalion Cameron Highlanders in 1913. His First War service began in France, where he was wounded in 1915. Attached to Coke's Rifles (Frontier Force) in India, he transferred to the Duke of Connaught's Lancers in 1916. Serving in Afghanistan and Waziristan, he was admitted to the DSO in 1919.

Married in 1922, Bucher attended the Staff College, Camberley, 1926–1927, and was Deputy Assistant Adjutant General, Deccan District, 1930–1932. Back with his regiment for the remainder of the 1930s, he commanded the 12th (Sam Browne) Cavalry Regiment 1939–1940. A colonel at war's beginning, he had numerous staff appointments at Army HQ, India, and was made Assistant QMG to British forces in Iraq in June 1941. Next year he was made Major General i/c Administration Southern Army, India, and he remained in this post until 1945.

In the lead-up to Indian independence and partition, Bucher served briefly as GOC-in-C Eastern Command and as Chief of Staff at Army HQ. Knighted in 1948, he was seconded C-in-C Army of India, from 1948–1949, when he retired from the army.

Sometime Chairman of the Royal British Legion, and for many years Chairman of the Anglo-Polish Society, Bucher, a keen cricketer, was made DL for the North Riding of Yorkshire in 1962

BUCKLEY, Major General Sir Hugh Clive
(1880–1962), KCIE, CSI, MD, FRCS
After studying Medicine at the University of Edinburgh, Buckley, a qualified surgeon, joined the Indian Medical Service in 1905. A major in 1915 and a colonel in 1933, he was, as major general, Surgeon General with the Government of Bombay 1937–1940.

Retired that year, and made CSI, Buckley was re-employed 1941–1946 as Principal of the Medical College at Agra. Knighted, he returned to Scotland and sat, for a number of years, as medical member on pension tribunals.

BUCKLEY, Major General John *(1883–1972), CBE, DSO, MC*
Born in Co. Killarney, Buckley ran away from school, lied about his age and joined the Royal Dragoons to serve in the South African War. Later with his regiment in India, he was a keen sportsman and became the Indian Army heavy-weight boxing champion. Leaving the army in 1910, he joined the Indian Civil service, but re-enlisted in 1914 in the King's Own Yorkshire Light Infantry. Commissioned in 1915, his First War service was in France, where he was awarded the MC and admitted to the DSO.

Married in 1917, and leaving the army, Buckley made his living as an independent business consultant. Re-commissioned in 1939, and appointed Controller General of Economy at the War Office in 1941, he retired in 1945 as a major general, having held every rank in the army beneath that grade save sergeant.

A director of the Beecham Group in 1946, Buckley was Managing Director from 1949 until illness forced his retirement in 1951. A racehorse owner and traveller, he died in his ninetieth year.

BUCKNALL, Lieutenant General Gerard Corfield *(1894–1980), CB, MC*
Educated at Repton and RMC, Sandhurst, Bucknall was commissioned in the 1st Battalion the Middlesex Regiment in 1914. His First War service was in France. Awarded the MC and bar, he was mentioned in despatches and, convalescing from wounds, served on the General Staff.

A brevet major in 1918, 'Jerry' Bucknall was a brevet lieutenant colonel in 1939. In between times he served in Sudan with the Egyptian Army 1920–1922, attended the Staff College, Camberley, 1928–1929, and served on the General Staff of the Canadian Army 1937–1938. At war's outbreak in 1939 he was commander of the 2nd Battalion Middlesex Regiment.

Kicking his heels in the War Office for more than a year, 'Jerry' Bucknall was placed in command of 53rd (Welsh) Division in 1941. Frustrated with training troops, his chance came in August 1943 when he was appointed GOC 5th Division, then involved in the Sicilian campaign. As a former student of Montgomery's at Staff College, it was Montgomery's patronage that had helped him up the ladder. Begging to follow his leader, he was transferred from Italy to 21st Army Group in January 1944 and placed in command of XXX Corps in preparation for D-Day.

Bucknall did badly. At any rate he was 'carted' for his corps's inability to exploit enemy disorganization west of Caen. Lacking the 'aggressiveness and determination to retain the initiative' at Villers-Bocage (D'Este, 2001, 192), he was sacked in July 1944. While Montgomery, in a rare admission, reported that Bucknall's appointment to corps command had been 'a mistake' (French, 1996, 198), employment was found for him the next year as GOC Northern Ireland District. He held this post until his retirement from the army in 1947.

A keen cricketer and member of the MCC, Bucknall was Colonel of the Middlesex Regiment 1952–1959 and Lord Lieutenant of Middlesex 1963–1965. He weathered local government reorganization sufficient to be appointed Assistant Lieutenant for Greater London 1965–1970.

Married in 1925, he fathered a daughter and two sons, the youngest of whom was killed in Korea while serving with the Sherwood Foresters.

BULLEN-SMITH, Major General Charles *(1898–1970), MC*
Few personal details of this 'hugely built Lowland Scot' (Hamilton, 1983, 715) are known. Commissioned in the King's Own Scottish Borderers during the First War, Bullen-Smith served on Montgomery's staff in 3rd Division 1939–1940 and, on his own initiative, Montgomery promoted him to command a battalion of the KOSB in June 1940.

Known as an 'outstanding trainer of troops' (Chandler & Collis (eds.), 1994,) with Home Forces, Bullen-Smith briefly commanded 15th Division in 1943, before being transferred to command 51st (Highland) Division on its return to Britain from Italy.

His task, to train the division for the invasion of France, was not made easy by the manner in which his predecessor, the popular and eccentric Wimberley, had been removed. Resented by many of his senior officers, the logistical difficulties of forming his command in France, coupled to some unexpectedly hard German resistance in the bocage country around Caen, led to negative reports on the division being 'too slow, too cautious and unwilling to take risks' (D'Este, 2001, 274). In mid-July Montgomery, though he recognized Bullen-Smith's 'many fine qualities', ordered his removal and judged him unfit 'to command any other division' (Hamilton, 1983, 715).

BURCH, Major General 'Eric' Frederick Whitmore
(1893–1977), CSI, CIE, MC
Educated at Framlingham, Burch's First War service was in France, Egypt and India. Enlisting with the East Riding of Yorkshire Yeomanry in 1914, he was commissioned in the East Yorkshire Regiment the same year. Wounded, mentioned in despatches and awarded the MC in 1916, he transferred to the Indian Army, joining the 7th Gurkha Rifles before transferring again to the 18th Royal Garwhal Rifles.

A captain in 1919, Burch served in the Third Afghan War 1919–1920. Married in 1929 and a brevet major in 1930, he was Deputy Assistant QMG, AHQ India, in 1936 and Deputy Director of Movements and Quartering, AHQ India, in 1937. A brevet lieutenant colonel in 1938, he was Assistant Military Secretary to the C-in-C, India, in 1939. A major general in 1942, he was Director of Staff Duties, General Staff, India, 1942–1943. He was, in addition, commander of the Indian Army Liaison Mission to the Middle East and Mediterranean 1944–1945. In 1946 he organized India's victory celebrations in New Delhi.

Made CSI in 1946, Burch retired from the army in 1949. Settling in Essex he was Chairman of Lexden and Winstree RDC 1959–1963 and, from 1968 to 1973, was Treasurer of the Chelmsford Diocesan Board of Finance.

BURNHAM, see LAWSON

BURROWS, Lieutenant General Montagu Brocas
(1894–1967), CB, DSO, MC
The son of an Indian Civil Servant, Burrows was educated at Eton and Oxford University. Commissioned in the 5th Dragoon Guards in 1914, he was taken prisoner during the retreat from Mons. Having taught himself Russian in captivity, he served with the North Russian Expeditionary Force 1918–1919, was twice mentioned in despatches, awarded the MC and admitted to the DSO.

Adjutant of the Oxford University OTC 1920–1922, 'Brocas' Burrows was an instructor at Sandhurst for the next three years. He attended the Staff College, Camberley, 1925–1926, before spending three years in India first at Army HQ and then as Brigade Major with the Nowshera Infantry Brigade. At Aldershot Command, 1930–1932, he was Brigade Major with the 1st Cavalry Brigade. On the staff at the War Office, 1935–1938, he was Military Attaché in Rome, Budapest and Tirana from 1938 to 1940.

Benefiting from Brooke's patronage, having been his student at Camberley, Burrows was promoted major general in 1940 and made commander of 9th Armoured Division. In this training role he was switched, in mid-1942, to command 11th Armourted Division. A good games player, and known as 'a bit flashy' (Roberts, 1987, 153), he was appointed to head the British Military Mission to Moscow in February 1944. There, despite – or perhaps because of – his fluency in Russian, his hosts asked for his removal (Danchev & Todman, 2001, 607). Appointed GOC-in-C West African Command in 1945, he retired from the army in 1946.

Having married the daughter of an iron and steel manufacturer, Burrows had a flourishing post-war business career. He held numerous directorships in industry and insurance.

BUTLER, Major General Stephen Seymour *(1880–1964), CB, CMG, DSO*
The son of a clergyman and educated at Winchester, Butler joined the Northumberland Fusiliers in 1897 and was commissioned in the Royal Warwickshire Regiment in 1899. He fought in South Africa, but became famous as an explorer of Northern Arabia. From 1909–1915 he was attached to the Egyptian Army.

Butler's First War Service was in Egypt, Gallipoli and France. Admitted to the DSO in 1917, he was, whether 'equal to the task' or not (Marshall-Cornwall, 1984, 39), Deputy Chief Intelligence Officer at GHQ at war's end.

Head of Naval Intelligence in Constantinople, 1919–1920, 'Sammy' Butler was Assistant Military Secretary to General Birdwood in Northern Command, India, 1921–1923. A military attaché in Bucharest for the next three years, he was Inspector General of the West African Frontier Force 1926–1930 and commanded the Sudan Defence Force 1930–1935. He was brought home that year to command the 48th (South Midland) Division. He held this post for four years when, approaching his sixtieth birthday, he retired in 1939.

Re-employed at war's beginning, Butler was head of the Military Mission to Turkey 1939–1940 and head of the Military Mission to Ethiopia 1941–1943.

Finally retired in 1944, Butler and his wife settled in Hampshire. She died the year of their 50th wedding anniversary, he the year after.

BUTLER, Major General Hon. Theobald Patrick Probyn
(1884–1970), DSO
Born in Devon, the youngest son of Baron Dunboyne, Butler was educated at Winchester and RMA Woolwich and commissioned in the Royal Artillery. Seconded for service with the Egyptian Army in 1914, his First War service was in Palestine, Egypt and Sudan. Twice mentioned in despatches, he was admitted to the DSO.

Butler served on the staff of the Risalpur Brigade in India 1928–1930 and on the North-West Frontier in 1930, where he commanded a mountain artillery battery. Married in 1933, he commanded 1st Regiment Royal Horse Artillery 1935–1937. Promoted colonel and appointed Garrison Commander and Commandant at the Royal Artillery Depot at Woolwich in 1937, he was promoted major general and commanded Bombay District in India 1940–1941.

Retiring from the army in 1942, Butler returned to live in his native Devon.

BUTTERWORTH, Major General Donald Clunes *(1895- ?), DSO*
Few of this officer's personal details are known. A territorial in 1914, he was enlisted in the ranks and commissioned in the North Staffordshire Regiment in 1915. His First War service was in France, where he was wounded and mentioned in despatches.

Living on a captain's pay for most of the inter-war years, Butterworth was Adjutant to a Territorial Army formation 1930–1934 and, a brevet major in 1936, a staff officer with Aldershot Command 1937–1939. He commanded the 2nd Battalion of the North Staffords, 1939–1940.

With his battalion in France with the BEF 1939–1940, Butterworth was admitted to the DSO after Dunkirk. An acting major general in 1942, he was GOC 38th (Welsh) Division, under Home Forces, from April 1944 until the formation was broken up in September 1944.

C

CADELL, Lieutenant General Charles Alexander Elliott
(1888–1951), CBE, MC
Educated at Cheltenham College and RMA, Woolwich, Cadell was commissioned in the Royal Artillery in 1908. First War service was with the Royal Field Artillery in India, Egypt, Malaya and France, where he was mentioned three times in despatches and awarded the MC.

Married in 1920, Cadell was one of those officers who lived on a captain's pay for most of the inter-war years. A battery commander on the North-West Frontier 1927–1931 and an instructor at the School of Artillery in India 1935–1938, he was CRA Singapore in 1938 and CRA Malaya 1939–1940, before returning to England to serve in Anti-Aircraft Command.

A major general in 1940, when he commanded an AA division, he later commanded an AA corps. An accomplished fisherman, first-class shot and fine billiards player, Cadell retired from the army in 1944. He died in his sixties in a Jersey nursing home after a long illness.

CALLANDER, Lieutenant General Sir Colin Bishop
(1897–1979), KCB, KBE, MC
Born in Somerset and educated at West Buckland and RMC, Sandhurst, Callander was commissioned in the Royal Munster Fusiliers in 1915. Thrice wounded in the First War, he was awarded the MC in 1917. Transferring to the Leicestershire Regiment in 1922, he married in 1923.

A captain in 1925, Callander was a major in 1936. In between times he had fathered two children and been mentioned in despatches for service on the North-West Frontier. A lieutenant colonel in 1940, he rose from battalion to divisional command in 1943, when he was appointed to command the 54th (East Anglian) Division, then in the process of being broken up. In 1944 he was appointed to command the 4th Division and saw service in Greece 1945–1946.

Director of Military Training at the War Office 1948, and again 1952–1954, Callander commanded the 2nd Division in Germany 1949–1951. Knighted in 1952, he was Military Secretary to the Secretary of State for War 1954–1956, before retiring from the army, with his knighthood enhanced, in 1957.

Settling in Kent, Callander was Colonel of the Leicestershire Regiment 1954–1963.

CAMERON, Lieutenant General Sir Alexander Maurice
(1898–1986), KBE, CB, MC
Of military family and educated at Wellington, Cameron was commissioned in the Royal Engineers in 1916. First War service was in France, where he was wounded, mentioned in despatches and awarded the MC. He also saw service in Iraq, Kurdistan and Persia (Iran) 1919–1921.

After graduating from the Staff College, Camberley, in 1929, Cameron, a captain for most of the inter-war years, attended the RAF Staff College in 1939. A brigadier in 1940, he liaised between the AASF and the BEF in France and was CRE 8th Army in Italy in 1943. On the staff of SHAEF 1944–1945, he was Deputy QMG at the War Office 1945–1948.

In 1948 Cameron was appointed Major General i/c Administration MELF and in 1951 was made GOC East African Command. Knighted in 1952, he retired from the army in 1954 and, 1955–1960, was Director of Civil Defence for the South-Eastern Region.

CAMPBELL, Major General John Charles *(1894–1942), VC, DSO, MC*
Born in Scotland and educated at Sedburgh, Campbell enlisted in the Honourable Artillery Company in August 1914. In July 1915 he was commissioned from RMA, Woolwich. Twice wounded in 1916, and by 1917 a captain in the Royal Horse Artillery, he was awarded the MC.

Devoted to horses and married in 1922, 'Jock' Campbell, between the wars was an equitation instructor at Woolwich and later at the Cavalry School, Weedon. A member of the Royal Artillery Polo team, he left his heart, it is said, 'on the polo field' (Pyman, 1969, 38). A major in 1939, Campbell was sent with his regiment to Egypt and was appointed to command the 3rd Regiment Royal Artillery in 1940.

Distinguishing himself in the retreat from the Libyan border in September 1940, Campbell developed a tactical means of probing at Italian weaknesses by fusing lorried infantry and tractor-towed artillery into mobile groups. Thus hindered, the Italians formed the impression that British forces in Egypt were much stronger than they were. These 'Jock' columns were used to good effect in the advance into Cyrenaica in December 1940, and the courage and dash of their leader, who alternated as commander of 3rd and 4th Regiments, RHA, was much admired by those of a privateering military inclination.

Admitted to the DSO in late 1940, with Bar attached in early 1941, the climax to Campbell's career came in the CRUSADER battles of that autumn. Promoted brigadier and placed in command of the 7th Armoured Division's Support Group, his leadership at the battle of Sidi Rezegh, when he was 'the heart and soul of the defences', became 'an epic of the war' (DNB). Though wounded, he refused to be evacuated and, from the roof of his staff car, personally led his tanks in the charge.

55

Awarded the Victoria Cross – surely one of the oldest recipients of that honour – Campbell was promoted major general in February 1942 and appointed to command 7th Armoured Division. Within a month he was dead. The staff car in which he was being driven crashed and overturned at the Halfaya Pass, killing him instantly. His fame was assured. Sidi Rezegh may have been an 'untidy battle' (Bidwell & Graham, 1985, 226), and the 'Jock' column, for all its emphasis on dispersal and manoeuvre, was, perhaps, of limited tactical value in the desert war. All the same, at a time in the war when the British public needed a hero, Campbell fitted the bill.

CANDY, Major General Ronald Herbert (1888–1972), CIE
The son of a professor of medicine, Candy was born in London. Educated at the City of London School and the London Hospital, he entered the Indian Medical Service in 1910. Married in 1912, his First War service was in Mesopotamia and on the North-West Frontier.

Candy's service record was made up of numerous Indian area postings, usually in base hospitals. In the 1930s he was Deputy Director Medical Services, Agra District, 1934–1936, and in 1937 he was made CIE and appointed Deputy Director Medical Services, Eastern Command. Superintendent of numerous hospitals during the war years, he retired from the army in 1944.

CANTLIE, Lieutenant General Sir Neil
(1892–1975), KCB, KBE, MC, MB, ChB, FRCS
Educated at Robert Gordon's College and graduating from Aberdeen University in 1914, Cantlie entered the Royal Army Medical Corps the same year. His First War service was in France. Awarded the MC, he was elected a Fellow of the Royal College of Surgeons in 1920.

Seconded for service with the Egyptian Army that year, Cantlie later served with the Sudan Defence Force. Married in 1930 and a lieutenant colonel in 1935, his Second War service was as Assistant Director Medical Services with the 46th Division, and later Deputy Director Medical Services with V Corps in North Africa and Italy. A major general in 1944, he was Deputy Director Medical Services, Southern Command, 1946–1948. As lieutenant general he was Director General of the Army Medical Services 1949–1952. With his knighthood enhanced, he retired from the army that year.

Retired to the Isle of Wight, Cantlie was House Governor and Medical Superintendent of the King Edward Convalescent Home for Officers, 1952–1958.

CARPENTER, Major General John Owen (1894–1967), CB, MC
Born in Bexhill-on-Sea and educated at Bradfield and RMC, Sandhurst, Carpenter was commissioned in the East Surrey Regiment in 1914. First War service was in France, where he was wounded, mentioned in despatches and awarded the MC, and later in Egypt and Macedonia.

A brevet major in 1918, Carpenter was a staff captain with the Army of the

Black Sea, and was employed with the Egyptian Army 1920–1922. Married in 1922, he spent the next dozen years a captain. An instructor at the Small Arms School, India, 1933–1936, he was a battalion commander in 1937 and an instructor at the Small Arms School, Netheravon, 1938–1939. A colonel in 1939 and a brigadier in 1941, he commanded 214th Independent Brigade before being appointed GOC of a training formation, 61st Division, in Northern Ireland in September 1942. Removed from that post in May 1943, he commanded Catterick sub-area 1944–1945. Appointed CB he retired from the army in 1946.

A widower in 1944, Carpenter re-married in 1948, only for his second wife to die in 1952. There were two sons from the first marriage.

CARR, Lieutenant General Laurence *(1886–1954), CB, DSO, OBE*

Educated at Uppingham and RMC, Sandhurst, Carr was commissioned in the Gordon Highlanders in 1904. A captain in 1914, his First War service was in France where he was twice wounded, mentioned in despatches and admitted to the DSO.

Married in 1916, Carr's regimental duties in the 1920s were various after he attended the Staff College, Camberley, in 1919, including a long spell of service in India where, between 1923 and 1926, he was an instructor at Quetta. Staff duties at the War Office in the late 1920s, and again 1931–34, led to his appointment as an instructor at the Imperial Defence College 1934–1936. Commander of 2nd Infantry Brigade at Aldershot in 1936, he saw service in Palestine and Transjordan over the next two years. He was Director of Staff Duties at the War Office 1938–1939. It was thanks to him, it is said, that the Bren light machine gun (originally manufactured in Czechoslovakia) was adopted by the British Army.

With a career thus far nicely balanced between staff duties and field commands, Carr, shortly after war's beginning, was appointed Assistant Chief of the Imperial General Staff. When Dill replaced Ironside as CIGS in June 1940, he was made GOC 1st Corps, and, a year later, GOC-in-C Eastern Command. Something happened. At any rate, he fell out so badly with one of his divisional commanders, Irwin, who, in telling Carr 'that he had no confidence in him' (French, 1996, 1195), practically refused to serve under him. Brooke, the CIGS, who had himself decided that Carr 'did not turn out to have the right qualities' (Danchev & Todman, 2001, 148) decided both would have to be moved.

Whereas Irwin was sent to command a corps in India, Carr was, humiliatingly, made Senior Military Assistant at the Ministry of Supply. He retired from that job and the army in 1944.

A keen all-round sportsman, member of the MCC and gardener, Carr lived out his final years in Surrey where he was chairman of the Roehampton Club.

CARRINGTON, Lieutenant General Sir Robert Harold
(1882–1964), KCB, DSO

The son of a clergyman and educated at Winchester, 'Freddy' Carrington was commissioned into the Royal Field Artillery in 1901, He served in the South

African War and with the Royal Horse Artillery from 1908 to 1916. Four-times mentioned in despatches and admitted to the DSO in 1916, he ended the war a brevet lieutenant colonel on the staff of 57th Division.

After attending the Staff College, Camberley, in 1920, Carrington married and performed regimental duties at home and abroad. On the staff of 4th Division 1931–32, he was CRA of the same formation 1932–1934. From 1936 until the outbreak of war he was Major General, Royal Artillery, at Army HQ, India.

Deputy Adjutant General at the War Office in 1939, Carrington was GOC-in-C Scottish Command and Governor of Edinburgh Castle the next year. His retirement on reaching the age of sixty was not inevitable, but 'bitterly hurt' though he was (Lindsay, 1987, 157), it was made necessary by the need to create vacancies for other displaced area commanders. Considered 'not a man of great ability' (Dill, 2nd acc., 9, LHCMA), and seen to be 'very lost without work' (Danchev & Todman, 2001, 178), he was knighted and found some employment with the Ministry of Supply 1942–1945.

Colonel Commandant of the Royal Artillery 1940–1950, Carrington was made DL for Suffolk in 1952 and High Sheriff of that County the following year.

CARTON DE WIART, Lieutenant General Sir Adrian
(1880–1963), VC, KBE, CB, CMG, DSO
Born in Brussels, brought up in Cairo and educated at the Oratory School, Edgbaston, Carton de Wiart abandoned his studies at Oxford to enlist in Paget's Horse in 1899. Wounded in South Africa, he ended the Boer War as a subaltern in the 4th (Royal Irish) Dragoons. Seconded to the Somali Camel Corps in 1914, he was wounded in the campaign to track down Mahomed bin Abdillah Hassan, the 'Mad Mullah', and, admitted to the DSO, was invalided home the next year.

Having had his left eye removed, Carton de Wiart rejoined his regiment in France. But he was to return wounded so often to the same hospital that, it is said, silk pyjamas with his name on were reserved for him (Sheffield in Keegan, 1991, 325). Losing his left hand in 1915, he was awarded the VC in 1916, only to be wounded again. He was, by war's end, a brigadier and a celebrity in the army. His eye-patch and empty sleeve invited the inevitable nickname, 'Nelson'.

Appointed second-in-command, and later head, of the British Military Mission to Poland in 1919, Carton de Wiart witnessed a good deal of military activity but was unable to exert much political influence. However, he fell in love with the place and its people sufficient to be loaned an estate near the Soviet border and settle there after resigning his commission in 1924.

His life as a Polish country gentleman, 'happily shooting duck' (DNB), was interrupted in 1939. Again made head of the British Military Mission, he could do nothing save evacuate his staff and their families from Warsaw to Romania. Back in England, although in his sixty-first year, he was appointed to command the 61st (Territorial) Division based in Oxford, while in April 1940 he was chosen to command MAURICEFORCE for the campaign in Norway. Landed at Namsos with a small staff, supposedly to co-ordinate a pincer-attack on

Trondheim, it was not long before Carton de Wiart realized that German air superiority rendered his position untenable and recommended evacuation. Had a less famously brave man made the request, it might not have been listened to. As it was MAURICEFORCE was evacuated with very few casualties.

Norway was Carton de Wiart's last active command. Appointed Head of the British Mission to Yugoslavia in April 1941, his aircraft crashed off North Africa en route and he was taken prisoner. Imprisoned near Florence and thrown into the company of other captured British senior officers, he proved himself 'a delightful character [who] must hold the world record for bad language' (Ranfurly, 1994, 123). Escaping, only to be re-captured, his Italian captors sent him to Lisbon in August 1943 hoping that, as an unwitting inter-mediary, Carton de Wiart might secure favourable armistice terms.

In one of his more eccentric decisions Churchill had Carton de Wiart promoted lieutenant general and made him, less than a month after his return to Britain, his personal representative to the Chinese generalissimo, Chiang Kai-shek. It was a position requiring more tact and delicacy that Carton de Wiart possessed, especially as, never having been to China, he imagined it full of 'whimsical little people . . . who . . . worshipped their grandmothers' (Carton de Wiart, 1950, 235). Developing a fondness for Chiang and his wife, and disagreeing with Mountbatten when he was supposed to be liaising with him, he appeared before the cabinet in January 1945, only to deliver a report on the China situation that lasted a full six-and-a-half minutes.

But Carton de Wiart's inadequacies as a diplomat tended to enhance his repu-tation as a man of action and inspired leader of men. Regarded with enormous affection as a *beau sabreur* (French, 1991, 1200), almost a throwback from a previous age, he was, it is said, the model for Evelyn Waugh's Ritchie-Hook character in *Men at Arms*.

Finally retired in 1947, Carton de Wiart wrote his entertaining memoirs, *Happy Odyssey* and, a widower in 1949, married again in 1950. Living in the west of Ireland and still waging his personal war against the local duck popula-tion, he received honorary degrees from Aberdeen and Oxford Universities.

CARY, Major General Rupert Tristram Oliver *(1896–1980), CB, CBE, DSO*
Commissioned into the Royal Corps of Signals in 1916, Cary's First War service was in France, where he was wounded, and in India. Awarded the MBE in 1919, he advanced in rank no higher than major over the next twenty years.

Noticed by Auchinleck in Norway in 1940, and considered 'excellent . . . and worth pushing on' (Dill, 2nd. acc. 11, LHCMA), Cary, by now attached to Middle East Command, was involved in operations in Iraq in 1941 and Persia (Iran) in 1943. Awarded the CBE that year, he became Deputy Chief Signal Officer with the Eighth Army in Italy and was admitted to the DSO.

Promoted major general and brought home in 1944, Cary was Commandant of the School of Signals in 1945. Commander of the Catterick sub-district in 1946, he retired from the army in 1949 and, with his second wife, settled in the Channel Islands.

CASEMENT, Major General Francis *(1881–1967), DSO*

Born in Ballycastle, Co. Antrim and educated at the Academical Institution, Coleraine, and Trinity College, Dublin, Casement completed his medical studies in 1906 and played rugby for Ireland.

First War service was with the Naval Division at Gallipoli, and later in France where, he was admitted to the DSO in 1917. Married in 1916, with one son and a daughter, Casement was Assistant Director of Pathology and Hygiene, Western Command, 1933–1935, and Assistant Director General of Army Medical Services at the War Office 1935–1936. Deputy Director General of Army Medical Services, 1937–1938, he was Deputy Director of Medical Services Southern Command, 1938.

Surgeon to the King 1940–1941, Casement retired from the army in 1941. He was High Sheriff for Co. Antrim in 1951.

CASSELS, Field Marshal Sir Archibald James Halkett
(1907–1996), GCB, KBE, DSO

The son of a general attaining general officer rank is a not unusual occurrence. What was unusual in 'Jim' Cassels's case was that he and his father should both be generals on the active list in the same war.

Born in Quetta, the only son of an Indian Army officer (then serving with the 32nd Lancers), Cassels was educated at Rugby and RMC Sandhurst. Commissioned in the Seaforth Highlanders in 1926, he was ADC to his father (who was then GOC Northern Command, India) from 1930–1931. Regimental duties then took him to Palestine and back to England in 1934. Married in 1935, he was again ADC to his father (who by now had become C-in-C in India) from 1935–1938.

At Fort George, Inverness, when war broke out in 1939, Cassels served with 52nd Lowland Division in France south of the Somme, his brigade being evacuated from Cherbourg in June 1940. Mentioned in despatches, he attended a shortened course at the Staff College, Camberley, before serving on the staff at the War Office. Returning to his division in 1942, he was BGS 21st Army Group in 1944, preparing for the opening of the second front. Made acting brigadier in July 1944, he commanded 152nd Brigade as part of 51st (Highland) Division during the latter part of the campaign in Normandy. Admitted to the DSO, he served with the division throughout the fighting in North-West Europe and was appointed to its command in May 1945.

Cassels's post-war career was long and illustrious. Posts included that of Director of Land and Air Warfare at the War Office 1948–1949, divisional command during the Korean War, and Director of Military Training 1954–1957.

C-in-C British Army of the Rhine 1960–1963, Cassels was promoted field marshal in 1968, the day after he had ceased being Chief of the General Staff. Though 'ill-suited to the Whitehall environment' (Heathcote, 1999, 81), he was appropriately honoured. Retired to his home in Morayshire, he held numerous honorary colonelcies and re-married after the death of his first wife in 1978.

CASSELS, General Sir Robert Archibald *(1876–1959), GCB, GCSI, DSO*
Born in India and educated at Sedbergh and RMC, Sandhurst, Cassels was commissioned in 1896 and was gazetted into the Indian Army the following year. First in the infantry and later with the 32nd Lancers, he spent most of his service life in India and the Middle East. His First War service was largely in Mesopotamia, where he was admitted to the DSO. A major general in 1919 and a general in 1929, Cassels commanded Peshawar District 1923–1928.

Adjutant General in India 1928–1930, Cassels was GOC-in-C Northern Command, India 1930–1934 and was appointed C-in-C of the Army in India in 1935. Though nearing retirement age and considered a 'bad choice' in that post by Hore-Belisha (Liddell Hart, 1965, 78), he was allowed to stay in it until 1941. Brusquely hardbitten and with a temper that was 'legendary' (Greacan, 1989, 139), he was, at the age of sixty-five, induced to get out from under the 'pagoda tree' and retire to make way for Wavell. Denied a field marshal's baton – unlike his son who acquired his – Cassels returned to England and lived out his retirement in Sussex, where 'he took a prominent and useful part in local affairs' (DNB).

CHEETHAM, Major General Geoffrey *(1891–1962), CB, DSO*
Educated at Wellington College and commissioned in the Royal Engineers in 1914, Cheetham's First War service was in France, where he was wounded, twice mentioned in despatches and admitted to the DSO, and in West Africa, where he was awarded the MC.

Engaged in survey work in the Gold Coast (Ghana) 1920–1924, Cheetham was an assistant instructor at the School of Military Engineering 1924–1924, later serving on the staff at the War Office. A lieutenant colonel in 1935, he was Chief Instructor of Survey at Chatham before being promoted colonel in 1938. A major general in 1943 he was, until his retirement from the army in 1949, Director General Ordnance Survey.

Married, with a son and two daughters, Cheetham was, for many years, Chairman of the Inland Water Survey Committee. He lived in his retirement near Newbury.

CHILTON, Lieutenant General Sir Maurice Somerville
(1898–1956), KBE, CB
Born in Liverpool and educated at Rugby and RMA, Woolwich, Chilton was commissioned in the Royal Artillery in 1915. He served in France in the First War and, transferring to the Royal Horse Artillery, served in India 1919–1924, before attending the Staff College, Camberley, 1930–1931. A married man with a son and two daughters, he was nominated to attend the Imperial Defence College course in 1940. Instead he served as a divisional staff officer with the BEF in France. He was Deputy Director of Military Training at the War Office 1941–1942 and CRA 44th Division 1941–1943.

In 1944 Chilton was Chief of Staff to Dempsey, GOC-in-C of the British Second Army and, next year, was appointed Deputy Adjutant General to 21

Army Group. Director of Air at the War Office 1946–1948, he commanded the East Anglian District 1948–1950.

Vice QMG 1950–1953, Chilton was GOC-in-C Anti-Aircraft Command 1953–1955. Knighted in 1954, he had just taken up the appointment of QMG when he died at his home of a heart attack.

CHRISTIE, Major General Campbell Manning *(1893–1963), MC*

Born in the Punjab, the son of an Indian Civil Servant, Christie was educated at Clifton and RMA, Woolwich. Commissioned in the Royal Artillery in 1913, and married in 1914, his First War service was in France and Macedonia, where he was awarded the MC.

An instructor at Woolwich 1923–1926, Christie, in common with so many of his contemporaries, spent many years on a captain's pay and endured the double-bind of spells on half pay when promoted. With his wife, he began to write plays. When *Someone at the Door* and *Family Group* were first performed in 1935, he was a gunnery instructor at the School of Artillery, Larkhill.

Chief Instructor at the School of Artillery 1939–1940, Christie was CRA 53rd (Welsh) Division 1940–1941 and, promoted major general, was CRA VIII Corps 1941–1942. Major General RA, Malta, 1942–1944 (re-styled GOC Anti-Aircraft Defences), he retired from the army in 1946.

Success on the London stage followed, with several long-running plays, one of which, *Carrington VC*, was made into a film. Christie, a 'tall, spare, clean-shaven man' who, according to his obituarist, 'could pack a punch . . . packed in wit', experienced the despair of no longer being in fashion as the 1950s progressed. Aged sixty-nine he was found dead in the 'gas-filled kitchen of his home in West Byfleet, Surrey'.

CHRISTISON, General Sir Alexander Frank Philip
4th Bt. (1893–1993), GBE, CB, DSO, MC

Born in Edinburgh and educated at Edinburgh Academy and Oxford University, Christison had more thoughts about pursuing a career in medicine than the army (Hickey, 1998, 96). But, like so many of his generation, the events of August 1914 saw him in uniform. Commissioned in the Cameron Highlanders, he was a captain in 1915, the same year as he was awarded the MC after the Battle of Loos.

Married in 1916 and with a wife and three children to support on a captain's pay, Christison attended the Staff College, Camberley, 1927–1928. A brevet major in 1930, he instructed at the Staff College, Quetta, and, unusually for a non-Indian Army officer, commanded a battalion of Gurkhas, An instructor at Camberley 1936–1937, he transferred to the Duke of Wellington's Regiment in 1937. Returning to Quetta, he commanded an infantry brigade and, 1940–1941, was Commandant of the Staff College.

Balancing his teaching commitments with a passion for ornithology, Christison commanded 15th Division with Home Forces from 1941–1943. His war in the Far East began after his son had been killed in action in Burma.

Promoted lieutenant general, he was appointed to command XXXIII Corps. Further reorganization resulted in him switching to command XV Corps, with responsibility for the re-conquest of the Arakan. Knighted in the field in 1944, the part Christison played in the re-conquest of Burma was considerable, especially when it came to amphibious operations. Whether, indeed, he was known by Indian troops as the 'Smiling General Sahib', his cheerfulness was well-known. Though it was Slim who stole the limelight, Leese, an old friend from Camberley days, was 'very pleased' (Ryder, 1987, 237) with Christison's handling of XV corps. Admitted to the DSO in 1945, after personally rallying his troops during an attack, he succeeded to his half-brother's baronetcy the same year.

Told by Leese that he was to succeed Slim as C-in-C XIV Army in 1945, Christison found himself succeeding Leese as C-in-C Allied Land Forces South East Asia and, 1945–46, held the appointment of allied commander in the Dutch East Indies. After co-authoring a book on the birds of the Arakan, he returned to Britain. GOC-in-C Northern Command in 1946, he was GOC-in-C Scottish Command from 1947 until his retirement from the army in 1949.

Christison's retirement was active, with a number of directorships, a swathe of honorary colonelcies, and a vice-presidency of the Burma Star Association. A fruit farmer and author of the Scottish National Trust's Bannockburn guidebook, he was DL for Roxburghshire in 1956. Though he wrote no memoirs he corresponded frequently with former comrades and historians. Allegedly fluent in Gaelic and a keen bagpipes player, he was widowed in 1974. He re-married that year and, outliving his second wife, died one month after his hundredth birthday in a Melrose nursing home.

CLARK, Lieutenant General John George Walters *(1892–1948), CB, MC*
Born in Paisley and educated at Winchester and RMC, Sandhurst, Clark was commissioned in the 16th (Queen's) Lancers in 1911. First War service was in France, where he was wounded, mentioned thrice in despatches and awarded the MC.

Married in 1915, Clark served in India, attended the Staff College, Camberley, 1926–1927 and commanded the 16th/15th Lancers 1933–1936. After a period as a staff officer at the War Office, he commanded the 12th Infantry Brigade and was Deputy Constable of Dover Castle 1938–1939. Appointed to command the 1st Cavalry Division in Palestine in 1940, he commanded HABFORCE the next year, in which a series of columns drove through the desert to help suppress the Raschid Ali revolt in Iraq. The 'quiet little man who recoiled when spoken to' (de Chair, 1994, 246) was, nevertheless, able to report that 'the Iraqis have asked for a flag of truce. Allah be praised' (Wilson, 1948, 108). After securing Baghdad, his division then participated in operations in Syria.

As the Cavalry Division's mechanization programme left Clark, a cavalryman, functionally redundant, his tenure of command of the 10th Armoured Division, then forming in Egypt, was not destined to last long. Made GOC Lines of Communication at Allied Forces HQ in Algiers late in 1942, his standard of comfort was, apparently, 'as high as ever' (Penney Diary, 3/2, LHCMA). Briefly Deputy Governor of Sicily in 1943, he was appointed Chief Administration Officer, AFHQ in January 1944. Made head of the SHAEF Mission to the Netherlands in 1945, he headed the British Economic Mission to Greece 1945–1946. Tiring of the work, he retired from the army that year.

Not much honoured in his own country, though decorated abroad (US Legion of Merit, French Légion d'Honneur, etc.) Clark died in his fifties after a short illness.

CLARKE, Major General Sir Edward Montagu Campbell
(1885–1971), KBE, CB
Educated at Rugby and RMA, Woolwich, Clarke was commissioned in the Royal Garrison Artillery in 1905. Married in 1914, his First War service was in France. A brevet major in 1925, he was promoted colonel in 1933. In 1936 he was appointed Deputy Superintendent of the Design Department at the Royal Arsenal. Senior military member of the Ordnance Committee 1936–1937, and later Vice-President, he was promoted major general in 1938 and made Director of Artillery at the War Office and Military Adviser to the Ministry of Supply

Director of the School of Artillery at Larkhill, 1939–1942, Clarke was Director General of Artillery at the War Office 1942–1945 and, knighted, retired from the army in 1946.

CLEWER, Major General Donald *(1892–1945) CB*
Educated in Brighton and, having completed his medical studies at Guy's Hospital, Clewer was commissioned in the RAMC as a dentist in 1914. A captain in 1921, he transferred to the newly-formed Army Dental Corps, rising in rank and status to become Inspector of Army Dental Services, India, 1936–1937. Director of the Army Dental Service at the War Office 1937–1942, he was the first Dental Corps officer to reach the rank of major general.

President of the Allied Forces Dental Society 1942–1943, illness induced Clewer's retirement from the army. He died in hospital in 1945.

CLOWES, Major General Norman *(1893–1980), CBE, DSO, MC*
An Australian, Clowes was educated at Toowomba Grammar School and RMC, Duntroon. Commissioned in the Australian Staff Corps in 1914, his First War service was with the AIF in Egypt, Gallipoli and France. Wounded, he was awarded the MC in 1915 and admitted to the DSO in 1918.

A graduate of the Staff College, Camberley, in 1920, Clowes, following exchange duty with the Indian Army, 1927–1930, transferred to the British Army in 1931. A staff officer with 46th (North Midland) Division in 1932, and Northern Command 1933–1936, he was Deputy Adjutant and QMG, Northern Command, 1936–1937. As commander of the 1st Battalion the Manchester Regiment, he served in Palestine 1937–1938.

A colonel in 1939, Clowes was chief staff officer with the British Military Mission in Egypt 1939–1940. A brigadier in 1941, he was BGS British troops in Egypt 1941–1943 and, promoted major general, was a District commander in North Africa 1944–1945.

CLUTTERBUCK, Major General Walter Edmond *(1894–1987), DSO, MC*

Educated at Cheltenham and RMC Sandhurst, Clutterbuck was commissioned in the Royal Scots Fusiliers in 1913. First War service was in France, Gallipoli, Egypt and Palestine. Twice wounded, mentioned in despatches and awarded the MC (with Bar), he served in southern Russia in 1919.

Married that year, Clutterbuck spent the next fifteen years on a captain's pay. A brevet lieutenant colonel in 1939, he commanded the 1st Battalion Royal Scots Fusiliers in France with the BEF, and commanded the 10th Infantry Brigade 1940–1941. Promoted major general, he was appointed to command 1st Division with Home Forces 1942–1943. In Tunisia in March 1943 he was judged 'rather muddled' (Allfrey, 3/1/ LHCMA), but he led his division in the assault on the island of Pantelleria, when, at the cost of ten casualties, the Italian garrison of 14,000 men was induced to surrender.

Admitted to the DSO, Clutterbuck was sent back to Britain where for the next year he commanded 55th Division. Not given a command in North-West Europe, he was sent instead to Egypt where, 1945–1946, he was head of the British Military Mission.

Retired from the army in 1946, Clutterbuck farmed in North Yorkshire, was a local councillor and, keen on field sports, was Chairman of the Bedale Hunt for a number of years.

COLLIER, Major General Angus Lyell *(1893–1971), CBE, MC*

Educated at Sedbergh and Oxford University, Collier was commissioned in the Cameron Highlanders in 1914. First War service was in France, where he was twice mentioned in despatches and awarded the MC, in the Balkans and in South Russia.

A regimental officer for most of the 1920s, Collier married in 1922 and attended the Staff College, Camberley, 1927–1928, where 'he liked everybody and enjoyed a joke' (Greacan, 1989, 98). A brevet lieutenant colonel in 1936, he was Deputy Assistant Military Secretary at the War Office 1937–1939 and, at the time of the outbreak of war a staff officer in Scottish Command.

Appointed briefly to command 207th Independent Brigade, Collier's war thereafter was confined to staff duties. Military Secretary to GHQ Middle East 1941–1942, he was District Commander in Cyrenaica in 1943, a district commander in Italy the following year and commanded the Highland District 1944–1946.

Retired from the army in 1946, Collier settled in his native Inverness-shire. Indulging in his passion for rock gardens, he was DL for the county in 1950 and a JP from 1953.

COLLINGS, Major General Wilfred d'Auvergne *(1893–1984), CB, CBE*
Born in Guernsey, the son of a doctor, Collings was educated at Elizabeth College and RMC, Sandhurst. Commissioned in the Army Service Corps in 1914, his First War service was in France, Gallipoli and Mesopotamia. He was twice mentioned in despatches.

Seconded to the Egyptian Army 1923–1924, and to the Sudan Defence Force 1925–1930, Collings married in 1928 and served in Palestine 1937–1939. Assistant Director Supplies and Transport to the Western Desert Force 1940–1941, he was Director of S and T for 'W' Force during the Greek campaign. Made CBE, he was DDS and T 8th Army in North Africa 1941–1942 and DS and T Persia (Iran) and Iraq Command 1942–1943. Made DS and T 21st Army Group, North-West Europe 1944–1945, he was DS and T for the British Army of the Rhine 1945–1946.

Appointed CB and retired from the army in 1948, Collings was Chief of Supply and Transport for the UN Relief and Works Agency in the Near East 1949–1953. He retired to his native Guernsey.

COLLINS, Major General Sir Dudley Stuart *(1881–1959), KBE, CB, DSO*
Born and brought up in Australia, and educated at Haileybury, Collins was drawn into the British Army after volunteering for service in the South African War. Commissioned in the Royal Engineers in 1904, he married in 1909 and his First War service was in Gallipoli and France. Wounded, twice mentioned in despatches and admitted to the DSO (with bar), he was a brevet lieutenant colonel in 1918.

Sometime Chief Instructor at the School of Electrical Lighting, Collins was Assistant Director of Works at the War Office 1928–1931 and Chief Engineer, Southern Command, 1931–1935. He was Director of Fortifications and Works at the War Office 1935–1939. Made Deputy QMG and Controller of Engineer Services at the War Office in 1939, he retired from the army in 1941.

COLLINS, Major General Robert John *(1880–1950), CB, CMG, DSO*
Educated at Marlborough, Collins joined the Warwickshire Militia in 1897 and was commissioned in the Royal Berkshire Regiment in 1899. After service in the South African War he was seconded to the Egyptian Army in 1904 and was, for two years, ADC to the Sirdar. Married in 1912, he attended the Staff College, Camberley, that year and the next. Collins's First War service was in France, where he was admitted to the DSO in 1916. He was eight times mentioned in despatches.

An instructor at the Staff School, Cambridge, in 1918, 'Jack' Collins was an instructor at Camberley 1919–1923 and Director of Military Training, India, 1924–1926. Colonel Commandant of the 9th Infantry Brigade 1926–1927, his appointment as Colonel Commandant of the 7th Infantry Brigade and Experimental Armoured Force in 1929 provoked Fuller, it is said, into contemplating resigning from the army. As an 'orthodox infantryman' (Bond, 1980, 140), he was Commandant at the Small Arms School, Netheravon, 1929–1932.

Promoted major general in 1932, he subsisted on half-pay until appointed Commander of Meerut District and GOC 3rd Indian Division in 1934. Said to be 'a man of tremendous mental energy . . . he received no further promotion, and to the astonishment of all who knew him, his great abilities were [scarcely] utilised by the Army during the war' (Beauman, 1960, 83). He retired in 1938.

Re-employed at the outbreak of war, Collins was appointed to command 61st Division, until made Commandant of the Staff College, Camberley. Reverting to retired pay in 1941, he was Deputy Regional Commissioner for the Southern Region 1942–1944 and, over the same period, was Editor of the *Army Quarterly*. Living near Newbury, he was DL for Berkshire in 1949.

CORBETT, Lieutenant General Thomas William
(1888–1981), CB, MC and Bar
Corbett's reticence about himself is matched by the modesty of his reputation. Gazetted into the Indian Army in 1908, he joined the 2nd Royal Lancers (Gardner's Horse). A captain in 1915, the year he married, he was awarded the MC for his part in the campaign in Palestine.

A brevet major in 1919, Corbett graduated from the Staff College, Camberley, in 1922. Of the little that is known about his peacetime career, all that can be established is that, a colonel in 1935, he returned to the Staff College, Quetta, as an instructor after his wife had been badly injured in the earthquake. Quite why his enthusiasm for polo and enjoyment of colonial military service should have rendered him 'unfitted to direct the staff of a modern army' (Hamilton, 1981, 258) is a mystifying judgement. Promoted major general in 1940, he was made Inspector of Cavalry in India.

Sent by Auchinleck, then C-in-C India, to command Indian troops in southern Iraq in April 1941, Corbett played his part in the crushing of the Raschid Ali revolt and so impressed his superior that when Auchinleck was made C-in-C Middle East he appointed him, duly promoted lieutenant general, as his CGS.

It is difficult to judge how adequately Corbett performed his duties. His name, however, occurs frequently when Auchinleck is discussed as a 'poor picker of men'. Certainly he was widely disliked. Said, on the one hand, to be a man 'of considerable talent' who created plans 'too complex to be administered by anyone except himself' (Warner, 1982, 300), he was, on the other, adjudged 'a complete fathead' (Hamilton, 1981, 571), and 'the stupidest officer in the Indian Army' (Carver, 1989, 131). Nicknamed 'Aunt Blanche' at Cairo GHQ (Richardson, 1985, 103), he may have ordered the burning of documents culminating in the notorious June 1942 'Ash Wednesday'. It was, perhaps, 'Chink' Dorman-Smith (another of Auchinleck's 'unfortunate' appointments) who made the most penetrating appraisal. Corbett, he described as a 'small sound nut of a man, but emotional and humourless and at sea in a big HQ, sharing the Auk's Indian Army inferiority complex' (Greacen, 1989, 195).

No doubt Indian Army dominance in key posts in the Middle East Command caused resentment in sections of Eighth Army. There is as little doubt that

Brooke, the CIGS, was as dissatisfied with the Auchinleck-led Cairo regime as he was determined to promote his own protégés. Hence Corbett, instead of being appointed to command 8th Army, as Auchinleck suggested, was the first casualty of the Brooke-Churchill 'Cairo purge' of August 1942. Dismissed by Brooke as 'small' and 'a poor specimen of a man' (Danchev & Todman, 2001, 297) he was sent back to India.

There, despite doing a 'magnificent job' training 7th Indian Division, a 'security lapse brought down on his head the wrath of Higher Command' (Maule, 1961, 216). Removed from his position, he retired from the army in 1943.

Beyond settling in Sussex, re-marrying in 1952, after the death of his first wife, and listing his recreation as painting, it is not known how Corbett, described in his *Times* obituary as a 'brave, modest and kindly man', spent the remaining 38 years of his life.

COSTIN, Major General Eric Boyd *(1889–1971), DSO*

The son of a soldier and educated at Christ's Hospital, Hertford and London, Costin was commissioned in the West Yorkshire Regiment in 1914. First War service was in France with the Royal Canadian Regiment and later attached to the Machine Gun Corps in Salonika. Mentioned in despatches and admitted to the DSO, he was a brevet major in 1918.

After attending the Staff College Camberley 1921–1922, Costin married in 1922 and transferred to the Manchester Regiment. He was an instructor at the Small Arms School, Netheravon, 1923–1924, and Brigade Major Lahore Area, India, 1925–1926. Assistant Military Secretary to the C-in-C, India, 1926–1928, he was an instructor at the Small Arms School, India, 1928–1929, and returned to England to endure a year on half-pay before serving on the staff at the War Office 1931–1935. He commanded the 2nd Battalion, Manchester Regiment, 1935–1938 and was Assistant QMG, Southern Command, India, 1938–1939. Briefly a brigade commander in 1940, he held Area command in India before being made Major General i/c Administration at GHQ, India.

Retired from the army in 1946, Costin, a keen yachtsman, lived in Cornwall. He was Colonel Commandant of the Manchester Regiment 1949–1954.

COTTAM, Rev. Major General Algernon Edward
(1893–1964), CB, CBE, MC

Born in Hertfordshire and educated at Highgate School, Cottam enlisted in the Artists Rifles in 1912. First War service was in France where, transferring to the East Surrey Regiment in 1915, he was commissioned and awarded the MC in 1918.

Transferring again to the South Staffordshire Regiment in 1926, he served with the Sudan Defence Corps from 1928–1938. After holding various staff appointments in East Africa Command 1940–1943, he was head of the British Military Mission to Ethiopia 1943–1949. In Addis Ababa he worked particularly hard on behalf of orphaned children.

Retired from the army in 1949 Cottam, a married man with three children, decided to enter the Church. After attending a theological course at St George's, Windsor Castle in 1952, he was ordained the next year. A Curate in Sussex for a year and a priest in 1954, he was Rector of Bodiam, also in Sussex, 1955–1963.

COWAN, Major General David Tennant
(1896–1983), CB, CBE, DSO (and Bar), MC
Educated at Reading School and Glasgow University, Cowan was commissioned in the Argyll and Sutherland Highlanders in 1915. First War service was in France, where he was mentioned in despatches and awarded the MC, and in India.

Transferring to the Indian Army in 1917, 'Punch' Cowan was mentioned in despatches while serving with 6th Gurkha Rifles in the Third Afghan War. He was also captain and manager of the Indian Army Hockey tour of Australia and New Zealand in 1926. After attending the Staff College, Quetta, 1927–1928, he was an instructor at the Indian Military Academy 1932–1934. Commandant of the 1/6 Burma Rifles 1939–1940, he was Deputy Director Military Training, GHQ India, 1941 and officiating DMT 1941–1942.

Appointed BGS to Smyth, GOC 17th Indian Division in February 1942, Cowan was involved in the retreat from Burma. After the disaster of the Sittang Bridge, when the bridge was blown up leaving a brigade stranded, the sick Smyth was relieved of his command and Cowan was appointed GOC of the Division in his stead. As part of Slim's 'Burcorps', Cowan was admitted to the DSO after bringing his Division through the long retreat to Imphal.

Among 'the finest fighting commanders ever produced by the old Indian Army' (Lunt, 1989, xviii) Cowan was to achieve legendary fame in the re-conquest of Burma. Regarded by Slim as 'the greatest morale-raiser I have ever met' (Slim, 1986, 26), his Division played a crucial role in the defensive victory of Imphal and, in capturing the town of Meiktila, opening the road to Mandalay.

His son was killed while serving with the Gurkhas in 1945. 'Punch' Cowan was awarded the CB, CBE and a bar to his DSO that year. He retired from the army in 1947 after serving with occupation forces in Japan. Commandant of the Devon Army Cadet Force 1948–1958 he was DL for Devon 1953–1963. In 1958 he was Honorary Commandant of the Empire Village at the Commonwealth Games in Cardiff.

COWELL, Major General Sir Ernest Marshall
(1886–1971), KBE, CB, DSO, TD
Educated at Steyning Grammar School and London University, Cowell was a qualified surgeon and FRCS in 1910. Married in 1912 and a surgeon in France with the RAMC 1915–1918, he was twice mentioned in despatches and admitted to the DSO in 1918.

Commandant of 1st Army School of Instruction, RAMC, Cowell left the corps in 1922 to become surgeon at Croydon General Hospital. Surrey County

Controller of the British Red Cross and DL for the county from 1927, he joined the Territorial Army and was Assistant Medical Director 44th (Home Counties) Division 1934–1940.

Author of numerous pamphlets on First Aid and Deputy Director Medical Services for III Corps in France with the BEF 1939–1940, Cowell was DDMS II Corps 1940–1942 and Director of Medical Services, Allied Forces North Africa in 1942. He was DDMS Northern Command in 1944.

Knighted in 1944 and Public Medical Officer for the Control Commission, Germany, in 1945, Cowell was a member of the UNRRA Mission to Greece. Re-married in 1963, he lived on Guernsey.

COX, Major General Lionel Howard *(1893–1949)*, CB, CBE, MC

Born in Gloucestershire, the son of a doctor, Cox was educated at Lancing and RMC, Sandhurst. Commissioned in the Gloucestershire Regiment in 1912, his First War service was in China and France. Attached to the Machine Gun Corps, he was twice mentioned in despatches and awarded the MC in 1918 he was a brevet major during operations in Iraq 1919–1920.

A regimental officer for most of the inter-war years, Cox attended the Staff College, Quetta, 1928–1929 and, after a spell as Officer i/c the regimental depot in Bristol, commanded the 2nd Battalion of the Glosters 1935–1936. He attended the Imperial Defence College in 1937 and in 1939 he was serving on the staff at the War Office, when, as a brigade commander, he was posted to Malta.

Married in 1940, Cox endured conditions on Malta until 1941 when he was appointed commander of the North Wales District. Made GOC of the 38th Infantry (reserve) Division in 1942 and promoted major general in 1943, he was made GOC Singapore District in 1945 and retired from the army in 1948. He was the UK delegate on the UN special committee on the Balkans in 1948, but died as a result of a heart attack in Athens the following year.

COXWELL-ROGERS, Major General Norman Annesley
(1896–1985), CB, CBE, DSO

The son of an officer in the Royal Irish Constabulary, Coxwell-Rogers was educated at Cheltenham and RMA, Woolwich. Commissioned in the Royal Engineers in 1915, his First War service was in France, where he was wounded and twice mentioned in despatches.

Married in 1928, Coxwell-Rogers experienced a variety of postings in Britain, Gibraltar and, for most of the 1930s, India. For his part in constructing the Gandab road, during Mohmand Operations in 1933, he was awarded the OBE. As lieutenant colonel he was made CRE in Mohmand Operations in 1935.

In 1939 Coxwell-Rogers was sent to France as Commander RE 4th Division with the BEF. Despite, or perhaps because of, his reputation as a 'boot-slapping *beau sabreur* who excelled in the show-jumping and hunting fields' (Richardson, 1985, 63), he was admitted to the DSO for his part in demolition work prior to evacuation. A colonel in 1941, he saw service in North Africa, Sicily and Italy. In late 1943 he was promoted major general and appointed Chief Engineer Allied Forces in Italy. Twice mentioned in despatches, he was admitted to the American Legion of Merit in 1945.

Retired from the army in 1946, Coxwell-Rogers lived in Gloucestershire. He was Colonel Commandant of the Royal Engineers 1956–1961.

CRAWFORD, Major General John Scott (1889–1978), CB, CBE

Educated in Liverpool and at Campbell College, Belfast, Crawford was a qualified mechanical engineer before being commissioned in the Royal Army Service Corps in 1915.

Transferring to the Royal Army Ordnance Corps in 1928, Crawford was made Director of Mechanization when the Ministry of Supply was formed in 1939. He was Deputy Director General of Tanks and Transport 1940–1943 and, until 1945, Director General of Armaments Production.

Retired from the army in 1947, Crawford was, for a number of years, a member of the Institute of Mechanical Inspection and was President of the Rubber Research Association 1952–1954. A Fellow of the Institute of Mechanical Engineering, and a keen golfer and fisherman, he lived in Richmond, Surrey.

CRAWFORD, General Sir Kenneth Noel (1895–1961), KCB, MC

The son of a Ceylon Civil Servant, Crawford was educated at Clifton and RMA, Woolwich. Commissioned in the Royal Engineers in 1915, his First War service was in Gallipoli, in Egypt and in France, where he was mentioned in despatches and awarded the MC.

A captain in 1918, Crawford, a keen Rugby player, married in 1921 and attended the Staff College, Camberley, 1929–1930. The father of two sons and a daughter, the slow rate of promotion in peacetime ensured that it took a further twenty years' army service for him to reach the rank of colonel. However, under wartime conditions his progress was more rapid. On the staff of 3rd Division in France with the BEF 1939–1940, he was Commandant of the Army Gas School in 1940 and BGS Northern Ireland District 1941–1942. Director of Air (including Airborne Forces) at the War Office 1942–1946, he was GOC Land Forces, Greece, 1946–1947.

Knighted in 1948, Crawford was Deputy CIGS 1947–1949 and Controller of Supplies (Munitions) at the Ministry of Supply from 1949 until his retirement from the army in 1953.

In retirement Crawford held down a number of directorships and honorary colonelcies and was Vice President of the Parachute Regimental Association.

CREAGH, Major General Sir Michael O'Moore (1892–1970), KBE, MC

Of Anglo-Irish military stock and educated at Wellington and RMC Sandhurst, Creagh was commissioned in the 7th (Queen's Own) Hussars in 1911. First War service was with Home Forces and in France, where he was mentioned in despatches and awarded the MC.

A staff officer with the British Army of the Rhine in 1919, Creagh was Adjutant to his regiment 1919–1922 and, after attending the Staff College, Camberley, 1924–1925, transferred to the 15th/19th Hussars. A brigade major with Southern Command 1927–1929, he served on the staff at the War Office 1929–1931 and was appointed to command the 15th/19th Hussars in 1934. A colonel in 1938, he was an instructor at the Senior Officers' School, Sheerness, and, at war's outbreak, was back at the War Office as Inspector of the Royal Armoured Corps.

Sent out to Egypt to replace Hobart as commander of the Mobile Division, 'Dickie' Creagh became, through a process of redesignation, the first GOC of 7th Armoured Division. He led it in the Western Desert during O'Connor's 'five day raid' on the Italian garrison at Sidi Barrani which, in developing into operation COMPASS, led to a stunning series of victories in Cyrenaica. Though suffering from an abscess on his tongue, Creagh was there when 'the fox was killed in the open' at Beda Fomm.

Twice mentioned in despatches and knighted in 1941, it was as though the luck that had thus far brought success turned against Creagh. From being 'on the best of terms' with his fellow-commanders in the little Western Desert Force (Bidwell & Graham, 1985, 242), the size of later operations left him isolated and friendless. Held responsible, along with Beresford-Pierse, for the failure of operation BATTLEAXE in June 1941, Creagh was recalled to Britain. Brooke, 'convinced he was not up to it' (Danchev & Todman, 2001, 179), did not, at Dill's suggestion, appoint him to command the newly-formed 42nd Armoured Division. Instead he was put briefly in charge of a paper formation, the 3rd Armoured Group. In this redundant role he lectured occasionally and, with his knighthood something of an embarrassment, was appointed to command the Hampshire and Dorset District in 1942.

Retired from the army in 1944, Creagh worked for the United Nations Relief and Rehabilitation Administration (UNRRA) 1944–1946 and was, briefly, Deputy Head of the British Mission to Greece. Letters to *The Times* after his death challenged the brevity as well as the tone of his obituary. But for all that he was 'charming and courageous', his reputation remains saddled with the stigma of the so-called cavalry mentality.

CROCKER, General Sir John Tredinnick *(1896–1963), GCB, KBE, DSO, MC*
Enlisting as a private soldier in 1915, Crocker's First War service began with the Artists Rifles in France before he was commissioned in the Machine Gun Corps. Awarded the MC in 1917, he was admitted to the DSO in 1918.

Demobilized in 1919, Crocker married in 1920, but so disliked his solicitor's training that he re-joined the army that year. Commissioned in the Middlesex Regiment, he transferred to the newly-formed Royal Tank Corps in 1923 and was a graduate of the Staff College, Quetta, in 1929. When the first tank brigade was formed on a permanent basis in 1934 Crocker was Brigade Major. An instructor at the Senior Officers' School, Sheerness, 1935–1937, he moved on to staff duties with the Mobile Division in 1937 and was appointed to command 3rd Brigade within 1st Armoured Division in 1939.

Sent to France in late May 1940, 1st Armoured Division fared badly in actions north and south of the Somme. But after evacuation from Cherbourg Crocker became GOC 6th Armoured Division. Made GOC 2nd Armoured Group in Eastern Command in 1941, he was appointed to command IX Corps the next year. Earmarked for service in North Africa, he landed in Tunisia in March 1943.

His stay in North Africa was short. Wounded during a demonstration of the new PIAT anti-tank weapon, Crocker was invalided home. It says a lot about his reputation as an officer of 'outstanding ability' (Carver, 1989, 32) that, despite his taciturnity and lack of operational experience, 'Honest John' Crocker was placed in command of 1st Corps in the autumn of 1943. Brooke, who remembered him from Mobile Division days, thought highly of him. Thus the D-Day corps commander was knighted and, but for a brief argument with Crerar, the commander of First Canadian Army who wanted him dismissed 'on the spot' (Hastings, 1984, 351), saw the campaign in North-West Europe through to the surrender of German forces in May 1945 without attracting much attention to himself. His son, serving with a tank regiment, was killed in action that year.

GOC Southern Command 1945–1947, Crocker was C-in-C Land Forces Middle East 1947–1950. Said to possess 'a most penetrating insight into character and behaviour' (Pyman, 1971, 61), he was not made successor to Montgomery as CIGS, but became instead Adjutant General. Retired from the army in 1953, he was Vice-Chairman of the Commonwealth War Graves Commission 1957–1963 and was appointed Lord Lieutenant of Middlesex in 1961.

CROSSMAN, Major General Francis Lindisfarne Morley
(1888–1947), CB, DSO, MC
Born in Edinburgh and educated at Wellington and RMA, Woolwich, Crossman was commissioned in the Royal Field Artillery in 1907. A captain in 1914, his First War service was in Gallipoli and in France. Mentioned in despatches five times, he was awarded the MC in 1916 and admitted to the DSO in 1918.

Married in 1919, Crossman spent many of the inter-war years serving in India. A colonel in 1936, he commanded the 54th Artillery Field Brigade and was an instructor at the School of Artillery, Larkhill, 1936–1937. In 1938 he was appointed CRA Aldershot Command and the next year, with so much of the expanding Territorial Army being channelled into air defence, he was appointed to command 1st AA Division. Having been responsible for the AA defence of London during the early stages of the Blitz, he moved to command 2nd AA Division in November 1940.

Retired in 1942, Crossman lived out the last years of his life in Berwick-on-Tweed. Lord of the Manor of Holy Island, he died after a short illness on his fifty-ninth birthday.

CUFF, Major General Brian *(1889–1970), CB, CBE*

The son of a doctor and educated at Malvern and Oxford University, Cuff was commissioned in the West Yorkshire Regiment in 1910 His First War service was in France, Salonika and, latterly, with the Army of the Black Sea.

Transferring to the Cheshire Regiment, Cuff married in 1923, attended the Staff College, Camberley, 1924–1925 and served on the staff with Northern Ireland District and at the War Office 1926–1929. A major in 1927, he was Deputy Assistant Adjutant and QMG in Malaya 1932–1935 and commanded the 1st Battalion of the Cheshire Regiment 1936–1938. A staff officer at the War Office 1938–1940, he served in France with the BEF 1939–1940. Mentioned in despatches and made CBE, he was Chief Administrative Officer, Northern Command, from 1942 until his retirement from the army in 1945.

Appointed CB in 1945, Cuff lived out his retirement in Herefordshire.

CUNNINGHAM, General Sir Alan Gordon
(1887–1983), GCMG, KCB, DSO, MC

The son of a professor of anatomy and younger brother of the famous admiral, Cunningham was educated at Cheltenham and RMA, Woolwich. Commissioned in the Royal Artillery in 1906, his First War service was with the RHA in France. Mentioned five times in despatches, he was awarded the MC in 1915 and admitted to the DSO in 1918.

A staff officer with the Malay Straits Settlement force 1919–1921, Cunningham graduated, unusually, from the Naval Staff College in 1925. A brevet lieutenant colonel in 1928, he was an instructor at the Machine Gun School 1928–1931. After attending the Imperial Defence College in 1937, he was CRA 1st Division 1937–38, before being promoted major general and appointed to command 5th AA Division.

GOC 66th Division in January 1940, Cunningham, after being transferred to command first 9th and then 51st Division with Home Forces, was sent to Kenya in October 1940 to assume command of East African Forces. There he led the southern force in the successful invasion of Abyssinia and Italian Somaliland. Showing great logistical skill in harsh terrain, he took the surrender of the Duke of Aosta at Amba Alagi in May 1941. Knighted that summer, he was chosen by Auchinleck in August to command the newly-created 8th Army in the western desert.

An acknowledged master of mobile operations, Cunningham looked the part. Dill thought he would 'fill the bill as GOC in the western desert' (Dill, 2nd acc. LHCMA), though his 'touchiness of temper' (Barnett, 1983, 84) was noted as, with 650 tanks at his disposal, he prepared for the CRUSADER offensive. Having 'worked himself to the edge of physical and nervous exhaustion' (Bierman & Smith, 2002, 100), and making 'no attempt to exude confidence'

(Belchem, 1978, 98), early reverses in the battle so undermined his spirit that, against the advice of his corps commanders, he wished to break off the offensive. Auchinleck, flying in from Cairo, found him in a 'very shaky condition' (Warner, 1982, 139) and, after countermanding his army commander's orders, had him replaced and admitted, under an assumed name, to a hospital in Alexandria.

Cunningham was sent home 'very depressed and hard to comfort' (Danchev & Todman, 2002, 211). Made Commandant of the Staff College, Camberley, he was appointed GOC Northern Ireland District in 1943 and GOC-in-C Eastern Command in 1944. Promoted general in 1945, he succeeded Gort as High Commissioner and C-in-C Palestine. He held that post throughout the process of British withdrawal and, elevated in the knighthood, retired from the army in 1948.

Colonel Commandant of the Royal Artillery 1954–1954 and President of the Council of Cheltenham College 1951–1963, Cunningham was also DL for Hampshire. A keen fisherman who lived to the age of 95, he was in the news a month before his death denouncing Menachem Begin, the incoming Israeli Prime Minister, as a 'fanatical terrorist'.

CURSETJEE, Major General Sir Heerajee Jehangir Manockjee
(1885–1964), KCIE, CSI, DSO
Born in Bombay and educated in India, Cambridge University and London Hospital, Cursetjee, a Parsee, joined the Indian Medical Service in 1912. First War service was in Egypt and Gallipoli, where he was twice mentioned in despatches and badly wounded, and finally in Mesopotamia. Admitted to the DSO in 1918, he served on in Iraq and Kurdistan 1919–1921.

Known as 'Charlie', Cursetjee, who stood at a little under five feet tall, took part in campaigns along the North-West Frontier throughout the 1920s. A major in 1924, he was a colonel in 1938 and officer i/c Lucknow District hospitals. Said to be 'a terror' when inspecting hospital, he ran his 'white-gloved finger along all the spaces where dust might collect' (Chevenix Trench, 1988, 90). Promoted major general in 1941, he spent the next two years as a liaison officer based at GHQ, India, but visiting all the fronts where Indian troops were serving. Deputy Director Medical Services for the North-Western Army 1943–1945, he retired in 1946.

Living in England, Cursetjee, a fine polo player and keen huntsman, was a popular figure. One month short of his eightieth birthday he was killed in a car crash.

CURTIS, Major General Alfred Cyril *(1894–1971), CB, DSO, MC*
Leaving RMC, Sandhurst, in 1914, and joining the Indian Army in 1915, Curtis was gazetted into the 11th Sikh Regiment. His First War service was on the North-West Frontier and in Mesopotamia where he was awarded the MC. A captain in 1918, he attended the Staff College, Camberley, 1927–1928.

Brigade Major Rawalpindi Brigade 1932–1934 and second-in-command of the Rattray Sikhs in 1936, Curtis commanded the 2nd Battalion of the 11th Sikh Regiment in 1938. A colonel in 1940, he commanded 13th Infantry Brigade during the retreat from Burma. Admitted to the DSO in 1942, he assumed command of the newly-formed 14th Indian Division in 1943. Promoted major general, he was Commander Lucknow District 1943–1944. He retired from the army in 1948.

CURTIS, Major General Henry Osborne
(1888–1964), CB, DSO, MC, DSM (US)
Educated at Eton and RMC, Sandhurst, Curtis was commissioned in the King's Royal Rifle Corps in 1908. First War service was in France, Salonika and in Palestine. Thrice mentioned in despatches and wounded three times, he was awarded the MC in 1917 and admitted to the DSO in 1919.

Ending the war as commander of the 4th Battalion KRRC, Curtis attended the Staff College, Quetta, in 1920, and served on the staff at Middle East HQ 1922–1926. On the directing staff at Camberley in the later 1920s, he returned to his regiment, commanding the 1st Battalion 1931–1934. After two years commanding British troops in Palestine, he served again on the staff at Camberley before commanding 3rd Infantry Brigade 1938–1939.

Sent home from France in December 1939 to assume command of 46th Division, Curtis rejoined the BEF in April 1940. Evacuated from Dunkirk, he was appointed to command 49th Division in June 1940 which, at a reduced establishment, was detailed to occupy Iceland. This done, Curtis spent the next two years nominally in charge of his Division based in Scotland from his office in Reykjavik. Known as 'Squeak', Curtis relied heavily on his senior brigade commander – and later GOC 49th Division – 'Bubbles' Barker. Made commander of Salisbury Plain District 1943, he was appointed commander of the Hampshire Distinct in 1944 and the Dorset District 1945. He retired from the army in 1946.

Commandant of 1st Battalion KRRC 1946–1954, Curtis was DL for Dorset in 1953 and President of the Dorset British Legion the same year. Married in 1918, two of his four sons were killed in the war.

D

DALBY, Major General Thomas Gerald *(1880–1963), CB, DSO*
Educated at Eton and RMC, Sandhurst, Dalby was commissioned in the 60th Rifles in 1899. Wounded while serving in the South African War, he campaigned in Somaliland in 1904. His First War service was in France, where he was

wounded twice, four times mentioned in despatches and admitted to the DSO in 1917.

Married in 1917, Dalby spent most of the 1920s as a brevet lieutenant colonel. Deputy Commandant at the Small Arms School, Hythe, 1922–1924, he commanded the 2nd Battalion of the Rifle Brigade 1928–1931 and the 3rd Infantry Brigade at Aldershot 1931–1935. Retiring from the army in 1937 as an honorary major general, he was re-employed in August 1939 as GOC 18th Division, then a second-line Territorial Army formation.

Retired in December 1939, Dalby spent most of the war years in Devon. He married again in 1948, his first wife having died the previous year. He was DL for the County of London 1945–1951. In his tribute to Dalby, published in *The Times*, Liddell Hart wrote warmly of him as 'a pioneer in the reform and modernization of infantry tactics'.

D'ARCY, Lieutenant General John Conyers *(1894–1966), CB, CBE, MC*

The son of the Archbishop of Armagh, D'Arcy graduated from RMA, Woolwich, in 1913 and, commissioned in the Royal Garrison Artillery, served in the First World War in France. Twice wounded and awarded the MC, he was wounded again while campaigning against Afridi tribesmen on the North-West Frontier in 1931.

A staff captain in Palestine in 1921, a major in 1934 and a colonel in 1940, D'Arcy was appointed acting GOC 9th Armoured Division in August 1942, only to be promoted major general the next month. With his command confirmed, he spent the next two years training his troops. When the Division was broken up in July 1944, he was promoted lieutenant general and made GOC British troops in Palestine.

Retired from the army in 1946, D'Arcy spent the remaining twenty years of his life living in the West of Ireland. His most treasured possession, apparently, was his leather-bound game book, in which 'he had recorded every round fired since his earliest youth . . . and the stupendous tonnage of blood shed' (Bond, 1980, 66).

DAVIDSON, Major General Alexander Elliott *(1880–1962), CB, DSO*

Educated at Blackheath School and RMA, Woolwich, Davidson was commissioned in the Royal Engineers in 1899 and served in South Africa. Secretary to the Mechanical Transport Committee at the War Office 1910–1914, he married in 1911 and his First War service was in France. Mentioned in despatches and admitted to the DSO in 1916, he was a brevet lieutenant colonel in 1918.

Chief Inspector of RE stores 1920–1924, Davidson was Deputy Assistant Director of Fortifications and Works 1924–1925. Chairman of the Technical Committee of the Mechanical Warfare Board 1927–1931, he was Assistant Director of Works at the War Office 1931–1935. Appointed Director of Mechanization at the War Office 1936, he retired from the army in 1940.

Colonel Commandant of the Royal Engineers in 1940, Davidson was also President of the Diesel Engine Users Association in 1950.

DAVIDSON, Major General Francis Henry Norman
(1892–1973), CB, DSO, MC (and Bar)
The younger son of a knight, Davidson was educated at Marlborough and RMA, Woolwich. Commissioned in the Royal Artillery in 1911, his First War service was in Gallipoli and France where he was wounded, mentioned four times in despatches and awarded the MC (and Bar).

Admitted to the DSO in 1919, Davidson spent most of the 1920s on a captain's pay. A graduate of the Staff College, Quetta, in 1924, he was a staff officer at Army HQ, India, 1925–1927, and Brigade Major to the 12th Indian Infantry Brigade 1927–1929. After a four-year period of staff duties at the War Office, he attended the Imperial Defence College in 1935, before being appointed an instructor at the Staff College, Camberley. A colonel in 1938, he was Chief of Staff to 2nd Division at Aldershot 1938–1939 and was a member of the Allied Military Mission to Moscow just prior to the outbreak of war.

Appointed CRA I Corps with the BEF in France, Davidson briefly commanded 2nd Division during the retreat to Dunkirk and was BGS with X Corps in the summer of 1940 before being promoted major general and appointed Director of Military Intelligence at the War Office. Described as 'a dour Scot' (Pimlott (ed.), 1986, 120), he was a key figure in the re-creation of the Intelligence Corps. Sent to Washington in 1944, he served as Deputy head of the British Army Staff before retiring from the army in 1946.

Colonel Commandant of the Intelligence Corps 1952–1960, Davidson, married and the father of two sons, lived out his last years in London.

DAVIES, Major General Henry Lowrie *(1898–1975), CB, CBE, DSO, MC*
Of military family and educated at Dover College and RMC, Sandhurst, 'Taffy' Davies joined the Royal Garhwal Rifles in India in 1916. First War service was in Mesopotamia, where he was awarded the MC, and, in 1919, with the Army of the Black Sea.

Returning to India in 1920, Davies took part in operations in Waziristan 1922–1923 and, graduating from the Staff College, Quetta, in 1929, served on the staff of Northern Command, India, 1931–32. Brigade Major, Peshawar Brigade, 1933–1935, he was admitted to the DSO for his part in the 1934 Mohmand expedition.

Posted to the Military Department of the India Office in London in 1937, Davies's war took a strange turn in 1940 when he served on the staff of the Iceland occupation force before returning to India at the end of 1941. BGS under Hutton, then Slim, in BURCORPS, the 'tall, thin, emaciated Welshman . . . combined driving energy with a first-class tactical brain' (Lunt, 1989, 98) to keep the 'scratch headquarters working' (Slim, 1986, 25) during the retreat from Burma. Appointed to command 25th Indian Division in 1943, he served under

Christison in the Arakan before being appointed Deputy CGS at GHQ, India, in 1944.

Made Commandant of the Staff College, Quetta, in 1945, Davies served briefly as Deputy CGS to the Pakistan Army before retiring from the army in 1948. An Assistant Director in the Investigations Division of the Ministry of Agriculture 1948–1962, he also worked with the Historical Section of the Cabinet Office. Married, with one son and a daughter, Davies, though in poor health, was a keen golfer. He lived in Kingston-on-Thames until his death.

de BURGH, General Sir Eric (1881–1973), KCB, DSO

Of military family and born in Co. Kildare, de Burgh was educated at Marlborough. A subaltern with the Royal Dublin Fusiliers (Militia), he served in the South African War before being commissioned in the Manchester Regiment in 1903. Transferring to the Indian Army in 1904, he joined Hodson's Horse and attended the Staff College, Camberley, 1913–1914. His First War service was in France and Mesopotamia, where he was admitted to the DSO in 1918.

A brevet lieutenant colonel in 1919, de Burgh's peacetime soldiering was real enough. Mentioned in despatches for service on the North-West Frontier and in operations in Waziristan in the early 1920s, he married in 1923 and was an instructor at the Staff College, Quetta, 1928–1930. Appointed to command 1st Risalpur Cavalry Brigade 1931–1934, he commanded Lahore District 1934–1935. After attending the Imperial Defence College he was appointed Deputy CGS at Army HQ, India, in 1935. While commander of Rawalpindi District, 1936–1938, he was appointed to command 1st Indian Division during operations in Waziristan in 1937.

Chief of the General Staff, India, 1939–1941, de Burgh retired that year on his sixtieth birthday. Knighted, he and his wife settled in Co Wexford. Socially active, he led, for many years, the British Legion march-past in Whitehall on Remembrance Day.

DEEDES, Lieutenant General Sir Ralph Bouverie
(1890–1954), KCB, OBE, MC

Educated at Haileybury and RMC, Sandhurst, Deedes was gazetted into the Indian army on the unattached list in 1910, joining the 31st Punjab Regiment the following year. A captain in the 2nd/16th Punjabis in 1915, his First War service was in India and Mesopotamia, where he was awarded the MC. He was made OBE for services during operations in Kurdistan in 1920.

A major in 1926, Deedes graduated from the Staff College, Camberley, in 1926 and thereafter served on the staffs of numerous area commands in India. He commanded 2nd (Rawalpindi) Infantry Brigade in 1936 and was mentioned in despatches during operations in Waziristan in 1937. Deputy Military Secretary, AHQ, India, 1937–1939, he commanded an infantry brigade in England 1939–1940, before being promoted major general and appointed to command Waziristan District in 1941. Military Secretary to the C-in-C India in 1943, he was appointed Adjutant-General, India, in 1944.

Knighted in 1945, Deedes retired from the army in 1946 and settled near Guildford in Surrey.

de FONBLANQUE, Major General Philip *(1885–1940), DSO*

Born in Bombay and educated at Rugby and RMA, Woolwich, de Fonblanque was commissioned in the Royal Engineers in 1905. A captain in 1914, his First War service was in France, where he served on the staff of Second Army, and Italy, where he was admitted to the DSO.

Married in 1916, de Fonblanque attended the Staff College, Camberley, 1920–1921, and was Deputy Assistant QMG, Eastern Command, 1923–1925, before being appointed DAQMG at the War Office. Assistant Adjutant and QMG for 2nd Division 1934–1937, he was Brigadier i/c Administration, Scottish Command, 1937–1939.

Promoted major general in 1939, de Fonblanque, though past retiring age, was appointed GOC Lines of Communication for the BEF in France. Despite his having no contact with the main part of the BEF, and having no 'combatant experience or war training' (Karslake, 1979, 39), he was able, from his HQ near Le Mans, to organize scratch forces in an attempt to stem the German advance south of the Somme. Replaced, then reinstated, his 'unique knowledge of the intricate machinery of the L of C' (Beauman, 1960, 138) was a positive asset in the usually successful evacuation of British forces from western French ports in June 1940.

Within a month de Fonblanque was dead. Suffering from 'a long illness' (presumably cancer) he was admitted to a Cambridge nursing home within days of his return to England. He left a widow, a son and two daughters.

de GUINGAND, Major General Sir Francis Wilfred
(1900–1979), KBE, CB, DSO

Born in West London, the son of a briar-root pipe manufacturer, de Guingand was educated at Ampleforth and RMC, Sandhurst. Commissioned in the West Yorkshire Regiment in 1919 the 'wildly handsome subaltern' (Hamilton, 2001, 148) quickly got bored with regimental soldiering and, requiring the income necessary to finance his expensive lifestyle, volunteered for service with the King's African Rifles in Nyasaland (Malawi).

Five years later, in 1932, he returned to his regiment in Egypt, where, noticed apparently by Montgomery, he was encouraged to apply for a place at the Staff College, Camberley. Graduating from there in 1936, he was appointed Brigade Major at the Small Arms School, Netheravon before being picked by the War Secretary, Hore-Belisha, to become his Military Secretary in June 1939.

Moved on, at his own request, after Hore-Belisha's dismissal in January 1940, 'Freddie' de Guingand, now a lieutenant colonel, became an instructor at the newly-formed Middle East Staff College at Haifa. Like the Commandant there, 'Chink' Dorman-Smith, he was 'ambitious and very capable' (Richardson,

1987, 44). Lacking 'Chink's' genius for making enemies, 'Freddie', it seems, could deploy his charm with emollient ease. A member of the joint planning staff in Cairo for most of 1941, Auchinleck was so impressed with his abilities that he made him his Director of Military Intelligence in 1942. Surviving the 'Cairo purge' that August, Montgomery, the incoming C-in-C 8th Army, selected him as his Chief of Staff.

It was thus that 'Freddie' of the 'quick and fertile brain' (Montgomery, 1958, 56) achieved his degree of fame. As the supposed 'perfect foil for Montgomery' (Richardson, 1987, 239) he was often ill, but when fit he campaigned at his master's side in North Africa, Italy and in North-West Europe. He was the bon viveur who, supposedly, provided those qualities of worldliness and tact which Montgomery so evidently lacked but which were so necessary in keeping inter-Allied relations smooth. Admitted to the DSO in 1942, he acquired such an 'enviable reputation and standing in the entire Allied force' (Eisenhower, 1948, 314), that, still a brigadier, he was knighted in 1944. It was probably his inter-vention that dissuaded Eisenhower from demanding Montgomery's dismissal in December of that year.

Because cast so heavily in Montgomery's shadow, it is difficult to reach an independent assessment of de Guingand's qualities as staff officer and confidant of the great commanders. Americans thought highly of him, though relations between 'Freddie' and 'Monty' did cool in the final months of the war. Montgomery seems to have transferred his affections from the now married 'Freddie', and a number of petty slights soured the post-war relationship. Excluded from the surrender ceremony at Lüneberg Heath, de Guingand, against medical advice, took up the post of Director of Military Intelligence at the War Office, hoping Montgomery would honour his pledge to make him VCIGS. But, finding that Simpson, not he, was installed instead, he accepted promotion to major general and retired from the army in 1946.

Resolving to go into business, de Guingand's first book of memoirs, *Operation Victory* (1946), was one of the first authoritative accounts of the war and was well received. Thereafter he applied his 'shrewdness, quick intelligence and charismatic personality' (Richardson, 1987, 234) to the good things of life, buttressed by a successful business career in South Africa. As a director of the Rothmans tobacco company he was able to live according to his chosen lifestyle. He survived the break-up of his marriage and declining health long enough to die, appropriately enough, in his flat in Cannes.

DEMPSEY, General Sir Miles Christopher
(1896–1969), GBE, KCB, DSO, MC
Born in Cheshire of non-military family and educated at Shrewsbury and RMC, Sandhurst, Dempsey was commissioned in the Royal Berkshire Regiment in 1915. First War service was in France where, in addition to being wounded, mentioned in despatches and awarded the MC, he commanded a company at the age of nineteen. Though badly gassed in 1918, he served in operations in Iraq 1919–1920.

Save for his renowned map-reading abilities, Dempsey was an unexceptional regimental officer for most of the inter-war years. A keen sportsman with a pleasant singing voice, he attended the Staff College, Camberley, 1930–1931, served for two years on the staff at the War Office and, in 1938, was placed in command of his regiment's 1st Battalion. Posted to Palestine he served in 6th Division under Wavell's command. Sent to France with the BEF at the outset of war, he was appointed to command 13th Infantry Brigade in Franklyn's 5th Division.

Admitted to the DSO for his part in covering the withdrawal to Dunkirk, Dempsey served as BGS to the 1st Canadian Division 1940–1941. Promoted major general and appointed to command 46th Division he came, once again, into contact with Montgomery who, as his Corps Commander, had him transferred to the newly-formed 42nd Armoured Division in June 1942.

Within six months Dempsey was in North Africa. Montgomery, having 'demanded' (Danchev &Todman, 2001, 323) his presence in 8th Army, made him commander of XIII Corps after El Alamein. Thus Dempsey was in the van of the pursuit of the retreating German forces. Though elements of his corps were badly mauled during the assault on the Mareth Line in March 1943, Dempsey was able to enter Tunis in triumph before turning his attention to the invasion of Sicily. There progress up the eastern side of the island was slower than expected. It was equally so during the invasion of Italy. Stalled south of Naples XIII Corps did, however, force the crossing of the River Sangro.

Summoned by Montgomery from England in December 1942, Dempsey was called back to London by Montgomery in December 1943 and made commander of the British Second Army. Once ashore in Normandy, he directed the 'writing-down' of German troops before Caen and was knighted in the field. Described as a man who 'hated publicity' (Horrocks, 1960, 186), he nevertheless criticized the handling of the American 1st Army in a newspaper interview (Irving, 1981, 245).

Possessing the 'charming manners' of the 'perfect British officer' (Pyman, 1971, 68), 'Bimbo' Dempsey, the 'ideal subordinate to Montgomery', played a subordinate part in the allied advance across North-West Europe. Neither blamed for the failure of MARKET GARDEN nor praised for the Rhine crossing in March 1945, his knighthood was upgraded to KBE.

The European war over, Brooke, who thought Dempsey suffered from a 'swollen head' (Danchev & Todman, 2001, 702), appointed him commander of XIV Army in readiness for the reconquest of Malaya. Succeeding Slim as C-in-C Allied Land Forces in South-East Asia, he was promoted General. C-in-C Middle East in 1946, he retired from the army that year. The least flamboyant of Montgomery's numerous protégés, Dempsey, whether swollen-headed or not, had nonetheless risen highest.

Made Chairman of the Racecourse Betting Control Board in 1947, Dempsey married in 1948. Holding down a number of directorships, he and his wife lived at Yattendon, within easy reach of Newbury racecourse.

DENNING, Lieutenant General Sir Reginald Francis Stewart
(1894–1990), KCVO, KBE, CB
Born in Hampshire and educated privately, Denning was commissioned in the Bedfordshire Regiment in 1915. First War service was in France where he was mentioned in despatches and severely wounded.

Adjutant to the 1st Battalion of the Bedfordshire and Hertfordshire Regiment 1922–1925, Denning filled the same post at the regimental depot with the 2nd Battalion for the next five years. Married in 1927, he was student at the Staff College, Camberley, 1929–1930. A brevet major in 1934, he was a brevet lieutenant colonel at war's outbreak in 1939.

Staff duties at the War Office and in Western Command occupied Denning for the first three years of the war. In 1943 he was appointed Major General i/c Administration with Eastern Command and the next year was made Principal Administrative Officer to Mountbatten, the Supreme Allied Commander South-East Asia.

Returning to Britain in 1946, Denning was knighted and was Chief of Staff, Eastern Command, 1947–1949. Appointed GOC Northern Ireland in 1949 he retired from the army in 1952. He held numerous honorary colonelcies and was the first colonel of the Anglian Regiment. A keen sportsman and member of the MCC, he was DL for Essex 1959–1968.

DENNIS, Major General Meade Edward *(1893–1965), CB, CBE, DSO, MC*
Of military family and educated at Haileybury and RMA, Woolwich, Dennis was commissioned in the Royal Field Artillery in 1913. First War service was in France, where he was wounded and mentioned in despatches, and in Palestine, where he was awarded the MC.

A brevet major in 1919, Dennis was attached to the Egyptian Army in the Sudan 1920–1924. After spells of duty with various home commands, he married in 1930, served briefly on the North-West Frontier, was a gunnery instructor at the School of Artillery, Larkhill, 1933–1934, and was back in India in 1939.

Dennis commanded the artillery of 6th Indian Division in Persia (Iran) in 1941 before being transferred to the western desert. Commander of XXX Corps Artillery 1941–1943, he was described by Montgomery as 'magnificent . . . a high class gunner' (Hamilton, 1983, 48), and admitted to the DSO after Alamein. Awarded the CBE in Sicily, he was promoted major general in 1944. He commanded the Royal Artillery 21st Army Group in North-West Europe 1944–1946.

Retiring from the army in 1947, Dennis and his wife settled in Co. Wicklow.

DEWING, Major General Richard Henry *(1891–1981), CB, DSO, MC*
Born in Suffolk and educated at Haileybury, Dewing was commissioned in the Royal Engineers in 1911. Joining the Queen Victoria's Own Sappers and Miners in India, his First War service was in Mesopotamia, where he was awarded the

MC in 1915, and Persia, where he was admitted to the DSO in 1917. After a year in Iraq he served on operations in the North-West frontier 1920–1921.

After graduating from the Staff College, Camberley, in 1924, Dewing was seconded to the directing staff of the Royal Military College, Canada, 1927–1929. He commanded a field company based in Wiltshire before serving on the staff of Southern Command 1931–1933. After attending the Imperial Defence College in 1934, he was posted to Malta for a year and then served on the staff at the War Office 1936–1937. The last years of peace were spent as an instructor at the Imperial Defence College.

Promoted major general in 1939, 'Dick' Dewing was appointed Director of Military Operations at the War Office. Despite, or perhaps because of, being considered 'singularly stupid and unhelpful' in that role (Bond (ed.), 1972, 323), he was made Chief of Staff, Far East, in the summer of 1940. Judged to be 'able, hard-working, but a bit too rigid' by Dill (Dill, 2nd. acc., 9, LHCMA), he was sent to Washington in December 1941 to act as deputy to Dill on the Joint Military Mission. Chief of Army-RAF Liaison Staff in Australia 1943–1944, he was recalled to the European theatre and, thanks to Eisenhower's regard for his 'ability and integrity' (Butcher, 1946, 36), was made head of the SHAEF Mission to Denmark in 1945. He was a member of the Allied Control Commission, Berlin, from 1945 until his retirement in 1946.

Married in 1920, Dewing outlived his wife and all three of his children. His elder son was killed in action in Libya.

DICKINSON, Major General Douglas Povah
(1886–1949), CB, DSO, OBE, MC

Educated at Cheltenham and RMC, Sandhurst, Dickinson was commissioned in the Welch Regiment in 1906. A captain in 1914, his First War service was in France where he was five times mentioned in despatches, awarded the MC and admitted to the DSO in 1917.

A brevet major at war's end, Dickinson graduated from the Staff College, Camberley, in 1920. On the directing staff at Camberley 1925–1928, he was appointed OBE for his service with the Iraqi Army in Kurdistan 1931–1932. A lieutenant colonel in 1933, he commanded the 1st Battalion the Welch Regiment, 1934–1936 and was Commandant of the Nigeria Regiment, 1938–1939.

Promoted major general at war's beginning, Dickinson was appointed commander of East African forces in Nairobi. Unsuccessful in his efforts to raise irregular forces, and 'tired and in need of a rest' (Mockler, 1984, 299), he was recalled home in early 1941, where it was found 'difficult to find a job' for him (Dill 2nd. acc., 9, LHCMA). Appointed Major-General i/c Administration, Western Command, he was also Colonel of the Welch Regiment until his retirement from the army in 1944.

Married with two daughters, Dickinson was Secretary of the National Rifle Association from his retirement until his death.

DILL, Field Marshal Sir John Greer

(1881–1944), GCB, KCB, CB, CMG, DSO, American DSM (posthumous)

The son of a bank manager, Dill was born in Lurgan, Co. Armagh and educated at Cheltenham and RMC, Sandhurst. Commissioned in the Leinster Regiment in 1901, he saw war service in South Africa and, risking the disapproval of his superiors, married in 1907 when he was a battalion adjutant. A student at the Staff College, Camberley, 1913–1914, he became brigade major of the 25th Infantry Brigade in France after the retreat from Mons.

Admitted to the DSO in 1915, Dill's First War service consisted of a succession of staff appointments. Eight time mentioned in despatches, he was judged 'the guiding brain of GHQ in the last year of the war' (Liddell Hart, 1965, 238). Promoted Brigadier General to the General Staff in 1918, he became a chief instructor at Camberley the next year.

There was, it is said, 'an aura of integrity which wrapped Dill like a mantle' (Kennedy, 1957, xvii). Tipped already as a future CICS, he commanded the Welsh Border Brigade in 1922 and moved to command 2nd Brigade at Aldershot the following year. In 1926 he was appointed to the staff of the new Imperial Defence College and, three years later, became Brigadier General Staff, Western Command, India. Promoted major general in 1931, Dill returned to England and, for the third time in his professional life, landed back in Camberley, this time as Commandant.

A 'successful and popular commandant' (DNB), Dill was in an ideal position to know, and be known by, a generation of army officers. Slim and dapper, and regarded highly by his peers, he seemed to have no enemies. Made Director of Military Operations at the War Office in 1934, he was promoted lieutenant general in 1936 and appointed to command British troops in Palestine. Returning to England the next year, he was knighted and made GOC-in-C Aldershot Command, then the British Army's chief training area.

Hitherto Dill had climbed the ladder steadily and without apparent effort. Hore-Belisha's decision to appoint the younger and less senior Gort CIGS in 1937 was, however, a check to his progress. Dill may have been 'the ablest administrator and [possessed] the keenest mind in the senior military hierachy', but when, in another 'disastrous decision' (Hamilton, 1981, 319), Ironside was made CIGS in September 1939, Dill could do nothing save hide his disappointment and travel to France as GOC I Corps with Gort's BEF.

Though promoted general in October 1939 Dill's spell of field command was short and laden with anxiety. Having 'failed to make Gort realize the risks he was running with the BEF' (Danchev & Todman, 2001, 16), he felt, in common with other senior officers in France, that the CIGS 'was not giving them the support that they had the right to expect' (Bond (ed.), 1972, xxvii). Whether or not this was true, Ironside's position in the War Office was so consistently undermined that in April 1940 Dill was recalled to London to take on the newly-created post of Vice-CIGS. The next month, at the height of the Dunkirk evacuaton, Dill 'ultimately achieved his ambition' (Karslake, 1979, 29) and succeeded Ironside as CIGS.

In that Dill was universally respected and held the confidence of the army, his was the ideal appointment, however dire the strategic situation. However, the protacted illness of his wife caused great personal strain. Her death in December 1940 was a happy release. He re-married in October 1941.

Though Dill did his best to stand up to Churchill's strong personality, he found the combined strain of Britain's desperate strategic position and Churchill's confrontational style all but unbearable. The cautionary advice Dill gave as CIGS was 'at once desperately necessary and singularly unpalatable' (Danchev in Keegan (ed.), 1991, 65) to a prime minister eager for offensive action. For his part Churchill came to regard Dill as unimaginative and obstructionist. He questioned his fighting spirit, nicknamed him 'Dilly-Dally' and, in increasing disagreement with his CIGS on strategic priorities, brushed aside the advice that sending troops to Greece would neither help in that country's defence nor improve military prospects in the Western Desert.

Whatever personal comfort Dill may have drawn from being proved right, Churchill was determined to remove him. Introducing a new rule that a CIGS should retire on reaching the age of 60, Dill was made a field marshal in November 1941 and nominated Governor of Bombay.

With his career seemingly over, it was the Japanese who rescued 'Jack' Dill from a dignified retirement. Travelling to Washington with Churchill to discuss joint planning with the Americans in December 1941, he was left there as head of the British Joint Staff Mission. By every account he was extraordinarily successful in this quasi-ambassadorial role. His 'sincerity, modesty and transparent integrity' combined, apparently, to win 'all hearts' (Ismay, 1960, 244). Establishing good relations with President Roosevelt, and particularly close ties with General Marshall, Chief of Staff of the United States Army, his part in maintaining and coordinating the alliance was crucial. He and Marshall lunched together regularly and became adept at defusing inter-allied difficulties, as well as heading off various imaginative yet impractical projects proposed by their political masters.

There is the slight suggestion that Dill 'went native' in Washington. Lukewarm towards the Mediterranean strategy, he 'hated' Operation TORCH (Harvey (ed.), 1978, 154), and became less a representative of British views in America than a relayer of American strategic ideas to his British superiors. Perhaps his achievement was to play his part in managing the decline of British influence in the Grand Alliance with grace and finesse. At any rate, nursing his declining health, he had no plans to return to Britain after the war. With Churchill not responding to Brooke's efforts to secure him a peerage, the only further British honour Dill received was his 1942 appointment as Colonel Commandant of the newly-raised Parachute Regiment. It was quite different in the United States. When Dill died in Washington, of aplastic anaemia, in November 1944, he was buried with full military honours in Arlington National Cemetery. As one witness of the ceremony recorded, he had 'never seen so many men so visibly shaken. Marshall's face was truly stricken'. (Danchev in Keegan (ed.), 1991, 68).

DIMOLINE, Major General William Alfred
(1897–1965), CB, CMG, CBE, DSO, MC
Born in Birkenhead and educated there and at a school in Cheltenham, Dimoline volunteered for service with the East Surrey Regiment in 1914. Commissioned during the war, during which he was mentioned twice in despatches and awarded the MC, he was on the staff of the British Army of the Rhine in 1919.

Transferring to the Royal Signals in 1920, Dimoline served in India and Iraq in the early 1920s. Married in 1922, he spent the next six years in Nigeria. A student at the Staff College, Camberley, 1933–1934, he spent the next two years in India on recovery work after the Quetta earthquake. Made o/c British troops in Northern Rhodesia (Zambia) in 1937, he went on to become a member of the Colony's Legislative Council before the outbreak of war.

A brigade commander in 1940, 'Dimmo' Dimoline served in the Abyssinian campaign and led 22nd East African Brigade during the capture of Madagascar in May 1942. In Burma from 1944, in command of the 28th East African Brigade, he wrote a long letter to Slim pressing his case for promotion (Dimoline, 4/2, LHCMA). Slim, needing to make changes among his divisional commanders, obliged and appointed him to command 11th East African Division in February 1945 on the grounds that he was 'very popular' with African troops (Slim, 1986, 440). The next year he was admitted to the DSO.

GOC East Africa, 1946–1948, Dimoline was Commander of Aldershot District, 1948–1951 and was UK representative on the Military Staff Committee of the UN from 1951 until his retirement from the army in 1953.

A widower in 1943, Dimoline re-married in 1948. He was Colonel Commandant of the King's African Rifles, the Northern Rhodesian Regiment and the Rhodesian African Rifles, as well as being, for a number of years, Secretary for Overseas Organization, Duke of Edinburgh's Award Scheme.

DIXON, Major General Bernard Edward Cooke *(1896–1973), CB, MC*
The son of a doctor, Dixon was educated at Bedford School and RMA Woolwich. Commissioned in the Royal Engineers in 1915, his First War service was in France where he was mentioned in despatches and awarded the MC in 1917.

Married in 1923, Dixon was Adjutant to 53rd (TA) Division 1923–1925 and an assistant instructor at the School of Electrical and Mechanical Engineering 1925–1926. He was Senior Instructor there 1927–1929. A major in 1932, and a lieutenant colonel in 1939, he served on the staff of GHQ Middle East from 1940.

Twice mentioned in despatches during the North African campaign, Dixon served in Italy 1943–1944 and, promoted major general, was Engineer-in-Chief, GHQ Middle East Command, 1944–1947. Chief Engineer, HQ Western Command, 1947–1948, he retired from the army in 1948.

DOBBIE, Lieutenant General Sir William George Sheddon
(1879–1964), GCMG, KCB, DSO

The son of an Indian Civil Servant, Dobbie was educated at Charterhouse, where he was a classical scholar, and at RMA, Woolwich. Commissioned in the Royal Engineers in 1899, he served in the South African War. Married in 1904, he was a student at the School of Engineering, Chatham, and attended the Staff College, Camberley, in 1911. First War service was in France, where he was seven times mentioned in despatches and admitted to the DSO in 1916.

A colonel in 1926, Dobbie served on the staff at the War Office 1926–1928 and, after a brief spell as Engineer-in-Chief, Western Command, was appointed to command an infantry brigade in Egypt. Between 1933 and 1935 he was, variously, Inspector of the Royal Engineers, Commander of the Chatham Area, Commandant of the School of Military Engineering and Officer Commanding the Royal Engineers Depot at Chatham. In 1935 he was appointed GOC Malaya, a post he held until his retirement in 1939.

Re-employed at war's beginning, Dobbie was promoted major general in 1940 and appointed Governor of Malta. With fewer than 5,000 men available for the defence of the islands and, initially, with only three obsolete aircraft at his disposal, Dobbie, a deeply religious man, bore the responsibility for withstanding the intensive siege conditions of the next two years. He gave bible readings, shared the same hardships as the civilian population, and, allegedly, banned troop-training and dock labour on Sundays. He was knighted in 1941.

Believed to be 'very tired and worn out' (Danchev & Todman, 2001, 257), Dobbie was recalled to London in May 1942. Though not bitter at being replaced by Lord Gort, and maintaining that 'I could have stayed perfectly well' (Kennedy, 1957, 231), he enjoyed his elevation in the knighthood and the publicity attendant on the lecture tour he embarked on in the United States.

Colonel Commandant of the Royal Engineers 1940–1947, Dobbie's retirement to 'well-earned obscurity' (Bierman & Smith, 2002, 341) involved the writing of books with such titles as *Active Service with Christ*. Outliving his wife by two years, he died in London.

DORMAN-SMITH (O'GOWAN), Major General Eric Edward
(1895–1969), MC

Born in Co. Cavan and educated at Uppingham and RMC, Sandhurst, Dorman-Smith was commissioned in the Northumberland Fusiliers in 1914. First War service was in France, where he was thrice wounded and awarded the MC in 1916, and in Italy.

Adjutant to his battalion 1919–1922, he saw service in Ireland and Germany before becoming an instructor at Sandhurst in 1924. There, allegedly, he hit on the idea of the beret as headgear for members of the Royal Tank Corps (Greacen, 1989, 95). Passing into the Staff College, Camberley, in 1926, he acquired the reputation of being conceited and arrogant. Falling foul of one of the instructors, Montgomery, he ostentatiously burned his lecture notes on graduation.

Married in 1927, 'Chink' Dorman-Smith was an instructor at the School of Engineering, Chatham, 1929–1931, and was Brigade Major under Wavell in the 6th Experimental Brigade at Blackdown 1931–1932. A determined modernizer contemptuous of most of his 'amateur' peers, he was for the next three years on the staff at the War Office. In 1936 he returned to Camberley as an Instructor. Commander of the 1st Battalion Northumberland Fusiliers in Egypt 1937–1938, he was appointed Director of Military Training in India in 1938. There he worked closely with Auchinleck, then Deputy Chief of Staff. Each was, in his own way, a zealous advocate of mechanization and they shared a 'horror of military backwardness' (Clayton & Craig, 2002, 66).

By 1939 'Chink' Dorman-Smith had come far and fast. In the peacetime conditions of desperately slow promotions he had, between 1932 and 1938, occupied every brevet position from captain to brigadier. His famously 'fertile brain' was recognized, though, unable to conceal his brilliance, his inability to tolerate the mediocrity of those around him marked him as a man with 'a talent for making enemies' (Bidwell & Graham, 1985, 243).

Made commandant of the newly-formed Middle East Staff College at Haifa in 1940, Dorman-Smith was restless in that post. Gravitating towards Cairo, he was able to advise Wavell and O'Connor on tactics and be on hand to draft the victory signal from Beda Fomm. Serving briefly as Director of Military Operations in Cairo, it was not until Auchinleck was made C-in-C Middle East in 1941 that he felt his abilities were being put to their fullest use. Auchinleck, conscious that Dorman-Smith was not universally popular, made unofficial use of his friend from Indian days and received from him much negative advice on the shortcomings of 8th Army commanders, in particular, as he quipped, 'l'embarras du Ritchie'. Appointed Deputy Chief of Staff in May 1942, his position at the hub of the planning system in the desert war was acknowledged when Auchinleck assumed personal command of 8th Army after the fall of Tobruk, taking Dorman-Smith with him as personal Chief of Staff.

In falling back to the Alamein position and blunting Rommel's June and July 1942 attacks, Auchinleck and Dorman-Smith together saved Egypt. Moreover, in his 'appreciation' of the military situation, written in late July, Dorman-Smith correctly anticipated the timing and path of Rommel's next assault and provided a blueprint for a counter-offensive. But this was both too early and too late. Dismissed, along with his chief, during the 'Cairo purge' of August 1942, 'Chink' reverted to his substantive rank and was sent to England to command an infantry brigade. It was his misfortune that Ritchie, the man he had criticized so much in the desert, was made his Corps Commander in October 1943. Removed from his post, Dorman-Smith remained unemployed for six months before being appointed to command a brigade in Italy. His tactical acumen seemed unimpaired during the break-out from the Anzio beach-head, but his battalion commanders so expressed their dislike of his style of leadership that the divisional commander, Penney, sacked him on the grounds that he was 'unfit for brigade command' (Barnett, 1983, 341).

Dismissed from the army in November 1944, Dorman-Smith, now divorced and re-married, stood unsuccessfully as a Liberal candidate in the 1945 general election and retired to his estate in Ireland. Changing his name to O'Gowan, his threats of legal action obliged Churchill and Montgomery to revise later editions of their memoirs. While allowing units of the Official IRA to train in his grounds, he would 'regale anyone who would listen' to his version of how the 'Military Establishment' had done him down' (Stewart, 1999, 40). One sympathetic listener was Correlli Barnett, whose *Desert Generals*, first published at a time when the Montgomery myth was at its height, helped to fuel controversy about the desert war.

The Barnett-inspired view of Dorman-Smith is that he was a 'brilliant and unorthodox theorist' and a commander of 'outstanding ability' (Barnett, 1983, 341), brought down by lesser men. To others he was either a phoney, the 'rabbit-toothed eminence grise' (Hamilton, 2001, 520) whose 'rhetoric, amply larded with his native blarney, seldom seemed based on any study of the problem' (Richardson, 1985, 77), or positively dangerous in the way he 'mesmerized' Auchinleck with his 'fertile imagination' (Carver, 1989, 127). The view, often expressed, that Auchinleck was a poor picker of subordinates is, in itself, a coded way of saying Dorman-Smith's influence was malign. A more balanced view, perhaps, would be that he fell some way short of the military genius as described by Barnett, but was not responsible for all the bad habits picked up by the 8th Army. To Tuker the 'intriguing' question was how 8th Army would have fought in May-June 1942 had 'the unorthodox Dorman-Smith been on its staff' (Tuker, 1963, 142).

That he was shabbily treated suggests, ultimately, that Dorman-Smith was unlucky in his choice of patrons. Able to exert influence on commanders like Wavell and Auchinleck, who knew him and were selectively receptive to his ideas, he could not survive their demise, nor flourish under the grimmer, more dour, Brooke-Montgomery regime. They were the military 'winners' in the war and wrote, or had written for them, their own triumphal histories. As a 'loser', 'Chink' Dorman-Smith was but one of the eggs that got broken and trodden underfoot in the process.

DOWLER, Lieutenant General Sir Arthur Arnhold Bullick
(1895–1963), KCB, KBE
Educated at Tonbridge School and RMC, Sandhurst, Dowler was commissioned in the East Surrey Regiment in 1914. First War service was in France, where he was mentioned in despatches.

A brevet major in 1918, Dowler married that year. Regimental duties in the 1920s gave way to a place at the Staff College, Camberley, 1931–1932, after which he was a battalion adjutant before returning to Camberley as an instructor in 1937. Commander of the 1st Battalion, East Surrey Regiment, in 1939, he served on the staff of 49th Division. Sent to Norway, he was considered 'quite first-class . . . I would take him anywhere', by Auchinleck (Dill, 2nd. acc., 9, LHCMA).

Made BGS of V Corps in the summer of 1940, Dowler was moved from that post by Montgomery, but, promoted major general, was appointed to command the 38th (Welsh) Division in 1941. Six months later he was made Major General i/c Administration, Southern Command, a post he held until 1943 when he was sent to command Tunis District. In 1944 he commanded the base area in Cairo.

Appointed Chief of Staff to the British Army of the Rhine in 1946, Dowler was knighted that year. Director of Infantry at the War Office 1947–1948, he ended his army career in 1951, having spent three years as GOC East Africa.

Colonel Commandant of the East Surrey Regiment 1946–1954, Dowler was made DL for Surrey in 1958. He was active in charity work until his death.

DOWN, Lieutenant General Sir Ernest Edward *(1902–1980), KBE, CB*

Born in Cornwall and educated in Plymouth, at Kelly College and RMC, Sandhurst, Down was commissioned in the Dorset Regiment in 1923. Seconded to the Royal West African Frontier Force in 1925, he spent seven years in Africa. On his return he transferred to the King's Shropshire Light Infantry. A brigade major from 1937, he was on a posting in Jamaica when war broke out in 1939.

Appointed to command the 1st Parachute Battalion in 1941, Down founded his wartime reputation on the training of airborne troops. In command of 2nd Parachute Brigade in 1942, he assumed temporary command of 1st Airborne Division in 1943. In 1944 he was sent to India to train the 44th (1st Indian) Airborne Division for future operations

Commander of the British Military Mission to Greece 1948–1949, Down was Commander of Mid-West District and 53rd (Welsh) Division 1949–1952. He was GOC-in-C Southern Command from 1952 until his retirement from the army in 1955. For the remaining 25 years of his life he lived in Andover, Hampshire.

DREW, Major General Sir James Syme *(1883–1955), KBE, CB, DSO, MC*

Born in Edinburgh and educated at Harrow, Drew was commissioned in the Queen's Own Cameron Highlanders in 1902. A captain in 1914, his First War service was in France, where he was mentioned in despatches, awarded the MC and admitted to the DSO in 1917.

A brevet major in 1918, the year he married, Drew attended the first post-war course at the Staff College, Camberley. He commanded the 2nd Battalion Cameron Highlanders 1927–1929 and was Assistant Commandant and Chief Instructor at the Small Arms School, Netheravon, 1929–1932. Assistant Director of the Territorial Army at the War Office 1932–1935, he was BGS Southern Command in 1936, before being promoted major general in 1938 and appointed to command 52nd (Lowland) Division.

Instead of being sent to France to join the BEF, the 52nd Division was held back in Scotland to train as mountain troops. However, after the Dunkirk evacuation it was landed piecemeal in France with the contradictory intention of bolstering French morale and, as proved necessary, screening the evacuation of British line of communication troops. Mentioned in despatches, Drew was moved from his divisional command to become Major General i/c Training,

Combined Operations. Appointed Director General of the Home Guard and Territorial Army in 1944, he retired from the army in 1945.

Colonel of the Cameron Highlanders 1943–1951, Drew was made DL for Perthshire in 1947. He died at his home near Pitlochry.

DUFF, Major General Alan Colquhoun (1896–1973), CB, OBE, MC
The son of a Cambridge Fellow and educated at Wellington and RMA Woolwich, Duff was commissioned in the Royal Engineers in 1915. His First War service was in Gallipoli and Serbia, where he was awarded the MC, and in Macedonia and Palestine.

A captain in 1918, Duff attended the Staff College, Camberley, 1926–1927. Attached to the Nigeria Regiment, 1930–1935, he married in 1935 and was a lieutenant colonel attached to the King's African Rifles by 1939.

Active in operations in East Africa, 1941–1942, Duff was twice mentioned in despatches. He was Deputy Quartermaster General at the War Office, 1943–1944 and, after a brief spell as Deputy QMG Allied Forces HQ in Italy, was made Chief Administrative Officer to Alexander in 1945.

Major General i/c Administration, Southern Command, 1946–47, Duff retired from the army in 1947. General Manager, Stevenage Development Corporation, 1947–1957, he deployed the writing skills he had acquired as a young man (he had written three novels under a nom de plume) to write, in 1961, a book on Britain's New Towns.

DUGUID, Major General Derek Robertson (1888–1973), CB, MBE
Born in Bo'ness and educated at Bo'ness Academy and Heriot-Watt College, Edinburgh, Duguid was an assistant engineer in the family business until, as a volunteer, he joined the army in 1915. He served with the Army Ordnance Corps as Inspector of Ordnance Machinery 1915–1919, in France, Salonika and South Russia.

Married in 1918 and resolved to make the army his career, Duguid was five years in Germany with the Inter-Allied Control Commission. He was Ordnance Mechanical Engineer, Western Command, 1924–1925, and Assistant Director of Guns and Carriages at Woolwich 1925–1929. By this time a lieutenant colonel, Duguid was Officer Commanding RAOC Workshops, Woolwich Arsenal, 1929–1932, and was o/c Ordnance Workshops, Quetta Arsenal, India, 1932–1937. Returning to England he was o/c RAOC Depot Workshops, Chilwell, 1937–1939.

Officer Commanding the BEF's Advanced Base Workshops in France 1939–1940, Duguid was Deputy Director of Mechanical Engineering at the War Office 1941–1943. There, at the creation of the Royal Electrical and Mechanical Engineers, he was promoted major general and appointed Director of Mechanical Engineering, India, in 1943. He retired form the army in 1946 as head of the Corps of Indian Electrical and Mechanical Engineers.

The father of three sons, Duguid retired to live in Dundee. He was made a Fellow of Heriot-Watt College in 1951.

92

DURNFORD, Lieutenant General Cyril Maton Periam
(1891–1965), CB, CIE

Born and educated in Bristol, Durnford joined the Indian Army Officer Reserve in 1914. Mobilized and commissioned in the 6th Rajputana Rifles, his First War service was in France, Mesopotamia and in Palestine. As with so many Indian Army officers, engagement in operations in Iraq and the North-West Frontier was constant throughout the 1920s.

Mentioned in despatches four times, Durnford attended the Staff College, Camberley, 1924–1925. A United Service Institution of India essay prize-winner in 1926 and 1935, he attended the Royal Naval College, Greenwich, in 1930 and, after serving on the staff of Northern Command, India, for four years, attended the Imperial Defence College in 1938. He commanded the 3rd Batalion 7th Rajputs 1938–1939.

Durnford's career trajectory in wartime did not quite match up to his impressive educational record. He was Chief-of-Staff, Northern Command, India, 1940–1942, served as Adjutant General and QMG, AHQ, India, in 1942, and was major-general i/c Administration Central Command, India, 1943–1945. Promoted lieutenant general, he was QMG India 1945–1946.

Retired from the army in 1947, Durnford lived the remaining years of his life in Bath.

E

EASTWOOD, Lieutenant General Sir Thomas Ralph
(1890–1959), KCB, DSO, MC

Of military family and educated at Eton and RMC, Sandhurst, Eastwood was commissioned in the Rifle Brigade in 1910. In New Zealand, as ADC to the Governor General, when war broke out in 1914, his First War service was in Samoa, Egypt, Gallipoli and in France. Mentioned in despatches seven times and awarded the MC in 1918, he was admitted to the DSO in 1919, after serving on Lord Rawlinson's staff with the Allied Relief Mission in North Russia.

A brigade major at Aldershot and in Ireland 1919–1921, Eastwood married in 1921 and attended the Staff College, Camberley, 1921–1922. A staff officer at the War Office 1923–1927, he served on the staff at Camberley 1928–1931 and commanded the Rifle Brigade Depot 1931–1934. By now a lieutenant colonel, 'Rusty' Eastwood commanded the 2nd Battalion KRRC 1934–1935 and served on the staff of 2nd Division 1936–1938. He was Commandant RMC, Sandhurst 1938–1939 and served on the staff of GHQ, BEF, 1939–40.

Appointed Chief of Staff to Brooke in June 1940, Eastwood helped in the evacuation of line of communication troops south of the Somme and, promoted major general on his return from France, was appointed to command 4th Division. In October 1940 he was made Director General of the Home Guard. Favoured by Brooke but described by Montgomery as 'no good . . . his ceiling is a Divisional Command' (Hamilton, 1982, 773), he was GOC-in-C Northern Command 1941–1944. He was Governor and C-in-C, Gibraltar, from 1944 until he retired from the army in 1947. Settling in Gloucestershire, he was a JP from 1951.

EDGCUMBE, Major General Oliver Pearce *(1892–1956), CB, CBE, MC*
The son of a knight, Edgcumbe was educated at Winchester and RMC, Sandhurst. Commissioned in the Duke of Cornwall's Light Infantry in 1911, his First War service was in France where he was awarded the MC in 1915.

Transferring to the Royal Signals in 1920, Edgcumbe attended the Staff College, Camberley, 1927–1928. Married in 1935, he was Director of Organization at the War Office 1941–42. While there he was instrumental in the formation and organization of the Royal Electrical and Mechanical Engineers (REME). After a brief period commanding the East Kent sub-District, he was appointed Commissioner for the Allied Control Commission, Hungary, in 1945. He held that post until he retired from the army in 1947.

Settling in Kent, Edgcumbe suffered frequent periods of ill-health before his relatively early death. Tributes to him, however, were numerous and warm.

EDWARD-COLLINS, Major General Charles Edward
(1881–1967), CB, CIE
Born in Cornwall and educated at Marlborough and RMC, Sandhurst, Edward-Collins was commissioned in the Devon Regiment in 1900. After service in the South African War, he married in 1907 and, seconded for service with the Indian Supply and Transport Corps, transferred to the Indian Army in 1909. Mentioned in despatches for his part in the Abor Expedition 1911–1912, his First War service was in Egypt, Mesopotamia and Palestine.

Mentioned in despatches during operations in southern Persia (Iran) in 1919, Edward-Collins spent the rest of his service career in India. Assistant Director of Supplies and Transport, India, in 1923–1924, he was Commandant of the Indian Army Service Corps 1927–1930. Deputy Director of Cavalry Remounts at AHQ 1934–1935 and Director of Supplies and Transport, India, 1935–1937, he was promoted major general in 1937 and retired from the army in 1940.

Commander of the North Cornwall Group Home Guard, 1942–1945, Edward-Collins outlived his wife and was appointed High Sheriff of Cornwall in 1955.

EDWARDS, Major General John Keith *(1896- ?), DSO, MC*
Commissioned in the Scots Guards in 1915, Edwards' First War service was in France, where he was wounded and awarded the MC.

A captain in 1920, Edwards commanded the London District School of

Instruction (TA) 1926–1928 and was a brigade major in Palestine in 1931. A student at the Staff College, Camberley, 1932–1933, he was Brigade Major with Cairo Brigade, Egypt, 1933–1935. From 1936 to 1939 he served on the directing staff of the Staff College, Quetta.

A staff officer in Palestine and Transjordan 1939–1940, Edwards was BGS East African Command 1940–1942. Admitted to the DSO, he commanded 148th Brigade in 1942. Promoted major general, he was GOC 45th Division, under Home Forces, from January 1943 to September 1944. Made head of the SHAEF Mission to the Netherlands, he retired from the army in 1947.

ELDRIDGE, Lieutenant General Sir William John
(1898–1985), KBE, CB, DSO, MC
Educated privately and commissioned in the Royal Artillery in 1915, Eldridge's First War service was in France, where he was twice wounded, mentioned in despatches and awarded the MC. He was admitted to the DSO in 1919 after service on operations in southern Iraq.

A graduate of the Staff College, Camberley, in 1934, Eldridge was on the directing staff at the RAF Staff College 1936–1938 and Chief Staff Officer with Anti-Aircraft Command 1939–1941. Little is known about his subsequent war service, other than that he served at the War Office as Director of Anti-Aircraft and Coast Defence 1941–1942 and as Deputy Director General of Artillery 1942–1944. He had a Bar added to his DSO in Italy in 1944 and was appointed Director General of Artillery, Ministry of Supply, in 1945. He held that post for three years.

Eldridge was Commandant of the Military College of Science 1948–1951, GOC Aldershot District 1951–1953 and Controller of Munitions at the Ministry of Supply until his retirement from the army in 1957. A company chairman 1957–1968, he married in 1954 only for his wife to die within two years.

ELLIOTT, Major General James Gordon *(1898–1990), CIE*
Born in Mid-Wales and educated at Blundell's, Elliott was gazetted into the Indian Army in 1916, joining the 1st Punjab Regiment in 1922. After more than a decade of regimental soldiering in India, interrupted by attendance at the Staff College, Camberley, 1929–1930, he served as an instructor at the Staff College, Quetta, 1935–1937, before joining the Directorate of Military Training in 1938.

Director of Military Training, India, 1942–1943, Elliott commanded a brigade in Burma 1943–1944. After serving briefly as Deputy Adjutant General, he was Deputy Welfare General, India, 1945–1946. Deputy Military Secretary to the Defence Committee, India, in 1947, he retired from the army in 1948 and settled in Exmouth.

'Jim' Elliott married in 1931 and fathered a son and a daughter. In his long retirement he wrote a number of books on military subjects, perhaps the best-known being *The Story of the Indian Army 1939–1945* (1965). Until just before his death he was working on a biography of Auchinleck.

ERSKINE, General Sir George Watkin Eben James
(1899–1965), GCB, KBE, DSO
The son of a general and educated at Charterhouse and RMC, Sandhurst, Erskine was commissioned in the King's Royal Rifle Corps in 1918. His First War service was brief, but promotion in peacetime was reasonably rapid.

Promoted captain in 1928, the year he married, Erskine graduated from the Staff College, Camberley, in 1930 and, Deputy Adjutant and QMG Eastern Command 1937–1939, was promoted major in 1938. Serving on the staff of 1st London (Territorial) Division in 1939, he commanded 2nd Battalion KRRC 1940–1941 and, 'as imperturbable an officer as could be found anywhere' (Maule, 1961, 116), commanded 69th Infantry Brigade in North Africa in 1942. Judged by Auchinleck 'a better staff officer than commander' (Dill, 2nd acc., LHCMA), he was made BGS XIII Corps in 1942 and, under Montgomery, served as BGS 8th Army during de Guingand's quite frequent absences. His mind, it is said, was 'not as acute as Freddie's but he had a great capacity for friendship' (Richardson, 1985, 134).

Admitted to the DSO after Alamein, and by now very much a Montgomery man, 'Bobby 'Erskine was promoted major general in January 1943 and appointed to command 7th Armoured Division. A 'cheerful, extrovert character' (Carver, 1989, 150), he led the 'Desert Rats' through the final stages of the campaign in Tunisia and at the Salerno landings in September 1943.

Recalled to Britain in January 1944, Erskine's preparations for operations in North-West Europe were not sufficient to enable 7th Armoured Division to overcome the difficult fighting conditions in Normandy. Dempsey, angered by Erskine's 'very poor show' (D'Este, 2001, 272) and the 'almost insubordinate' letter he wrote to O'Connor, his Corps Commander, (Baynes, 1989, 209), recommended his removal. Sacked by Montgomery for being 'very sticky' (Hamilton, 1983, 804), he was made head of the SHAEF Mission to Belgium, before being briefly appointed to command 43rd Infantry Division in late 1945.

Made Deputy Chief of Staff to the Control Commission, Germany, 1945–1946, Erskine was briefly GOC Land Forces, Hong Kong. Director General of the Territorial Army 1948–1949, he was GOC British Troops in Egypt and Mediterranean Command 1949–1952. Knighted that year, he was GOC-in-C Eastern Command 1952–1953, C-in-C East Africa 1953–1955, and GOC-in-C Southern Command 1955–1958.

Retired that year, with knighthood enhanced, Erskine was Lieutenant Governor of Jersey 1958–1963.

EVANS, Major General David Sydney Carlyon *(1893–1955), CBE*
Educated at St Paul's and RMA, Woolwich, Evans was commissioned in the Royal Artillery in 1913. First War service was with the Royal Garrison Artillery in France.

A captain in 1918, Evans was an Instructor at the School of Artillery, Larkhill, 1922–1926, and an Assistant Inspector in the RA Inspection Department 1928–1930. An Experiments Officer at the Admiralty Research

Laboratory 1930–1934, he was Assistant Superintendent of the Design Department 1935–1939. A colonel in 1939, he was Secretary of the Ordnance Board at the War Office when war broke out.

Evans was Assistant Director of Artillery 1939–1942. Vice-President and Senior Military Member of the Ordnance Board 1942–1947, he retired from the army in 1947.

EVANS, Lieutenant General Sir Geoffrey Charles
(1901–1987), KBE, CB, DSO (two Bars)
Of military family, Evans was educated at Aldenham School and RMC, Sandhurst. Commissioned in the Royal Warwickshire Regiment in 1920, he was Adjutant of the 1st Battalion 1926–1929 and the 7th (Territorial) Battalion 1934–35. Married in 1928, he attended the Staff College, Camberley, 1936–1937.

Having transferred to the Royal Sussex Regiment, Evans, a brigade major in 1941, was admitted to the DSO for his 'forceful leadership' (Maule,1961, 264) at Keren and throughout the campaign in Abyssinia, and commanded the 1st Battalion Royal Sussex Regiment in North Africa 1941–1942. Made Commandant of the Staff College, Quetta, in 1942, he was BGS IV Corps in Burma 1943–1944. Commander of 123rd Indian Brigade there in 1944, he was awarded the second Bar to his DSO for his 'inspiring leadership' (Hickey, 1998, 104) during the battle of the 'Admin.Box' at Sinzweya. Promoted major general, his stay as GOC 5th Indian Division was curtailed through illness, but in December 1944 he was appointed to command 7th Indian Division. Surviving the 'fiasco' of the Irrawaddy River crossing (Allen, 2002, 417), his part in the capture of Meiktila was central to the success of operations in central Burma.

GOC Allied Land Forces, Siam (Thailand), 1945–1946, Evans returned to Britain to assume command of 42nd Division and of North-West District. Director of Military Training at the War Office 1948–1949, he was GOC 40th Division, Hong Kong, 1949–1951, and Temporary Commander British troops in the Crown Colony 1951–52. Made Assistant Chief of Staff, Allied Powers Europe in 1952, he was GOC Northern Command from 1953 until he retired from the army in 1957.

As well as holding down a series of honorary colonelcies, Evans was Vice-President of the National Playing Fields Association, Commander of the Royal Hospital Chelsea 1968–1976 and DL for Greater London 1970–1976. He was also a prolific writer, with interests ranging from field sports to military history, via antiques. Perhaps his best known work was *Slim as Military Commander* (1969).

EVANS, Major General Roger *(1886–1968) CB, MC*
Little is known about Evans's early life. Commissioned in the 7th Hussars in 1907, he served in Mesopotamia 1917–1918. He was mentioned in despatches and awarded the MC in 1918. Married in 1919, he had to bring up his son after the death of his wife in 1921.

After attending the Staff College, Camberley, 1920–1921, Evans returned to regimental duties. On the directing staff at Camberley 1924–1927, and at the War Office, 1927–1929 he re-married in 1931. He commanded 5th Royal Inniskilling Dragoon Guards 1929–1933, attended the Imperial Defence College in 1934, and was BGS Army HQ, India, 1935–1938. Promoted major general in 1938, he briefly commanded the Mobile Division and was appointed Deputy Director of Military Operations at the War Office. The same year, in what appeared to be 'a deliberate snub to qualified Tank Corps major generals' (Bond, 1980, 180), he was appointed to command 1st Armoured Division, presumably on the grounds that only a cavalryman could 'sell' an armoured command to his cavalry peers. Working his division up, Evans was ordered to France in May 1940 to try and stem the German advance on the Channel ports and 'fight to the last extremity in order to give the French no excuse to abandon the struggle' (Marshall-Cornwall, 1984, 139).

Failing on both counts, Evans returned to England and was removed from his command in August 1940. After an 'unpleasant interview' with Brooke (Danchev & Todman, 2001, 101), he was made Commander of Aldershot District. His son, by his first marriage, died on active service in 1942 and he retired from the army in 1944.

A Somerset JP from 1947, Evans was High Sheriff 1955–1956 and a County Alderman from 1957.

EVANSON, Major General Arthur Charles Tarver *(1895–1957), CB, MC*
Educated at Haileybury and RMC, Sandhurst, Evanson was commissioned in the East Surrey Regiment in 1914. His First War service was in France, latterly with the Machine Gun Corps. He was mentioned in despatches and awarded the MC.

Married in 1922, and an instructor at the Small Arms School, Netheravon, 1924–1928, Evanson, in common with so many army officers during the inter-war years, suffered the blight of slow promotion and periods on half-pay. A major in 1935, he commanded the 198th Brigade 1941–1943, the 220th Brigade 1943–1945 and the 141st Brigade in 1945. Appointed CB, he retired from the army in 1947.

EVELEGH, Major General Vyvyan *(1898–1958), CB, DSO, OBE*
Of military family and educated at Wellington, Evelegh was commissioned in the Duke of Cornwall's Light Infantry in 1917. His First War service was in France, and in 1919 he was wounded while serving with the Allied Relief Mission in North Russia.

After regimental duties in Ireland, India and Gibraltar, Evelegh, in 1939, was a battalion commander with the BEF in France when he was posted home to serve as an instructor at the Staff College, Camberley. Awarded the OBE, although he missed out on the fighting in France, he commanded 11th Brigade under Home Forces 1940–1941. Promoted major general in 1942, he was briefly

Assistant Commandant at Camberley and was appointed GOC of the newly-formed 78th Division, which formed part of First Army in Tunisia. Possessing 'a genial nature . . . he could be scathing in his criticism, which lost no impact from an occasional stutter' (Blaxland, 1977, 40).

In common with most First Army senior officers, Evelegh had to live with the prejudices of Montgomery and, later, Leese, as 8th Army commanders. Hence, after the campaigns in Sicily and southern Italy, command of 78th Division passed to Keightley, while Evelegh, who Montgomery did 'not recommend for a Corps' (Hamilton, 1983, 427), had to wait for his new command, 6th Armoured Division, to be shipped-up piecemeal from Tunisia.

Admitted to the DSO after serving as Deputy to Lucas at Anzio, Evelegh assumed command of his Division in February 1944, only to relinquish it in July, having, it is said, 'been unable to make amends for the bad start made by 6th Armoured in the exploitation of the Hitler Line' (Blaxland, 1979, 166).

Made Assistant Chief of Staff at the War Office, illness caused Evelegh to take 18 months' sick leave. Made Commander of North-West District in 1947, he retired from the army in 1950. He was Colonel Commandant of the DCLI from 1953 until his death.

EVETTS, Lieutenant General Sir John Fullerton
(1891–1988), KBE, CB, CBE, MC
Of military family and educated at Lancing and RMC, Sandhurst, 'Jack' Evetts was commissioned in the Cameronians (Scottish Rifles) in 1911. A captain in 1915, his First War service was in France, where he was mentioned in despatches and awarded the MC. By war's end he was a temporary major with the Machine Gun Corps.

Married in 1916, Evetts attended the Staff College, Camberley, 1922–1923, and was seconded to the Iraqi Army 1925–1928. Deputy Assistant Adjutant General at the War Office 1932, he transferred to the Ulster Rifles in 1934 and was a battalion commander in Palestine in 1936. After a brief spell of staff duties there, he was appointed to command 16th Infantry Brigade in Palestine and Transjordan. Mentioned in despatches he, as reported by Montgomery, 'require[d] no urging . . . to kill [Arab] rebels' (Hamilton, 1981, 297).

Sent to India, Evetts was BGS, HQ Northern Command, 1939–1940 and was GOC, Western District, 1940–1941. Acknowledged as having 'a most versatile mind' (Pile, 1949, 36), and promoted major general that year, he was appointed to command 6th Division, and was mentioned in despatches after operations in Syria. It was about this time that Auchinleck, planning to send 6th Division to Tobruk by sea, became worried about 'Jack' Evetts. He was, the C-in-C wrote to Dill, 'suffering some form of breakdown . . . [and] making a fool of himself with Druze women in Syria' (Dill, 2nd. acc., 4, LHCMA).

Hospitalized and sent home, a post was created for Evetts as Assistant CIGS. Assistant Military Adviser to the Minister of Supply 1944–1946, he retired from the Army that year

Head of the British Ministry of Supply Staff in Australia 1946–1951, Evetts was Chief Executive Officer for the Joint UK-Australia Long Range Weapons Board 1946–1951. Knighted upon his return to Britain, he and his wife lived in Tewkesbury, where he was a successful businessman for a number of years.

F

FAIRTLOUGH, Major General Eric Victor Howard
(1887–1944), DSO, MC
Of military family, Fairtlough was educated at Marlborough and RMA, Woolwich. Commissioned in the Royal Artillery, his First War service was in France and Salonika. Awarded the MC in 1915, he was four times mentioned in despatches and admitted to the DSO in 1918.

Married in 1928 and a lieutenant colonel in 1939, Fairtlough's Second War service was as CRA 3rd Division with the BEF in France 1939–1940 and with Anti-Aircraft Command. He was GOC 7th Anti-Aircraft Division 1940–1942. Made major general in 1941, ill health forced him to retire from the army the next year. He died at his home in Dorset.

FANSHAWE, Major General Sir Evelyn Dalrymple
(1895–1979), KBE, CB, CBE
The son of a general and educated at King's School, Canterbury, and RMC, Sandhurst, Fanshawe was commissioned in the Queen's Bays in 1914. First War service was in France, Egypt, Palestine, Mesopotamia, Persia, Russia and Syria; from 1915 he had been seconded to the Royal Flying Corps.

Returning to his regiment as Adjutant in 1919, Fanshawe married the next year. A lieutenant colonel in 1935, he served with the 20th Mechanized Cavalry Brigade in 1939, before being appointed to command the 20th Armoured Brigade in 1940. Briefly made acting GOC 6th Armoured Division that year and promoted major general in 1942, he was appointed to command the Royal Armoured Corps Training Establishment. He held that post until 1945 when he retired from the army.

Director of the United Nations Relief and Rehabilitation Administration (UNRRA) in the British zone of Germany, 1945–1948, Fanshawe was Director of the International Refugee Organization in the British zone of Germany 1948–1952. Knighted in 1951 he was active thereafter with the Northamptonshire Territorial Army Association, the County Cricket Club and the Northamptonshire Spastics Society. He was also Chairman of the Kettering Conservative and Unionist Association 1952–1967. A keen huntsman, he listed his other recreations as polo, yachting, shooting, fishing, racing and flying.

FEILDEN, Major General Sir Randle Guy *(1904–1981), KCVO, CB, CBE*
Educated at Eton and Cambridge University, Feilden was commissioned in the
Coldstream Guards in 1925. Married in 1929, he was ADC to the GOC London
District 1933–1936 and Regimental Adjutant 1936–1939.

A staff captain with 7th Guards Brigade 1939–1940, Feilden was Deputy
Assistant QMG with 3rd Division from April to September 1940. Having come
to the notice of Montgomery, he followed him to V Corps that autumn as QMG.
He was Assistant Adjutant and QMG, Guards Armoured Division, 1941–1942.
He was Deputy QMG, Home Forces in 1943 and, promoted major general,
occupied the same role with 21st Army Group, 1943–1945.

QMG of the Rhine Army 1945–1946, Feilden was appointed CB and was
Vice-QMG at the War Office from 1947 until his retirement from the army in
1949. A steward of the Jockey Club in 1952, he was knighted in 1953 and went
on to be senior steward for many succeeding years. Responsible for the intro-
duction of starting stalls, he was Chairman of the Turf Board from
1965–1967. High Sheriff of Oxfordshire in 1971, he was DL for the county
from 1975.

FESTING, Field Marshal Sir Francis Wogan *(1902–1976), GCB, KBE, DSO*
Born in Dublin, the son of an army captain (later Brigadier General), Festing
was educated at Winchester and RMC, Sandhurst. Commissioned in the Rifle
Brigade in 1921, he served at Chanak and then Aldershot. Regimental duties
included a three-year spell as ADC to General Sir John Burnett-Stuart. After
attending the Staff College, Camberley, 1933–1934, he served on the staff at
Eastern Command, married in 1937 and returned to Camberley as an instructor
the next year.

A battalion commander with the East Lancashire Regiment in 1939, Festing
served briefly as Air Liaison Officer during the campaign in Norway before
being posted to the staff at the War Office. In 1942 he was appointed to
command 29th Infantry Brigade and was admitted to the DSO for his part in
the invasion of Madagascar. Promoted major general, he was posted to India
and assumed command of the newly-formed 36th Division. After several
months, jungle training, 'Frankie' Festing led his division in the second Arakan
offensive and in the advance on Rangoon. Said to be 'an inspiring leader'
(Heathcote, 1999, 119), he at one time took command of a platoon whose leader
had been killed.

Made GOC Land Forces, Hong Kong, in 1945, Festing was Director of
Weapons and Development at the War Office 1947–1949. He returned to Hong
Kong that year, this time as Commander of British Forces, but illness forced
him to return home. President of the Regular Commissions Board 1950–1951,
he was Assistant Chief of Staff, Supreme Headquarters Allied Powers in Europe
1951–1952, GOC British troops in Egypt 1952–1954 and GOC Eastern
Command 1954–1956. Appointed C-in-C Far East Land Forces in 1956, he
became CIGS in 1958. It fell to him to implement the government's policy of

ending conscription and reducing the size of the army. Twice knighted, he retired, a field marshal, in 1961. Careless of his appearance and a much beloved 'character', it had given him great pleasure, so it is said, to have been the first practising Roman Catholic to have headed the British Army since the reign of James II.

Active in his retirement, Festing was Honorary Colonel of the Royal Northumberland Fusiliers, received an honorary degree from the University of Newcastle in 1964 and was an ardent collector of early weapons and Japanese swords. He was DL for Northumberland in 1962.

FINCH, Major General Lionel Hugh Knightley
(1888–1982), CB, DSO (Bar), OBE
Of military family, Finch was educated at Cheltenham and Birmingham and London Universities. Joining the Royal Sussex Regiment as a volunteer in 1914, he was commissioned in the Lancashire Fusiliers in 1915, was mentioned in despatches and admitted to the DSO in 1916 (Bar 1917).

Post-war, serving with occupation forces in Germany, Finch made two decisions: to marry and to remain a soldier. He attended the Staff College, Camberley, 1924–1925, and served on the staff at HQ, Northern Command, 1926–1927. For the next two years he was Deputy Assistant Adjutant and QMG in the Northumberland District and, transferring to the Cheshire Regiment, commanded the regimental depot 1930–1933. Posted to India in 1934, he was briefly Deputy Assistant Adjutant General, Army HQ, India, before commanding the 1st Battalion Lancashire Fusiliers in Shanghai. Returning to England in 1936, he was Assistant Adjutant General at the War Office until the outbreak of war.

Made Director of Recruiting at the War Office, Finch reverted briefly to being Deputy Adjutant General in 1940 and served, even more briefly, as GOC 18th Infantry Division in June 1940. Disliked by Brooke, who thought him 'an even more poisonous specimen than I first thought he was' (Danchev & Todman, 2001, 113), he was reduced to chairing various War Office committees. Appointed CB in 1941, he was a District Commander with Home Forces until he retired from the army in 1943.

Still in his fifties by war's end, Finch lived out the remaining forty years of his life in Sussex.

FINNIS, General Sir Henry *(1890–1945), KCB, CB, MC*
The son of an Indian Army officer, Finnis was educated at Wellington and RMC, Sandhurst. He joined the Indian Army in 1909 and was commissioned in the 13th Frontier Force Regiment. First War service was in Egypt, Aden and Mesopotamia, where he was twice wounded and awarded the MC.

Married in 1917, Finnis served as a staff officer, Northern Command, India, 1922–1923, was Assistant Military Secretary, GHQ India, 1926–1930, and commanded a battalion of the Frontier Force Regiment in 1934. An instructor at the Senior Officers' School, Belgaum, 1936–1938, he commanded the Khojak brigade in Baluchistan 1938–1939. Commander of Baluchistan Area 1939–1941, he was promoted major general in 1940, and was Military Secretary GHQ, India, 1941–1943. That year he was appointed GOC-in-Chief North-Western Army, India. Knighted in 1945 and promoted general, he died suddenly in May that year, at his desk in his Rawalpindi HQ.

FINNY, Major General Charles Morgan (1886–1955), OBE

The son of a Dublin doctor and educated at Shrewsbury and Trinity College, Dublin, Finny studied medicine and qualified in 1910. Joining the RAMC in 1911, he was a captain in 1914 and his First War service was in France, India and Persia (Iran).

Elected a Fellow of the Royal College of Surgeons in 1921 and made OBE in 1927, Finny married in 1928. A lieutenant colonel in 1934, he was Assistant Professor of Military Surgery at the Royal Army Medical College 1937–1938. Deputy Director Medical Services, 3rd Division, in France with the BEF in 1940 and DDMS III Corps 1940–1941, he was promoted major general and made DDMS Northern Command. He retired in 1942 and thereafter lived in Camberley.

FISHER, Lieutenant General Sir Bertie Drew
(1878–1972), KCB, CMG, DSO

Educated at Marlborough and Oxford University, Fisher was commissioned in the 17th Lancers in 1900. He campaigned in the South African War and was a brigade major in India 1909–1910. A major in 1914, his First War service began for him on the staff in the Military Aeronautics Department. Returning to his regiment in France, he was twice wounded, four times mentioned in despatches and admitted to the DSO in 1915.

Married in 1918 and a lieutenant colonel in 1919, Fisher attended the Staff College, Camberley, 1922–1923. ADC to the King 1926–1931, he commanded 2nd Cavalry Brigade 1923–1927 and was Commandant of the Senior Officers' School, Sheerness, 1927–1930. BGS Aldershot Command 1930–1931, he was Director of Recruiting and Organization at the War Office 1932–1934. Commandant RMC, Sandhurst 1934–1937, he was knighted and retired from the army in 1938.

Recalled to service at war's beginning, Fisher was appointed GOC Southern Command, a post he held until June 1940. Living near Basingstoke and a near neighbour to Brooke, he made himself an agreeable weekend shooting companion to the CIGS. He was Colonel of the 17th/21st Lancers 1938–1947.

FISHER, Major General Donald Rutherford Dacre
(1890–1962), CB, CBE, DSO

Born in North Wales and educated at Clifton and RMA, Woolwich, Fisher was commissioned in the Royal Field Artillery in 1909. His First War service was in

France, where he was twice wounded, mentioned twice in despatches and admitted to the DSO in 1917.

Regimental duties, with a variety of postings at home and abroad, occupied Fisher throughout the 1920s. Married in 1934, he attended the Staff College, Camberley, 1934–1935 and, a colonel in 1938, he served on the staff at the War Office. Promoted major general in 1941, he was Director General Army Requirements at the War Office 1942–1946. Appointed CB in 1945, he retired from the army in 1947.

Outliving his wife by six years, and with his son and daughter scarcely grown up, Fisher was a JP in Wiltshire before spending his final years in his native North Wales.

FITZGERALD, Major General Gerald Michael (1889–1957), CB, MC

Born in Canada of Anglo-Irish parents, FitzGerald was educated at Cheltenham and RMC, Sandhurst. Attached to the 1st Battalion South Lancashire Regiment 1910, he was gazetted into the 19th Lancers (Fane's Horse), Indian Army, in 1911. First War service was in France, where he was mentioned in despatches and awarded the MC in 1916, and, with the Indian Expeditionary Force, in Egypt and Palestine.

A brigade major in Egypt with the 11th Cavalry Brigade 1919–1922, FitzGerald attended the Staff College, Camberley, 1924–1925, and was Brigade Major with the 2nd Cavalry Brigade in India 1929–1931. He commanded the 19th (King George's Own) Lancers 1936–1938. Assistant Adjutant and QMG Eastern Command, India, 1938–1939, he commanded the Lahore Brigade 1939–1941 and, promoted major general, was appointed to command Lucknow District in 1941.

Appointed CB in 1943, FitzGerald retired from the army in 1944 and settled in the family home in Co. Cork.

FITZHERBERT, Major General Edward Herbert
(1885–1979), CBE, DSO, MC

Of military family, Fitzherbert was educated at Rossall and RMC, Sandhurst. Commissioned in the Army Service Corps in 1905, he studied mechanical engineering at the LSE and was a captain in 1914. First War service was in France, where he was thrice mentioned in despatches, awarded the MC in 1917 and admitted to the DSO in 1918.

Deputy Assistant Director of Supplies and Transport with the Rhine Army in 1929, Fitzherbert was Commandant of the Mechanical Transport School of Instruction and Chief Inspector of Subsidized Transport 1930–1934. A colonel in 1935, he was Deputy Adjutant and QMG at the War Office 1935–1937. He was Assistant Director of Supplies and Transport 1937–1939 and was appointed Assistant Inspector Royal Army Service Corps when war broke out in 1939.

Appointed Inspector RASC in 1940, Fitzherbert was promoted major general in 1941, only to retire from the army in 1943. A keen golfer, good shot and member of the MCC, he lived out his long retirement in London.

FLADGATE, Major General Courtenay William *(1890–1958), CBE*
The son of a knight, Fladgate was educated at Harrow and RMC, Sandhurst. Commissioned in the King's Royal Rifle Corps in 1910, his First War service was in France and Italy, where he was wounded.

A staff officer at the War Office 1919–1923 and married in 1922, Fladgate transferred to the Royal Corps of Signals the same year. Chief Signal Officer, Northern Command, 1936–1938, he was promoted colonel and made CSO Aldershot Command 1938–1939.

Chief Signal Officer with the BEF in France 1939–1940, Fladgate was CSO Northern Command after Dunkirk and Deputy Director of Signals at the War Office 1941–1942. He was Director of Signals 1942–1943. CSO Middle East in 1943, he was considered by Penney as 'not strong enough to exert control' over American subordinates (Penney Diary, 3/2, LHCMA). He was ADC to the King 1944–1946, the year in which he retired from the army, and was Colonel Commandant of the Royal Signals 1947–1955.

FLOYER-ACLAND, Lieutenant General Arthur Nugent
(1885–1980), CB, DSO, MC
Born in Dorset and educated at Blundell's School, Acland (the Floyer was added in 1927) was gazetted into the Duke of Cornwall's Light Infantry in 1907. Married in 1913, his First War service was in France and Italy, where he was six times mentioned in despatches, awarded the MC and admitted to the DSO.

A graduate of the Staff College, Camberley, in 1921, Floyer-Acland was a brevet lieutenant colonel in 1927 and commanded 1st Battalion DCLI 1931–1934. Assistant Adjutant General at the War Office 1934–1936, he spent the next two years in India. There he commanded the 3rd (Jhelum) Infantry Brigade and was mentioned in despatches for his part in operations in Waziristan 1937–1938.

Promoted major general, Floyer-Acland was appointed GOC 50th (Northumberland) Division in 1938, before moving to command 43rd (Wessex) Division at war's beginning. Military Secretary to the War Secretary 1940–1942, he was promoted lieutenant general in 1941, only to find himself put out of a job by Brooke the next year, 'until such time as we can find work for him' (Danchev & Todman, 2001, 258). For the remainder of the war he served on various War Office committees.

Retired from the army in 1945, Floyer-Acland returned to the Dorset estate he had inherited. High Sheriff of the County in 1953, he was DL in 1957 and outlived his wife by seven years.

FORTUNE, Major General Sir Victor Morven *(1883–1949), KBE, CB, DSO*
Born in the Scottish Lowlands and educated at Winchester and RMC, Sandhurst, Fortune was commissioned in the Black Watch in 1903. First War service was in France, where he was mentioned in despatches and admitted to the DSO in 1916.

Fortune attended the Staff College, Camberley, 1920–1921, and was an instructor at Sandhurst for the next three years. Married in 1923, he commanded 1st Battalion Seaforth Highlanders 1927–1929. A staff officer with 5th Division 1930–1932, he commanded 5th Infantry Brigade 1932–1935. Promoted major general in 1935, he was temporary commander of 52nd Lowland Division 1935–1936, Commander South-West Area 1937 and appointed GOC 51st Highland Division in 1937.

Stationed at Aldershot during the latter part of 1939, 51st Division arrived in France to join the BEF in January 1940. Brooke, GOC II Corps, was unimpressed with the new arrival, doubting whether he was 'up to requirements' (Danchev & Todman, 2001, 33). Whatever Fortune's view of Brooke, he took his Division to the so-called Saar front, in front of the Maginot Line, in April 1940, and was thus separated from the BEF when the German attack in the West began. Withdrawing successfully westwards, as far back as the Somme, Fortune, ever the 'experienced, determined and very able commander' (Beauman, 1960, 142), came under the command of General Altmayer's Tenth French Army. Hemmed in on the Le Havre peninsula, waiting for an evacuation that was planned but not instigated, he surrendered his Division (less one brigade) to General Rommel at St Valéry-en-Caux in June 1940.

A prisoner of war for the next five years, Fortune, deemed by his captors to be in sufficient ill-health to be worthy of repatriation, refused three times to be sent home. He was in hospital in Limburg when he was liberated by units of the American First Army in April 1945. Knighted, he retired immediately from the army. Much honoured by his regiment and DL for Perhshire in 1947, his health never recovered. He died at his home in Kirkcubrightshire.

FOWKES, Major General Charles Christopher
(1894–1966), CBE, DSO, MC
Educated at Dulwich College and RMC, Sandhurst, Fowkes was commissioned in the South Wales Borderers in 1914. His First War service was in France, where he was four times wounded and awarded the MC. He then served in Egypt and, latterly, North Russia.

A captain for fifteen years in the peacetime army, Fowkes spent many years in West Africa and married in 1928. Serving on the staff of the Sudan Defence Force in the mid-1930s, he rose from commanding a battalion to command the Southern Brigade, King's African Rifles, in little more than a year.

Made acting GOC 2nd (later 12th) African Division in 1940, 'Fluffy' Fowkes was admitted to the DSO for his part in the Gondar battles during the latter stages of the campaign in Ethiopia. A major general in 1941, he was appointed to command the newly-formed 11th East African Division in 1942, which he spent eighteen months training. Upon arrival in Burma Slim was 'very favourably impressed' (Slim, 1986, 353) with Fowkes's Division after its part in the advance down the Kabaw Valley. Taken ill in January 1945, he was relieved of his command and hospitalized. He retired from the army in 1946 and lived the rest of his life in Kenya.

FRANKLYN, General Sir Harold Edmund *(1885–1963), KCB, DSO, MC*
The son of a lieutenant general, Franklyn was educated at Rugby and RMC, Sandhurst. Commissioned in the Green Howards in 1905 and married in 1913, he was a captain in 1914. First War service was in France, where he was six times mentioned in despatches, awarded the MC and admitted to the DSO in 1918.

A brevet major in 1916, Franklyn was a brevet lieutenant colonel in 1925. After attending the Staff College, Camberley, he was Inspector General of West Indian Land Forces in 1930 and commanded the 1st Battalion of the West Yorkshire Regiment 1930–1933. A staff officer with the Sudan Defence Force 1933–1935, he was Commandant of the Sudan Defence Force 1935–1938. Promoted major general in 1938, he was appointed to command 5th Division.

In France with the BEF from late 1939 5th Division was temporarily attached to Brooke's II Corps. Brooke liked him, finding him 'a more attractive type of individual than Montgomery' (Danchev & Todman, 2001, 29). Playing an outstanding part in the Arras counter-attack and in covering the BEF's withdrawal to Dunkirk, it was Franklyn Pownall had in mind as the outstanding divisional commander when he wrote to Montgomery that he, Montgomery, had come out of the campaign 'a good second' (Hamilton, 1982, 395).

Appointed to command 8th Corps in July 1940, Franklyn trained his troops for their allotted anti-invasion role. Promoted lieutenant general in 1941, when he re-married, he was made GOC British troops in Northern Ireland. Considered by now rather old for field command (though only two years older than Montgomery), he was knighted, promoted general and, in a complicated series of command reorganizations, made C-in-C Home Forces in November 1943. He held this post until he retired from the army in 1945. Described as 'extremely intelligent' but 'an unlucky soldier' (Pile, 1949, 35), his only son was killed in action in 1944.

FRASER, Major General Alexander Donald *(1884–1960), DSO (Bar), MC*
The son of a clergyman, Fraser was educated at Aberdeen Grammar School and Aberdeen University. A qualified doctor in 1906, he joined the Royal Army Medical Corps in 1907. Seconded to the Colonial Office, he was employed in investigating sleeping sickness in Uganda 1908–1911. First War service was in France, where he was mentioned in despatches, awarded the MC and admitted to the DSO in 1917. A bar was added to the DSO in 1918.

Serving with the North Russia Relief Force in 1919, Fraser's later postings were more appropriate to his expertise in tropical medicine. He served in Iraq, Palestine and Egypt before becoming commander of the RAMC depot and training establishment at Aldershot in 1934. A major general in 1937, he was Deputy Director Medical Services Southern Command, India, 1937–1941. He retired from the army that year.

Settling in his native Banffshire, Fraser married in 1942 and, though well into his sixties, fathered three daughters.

FRASER, Major General William Archibald Kenneth
(1886–1969), CB, CBE, DSO, MVO, MC
The son of an Indian Army Medical Officer, Fraser was gazetted into the Indian Army in 1906. First War service was in France and Mesopotamia, where he was awarded the MC and admitted to the DSO.

An Assistant Adjutant and QMG, India, 1918–1919, and married in 1920, Fraser was Inspector General Soutb Persia Rifles 1920–1921 Military Attaché at Kabul 1922–1924, he performed the same function at Teheran over the next four years. A first-class interpreter in French, he was Military Secretary to the Governor of Bengal 1930–1932 and commanded Sam Browne's Cavalry in India 1933–1935. Commander of 10th (Jubbulpore) Brigade, India, in 1936, he served on the staff in Lahore District 1936–1937. A brigade commander in Mhow Area, India, in 1937, he was a divisional commander in India in 1941 and was GOC 10th Indian Division in Iraq before retiring from the army that year. He was, however, re-employed for the remaining war years as Military Attaché in Teheran and, appointed CB, finally retired in 1945.

FREELAND, Major General Rowan Arthur Bayfield *(1895–1970), MC*
Gazetted into the 13th Frontier Force Rifles in 1915, Freeland's First War service was in India and Mesopotamia, where he was awarded the MC.

A graduate of the Staff College, Quetta, in 1931, Freeland was Assistant Military Secretary, AHQ, India, 1933–1935, and was Brigade Major, Zhob Area, 1935–1938. He Commanded the 2nd Battalion of 13th Frontier Force Rifles 1938–1940. Chief Staff Officer, Waziristan District, 1940–1941, he commanded the Razmak Brigade 1941–1943 and commanded Delhi District from 1944 until his retirement in 1946.

FREEMAN-ATTWOOD, Major General Harold Augustus
(1897–1963), DSO, OBE, MC
Of military family and educated at Marlborough and RMC, Sandhurst, Freeman-Attwood was commissioned in the Royal Welch Fusiliers in 1915. First War service was in France, where he was awarded the MC, and in Italy.

Married in 1921, Freeman-Attwood took part in operations in Waziristan 1921–23. Adjutant to his regiment's territorial battalion 1924–1928, he attended the Staff College, Camberley, 1928–1930. Commanding British troops in Cyprus 1931–1932, he was awarded the OBE for his part in suppressing a Greek Cypriot rebellion. After serving on the staff at the War Office 1932–1934, he was a brigade major in Khartoum 1934–1936. At the outbreak of war in 1939 he was a staff officer with the 50th (Northumbrian) Division.

After evacuation from Dunkirk Freeman-Attwood was made a brigade commander in July 1940. Promoted major general in November 1941, he assumed command of 46th Division which, from January 1943, formed part of First Army in Tunisia. Although regarded as 'not up to it' by his Corps Commander (Allfrey Diary 3/1/ LHCMA), his handling of his division in the assault on Djebel Abiod in March led to him being admitted to the DSO.

A few months later, just as 46th Division was being made ready for operations in Italy, something went wrong. Freeman-Attwood was removed from his command in August 1943 and his service with the army was terminated that October. He was court-martialled for sending letters to his wife, and other women, disclosing details of future military operations (PRO WO 71/1092). Thereafter he joined ICI, rising to the post of Staff Manager ICI (India) in 1949.

Re-married in 1946, his first marriage having ended in divorce, Freeman-Attwood retired to Nottinghamshire. He was active in the East Midlands area for the Conservative party and listed his recreations as hunting, shooting, gardening and stamp collecting.

FRITH, Major General Osmund Townley (b.1890), CBE

Commissioned in the Royal Artillery in 1910, Frith was employed with the West African Frontier Force in 1913 and served in Cameroon and Nigeria for his first two years of war service before being posted to France, where he was mentioned in despatches.

Serving thereafter largely in India, Frith was an instructor at the School of Artillery, India, 1931–1935, and commanded a brigade area 1936–1938. He was GOC 5th Anti-Aircraft Division in 1942.

FULLBROOK-LEGGATT, Major General Charles St Quentin Outen (1889–1972), CBE, DSO, MC

Educated at Bath College and RMC, Sandhurst, Fullbrook-Leggatt was commissioned in the Royal Berkshire Regiment in 1909. A captain in 1915, his First War service was in France. Admitted to the DSO in 1914, he was twice wounded, four times mentioned in despatches and awarded the MC.

Married in 1917, Fullbrook-Leggatt was a brevet major by war's end. After attending the Staff College, Camberley, 1922–1923, he commanded the 2nd Battalion Royal Berkshire Regiment 1932–1936 and was an instructor at the Senior Officers' School Sheerness 1936–1939.

Commander of a Territorial Infantry Brigade for the first two years of the war, Fullbrook-Leggatt was promoted major general in 1941 and appointed to command 61st Division, then stationed in Northern Ireland. Posted to Tunisia in May 1943, he served on the staff of Supreme Allied Headquarters before becoming an area commander in Italy in 1944.

Retired from the army in 1946, Fullbrook-Leggatt lived out the rest of his life in Cromer, Norfolk.

G

GAIRDNER, General Sir Charles Henry

(1898–1983), GBE, KCMG, KCVO, CB

Of Anglo-Irish parentage, and educated at Repton and RMA, Woolwich, Gairdner was commissioned in the Royal Artillery in 1916. Wounded in France that year, he stayed in the army after the armistice and, transferring to the Cavalry, remained a captain throughout the 1920s. After attending the Staff College, Camberley, 1934–1935, he commanded the 10th Royal Hussars 1937–1940.

A staff officer with the 7th Armoured Division in North Africa 1940–1941, Gairdner was briefly Deputy Director of Plans, Middle East, in 1941, before being recalled to England, promoted major general and appointed to command 6th Armoured Division. Within six months Gairdner was back in North Africa, this time as Commandant of the Auchinleck-inspired Higher Commanders' School. Appointed GOC 8th Armoured Division in August 1942, there was talk of him leading a Corps de Chasse after Alamein, but instead all that was left to him was the task of winding-up his divisional command in January 1943. Made CGS North Africa that year, he had a hand in the planning of operation HUSKY until Montgomery delivered another of his 'he is useless . . . and completely out of his depth' pronouncements (Richardson, 1985, 152). Effectively unemployed for a year and feeling that everything [he] touched had a Hoodoo on it' (Kennedy, 4/3, LHCMA), he was made Major General i/c Armoured Fighting Vehicles, India, in 1944.

A lieutenant general in 1944, Gairdner headed the UK Liaison Mission in Japan 1945–1946 and was Attlee's special representative in the Far East 1945–1948. Governor of Western Australia 1951–1963, he was Governor of Tasmania 1963–1968. In addition to numerous honorary colonelcies, he was the recipient of several honorary degrees from Australian Universities. He and his wife settled in Perth.

GALE, Lieutenant General Sir Humfrey Myddelton

(1890–1971), KBE, CB, MC

The son of an architect and educated at St Paul's School, Gale studied at the Architectural School, Westminster, for two years before being accepted as a

110

cadet at RMC, Sandhurst. Not passing out high enough to gain entry to the Indian Army, he joined the Army Service Corps in 1911. First War service was in France, where he was twice mentioned in despatches and awarded the MC. He married in 1917.

Employed on regimental duties at home and in Egypt during the early 1920s, Gale also had numerous spells at the War Office. He attended the Staff College Camberley, 1924–1925, and the Naval College at Greenwich in 1928. He joined the directing staff at Camberley in 1934. A colonel in 1937, he served as Assistant Director of Supplies and Transport at the War Office while bringing up two teenage daughters after the death of his wife. A brigadier in 1940, he was Deputy Assistant QMG with III Corps in the BEF, being awarded the CBE for his 'energetic leadership and practical improvisation' during the Dunkirk evacuation (DNB).

Promoted and made Major General i/c Administration, Scottish Command, in 1941, Gale served briefly as chief administrative officer to Brooke at GHQ Home Forces until selected as Eisenhower's Deputy Chief of Staff and Chief Administrative Officer in preparation for the 1942 TORCH landings. He continued working under Eisenhower throughout 1943 in North Africa, Sicily and Italy. Knighted that year, he returned with Eisenhower to Britain in January 1944 to prepare for OVERLORD. The 'widely experienced and extremely able' Gale (Eisenhower, 1948, 259) continued to serve the Supreme Commander at SHAEF until the end of the war in Europe. Like a number of British officers who worked closely with Americans, Gale suffered the criticism of 'going native' (Irving, 1981, 287). This might explain why Montgomery considered he had 'no character and is useless in his present job' (Hamilton, 1986), why the only honours conferred on him after 1943 were American decorations and why his army career ground to a halt after 1945. Made personal representative in Europe of Herbert Lehman, the Director General of UNRAA, he retired from the army in 1947.

Re-married in 1945 and with business connections with the Anglo-Iranian oil company, Gale, apparently on Harold Macmillan's recommendation, was made Chairman of Basildon New Town Development Corporation in 1954. He was Colonel Commandant of the RASC 1944–1954 and Colonel Commandant of the Army Catering Corps 1946–1948. He lived out his last years in Switzerland.

GALE, General Sir Richard Nelson *(1896–1982), GCB, KBE, DSO, MC*
Born in London and spending much of his early childhood in Australia, Gale was educated at Merchant Taylors' and Aldenham School. Beginning work in the City, he passed the Sandhurst entrance examination in 1915 and, after a shortened course, was commissioned in the Worcester Regiment that year.

Gale's First War service was in France, where he joined the Machine Gun Corps and was awarded the MC in 1918. Ending the war a company commander, reversion to his peacetime seniority meant he spent the next dozen years a subaltern. Married in 1924, he served mainly in India, where he commanded a company of the Duke of Cornwall's Light Infantry in 1930 and attended the Staff College, Quetta, 1930–1931. Promoted major in 1938, he transferred to the Royal Inniskilling Fusiliers only to find himself posted to staff duties at the War Office.

Given command of a Territorial Army battalion, the 5th Leicesters, in 1940, 'Windy' Gale impressed Brooke enough as a trainer of troops to be promoted and appointed to command 1st Parachute Brigade. He thus became a central figure in the development of airborne forces, being appointed commander of 6th Airborne Division in April 1943. Prominent in the Normandy landings in June 1944, when his airborne troops secured the left flank of the invasion beaches, his division was not deployed for the disastrous MARKET GARDEN operation, but was used -on the ground – to help counter the German Ardennes offensive at the end of 1944. Admitted to the DSO, he was promoted lieutenant general after his division had participated in the successful Rhine crossing of March 1945. Made Deputy Commander 1st Allied Airborne Army, he was also appointed commander of the 1st British Airborne Corps.

Selected to command 1st Division in Palestine 1946–1947, Gale was GOC British troops in Egypt and the Mediterranean 1948–1949. Director General of Military Training at the War Office 1949–1952, he was C-in-C Northern Army Group, Allied Land Forces Europe and BAOR, from 1952 until his retirement from the army in 1957. Suitably honoured, and honorary Colonel of the Worcestershire and Parachute regiments, Gale returned to duty in 1958, succeeding Montgomery as Deputy Supreme Allied Commander, Europe.

Re-married, after the death of his first wife, in 1953, Gale wrote his auto-biography, *Call to Arms* (1968) and lived out his final years in a flat in Hampton Court Palace. He died in hospital in Kingston-on-Thames.

GALLOWAY, Lieutenant General Sir Alexander
(1895–1977), KBE, CB, DSO, MC

The son of a Church of Scotland minister, Galloway was educated at King William's College, Isle of Man. Ready to go to Cambridge in 1914, he volunteered instead for the army. Commissioned in the Cameronians (Scottish Rifles) on the basis of his enrolment in his school OTC, his First War service was in Gallipoli, Egypt, Palestine and France. There he was awarded the MC in 1918.

A subaltern for most of the 1920s, Galloway married in 1920. As his regiment's adjutant 1925–1926 he was a 'somewhat frightening person', known generally as 'PR', or 'perpetual rage' (Baynes, 1989, 34). He attended the Staff College, Camberley, 1928–1929, and was remembered there as 'a deadly fast bowler' (DNB). Returning to Camberley in 1937, this time as an instructor, he commanded the 1st Battalion of the Cameronians at war's outbreak in 1939.

Appointed Commandant of the newly opened Middle East Staff College at Haifa in February 1940, 'Sandy' Galloway served briefly as BGS to Wilson in Palestine and in Greece before becoming BGS to Cunningham, the newly installed 8th Army commander. A 'keen, hard man . . . equipped with a caustic sense of humour' (Barnett, 1983, 33), and 'very popular' (de Guingand, 1947,

169), it was he, allegedly, who, in the early stages of the CRUSADER offensive, realized that Cunningham had already lost the battle in his mind and called on Auchinleck to intervene (Belchem, 1978, 99). Promoted, admitted to the DSO and sent to the USA to select equipment for 8th Army, he was recalled to London to serve as Director of Staff Studies at the War Office.

Appointed to command 1st Armoured Division in July 1943, Galloway spent several months training his troops in North Africa. Made temporary GOC 4th Indian Division in early 1944, he took part in the assault on Monte Cassino while awaiting the arrival of his armoured division. In ill-health, and eventually hospitalized, he was removed from his command that August and returned to England. Restored to health, he joined the staff of 21st Army Group in North-West Europe, briefly commanded 3rd Division in early 1945 and, promoted lieutenant general, was appointed commander of XXX Corps, BAOR, in 1946.

Described as 'a little rash, . . . very outspoken, very loyal, and a very brave and able soldier (Pile, 1949, 36), Galloway was appointed GOC-in-C Malaya Command in 1946. He was appointed High Commissioner and C-in-C British troops in Austria the next year. He held that post until he retired from the army in 1950. Suitably honoured, he was Chairman of the Jordan Development Bank 1951–1952 and subsequently joined the building and civil engineering firm Costain. Outliving one of his three sons, he lived out his retirement in Norham, Northumberland.

GAMBIER-PARRY, Major General Michael Denman *(1891–1976), MC*

Educated at Eton and RMC, Sandhurst, Gambier-Parry was commissioned in the Royal Welch Fusiliers in 1911. A captain in 1914, his First War service was in Gallipoli and Mesopotamia, where he was mentioned six times in despatches and awarded the MC in 1916.

Married in 1918, Gambier-Parry attended the Staff College, Camberley, 1923–1924, and transferred to the Royal Tank Corps in 1924. A lieutenant colonel in 1935 and a colonel in 1936, he commanded the Malaya Infantry Brigade 1938–1940.

Promoted major general in 1940, Gambier-Parry headed the Military Mission to the Greek army that year and was appointed to command 2nd Armoured Division in Cyrenaica in February 1941. It fell to him to try to 'fit an incomplete force which he did not know at all well into an unrealistic defence system' (Pitt, 1988, 249). Whether this meant he lacked 'a sense of urgency and grip of the situation' (Baynes, 1989, 135) and was 'a conventional and slow- minded soldier who couldn't cope with the unexpected' (cited in French, 2000, 231), he was overwhelmed by the speed and boldness of Rommel's attack from El Agheila. Trying to retire eastwards he, along with most of his divisional HQ staff, was captured in April 1941.

A prisoner of war in Italy, eventually in Campo 12 near Florence alongside numerous other captured *prominenti*, 'GP', an 'ardent musician' (Neame, 1947, 304), led the choir in Sunday Church services, copied maps for would-be escapees and, allegedly, played poker 'extraordinarily badly' (Ranfurly, 1998,

123). Released by his captors in the autumn of 1943, he was, for a while, given refuge in the Vatican. Brought back to England in the summer of 1944, he retired from the army the same year.

Made a member of the Council, Royal College of Music, in 1951, Gambier-Parry was DL for Wiltshire 1952–1954. He was elected a Fellow of the Royal College of Music in 1961 and spent his final years living in Sussex.

GAMMELL, Lieutenant General Sir James Andrew Harcourt
(1892–1975), KCB, DSO, MC

The son of a knight and educated at Winchester and Cambridge University, Gammell was commissioned in the Royal Field Artillery in 1912. His First War service was in France, where he was mentioned seven times in despatches, awarded the MC in 1915 and admitted to the DSO in 1917.

Married in 1919, Gammell attended the Staff College, Camberley, 1921–1922, and was a staff officer with Aldershot Command in 1924. Promoted major, he transferred to the Cameron Highlanders in 1927. An instructor at Camberley 1930–1935 he commanded the 1st Battalion Cameron Highlanders 1935–1938. He attended the Imperial Defence College that year and was appointed to command 48th Infantry Brigade.

Held at home to train for possible operations in Scandinavia, Gammell's brigade was sent to Norway as part of the force investing Narvik. There he served as Chief of Staff. Auchinleck considered he 'work[ed] like a slave . . . but [was] not in the first flight' (Dill 2nd. acc. 6/2 LHCMA). Promoted major general in 1940, he was appointed to command 3rd Division which came under Montgomery's command in V Corps and, with Montgomery considering him 'young and virile' (Hamilton, 1982, 773) he was, for a while, acting commander of XII Corps. Not considered for field command in North Africa, he was promoted lieutenant general and appointed GOC Eastern Command in 1942. Made Chief of Staff to Wilson, the Supreme Allied Commander in the Mediterranean, in 1944, he was knighted and made Head of the British Military Mission in Moscow in 1945.

Retiring from the army in 1946, Gammell returned to his native Scotland. DL for Angus, 1946, his wife died in 1960 and he re-married in 1964.

GARTLAN, Major General Gerald Ion *(1889–1975), CBE, DSO, MC*

Born in Co. Down and educated at Downside and RMC, Sandhurst, Gartlan was commissioned in the Royal Irish Rifles in 1909. A captain in 1915, his First War service was mainly as a staff officer in France. Twice wounded, he was awarded the MC and admitted to the DSO in 1919 after service with the Plebiscite Commission in Upper Silesia.

A brevet major in 1918, Gartlan attended the Staff College, Camberley, 1924–1925, and, after staff duties in the War Office, commanded the Depot of the Royal Ulster Rifles 1929–1933. Married in 1933, he commanded 2nd Battalion Royal Ulster Rifles 1933–1936 and attended the Imperial Defence

114

College in 1937. Appointed to command 5th Infantry Brigade in 1938, he took it to France in 1939 as part of Loyd's 2nd Division in the BEF.

Made CBE for his part in the withdrawal to Dunkirk, Gartlan was promoted major general and appointed to the staff of Northern Command. He remained at the command's York HQ until his retirement from the army in 1944.

With his two daughters scarcely grown up, Gartlan returned to Northern Ireland. A keen sportsman, he was DL for Co, Down in 1952, High Sheriff of the County in 1954 and a JP from 1955.

GATEHOUSE, Major General Alexander Hugh *(1895–1964), DSO, MC*
Educated privately and at RMC, Sandhurst, Gatehouse was commissioned in the Northumberland Fusiliers in 1915. As his Who's Who entry has him commanding a battalion of tanks in the 'European War, 1914–1918'; and commanding 'a battalion of tanks in 1939', it appears he regarded his inter-war army service as a period of marking time. Actually he transferred to the Royal Tank Corps in 1916, was awarded the MC at Cambrai, was an instructor at Sandhurst 1924–1927 and was Commandant of the Mechanization Experimental Establishment at Farnborough 1933–1937. A keen sportsman and noted boxer, he reached the ABA middle-weight final in 1920. He sailed for France in 1939 as second-in-command of 7th Armoured Brigade.

'Alec' Gatehouse's reputation as a tank specialist was made and broken in North Africa. While not known as a theorist, he 'thoroughly understood armoured warfare' and his mind 'was uncluttered by equestrian foppery' (Bierman & Smith, 2002, 104).His brigade led the assault on Sidi Barrani and he was present when 'the fox was killed in the open' at Beda Fomm. He commanded 4th Armoured Brigade in 1941 and his criticisms of Beresford-Pierse's leadership during BATTLEAXE did him no harm. At Sidi Rezegh, during the CRUSADER battles, he led his men from an armchair strapped to the roof of his tank. Admitted to the DSO, with a bar added within two weeks and appointed GOC 10th Armoured Division in June 1942, he was praised for his handling of tanks in the defence of the Alam Halfa position in August, but damned for his 'display of poor leadership' (Hamilton, 1983, 41) in the first phases of the Alamein battle and, particularly, during the pursuit. Showing, allegedly, no desire to push his tanks forward, Montgomery relieved him of his command. In this way Gatehouse, the 'old desert hand', was, along with Lumsden, his Corps Commander, made scapegoat for 8th Army's inability to finish-off their German-Italian opponents in November 1942, Gatehouse himself maintaining that it had been Montgomery's caution that had allowed Rommel to retire in good order.

Sent back to England, Gatehouse had his rank of major general confirmed. He lectured on tank tactics, was sent to Washington as Major General Armoured Fighting Vehicles and was made British Army Attaché to Moscow in 1946. He retired from the army in 1947. The cryptic brevity of his Who's Who entry and the almost complete lack of personal detail suggests a man nursing a grievance at odds with the establishment. Incapacitated by a stroke in 1961, he died in a Swedish nursing home.

GATTIE, Major General Kenneth Francis Drake *(1890–1982), DSO, MC*
Educated at Tonbridge School, Gattie was commissioned in the Monmouthshire Regiment in 1910. His First War service was in France, where he was a captain with the South Wales Borderers and a staff officer at GHQ. Mentioned five times in despatches, he was awarded the MC in 1916 and admitted to the DSO in 1917.

A Brigade major with the British Rhine Army, 1919, Gattie served in India 1919–1922 and attended the Staff College, Camberley, 1922–23. After a further brief spell of duty in India, he served on the staff at the War Office 1924–1926. A brigade major with the Rhine Army in 1927, he was an instructor in tactics at the School of Artillery, Larkhill, 1929–1931. Deputy Assistant Adjutant and QMG, Highland Area 1931–1935, he was on the staff of 43rd (Wessex) Division 1934–1937. Made commander of 1st Battalion Queen's (West Surrey) Regiment in 1937, he was appointed to command 2nd (Rawalpindi) Brigade on the North-West Frontier in 1938.

Promoted major general in 1941, Gattie was commander of Rawalpindi District in India from 1942 until his retirement from the army in 1945. Returning to Wales, he lived in Brecon and was DL for Becknock in 1954.

GEAKE, Major General Clifford Henry *(1894–1982), CB, CBE*
Commissioned in the Royal Artillery in 1913, Geake's First War service was in France, where he was wounded and mentioned in despatches.

Transferring to the Royal Army Ordance Corps in 1923, Geake was an instructor at the RAOC School 1927–1930. Deputy Assistant Director of Ordnance Services at the War Office 1932–1936 and a brigadier in 1939, he was ADOS North China Command 1939–1940 and thereafter with Home Forces. Director of Clothing and Stores at the War Office 1942–1943, he was DOS in the Middle East and in Italy 1943–1945. Mentioned in despatches, awarded the CBE in 1944 and appointed CB in 1945, he retired from the army in 1946, settling near Guildford in Surrey.

GEPP, Major General Sir Ernest Cyril, *(1879–1964), KBE, CB, DSO*
The son of a clergyman, Gepp was educated at Marlborough. Enlisting for the South African War in 1900, he was commissioned in the Duke of Cornwall's Light Infantry in 1901, served in Somaliland 1910–1911 with the King's African Rifles and left the army in 1911. Re-enlisting in 1914, he was commissioned in the Oxfordshire and Buckinghamshire Light Infantry. First War service was in France, where he was five times mentioned in despatches and admitted to the DSO in 1916 (Bar 1917).

After attending the Staff College, Camberley, in 1920, Gepp married and spent many years serving in India. He commanded 4th (Quetta) Infantry Brigade 1929–1930 and was BGS Western Command, India, 1930–1932.

Commandant of the Small Arms School, Netheravon, 1932–1936, he was promoted major general in 1935. Appointed Major General i/c Administration, Northern Command, in 1937, he retired from the army in 1941, only to be re-employed almost immediately as Director of Prisoners of War at the War Office. He held this post until 1945.

Re-married in 1944 and knighted in 1946, Gepp retired to settle in Bath, where he lived until well into his eighties.

GIFFARD, General Sir George James (1886–1964), GCB, DSO

Educated at Rugby and RMC, Sandhurst, Giffard was commissioned in the Queen's (West Surrey) Regiment in 1906. Seconded to the King's African Rifles in 1911, he saw active service in East Africa before the outbreak of war with Germany. His First War service was in East Africa, where he was wounded, five times mentioned in despatches and admitted to the DSO in 1917.

Married in 1915, Giffard was selected for the first post-war course at the Staff College, Camberley. Serving on the staff of the Royal West African Frontier Force 1920–1925, he was on the directing staff at Camberley 1928–1931. After attending the Imperial Defence College in 1932, he commanded 2nd Battalion Queen's Regiment for a year. He then served on the staff of 2nd Division at Aldershot, under Wavell 1933–1936. Promoted major general, he was Inspector General African Colonial Forces 1937–1939 and, after a brief period as Military Secretary to the Secretary of State for War, was made GOC British troops in Palestine and Trans-Jordan in 1940.

This too was a brief appointment. In June 1940 Giffard returned to West Africa, this time as C-in-C of the newly created West Africa Command. Knighted and promoted general in 1941, he supervised the expansion of African military formations so that over 200,000 men were trained and equipped for service at home or abroad. No one but Giffard, it is said, 'could have accomplished what was done' (Swinton, 1958, 199). In April 1943 Wavell, who knew him well, asked for him to be sent to India, there to replace Irwin as commander of Eastern Army.

From the start Giffard was intent on re-building troop morale after the demoralizing series of defeats at the hands of the Japanese. Instituting better organization, intensive jungle training and improved health measures, he also took steps to render supply of forward troops by air a practical reality. His willingness, it is said, to 'back subordinates . . . stamped him as an ideal commander for the recovery of Eastern Army' (Hickey, 1998, 81).

When South-East Asia Command was set up under Mountbatten 'Pop' Giffard was made C-in-C 11th Army Group, which comprised Slim's XIV Army and, on paper at least, the Chinese forces in northern Burma. Disliked by Stillwell, predictably enough, for being 'timid and inept' (Zeigler, 1985, 237), and finding the relationship with Wingate 'pretty nearly intolerable' (Bond (ed.), 1974, 150), he nonetheless enjoyed a good working relationship with Slim. But, quite quickly, he fell out with Mountbatten, whether on the siting of GHQ, the interpretation of intelligence or over mounting operations through the monsoon. Told by Mountbatten in May 1944 that he had lost the Supreme Commander's confidence and that he must have 'a younger, more aggressive commander' (DNB), he enjoyed a six-month stay of execution before a replacement could be found. During that time the defensive victories at Kohima and Imphal were won, fully justifying his cautious strategic approach and careful rebuilding of the army. Mountbatten conceded that he had been 'a pleasant colleague' (Mountbatten, C50/24) and, as Slim generously put it, those who succeeded him 'often received credit that should justly have been his' (Slim, 1986, 164).

Probably the least known of all British general who held high command in the Second World War, Giffards's dislike of publicity was, by all accounts, genuine. The self-publicizing Montgomery, with characteristic lightness of touch, pronounced him 'a very great gentleman, but he is not really any good' (Hamilton, 1983, 610). Elevated in the knighthood and told he was too old to succeed Adam as Adjutant General, he retired from the army in 1946. He and his wife settled in Winchester, from where he was an active president of the Army Benevolent Fund, Colonel of the Queen's Regiment and Colonel Commandant of the King's African Rifles, the Royal West African Frontier Force and the Northern Rhodesian Regiment 1945–1954. He grew apples, kept bees and, after a coronary thrombosis curtailed activity, took up tapestry and rug-making. Husband and wife died within a fortnight of one another.

GILL, Major General John Galbraith (1889–1981), CBE, DSO, MC

Born in India and educated at Brentwood and Edinburgh University, Gill was commisioned in the Royal Army Medical Corps in 1915, the year he married. First War service was in France where he was awarded the MC in 1917 and in Italy, where he was admitted to the DSO in 1918.

Deputy Assistant Director of Hygiene and Pathology, Northern Ireland District, 1924–1925, Gill was DAD Hygiene in India 1933–1936. Assistant Director of Hygiene and Pathology, India, 1936–1938, he was AD of H in Norway in 1940.

Assistant (later Deputy) Director Medical Services, Home Forces, 1940–1942, Gill was DMS Iraq and Persia (Iran) Command 1942–1944. DDMS Home Forces in 1944, he retired from the army in 1946. Therafter he lived in Hampshire.

GLOVER, Major General Sir Guy de Courcy
(1887–1967), KBE, CB, DSO, MC

Of military family and educated at Cheltenham and RMC, Sandhurst, Glover was commissioned in the South Staffordshire Regiment in 1907. A captain in 1914, his First War service was in France, where he was six times mentioned in despatches and awarded the MC, and latterly in Italy.

Admitted to the DSO in 1918, the same year as he married, Glover attended the Staff College, Camberley, 1920–1921 and commanded the second battalion of his regiment 1931–1934. He was an Assistant Adjutant General at the War

Office 1934–1938. Commander of Bombay District, India, 1938–1940, he was promoted major general and made Director of Recruiting and Organization at Army HQ, India, in 1940. He was Deputy Adjutant General in India from 1940 until his retirement from the army in 1946.

Colonel of the South Staffordshire Regiment 1946–1954, Glover and his wife settled on the Isle of Wight.

GLOVER, Major General Malcolm (1897–1970), CB, OBE

Educated at Birkenhead school, Glover volunteered for service in 1914 and was commissioned in the South Lancashire Regiment in 1915. After First War service in France, he transferred to the Indian Army in 1919.

A regimental officer with the 14th Punjabis for most of the 1920s, Glover attended the Staff College, Quetta, 1932–1933. Deputy Assistant Director of Ordnance Services, India, 1937–1939, he was an assistant military secretary at GHQ, India, in 1940, before being appointed Assistant Master General of the Ordnance. BGS North Western Army HQ 1941–1943, he commanded 3rd Indian Infantry Brigade 1943–1944. Promoted major general in 1944, he was appointed Director of Organization, GHQ, India. Made Deputy Adjutant General in 1946, he retired from the army in 1948 and settled in Budleigh Salterton in Devon.

GODDARD, Lieutenant General Eric Norman
(1897–1992), CB, CIE, CBE, MVO, MC

The son of a chartered accountant, Goddard entered the Indian Army in 1915. Gazetted into the 12th Frontier Force Regiment, his First War service was in Mesoptamia, where he was twice mentioned in despatches and awarded the MC. For service in Persia and Kurdistan in 1919, he was awarded the OBE.

On the staff of Army HQ, India, 1923–1925, Goddard saw service on the North-West Frontier with his regiment's 3rd Battalion. He attended the Staff College, Quetta, 1928–1929 and was subsequently brigade major with the Nowshera Brigade. He was mentioned in despatches for his part in the Chitral relief expedition, and for operations against the Mohmands in 1933 had a bar added to his MC. He served on the staff of Eastern Command, India 1934–1936 and commanded 4th Battalion 15th Punjab Regiment in 1936.

Made Colonel i/c Administration, Burma Army in 1939, the year he married, Goddard commanded a brigade in 1940. He was Major General i/c Administration of the Army in Burma in 1941. It was, it is said, due largely to his 'drive, administrative skills and willingness to ride roughshod over all bureaucratic opposition' that the retreat was made possible (Lunt, 1989, 164). He served in Burma for the next four years as Major General i/c Administration to 11th Army Group and Allied Land Forces South-East Asia.

Made GOC-in-C Southern Command, India, in 1947, Goddard retired from the army in 1948 with the honorary rank of lieutenant general. He worked with the Control Commission in Germany 1949–1953 and was Director of Civil

Defence, North-Western Region (Manchester), 1955–1963. He was also President of the East Lancashire British Red Cross Society 1964–1966.

GODWIN-AUSTEN, General Sir Alfred Reade
(1889–1963), KCSI, CB, OBE, MC

Of military family and educated at St Lawrence College, Ramsgate, and RMC, Sandhurst, Godwin-Austen was commissioned in the South Wales Borderers in 1909. First War service was in Gallipoli, Palestine and Mesopotamia, where, on the staff of 13th Division, he was twice mentioned in despatches and awarded the MC.

A student at the Staff College, Camberley, 1924–1925, Godwin-Austen served in a variety of staff appointments at the War Office and was an instructor at Sandhurst. He commanded the 2nd Battalion the Duke of Cornwall's Light Infantry 1936–1937 and was employed with the British Military Mission to the Egyptian Army 1937–1938. Appointed to command 14th Infantry Brigade in Palestine 1938–1939, he was promoted major general in 1939.

At war's beginning Godwin-Austen was in command of 8th Infantry Division on internal security duties in Palestine. When that command was wound up in 1940 he was diverted, while en route to Mombasa to take-up the command of 2nd African Division, to Berbera in Somaliland and ordered to defend the territory against Italian invasion. There, with five infantry battalions pitted against a large Italian force, he was 'a tower of strength' in screening the withdrawal to the coast and in the successful evacuate his troops (Kennedy Diary. 4/3, LHCMA). Returning to his original command, 2nd African Division, he took part in the Abyssinian campaign and the conquest of Italian Somaliland in 1941.

Auchinleck, who at this stage considered Godwin-Austen 'good', and 'with sound views' (Dill 2nd. acc. 11/1/ LHCMA), appointed him commander of XIII Corps in the newly-formed 8th Army in September 1941. In the opening phases of the CRUSADER offensive, when Cunningham, the army commander, showed signs of losing his nerve, it was Godwin-Austen's 'solid and 'robust' qualities, coupled to 'his renowned fog-horn voice' (Barnett, 1983, 111) that probably saved a delicate situation making him 'the real victor of Crusader' (Bidwell & Graham, 1985, 242).

Knowing this, it seems likely that Godwin-Austen came to resent Ritchie, Cunningham's successor, as 8th Army commander. When Rommel attacked again in Cyrenaica in January 1942, he showed his usual qualities of 'courage, determination and robust optimism' (Carver, 1978, 89), but reacted in high-handed fashion to Ritchie's orders to counter-attack before Benghazi. Obliged to retreat and aggrieved that 'he had asked for bread and been given a stone' (Tuker, 1963, 65), he asked, in a manner that seemed to Auchinleck to betray 'a lack of balance' (Dill, 2nd. acc. 6/2/ LHCMA), to be relieved of his command.

With Churchill muttering that he should suffer the same fate as Admiral Byng and told by Brooke that 'he was unlikely to be employed again' (Danchev & Todman, 2001, 244), work was found for him in the Directorate of Tactical Research at the War Office. He was also, briefly, Assistant Commandant of the

Staff College, Camberley, in late 1942. From there he proceeded to the post of Vice QMG at the War Office 1943–1944 and, possibly to spite Auchinleck, was appointed QMG, India, in 1945. Principal Administrative Officer, India Comamnd, 1945–1946, he retired in 1947, having been promoted general and knighted the year before.

A bachelor and keen tennis-player, Godwin-Austen was Chairman of the South-West Division of the National Coal Board 1946–1948 and Colonel of the South Wales Borderers 1950–1954. He died after a long illness in hospital in Maidenhead.

GOLDNEY, Major General Claude Le Bas *(1887–1978), CB, CBE, MC*

Of military family, Goldney was eductaed at Dover College, Portsmouth Grammar School and RMA, Woolwich. Commissioned in the Gloucestershire Regiment in 1906, he transferred to the Army Service Corps in 1910. First War service was in France, where he was mentioned in despatches and awarded the MC.

For the rest of his military career Goldney was able to specialize in supply and transport. He was Assistant Director of S & T, Egypt, in 1938, the year he married, and was Assistant Director S & T, Aldershot Command, in 1939. At war's beginning he was made Deputy Director S & T with I Corps in the BEF in France and at the time of Dunkirk he fulfilled the same function with III Corps.

Awarded the CBE for his part in the campaign in France and Flanders, Goldney was promoted major general in 1941 and was Director S & T, GHQ Middle East, from then until his retirement from the army in 1944. Outliving his wife by ten years, he spent a goodly part of his long retirement in Surrey fishing.

GORDON-FINLAYSON, General Sir Robert *(1881–1956), KCB, CMG, DSO*

Entering the army from the Suffolk Artillery Militia in 1900, Gordon-Finlayson was a captain in 1908 and, after marrying in 1912, a major in 1914. His First War service was with the Royal Artillery in France, where he was eight times mentioned in despatches and admitted to the DSO in 1915, and latterly in North Russia. For service there, 1918–1919, he was awarded the CMG.

Appointed Military Secretary to Sir Henry Wilson, the CIGS, in 1921, after he graduated from the Staff College, Camberley, 'Copper' Gordon-Finlayson was a staff officer at the War Office 1922–1925. On the directing staff at Camberley 1925–1927, he was CRA 3rd Division 1927–1930. Commander of Rawalpindi District 1931–1934, he was GOC 3rd Division 1934–1936. Knighted and promoted general in 1937, he was C-in-C British troops in Egypt 1938–1939.

Adjutant General to the Forces 1939–1940, Gordon-Finlayson was earmarked to command an army in France, once the BEF reached sufficient size to merit the reorganization. Instead, he was appointed GOC-in-C Western Command 1940–1941 when, not without him protesting, and with his wife insisting there was an 'intrigue' against him (Marshall-Cornwall, 1984, 196), he was placed, at the age of 60, on the retired list. As stories of 'dear old Copper's rusty brain slowly creaking around' abounded (Macksey, 1967, 136), he spent the best part of the next two years pestering those in authority for higher decorations and a job. Brooke described him as 'snooping around [the War Office] to push himself as C-in-C India' (Danchev & Todman, 2001, 218). But, as Dill confided, 'no-one can say he is a superman' (Dill, 2nd. acc. 6/11/ LHCMA) and he was made instead Special Commissioner for the Imperial War Graves Commission in 1942.

Retired to West Suffolk, Gordon-Finlayson was Colonel Commandant of the Royal Artillery 1936–1946 and Colonel Commandant of the Royal Horse Artillery 1937–1947. A West Suffolk County Councillor from 1949, he was also DL for the County in 1950. His younger son, after a distinguished wartime career in the army, went on to become a general.

GORT, Field Marshal the Lord, John Standish Surtees Prendergast Vereker, 6th Viscount Gort *(1886–1946), VC, GCB, CB, CBE, DSO, MVO, MC*

The elder son of the 5th Viscount Gort (Irish peerage) Vereker was born in London and succeeded as 6th Viscount in 1902 while still at Harrow. After attending RMC, Sandhurst he was commissioned in the Grenadier Guards in 1907. In 1911 he married his second cousin, fathering two sons and a daughter.

Gort's record of service in France the First War was outstanding. Four times wounded, his convalescent spells seldom kept him long from the front. Awarded the MC in 1915 and admitted to the DSO in 1916 (bar 1917), he was awarded the VC in 1918.

Graduating from the first post-war course at the Staff College, Camberley, in 1919, Gort was an instructor there 1921–1923. Through showing an interest in flying and corresponding with the influential military writer Liddell Hart, he gained a reputation as a progressive at about the same time (1925) as he divorced his wife on the grounds of her adultery. Following a two-year spell at the Senior Officers' School, Sheerness, a series of staff posts followed in quick succession. A brigadier in 1932, he was Director of Military Training, India, 1932–1936. When he returned to England he went, for the third time, to Camberley, this time as Commandant. He was already a major general.

By peacetime standards this was rapid promotion. More was to follow. When the ambitious Hore-Belisha became War Secretary in May 1937, instructed by Neville Chamberlain to stir 'the old dry bones' of the War Office (Macleod, 1961, 284), he determined to promote younger and less conservative men. Gort benefited from this. Made Military Secretary to the Army Council, his progress became so accelerated as to seem to contemporaries almost indecent. An acting Lieutenant General in September 1937, he was a substantive general by Christmas when, in an axe-wielding flourish, Hore-Belisha, advised by Liddell Hart, induced the existing CIGS, Sir Cyril Deverell, to retire and appointed the fifty-one-year-old Gort in his stead. As the youngest soldier ever to hold that post, Gort courted publicity to the extent that he continued to fly his Moth aeroplane. Privately he resolved to devote four hours of each day to the study of military history (Strachan, 1997, 153).

Yet those qualities and circumstances that had made Gort's rise so inexorable and apparently effortless thus far worked against him thereafter. As soldier he was a brave leader of men who had never commanded in the field above battalion level. As political general he was sensitive and jealous. Not such a progressive after all, he could be as vindictive as he was naïve. For all that Liddell Hart's 'partnership' with Hore-Belisha was short-lived, it served, for as long as it had any semblance of actuality, to alienate Gort from his political chief and sour relations with his former mentor. Feeling left out, Gort came to hate Hore-Belisha for his self-advertising ways and for those 'characteristics which inevitably but inexplicably make Jews unpopular' (Colville, 1985, 76). When war was declared in September 1939 War Secretary and CIGS had scarcely been on speaking terms for nearly a year.

In a move that surprised many, but which probably stemmed from Hore-Belisha's simple wish to get Gort out of the War Office, he was made C-in-C of the BEF. Likened to a 'schoolboy going off on his holidays' (Kennedy, 1957, 20), he established a notoriously Spartan regime at his Arras GHQ. From there, for all that he established good relations with French generals and was loyally served by his Chief of Staff, Pownall, he failed to win the respect of his corps commanders, Dill and Brooke. Irritated by his childish sense of humour, fussy attention to detail and lack of vision, they judged any level of command higher than a battalion as being 'beyond his mental ceiling' (Bond, 1980, 331). While Pownall put it about that Gort's nickname was 'Tiger', the men continued to refer to him as 'Fat Boy' (Harris, 1980, 16). The most popular act he performed as C-in-C of the BEF was, via the 'pill-box affair', his part in Hore-Belisha's removal from the War Office in January 1940. It was a squalid episode, reeking of class snobbery and tinged with anti-semitism, and compounded by Gort's confusion of principle with prejudice. Nevertheless, great was the joy at GHQ when news of Hore-Belisha's removal arrived. It was, as Brooke noted, 'the most cheerful bit of news in months' (Danchev & Todman, 2001, 28).

Brooke, neither then nor later, had a good word for his C-in-C. However, he fully agreed that the BEF should advance into Belgium should the Germans launch their attack in the west. When that attack came in May 1940 the advance was made easily enough, though what began as an orderly withdrawal towards all those pill-boxes built in vain the previous winter was turned into an unseemly retreat by the speed of the German advance to the south and the disintegration of Belgian forces to the north. Once the improvised attempt at a break-out at Arras failed, the scramble towards the coast continued. The only port available to allied troops caught in the northern pocket was Dunkirk.

Praised in some quarters for having the realism and 'mental toughness' to see that the only alternative to mass surrender was evacuation (Horrocks, 1960, 56), Gort nevertheless turned a blind eye to orders from London and deceived his French allies about his intentions. He may have 'saved the BEF' (Colville, 1976, 226), but his frequent absences from GHQ helped reduce command during the retreat to a shambles. His orders were infrequent but contradictory and his reliance on improvised scratch forces was of as dubious military value as it was disruptive of intelligence gathering. By the end command in the BEF, such as it existed, was carried out at corps and divisional level. As withdrawal into the Dunkirk perimeter was effected, Gort, described by Montgomery as 'incapable of grasping the military situation' (Hamilton, 1982, 388), was ordered home.

Churchill's 'gallant Lord Gort' was quickly sidelined to write his despatches. Dill, now CIGS, created a post for him – Inspector General to the Forces – and in April 1941 he was made Governor and C-in-C of Gibraltar. There he superivized more tunnelling, lengthened the colony's airstrip and learned of his son's suicide. In May 1942 he was made Governor and C-in-C of Malta. The island was then a war zone and Gort, though by now a lonely and embittered man, rose to the challenge. Living off the same rations as the islanders, with a bicycle as his means of transportation, he became popular. His daily rapid march up and down the Government House cement tennis court 'for about twenty minutes' (Coward, 1987, 447) doubtless contributed to his losing two stone in weight. Churchill who, until dissuaded by Brooke (now CIGS), had toyed with the idea of making him C-in-C Middle East in Auchinleck's stead, had the grace to recommend promotion to Field Marshal in January 1943.

Gort was by now a tired and sick man. Retirement was in order. But as the policy was to keep 'failed' commanders far from London, a job was found for him in what had become the military backwater but political headache of Palestine. Taking up his duties as Commissioner and C-in-C in October 1944, he was invalided home in less than a year. The cancer from which he suffered was declared inoperable and he died at the home of his son-in-law in March 1946.

Gort's reputation is strangely shaped. The trajectory of his career makes it so. So much early progress was followed by the hiatus at the War Office. The credit afforded him for having saved the BEF is offset by the damning verdicts of his then subordinates. He may not have had the intelligence of a great commander but he could read a battle as well as any British general. A 'misfit as CIGS' he may have been (Kennedy Diary, 4/2/2, LHCMA), but so too was Montgomery when he held that post. He was not over-promoted and all the talk that he had a 'schizoid personality . . . with a curious feral expression around the eyes' (Harvey, 1994, 746) amounts to is that he was not photogenic. The resentment he exhibited during the wearying spells of duty in Gibraltar and on Malta was the natural, and perhaps reasonable, reaction of a man who felt himself ill-used. Dill he outlived. But of those who had served under him in France, it was the 'winners', the Brookes and the Montgomerys, who wrote the history. Gort, the 'loser', died before he could write his.

GOSCHEN, Major General Arthur Alec (1880–1975), CB, DSO

Educated at Eton and commissioned in the Royal Artillery in 1899, Goschen served in the South African War and was admitted to the DSO. Married in 1908 and a major in 1914, his First War service was in France, where he was wounded and had two bars added to his DSO.

A graduate of the Staff College, Camberley, in 1920, 'Jumbo' Goschen was an instructor at the Staff College, Quetta, 1925–1928. After some months on half pay, he was Garrison Commander and Commandant of the Royal Artillery Woolwich Depot and was Brigadier RA Aldershot Command 1931–1934. Appointed Commandant of RMA, Woolwich, in 1934, he retired from the army in 1938, only to be recalled in 1939 and made Commander of Chatham Area.

Finally retired in 1941, Goschen was Colonel Commandant of the Royal Horse Artillery 1942–1948 and Colonel Commandant RA 1941–1948. Living near Cirencester, he was DL for Gloucestershire in 1953.

GOTT, Lieutenant General William Heny Ewart
(1897–1942), CB, CBE, DSO, MC
The son of a soldier and grandson of a bishop, Gott was educated at Harrow. Commissioned in the King's Royal Rifle Corps in 1915, his First War service was in France, where he was wounded and awarded the MC.

A captain in 1918, Gott's peacetime soldiering consisted mainly of regimental duties. Adjutant to the 13th London Regiment (TA) between 1925 and 1928, he attended the Staff College, Camberley, 1930–1931. Married in 1934, he commanded 1st Battalion KRRC in 1938 which formed part of the Mobile Division commanded by Brooke.

In Egypt in 1939 Gott's battalion became the nucleus of the support group for the embryonic 7th Armoured Division. A brigadier in 1940, he played his part in O'Connor's 'five-day raid' which developed into the highly successful operation COMPASS and it was at Beda Fomm that he acquired the nickname, a rather sophisticated one by army standards, 'Strafer'. Appointed to command 7th Armoured Division in September 1941, he was admitted to the DSO after the CRUSADER battles and in February 1942 was appointed to command XIII Corps in the western desert after Godwin-Austen, at his own request, had been relieved of his command.

By this time Gott had acquired an enviable reputation. Handsome enough, as well as being 'young, energetic, large, religious, relentless, humorous and kind' he had too, it is said, the kind of 'frightening profundity' (Pyman, 1971, 35) that made men look to him for the final word in a discussion. The veteran's veteran in the Western Desert by mid-1942, his influence among his peers was, by all accounts, as strong as it is difficult to define. He wrote no papers, nor did he bequeath any set of ideas on tactical doctrine. Indeed, he had been 'involved in, if not responsible for, a string of failures' (Bidwell & Graham, 1985, 243). And yet 'Strafer' Gott commanded universal respect and affection. Having extricated XIII Corps from the 'Cauldron' of Gazala and taken it back to the Alamein position, he became, in Churchill's mind, the ideal man to take over the leadership of 8th Army.

Gott was duly appointed to this command as part of the 'Cairo purge' of August 1942. He was, however, killed when the aircraft carrying him from the desert to Cairo was shot down (in some accounts he died on the ground while trying to help the wounded from the wrecked plane). The father of two daughters, he never saw the younger.

Yet, far from ending at this point, the Gott story has a curiously fashioned sequel to it. His death, although for form's sake conceded as 'unfortunate for him and those who loved and respected him' (Carver, 1998, 233), is rendered neither sad nor tragic, rather 'a blessing in disguise' (Hamilton, 1982, 581). It is as though, in removing himself from the scene, Gott performed his greatest service in allowing, 'the right man', Montgomery, to take the stage 'at the right place and at the right moment' (Stewart, 1999, 41) and assume command of 8th Army.

Montgomery was characteristically categoric and ungenerous in his memoirs: the 'appointment of Gott to command 8th Army at that moment would have been a mistake' (Montgomery, 1958, 83). Gott, he claimed was a tired man who had been in the desert too long and who had tried 'every club in the bag' and failed. Brooke was not only of the same opinion but, in a queer Gott strafe Gott frame of mind, discerned 'the part that the hand of God had taken' in removing him from the scene (Danchev & Todman, 2001, 674). In his ghosted biography, though not in his diaries, he has Gott opening 'out his heart to me' on his own tiredness and the need 'for someone with new ideas and plenty of confidence' to command in the desert (Bryant, 1957, 443). Gott's memorial, we are therefore led to believe, lay in his own realization of his staleness-induced unfitness to command and his insight that 'new blood' was necessary for 8th Army to win its desert victory. It seems an extraordinary way to treat a dead man – to say, in effect, that the finest thing he did was to get himself killed – but there we have it. Gott's death, apparently, 'far more than his life, was the origin of historic events in European history' (Mason, 1978, 112).

GRACEY, General Sir Douglas David *(1894–1964), KCB, KCIE, CBE, MC*
The son of an Indian Civil Servant, Gracey was educated at Blundell's and RMC, Sandhurst. Entering the Indian Army in 1914, his First War service was in France with the Royal Munster Fusiliers and later with a Gurkha battalion in Palestine and Syria. He was twice wounded and awarded the MC in 1917.

An instructor at Sandhurst 1925–1927, Gracey attended the Staff College, Quetta, 1928–1929. Married in 1931, he was a staff officer at AHQ, India, 1930–1934 and served on the staff in Western Command, India, 1936–1937. In 1938 he was BGS Western Command. In 1939, as a brevet lieutenant colonel, he commanded a Gurkha battalion in operations on the North-West Frontier and was Assistant Commandant of the Staff College, Quetta, 1940–1941.

In 1941 Gracey commanded 17th Infantry Brigade on operations in Iraq and Syria. There he was awarded the OBE. The next year he was appointed to command 20th Indian Division which, from November 1943, fought as part of XIV Army in Burma. Described by Slim as 'full of energy and ideas' (Slim, 1986,

146), he was nearly captured when the Japanese began their Imphal offensive across the Chindwin, but, having helped blunt the Japanese advance at Kohima, he led his division during the re-conquest of Burma.

With a CB to his credit, Gracey commanded Allied Land Forces in Indo-China 1945–1946 and was officiating GOC-in-C Northern Command, India, in 1946. Commander of I Indian Corps 1946–1947, he was Chief of Staff of the Pakistan Army 1947–1948, being appointed Commander in Chief in 1948.

Retired in 1951, Gracey was knighted and settled in Surrey. A keen cricketer and member of the MCC, he was, in the years before his death, Chairman of the Royal Hospital and Home for Incurables, Putney.

GRAHAM, Major General Douglas Alexander Henry
(1893–1971), CB, CBE, DSO, MC
Though famous in his way, few personal details are known about this officer. Commissioned in the Cameronians (Scottish Rifles) in 1914, Graham's First War service was in France. A captain in 1916, he was wounded, twice mentioned in despatches and awarded the MC.

A graduate of the Staff College, Camberley, in 1925 and a major in 1930, Graham served in Palestine 1936–1939, where he commanded a battalion. Said to have played a 'distinguished part' in the desert campaign (Pitt in Chandler (ed.), 1994, 282), he was admitted to the DSO before being appointed commander of 56th (London) Division in May 1943. Wounded in Italy just before the Volturno crossing, when he drove his jeep into a shell-crater, he convalesced in England and was appointed to command 50th (Northumbrian) Division in January 1944. His Division was part of the assault wave on D-Day which, of all Allied formations put ashore that day, came closest to meeting its objectives. With his 'firm religious convictions' and indomitable courage' he was, as his obituarist wrote, the 'ideal leader' for the campaign in North-West Europe.

Much decorated by foreign governments, Graham retired from the army in 1947. Said to be 'the epitome of the Lowland Scottish Covenanters', and an 'old war horse never far from the scene of battle' (Horrocks, 1960, 182), he settled in his native Brechin just south of the Highland Line. A councillor for the Burgh for a number of years, he was Colonel of the Cameronians from 1954 to 1958.

GRAHAM, Major General Sir Miles William Arthur Peel
(1895–1976), KBE, CB, MC
Of military family, Graham was educated at Eton,where he was a scholar, and Cambridge University. Commissioned in the 2nd Life Guards in 1914, his First War service was in France, where he was twice wounded, twice mentioned in despatches and awarded the MC.

Having married in 1918 and left the army in 1919, Graham retained his status as a reserve officer and rejoined the Life Guards in 1939 as a captain. On the staff with 1st Cavalry Division in Palestine 1939–1941, he was 'a gifted amateur', with 'shrewd imagination' (Richardson, 1985, 174), who had the good fortune to catch Montgomery's eye after the 'Cairo purge'of August 1942. A great friend of de Guingand and Robertson, he was Chief Administrative Officer with 8th Army 1942–1943 and, despite his lack of field experience, was promoted major general and was Chief Administrative Officer 21st Army Group, North-West Europe, 1944–1945. Re-married in 1943, his son from his first marriage was killed in action in 1944.

Much decorated during the war and knighted immediately after, Graham retired from the army in 1946. He immediately joined the board of Times Publishing, Ltd. and thereafter held a number of directorships. He was a Nottinghamshire County Councillor and DL for the county in 1973.

GRANT, General Sir Charles John Cecil *(1877–1950), KCB, KCVO, DSO*

The son of a general, Grant was commissioned in the Coldstream Guards in 1897. Wounded in the South African War, he married in 1903 and was Brigade Major, Brigade of Guards, 1909–1912. His First War service was in France and Italy. He was wounded, seven times mentioned in despatches and admitted to the DSO.

Brigadier General, General Staff, 1918–1919, Grant commanded the 3rd Battalion Coldstream Guards 1919–1921. A staff officer in Egypt 1921–1925, he commanded 137th (Staffordshire) Brigade 1925–1927 and 8th Infantry Brigade 1927–1930. From 1930 to 1932 he was GOC 53rd (Welsh) Division and was GOC London District 1932–1934.

Knighted and promoted lieutenant general, Grant spent several months on half-pay before being appointed GOC-in-C Scottish Command and Governor of Edinburgh Castle in 1937. He held these posts until his retirement in 1940.

Colonel of the King's Shropshire Light Infantry 1931–1946, Grant lived in Shropshire. A JP, he was DL for the county in 1946.

GRANT, Major General Ian Cameron *(1891–1955), CB, CBE, DSO*

Born in Inverness and educated at Cheltenham and RMC, Sandhurst, Grant was commissioned in the Cameron Highlanders in 1910. His First War service was in Gallipoli and France where he was thrice mentioned in despatches, twice wounded and admitted to the DSO in 1916. While convalescing, he married and acted as Assistant Private Secretary to the Minister of Labour 1917–1918.

A brevet major in 1919, Grant was Deputy Assistant QMG to the 52nd Lowland Division (TA) 1924–1928 and commanded the 1st Battalion of the Cameron Highlanders 1931–1935. After service in India and the Sudan, he was made Commander of 160th (South Wales) Brigade 1935–1938 and was in Egypt at the outbreak of war, commanding the Cairo Infantry Brigade.

An acting major general in 1941, Grant's career in wartime was dogged by ill-health. In 1944 he was invalided out of the army. Retiring to his native Inverness, he was a town councillor in 1949, Baillie to the Royal Burgh in 1950 and DL for the County in 1952. He was also a director of a local food-processing firm.

GRASETT, Lieutenant General Sir Arthur Edward
(1888–1971), KBE, CB, DSO, MC
Of Canadian parentage, Grasett was educated at Upper Canada College, Toronto, and RMC, Kingston, Ontario. Commissioned in the Royal Engineers in 1909, his First War service was in France, where he was five times mentioned in despatches, awarded the MC in 1915 and admitted to the DSO in 1918.

After attending the Staff College, Camberley, in 1920, Grasett served in operations on the North-West Frontier and attended the Imperial Defence College in 1931. Married in 1935, he was on the directing staff of the Staff College, Camberley, 1935–1937 and was BGS Northern Command 1937–1938. There then followed a three-year posting to Shanghai, where he was GOC British troops.

One of Brookes 'oldest friends', Grasett was appointed to command 48th (South Midland) Division in October 1941. Within six weeks he was promoted lieutenant general and made commander of VIII Corps under Home Forces. Regarded by Dill as 'educated and quite charming' (Alanbrooke, 6/2/2, LHCMA), and 'disappointed' to be told just before Christmas 1943 that he was being put in charge of Allied Forces (i.e. Czech, Polish, etc.) in the UK (Danchev & Todman, 2001, 352), he was attached to SHAEF 1944–45.There he was regarded by Montgomery as 'all bluff and eye-wash' (Hamilton, 1986, 363). He was Lieutenant Governor and C-in-C Jersey 1945–1953.

Knighted in 1945, Grasett retired from the army in 1947. When the Jersey appointment ended, he and his wife settled in Oxfordshire.

GREEN, Major General William *(1882–1947), CB, DSO*
Of military family and educated at Fettes and RMC, Sandhurst, Green was commissioned in the Black Watch in 1900. He fought in the South African War, married in 1914 and was, by 1915, a major. His First War service was in France where he commanded a battalion of the Royal Scots. He was five times mentioned in despatches and admitted to the DSO in 1916.

After graduating from the Staff College, Camberley, in 1920, Green won the Army Golf championship for the second time in 1921 and commanded 2nd Battalion the Loyal (North Lancashire) Regiment 1928–1931. A staff officer with Scottish Command 1931–1933, he commanded 9th Infantry Brigade 1933–1935.

Made commander of the South-Western Area in 1938, Green's fate was sealed after an inspection by Brooke (then GOC-in-C Southern Command) in July 1940. Deemed not to have 'the required qualities', Brooke determined that 'Green I am afraid must go' (Danchev & Todman, 2001, 91). Go he did. He retired from the army in 1940.

GREEN, Lieutenant General Sir Wyndham William
(1887–1979), KBE, CB, DSO, MC
Of military family and educated at Malvern and RMA, Woolwich, Green was commissioned in the Royal Artillery in 1907. His First War service was in

France where he was awarded the MC (and Bar) and, in 1918, admitted to the DSO.

A student at the Staff College, Camberley, 1920–1921, and re-marrying in 1924, after the death of his first wife, Green was a brevet lieutenant colonel in 1929. Mentioned in despatches for his part in operations on the North-West Frontier in 1930, his elder son died the next year. He was CRA Gibralter 1934–1936, Chief Instructor (Equipments) at the School of Artillery 1937–1938 and Commandant of the Military College of Science, Woolwich, in 1938.

Serving briefly as Deputy Governor of Malta in 1941, Green was Deputy GOC, Gibraltar, 1941–1942. Returning home, he assumed command of an Anti-Aircraft Division in 1942 and commanded 5th and 6th Anti-Aircraft Groups 1943–1945. Appointed GOC Anti-Aircraft Command in 1945, he was knighted and retired from the army in 1946.

Honorary Colonel of 410 Coast Regiment (Kent) 1949–1956, Green was Colonel Commandant of the Royal Artillery 1947–1952 and Chairman of the Kent Territorial and Auxillary Forces Association 1952–1954. Chairman of the Canterbury Diocesan Board of Finance 1953–51, he was DL for Kent in 1949 and a Governor of Dover College 1959–1972.

GREGSON-ELLIS, Major General Philip George Saxon
(1898–1956), CB, OBE

Of military family and educated at Eton and RMC, Sandhurst, Gregson-Ellis was commissioned in the Grenadier Guards in 1917. After attending the Staff College, Camberley, 1928–1929, he was Brigade Major 5th Infantry Brigade in 1931, and with 1st Guards Brigade 1932–1934. He was an instructor at Camberley 1937–1939.

An 'extremely able' (Ryder, 1987,72) staff officer at GHQ with the BEF in France 1939–1940, Gregson-Ellis was awarded the OBE for his part in the with-drawal to Dunkirk. Commander of 2nd Battalion Grenadier Guards in 1940, he was BGS Northern Command 1941. Made Deputy Chief of Staff at GHQ Home Forces in 1942, his wish for a field command was granted in 1943 when he was appointed to command 30th Armoured Brigade. He arrived in Italy just after Christmas that year.

Made commander of 5th Division in January 1944, Gregson-Ellis was sent to reinforce the Anzio beach-head in March. Said by the American general, Mark Clark, to have 'no offensive spirit' (Ellis, 1984, 432), but described elsewhere as 'an outstanding divisional commander who could impress his personality on his own men and American colleagues' (Vaughan-Thomas, 1961, 213), he devised a catapult for throwing bombs into German strongpoints. Invalided home in November 1944, he was appointed CB and made Commandant of the Staff College, Camberley, 1945–1946.

Re-assuming command of 5th Division in 1946, Gregson-Ellis went on to command 44th (Territorial) Division in 1947. He retired from the army in 1950. Settling in Kent, he was DL for the County in 1954.

GRIFFIN, Major General John Arnold Atkinson *(1891–1972), DSO*
The son of a naval officer, Griffin was educated at Sherborne and RMC, Sandhurst. Commissioned in the Lincolnshire Regiment in 1911, his First War service was in first in France, where he was thrice mentioned in despatches, and later Italy, where he was admitted the DSO in 1918.

An instructor at the Small Arms School, India, 1921–1923, Griffin was Adjutant to 52nd (Lowland) Division 1923–1927. He commanded the 1st Battalion of the Lincolnshire Regiment 1935–1939 and served in France with the BEF. Seeing service in Hong Kong and India, he commanded 11th Independent Brigade in Italy 1943–1944. He retired from the army, a major general, in 1945.

Colonel of the Lincolnshire Regiment 1948–1958 and a keen sailor and member of the Royal Lymington Yacht Club, Griffin, a widower after a fifty-year-long marriage, re-married barely a year before his own death.

GRIMSDALE, Major General Gordon Edward *(1893–1950), CB*
Educated at Cheltenham and RMA, Woolwich, Grimsdale was commissioned in the Royal Engineers in 1913. His First War service was in France, latterly serving on the staff of Second Army.

A captain in 1917, Grimsdale served in Ireland 1919–1921. Posted as Adjutant to the Engineers of the 47th London (Territorial) Division in 1923, he attened the Staff College, Camberley, 1925–1926. He then served on the staff at the War Office, 1927–1929, and was Deputy Assistant Adjutant General, Scottish Command, 1930–1932. Promoted lieutenant colonel in 1936, he served on the staff of Northern Command and in numerous postings abroad before being appointed Chief Staff Officer in Hong Kong in 1939.

Promoted major general in 1942, Grimsdale was appointed Military Attaché to the British Embassy in Chungking and in the same year was made head of the British Military Mission in China. Judged by Carton de Wiart to have been 'out there too long' and 'no longer ha[ving] what it takes to run the mission' (Mountbatten C50/19), he retired in 1945 and was briefly Colonel Commandant of the Royal Engineers before he died after a short illness.

GROVER, Major General John Malcolm Lawrence *(1897–1979), CB,MC*
The son of a general, Grover was educated at Winchester and RMC, Sandhurst. Commissioned in the King's Shropshire Light Infantry in 1914, his First War service was in France, where he was three times wounded and awarded the MC (and bar).

A captain for most of the 1920s, Grover married in 1930, was Deputy Assistant QMG, India, and saw service on the North-West Frontier 1930–1931, before attending the Staff College, Quetta, 1932–1933. After serving on the staff at Aldershot Command and a spell commanding the regimental depot at Shrewsbury, he commanded the 1st Battalion KSLI 1938–1939. He was a staff officer with 5th Division in the BEF in France 1939–1940. In command of 11th Brigade 1940–1941, he was appointed GOC 2nd Division in September 1941.

Attached to Home Forces for the next six months, 2nd Division was sent to India in mid-1942 where, for a year, Grover supervised training in amphibious operations 'to a high pitch of efficiency' (Hickey, 1998, 260).

Thrown into the fighting around Kohima in April 1944, 2nd Division bore the brunt of the Japanese offensive. Amidst some of the bitterest fighting of the Burma campaign, Stopford, Grover's Corps Commander, became impatient at 2nd Division's progress and, in a move that 'still rankles with the veterans of Kohima' (Rooney, 1992, 105), asked Slim to relieve him from his command.

Sacked in July 1944, Grover returned to England to take up duties as Director of Welfare Services at the War Office. Retiring from the army in 1948, he was General Secretary of the Officers' Association 1948–1951. Colonel of the KSLI 1947–1955, he was Commissioner for the Royal Hospital, Chelsea, 1957–1966.

GROVE-WHITE, Lieutenant General Sir Maurice Fitzgibbon
(1887–1965), KBE, CB, DSO

Of Anglo-Irish military parentage, Grove-White was educated at Wellington and RMA, Woolwich. Commissioned in the Royal Engineers in 1907, he was a captain in 1914. First War service was in France, where he was four times mentioned in despatches and admitted to the DSO in 1917.

Married in 1919, Grove-White served for two years on the staff at the War Office and in the Frederated Malay States 1925–1929. A student at the Staff College, Camberley, 1928–1929, he served on the staff at the War Office in the mid-1930s. Appointed to command 2nd Anti-Aircraft Division in 1939, he commanded an Anti-Aircraft Corps in 1940. He served in wartime postings in Malaya and the West Indies, took part in the Dumbarton Oaks 'conversations' and retired from the army in 1945 with a knighthood and the honorary rank of Lieutenant General. Colonel Commandant of the Royal Engineers 1946–1953, his elder son was killed in action in France in 1940.

GUBBINS, Major-General Sir Colin McVean
(1896–1976), KCMG, DSO, MC

Born in Tokyo, the son of a diplomat, and educated at Cheltenham and RMA Woolwich, Gubbins was commissioned in the Royal Field Artillery in 1914. His First War service was in France, where he was wounded and awarded the MC, and with the North Russian Relief Force in 1919.

A brigade major in Ireland 1921–1922, Gubbins served on the staff at Army HQ, India, 1924–1925. After attending the Staff College, Quetta, 1928–1929, he joined the staff of the Russian section at the War Office in 1931, moving on in 1934 to the military training directorate where, something of a linguist, he developed an interest in irregular warfare.

Appointed Chief of Staff to the Military Mission to Poland in September 1939 and continuing to liaise with Polish officers in Paris after the fall of Warsaw,

Gubbins was recalled to London in March 1940 to raise 'independent companies' for use in operations in Scandinavia. Although the men he commanded made little impression when the Germans invaded Norway in April, Auchinleck considered him 'a first-class man' (Alanbrooke, 6/2/9, LHCMA). He was admitted to the DSO, accredited with the inventions of Commandos and promoted brigadier. He raised and commanded Auxiliary Units in Britain from June 1940, under GHQ Home Forces. These units were to operate behind enemy lines in the event of invasion.

Seconded to the Special Operations Executive (SOE) in late 1940, Gubbins sought to 'set Europe ablaze'. Thanks to him European Resistance groups scored some notable successes against a background of frustrating failure. As executive head of SOE from 1943, Gubbins, a 'still waters running deep sort of man' (Pimlott, 1985, 304), was protected by his ministerial chief, Dalton, but had to fend off the criticisms, and sometimes outright hostility, of other Whitehall departments. However, in North-West Europe, where SOE's influence was strongest, General Eisenhower estimated after the war that the contribution of the French Resistance to Allied victory had been the equivalent of six divisions (DNB). His elder son was killed in action in Italy in 1944, the same year as his marriage was dissolved.

Retiring from the army in 1946, Gubbins was knighted, was much honoured by foreign governments, and, though in fact became a director of a carpet and textile manufacturing firm, emerged in fiction as the model for many a spy-thriller writer's underground controller. Re-married in 1950, he lived on the Isle of Harris in the Hebrides. A keen shot and fisherman, he was DL for the Islands Areas of the Western Isles in 1975.

GURDON, Major General Edward Temple Leigh
(1896–1959), CB, CBE, MC
The son of a bishop, Gurdon was educated at Rugby and RMC, Sandhurst. Commissioned in the East Yorkshire Regiment in 1914, he transferred to the Rifle Brigade the next year. Most of his First War Service was in East Africa, where he was mentioned in despatches and awarded the MC.

Private Secretary to the Governor of Uganda 1919–1920, Gurdon transferred to the Black Watch in 1922. Married the next year, he attended the Staff College, Camberley,1929–1930 and was an instructor at Camberley from 1937 to 1940.

A lieutenant colonel in 1938, Gurdon commanded the 1st Battalion the Black Watch in 1940. Attached to 51st Division with the BEF, he was fortunate not to have been taken prisoner at St Valéry that June. Commander of 25th Infantry Brigade in 1941, he was appointed BGS IV Corps in Burma the same year, and was a District Commander as well as BGS Eastern Army, India, 1942–1943. For the remainder of the war he was Director of Military Training, India.

Made Major General, General Staff, Home Forces, in 1945, Gurdon commanded a division in the British Army of the Rhine 1945–1946. He ended his career in the army in 1948 as District Commander, Salisbury Plain.

GURNEY, Major General Russell *(1890–1947), CB*

The son of a clergyman and educated at Clifton College, Gurney volunteered for the army in 1914 and was commissioned in the Northamptonshire Regiment in 1915. His First War service was in France and Italy.

A regimental officer for most of the inter-war years, Gurney attended the Staff College, Camberley, 1921–1922 and married in 1928. He wrote a history of the Northamptonshire Regiment in 1935 and promptly transferred to the Suffolk Regiment. He commanded the 1st Battalion in 1937. Made Commandant of the Small Arms School, Netheravon, in 1938, he served as Senior Umpire, Home Forces in 1941 and was briefly seconded to the War Cabinet Secretariat in 1942.

Promoted major general, Gurney was appointed Director of Personnel Services at the War Office in 1943. He held that post until his retirement from the army in 1947. He died that year after a short illness at his home in Devon.

GWATKIN, Major General Sir Frederick *(1885–1969), KCIE, CB, DSO, MC*

Of military family, Gwatkin was educated at Clifton and RMC, Sandhurst, from where, via the unattached list, he joined the 19th King George's Own Lancers (Indian Army) in 1905. A cavalryman, his First War service was in France, where he was awarded the MC and Mesopotamia, where, in 1919, he was admitted to the DSO.

Married in 1920, upon graduation from the Staff College, Camberley, Gwatkin's spells of regimental duties in India were interrupted by transferring to the Royal Deccan Horse, instructing at the Equitation School and at the Staff College, Quetta, 1927–1930, followed by attendance at the Imperial Defence College in 1933. He commanded the Royal Deccan Horse 1931–1933 and 2nd (Sialkot) Cavalry Brigade 1934–1938. From then until his retirement from the army in 1943 he was Military Adviser-in-Chief to Indian States Forces. Both his sons were killed in action in Burma in 1945.

H

HAIG, General Sir Arthur Brodie *(1886–1957), KCB, MC*

Educated at Winchester and gazetted into the 24th Punjab Regiment (Indian Army) in 1906, Haig's First War service was in Egypt where he was twice mentioned in despatches and awarded the MC and later in Mesopotamia where he was taken prisoner at Kut-Al-Amara.

Married in 1919, Haig was a staff officer at Army HQ, India, 1920–1922 and an instructor at the Staff College, Quetta, 1923–1926. Promoted lieutenant colonel in 1930, the year after he had attended the Imperial Defence College, he commanded the 4/14th Punjabis 1930–1932, before serving again on the staff at Army HQ, India. Appointed to command 7th Dehra Dun Infantry Brigade in 1933, he was made Deputy Adjutant and QMG Eastern Command, India, in 1936. Commandant of the Staff College, Quetta, from 1937 to 1940, he was Adjutant General, India, in 1941.

Haig's Second War service was relatively brief. Made GOC-in-C Southern Command, India, in 1941, he retired from the army the next year. Staying on in India until 1945, he and his wife eventually settled in Jersey. He died in a Torquay nursing home.

HAINING, General Sir Robert Hadden (1882–1959), KCB, DSO

The son of a doctor and educated at Uppingham and RMA, Woolwich, Haining was commissioned in the Royal Artillery in 1900. A captain in 1914, his First War service was in France, where he was six times mentioned in despatches and admitted to the DSO in 1915.

Qualified as a barrister in 1919, Haining never practised. Instead, he attended the Staff College, Camberley, 1920–1921. A colonel in 1922, he was an instructor at Camberley, 1922–1924, attended the Imperial Defence College in 1927 and was Assistant Adjutant and QMG, Aldershot, 1928–1929. A staff officer with 4th Division at Colchester 1930–1931, he served on the staff at the War Office before being appointed Deputy Director of Military Operations and Intelligence in 1933. Commandant of the Imperial Defence College 1935–1936, he was Director of Military Operations and Intelligence from 1936 to 1938. GOC British Forces in Palestine and Trans-Jordan 1938–1939, he was appointed GOC-in-C Western Command in September 1939.

Knighted in 1940, Haining took up the post specifically created for Dill in April 1940, that of Vice-CIGS, when Dill became CIGS in May. Perhaps there was not enough work for him to do, for Dill, who never thought much of 'Bob' Haining as a commander, 'in spite of his abilities', became 'very tired of him as VCIGS because he really has odd ideas on loyalty' (Dill, 2n.acc. 15, LHCMA). Brooke quickly came to consider him 'quite useless', understanding 'nothing of military matters and mess[ing] everything up' (Danchev & Todman, 2001, 140). Made Intendant-General, Middle East, in 1941, Haining, having reached the age of 60, retired from the army in 1942.

Settling in Surrey, Haining was Colonel Commandant of the Royal Artillery 1939–1950 and was made Chairman of the Farnham bench of JPs in 1943.

HAKEWILL SMITH, Major General Sir Edmund
(1896–1986), KCVO, CB, CBE, MC

Born in Kimberley, South Africa, and educated at Diocesan College, Cape Town and RMC, Sandhurst, Hakewill Smith was commissioned in the Royal Scots Fusiliers in 1915. His First War service was in France, where he was twice wounded and awarded the MC.

After serving with the British Military Mission in South Russia 1919–1920, Hakewill Smith was ADC to the Governor of Bengal 1921–1922 and was

Adjutant to his regiment's second battalion 1927–1930. Married in 1928 and a student at the Staff College, Quetta, 1932–1933, he was a staff captain at the War Office 1934–1936. Employed on Air Staff duties with the RAF 1936–1937, he was a Deputy Assistant Adjutant General 1938–1940.

Commander of 5th Battalion the Devonshire Regiment in the summer of 1940, Hakewill Smith reverted to his own regiment and assumed command of 4th/5th RSC in 1941. Promoted brigadier, he commanded 157th Infantry Brigade 1941–1942 before being made Director of Organization of the War Office. Commander of 155th Infantry Brigade in 1943, he was appointed GOC 52nd (Lowland) Division that November. Training in Scotland, first for mountain warfare and then as airborne troops, the Division was never deployed in either capacity, but was sent to France in October 1944 to form part of First Canadian Army. There an 'elderly' and 'pedestrian' Hakewill Smith led his troops in the assault on Walcheren (Carver, 1989, 215).

Appointed CB in 1945, Hakewill Smith was Commander of the Scottish Lowland District in 1946 and was President of the Military Court trying Albert von Kesselring for war crimes in 1947. He retired from the army in 1949.

Colonel of the Royal Scots Fusiliers 1946–1957 and Commandant of the Berkshire Army Cadet Force 1952–1957, Hakewill Smith was a Berkshire JP and Governor of the Military Knights of Windsor 1951–1978. He was Deputy Constable of Windsor Castle 1964–1972 and, a widower, lived out his last years in a flat in Hampton Court Palace.

HALL, Major General Henry Ronald *(1895- ?)*, DSO, MC
Commissioned in the Royal Artillery in 1914, Hall's First War service was in France, where he was awarded the MC and admitted to the DSO.

A staff captain in India 1920–1922, Hall graduated from the Staff College, Quetta, in 1927 and served on the staff at the War Office over the next four years. A brevet major in 1933, he served on the staff in Malaya 1933–1936. Spending several months on half-pay in 1936, he served on the staff with Home Forces 1937–1940.

Hall was CRA 44th Division in North Africa 1942–1943, and was GOC Aegean Islands over the period of the ill-fated Dodecanese campaign of 1943.

HALSTED, Major General John Gregson *(1890–1980)*, CB, OBE, MC
Commissioned in the Loyal (North Lancashire) Regiment in 1910, Halsted, a captain in 1915, served in France in the First War. Twice wounded and twice mentioned in despatches, he was awarded the MC.

A student at the Staff College, Camberley, 1923–1924, a major in 1928 and a lieutenant colonel in 1935, Halsted commanded the 1st Battalion of the Loyals in Palestine 1936–1937, where he was mentioned in despatches and made OBE. He was Assistant QMG, Aldershot Command, 1938–1939.

On the staff at GHQ of the BEF in France 1939–1940 and appointed CB for his part in the withdrawal to Dunkirk, Halsted was Major General i/c Administration, Southern Command, in 1941. Spells on the staffs of various home commands followed and he was Vice-QMG at the War Office in 1945. He retired from the army the following year.

HAMILTON, Major General William Haywood
(d. 1955), CB, CIE, CBE, DSO, FRCS
The son of an Indian Civil Servant, Hamilton was educated at Tonbridge School and St Bartholomew's Hospital.

A keen sportsman and excellent shot, Hamilton joined the Indian Medical Service in 1905. An ophthalmic specialist, he was Deputy Assistant Director of Medical Services, Lucknow District, 1911–1915 and Deputy Director of Medical Services at GHQ in Mesopotamia from 1915–1922. Mentioned eight times in despatches, he was admitted to the DSO in 1916.

Much decorated for his part in operations in Kurdistan, Persia (Iran) and the North-West Frontier in the 1920s, Hamilton won the Iraq open tennis championship in 1922 and was appointed CB after military operations in Waziristan in 1937. Assistant Director of Medical Services, Meerut District, in 1938, he was Director of Medical Services Northern Command, India, 1939–1940.

Made Director of Medical Services, India, in 1941, Hamilton retired from the army the same year.

HAMMOND, Major General Arthur Verney *(1892–1982), CB, DSO*
The son of a highly decorated army officer and educated at Wellington and RMC, Sandhurst, Hammond was commissioned in the Royal West Kent Regiment in 1911. Transferring to the Corps of Guides in India the next year, his First War service was in Mesopotamia and France, where he was mentioned in despatches. He married in 1919.

After serving on operations in North-West Persia (Iran) 1920–1921, Hammond graduated from the Staff College, Quetta, in 1927. A brigade major in the early 1930s, he attended the Senior Officers' School, Belgaum, in 1934, and, a lieutenant colonel in 1936, commanded the Guides Cavalry 1937–1939.

At war's beginning in 1939 Hammond was a staff officer at the War Office. Appointed to command an infantry brigade in 1941, he served on the staff of GHQ, India, in 1942, in Burma 1942–1943 and was admitted to the DSO for his part in the 1942 Arakan offensive. Promoted major general in 1942, he commanded Lucknow District 1944–1945.

Retiring from the army in 1947 Hammond, having divorced his wife, remarried the same year.

HANCE, Lieutenant General Sir James Bennett
(1887–1958), KCMG, KCIE, OBE, MA, FRCSE, MRCS
The son of a barrister and born in Cheshire, Hance was educated at Oundle, Cambridge University and Guy's Hospital. A House Surgeon in the Royal Surrey County Hospital, he joined the Indian Medical Service in 1912. Attached to the 7th Meerut Division, his First War service was in France and Persia (Iran), where he was twice mentioned in despatches.

An Agency Surgeon with the Foreign and Political Department, Government of India, from 1919, Hance was Principal Medical Officer in Jodhpur, 1925–1928 and Chief Medical Officer for the States of Western India 1928–1923. Resident Surgeon in Mysore 1933–1940, he was Inspector General of Civil Hospitals, Central Provinces, 1940–1942. Made Deputy Director General Indian Medical Services in 1942, his 'very job of work' coping with the Bengal Famine (Moon, 1973, 36) preceded his appointment as Director General in 1943.

Retired from the army in 1946, Hance became Medical Adviser and President of the Medical Board in the Commonwealth Relations Office. Re-married in 1938, there were two daughters from his first marriage.

HARDING, Field Marshal Allan Francis (John)
(1896–1989), 1st Baron Harding of Petherton, GCB, CBE, DSO, MC

The son of a solicitor's clerk, Harding was educated at Illminster Grammar School and, travelling to London, joined the Post Office Savings Bank as a boy clerk in 1911. Aged 18 he joined a territorial battalion of the London Regiment in 1914. Attached to the newly-formed Machine Gun Corps in 1915, his First War service was in Gallipoli, where he was wounded, and in Egypt and Palestine, where he was awarded the MC.

Commissioned in the Somerset Light Infantry, Harding stayed with the Machine Gun Corps until its disbandment in 1921. By this time he had dropped 'Allan' and had become 'John'. Adjutant to his battalion in India 1922–1925, he married in 1927 and attended the Staff College, Camberley, 1928–1929, where, 'independent of mind and short of stature' (Greacen, 1989, 101), he impressed his fellow student Dorman-Smith. On the staff of Southern Command 1931–1933, he became Brigade Major of 13th Infantry Brigade at Catterick and in 1935 began a three-year spell at the War Office, serving on the staff of the Directorate of Military Operations. On the eve of war in 1939 he was appointed to command the 1st Battalion Somerset Light Infantry.

Mentioned in despatches for his part in operations on the North-West Frontier in 1940, Harding was sent as a staff officer to GHQ Middle East. BGS to O'Connor during Operation COMPASS, he assumed temporary command of the Western Desert Force in April 1941 when both O'Connor and Neame were taken prisoner. It was he who was responsible for the initial decision to hold Tobruk. Admitted to the DSO in June 1941, he remained as BGS XIII Corps until February 1942, when he was made Director of Military Training at GHQ in Cairo. In this role Auchinleck found him so 'wholly admirable' (Dill 2nd. acc., 6/2/14, LHCMA), that he not only survived the 'Cairo purge' of August 1942 but was promoted to command 7th Armoured Division in September. In that capacity, it is said, he 'infused the whole division with his own energy, enthusiasm and commonsense' (Carver, 1989, 139). Awarded a second bar to his DSO for his conduct at El Alamein and during the pursuit of the Axis forces, he was badly wounded in January 1943 when, in the drive to take Tripoli, a shell exploded in front of his command tank.

Losing three fingers from his left hand, Harding was invalided home. Promoted acting lieutenant general, he was given command of VIII Corps in November 1943 only to be assigned as Chief of Staff to Alexander, the Allied commander in Italy, a month later. There, it is said, his influence was 'thoughtful and profound' in transforming a campaign sinking into a series of attritional battles into concentrating forces for a 'complete breakthrough' (Nicolson, 1973, 283/4).

Knighted in 1944 – officially as Sir Allan, but unofficially as Sir John as he and his wife preferred – Harding was appointed to command XIII Corps in Italy in March 1945. He occupied Trieste and remained there during the period of strained relations with erstwhile Yugoslav allies. In 1946 he became Commander, Central Mediterranean Force, the successor to 8th Army in Italy.

Harding was GOC-in-C Southern Command 1947–1948, C-in-C Far East Land Forces 1948–1951 and C-in C British Army of the Rhine 1951–1952. He succeeded Slim as CIGS in 1952, was promoted Field Marshal in 1953 and, in 1955, was appointed Governor of Cyprus. There he conducted a successful two-year counter-insurgency campaign against the Greek Cypriot terrorist organizxation EOKA.

Raised to the peerage as Baron Harding of Petherton in 1958, Harding was a director of several large companies and, in 1961, was made Chairman of the Horse Race Betting Levy Board. He held numerous honorary colonelcies, was Gold Stick to the Queen 1953–1960 and received an honorary doctorate from Durham University. Outliving his wife, and much sought after by military historians for interviews, he died at his home near in Sherborne in Dorset.

HARE, Major General James Francis *(1897–1970), CB, DSO*
The son of a major general and educated at Malvern and RMC, Sandhurst, Hare was commissioned in the King's Royal Rifle Corps in 1915. His First War service was in France and in Egypt, where he was mentioned in despatches.

Adjutant to his battalion 1920–1923, Hare attended the Staff College, Camberley, 1928–1929. Appointed an instructor at the Army Technical School in 1930, he resigned his commission soon after to pursue a career in Law. Called to the Bar in 1933, he married in 1935 and, settling in Kenya, was re-commissioned in the King's African Rifles in 1939. The next year his wife died and he was admitted to the DSO during operations in Abyssinia. Deputy Director of Supplies and Transport, East Africa, 1940–1943, and a major general in 1944, he re-married in 1945 and retired from the army in 1946.

Secretary of King George's Jubilee Trust 1949–1956 and Assistant Secretary 1956–1960, Hare was Secretary of Atlantic College (UK) Ltd. 1960–1963.

HARRISON, Major General Desmond *(1896–1984),CB, DSO, FICE*
Educated at Mountjoy School, Dublin, RMA, Woolwich, and Cambridge University, (young officers' course), Harrison was commissioned in the Royal Engineers in 1916. His First War service was in France.

Subsisting on a captain's pay for more than fifteen years, Harrison was a staff captain at AHQ, India, 1935–1937. Commandant of the School of Military Engineering in 1942 and Engineer-in-Chief, South-East Asia Command in 1943, he was promoted major general in 1944 and was Director of Fortifications and Works at the War Office in 1946.

Retired from the army in 1947, Harrison was employed by the Ministry of Food. A member of the Overseas Food Corporation 1947–1949, he was general manager of the ill-fated groundnuts scheme, whereby, it was envisaged, three million acres of East African bush could be cleared and nuts grown from which edible fats and oils would be extracted. Resigning from the job on health grounds, Harrison thereafter held numerous civil engineering consultancies. Married in 1920, his only son was killed in action in North-West Europe in 1945.

HARRISON, Major General Eric George William Warde
(1893–1987), CB, CBE, MC
The son of an Indian Army officer, Harrison was educated at Cheltenham and RMA, Woolwich. Commissioned in the Royal Artillery in 1913, his First War service was in France, where he served on the staff at divisional and corps level, was four times mentioned in despatches and awarded the MC in 1915.

A keen sportsman, Harrison played rugby for the Army in 1920 and represented Britain in the High Hurdles in the 1914 and 1924 Olympic Games. Thereafter he turned to shooting big game, foxhunting and other field sports. After attending the Staff College, Camberley, 1926–1927, he served on the staff in Lahore District, India, 1928–1932. In India he was 'a fearless pig-sticker'. A brevet lieutenant colonel in 1931, he commanded Oxford University OTC 1934–1938, before commanding an infantry battalion in Palestine with Montgomery as his divisional commander. There, as Montgomery put it, having 'loosed' 'Dreadnought' Harrison 'on the task of killing rebels' . . . he 'require[d] no urging in this respect' (Hamilton, 1982, 297).

A colonel in 1939, Harrison was made CRA 12th Division in Northern Ireland. He did not accompany the division to France in 1940 as, bereft of artillery, the troops were assigned to labour duties. Made commander Surrey and Sussex District in 1941, he was CRA 5th Division in North Africa and Italy 1943–1944 and CRA Allied Forces HQ 1944–1945. Promoted major general in 1944, he retired from the army in 1946.

Active in his retirement, Harrison wrote books on riding, gardening and dog ownership, and was a JP in Cornwall from 1951. DL for the County in 1953, he was High Sheriff in 1958, and Chairman of St Lawrence Hospital Management Committee 1952–1956. Master of the North Cornwall Hounds and married in 1961, he outlived his wife by twenty years.

HARRISON, Major General James Murray Robert *(1880–1957), CB, DSO*
Commissioned in the Royal Artillery in 1900, Harrison served in the South African War. A captain in 1910 and a major in 1914, his First War service was in France, where he was admitted to the DSO in 1916, and latterly in Italy.

A brevet lieutenant colonel in 1919, 'Jimmy' Harrison graduated from the

140

Staff College, Camberley, in the first post-war course, and spent most of the decade on regimental duties in India. Married in 1924, he was CRA 55th (West Lancashire) TA Division 1930–1932 and Commandant of the School of Artillery at Larkhill 1932–1934. Promoted major general, he was MGRA Army Headquarters, India, 1935–1936, and was GOC 2nd Anti-Aircraft Division 1936–1939.

Made Lieutenant Governor of Jersey in 1939, 'Jimmy' Harrison was evacuated in 1940. As no further employment was found for him, he retired from the army in 1941 and, thereafter, sometimes alone and sometimes with their wives, he and Brooke had fairly frequent lunches together. Re-married in 1945, he fathered a daughter by his second marriage.

HARTER, Major General James Francis (1888–1960), DSO, MC

Volunteering for service in 1914, Harter was commissioned in the Royal Fusiliers in 1915. His First War service was in France, where he was five times mentioned in despatches, awarded the MC and admitted to the DSO.

Married in 1917 and the father of a son and two daughters, Harter attended the Staff College, Camberley, 1924–1925, but resigned his commission in 1926 and took up fruit farming. Re-commissioned in 1938, he commanded the 5th Battalion of the Suffolk Regiment (TA) in 1939 and was made Garrison Commander of Portsmouth in 1940. A major general in 1942, he commanded the Northern Midland District in 1942.

Retired from the army in 1943, Harter was Colonel of the Royal Fusiliers 1947–1954. He was also DL for Essex in 1949.

HARTGILL, Major General William Clavering (1888–1968), CB, OBE, MC

Born and brought-up in New Zealand, Hartgill graduated from the London Hospital in 1914 and was commissioned in the Royal Army Medical Corps the same year. His First War service was in France, where he was mentioned in despatches and awarded the MC.

A captain in 1918, Hartgill took part in the Somaliland campaign of 1920 and married in 1922. A major in 1926, he was a lieutenant colonel in 1939, having spent a number of years serving in India.

Appointed OBE in 1940, after service with the BEF in France, Hartgill chaired the War Office Committee on Reorganization of Medical Services in the Field in 1943. Promoted major general in 1943, he retired from the army in 1947. He and his wife settled in his native New Zealand.

HARTLEY, General Sir Alan Fleming (1882–1954), GCIE, KCSI, CB, DSO

The son of a doctor, Hartley was educated at Charterhouse and RMC, Sandhurst. Commissioned in the Durham Light Infantry in 1901, he served in the South African War. Transferring to the Bengal Lancers (Probyn's Horse) in 1905, he married in 1914 and his First War service was in France, Salonika and Iraq. Twice mentioned in despatches, he was admitted to the DSO in 1917.

A staff officer at Army HQ, India, 1921–1923, Hartley, having attended the

Staff College, Quetta, in 1920, was an instructor there from 1924 to 1925. Commandant of Probyn's Horse 1927–1930, he was mentioned in despatches for his part in operations on the North-West Frontier. After attending the Imperial Defence College in 1931, he commanded the 4th (Secunderabad) Cavalry Brigade 1932–1933. Made Director of Military Operations and Intelligence, Army HQ, India, in 1933, he was promoted major general in 1936 and appointed to command Waziristan District in 1937. It fell to him to supervise the campaign aimed at finding, or at least suppressing the activities of, one of 'the kind who had always been the plague of the Frontier' (Chenevix Trench, 1988, 126), the Fakir of Ipi.

Commander of Rawalpindi District 1939–1940, Hartley was promoted lieutenant general in 1940 and appointed GOC-in-C Northern Command, India. A general in 1941, he was C-in-C India for three months in 1941, before making way for Wavell and, later, Auchinleck. Deputy C-in-C, India, 1942–1944, he retired from the army in 1944.

HARTWELL, Major General John Redmond (1887–1970), CB, DSO
Educated at Radley and RMC, Sandhurst, Hartwell was commissioned in the Royal Irish Fusiliers in 1906. Transferring to the 4th Gurkha Rifles the next year, he began his career in the Indian Army and a twenty-year association with the Gurkhas. Married in 1911, his First War service was in Gallipoli, Egypt and in France. He was wounded, mentioned in despatches and admitted to the DSO in 1916.

Serving on the staff at AHQ, India, 1919–1924, Hartwell, by now divorced, was a noted sportsman, winning the Indian Army Tennis Championship (singles) in 1924 and 1925. Deputy Assistant QMG in the Shanghai Defence Force in 1927, he re-married and attended the Staff College, Quetta, 1929–1930. A lieutenant colonel in 1931, he commanded the 1st Battalion, 18th Garwhal Rifles, 1931–1934, and was an instructor at the Senior Officers' School, Belgaum, 1935–1938. He commanded the Sind Brigade Area, Karachi, in 1938. Promoted major general in 1941, he commanded Kohat District, North-West Frontier, until his retirement from the army in 1943.

Upon the death of his second wife in 1945, Hartwell re-married the next year. He and his wife lived in London

HARVEY, Major General Sir Charles Offley
(1888–1969), CB, CVO, CBE, MC (Bar)
The son of a clergyman, Harvey was educated at Marlborough and RMC, Sandhurst. Commissioned in the Highland Light Infantry in 1908, he transferred to the Central India Horse in 1909. First War service was in Egypt and Palestine, where he was awarded the MC (and bar).

Assistant Military Secretary to the Prince of Wales during his Indian tour 1921–1922, Harvey attended the Staff College, Quetta, and was Military Secretary to the Viceroy 1926–1931. Married in 1931 and Commandant of the Central Indian Horse 1931–1936, he commanded the Indian contingent at the coronation of George VI in 1937. A staff officer in Meerut District 1936–1939, and commander of Wana Brigade 1939–1940, he was GOC 8th Indian Division 1940–1942.

Military Adviser-in-Chief to Indian States Forces 1943–1946, Harvey retired from the army in 1946.

Colonel of the Central India Horse 1945–1952, Harvey settled in Dublin and was Assistant Managing Director of the Guinness brewing concern 1946–1961. He spent the last years of his life as Chief Steward of Hampton Court Palace.

HASTED, Major General William Freke
(1897–1977), CB, CIE, CBE, DSO, MC

Born in Sussex, Hasted was educated at Cheltenham, Cambridge University and RMA, Woolwich. Commissioned in the Royal Engineers in 1915, his First War service was with 2nd Division in France 1916–1918. Mentioned in despatches, he was awarded the MC in 1918.

Married in 1920 and an England Hockey international in 1923, Hasted was an instructor at RMA, Woolwich, 1924–1926. An instructor at the Canadian RMC, Kingston, Ontario, 1926–1930, he was o/c Irish Free State Treaty Ports Coast Defences 1932–1936 and served with the Bengal Sappers and Miners (Peshawar Brigade) 1936–1937. Attached to the HQ staff Northern Command, India, in 1937, he was mentioned in despatches and admitted to the DSO for his part in operations in Waziristan. Continuing to serve on the North-West Frontier until 1940, he was appointed Deputy Chief Engineer Tenth Army (Iran) 1941–1942.

Promoted major general, Hasted was Deputy Engineer-in-Chief (Air), GHQ, India, 1942–1943, and Chief Engineer XIV Army in Burma 1944–1945. Slim regarded the 'quietly-spoken' Hasted as 'one of the heroes of the campaign' (Slim, 1986, 397–8). Chief Engineer Allied Land Forces South-East Asia 1945–1946, he was Engineer-in-Chief, India, 1946–1947.

Retired from the army in 1947, Hasted was President of Loughborough College in 1951 and Controller of Development in Kuwait, 1951–52. Outliving his wife by fifteen years, he died in London.

HAUGH, Major General James William Norris *(1894–1969), CB*

Born in Glasgow and a territorial soldier, Haugh was commissioned in the Cameronians (Scottish Rifles) in 1914. His First War service was in France, where he was wounded.

Adjutant to his regiment's 2nd Battalion in 1921, Haugh served for many years in India. He graduated from the Staff College, Quetta, in 1929 and was a staff officer at the School of Artillery, Larkhill, 1931–1933. Brigade Major with 6th Infantry Brigade 1933–1935, he was Brigade Major with 13th Infantry Brigade in Egypt in 1936 and served on the staff of 5th Division 1936–1937 in Palestine and in England. He was a staff officer with Northern Command 1937–1939.

A brigade commander under Home Forces 1941–1942, Haugh was BGS

Northern Ireland District 1942–1943 and was Deputy Chief of Staff, Middle East Command, 1943–1944.

Made Deputy QMG at the War Office in 1945, Haugh retired from the army in 1948. He lived in Putney.

HAUGHTON, Major General Henry Lawrence *(1883–1955), CB, CIE, CBE*
Of military family and educated at Winchester and RMC, Sandhurst, Haughton was commissioned in the Wiltshire Regiment in 1902. Transferring to the Indian Army, he was gazetted into his father's old regiment, the 34th Sikhs, in 1903. A captain in 1911 and married the next year, his First War service was on the North-West Frontier and later in Mesopotamia.

Attached to the India Office in London 1920–1922, Haughton was Commandant of 11th Sikh Regiment in 1927 and was appointed CBE for his part in operations on the North-West Frontier in 1930. Deputy Military Secretary Army HQ, India, 1931–1933, he commanded 1st (Abbottabad) Infantry Brigade, 1933–1936. Promoted major general in 1936, he commanded Kohat District from then until his retirement from the army in 1940. Re-employed, he continued to command the District until 1943.

A keen sportsman and author of a book on big game shooting in the Himalayas, Haughton and his wife settled in North Berkshire.

HAWES, Major General Leonard Arthur *(1892–1986), CBE, DSO, MC*
Born in Hertfordshire and educated at Bedford School and RMA, Woolwich, Hawes was commissioned in the Royal Garrison Artillery in 1911. A captain in 1916, his First War Service was in France and Italy, where he was awarded the MC and admitted to the DSO in 1918.

A temporary major in 1917, it took twelve years of peacetime soldiering for Hawes to attain that substantive rank. In between times he married and graduated from the Staff College, Camberley, in 1926. An Assistant Adjutant and QMG at the War Office 1932–1935 and a colonel in 1938, his 'admirable work' at the Directorate of Staff Duties helped in the movement of the BEF to France (Bond (ed.), 1972, 171).CRA 5th Division with the BEF in France 1939–40 and appointed CBE in 1940, he was BGS Eastern Command in 1941 and Major General i/c Administration Home Forces 1942. Appointed to command South Midland District in 1943, he held that post until his retirement from the army in 1945.

An active member of the British Red Cross Society, Hawes was the Controller of the Home Department 1947–1957. A widower in 1970, he re-married in 1972. He and his second wife lived in Sussex.

HAWKESWORTH, Lieutenant General Sir Ledlie Inglis
(1893–1945), KBE, CB, CBE, DSO (Bar)
Educated at St Bee's School and Oxford University, Hawkesworth was commissioned in the East Yorkshire Regiment in 1914. First War service

was in France. A captain in 1916, he was three times wounded.

Admitted to the OBE after service with the North Russia Relief Mission in 1919, 'Ginger' Hawkesworth served on the staff at the War Office 1920–1923. A student at the Staff College, Camberley, 1927–1928, he was BGS Northern Command 1930–1932. Deputy Assistant Adjutant General 1932–1934, he served on the directing staff at Camberley 1934–1937.

Commander of 12th Infantry Brigade with the BEF in France 1939–1940, and appointed CBE after Dunkirk, Hawkesworth was made Director of Military Training at the War Office in 1940, Placed in command of 4th Division in 1942, this ' master of infantry tactics' (Blaxland, 1979, 228) served in Tunisia with First Army and was admitted to the DSO.

Appointed GOC 46th Division in August 1943, Hawkesworth took part in the Salerno landings, the capture of Naples and the breaching of the Gothic Line. Transferring briefly to 1st Division in the Anzio beachhead in May 1944, he was promoted lieutenant general and placed in command of X Corps in November 1944. Detached from 8th Army to command British troops in Greece, he was knighted and returned to Italy. But, suffering from heart trouble, was booked for an early passage home.

The end came swiftly and sadly. Embarked on a troopship bound for England on 29 May 1945, Hawkesworth suffered a fatal heart attack while the ship lay at anchor in Gibraltar harbour. He left a widow and a son.

HAWKINS, Major General Edward Brian Barkley (d. 1966), DSO, OBE
Born in Surrey and educated at Winchester and RMC, Sandhurst, Hawkins was commissioned in the West Yorkshire Regiment in 1909. After a long spell of service on Malta, he was a captain in 1914. First War service was in East and southern Africa, where he was wounded and admitted to the DSO in 1918.

A brevet lieutenant colonel in 1918, Hawkins served on in Africa after the Armistice. Consul for south-western Ethiopia 1920–1922, he developed 'a great love for Africa, and became a great expert in its people, the country and its game'. Returning briefly to his regiment's Yorkshire depot 1924–1925, he returned to Africa to assume command of the 1st Battalion King's African Rifles in Nyasaland 1926–1931. Said to be an 'excellent commanding officer' with an 'imaginative approach to training' (Richardson, 1987, 25/6), he supplemented his pay by selling the ivory from the elephants he shot.

Returning to Britain in 1936, Hawkins commanded the 2nd Battalion, the West Yorkshire Regiment, 1936–1939 and, promoted major general in 1940, was made GOC British troops in West Africa. An experienced trainer of troops, he served briefly as Giffard's Chief of Staff in West African Command in 1941. He was made GOC Nairobi in 1945.

Retiring from the army in 1946, Hawkins and his French-born wife farmed for a number of years in Kenya, before settling in the villa she had inherited at Le Touquet, Pas de Calais.

HAWKINS, Major General George Ledsam Seymour
(1898–1978), CB, MC
Commissioned in the South Staffordshire Regiment in 1914 and transferring to the Royal Field Artillery in 1915, Hawkins's First War service was in France, where he was awarded the MC.

Married in 1921, Hawkins transferred to the Indian Army in 1925. Commandant of the Indian Army Ordnance Corps School 1928–1933, he was Assistant Director of Ordnance Services, India, 1936–1937, and was mentioned in despatches for his part in operations in Waziristan in 1937. He was Ordnance Consulting Officer at the India Office 1937–1941.

Promoted major general in 1941, Hawkins was Director of Ordnance Services, India, until his retirement from the army in 1945. Colonel Commandant of the Indian Army Ordnance Corps 1945–1956, he was Director, Southern Region, Ministry of Works, 1945–1957.

Outliving his wife by more than twenty years, Hawkins lived in Norfolk.

HAWTHORN, Major General Douglas Cyril *(1897–1974), CB, DSO*
Commissioned in the King's Own Yorkshire Light Infantry in 1917, Hawthorn transferred to the 1st Punjab Regiment, Indian Army, in 1918.

Married in 1919 and captain throughout the 1920s, regimental duties took Hawthorn to Palestine, the North-West Frontier and Baluchistan. A student at the Staff College, Quetta, 1930–1931, he took part in Mahsud and Waziristan operations in the later 1930s.

Commandant and Chief Instructor at the Tactical School, India, 1941–1942, Hawthorn commanded 62nd Indian Infantry Brigade 1942–1943 and was Chief of Staff to Christison's XV Corps in the Arakan 1943–1944. Admitted to the DSO in 1945, he was appointed GOC 23rd Indian Division in the latter stages of the campaign in Burma.

Commander of British troops on Java 1945–1946, Hawthorn, appointed CB in 1946, was Director of Military Training, India, 1946–1947. Deputy CGS, India, in 1947, he retired from the army in 1948 and was Chairman of the Burma Star Association 1949–1955.

HAY, Major General Arthur Kenneth *(d.1949), DSO, OBE*
The youngest son of a major general, Hay was educated at the United Services College, Westward Ho! and RMA, Woolwich. Joining the Royal Field Artillery in 1902 and a captain in 1914, his First War service was in France. There he was four times mentioned in despatches, admitted to the DSO in 1917 and appointed OBE after service in the North Russian Relief Force in 1919.

A student at the Staff College, Camberley, 1919–1920, Hay, a lieutenant colonel in 1929, was an Assistant Adjutant General at the War Office 1931–1933 and BGS 2nd Division, Aldershot, 1934–1935. Commander of 8th Infantry Brigade, India, 1935–1938, he retired from the army in 1938, married that year and fathered a daughter.

Re-employed in 1939, Hay served in the War Office. In February 1941, as acting major general, he was GOC of the Lincolnshire County Division. When the Division was disbanded that November, he reverted to retired pay, and lived with his wife and infant daughter near Peterborough.

HAY, Lieutenant General Sir Robert *(1889–1980), KCIE, MB*

Educated at George Watson's College, Edinburgh, and Edinburgh University, Hay, already a qualified doctor, joined the Royal Army Medical Corps Special Reserve in 1914. His First War service was in Egypt, Mesopotamia and France until he was commissioned and transferred to the Indian Medical Service in 1917.

Service in Kurdistan in 1919 was followed by a two-year spell in Iraq. There were later postings on the North-West Frontier, with higher degrees, conferred by Glasgow and Liverpool universities; along the way Hay held residency surgeoncies in several hospitals. Married in 1928, his young son was killed in the Quetta earthquake.

Appointed Inspector General of Civil Hospitals in the Punjab in 1943, Hay became the last Director of Indian Medical Services in 1946. Knighted in 1947, he retired from the army in 1948. Returning to Edinburgh he found the newly-constituted National Health Service uncongenial and retired to live in Hawick.

HAYDON, Major General Joseph Charles

(1899–1970), CB, DSO (and Bar), OBE

Educated at Downside and RMC, Sandhurst, Haydon was commissioned in the Irish Guards in 1917. Serving in France, he was mentioned in despatches in 1918.

Spending a good part of the inter-war years a captain, Haydon married in 1926 and attended the Staff College, Camberley, 1935–1936. Military Secretary to the Secretary of State for War in 1938, he was promoted lieutenant colonel and commanded the 2nd Battalion, Irish Guards, in 1939.

While still a lieutenant colonel Haydon took his battalion to the Hook of Holland in mid-May 1940 and helped ensure the safe passage to England of the Dutch Royal Family. He also assisted in the defence of Boulogne later in the month. Admitted to the DSO and a brigadier in 1941, he commanded the newly-constituted Special Service Brigade (better known as Commandos) 1940–1942. Vice-Chief of Combined Operations in 1942, he helped plan the ill-fated Dieppe raid and, among other achievements, sacked Evelyn Waugh 'on the spot for insubordination' (Hastings, 1995, 451). After commanding 1st Guards Brigade in Italy in 1944, he was promoted major general and made a member of the British Joint Services Mission in Washington from July 1944 until the end of the war in Europe.

Appointed British Army Representative to the Joint Chiefs of Staff in Australia 1946–1947, Haydon was Chief of the Intelligence Division, Control Commission, Germany, 1948–1950. Retiring from the army in 1951, he served in the Foreign Office for the next seven years.

147

A widower from 1957, Haydon was a director of a light aircraft company in Sussex until two years before his own death.

HAYES, Major General Eric Charles *(1896–1951)*, *CB*
Educated at Sleaford School and RMC, Sandhurst, Hayes was commissioned in the Royal Norfolk Regiment in 1915. His First War service was in France, where he was mentioned in despatches.

Volunteering for service in Russia in 1919, Hayes served on the staff of the Anglo-Russian Brigade based in Vladivostok. Held prisoner by the 'Reds' for some ten months, he spent most of the remaining inter-war years on a captain's pay. He married in 1924, attended the Staff College, Camberley, 1927–1928 and, a lieutenant colonel in 1938, commanded the 2nd Battalion the Royal Norfolk Regiment in France with the BEF 1939–1940.

Made Commandant of the Company Commander's School in 1940, Hayes was briefly appointed to command 169th Infantry Brigade in 1941, before, even more briefly, being given command of the Yorkshire County Division. Made GOC of 3rd Infantry Division in December 1941, he was appointed to an area command in Nigeria in December 1942. Commander of East Central District, England, 1943–1944, he was appointed Head of the British Military Mission to China. For this period of service he was appointed CB in 1946.

Retired from the army in 1947, Hayes, a keen golfer and gardener, lived in London. Colonel of the Royal Norfolk Regiment in 1951, he died the same year after a short illness.

HAYMAN-JOYCE, Major General Hayman John *(1897–1958)*, *CBE, DSO*
Educated at Radley and RMC, Sandhurst, Hayman-Joyce was commissioned in the Border Regiment in 1915. His First War service was in France. Inter-war regimental duties took him to India, Sudan and to China with the Shanghai Defence Force.

After attending the Staff College, Camberley, 1933–1934, Hayman-Joyce spent four years on staff duties at the War Office. A lieutenant colonel in 1939, he commanded the 5th Battalion, King's Own Royal Regiment in France with the BEF. Admitted to the DSO for his part in 44th Division's withdrawal to Dunkirk, he was appointed to command 12th Infantry Brigade in 1941.

A trainer of troops over the next two years, Hayman Joyce was appointed GOC 4th Division in September 1943. Posted first to Egypt, he was made an area commander there just as his division was embarking for active service in Italy.

Retired from the army in 1947, Hayman-Joyce settled on Exmoor.

HEATH, Lieutenant General Sir Lewis Macclesfield
(1885–1954), *KBE, CB, CIE, DSO, MC*
The son of an Indian Civil Servant and educated at Wellington and RMC, Sandhurst, Heath was gazetted into the 11th Sikh Regiment (Indian Army) in 1906. A captain in 1914 and married in 1915, his First War service was as an

artilleryman in Egypt and Mesopotamia, where he was mentioned in despatches and awarded the MC in 1917. Badly wounded, he lost an eye and suffered permanent injury to his left arm.

Appointed CIE for his part in operations in Afghanistan and East Persia (Iran) 1919–1922, 'Piggy' Heath commanded a mountain artillery battery on the North-West Frontier, for which he was mentioned in despatches and admitted to the DSO in 1933. He was an instructor at the Senior Officers' School, Belgaum, 1934–1936, and Commander of the Wana Brigade, India, 1936–1939. He was Commander of Deccan District when war broke out in 1939.

Promoted major general, Heath was appointed to command 5th Indian Division in 1940 and, arriving at Port Sudan, joined with Platt and Cunningham in the conquest of Abyssinia. Said to be a soldier of 'immense resolution and toughness' (Maule, 1961, 170) and 'very highly regarded in Indian circles' (Warren, 2002, 29), he planned and executed the assault on the Eritrean mountain fortress of Keren in 1941.

Knighted and returned to India, Heath, 'a handsome widower' and father of three sons and two daughters, re-married. Promoted lieutenant general and appointed to command III Indian Corps, he was entrusted with defending northern Malaya against Japanese invasion. Unable to use his own plans for 'forward defence' and powerless to stop the Japanese advance, his 'ideas on the conduct of the campaign were at variance' with Percival's (Kinvig, 1996, 227).

Taken prisoner when Singapore fell, Heath endured the privations and humiliations of captivity on Formosa with considerable stoicism. Separated from his wife, herself interned and nursing their infant son, he retired from the army upon his release from captivity. In declining health he spent his last years living in Bath.

HERBERT, Major General William Norman *(1880–1949), CB, CMG, DSO*
Gazetted into the Northumberland Fusiliers in 1900, Herbert served in the South African War and was seconded to the West Africa Frontier Force 1904-07. He was decorated for his service on operations in northern Nigeria in 1906. A captain in 1914, his First War service was in France, where he was mentioned in despatches and admitted to the DSO.

After a further spell of active service in Iraq in 1920, Herbert was a staff officer in Rawalpindi District, India, 1920–1921, attended the Staff College, Camberley, married in 1925, and, returning to India, was Assistant Director of Auxiliary and Territorial Forces 1922–1923. He was a staff officer attached to Northern Command 1930–1932 and commanded 10th Infantry Brigade at Shorncliffe 1932–1934. He was promoted major general and appointed to command 50th (Northumbrian) Division in 1935. Colonel of the Royal Northumberland Fusiliers 1935–1947, he retired from the army in 1939 only to be re-employed and appointed GOC 23rd (Northumbrian) Division.

Sent to France, with his men deployed as labour battalions in the BEF's base areas, 23rd Division was so badly cut up by the German advance that it was disbanded in June 1940. Herbert retired to his home in Worcestershire. DL for the County in 1946, he died three years later.

HEWER, Major General Reginald Kingscote *(1892–1970), CB, CBE, MC*
Educated at Haileybury and Oxford University, Hewer volunteered for service in 1914 and served in France with the Royal Artillery 1914–1918. By now commissioned, he was mentioned in despatches and awarded the MC in 1917.

Transferring to the 7th Dragoon Guards in 1921 and the 7th Hussars in 1925 'Rex' Hewer married in 1925, was a major in 1935 and, as lieutenant colonel, was Assistant QMG with the BEF in France. An acknowledged 'movement' specialist, he was appointed OBE in 1940 for his part in organizing the Dunkirk evacuation. A brigadier in 1940, he was made CBE in North Africa in 1942. A major general in 1943, he was appointed CB in 1945. Retiring from the army that year he became Deputy Director of the European Central Inland Transport Organization. His job, a difficult one, was to try and get Europe's railway network running.

A keen huntsman and good shot, Hewer, the father of two sons and a daughter, retired in 1947 to his native Wiltshire.

HEYDEMAN, Major General Cecil Albert *(1889–1967), CB, MC*
Of the little that is known about this officer, it can be said he was of military family and educated at Harrow. Commissioned in the 2nd Dragoon Guards (Queen's Bays) in 1909, Heydeman's First War service was in France, where, as a machine gun instructor, he was mentioned in despatches and awarded the MC.

A brigade major with the Rhine Army in 1919, Heydeman attended the Staff College, Camberley, 1922–1923. A staff officer at the War Office 1924–1926, he was Assistant Adjutant and QMG with 1st Division at Aldershot 1933–1935 and commanded the 2nd Cavalry Brigade 1935–1936. Commander Presidency and Assam District, Calcutta, 1939–1941, he commanded a training division in India, 1941–1943, before being transferred to a District Command in the Mediterranean in 1943.

A keen sportsman, Heydeman was President of the Army Polo Association in 1939. He married in 1941 but divorced as soon as was legally possible. He retired from the army in 1946.

HEYWOOD, Major General Thomas George Gordon
(1886–1943), CB, OBE
Born in France, Heywood was commissioned in the Royal Artillery in 1905. A captain in 1914, his First War service was in Gallipoli, Egypt, France (where he was twice mentioned in despatches) and Macedonia. He was appointed OBE in 1919 for service in the British Salonika Army.

A student at the Staff College, Camberley, in 1919, and brevet lieutenant colonel in 1923, Heywood was an outstanding linguist. He served with the Army of the Orient in Turkey, the Shanghai Defence Force in the later 1920s and was

Military Attaché attached to the Paris Embassy 1932–1936. Brigadier RA, Aldershot Command, 1936–1939, he was promoted major general in 1939 and appointed GOC 7th Anti-Aircraft Division before being appointed Army Representative on the British Military Mission to Moscow.

Appointed CB in 1940 and Head of the British Military Mission to Holland, Heywood was then posted to Athens as head of the British Military Mission there. Described as 'intelligent, but not very wise' (Beevor, 1991, 8) the be-monocled Heywood was duly evacuated to Crete, where he helped ensure the safe passage of the King of the Hellenes before himself being evacuated to Egypt. Made Commander of the Presidency and Assam District, India, in 1941, he was GOC 26th Indian Division 1942–1943. Retiring from the army in 1943, he took up a post with the Supply Department in New Delhi, only to be killed in a plane crash in August that year. He left a widow and two daughters from his first marriage.

HIBBERT, Major General Hugh Brownlow (1893–1988), DSO
The son of an admiral and educated at Uppingham and RMC, Sandhurst, Hibbert says nothing about himself other than that he married in 1926, was admitted to the DSO in 1940, and, retiring from the army in 1946, lived in Shropshire. He commanded 148th Brigade 1941–1942 and was GOC 55th Division (Home Forces) between May 1942 and August 1943.

Commissioned in the King's Own Yorkshire Light Infantry in 1913, Hibbert's First War service was in France, where he was admitted to the DSO and taken prisoner. A keen sportsman, he played rugby for the army and tennis for his regiment. He was a staff officer in India in 1919 and graduated from the Senior Officers' School, Sheerness, in 1938.

HICKES, Major General Lancelot Daryl (1884–1965), CB, OBE, MC
Educated at Blundell's, Bedford School and RMA, Woolwich, Hickes was commissioned in the Royal Artillery in 1903. He served with the West African Frontier Force 1908–1909 and his First War service was in West Africa, Gallipoli, France and in Egypt. He was four times mentioned in despatches and awarded the MC. He was appointed OBE in 1919 after service with the North Russia Relief Mission.

Married in 1915 and a Deputy Assistant Adjutant at the War Office 1919–1920, Hickes was a graduate of the Staff College, Camberley, in 1921. A staff officer in India 1922–1926, he was Deputy Assistant Adjutant Southern Command 1932–1933 and DAAG and QMG, Eastern Command, 1933–1935. A colonel in 1936, he was an instructor at the Senior Officers' School, Sheerness, 1936–1937. A major general in 1938, he was, briefly, Assistant Director of the Territorial Army and GOC 3rd Anti-Aircraft Division 1938–1940. GOC 5th Anti-Aircraft Division 1940–1941, he was for three months Director of Staff Duties at the War Office.

Retired from the army in 1942, Hickes re-married in 1962.

HICKMAN, Major General Henry Temple Devereux
(1888–1960), CB, OBE, MC
The son of an Indian Army officer, Hickman was educated at Wellington and RMC, Sandhurst. Gazetted into the 34th Sikh Pioneers (Indian Army) in 1906, he served in operations against the Mohmands in 1908 and, married in 1913, was a captain in 1914. His First War service was in France, in Mesopotamia, where he was awarded the MC, and in Palestine.

A graduate of the Staff College, Quetta, in 1929 and made OBE after operations in Iraq in 1930, Hickman was Assistant Adjutant and QMG, Kohat District, 1933–1935. He also served in operations in Waziristan 1935–1937, where he commanded the 2nd Battalion of the Sikh Corps. Commanding the Kotal Brigade, India, 1937–1940, he was promoted major general and commanded Lahore District until his retirement from the army in 1944.

Appointed CB, Hickman settled in Kenya and farmed near Nairobi until his death.

HILL, Major General Sir Basil Alexander *(1880–1960), KBE, CB, DSO*
Educated in Heidelberg, Hill was gazetted into the Royal Marine Artillery in 1897. An England Rugby international between 1903 and 1907, he married in 1907 and joined the Army Ordnance Department the following year. First War service was in Gallipoli, Egypt and Palestine, Twice mentioned in despatches, he was admitted to the DSO in 1917.

Making a career in the RAOC, Hill was President of the Rugby Football Union 1937–1938 and rose to become Controller of Ordnance Services at the War Office 1939–1940. Before he retired from the army in 1941, he had helped in the formation and organization of the Royal Electrical and Mechanical Engineers.

Knighted in 1941, Hill was Colonel Commandant of the RAOC 1936–1947 and became the first Colonel Commandant of REME in 1942. Director of Hand Tools at the Ministry of Supply 1944–1945, he had an active retirement (golf, fishing, shooting, etc,), and was also was a Surrey JP.

HILL, Major General Leslie Rowley *(1884–1975), OBE*
Born near Edinburgh, the fifth son of a lieutenant colonel, Hill was educated at Wellington and RMA, Woolwich.

Commissioned in the Royal Artillery in 1904, Hill spent four years in Japan as a student at various military academies. His First War service was in France, where he was wounded in 1916, Married the same year, he served on the General Staff from 1917–1921. After attending the Staff College, Camberley, 1923–1924, he was Military Attaché at the Tokyo Embassy 1925–1930 and, a colonel in 1933, served on the staff at the War Office 1934–1936. Commander of 28th (Thames and Medway) Anti-Aircraft Group 1936–1938, he was promoted major general in 1938 and became Director of Training and Organization (Anti-Aircraft) at the War Office.

Briefly GOC 3rd Anti-Aircraft Division in 1940, Hill retired from the army that year. He lived in Alton, Hampshire, and died a few months before his illustrious near neighbour, Montgomery.

HIND, Major General Neville Godfray *(1892–1973), CSI, MC*
Born on Jersey, the son of a distinguished surgeon, Hind was educated at Winchester and RMA, Woolwich. Joining the Indian Army in 1911, he was gazetted into the 2nd Gurkha Regiment in 1914.

Hind's First War service was in France, Egypt and Baluchistan. Mentioned in despatches, he was again mentioned in despatches while serving on operations in Waziristan in 1919 and awarded the MC. After graduating from the Staff College, Quetta, in 1924, he served on the staff of Northern Command, India, 1925–1926. Assistant Secretary to the Committee of Imperial Defence in 1930, he returned to India a lieutenant colonel and assumed command of his Gurkha regiment in 1935. Made Deputy Secretary to the Defence Department, India, in 1938, he was Commander Jubbulpore Area in 1940.

Commander of Sind District in 1942, Hind was promoted major general the next year. Retiring from the army in 1945, he and his wife settled in his native Jersey. After the death of his wife in 1953, he married again in 1958.

HOBART, Sir Percy Cleghorn Stanley *(1885–1957), KBE, CB, DSO, MC*
Born in India, the son of an Indian Civil Servant, Hobart was educated at Clifton and RMA, Woolwich. A moderate sportsman, he captained the 'Shop's' 2nd Rugby XV and was commissioned in the Royal Engineers in 1904. Transferring to the 1st Sappers and Miners in 1906, he saw service in the Mohmand Expedition in 1908 and served on the staff of the Dehli Durbar in 1911.

'Hobo' Hobart, known as Patrick to his family, served in France in the First War, where he was awarded the MC in 1915, and latterly in Mesopotamia. There he became something of a specialist in aerial reconnaissance, was admitted to the DSO in 1916 and, six times mentioned in despatches, was briefly taken prisoner in 1918.

Appointed OBE in 1919, Hobart attended the Staff College, Camberley, in 1920, and returned to India to see active service on the North-West Frontier. While serving on the staff of Eastern Command, India, he became an ardent advocate of armoured warfare and duly converted to the Royal Tank Corps in 1923. An Instructor at the Staff College, Quetta, 1923–1927, he gained a reputation as a seducer of women and a brilliant trainer of troops. It was at this time that his sister, Betty, herself a widow with two children, married Montgomery.

Second-in-command of the 4th Battalion of the Tank Corps at Catterick 1927–1930, Hobart commanded the 2nd Battalion 1931–1933. By now a colonel, he was Inspector of the RTC 1933–1936, during which time he founded and led 1st Tank Brigade. In 1937 he was, briefly, Deputy Director of Staff Duties at the War Office, before being promoted major general and, as part of a complicated series of changes instigated by Hore Belisha at the War Office, appointed Director of Military Training.

By now Hobart was the army's 'most senior and experienced expert in mechanization' (Macksey, 1967, 152). As DMT he was in the best possible position to put through his cherished ideas on mechanization. However, he was not a success in the post. It is tempting to depict him as the outspoken prophet undermined by dim reactionaries, but it has to be said that Hobart was never easy to work with. Temperamentally unsuited to working as a member of a team, his impatience and lack of tact made enemies of colleagues he should have befriended. Moreover, his unconventional route to marriage (having been cited as co-respondent by the brother officer husband of his future wife) was not well regarded.

Sent to Egypt in mid-1938, with an ill-defined brief to form armoured units in the event of Italian invasion, Hobart was in his element. He raised and trained the mobile force that became 7th Armoured Division. However, he contrived to antagonize first Wilson, who considered he could not 'be relied on to discard his own ideas and carry out instructions . . . in a spirit of loyalty and co-operation' (Macksey in Keegan (ed.), 1991, 247), and later made an enemy of Wavell.

Appointed CB, sent back to England and effectively cashiered, Hobart joined the Chipping Campden Home Guard in 1940. He moved from being a Lance Corporal to Deputy Area Organizer quite quickly and put it about that he was appealing to the King to be reinstated. Churchill, it seems, rescued him from obscurity. It is worthwhile to record, though, that he had very few friends in the army. Regarded as a 'loose cannon', a confidential report described how 'on various occasions in his military career, he has been reported as impatient, quick-tempered, hot-headed, intolerant and inclined to see things as he wished them to be, instead of as they were' (Dill, 2ndacc., 7, LHCMA). If Hobart was to be reinstated, he would have to be held on a short leash.

Work was found for him as GOC of the newly-formed 11th Armoured Division in March 1941. Showing himself 'merciless' in his training methods, the only way a subordinate could earn his respect was to 'stand up to his bullying' (Carver, 1989, 47). Bitterly disappointed that he was considered too old to command his Division in the field – he was two years older than Montgomery and two years younger than Brooke – he was transferred to command 79th Armoured Division in 1942.

Knighted in 1943, Hobart developed his 'funnies'; specialized AFVs designed to clear mines with flails, lay down carpets of chicken wire and breach obstacles with flame and explosive. In this way Hobart made a significant contribution to the success of OVERLORD in June 1944. Yet, interesting and ingenious though his 'funnies' were, his role was a far cry from the position he had imagined for himself of leading vast tank armies into battle. His specialized tanks were farmed out to other formations, and for all that Brooke was 'delighted' that 'Hobo' was 'doing wonders' (Danchev & Todman, 2001, 517), there was no Brooke-Montgomery-Hobart triumvirate. By the end of the war in Europe 79th Division was broken up. Made Commandant of the Specialized Armoured Experimental Establishment, he retired from the army in 1946.

Acting as military adviser to the Nuffield Organization, and seeking, unsuccessfully, to be made Professor of Modern History at Oxford University, Hobart was Colonel Commandant of the Royal Tank Regiment 1948–1951 and Lieutenant Governor of the Royal Hospital Chelsea 1948–1953. Happy to be a grandfather, the cancer that was to kill him was diagnosed in 1955.

HODGEN, Major General Gordon West *(1894–1968), CB, OBE*
Commissioned on the unattached list in 1915 and gazetted into the Indian Army Service Corps the following year, Hodgen served in Egypt and Mesopotamia in the First War. Appointed OBE for services in Southern Persia (Iran) in 1921, he was Assistant Director Supplies and Transport, Meerut District, in 1937 and ADS and T, AHQ India, from 1937 to 1940.

Deputy Director Supplies and Transport, India, 1940–1941, Hodgen was Director General of Lands, Hirings and Disposal at Army HQ, India, 1942–1945. He was Chief Administration Officer, Southern Command, India, 1945–1946. Appointed CB and made President of the Claims Commission, India, in 1946, he was Colonel Commandant of the Royal Indian Army Service Corps from 1945 to 1947 and retired from the army that year. Married in 1949, he spent his remaining years living in Spain.

HOGG, Major General Douglas McArthur *(1888–1965), CBE, MC*
The son of a general and educated at Cheltenham and RMA, Woolwich, Hogg was commissioned in the Royal Engineers in 1906. A captain in 1914, his First War service was in Egypt and Mesopotamia, where he was thrice mentioned in despatches and awarded the MC. He also saw service in Siberia.

Married in 1921 and a student at the Staff College, Quetta, 1922–1923, Hogg was a founder-member of the Kandahar Ski Club. A brevet lieutenant colonel in 1931, he was Brigadier i/c Administration, Anti-Aircraft Command, 1938–1940.

Made o/c Åndalsnes, Norway, in April 1940, Hogg's request for speedy evacuation probably saved many lives and earned him a CBE. Major General i/c Administration, Northern Command, in 1941, he retired from the army in 1942 and joined the John Lewis partnership. He was General Manager, Peter Jones, 1943–1945.

HOLDEN, Major General William Corson *(1893–1955), CSI, CBE, DSO, MC*
Born in the Bahamas, the son of an official in the Imperial Lighthouse Service, and educated at Nassau Grammar School, Holden joined the Royal Artillery from the Special Reserve in 1913. His First War service was in France, where he was awarded the MC, and in Egypt, Palestine and Macedonia.

Admitted to the DSO in 1919, Holden married in 1920 and attended the Gunnery Staff Course 1920–1921. He was an instructor at the School of Artillery 1922–1925. After attending the Staff College, Camberley, 1926–1927, he was a brigade major before being seconded to the staff of an RAF Group in 1930. A staff officer at the War Office 1932–1936, he attended the Imperial

Defence College in 1937. Further staff duties at the War Office 1938–1939 gave way to him being appointed BGS I Corps with the BEF in France.

Appointed CBE and made BGS Home Forces in June 1940, 'Bill' Holden was promoted major general and, judged 'not a very easy fellow to place' (Alanbrooke, 6/2/6, LHCMA), was sidelined into Home Guard duties in 1941. In 1942 he was sent to India as Military Member of the Eastern Group Supply Council, which meant he travelled massively throughout the Far East and Australasia. Deputy Chief of the General Staff, India, in 1944, he was appointed Deputy Master General of the Ordnance, India, in 1944.

Retiring from the army in 1946, Holden re-married the following year. A keen yachtsman, he and his wife lived on the Hampshire coast. He died in his early 60s after a short illness.

HOLLAND, Major General John Charles Francis *(1897–1956), CB, DFC*
The son of an Indian Civil Servant, Holland was educated at Rugby and RMA, Woolwich. Commissioned in the Royal Engineers in 1915, his First War service saw him attached to the Royal Flying Corps in France, for which, as a pilot, he was awarded the DFC.

Married in 1924, Holland served with the Bombay Sappers and Miners in India and attended the Staff College, Quetta, 1932–1933. He spent much of the 1930s as a staff officer at the War Office. Nominated to attend the 1940 Imperial Defence College course, he was in at the beginning of building up a clandestine intelligence operations staff. A colonel in 1940, he served on numerous divisional staffs as CRE. Deputy Engineer-in-Chief at the War Office 1942–1943, he was Major General RE, Mediterranean Theatre 1944–1945.

Appointed CB in 1945, Holland was Chief of Staff, Western Command, 1947–1948 and was 'specially employed' 1949–1950. He retired from the army in 1951.

HOLMES, Major General Sir Noel Galway *(1891–1982), KBE, CB, MC*
Born in Galway and educated at Bedford School, Holmes was commissioned in the Royal Irish Regiment in 1912. After two years in India, his First War service was in France, where he was wounded, four times mentioned in despatches and awarded the MC in 1917.

Married in 1920 and a temporary lieutenant colonel, Holmes was Assistant Adjutant and QMG, British Forces in Upper Silesia, 1921–1922. Transferring to the East Yorkshire Regiment in 1922, he attended the Staff College, Camberley, 1926–1927, and was stationed at Dover Castle 1929–1931. Duties there did not prevent him from being a member of the Ireland Davis Cup Tennis team in 1930. A staff officer with Southern Command, India, 1933–1937, he commanded the 1st Battalion East Yorkshire Regiment 1938–1939.

Director of Movements at the War Office 1939–1943, Holmes attended many of the major allied conferences of the war. Promoted major general in 1943, he was Deputy QMG at the War Office 1943–1946. Made commander Aldershot and Hampshire District in 1946, he retired from the army that year.

Chairman of the North-East Divisional Coal Board 1946–1957, Holmes retired to Hove in Sussex. Living well into his nineties, he re-married in 1979, a year after his first wife's death.

HOLMES, Lieutenant General Sir William George
(1892–1969), KBE, CB, DSO

The son of an Aberdeen doctor, Holmes was educated at Gresham's School and commissioned in the Royal Welch Fusiliers in 1912. His First War service was first in France, where he was four times mentioned in despatches and admitted to the DSO in 1917, and later in Italy.

A brevet lieutenant colonel at war's end, it took more than ten years before Holmes reached that substantive rank. Meanwhile he served on the North-West Frontier, attended the Staff College, Camberley, 1928–1929, and commanded the 2nd Battalion of the East Lancashire Regiment. A colonel in 1933, he served on the staff of Northern Command 1934–1935 and commanded 8th Infantry Brigade 1935–1937. Promoted Major General in 1937, he was appointed to command 42nd (East Lancashire) Division the following year.

Sent to France in April 1940, to form part of III Corps of the BEF, 42nd Division had scarcely time to acclimatize itself to new surroundings before the German onslaught in the west began. The BEF's youngest divisional commander, Holmes was the first to be promoted lieutenant general after Dunkirk and given a Corps. Placed in command of VII Corps with Home Forces, he was appointed to command X Corps in North Africa in 1941. There, two days after his arrival, 'he ate a bad prawn' (Kennedy, 4/3, LHCMA), was hospitalized and on recovery found that as his command had been stripped of most of its troops and, he was being sent to Syria. His first action with 8th Army in 1942, as ordered by Ritchie, was to form a garrison at Mersa Matruh and then, as ordered by Auchinleck, to break out and retire eastward to the Alamein position. The disorder of his retreat 'seems to have made a greater impact than the reasons for it' (Blaxland, 1977, 25) and thereafter he was sidelined. Regarded as a 'problem' and judged 'extraordinarily ignorant of the various arms other than infantry' (Alanbrooke, 6/2/12, LHCMA), he was sent back to the Delta to prepare defences there and later assumed command of Ninth Army in Syria.

Returned to England and knighted in 1943, Holmes was briefly attached to the British Mission to Athens in 1945. He retired from the army the same year, settling eventually in the United States.

HOLWORTHY, Major General Alan Wilmot Wadeson
(1897–1983), DSO, MC

The son of a commissioner in the Chinese Customs Service, Holworthy passed out of RMC, Sandhurst in 1916 and was gazetted into the 3rd Gurkha Rifles in 1917. His First War service was brief, but he was awarded the MC while campaigning in Mesopotamia.

A captain at war's end and married in 1921, 'Hol' Holworthy was an instructor at the Army School of Education, India, 1929–1931, and attended the

Staff College, Camberley, 1933–1934. A major in 1935, he commanded the 7th Gurkha Rifles in the late 1930s. In 1940 he was Assistant Commandant of the Senior Officers' School, Belgaum. Commander of 7th Indian Brigade in North Africa 1942–1943, he was said to be 'of cheerful and kindly disposition' (Blaxland, 1979, 156). Appointed GOC 4th Indian Division, after its mauling at Cassino, in July 1944 he led his command in successful assault on the Gothic Line and was admitted to the DSO.

HOOD, Lieutenant General Sir Alexander (1888–1980), GBE, KCB, KCVO

Born in Edinburgh and educated at George Watson's College and Edinburgh University, Hood was a House Surgeon, Royal Edinburgh Infirmary, 1910–1911. Commissioned in the Royal Army Medical Corps in 1912 and a captain in 1915, his First War service was in France.

Thereafter Hood's rise in his chosen profession appeared inexorable. Sometime Deputy Director of Medical Services in Palestine and Transjordan, he was a brigadier in 1940 and a lieutenant general a year later. Director General of Army Medical Services 1941–1948, he was Chairman of the Governors of the Star and Garter home for disabled servicemen in 1948.

Governor and C-in-C, Bermuda, 1949–1955, Hood re-married and settled there after his term of duty ended. In addition to his numerous honours, he was much decorated by foreign governments and received honorary degrees from Edinburgh and Durham universities.

HOPKINSON, Major General George Frederick (1896–1943), MC

Few of this officer's personal details are known. Commissioned in the North Staffordshire Regiment and awarded the MC during war service in France, Hopkinson graduated from the Staff College, Camberley, in 1931 and, a lieutenant colonel in 1940, commanded an armoured car reconnaissance unit in France with the BEF. He gained a reputation as 'a brave and fearless leader' (Smyth, 1957, 54).

Made commander of 31st Independent Brigade Group in 1941, 'Hoppy' Hopkinson transferred to airborne forces and, having learned to parachute, commanded 1st Airlanding Brigade 1941–1942. Appointed GOC 1st Airborne Division in May 1943, he led his men in the near-disastrous pre-invasion 'drop' in Sicily. He was fatally wounded by a sniper's bullet that September near Taranto.

HORNBY, Major General Alan Hugh (1894–1958), CB, CBE, MC

Educated at Winchester and RMA, Woolwich, Hornby was commissioned in the Royal Field Artillery in 1914. His First War service was in France, where he was wounded, mentioned in despatches and awarded the MC.

Hornby saw service in Iraq 1919–1920 and, married in 1923, attended the Staff College, Camberley, 1930–1931. A staff officer at the War Office 1938–1939, he was briefly Deputy Director of Combined Operations in 1940. Thereafter he served in the Middle East, Sicily and Italy. Appointed CBE in

1943, he was promoted major general in 1944 and commanded 2nd Anti-Aircraft Group 1945–1947.

Retired from the army in 1948, Hornby, a keen cricketer and sailor, was Commissioner of the Kent St John Ambulance Brigade and Honorary Colonel of the Kent Auxiliary Cadet Force. A Freemason for 33 years, he was also Colonel Commandant of the Royal Artillery from 1953 until his death.

HORROCKS, Lieutenant General Sir Brian Gwynne
(1895–1985), KCB, KBE, DSO, MC

Born in India, the son of an army doctor, Horrocks was educated at Uppingham and RMC, Sandhurst. A keen sportsman, he was commissioned in the Middlesex Regiment in 1914. His First War service was brief. Wounded and taken prisoner in October 1914, he learned French, German and some Russian while in captivity.

Repatriated in 1919 and, allegedly, with 'four years back pay spent in six weeks' (Shepperd in Keegan (ed.), 1998, 226), Horrocks volunteered for service in Russia. Serving with the Military Mission based in Vladivostok, he was awarded the MC and again taken prisoner. In appalling conditions and more than once seriously ill, he recovered his health on release sufficient to win the British Modern Pentathlon Championship and represent Britain in the 1924 Olympic Games.

Fifteen years a captain, Horrocks's regimental duties took him to Germany, Silesia and Wormwood Scrubs. Adjutant of 9th (TA) Battalion of the Middlesex Regiment in 1927, he married in 1928 and, as he put it 'lived in some twenty-six different houses in our first twenty years of married life' (Horrocks, 1960, 69). After attending the Staff College, Camberley, 1931–1932, he served on the staff at the War Office for two years before becoming Brigade Major to the 5th Infantry Brigade based at Aldershot. In 1938 he returned to Camberley as a member of the directing staff. It fell to him to anticipate the needs of war and organize short courses for would-be staff officers drawn from the Territorial Army. He, allegedly, 'rose to the occasion', while his students found him 'energetic, enquiring and imaginative' (Warner, 1985, 50).

Due to leave Camberley in May 1940 and assume command of the second battalion of his regiment, the German attack in the west so accelerated events that he arrived at the front aboard a dental truck. Promoted brigadier while still in France, he assumed command of 11th Brigade in July 1940. He had acquitted himself well enough during the withdrawal to Dunkirk, but more importantly he had done so in front of the two men who would become the most powerful patrons in Britain's wartime army: Brooke, who had commanded II Corps, and Montgomery, his divisional commander.

It was to be more than two years before 'Jorrocks' again heard a shot fired in anger. Made BGS Eastern Command in January 1941, he was promoted major general and appointed to command 44th (Home Counties) Division in June. With Montgomery as his GOC-in-C, and self-consciously styling himself an 'army commander', Horrocks was successful in ingratiating himself with his

159

chief. Ever bright, cheerful and eager, he did what he was told, did not 'belly-ache' and posed no intellectual challenge. He had the air, it is said, 'of a country town family solicitor at a tennis party' (Latimer, 2003, 109). Made commander of 9th Armoured Division in March 1942, he overcame any lingering prejudice against infantrymen commanding tanks and, because considered 'exactly what was wanted for the job which lay ahead' (Montgomery, 1958, 94), he was summoned to North Africa that August and placed in command of the 'infantry-heavy' XIII Corps. The battles of Alam Halfa and El Alamein over, he was appointed to command the 'tank-heavy' X Corps.

Lent to Anderson's 1st Army in April 1943, Horrocks commanded IX Corps during the final stages of the campaign in Tunisia. Badly wounded in Bizerta in June, when he was hit by fire from a lone German raiding aircraft, he was consoled by being appointed CB and having a bar added to his DSO. However, it was to be a year before he was re-assigned to a command. As one of Montgomery's favourites, he was once again used to substitute a general who had fallen into the great man's bad books. Hence, although still not fully fit, he replaced Bucknall as commander of XXX Corps in August 1944. In the manner of his patron he prided himself on his ability to register his personality and inspire his men by addressing them in forthright terms. Accordingly, the part he played in MARKET GARDEN was to lead his corps in the failed attempt to make the ground link-up with the airborne forces beleaguered at Arnhem. Sent home on compulsory sick-leave at the end of 1944, he was back to lead his Corps during the Rhine crossing in March 1945.

Knighted in 1945, Horrocks was GOC Western Command in 1946–1948 and GOC-in-C British Army of the Rhine 1948–1949. Invalided out of the army, he took up the post of Gentleman Usher of the Black Rod. Still handsome and dapper, he became something of a television personality in the 1960s and was a Director of Bovis Holdings from 1963 to 1977. Active in his charity work, his last years were marred by the death of his daughter, his only child. She was drowned while swimming in the Thames in 1979.

HOTBLACK, Major General Frederick Elliot *(1887–1979), DSO, MC*
Born in Norwich and educated at Rugby and RMC, Sandhurst, Hotblack was commissioned in the Royal Dragoons in 1907. A squadron commander in 1914, his First War service was in France. Five times wounded, he was mentioned in despatches, awarded the MC in 1916 and, having transferred to tanks, was admitted to the DSO in 1917 (bar 1918).

'Boots' Hotblack attended the Staff College, Camberley, 1920–1921, was Brigade Major 1st Brigade, Rhine Army, 1922–1923, and, after serving on the Upper Silesia Plebiscite Commission, transferred to the Royal Tank Corps in 1925. A staff officer at the War Office in 1927, he developed his interest in mechanization when appointed to the Directorate of Military Training. A lieutenant colonel and instructor at Camberley 1932–1935, he was Military Attaché at the British Embassy, Berlin, 1935–1937. Recalled to War Office duties and promoted brigadier, he was Assistant Director of Military Operations over the last two years of peace.

Named by Liddell Hart on his 'select list of commanders of outstanding promise' (Liddell Hart, 1965, 238), Hotblack was employed on liaison duties between GHQ of the BEF and the French GGQ in the autumn of 1939 and, promoted major general, was appointed to command the newly-formed 2nd Armoured Division in December. Called to London in April 1940 and told 'he might be needed in Norway' (Kennedy, 1957, 147), he was given command of an infantry brigade and two battalions of French *chasseurs alpins* prior to the planned seaborne assault on Trondheim. The evening before his intended departure he was found unconscious at the foot of the Duke of York steps. He had suffered a stroke.

Hospitalized for six months, Hotblack returned for duties at the War Office but was placed on the retired list in 1941. Living in Wimbledon, he performed no further military activities beyond membership of the Royal Tank Regimental Association.

HOWARD-VYSE, Major General Sir Richard Granville Hylton
(1883–1962), KCMG, DSO
Educated at Eton and commissioned in the Royal Horse Guards in 1902, Howard-Vyse was a captain in 1908. His First War service was in France, where he was admitted to the DSO in 1915, and in Palestine, where he was chief staff officer with 5th Cavalry Division 1917–1918.

Married in 1925, Howard-Vyse was the first officer of the Household Cavalry to graduate from the Staff College, Camberley. Commander of the Cairo Cavalry Brigade 1928–1930, he was Inspector of Cavalry and Commandant of the Equitation School, Weedon, 1930–1934. Promoted major general, he was Chief of Staff to the Duke of Gloucester on his visit to Australia and New Zealand 1934–1935. Retired from the army that year, he was knighted, made Sheriff of Buckinghamshire and re-employed in 1939 as Head of the Military Mission to the French High Command at Vincennes.

Retired again in June 1940, Howard-Vyse was Chairman of the POW Department of the British Red Cross 1941–1945. Chairman and later President of the British Legion from 1950 until his death, he was, in addition, Vice-Lieutenant of Buckinghamshire, a JP and Colonel of the Royal Horse Guards from 1951.

HOWELL, Major General Frederick Duke Gwynne
(1881–1967), CB, DSO, MC
Educated privately and at St Thomas's Hospital, London, Howell joined the Royal Army Medical Corps as a qualified surgeon in 1906. A captain in 1909, he married in 1912. His First War service was in France, where he was five times mentioned in despatches, awarded the MC and admitted to the DSO.

A lieutenant colonel in 1930, Howell was Assistant Director General Army Medical Services at the War Office 1933–1934. Deputy Director of Medical

Services Army HQ, India, 1934–1937, he was Deputy Director of Medical Services, Aldershot Command, 1937–1941. Retired from the army that year, he settled in his native mid-Wales. DL for Radnorshire in 1944, he was High Sheriff of the county in 1945.

HUDDLESTON, Major General Sir Hubert Jervoise
(1880–1950), GCMG, GBE, CB, DSO, MC

Born in Norfolk and educated at Felsted, Huddleston was commissioned in the Dorsetshire Regiment in 1900 and served in the South African War. Decorated for service in the Sudan, his First War service was in East Africa, where he was mentioned in despatches, awarded the MC and admitted to the DSO.

A brevet lieutenant colonel in 1918, Huddleston was GOC, Sudan, 1924–1930 in which role he is credited with founding the King's African Rifles. Married in 1928, he commanded 14th Infantry Brigade. 1930–1933. Promoted major general, he commanded the Presidency and Assam District, India, 1934–1935, and Baluchistan District 1935–1938.

Retired from the army in 1938, 'Pasha' Huddleston was Lieutenant Governor and President of the Royal Hospital, Chelsea, before being re-employed as GOC Northern Ireland District in 1940. He was Governor General of the Sudan, 1940–1947 and, finally retired, lived out his final years in London. He was Colonel of the Dorsetshire Regiment 1933–1946.

HUDSON, Major General Charles Edward
(1892–1959), VC, CB, DSO (and bar), MC

Of military family and educated at Sherborne and RMC, Sandhurst, Hudson was commissioned in the Sherwood Foresters in 1912. His First War service was in France and Italy. His record for bravery was outstanding. Awarded the MC and admitted to the DSO in 1917, he was awarded the VC in 1918 while fighting on the Asiago plateau. A bar was added to his DSO during operations in North Russia in 1919.

Married in 1920, Hudson attended the Staff College, Camberley, 1926–1927, and transferred to the King's Own Scottish Borderers in 1928. A staff officer in Malaya 1930–1932 and an instructor at Sandhurst 1933–1937, he commanded the 2nd Battalion KOSB in 1938.

Appointed to command 2nd Infantry Brigade in 1938, Hudson served under Alexander in 1st Division with the BEF in France. Appointed CB, and GOC 46th Division from December 1940 to May 1941, he reverted to the substantive rank of brigadier and commanded 182nd Brigade in Northern Ireland 1941–1943. As no employment was found for him in the final two years of the war, he was ADC to the King 1944–1946 and retired from the army that year. In common with many other officers highly decorated in the First War, he seems to have failed to impress his superiors with his capacity for field command in the Second.

Devon County Commissioner for the St John Ambulance Brigade 1949–1954, Hudson was a JP from 1949, and DL for Devon in 1956.

162

. Better looking than 'Monty'! Auchinleck in India, 1944. *(Tank Museum)*

2. General Sir John Crocker, known as 'Honest John'. (Tank Museum

Dill, Smith, Jacob, Lampson, Eden and Wavell in North Africa, February 1941.
(Tank Museum)

4. Ritchie and
   Dempsey in
   North-West
   Europe, 1945.
   (Tank Museum)

5. General Sir John Dill.

. Taciturn as ever, Wavell, in macintosh, having the situation explained to him.

(Tank Museum)

. Percy Hobart, 'Pip' Roberts and 'Monty' in Berlin in 1945.   *(Tank Museum)*

8. General
Vyvyan Pope.
(Tank Museum)

9. In America with their tank production hosts (in civilian clothes) Raymond Briggs, Sir John Dill, 'Alec' Gatehouse and Francis Davidson. *(Tank Museum*

10. Major-General J. S. Crawford.
(Tank Museum)

11. Major-General F. E. Hotblack.
(Tank Museum)

12. Major-General
'Willie' Ross.
(Tank Museum)

13. Major-General D. W. Richards.
(Tank Museum)

14. Major-General Raymond Briggs.
(Tank Museum)

15. Major-General A.
W. C. Richardson.
(Tank Museum)

HUGHES, Major General Henry Bernard Wylde
(1887–1953), CB, OBE, DSO

Born in Hampshire and educated at Cheltenham and RMA, Woolwich, Hughes was commissioned in the Royal Engineers in 1906. A captain in 1914, his First War service was in India and Mesopotamia, where he was twice mentioned in despatches and admitted to the DSO in 1917.

A brevet major in 1918, Hughes was mentioned in despatches during operations in Afghanistan in 1919 and made OBE in 1920 after service in Waziristan. After many years of service in India, he was CRE 2nd Division at Aldershot 1933–1935 and, a colonel in 1935, was an instructor at the Senior Officers' School, Sheerness, 1935–1936. An Assistant Adjutant General at the War Office 1936–1939, he was Chief Engineer, Western Command, 1939–1940.

Engineer-in-Chief, Middle East, 1940–1942, Hughes was promoted major general and served briefly as GOC British troops in Cyprus. Chief Engineer, Supreme HQ Allied Expeditionary Force, 1943–1944, he retired from the army in 1946.

Married, with two sons, Hughes was more honoured by foreign governments than his own (Legion of Merit, Légion d'Honneur, etc.).He lived out his retirement in Suffolk.

HUGHES, Major General Ivor Thomas Percival
(1897–1962), CB, CBE, DSO, MC

The son of a clergyman, Hughes was educated at Wellington and RMC, Sandhurst. Commissioned in the Queens Royal (West Surrey) Regiment in 1916, his First War service was in France, where he was mentioned in despatches and awarded the MC.

Mentioned in despatches during operations on the North-West Frontier 1920–1921, Hughes married in 1923 and was Adjutant to his regiment's 2nd battalion in India and the Sudan 1925–1928. After attending the Staff College, Camberley, 1929–1930, he learned to fly, served on the staff of Scottish Command 1932–1934 and was Brigade Major to the 12th Infantry Brigade at Dover 1934–1935. Leaving the regular army, he was Assistant Serjeant at Arms of the House of Commons 1935–1939. He also commanded 4th Battalion (TA) of the Queen's Regiment 1937–1939.

Re-employed in 1939 and sent to France with the BEF, Hughes commanded 1/6th Battalion of the Queen's. Admitted to the DSO, he was promoted brigadier and appointed to command 219th Brigade in June 1940 and 131st (Queen's) Brigade in 1941. Promoted major general, he commanded 44th (Home Counties) Division in mid-1942, prior to being sent to North Africa. Badly mauled at the battle of Alam Halfa, 44th Division was disbanded in early 1943 and Hughes was appointed to command XXV Corps, a training establishment with Home Forces. A member of the Military Liaison Mission in Greece, Yugoslavia and Albania, 1944–1945, he was appointed CB and retired from the army in 1947.

Chairman of the Surrey Territorial and Auxiliary Forces Association

1947–1949 and DL for the county in 1953, Hughes was Serjeant at Arms of the House of Commons from 1957 until his death. He noted in his *Who's Who* entry that he had been 'gazetted KCVO in 1962, but did not receive the accolade'.

HULL, Field Marshal Sir Richard Amyatt *(1907–1989), KG, GCB, DSO*
Of military family, Hull was educated at Charterhouse and Cambridge University. With a pass degree, he was commissioned in May 1928, joining the 17th/21st Lancers. A captain in 1933, he served with his regiment in India. Married in 1934, he was his regiment's Adjutant during the process of mechanization and was a Student at the Staff College, Quetta, 1938–1939.

A staff officer at the War Office 1939–1941, Hull briefly commanded his regiment before serving on the staff of the Canadian Armoured Division and No. 2 Group, RAC, in 1942. Given command of Blade Force before Operation TORCH, he led his men to the outskirts of Tunis in November 1942. Admitted to the DSO, he was appointed second-in-command of 26th Armoured Brigade and, as acting brigadier, assumed command of 12th Infantry Brigade in April 1943, before returning to 26th Armoured Brigade as its commander, just before the entry into Tunis.

Made Deputy Director of Staff Duties at the War Office in December 1943, Hull became an acting major general in 1944 and was flown out to Italy to assume command of 1st Armoured Division. Aged thirty-seven, he was considered 'stuffy' by some, (Roberts, 1987, 136), but was one of the youngest, if not the youngest, British divisional commander in the Second World War (Blaxland, 1979. 168).

Appointed Commandant of the Staff College, Camberley, in 1946, Hull was Director of Staff Studies at the War Office 1948–1950. An instructor at the Imperial Defence College 1951–1952, he was Chief of Staff to Middle East Land Forces 1953–1954 and GOC British troops in Egypt 1954–1956. Deputy CIGS 1956–1958, he was C-in-C Far East Land Forces 1958–1961. That year he became the last CIGS (the word 'Imperial' was dropped from the title in 1964), and in 1964 he became Chief of the General Staff, Ministry of Defence. Promoted field marshal in 1965, he retired from the army in 1967 and became a director of a large brewing company.

Appropriately honoured, Hull was Colonel of the 17th/21st Lancers 1947–1957, Colonel Commandant of the Royal Armoured Corps 1968–1971 and Honorary Colonel of the Cambridge University OTC. The father of three children, he lived at Pinhoe near Exeter.

HUTCHISON, Lieutenant General Sir Balfour Oliphant
(1889–1967), KBE, CB
Born in Kirkaldy and educated at Uppingham, Hutchison was commissioned in the Royal Artillery from the Supplementary Reserve in 1909. Transferring to the 7th Hussars in 1911, his First War service was in Mesopotamia, where he was four times mentioned in despatches.

Married in 1920, Hutchison attended the Staff College, Camberley,

1923–1924, and was Deputy Assistant QMG with the Shanghai Defence Force in 1927. Always with 'a happy smile for everyone' (Brownrigg, 1942, 63), he was Deputy Adjutant and QMG, Eastern Command, 1928–1929. Assistant Adjutant and QMG for the Mobile Division in 1937, he was Brigadier i/c Administration in Palestine 1938–1939.

Appointed CB and Made Deputy QMG, Middle East, in 1940, Hutchison, although regarded by Auchinleck as 'not a top-notcher' (Alanbrooke, 6/2/6, LHCMA), was promoted major general and appointed GOC Sudan and Eritrea in 1942. He was QMG, India, from 1944 until his retirement from the army in 1945.

Knighted in 1946, Hutchison lived out his retirement in Suffolk, having to bear the loss of two sons killed in the war.

HUTSON, Major General Henry Porter Wolseley
(1893–1991), CB, DSO, OBE, MC
Born in Colorado and educated at King's College School and RMA, Woolwich, Hutson was commissioned in the Royal Engineers in 1913. His First War service was in France, where he was awarded the MC, and in Egypt and Mesopotamia where he was admitted to the DSO in 1917.

A captain in 1917, 'Hutty' Hutson was appointed OBE for services in Iraq in 1919. Employed with the Egyptian Army 1920–1924, he married in 1922 and was employed by the Colonial Office as a road engineer in Nigeria 1926–1928. After service in Hong Kong, he was Chief Instructor at the Field Works and Bridging School of Military Engineering 1934–1936. His Second War service began in England with Home Forces and continued in North Africa under O'Connor and in Greece under Wilson. Briefly Chief Engineer Ninth Army in Syria 1941–1942, he also served in East Africa before being promoted major general in 1944 and appointed Deputy Engineer-in-Chief, India.

Made Deputy Engineer-in-Chief at the War Office in 1946, Hutson retired from the army in 1947. He was Chief Engineer for the Forestry Commission 1947–1958. In common with a surprisingly large number of British generals, he was a keen ornithologist. He also wrote books supporting the white regime in Rhodesia (Zimbabwe).

HUTTON, Lieutenant General Sir Thomas Jacomb
(1890–1981), KCIE, CB, MC
Educated at Rossall and RMA, Woolwich, Hutton was commissioned in the Royal Artillery in 1909. A captain in 1915, his First War service was in first in France, where he was three times wounded, mentioned four times in despatches and awarded the MC, and latterly in Italy.

A brevet major in 1918, Hutton was Assistant Military Secretary to Milne, the commander of the Army of the Black Sea, 1919–1920. Married in 1921, he attended the Staff College, Camberley 1922–1923, and was a Deputy Assistant Adjutant General at the War Office 1923–1924. Military Secretary to Milne (by now CIGS) 1927–1930, he attended the Imperial Defence College and served in the directorate of Military Operations 1933–1936. A staff officer with 1st Division in Palestine, 1936–1938, he was promoted major general and appointed GOC of Western Independent District, India, that year.

Made Deputy Chief of the General Staff, AHQ, India, in 1940, Hutton was so well thought of that Dill had to rebuke Auchinleck for his 'instinctive and entirely illogical feeling against him' (Dill, 2nd. acc., 4, LHCMA). Promoted lieutenant general in 1941 and appointed CB, he was made Chief of the General Staff, India. Known as a first-class staff officer with 'great organizational powers' (Slim, 1999, 10), he was appointed GOC Burma by Wavell in December 1941. Looking, it is said, 'more like a head gardener than a general' (Lunt, 1989, 82), but 'shrewd and cautious' (Allen, 2002, 34), he presided over the early disasters in the Burma campaign. With others holding him responsible for the apparent inability of his troops to fight and detecting 'a lack of drive and inspiration from the top' (Nicolson, 1976, 159), he was replaced by a general with more 'personality', Alexander, in March 1942.

After a period of sick leave Hutton was created Secretary of the War Resources and Reconstruction Committee, India, in 1942. Knighted in 1944, he retired from the army the same year. Active in his retirement, he was Colonel Commandant RA 1942–1952, was Secretary to the Planning and Development Department, India, 1944–1946, and a regional officer for the Ministry of Health 1947–1949. Thereafter he served on numerous Anglo-American bodies concerned with worker productivity and, as his surviving papers in the Liddell Hart archive show (LHCMA), retained a vigilant watching brief on anything written or broadcast about the retreat from Burma

If 'lacking in personality' equates with warmth, bravery, sympathy, modesty and kindness, Hutton was that man. He was a fine officer who, charged with achieving the impossible in Burma, had the wit to realize that the only way to fight the campaign was to conduct a fighting retreat. His reputation suffered in that, in the manner of Ritchie's and Percival's, first-rate staff officers do not, so they say, make effective fighting commanders. Making way for bigger or more illustrious men who went on to achieve fame, his main fault, perhaps, was his consistent aversion to self-advertisement.

HYLAND, Major General Frederick Gordon *(1888–1962), CB, MC*
Educated at Marlborough and RMA, Woolwich, Hyland was commissioned in the Royal Engineers in 1909. His First War service was in France, where he was five times mentioned in despatches and awarded the MC. Married in 1918, his wife died within a year.

A brevet major in 1919, Hyland married again in 1922 and attended the Staff College, Camberley, 1924–1925. An instructor at the School of Military Engineering, Chatham, 1926–1930, and Commander RE, Singapore, 1931–1934, he was Commander RE, 3rd Division, 1935–1936. Appointed to command 31st (North Midland) Anti-Aircraft Brigade in 1936, he was promoted major general and was GOC 6th Anti-Aircraft Division 1939–1941.

Responsible for Anti-Aircraft defences of London and the South-East, it is said that Hyland's 'kindly but firm character earned him the respect and affection of all under his command' (Pile, 1949, 31). Appointed CB in 1942 and Chief of Staff and Deputy Commander of Gibraltar 1942–1944, he retired from the army in 1946. He died in a London nursing home.

I

INGLIS, Major General Sir John Drummond *(1895–1985), KBE, CB, MC*
Of military family and educated at Wellington and RMA, Woolwich, Inglis was commissioned in the Royal Engineers in 1914. His First War service was in France and Salonika. Awarded the MC in 1916, he was a brevet major in 1918.

Married in 1919, Inglis spent most of the inter-war years on a captain's pay. A lieutenant colonel in 1937 and mentioned in despatches and appointed OBE for service in Palestine 1937–1939, he was Vice-President of the Mechanization Board 1940–1942. Promoted major general in 1943, Inglis was nearly placed under arrest for 'tr[ying] to beat the gun' and land in Sicily before receiving proper authorization (de Guingand, 1947, 184). But his impetuosity served him well. Made Chief Engineer 21st Army Group, he saw the campaign in North-West Europe through to its close. Appointed CB in 1944, he was knighted in 1945 and retired from the army that year.

Colonel Commandant of the Royal Engineers 1955–1960, Inglis lived in Eastbourne. He re-married in 1977 after the death of his first wife.

INSKIP, Major General Roland Debenham *(1885–1971), CB. CIE, DSO, MC*
The son of a clergyman and educated at Framlingham and RMC, Sandhurst, Inskip was gazetted into the 13th Frontier Force Rifles (Indian Army) in 1908. His First War service was in France and Mesopotamia, where he was awarded the MC and admitted to the DSO, and latterly in Palestine. Five times mentioned in despatches, he was a brevet major in 1918, the year he first married.

Inskip's 'real soldiering' in peacetime was active enough. He served on the North-West Frontier and, after attending the Staff College, Quetta, re-married in 1929, and commanded the 6th Battalion of the Frontier Force Rifles 1932–1934. After serving for a year on the staff of AHQ, India, he attended the Imperial Defence College in 1936. Commander of the 1st (Abbottabad) Infantry Brigade, 1937–1939, he was promoted major general.

A district commander in India 1939–1941, Inskip was GOC, Ceylon, 1941–1942. Retired from the army that year, he was re-employed for special duties at GHQ, India, 1942–1946. Chief of Staff Bhopal State Forces

1946–1947, he was Colonel of the 6th Battalion Frontier Force Rifles 1943–1946. One of his sons by his first marriage was killed in the war.

IRONSIDE, Field Marshal William Edmund,
Baron of Archangel and Ironside (1880–1959), GCB, CMG, DSO

Born in Edinburgh, the son of an army surgeon, Ironside was brought up by his widowed mother in straitened circumstances, often abroad. Educated at Tonbridge School and RMA, Woolwich, he was commissioned in the Royal Artillery in 1899 and served in the South African War. A captain in 1908, he served on various brigade staffs, played rugby for Scotland and won the army heavyweight boxing championship. He attended the Staff College, Camberley, 1913–1914.

A major in 1914 and married in 1915, Ironside's First War service was mainly as a staff officer in France. Admitted to the DSO in 1915 and briefly Commandant of the Machine Gun Corps, he commanded an infantry brigade before being sent to North Russia in September 1918 as Chief of Staff to the allied forces in Archangel. Within a month he was Commander-in-Chief of the Allied Relief Mission.

Knighted and a substantive major general in 1919, Ironisde was appointed head of the military mission to Hungary in 1920 and later commanded British forces in Turkey and North Persia (Iran). Badly injuring his legs in a plane crash in 1921, the re-setting operation necessitated him losing an inch in height. Still a full six feet, four inches tall, he was known inevitably as 'Tiny'. Commandant of the Staff College, Camberley, 1922–1926, he commanded 2nd Division at Aldershot 1926–1928. Between 1928 and 1931 he commanded the Meerut District in India and, promoted lieutenant general in 1931, spent some months on half-pay before assuming the appointment of Lieutenant of the Tower of London. Returning to India in 1933, he was QMG for the next three years and, promoted general, he returned to England to take up the post of GOC-in-C Eastern Command. In 1938 he was appointed Governor and C-in-C Gibraltar, a position which, but for the advent of war, would have taken him to retirement.

Told by Gort (then CIGS) that, in the event of war, he would be appointed to command the field force in France, he was recalled to England in May 1939 and made Inspector General of Overseas Forces. Travelling to Warsaw to assess the fighting qualities of the Polish Army, he reported that the military effort was 'prodigious' and that 'the Poles [were] strong enough to resist' a German invasion' (Mcleod & Kelly, 1962, 81–2). Back in England he assembled a small staff and, on the assumption that he was C-in-C designate of the BEF, awaited instructions. He was not alone in being surprised to learn that Gort, not he, was to command the field force, while he was to be the new CIGS.

As he was, by his own account 'not suited in temperament' for the post (DNB), accounts of Ironside's nine-month spell as CIGS are generally negative. Reputed to be something of a linguist, but also said to be incomprehensible in any language, he had a reputation as an intriguer. Said to be 'not liked in the Army' (Minney, 1991, 230) and 'complacent and optimistic' (Smart, 2003, 61), his numerous gaffes were 'gleefully recorded' by Pownall in his diary (Bond in Keegan (ed.), 1991, 21). Some contemporaries found him 'an engaging person-ality' (Marshall-Cornwall, 1984, 129), and 'amusing and stimulating' (Kennedy, 1957, 22), but the overall verdict on Ironside as CIGS is that he reduced the War Office organization to a state of chaos and so distracted himself with 'sideshows' that he starved the BEF of the resources necessary to play an effective role in the forthcoming campaign in France and Flanders.

These are harsh judgements. Overgrown bull-in-a-china-shop Ironside may have been, but the War Office's systems should have been robust enough to sustain the impact of one man. What is more, he did not starve the BEF of resources. As CIGS his responsibilities were wider than maintaining the field force in France and he was probably correct in siphoning what resources he could towards Egypt. Strategically no more wrong than anybody else on the allied side during the months of the phoney war, it was his political relationships that led to his downfall. At the start of the war he had enjoyed the support of Churchill. By the time Churchill became prime minister he had forfeited that support. Both men had sought to extend the war to Scandinavia in the winter of 1939–40, though neither had been especially successful in persuading their political and military colleagues to accept their proposals. Churchill thought 'big' about Scandinavia, though it has to be said that Ironside thought bigger still. Moreover, alone among the chiefs of staff, he was fully prepared to confront Churchill in argument. In temperament he was unsuited to assist an incoming prime minister as forceful and outspoken as himself, especially one whose powers as 'Minister of Defence' were so loosely defined.

Having made way for Dill in the newly-created post of Vice-CIGS in April 1940, Ironside did not complain when Dill replaced him as CIGS at the end of May. No more responsible than Churchill for military setbacks in Norway, he was made to bear the blame. Appointed C-in-C Home Forces, he spent less than two months in that post before retiring from the army in July 1940. Promoted field marshal, he withdrew 'in silence and dignity' (DNB) to tend the garden of his house in Norfolk. Raised to the peerage in 1941, he was sometime President of the South African Veterans Association and the author of two entertaining books on his Russian and East European experiences. Unconventional soldier and interesting man to the end of his days, Ironside was the supposed model for John Buchan's Richard Hannay character. For all that the verdict of the war's winners casts his reputation in a dull light, 'Tiny' was as imposing for his imag-ination and forcefulness as he was in his physique.

IRWIN, Lieutenant General Noel Mackintosh Stuart
(1892–1972), CB, DSO (two bars), MC
Born in India and educated at Marlborough and RMC, Sandhurst, Irwin was commissioned in the Essex Regiment in 1912. His First War service was in France. Mentioned five times in despatches and awarded the MC, he commanded a series of infantry battalions in 1918 and was admitted to the DSO (with bars).

Married in 1918 and a temporary colonel in 1919, Irwin, a keen sportsman, attended the Staff College, Camberley, 1924–1925. On the staff of the Rhine Army 1926–1927, he commanded a battalion of the Border Regiment in India 1929–1933. An instructor at Sandhurst 1933–1935, he attended the Imperial Defence College in 1936. A staff officer with British forces in North China 1937–1938, he commanded 6th Infantry Brigade in 1939.

In France with the BEF, Irwin, as senior brigadier in 2nd Division, assumed command when the GOC, Loyd, was taken ill during the retreat to Dunkirk in May 1940. Placed in charge of land forces for the Dakar expedition in August 1940, he played his part in the 'unavoidable misfortunes' (Hinsley, 1979, 158) that plagued the attempt to win the port over to de Gaulle's Free French cause. Appointed CB and with his rank of major general confirmed, he was appointed to command 38th (Welsh) Division that October. A lieutenant general in 1942 and made commander of XI Corps, he showed himself an 'outspoken character' (French, 2000, 193) by clashing with colleagues. Sent to India and made commander of VI Indian Corps, his 'egocentric and dictatorial temperament' notwithstanding (Allen, 2000, 94), he was appointed by Wavell to command the Eastern Army in Burma. In charge of the ill-fated Arakan offensive 1942–1943, he ran his subordinates very hard; sacking one divisional commander, Lloyd, and signalling to Slim that he was recommending his removal from command of XV Corps. Hearing, however, that he was to be replaced by Giffard as GOC Eastern Army, he was 'man enough' to signal to Slim: 'You're not sacked, I am' (Hickey, 1998, 79).

Distinctly 'unhappy about his fate' (Danchev & Todman, 2001, 510) and believing 'a long history of dysentery' had dogged his career (Mountbatten, C1 35/5), Irwin returned to England. Known for his 'powerful intellect and aggressive personality' (Lewin, 1999, 123), he remained unemployed for the rest of the war. He was GOC North Africa from 1946 until his retirement from the army in 1948. For fifteen years a farmer in Kenya, he decided after his wife's death to return to England and settle in Somerset. He may not have been lonely, but there were no decorations or honorary colonelcies to stir the memory. What shaped his reputation was less the failures of Dakar and the Arakan against his name than the memory of his clashes with Slim in Burma. He was probably correct in his critical appraisal of the Indian Army's fighting capabilities. But the fact that Slim saw him off and then went on to create victory from defeat consigned Irwin's name to the list of failures. He had been an energetic and intelligent soldier, but he was never lucky.

IRWIN, Major General Stephen Fenemore *(1895–1964), CB, CBE*
Of military family and educated at Tiffins, Kingston, Irwin volunteered for service with the London Irish Rifles in 1914. His First War service was in France, where he was commissioned in the East Surrey Regiment in 1915.

Transferring to the 1st Punjab Regiment (Indian Army) in 1918, Irwin married in 1921 and attended the Staff College, Camberley, 1927–1928. A staff officer at AHQ, India, 1932–1935, he was Chief Staff Officer, Eastern Command, India, 1940–1941.

A brigade commander in India 1941–1942, 'Steve' Irwin was appointed BGS to the newly-created XIV Army in 1943 and was thus Slim's right-hand man during the re-conquest of Burma. Slim wrote warmly of his 'loyalty, brilliance and imperturbable common sense' (Slim, 1999, 387). Made CBE and promoted major general, he made a lecture tour of the US and was Commandant of the Staff College, Quetta, 1945–1946.

Deputy Chief of the General Staff, India, in 1947, Irwin was appointed CB and retired from the army the next year. From 1951 to 1960 he was Assistant Under Secretary in the Civil Defence Department of the Home Office. He lived in Richmond, Surrey.

ISMAY, General Hastings Lionel
1st Baron Ismay of Wormington (1887–1965), KG, CH, GCB, CB, DSO

Born in India and educated at Charterhouse and RMC, Sandhurst, Ismay joined the Indian Army in 1905 and was gazetted into the 21st (Frontier Force) Cavalry in 1907. Seconded to the King's African Rifles in 1914, his First War service was in Somaliland, where he served with the Camel Corps. Distinguishing himself in operations against the 'Mad Mullah', he was admitted to the DSO.

Married in 1921, Ismay attended the Staff College, Quetta, 1921–1922. Serving briefly as Deputy Assistant QMG, AHQ, India, he attended the RAF Staff College, Andover, in 1924. Returning to India as a staff officer at AHQ, he was appointed Assistant Secretary to the Committee of Imperial Defence in London at the end of 1925. By 1930, having acquired 'an exceptional insight into the ways of Whitehall' (DNB), 'Pug' Ismay (he had, it is said, the pushed-in face of a pugilist) became 'wiser in its ways than any servant of the Crown' (Young (ed.), 1973, 586). Appointed CB in 1931, he was Military Secretary to the Viceroy of India, Lord Willingdon, 1931–1933, and served on the staff at the War Office 1933–1936 before returning to the CID, first as Deputy Secretary, then, in 1938, as Secretary.

A major general in 1939, Ismay became Chief of Staff to Churchill when wearing his Minister of Defence hat. He was also Deputy Secretary (military) to the War Cabinet, 1940–1945. In on the Ultra secret, he was Churchill's 'right-hand man and trusted confidant' (Lewin, 1978, 186). As all the papers between the Prime Minister and his service chiefs passed through Ismay's hands, his 'genius' lay in his discretion and in 'minimizing friction within the British military machine' (Boatner, 1996,253).

Promoted general in 1944, Ismay was appointed CH in 1945 and, upon his retirement from the army in 1947, a baron. Chief of Staff to Mountbatten, the last Viceroy of India, in 1947 he found the job 'the most distasteful assignment of his career' (DNB). Made Chairman of the Council of the Festival of Britain in 1948, he became a minister in Churchill's second government in 1951 as Secretary of State for Commonwealth Affairs. Sworn of the Privy Council that year, he was Secretary General of NATO 1952–1956 and Chairman of the North Atlantic Council 1956–1957. Appointed KG that year, he finally retired from public life. In addition to being Chairman of the National Institute for the Blind, Ismay held directorships in a variety of companies. His memoirs, published in 1960, were remarkable for their self-effacing blandness. Feline in his dealings but displaying canine loyalty to his chief, he allowed Churchill to so dominate the narrative that it ends with him saying, with no hint of Jeevesian irony, 'Sir, you were right, as always' (Ismay, 1960, 464).

J

JACOB, Lieutenant General Sir Edward Ian Claud *(1899–1993), GBE, CB*
The son of a field marshal, Jacob was educated at Wellington, RMA, Woolwich, and Cambridge University, where he attended a wartime course for young officers. Commissioned in the Royal Engineers in 1918, he spent the first ten years of his army career on a captain's pay with the Bengal Sappers and Miners.

After service in Waziristan 1922–1923, Jacob married the next year and attended the Staff College, Camberley, 1931–1932. A staff officer at the War Office 1934–1936, he was Brigade Major to the Canal Brigade, Egypt, 1936–1938. Assistant Secretary to the Committee of Imperial Defence in 1938, he was Assistant Secretary to the War Cabinet 1939–1946.

A man of 'tireless industry' who was known as 'Iron Pants' (Colville, 1985, 752), Jacob was one of Ismay's principal 'trusty deputies' (Ismay, 1960, 168) in handling relations between Churchill and the Chiefs of Staff. Accompanying Churchill on several of his foreign trips, it was he who delivered Churchill's August 1942 letter to Auchinleck telling him he had been sacked.

Knighted in 1946, Jacob retired from the army that year and joined the BBC. He was Controller of European Services in 1946, Director of Overseas Services in 1947 and, after a year's leave of absence working for the Ministry of Defence, was Director General of the BBC 1952–1960. One of his achievements in that role, apparently, was to effectively ban Malcolm Muggeridge from broadcasting. Besides holding down numerous directorships, he was a County Councillor of East Suffolk, a JP and DL for the county 1964–1968.

JARDINE, Major General Sir Colin Arthur *(1892–1957), CB, DSO, MC*
The second son of a baronet and educated at Charterhouse and RMA, Woolwich, Jardine was commissioned in the Royal Artillery in 1912. His First War service was in France, where he was thrice wounded, four times mentioned in despatches, awarded the MC and admitted to the DSO.

Married in 1919, Jardine served on the staff of Northern Command, India,

1920–1923. Succeeding his brother to the baronetcy in 1924, he was Brigade Major to 7th Indian Brigade at Razmak 1926–1927 and attended the Staff College, Camberley, 1927–1928. A staff officer at the War Office 1930–1934, he served in various area commands in the years leading up to the Second World War.

Military Secretary to Gort, the C-in-C of the BEF, 1939–1940, Jardine was appointed CB after Dunkirk. Made Deputy Fortress Commander, Gibraltar, in 1942, he again served under Gort. Promoted major general the next year, he was appointed Director of Army Welfare at the War Office and retired from the army in 1945.

Active in charity work in his retirement, Jardine was, at various times, Chairman of the Church Army Board, the Family Welfare Association and a member of the Church of England Assembly. He also took an active interest in the affairs of Toc H. Made DL for Hampshire in 1954, he was a near neighbour to Montgomery before he died on his sixty-fifth birthday.

JENKINS, Major General Frederick Arthur Montague Bertram
(1891–1986), DSO, OBE, MC
A territorial soldier at war's outbreak in 1914, Jenkins was commissioned in the Yorkshire Regiment in 1915. His First War service was in France and Mesopotamia. Awarded the MC, he transferred to the 2nd Punjab Regiment (Indian Army) in 1918.

Jenkins was an instructor at Kitchener College, India, 1929–1932 and, a major in 1934, he commanded his regiment's 2nd battalion in East Africa 1940–1941. Admitted to the DSO in 1941, he commanded 29th Indian Brigade in Palestine and Syria, 1942–1943 and in Italy 1943–1944. He was promoted major general in 1945 and was District Officer, Quetta and Baluchistan District, until his retirement in 1946.

JOHNSON, Major General Dudley Graham *(1884–1975), VC, CB, DSO, MC*
Of military family, educated at Bradfield and commissioned in the South Wales Borderers in 1913, Johnson's initial First War service was in Tsingtau, where he was mentioned in despatches and admitted to the DSO. He later served in Gallipoli and in France, where he had a bar added to his DSO, was awarded the MC and, right at the end of hostilities, was awarded the VC for his part in leading the crossing of the Sambre Canal.

Appointed Chief Instructor at the Small Arms School, Hythe, in 1919, Johnson attended the Staff College, Camberley, 1923–1924 and, a brevet lieutenant colonel in 1924, was Chief Instructor at the Machine Gun School, Netheravon, 1926–1928. A lieutenant colonel in 1928, he commanded the 12th (Secunderabad) Infantry Brigade in India 1933–1936 and was Commandant of the Small Arms School, Netheravon, 1936–1938. Promoted major general, he commanded 4th Division 1938–1940 and was appointed CB in 1939.

With the BEF in France, Johnson proved himself a 'charming, amiable officer . . . capable of evoking great loyalty' (Hamilton, 1982, 321). However, he was relieved of his divisional command after Dunkirk and appointed GOC Aldershot Command. Made Inspector of Infantry in 1941, he had little to do after that post was wound up.

Retired from the army in 1944, Johnson was Colonel of the South Wales Borderers, 1944–1949. Living in Hampshire, he spent the last 25 years of his life a widower.

JOLLY, Lieutenant General Sir Gordon Gray *(d. 1962), KCIE*
The son of a clergyman, Jolly was educated at Watson's College, Edinburgh, and Edinburgh University. A qualified doctor in 1907, he entered the Indian Medical Service the next year. First War service was in East Africa, where, a specialist radiologist, he was mentioned in despatches.

Married in 1920, Jolly was Medical Officer of Health, Delhi, in 1921, and Assistant Director of Public Health, Burma, 1922–1927. Director of Public Health, Burma, 1928–1933, he was Public Health Commissioner for the Government of India 1935–1936. Secretary-General of the National Association for Prevention of Tuberculosis 1936–1937, he was Inspector General of Civil Hospitals, Punjab, 1937–1939.

Promoted major general, Jolly was Director General of the Indian Medical Service from 1939 until his retirement in 1943. Under his stewardship the staff of the IMS quadrupled in numbers. Knighted in 1941, he was Chief Commissioner of the Indian Red Cross War Organization 1943–1946

Retiring to Cape Town in South Africa, Jolly re-married in 1949. He was a Fellow of the Royal Institute of Public Health and of the Royal Numismatic Society.

K

KARSLAKE, Lieutenant General Sir Henry
(1879–1942), KCB, KCSI, CB, CMG, DSO
Educated at Harrow and RMA, Woolwich, Karslake was commissioned in the Royal Artillery in 1898. Admitted to the DSO in 1902 at the end of the South African War, he married in 1905, was an instructor at Sandhurst 1907–1911 and, after attending the Staff College, Camberley, 1912–1913, was a brigade major in 1914. His First War service was in France, where he served mainly as a staff officer.

An acting brigadier general in 1918, Karslake reverted to his substantive rank of colonel in 1919. He served with the Rhine Army and with the Peshawar Brigade on the North-West Frontier. A staff officer at the War Office 1923–1925, he spent the next three years with Southern Command. Brigadier

RA, Western Command, India, 1928–1931, he was Major General RA, AHQ, India, 1931–1933. Commander of Baluchistan District 1933–1935, he was, 'entirely contrary to his own expectations' (Morgan, 1961, 100), promoted lieutenant general and appointed to direct reconstruction work after the Quetta earthquake.

Knighted in 1937, Karslake retired from the army in 1938. Having set up his 'personal establishment' in Hampshire (Karslake, 1979, 52), he was appointed GOC Lines of Communication, BEF, in May 1940. Sent to France, his actions were judged 'somewhat injudicious' and, 'having caused a certain amount of confusion' (Marshall-Cornwall, 1984, 151), he was ordered home by Brooke on 12 June. Taking no further active part in the war, he died in London aged 63.

KEIGHTLEY, General Sir Charles Frederic *(1901–1974), GCB, GBE, DSO*
The son of a clergyman, Keightley was educated at Marlborough and RMC, Sandhurst. Commissioned in the 5th Dragoon Guards in 1921, regimental duties over the next ten years took him to Palestine, Egypt and India.

Excelling at polo and Adjutant of the 5th Inniskilling Dragoon Guards 1930–1933, Keightley married in 1932, attended the Staff College, Camberley, 1935–1936, and was a staff officer serving the Director General of the Territorial Army in 1937. Brigade Major to the Cairo Cavalry Brigade 1937–1938, he was an instructor at the Staff College, Camberley, 1938–1940.

Made Assistant Adjutant and QMG to 1st Armoured Division in May 1940, Keightley served in the brief campaign in France south of the Somme and, 1941–1942, commanded 30th Armoured Brigade with Home Forces. Aged 40 he was promoted major general and put in charge of the RAC training establishment. Appointed to command 6th Armoured Division in May 1942, a formation of 'almost comprehensive battle-virginity' (Blaxland, 1977, 40), he led it throughout the Tunisian campaign. Regarded as 'definitely depressed . . . [and] over-impressed with the tiredness of our troops' (Allfrey Diary, 20.01.43, LHCMA), he nevertheless helped contain a German breakthrough at Kasserine and participated in the capture of Tunis.

Ever the urbane cavalryman, Keightley was appointed GOC 78th Division in December 1943. He was one of the few ex-First Army men to prosper under Montgomery's 8th Army regime in Italy. Admitted to the DSO and promoted lieutenant general, he was appointed to command V Corps in August 1944 by Leese, who predicted he would be 'first-class' (Ryder, 1987, 182). Seeing the Italian campaign through to its end, he was knighted in 1945. Director of Military Training at the War Office 1946–1947 and Military Secretary to the Secretary of State for War in 1948, he succeeded Horrocks as C-in-C BAOR the same year and was C-in-C Far East Land Forces 1951–1953. Appointed C-in-C Middle East Land Forces from 1953–1958, he was C-in-C of the Anglo-French forces that staged their assault on Suez in 1956. Militarily not unsuccessful, the operation ended in political humiliation. He ended his military career as Governor and C-in-C, Gibraltar, 1958–1962.

Colonel of the Inniskilling Dragoons 1947–1957 and Colonel Commandant of the Royal Armoured Corps (Cavalry Wing) 1958–1968, Keightley was DL for Dorset in 1970. One of his sons became a professional soldier and also attained general officer's rank.

KEMP, Major General Geoffrey Chicheley *(1890–1976), CB, MC*
Of military family and educated privately and at RMA, Woolwich, Kemp was commissioned in the Royal Field Artillery in 1910. A captain in 1916, his First War service was in France, where he was twice wounded, mentioned in despatches and awarded the MC.

Spending the next ten years on a captain's pay, Kemp married in 1927 and, promoted major, was an instructor at the School of Artillery, Larkhill, 1929–1932. A colonel in 1938, he briefly commanded 38th Anti-Aircraft Group and was Commandant of the School of Artillery 1938–1939.

Appointed to command the Orkney and Shetland Defences in 1939, Kemp was promoted major general in 1941 and appointed CB in 1942. From 1943 his job was to preside over various selection boards in Britain and the Middle East. A keen golfer, he retired from the army in 1946, settled in North Berwick and was Colonel Commandant of the Royal Artillery in 1948. The father of three daughters, he spent the last fifteen years of his life a widower.

KENNEDY, Major General Sir John Noble
(1893–1970), GCMG, KCVO, KBE, CB, MC
The eldest son of a clergyman, Kennedy was educated at Stranraer and RMA, Woolwich. Entering the Royal Navy in 1911, he applied for a transfer and was commissioned in the Royal Garrison Artillery in 1915. His First War service was in France, where he was wounded, mentioned in despatches and awarded the MC.

Mentioned in despatches during service with the British Military Mission in South Russia 1919–1920, Kennedy also served with the Allied Police Commission in Constantinople. A student at the Staff College, Casmberley, 1921–1922, he was a staff officer at the War Office 1923–1924 and was Brigade Major, RA, Southern Command, 1925–1926. Married that year, he spent the next four years on the staff at the War Office. On the directing staff at Camberley 1931–1934, he returned to staff duties at the War Office for the next two years. A major in 1936 and a colonel in 1938, he was appointed Deputy Director of Military Operations in 1938 before he was able to complete the course at the Imperial Defence College.

Director of Plans in 1939 and earmarked for duties in Scandinavia in early 1940, Kennedy, annoyed at the constant waiting, found himself 'better employed' digging [his] garden' (Kennedy, 1957, 50). Hospitalized after a road accident, he was briefly CRA with 52nd Division in France in June 1940. Appointed BGS Northern Ireland District in 1940, he was Director of Operations and Plans at the War Office 1940–1943. Re-married after the death of his first wife, he was Assistant CIGS (Operations and Intelligence)

1943–1945, in which role he spent much time attending high-level conferences and bird-watching with Brooke. He retired from the army in 1946.

Knighted in 1945, Kennedy was Governor of Southern Rhodesia (Zimbabwe) 1946–1954. Though in indifferent health himself, 'his wife's experience', apparently, 'made her particularly suitable' for the role (Richardson, 1987, 190). Sometime Chairman of the Central African Council and Defence Committee, he was Colonel Commandant of the Royal Artillery 1948–1958. His memoirs, *The Business of War* (1957), are among the most readable and informative of the post-war set. Chairman of the Rosehill Arts Trust, Whitehaven, 1959–1970, he wrote a number of *Times* obituaries and, living near Edinburgh, outlived his second wife by a year.

KERR, Major General Sir Harold Reginald *(1897–1974), KBE, CB, MC*
Educated at Bedford School and RMC, Sandhurst, Kerr was commissioned in the Army Service Corps in 1914. His First War service was in France, where he was awarded the MC in 1918.

Serving on the staff of the Rhine Army of Occupation 1919–1920, Kerr married in 1921 and was an instructor at RMC, Sandhurst 1924–1928. Adjutant to the RASC Training College 1929–1930, he attended the Staff College, Camberley, 1931–1932. A staff officer in the Sudan in 1934, he served on the staff of 3rd Division 1935–1936 and was Chief Instructor at the RASC Training Centre 1937–1939.

An instructor at Camberley 1939–1940, Kerr was appointed QMG, British Army Staff, Washington, in June 1941. Major General i/c Administration, Eastern Command, 1942–1943, he was Director of Supplies and Transport at the War Office 1943–1946.

Appointed CB in 1945 and knighted in 1946, Kerr was Major General i/c Administration, Far East Land Forces, 1946–1948. He retired from the army in 1949, and was Divisional Manager (Midlands) British Road Services 1949–1954. Colonel Commandant of the RASC 1949–1959, he was Chairman and General Manager, British Waterways, 1955–1962. Listing his hobby as four-in-hand driving, he lived in retirement in Lyme Regis.

KEY, Major General Berthold Wells *(1895–1986), CB, DSO, MC*
The son of a doctor, Key was educated at Dulwich College. Gazetted into the Indian Army in 1914, he joined the 45th Rattray Sikh Regiment. First War service was in India and Mesopotamia, where he was wounded and awarded the MC.

Married in 1917, Key served in Afghanistan in 1919, was mentioned in despatches during operations on the North-West Frontier in 1930 and attended the Staff College, Quetta, 1931–1932. Admitted to the DSO in 1937 for service in the Waziristan campaign, he was a lieutenant colonel commanding a battalion of the Sikh Regiment in 1939.

Commanding 8th Indian Brigade 1940–1941, 'Billy' Key served in Malaya. Retreating from the Kota Bharu beachhead in December 1941, he was judged

177

'the outstanding brigadier of the campaign to date' (Warren, 2002, 115), and in January 1942 was placed in command of the badly mauled 11th Indian Division. Advising Percival to capitulate, while 'the Japanese soldiers were still under the control of their officers' (Kinvig, 1996, 215), he was taken prisoner in Singapore in February 1942. Held first in Changi gaol and then on Formosa, to add to the 'unbelievable miseries' he suffered, he learned, while still in captivity, that his only son, an officer with the Sikh Regiment, had been killed in action in Italy.

Made ADC to the King in 1945, Key commanded Rawalpindi District in 1946 and Lahore District in 1947. Retiring from the army in 1947, he was appointed CB and was Colonel of the Sikh Regiment 1947–1962. A widower for 35 years, he won the Generals' Cup at golf in his seventies and lived well into his nineties near the golf course at Sandwich.

KING, Lieutenant General Sir Charles John Stuart *(1890–1967), KBE, CB*
Educated at Felsted and RMA, Woolwich, King was commissioned in the Royal Engineers in 1910. A captain in 1916, his First War service was in India where he was mentioned in despatches during operations against the Mohmands.

Appointed OBE after serving in Afghanistan in 1919, King married in 1920. Chief Instructor in Military Engineering at Woolwich 1929–1933, he served on the staff at AHQ, India, for the next five years. Appointed CB in 1939, he was Deputy Engineer-in-Chief of the BEF in France 1939–1940 and Chief Engineer, Home Forces, in 1940. Engineer-in-Chief at the War Office 1941–1944 and, promoted lieutenant general, he served on a special mission to promote the troops' welfare in India and South-East Asia Command from 1944 until his retirement from the army in 1946.

Knighted in 1945 and the father of three sons, King was Chairman of Festival Gardens Ltd., for the Festival of Britain in 1951. Living in Suffolk, he was Colonel Commandant of the Royal Engineers 1946–1956.

KIRBY, Major General Stanley Woodburn
(1895–1968), CB, CMG, CIE, OBE, MC (bar)
Educated at Charterhouse, Kirby was commissioned in the Royal Engineers in 1914. His First War service was in France and Macedonia, where, a captain in 1917, he was mentioned in despatches and awarded the MC.

An instructor at the Survey School of Military Engineering 1920–1923, Kirby was stationed in Singapore 1923–1926. Married in 1924 and appointed OBE in 1927, he attended the Staff College, Camberley, 1927–1928. A staff officer at the War Office 1931–1935, he attended the Imperial Defence College in 1936 and, promoted colonel, was Assistant Master General of the Ordnance 1937–1940.

Deputy Master General of the Ordnance, GHQ India, 1940–1941, Kirby was Director of Staff Duties, India, 1941–1942. Deputy Chief of the General Staff, India, 1942–1943, he was appointed CB and returned to Britain to take up the post of Director of Civil Affairs at the War Office. Deputy Chief of Staff for the Control Commission of Germany in 1945, he retired from the army in 1947.

One of a team writing the official history of the war against Japan (four volumes over a twelve-year period), Kirby was appropriately honoured. Re-married in 1955, he lived in Gloucestershire.

KIRKMAN, General Sir Sidney Chevalier *(1895–1982), GCB, KBE, MC*
Born in Bedford and educated at Bedford School and RMA, Woolwich, Kirkman was commissioned in the Royal Artillery in 1915. His First War service was in France, where he was twice wounded and mentioned in despatches, and in Italy, where he was awarded the MC in 1918.

A captain throughout the 1920s, Kirkman served in Egypt, Palestine, Malta and India. A student at the Staff College, Camberley, 1931–1932, he married in 1932 and served in Aldershot Command 1933–1935. In 1939, after 24 years of service in the army, he had risen no higher than major in rank.

Commanding a regiment of medium artillery 1940–1941, 'Kirkie' Kirkman was CRA 56th Division with Home Forces 1941. Appointed OBE, he was CRA XII Corps, South Eastern Command, 1941–1942. Having made a favourable impression on Montgomery, who described him as the 'best artilleryman in the British Army' (Montgomery, 1958, 103), his future was assured in the sense that 'Bernard would take . . . Kirkman with him wherever he went' (Hamilton, 1982, 485). Appointed Brigadier RA, 8th Army, 1942, he commanded the artillery at El Alamein and, appointed CBE, was made Brigadier RA, 18 Army Group, in Tunisia in 1943. Promoted major general, he was GOC 50th (Northumbrian) Division from April 1943 to January 1944, and, appointed CB, was commander of XIII Corps in Italy in 1944. A 'studious and humane man' (Blaxland, 1979, 23), he had some successes against German forces retreating north of Rome, but, assailed by arthritis, was invalided home in March 1945.

Knighted in 1945 and made GOC Southern Command, Kirkman was appointed to command I Corps of the BLA in Germany before the year was out. A member of the Army Council 1945–1950, he was Deputy CIGS 1945–1947. His last appointment before retiring from the army in 1950 was that of Quartermaster General.

Special Financial Representative to Germany, 1951–1952, Kirkman was Colonel Commandant of the Royal Artillery 1947–1957. Director General of Civil Defence 1954–1960, he was Chairman of the Fire Brigades Advisory Council for England and Wales 1957–1960. Much honoured by foreign governments, he lived in Hampshire.

L

LAMMIE, Major General George *(1891–1946), CBE, MC*
Born in Glasgow and educated at George Watson's College, Edinburgh, Lammie was gazetted from the London Scottish (Territorial Army) to the Royal Scots in 1914. His First War service was in France, where he was mentioned in despatches and awarded the MC.

Married in 1918, Lammie attended the Staff College, Camberley, 1924–1925, and transferred to the Seaforth Highlanders in 1930. Mentioned in despatches for his part in operations in Palestine 1936–1937, he served on the staff at the War Office 1938–1939.

A staff officer with Home Forces in 1940 and appointed to command 147th Infantry Brigade 1940–1941, Lammie endured garrison duties in Iceland for a year. Briefly Deputy Adjutant and QMG, Scottish Command, in 1941, he was Director of Quartering at the War Office 1941–1944. Commander of 3 District, Italy, Central Mediterranean Force, 1944–1945, he retired from the army in 1945.

LAMPLUGH, Major General Stephen *(1900–1983), CB, CBE*
Born in Yorkshire and educated at St Albans and RMA, Woolwich, Lamplugh was commissioned in the Royal Engineers in 1919. He served in the Near East 1922–1923, and on the North-West Frontier in 1930. After attending the Staff College, Camberley, 1935–1936, he was a staff captain with the Anti-Aircraft Corps 1937–1938. Married in 1937, he was Brigade Major to 2nd Anti-Aircraft Brigade 1938–1939.

Mentioned in despatches while serving in France with the BEF 1939–1940 and a brigadier in 1940, Lamplugh was BGS Anti-Aircraft Command 1940–1943. Promoted major general in 1942 and made CBE in 1943, he was Commander of the Rhine District, BAOR, 1952–1955. He retired from the army and became Chairman of the Joint War Office Treasury Committee in 1955. Director of Civil Defence, Northern Region, 1955–1964, he lived near Amesbury in Wiltshire.

LANE, Major General Sir Charles Reginald Cambridge
(1890–1964), KCIE, CB, CBE, MC
Born in Dorset and educated at Bradfield and RMC, Sandhurst, Lane was

commissioned on the unattached list in 1910 and joined the 19th Lancers (Fane's Horse), Indian Army, the following year. His First War service was in France, Egypt and Palestine. Twice mentioned in despatches, he was awarded the MC in 1917.

Married in 1915, Lane served on in Syria in 1919 and attended the Staff College, Camberley, 1922–1923. He held various staff appointments in India over the next ten years. A brevet lieutenant colonel in 1932, he commanded the 20th Lancers in India 1936–1938.

A brigadier in 1940, Lane commanded Bombay area. Major General i/c Administration, Southern Army, India, in 1941, he took part in operations in Iraq to depose the Raschid Ali regime. Made Deputy Adjutant and QMG of Tenth Army in Iraq in 1942 because 'he had wide administrative experience' (Wilson, 1948, 137), he commanded 303 L of C Area in India in 1943. Deputy Principal Administrative Officer, HQ Supreme Allied Commander South-East Asia, 1943–1944, he was the Representative in India of the SACSEA, 1944–1946.

Knighted in 1946 and retired from the army in 1947, Lane re-married in 1948 and was a Principal Regional Officer, Ministry of Health, 1947–1957.

LAURIE, Major General Sir John Emilius, 6th Bt *(1892–1983), CBE, DSO*
Educated at Eton and RMC, Sandhurst, and commissioned in the Seaforth Highlanders in 1912, Laurie's First War service was in France. Five times mentioned in despatches and admitted to the DSO in 1916 (bar 1918), he commanded a battalion at war's end.

Married in 1922, regimental duties took Laurie to Egypt and India. Commanding the 2nd Battalion Seaforth Highlanders 1934–1938, he succeeded to the baronetcy in 1936. Mentioned in despatches while commanding British troops in the Tientsin area of China 1939–1940, he was recalled to England to assume command of 157th Infantry Brigade.

Sent to France with the 52nd (Lowland) Division in June 1940, Laurie was appointed CBE on his return and made GOC of the Division in March 1941. Made Commandant of the Combined Operations Training Centre at Inveraray in 1942, he retired from the army in 1945.

A keen sportsman, Laurie was a member of the MCC. He lived in Wiltshire.

LAURIE, Major General Rufus Henry *(1892–1961), CB, CBE*
Educated at Dover College, Laurie joined the Royal Irish Rifles in 1912. A captain in 1916, the year he married, his First War service was in Gallipoli and France.

A staff officer with the Rhine Army 1918–1919, Laurie was an instructor at RMC, Sandhurst, 1919–1922. After attending the Staff College, Camberley, 1924–1925, he was a staff officer with 2nd Division in 1926 before being posted to serve on the staff with the Shanghai Defence Force in 1927. On the staff of Southern Command 1928–1929, he commanded the 1st Battalion Royal Ulster Rifles in 1930. A Deputy Assistant QMG at the War Office 1932–1933, he spent the next two years on the staff. Appointed to command the 2nd Battalion Royal Ulster Rifles in 1936, he was mentioned in despatches while serving in Palestine. Promoted colonel and appointed Assistant Adjutant and QMG 3rd Division in 1938, he travelled to France the next year as part of the BEF.

Appointed CBE for his part in the campaign in France and Flanders, Laurie was Assistant Adjutant and QMG, III Corps, 1940–1941. Major General i/c Administration, South Eastern Command, 1941–1942, he served with Home Forces 1942–1943, was appointed CB and made Major General i/c Administration, 21st Army Group in 1943. GOC Salisbury Plain District in 1944, he retired from the army in 1947.

LAWSON, Major General Frederick, 4th Baron Burnham
(1890–1963), CB, DSO, MC, TD
Educated at Eton and Oxford, where he played polo for the university and obtained a third-class degree, Lawson was commissioned in the Royal Buckinghamshire Hussars in 1914. His First War service was in Gallipoli and Palestine, where he was three times mentioned in despatches, awarded the MC and admitted to the DSO.

Married in 1920, Lawson returned to his press career with the *Daily Telegraph*. Colonel of the merged Berkshire and Buckinghamshire Yeomanry, he helped them convert to artillery and was made – unusually for a Territorial Army Officer – CRA to the 48th (South Midland) Division in 1938. In France with the BEF, he was appointed CB for his part in the retreat to Dunkirk. Appointed to command the newly-formed Yorkshire Division in 1941, he was Director of Public Relations at the War Office and Military Adviser to the Ministry of Information 1942–1945.

Succeeding his father in 1943, he was, as Lord Burnham, Managing Director of the *Daily Telegraph* 1945–1961. A successful racehorse owner and freemason, he was DL for Buckinghamshire in 1962.

LAYCOCK, Major General Sir Robert Edward
(1907–1968), KCMG, CB, DSO
Of military family and born in London, Laycock was educated at Eton and RMC, Sandhurst. Commissioned in the Royal Horse Guards in 1927, his duties were light enough to permit him to develop his scientific interests and sail around the world on a Finnish Windjammer.

Married in 1935 and a staff officer with the BEF's Chemical Warfare unit in France 1939–1940, Laycock was attending the Staff College, Camberley, at the time of Dunkirk. Volunteering for the Special Services Brigade in the summer of 1940, he was promoted lieutenant colonel and posted to the Middle East. Combining 'great qualities of leadership' with 'charm, arrogance and aristocratic self-assurance' (Hastings, 1995, 413), he found himself leading the first Commando raids in that theatre. In action in Libya his 'Layforce' suffered heavy casualties in 1941 when acting as the rearguard in Crete. With 'Layforce' broken up, 'Lucky' Laycock led another Commando group in an unsuccessful attempt to assassinate Rommel. Spending two months behind German lines, he was recalled to England to train Commando troops, and saw further action in Sicily and Salerno.

Admitted to the DSO, Laycock was promoted major general in 1943 and succeeded Mountbatten as Chief of Combined Operations. He held that post until 1947, having stood, unsuccessfully, as a Conservative candidate in the 1945 general election. Appointed CB, he retired from the army in 1947. Chairman of Windsor Group Hospital Management Committee 1953–1954, he was High Sheriff of Nottinghamshire in 1954. Knighted in 1954, he was Governor and C-in-C, Malta, 1954–1959, and a member of the Sheffield Regional Hospital Board 1960–1963.

A keen horseman and sailor and much decorated by foreign governments, Laycock was Colonel Commandant of the SAS Regiment 1962–1968 and of the Sherwood Rangers Yeomanry over the same period. Evelyn Waugh, who had been Intelligence Officer with 'Layforce' on Crete, dedicated the second volume of his war trilogy *Officers and Gentlemen* to him. This may have been ironic. Whatever, he 'that every man in arms should wish to be' died of a heart attack aged 60.

LEE, Major General Alec Wilfred *(1896–1973)*, CB, MC
Educated at Clifton and commissioned in the South Staffordshire Regiment in 1914, Lee's First War service was in France and Italy. He was six times mentioned in despatches and awarded the MC in 1915.

A captain in 1923, Lee graduated from the Staff College, Quetta, in 1927 and over the next four years served on the directing staff at Camberley. Transferring to the Royal Irish Fusiliers in 1937, he was promoted colonel in 1939, the year of his wife's death.

Serving on the staff of GHQ with the BEF, Lee was mentioned in despatches for his part in the campaign in France and Flanders. A brigadier, he served on the staff of HQ Middle East 1942–1943, and was, from 1944–1947, Deputy Commander of the British Army Staff, Washington.

Retired in 1947, Lee re-married that year. Colonel Commandant of the South Stafford Regiment 1954–1959 (and the Staffordshire Regiment 1959–1961), he was a keen sportsman who wrote pieces for *Encyclopaedia Britannica*. He married for a third time in 1970.

LEESE, Lieutenant General Sir Oliver William Hargreaves
3rd Bt (1894–1978), KCB, CBE, DSO
Born in London, the eldest son of a baronet, Leese was educated at Eton, where he excelled at games. Commissioned in the Coldstream Guards in August 1914, his First War service was in France. Wounded three times and twice mentioned in despatches, he was admitted to the DSO in 1916.

Unsure whether to continue in the army, it was a spell as Adjutant to the Eton OTC between 1920 and 1922 that decided Leese to take soldiering seriously. A student at the Staff College, Camberley, 1927–1928, he was a major in 1929 and

Deputy Assistant Adjutant General (London District) 1931–1933. Married in 1933, he served on the staff at the War Office 1934–1936 and assumed command of the 1st Battalion Coldstream Guards in October that year. Succeeding to his father's title in 1937, he was Chief Instructor at the Staff College, Quetta, 1938–1940.

Returning from India in the spring of 1940, Leese was placed in command of the newly-formed 32nd Brigade. Told to prepare for operations in Norway, he was sent instead to the BEF's GHQ in France. There, as Deputy CGS, his peaceful enjoyment of the mess's 'very good champagne and an excellent claret' (Ryder, 1987, 65) was short-lived.

Recalled as a model of cool, unruffled fortitude during the retreat to Dunkirk, it was probably Leese who, more than anyone, imposed some order on the BEF's withdrawal and evacuation. A tall, commanding figure who, though inclined to fits of temper, usually boomed with confidence, he existed, it is said, on a diet of caviar and champagne. Accompanying Gort, the C-in-C, back to London, dressed in a duffel coat over a pair of borrowed pyjamas, he was appointed CB and made commander of 29th Independent Brigade.

A trainer of troops over the next two years, Leese was promoted major general in 1941. He commanded, in the space of that year, the West Sussex County Division and the 15th (Scottish) Division before becoming GOC of the newly-formed Guards Armoured Division. Rejoicing at receiving 'such a marvellous command . . . a fascinating one to fashion, mould and train' (Ryder, 1987, 89), he registered his personality on subordinates as a fast-driving, hard-living, extrovert guardsman who, dressing with studied unconventionality, was 'mainly charming . . . especially to the young' (Fraser, 2002, 170).

Montgomery, who had taught Leese at the Staff College days and been impressed by his 'first-class' performance at Dunkirk (Hamilton, 1982, 388), summoned him to Egypt in September 1942. There, promoted lieutenant general, he assumed command of XXX Corps just as the German assault on the Alam Halfa position began. At Alamein his determination to maintain the momentum of the attack established his reputation as Montgomery's favourite corps commander. Though asked for by Alexander to replace Anderson as commander of First Army in Tunisia, Montgomery's insistence that Leese 'could not be spared' (Blaxland, 1977, 209) made him ever after an 8th Army man.

For his part Leese never bit the hand of his benefactor and 'greatest soldier of our age' (Ryder, 1987, 136). Always he did his master's bidding. Able to blame others for the setbacks XXX Corps suffered during the assault on the Mareth Line in March 1943, he adopted many of Montgomery's turns of phrase and mannerisms. Father Christmas-like, he distributed cigarettes to the troops and was a willing 'warm-up speaker' when the army commander gave his famous addresses. However, Leese was a better diplomat than Montgomery, being able to establish cordial relations with American field commanders.

Leading XXX Corps during operations in Sicily and southern Italy, Leese, taking an overdue spell of leave, hoped, probably, that he would be assigned to Montgomery's 21st Army Group, then assembling for the future cross-channel invasion of France. Instead, in December 1943 he learned that he was to be sent back to Italy as commander of 8th Army.

Few allied commanders emerged from the Italian campaign with reputations enhanced and Leese was no exception. Though it was hardly his fault to find himself in a theatre of war that, in strategic terms, had become something of a sideshow, his 'too methodical and deliberate' approach to operations won him few plaudits (Nicolson, 1986, 281). Being decorated by Polish generals and knighted in the field by George VI were forms of dignified recognition. Meanwhile the efficient parts of the supreme direction of the war had reached less positive conclusions. 'Leese', Brooke noted, was 'certainly not outstanding as a commander' (Danchev & Todman, 200, 582).

The obvious solution, transfer to a different theatre, was effected in October 1944. Mountbatten, the Supreme Commander South-East Asia, had been trying for some time to find a replacement for Giffard as land forces commander. When Leese's name came up, Mountbatten wrote delightedly to Montgomery, saying 'how grand' it was ' to get your principal disciple to carry on your doctrine' (Ziegler, 1985, 286). Thus, in tandem with another reject from the European theatre, 'Boy' Browning of Arnhem notoriety, Leese duly arrived in India to mastermind the re-conquest of Burma. He brought with him some thirty officers from 8th Army.

This was a mistake. Soldiers who had spent three years fighting the Japanese tended to resent this 'silk handkerchief-waving guardsman' thrusting '8th Army ways down their throats' (Slim, 1999, 385), and for all that Leese may have been right in thinking Slim had a chip on his shoulder, he failed to realize that XIV Army, like his own beloved 8th Army, had developed firm tribal loyalties. Equally, his impression of Mountbatten as 'a vain and dangerous man' (Hickey, 1988, 231) bode ill for future relations. Though sincere and vigorous in his 'Rangoon before the Monsoon' urgings, there was little constructive for Leese to do in the congested South-East Asia command set-up and what he did do was seen as interfering.

After the capture of Rangoon in April 1945 Leese, in an obscure series of manoeuvres, pushed for his friend Christison to become head of XIV Army, while the 'tired . . . continually belly-aching Slim' (Ryder, 1987, 227) would assume command of the newly-constituted Twelfth Army and mop up in Burma. He thought he had Mountbatten's approval for these changes, as well as Slim's agreement. When he found he had neither, and that Slim's XIV Army staff were in a state of near mutiny, Mountbatten back-tracked and Brooke, in London, had no hesitation in recommending Leese's dismissal.

With his career ruined and having, as he put it, 'carried the can for Dickie' (Hickey, 1988, 230), Leese returned to England. Appointed GOC Eastern Command, he retired from the army in 1946. Determined 'never to look back' (DNB), he became a successful horticulturalist and prominent figure in his adopted Shropshire. Honorary Colonel of the Shropshire Yeomanry 1947–1962, he was a JP and High Sheriff of the county in 1958. President of Warwickshire Cricket Club 1959–1975, he was President of the MCC

1965–1966. He was also Chairman of the Old Etonian Association 1964–1973. A widower for the last fourteen years of his life, he remained, although in declining health, much visited and outwardly cheerful to the end.

LE FANU, Major General Roland *(1888–1957), DSO, MC*
Educated in Germany before being apprenticed to a Glasgow engineering firm, Le Fanu followed the family tradition by joining the navy. Disliking that service, his father bought his discharge, he joined the Royal Irish Fusiliers and was commissioned in the Leicestershire Regiment in 1908. Regimental duties took him to India and his First War service was in France, where he was awarded the MC and admitted to the DSO.

After a number of staff appointments in India, Le Fanu attended the Staff College, Camberley, 1925–1926, and the Naval Staff College, Greenwich, 1931–1932. From 1935 to the outbreak of war he served on the staff at the War Office. Promoted major general and made GOC 15th (Scottish) Division in 1939, his career juddered to a halt in August 1940. Brooke, then C-in-C Home Forces, inspected the division and 'did not think much' of its commander (Danchev & Todman, 2001,97).

Retired before the end of 1940, Le Fanu settled in St Andrews. He was sometime JP for Fifeshire.

LE FLEMING, Major General Roger Eustace *(1895–1962), CB, OBE, MC*
Educated at Tonbridge School and RMC, Sandhurst, Le Fleming was commissioned on the unattached list in 1914 and, after brief service with the 3rd Battalion East Surrey Regiment in France, was gazetted into the 4th Bombay Grenadiers (Indian Army) in 1915. His First War service was on the North-West Frontier. Twice wounded and thrice mentioned in despatches, he was awarded the MC in 1918.

An instructor at the Indian Military Academy, Dehra Dun, 1932–1935 and an instructor at the Senior Officers' School, Belgaum, in 1936–1937, Le Fleming commanded the 2nd Bombay Grenadiers in 1938. He commanded a brigade in 1941 and, promoted major general, was District Officer commanding Waziristan District 1944–1948. He retired from the army in 1948 and settled in Sussex.

LEJEUNE, Major General Francis St David Benwell *(1899–1984), CB, CBE*
Educated at Bedford School and RMA, Woolwich, Lejeune was commissioned in the Royal Artillery in 1917. Mentioned in despatches during his First War service in France, he was seconded to the RAF in 1920, for service on operations in Somaliland and Iraq.

Married in 1927, Lejeune was a staff captain at the War Office in 1929 and, after serving as Assistant Military Attaché at the Washington Embassy 1932–1933, attended the Staff College, Camberley, 1934–1935. On special duties in Spain 1938–1939, he was a colonel at war's outbreak in 1939.

Attached to the British Military Mission to Greece 1940–1941, Lejeune later saw service in North Africa and Italy. Appointed CB in 1944, he served on the Staff of South-East Asia Command 1944–1945. Director of Technical Training at the War Office in 1946, he was President of the Ordnance Board in 1947.

Retired from the army in 1949, Lejeune, the father of two children, served on the International Staff at NATO HQ 1952–1962.

LENTAIGNE, Major General Walter David Alexander
(1899–1955), CB, CBE, DSO

The son of a judge, born in Burma and educated at the Oratory School, Birmingham, Lentaigne was gazetted into the 4th Gurkha Rifles in 1918. Peacetime soldiering consisted of long periods of active service on the North-West Frontier. Mentioned in despatches for service during operations in Waziristan in 1924, and again in 1927, he married in 1928, attended the Staff College, Camberley, 1935–1936, and was Deputy Assistant QMG, GHQ India, 1938–1941.

Commander of the 1st Battalion, 4th Gurkhas, in 1942, 'Joe' Lentaigne, though of 'somewhat donnish appearance' (Hickey, 1998, 120) was admitted to the DSO for the part he played in the retreat from Burma (during which he was said to have killed a Japanese officer with his own sword). A 'great talker, voluble and fond of his whisky' (Clay, 1992, 68), he was promoted brigadier and appointed to command 111th Brigade. He trained his troops in jungle fighting and, for all that 'he regarded Wingate as an upstart [and] held his theories in contempt' (Allen, 2002, 348), joined the special force officially known as 3rd Indian Division, but which was better known as the Chindits.

When the Chindits were already embarked on their second expedition in March 1944 (operation THURSDAY), Lentaigne learned that, due to Wingate's death in an air crash, Slim had appointed him to command on the grounds that he was 'the most balanced and experienced' Chindit officer' (Slim, 1999, 269). This may have been a mistake. The view that Lentaigne was an unworthy successor to Wingate, being neither physically nor temperamentally up to the job, is widespread (see Rooney, 1992, 134). He never established a good relationship with the American theatre commander, Stilwell, and it was said that he was 'drinking too much' (Royle, 1995, 316). Hence the notion that after Wingate's death 'the Chindits were villainously misused' has gained currency (Allen, 2002, 348). However, it seems just as likely that Slim, never more than lukewarm towards special forces and Wingate's ideas on long-range penetration, deliberately chose a commander who would assist in, or at any rate not obstruct, the disbandment of Wingate's Chindits.

Promoted major general and appointed CBE in 1945, Lentaigne was an instructor at the Imperial Defence College in 1946. He was Director of Military Operations, GHQ India, in 1947 and, re-married in 1948, was Commandant of the Indian Staff College 1948–1955. Within three months of his retirement, he died suddenly at his home in London.

LESLIE, Major General Robert Walter Dickson *(1883–1957), CB, CBE*
Born and brought up in South Africa and finishing his education at the Royal College of Surgeons, Dublin, Leslie joined the Royal Army Medical Corps in 1906. A captain in 1910 and married the next year, his First War service was in France. Mentioned in despatches, he was Assistant Director Medical Services in France, 1918–1919, and made OBE. He was a colonel in 1920.

Deputy Assistant Director Medical Services, India, 1930–1932 and briefly DDMS Palestine and Transjordan in 1936, Leslie was Commandant of the Queen Alexandra Military Hospital, Millbank, 1935–1937. A major general in 1937, he was DDMS Northern Command from 1937 until his retirement from the army in 1941.

A frequent contributor to army medical journals, Leslie was a Medical Officer with the Ministry of Health 1948–1954. He lived in Leicestershire.

LETHBRIDGE, Major General John Sydney *(1897–1961), CB, CBE, MC*
Of military family and educated at Uppingham, RMA, Woolwich, and Cambridge University (a young officers' course), Lethbridge was commissioned in the Royal Engineers in 1915. His First War service was in France and, from 1917, with the Aden Frontier Force.

Awarded the MC for service in Afghanistan in 1919, 'Tubby' Lethbridge married in 1925, attended the Staff College, Quetta, 1932–1933 and, at war's beginning in 1939 was a lieutenant colonel.

An acting brigadier in 1940, Lethbridge was CRA 59th Division, Home Forces, 1940–1941 and served on the staff at the War Office 1942–1943. Appointed CBE he was Commander of 220 Military Mission (effectively a committee to study and report on the prospects of military operations in the Pacific) 1943–1944. From 1944 to 1945 he was Chief of Staff to XIV Army in Burma and Malaya, in which role he combined 'the typical clear-headedness of an engineer with a broad humanity' (Slim, 1999, 387).

Chief of Intelligence, Control Commission for Germany and BAOR, 1945–1948, Lethbridge retired from the army in 1948. Commandant of the Civil Defence Staff College 1949–1952, ill-health forced him, the father of three children and a keen sportsman, into retirement. He lived in mid-Devon.

LEWIS, Major General Harold Victor *(1887–1945),CB, CIE, DSO, MC*
The son of a clergyman, Lewis was educated at Uppingham and RMC, Sandhurst. Commissioned on the unattached list in 1908, he was gazetted into the 18th Garwhal Rifles (Indian Army) in 1909. After service on the North-West Frontier and in Somaliland, he was a captain in 1914. First War service was in India and Mesopotamia, where he was four times mentioned in despatches, awarded the MC and admitted to the DSO in 1917.

Mentioned in despatches during operations in Waziristan in 1920, Lewis married in 1924. A student at the Staff College, Quetta, 1928–1929, he commanded the 4th Battalion of the 19th Hyderabad Regiment 1932–1933. Deputy Director of Staff Duties, AHQ India, 1933–1935, he was Assistant Adjutant and QMG, Peshawar Brigade Area, 1935–1937. Appointed to command the Razmak Brigade 1937–1940, he was promoted major general and made commander of Jullundur Area in the same year. A divisional commander in India in 1941, he retired from the army in 1942.

Colonel of the 4th/10th Baluch Regiment from 1940, Lewis died suddenly at his home in Buckinghamshire in September 1945.

LEWIS, Major General Sir Richard George *(1895–1965), KCMG, CB, CBE*
Of Anglo-Irish parentage and educated at St Columba College and Trinity College, Dublin, Lewis was intending to make a career in medicine before volunteering for service with the Leinster Regiment in 1914. His First War service was in France, where he received a regular commission in 1917 and was mentioned in despatches.

Married in 1918 and transferring to the Royal Tank Corps in 1920, 'Dick' Lewis attended the Staff College, Camberley, 1926–1927, and the Imperial Defence College in 1937. Later he was an 'excellent and imaginative' staff officer at the War Office (Macready, 1965, 89). Transferred from the BEF's GHQ staff in France in April 1940, he landed with the 148th Brigade in Åndalsnes, Norway, only to be evacuated within two weeks. A staff officer with Northern Command 1940, he served on the administrative staff of Anti-Aircraft Command in 1941. Deputy QMG at the War Office in 1942, he served on the staff of AFHQ, Algiers, in 1943 and at Alexander's HQ in Caserta 1944–1945.

Retired from the army in 1945, and appointed CB, Lewis was Deputy Director General (Finance) of UNRRA in Europe, and Personal Representative of the Director General of UNRRA 1947–1948. He was also Director General Foreign Office Administration of African Territories, 1949–1952. Knighted that year, he retired to live in Oxfordshire and held a number of directorships in engineering companies.

LIARDET, Major General Sir Claude Francis *(1881–1966), KBE, CB, DSO*
The son of a naval officer and educated at Bedford School, Liardet joined the Lancashire Artillery in 1899. A captain in 1905, he married in 1906 and, on the reorganization of the Territorial Army in 1909, transferred to the Lancashire and Cheshire Royal Garrison Artillery. His First War service was in France, where he was five times mentioned in despatches and admitted to the DSO in 1917.

As a Territorial Army Artillery Officer Liardet was a colonel in 1927. Remarried in 1928, he was made CRA of 47th Division in 1934 and promoted major general in 1938. GOC the London Division (TA) from 1938–1941, he retired from the army to become Inspector of Aerodrome Defences. Made Director General, Ground Defence, at the Air Ministry in 1942, he in effect founded the RAF Regiment and was its first Commandant 1942–1945. He was knighted in 1944.

A member of Lloyds and President of the Corporation of Insurance Brokers 1947–1951, Liardet was DL for the County of London in 1952. He lived in Surrey.

LIDDELL, General Sir Clive Gerard *(1883–1956), KCB, CMG, CBE, DSO*
Born in Huddersfield and educated at Uppingham and RMC, Sandhurst, Liddell was commissioned in the Leicestershire Regiment in 1902. A captain in 1908, he played rugby for the Army in 1912. Married in 1914, his First War service was in France, where he was mentioned in despatches six times and admitted to the DSO, and, from 1917, at the War Office, where he was an Assistant Adjutant General.

Re-married in 1918, 'Jock' Liddell graduated from the Staff College, Camberley, in 1919 and was an instructor there for the next two years. Deputy Administrator, British Empire Exhibition, 1923–1925, he attended the Imperial Defence College in 1927. Serving on the staff at the War Office 1928–1931, he commanded 8th Infantry Brigade 1931–1934. Promoted major general in 1933, he commanded 47th (2nd London) Division in 1935 and was GOC 4th Division, 1937. A lieutenant general in 1938, he was Adjutant General to the Forces 1937–1939.

Governor and C-in-C, Gibraltar, 1939–1941, Liddell was promoted general in 1941 and was Inspector General for Training (Home Forces) 1941–1942. He retired from the army in 1942.

Colonel of the Royal Leicestershire Regiment, 1943–1948 Liddell was Director of Ambulance, St John Ambulance Brigade over the same period. A governor of the Royal Hospital, Chelsea, 1943–1947, he held a number of directorships, including that of Southall and Wembley Laundries Ltd. A recipient of the Royal Humane Society Bronze Medal, he lived in Chelsea.

LINDSAY, Major General George Mackintosh
(1880–1956), CB, CMG, CBE, DSO
Educated at Radley, Lindsay joined the Royal Monmouthshire Royal Engineers (Militia) in 1898 and was commissioned in the Rifle Brigade in 1900. After service in the South African War, he was Army Middleweight Boxing Champion in 1905, a captain in 1906 and Adjutant to various territorial formations 1907–1913. An instructor at the School of Musketry, Hythe, 1913–1915, his First War service was with training commands and in France. Admitted to the DSO in 1917 and six times mentioned in despatches, he ended the war commanding a battalion of the Machine Gun Corps.

A student at the Staff College, Camberley, in 1920, Lindsay commanded an armoured car group in Iraq 1921–1923 and transferred to the Royal Tank Corps in 1923. For the next two years he was Chief Instructor at the RTC Central School, and was Inspector of the RTC at the War Office 1925–1929. BGS Egypt Command 1929–1932, he commanded 7th (Experimental) Infantry Brigade, Southern Command, 1932–1934. Regarded as 'the most intellectually sophisticated of the RTC radicals between the wars' (Harris, 1995, 198), he was promoted major general in 1934 and, as though to bring his career to a close, was shunted into obscurity by being appointed GOC Presidency and Assam District, India, in 1935.

Retired in 1939, Lindsay was re-employed at the outbreak of war and made GOC 9th (Highland) Division. In 1940 he was appointed Deputy Regional Commissioner for the South West Civil Defence Region, a post he held until his retirement in 1944. He was Commandant of the RTC 1938–1947, and Commissioner for the British Red Cross, North-West Europe, 1944–1946.

LINDSELL, Lieutenant General Sir Wilfrid Gordon
(1884–1973), GBE, KCB, DSO, MC
Of military family and educated at Victoria College, Jersey, and RMA, Woolwich, Lindsell was commissioned in the Royal Artillery in 1903. ADC to the Governor Generals of Tasmania and Western Australia 1910–1914, and a captain in 1914, his First War service was in France, where he was four times mentioned in despatches, awarded the MC and admitted to the DSO.

Married in 1916, Lindsell attended the short course at the Staff College, Camberley, in 1919 and was a Deputy Assistant Adjutant General at the War Office in 1920. An instructor at the School of Military Administration 1921–1923, he was on the instructing staff at Camberley 1925–1928. After attending the Imperial Defence College in 1929, he served on the staff at the War Office 1930–1933 and was Commandant of the Senior Officers' School, Sheerness, 1934–1935. Deputy Military Secretary at the War Office 1935–1936, he was CRA 4th Division 1937–1938. In the year before the outbreak of war he was Major General i/c Administration, Southern Command.

Made QMG of the BEF in 1939, 'Tommy' Lindsell, acknowledged as 'a master of his craft' (Brownrigg, 1942, 139), was knighted after the Dunkirk evacuation. Serving as Lieutenant General i/c Administration, Home Forces, in 1940, he was seconded to the Ministry of Supply in 1941, and was made Lieutenant General i/c Administration, Middle East, in 1942. Made Principal Administrative Officer to the Indian Command in 1943, he retired from the army in 1945, only to work for a further two years at the Board of Trade.

The recipient of many decorations and honorary degrees, Lindsell re-married in 1958 and lived well into his eighties in London.

LLOYD, Major General Wilfrid Lewis *(1896–1944), CBE, DSO, MC*
The son of an Indian Civil Servant and educated at Shrewsbury and Trinity College, Dublin, Lloyd was commissioned in the King's Shropshire Light Infantry in 1914. His First War service was in France until 1917 when, already the recipient of an MC, he transferred to the Indian Army.

Serving with the Kumaon Rifles on the North-West Frontier, Lloyd married in 1922 and attended the Staff College, Camberley, 1927–1928. A brigade major between 1930 and 1933, he commanded the 4th/19th Hyderabad Regiment 1936–1939. A staff officer at AHQ, India, in 1939, he was appointed to command a brigade of 4th Indian Division and served in the Middle East 1939–1941. Appointed CBE and admitted to the DSO in 1941 after taking part in operations in Syria, he returned to India to take up the post of Director of Military Training at GHQ. Appointed to command the newly-formed 14th Indian Division in 1942, he led it during the 'worst-managed British military effort of the war' (Hickey, 1998, 77), the ill-fated Arakan offensive. A 'conscientious but unlucky general' (Lewin, 1999, 122), he was removed from his command by Irwin, the army commander, in March 1943 and received Slim's sympathy and admiration for the manner in which he accepted his fate 'quite without bitterness' (Slim, 1999, 156).

Assuming command of 10th Indian Division in Egypt, Lloyd was killed in a motor accident near Cairo in January 1944. He left a widow and two children.

LOCH, Lieutenant General Sir Kenneth Morley
(1890–1961), KCIE, CB, MC
Of military family and educated at Wellington and RMA, Woolwich, Loch was commissioned in the Royal Artillery in 1910. His First War service was in France, where he was twice mentioned in despatches and awarded the MC.

A student at the Staff College, Camberley, 1923–1924, Loch served on the staff with various Territorial Army Air Defence formations 1926–1929. Married in 1929, he was an instructor at the Staff College, Quetta, 1932–1934. An instructor at the Anti-Aircraft School, Shoeburyness, 1934–1935, and Brigade Major 1st Anti-Aircraft Brigade in 1935, he served on the staff at the War Office 1935–1937. He was, as Brigadier Home Defence, attached to Fighter Command HQ, Northolt, 1937–1938.

Director of Anti-Aircraft and Civil Defence at the War Office 1939–1941, Loch, a softly spoken 'erudite man' (Colville, 1985, 404), was assigned to special duties in 1941. Appointed CB in 1942, he was Master General of the Ordnance in India 1944–1947 and retired from the army in 1947.

Knighted in 1946, Loch joined the British Council. Seconded to the Control Commission, Germany, 1948–1949, he retired in 1950.

LOCHNER, Major General Rupert Gordon *(1891–1965), MC*
Few of this officer's personal details are known. Commissioned in the South Wales Borderers in 1910 after leaving RMC, Sandhurst, Lochner's First War service was in Gallipoli and France. He was awarded the MC.

Commander of the 1st Battalion South Wales Borders in Rawalpindi 1938–1940, Lochner commanded a brigade, 1941–1942, and was Commander of the Basra area base, Persia (Iran)-Iraq in 1942. He was GOC of an Indian Division in 1944. Retired from the army in 1946, he was DL for Brecknock in 1948.

LOCKHART, General Sir Rob McGregor Macdonald
(1893–1981), KCB, CB, CIE, MC
Educated at Marlborough and RMC, Sandhurst, Lockhart was commissioned

in the Indian Army (unattached list) in 1913. Gazetted into the 51st Sikh Regiment (Frontier Force) in 1914, his First War service was on the North-West Frontier, in Egypt and in Mesopotamia, where he was awarded the MC in 1918.

Married in 1918, Lockhart spent most of the rest of his army career, save for a two-year stint at the Staff College Camberley, 1926–1927, in India. Brigade Major at Kohat 1929–1931, he was a general staff officer at AHQ 1932–1932 and Military Attaché at Kabul 1934–1935. Director of Staff Duties in 1939 and considered 'a real live wire' (Kennedy, 4/3, LHCMA), he was Military Secretary at the India Office 1941–1944. GOC Southern Command, India, 1945–1947, he was Acting Governor of North-West Frontier Province in early 1947, before becoming the last C-in-C of the Indian Army in the months leading up to independence and partition.

Knighted in 1946 and retired from the army in 1948, Lockhart was Director of Operations, Malaya, 1951–1952, and Deputy Director 1952–1953. DL for Surrey 1957–1966, he was Deputy Chief Scout for the Boy Scouts' Association 1951–1961 and President of the Greater London Scout's Association, 1965–1972. President of the Association of British Officers of the Indian Army 1969–1971, he lived until his late eighties, the last year of his life a widower.

LOEWEN, General Sir Charles Falkland *(1900–1986), GCB, KBE, DSO*

Born and raised in Vancouver and educated at Haileybury and the Canadian RMC, Kingston, Ontario, Loewen, too young for active service with the Canadian Army, travelled to Britain at his parents' expense and was commissioned in the Royal Field Artillery in 1918.

Spending most of the 1920s in India, Loewen was active in operations on the North-West Frontier and, a keen marksman, allegedly shot twelve tigers. Married in 1928 and a captain in 1931, he graduated from the Staff College, Quetta, in 1934. He was a brevet lieutenant colonel in 1939 and an instructor at the Staff College, Camberley, at war's beginning.

Mentioned in despatches for his part in the campaign in Norway in 1940, Loewen served on the staff of Northern Command 1940–1941 and in the Plans department of the War Office 1942–1943. Mentioned in despatches during the fighting on the Anzio beachhead, when he was CRA X Corps, he never lost 'the bustle and vigour of a Canadian' (Blaxland, 1979, 189). Commanding 1st Infantry Division during the latter phases of the war in Italy, where he was found to be 'forthright, foul-mouthed, tactless [and] efficient' (Greacan, 1987, 278), he was admitted to the DSO in 1945.

Loewen was appointed GOC Ist Armoured Division in 1947. After service in Trieste and Palestine, he commanded the Northumbrian District 1948–1949. GOC-in-C Anti-Aircraft Command 1950–1953, he was C-in-C Far East Land Forces 1953–1956. Adjutant General to the Forces 1956–1959, he retired from the army in 1959. Colonel Commandant of the Royal Artillery 1953–1963, he was much honoured in Britain and his native Canada as being the last general in the British Army to have been commissioned during the First World War.

LOFTUS-TOTTENHAM, Major General Frederick Joseph
(1898- ?), DSO, CBE
Few of this officer's personal details are known. Gazetted into the 2nd Gurkha Rifles in 1916, a captain in 1920 and a major in 1934, Loftus-Tottenham commanded the 10th Gurkha Rifles in 1939 and the 153rd Gurkha Parachute Battalion in 1942.

Commander of 33rd Indian Brigade 1943–1944, Loftus-Tottenham was GOC 81st West African Division in Burma 1944–1945. Admitted to the DSO in 1945 (and bar), his two sons, both officers with the Gurkhas, were killed in action, one in Italy in 1944, the other in Burma in 1945. He was made CBE in 1947 after service in Iraq.

LOMAX, Major General Cyril Ernest Napier
(1893–1973), CB, CBE, DSO, MC
Of military family and educated at Marlborough and RMC, Sandhurst, Lomax was commissioned in the Welch Regiment in 1913. His First War service was in France, where he was five times mentioned in despatches and awarded the MC, and in Italy, where he was admitted to the DSO in 1918.

Married in 1927, Lomax commanded the 2nd Battalion of the Welch Regiment 1936–1939, and commanded a brigade in North Africa in 1941. There he acquired the second bar to his DSO and was appointed CBE. Made commander of 16th Infantry Brigade in Burma in 1942, he assumed command of 26th Indian Division in March 1943, but before taking up the appointment was briefly made acting GOC of 14th Indian Division which had received a severe mauling during the ill-fated Arakan offensive. Impressing Slim with his 'calmness and professionalism' (Hickey, 1998, 79), he managed, in a 'near desperate situation' (Connell, 1969, 253), to stabilize his front and, with 'great skill and very little loss' (Slim, 1999, 161), extricate his troops. Regarded by Leese as 'intelligent and sound' (Ryder, 1987, 201), he was appointed CB in 1944, after his Division, as part of Christison's XV Corps, had finally cleared the Arakan of Japanese.

GOC East Anglia District 1946–1948, Lomax was President of the army's Regular Commission Board 1948–1949. Retired from the army that year, he lived in Sussex, outliving his wife by five years.

LONGDEN, Major General Harry Leicester *(!900–1981), CBE*
Commissioned in the Dorset Regiment in 1919, Longden attended the Staff College, Quetta, 1930–1931 and served on the staff at the War Office 1934–1938. He was Chief Staff Officer 43rd (Wessex) Division in 1940, though Percival, the divisional commander, regarded him as 'not a happy choice . . . as he has not been a bit popular with his regiment' (PRO WO 282/7). Assistant QMG, Southern Command, 1940–1941, he was Deputy Adjutant and QMG at the War Office 1941–1942. Brigadier i/c Q Operations at the War Office 1942–1943, he was Deputy QMG 21st Army Group, North-West Europe, 1944–1945. Made OBE in 1944, he was Director of Quartering at the War Office 1945–1947.

President of the War Crimes Court, Hamburg, in 1947, Longden retired from the army in 1948. A keen golfer, he lived in Sussex.

LORIE, Major General Reginald Harvey *(1891- ?)*
Serving for two years with the Royal North Down Militia and commissioned in the Roytal Irish Rifles in 1912, Lorie's First War service was in France, Gallipoli and Palestine.

An instructor at Sandhurst 1919–1921, Lorie transferred to the Royal Ulster Rifles in 1922, attended the Staff College, Camberley, 1924–1925 and was a staff captain with the Shanghai Defence Force 1927–1928. A staff officer with Southern Command 1928–1930, he served on the staff at the War Office for the next seven years. A lieutenant colonel in 1936, he commanded the 2nd Battalion Royal Ulster Rifles in 1937 and was Assistant Adjutant and QMG 3rd Division, in 1938. He was Brigadier i/c Administration, I Corps, in 1940.

LOUGHBOROUGH, Major General Arthur Harold *(1883–1967)*, CB, OBE
The son of a barrister and educated at Bradfield, Loughborough joined the Sussex Garrison Artillery (Militia) in 1900. After service in the South African War he was commissioned in the RGA in 1902. Married in 1906 and a captain in the Territorial Army in 1914, his First War service was in France, where he was mentioned in despatches and appointed to the OBE in 1919.

Re-married in 1921, Loughborough was Secretary to the Royal Artillery Committee in 1923 and Colonel and Superintendent of Experiments in 1932. Deputy Commandant of the Military College of Science 1932–1934 and a member of the Ordnance Committee in 1934, he was Commandant of the Military College of Science 1936–1938. Promoted major general in 1938, he was Vice President of the Ordnance Committee and President of the Ordnance Board in 1940. Retired from the army in 1942, he lived in Hampshire.

LOUP, Major General Louis Anthony *(1897–1991)*, CBE
A territorial soldier, mobilized in the ranks in 1915 and commissioned in the Nottinghamshire and Derbyshire Regiment the same year, Loup's First War service was in France.

Transferring to the Indian Army in 1919, Loup, a captain in 1920, was gazetted into the Indian Army Service Corps. A major in 1924, he graduated from the Staff College, Quetta, in 1932. A staff captain with Northern Command, India, and Deputy Assistant Adjutant General, AHQ India, 1935–1936, he was Deputy Assistant QMG, Northern Command, India, 1936–1940.

A lieutenant colonel in 1939, Loup was an instructor at the Senior Officers' School, Belgaum. in 1940. Made CBE in 1943, after the retreat from Burma, he was promoted major general in 1944 and retired from the army in 1947.

LOYD, General Sir Henry Charles *(1891–1973)*, GCVO, KCB, DSO, MC
Born in Hertfordshire and educated at Eton and RMC, Sandhurst, Loyd was commissioned in the Coldstream Guards in 1910. His First War service was in

France, where he was appointed to the DSO in 1914, wounded four times, thrice mentioned in despatches and awarded the MC. He ended the war a brevet lieutenant colonel and, at 27, was one of the army's youngest battalion commanders.

Selected for the first post-war course at the Staff College without examination, Loyd married in 1922 and returned to Camberley in 1925 as an instructor. A useful cricketer, he commanded the 3rd Battalion, Coldstream Guards, 1926–1932, and was o/c Coldstream Guards Regimental District 1932–1934. Serving on the staff at the War Office 1934–1936, he was promoted brigadier and appointed BGS at AHQ Cairo. Commander of 1st Infantry (Guards) Brigade 1938–1939, he was selected to command 2nd Division at Aldershot just before war's beginning.

In France with the BEF 1939–1940, Loyd led his division during the planned advance to the Dyle on 10 May 1940, but six days later fainted during a conference held to plan the withdrawal to the Scheldt. Hospitalized in Boulogne, he was evacuated just before the arrival of German forces.

Brooke, by now C-in-C Home Forces, remembered 'Budget' Loyd from Staff College days and made him his CGS in 1941. Supposedly 'quite recovered from his breakdown' (Dill, 2nd. acc., 4, LHCMA), he was promoted lieutenant general and appointed GOC-in-C Southern Command in 1942, in which role he, as a 'great Guardsman', gained, according to his obituarist, a 'notable reputation as a trainer of troops'. Knighted in 1943, he was GOC London District 1944–1947. Promoted General in 1946, he retired from the army in 1947.

A Norfolk JP in 1950 and DL for the County in 1954, Loyd was Colonel of the Coldstream Guards from 1945 to 1966. It was perhaps for this reason that his knighthood was enhanced in 1965.

LUMSDEN, Lieutenant General Herbert *(1897–1945), CB, DSO, MC*
Educated at Eton and RMA, Woolwich, Lumsden was commissioned in the Royal Artillery in 1915. His First War service was in France, where he was awarded the MC.

Married in 1923 and transferring to the 12th Royal Lancers in 1925, Lumsden rode in several Grand Nationals, won the Military Gold Cup at Sandown in 1926 and attended the Staff College, Camberley, 1929–1930. As a 'gay, charming, handsome, theatrical, highly-strung' cavalryman (Barnett, 1983, 278), it fell to him and his kind to mechanize the RAC in the 1930s. Brigade Major with 1st Cavalry Division 1932–1934, he was on the directing staff at Camberley 1936–1938.

In command of the 12th Lancers, now an armoured car regiment, 1938–1940, Lumsden did famous work covering the withdrawal of the BEF to Dunkirk. Admitted to the DSO, and promoted brigadier, he commanded a tank brigade with Home Forces 1940–1941 and was appointed GOC 1st Armoured Division in November 1941. Wounded in an air attack in North Africa in early 1942, he was wounded again that July during the first Alamein battle.

Regarded by now as a desert veteran and 'a leader of exceptional quality' (Carver, 1989, 100), Lumsden was appointed by Montgomery to command X Corps, 8th Army's supposed *Corps de Chasse* in September 1942. Unused to the pliant sycophancy Montgomery required of his subordinates and disposed to dispute orders he disagreed with, he often clashed with his army commander who, needing a scapegoat for 8th Army's dilatory pursuit of Rommel's Panzerarmee, sacked him and sent him home in December 1942. It is possible that Lumsden had been 'wilting under the strain' (Latimer, 2002, 314), though Montgomery's judgement that 'command of a corps in a major battle was above [his] ceiling' (Montgomery, 1958, 129) was neither just nor gracious. For his part, Lumsden exhibited his brand of comic showmanship by arriving at his London clubs wearing a bowler hat.

A corps commander with Home Forces for most of 1943, Lumsden, still a substantive major general, was appointed CB and sent by Churchill as his special representative on MacArthur's staff in the Pacific theatre in 1944. Observing the American bombardment of Lingayen Gulf on board the USS *New Mexico* in January 1945, he was killed when a Kamikaze plane struck the ship's bridge. He may have been, as MacArthur put it, 'England at its best' (Boatner, 1999, 330), he was certainly one of the very few British generals of the Second World War who was killed in action.

LUND, Lieutenant General Sir Otto Marling *(1891–1956), KCB, DSO*

Educated at Winchester and RMA, Woolwich, Lund was commissioned in the Royal Artillery in 1911. His First War service was with the RHA and RFA in France, where he was four times mentioned in despatches and admitted to the DSO.

From 1919 to 1922 Lund served as ADC to General Lord Rawlinson in North Russia, Aldershot and India. Married in 1922, he was Assistant Military Secretary, Eastern Command, 1923–1924, attended the Staff College, Camberley, 1924–1925 and served on the staff of Aldershot Command 1926–1927. Brigade Major to the 2nd Infantry Brigade 1928–1930, he was on the instructing staff at Camberley 1931–1934. Military Assistant to the CIGS 1934–1936, he attended the Imperial Defence College in 1936 and was a staff officer at the War Office 1937–1939.

A member of the British Military Mission to Turkey in 1939, Lund was Deputy Director of Military Operations the same year. Major General RA with Home Forces 1940–1943, he was regarded as 'a potential corps commander' (Dill 2nd, acc., 9, LHCMA) though he never reached that height. With 21st Army Group in the planning stages of OVERLORD, he was appointed Director of Royal Artillery at the War Office before June 1944.

Promoted lieutenant general and appointed GOC-in-C Anti-Aircraft Command in 1946, Lund, knighted in 1948, was unable to take up his post of GOC British troops in Egypt due to ill-health. Retired from the army in 1949, he was Colonel Commandant of the RHA 1947–1950.

LYNE, Majort General Lewis Owen *(1899–1970), CB, DSO*
Educated at Haileybury and RMC, Sandhurst, Lyne saw service in France in the latter stages of the First War and was commissioned in the Lancashire Fusiliers in 1921. A regimental officer for most of the inter-war years, he served in Ireland, Egypt, Gibraltar and North China, as well as with home commands. He attended the Staff College, Camberley, 1935–1936 and served on the staff at the War Office 1938–1940.

A brevet lieutenant colonel in 1940, 'Lou' Lyne commanded the 9th Battalion, Lancashire Fusiliers in France with the BEF. Chief Instructor at the Senior Officers' School, Sheerness, in 1941, he commanded 169th Infantry Brigade in England, Iraq, North Africa and Italy 1942–1944. Admitted to the DSO in 1943 for his part in the successful assault on Monte Camino, he was sent home, promoted major general and, in the space of six months, was appointed to command 59th (Stafford) Division, 50th (Northumbrian) Division and 7th Armoured Division in North-West Europe.

Appointed CB in 1945, Lyne was Military Governor, British Zone, Berlin, in 1945 and was Director of Staff Duties at the War Office 1946–1948. Retired from the army in 1949, he was Chairman (later Joint President) of the United Nations Association 1951–1957, was active in the Youth Clubs movement and held a number of directorships in the petroleum and petro-chemical industries. From 1950 until he death he was C-in-C of the St John Ambulance Brigade.

M

MacARTHUR, Lieutenant General Sir William Porter
(1884–1964), KCB, DSO, OBE
Born near Belfast, MacArthur received his medical education at Queen's University and joined the Royal Army Medical Corps in 1909. Posted to Mauritius, he developed a career-long interest in tropical medicine. First War service was with the RAMC in France. Wounded and admitted to the DSO in 1916, he was Commandant of the Army School of Hygiene, Blackpool, in 1919 and appointed Professor of Tropical Medicine at the Royal Army Medical College in 1922.

A consulting physician to the army 1929–1934, MacArthur was Deputy Director General Army Medical Services at the War Office 1934–1935. Commandant and Director of Studies, Royal Army Medical College, 1935–1938, he was Director General of Army Medical Services, 1938–1941.

Knighted in 1939, MacArthur was 'somewhat at sea in the hurly-burly of war'

(DNB), and retired from the army in 1941. Thereafter he pursued a distinguished academic career at Oxford University. Acquiring fame as a lecturer and keen on all things Gaelic, he was the recipient of numerous honorary degrees. He wrote pieces on the history of medicine, proved to his own satisfaction that Robert the Bruce had not been a leper and made a study of the Appin Murder. He was Colonel Commandant of the RAMC 1946–1951.

McCAY, Lieutenant General Sir Ross Cairns *(1895–1969), KBE, CB, DSO*
Born and raised in Australia and educated at Scotch College, Melbourne, and RMCA, Duntroon, McCay volunteered for the AIF in 1914 and saw service in Egypt, Gallipoli and France. Admitted to the DSO in 1917, he joined the Indian Army in 1918, being gazetted into the 17th Cavalry.

A captain in 1919, McCay was mentioned in despatches during operations on the North-West Frontier and transferred to the 6th Rajputana Rifles in 1924. Married in 1928, he attended the Staff College, Quetta, 1929–1930 and, a major in 1931, saw more service on the North-West Frontier. Brigade Major 10th (Jubbulpore) Infantry Brigade, 1934–1936, he was a staff officer with Northern Command, India, 1937–1938 and commanded the 2nd/6th Rajput Regiment 1938–1939.

Deputy Military Secretary, India, 1940–1941, McCay was BGS at the India Office in London 1941–1943. Commander 1st Indian Brigade in Burma in 1943, he was promoted major general and made Military Secretary, GHQ India, in 1944. Appointed CB in 1945, and an area commander in India that year, he commanded the Peshawar Brigade in 1947, before becoming Chief of Staff to the Pakistan Army in 1948.

Chief Military Adviser to the Pakistan Army 1951–1953, McCay was knighted in 1952 before retiring the next year to live in Surrey.

McCONNEL, Major General Douglas Fitzgerald *(1893–1961),CB, CBE, DSO*
Born in Basingstoke and educated at Winchester, where he was a keen footballer, and at RMA, Woolwich, McConnel was commissioned in the Royal Artillery in 1913. His First War service was in France and Palestine. Thrice mentioned in despatches and admitted to the DSO in 1917, he was a major by war's end.

Married in 1920 and a student at the Staff College, Camberley, 1925–1926, McConnel was Brigade Major to the Quetta Infantry Brigade 1927–1931. An instructor at RMA,, Baluchistan District, in the early 1930s, and Camberley in the later 1930s, he was chief staff officer to 8th Division in Palestine 1939.

Promoted major general in 1941, McConnel was GOC-in-C Palestine and Transjordan 1941–1944. Appointed CB, he was Commander of the Lowland District 1945–1946 and ADC to the King for a year before retiring from the army in 1947. Settling in Scotland, he was DL for Ayrshire in 1953. His daughter married the future Duke of Wellington.

MACDONALD, Major General Harry *(1886–1976), CB, CIE, DSO*
Born on the Isle of Skye and educated at Fettes and RMC, Sandhurst, Macdonald joined the Indian Army in 1906 and was gazetted into the 5th Bengal Lancers (Probyn's Horse) the following year. A captain in 1914, his First War service was in France, where he was admitted to the DSO in 1918.

A graduate in the first post-war course at the Staff College, Camberley, in 1919, Macdonald spent the remainder of the 1920s on regimental duties in India. A brevet lieutenant colonel in 1929, he served on the staff of Western Command, India, 1928–1931. Married in 1934, he commanded Probyn's Horse 1933–1935 and served on the staff in Lahore District 1935–1936. Appointed to command 1st (Risalpur) Cavalry Brigade in 1936, he was Major General i/c Cavalry 1939–1940. Appointed CB in 1940, he was from then until his retirement from the army in 1943 commander of the Meerut District.

Re-employed as Chief Civil Liaison Officer and Deputy Director of Recruiting, Northern Area, India in 1943, Macdonald served on in India until 1946. Returning to his native Scotland, he was DL for Inverness-shire in 1948 and Sheriff Substitute over much of the Highland area 1949–1971.

MacDOUGALL, Major General Alastair Ian *(1888–1972), CBE, DSO, MC*
Born in Edinburgh and educated at Wellington and RMC, Sandhurst, MacDougall was commissioned in the Royal Scots Greys in 1912. His First War service was in France and Palestine, where he was mentioned in despatches, awarded the MC and admitted to the DSO in 1919.

Married in 1922, MacDougall attended the Staff College, Camberley, 1923–1924 and commanded the Scots Greys 1928–1932. Commander of the 6th (Midland) Cavalry Brigade 1932–1934, he was an instructor at the Senior Officers' School, Sheerness, from 1934 to 1936. A staff officer at the War Office 1936–1939, he was an area commander at war's beginning and, promoted major general, was a Deputy CGS in 1940. A District Commander 1940–1944, he retired in 1944. His only son died of wounds in 1945.

MacDougall was Chairman of the Argyll TA Association, 1946–1955.

MACKESY, Major General Pierse Joseph *(1883–1956), CB, DSO, MC*
The son of a lieutenant general, Mackesy was educated at St Paul's and RMA, Woolwich. Commissioned in the Royal Engineers in 1902, he became a survey specialist in the Gold Coast (Ghana) in 1911. The first eighteen months of his First War service were in West Africa. Thereafter he served in France, where he was awarded the MC.

A staff officer with the North Russian Relief Force in 1919, he was admitted to the DSO before joining the Military Mission to South Russia in 1920. A student at the Staff College, Camberley, 1920–1921, he married in 1923 and, after a variety of postings at home and abroad, was appointed to command 3rd Infantry Brigade at Borden in 1935. In Palestine 1935–1938, he was promoted major general in 1937 and, appointed CB in 1938, was made GOC 49th (West Riding) Division and area. Adviser to the New Zealand government on defence.

In 1939 he returned to England at war's beginning and re-assumed command of his Division.

Destined to be sent to France to form part of Adam's III Corps of the BEF, 49th Division was instead held at home in readiness for operations in Scandinavia. As the Russo-Finnish 'winter war' only interested the British government to the extent that it offered a pretext for interrupting the traffic of iron ore to Germany, 'Pat' Mackesy, with his experience of war in arctic conditions, was an obvious choice as commander of an expeditionary force. In the event British intervention in Scandinavia happened not, as was planned, to forestall German action but as a response to the German invasion of Norway. Mackesy, with one infantry brigade, was sent to invest the port of Narvik.

Enraging Churchill by refusing to commit his troops to 'the sheer bloody murder' of an 'arctic Gallipoli' (Kersaudy, 1990, 127), Mackesy was recalled home and, amidst Churchillian mutterings about his 'feebleness and downright cowardice' (Harvey, 1992, 747), was spared a court martial but never held command again.

Retired from the army in November 1940, Mackesy served for a while on various War Office committees and was an occasional contributor to the *Daily Telegraph*. Considered a drunkard and a security risk by Brooke (Danchev & Todman, 2001, 456), his mail was regularly intercepted. A Southwold borough councillor from 1946, he was subsequently mayor of the town on two separate occasions, as well as being a member of the East Suffolk County Council.

MACLEOD, Major General Charles William *(1881–1944), CB, CMG, DSO*

Born in Edinburgh and educated at Dulwich and RMC, Sandhurst, Macleod was commissioned in the Army Service Corps in 1900. After service in the South African War, he was a captain in 1904 and a major in 1914, the year he married. His First War service was in France, where he was admitted to the DSO in 1915.

A lieutenant colonel in 1921 and a colonel in 1923, Macleod was Inspector of the RASC 1929–1933. Director of Supplies and Transport at the War Office 1933–1937, he was known as a 'walking encyclopaedia', able, apparently, to recall the name of every Scottish rugby international. He retired from the army in 1937.

An area officer in Scotland and London, responsible to the Director General of Munitions Production 1937–1939, Macleod was re-employed at war's beginning as Director of Supplies and Transport at the War Office. He reverted to retired pay in 1944.

McLEOD, Lieutenant General Sir Donald Kenneth
(1885–1958), KCIE, CB, DSO

The son of a general and educated at Wellington and RMC, Sandhurst, McLeod was gazetted into the Guides Cavalry Corps (Indian Army) in 1905. He served on the North-West Frontier and in the First War was wounded in Mesopotamia, mentioned three times in despatches in Palestine and admitted to the DSO in 1917.

A graduate of the Staff College, Camberley, in 1920, McLeod was a staff officer at the War Office 1921–1922 and, married in 1923, was an instructor at Camberley 1923–1926. He commanded the Guides Cavalry in India 1928–1932, attended the Imperial Defence College and, returning to India, commanded, in turn, the 4th and 1st Cavalry Brigades 1933–1936. A major general in 1936, he was Deputy Adjutant and QMG Northern Command, India, in 1937, and from 1938 to 1941 was GOC Burma.

Adjudged deficient in 'push and go' by Pownall (Bond (ed.), 1974, 67), and 'a nice old gentleman' by Wavell (Lunt, 1989, 70), McLeod was dismissed from his command at the same time as he was promoted lieutenant general and retired from the army in 1942. Knighted, he was Honorary Sheriff Substitute for Inverness-shire from 1942 and DL for the county from 1955.

MacLEOD, Major General Malcolm Neynoe *(1882–1969), CB, DSO, MC*
Born in India and educated at Rugby and RMA, Woolwich, MacLeod was posted to India in 1902 and served with the Military Works Services for two years before transfer to the Indian Army Service Corps and work on the Military Survey of India. His First War service was in France, where he commanded a Field Survey Battalion. He was awarded the MC in 1917 and admitted to the DSO in 1918.

Chief Instructor, School of Artillery, Larkhill, 1919–1923, MacLeod married in 1924 and worked at the Ordnance Survey, Southampton, 1923–1929. A staff officer at the War Office 1929–1932, he attended the Staff College, Quetta, 1932–1933 and was Director General Ordnance Survey from 1935 until his retirement from the army in 1943.

Colonel Commandant of the Royal Engineers 1941–1950, MacLeod, a keen tennis player even in retirement, was for many years President of the Southampton Tennis Association.

McMICKING, Major General Neil *(1894–1963), CB, CBE, DSO, MC*
Born in Dumfries and educated at Eton and RMC, Sandhurst, McMicking was commissioned in the Black Watch in 1913. His First War service was in France, with his battalion and as a staff officer. Three times wounded, five times mentioned in despatches and awarded the MC in 1916, he was admitted to the DSO in 1919, the year in which he commanded the tanks sent to General Deniken's army in South Russia.

Serving in Waziristan in 1920, McMicking was Adjutant to the 2nd Battalion the Black Watch 1921–1924 and was Deputy Assistant Adjutant and QMG at the regimental depot 1927–1928. Married in 1927, he attended the Staff College, Camberley, 1929–1930. A brigade major 1933–1934, he was Deputy Assistant Adjutant General, Scottish Command, 1934–1937. A lieutenant colonel in 1938, he was AA and QMG British Troops in Egypt 1937–1938 and commanded the 2nd Battalion Black Watch in Palestine 1938–1939.

Assistant QMG Western Desert Force in 1940, McMicking was Brigadier i/c Cairo Area in 1940, Deputy Adjutant and QMG, Egypt, 1941, and Deputy

Adjutant and QMG XIII Corps in 1942. A minor victim of the 'Cairo purge', he was sent to England at the end of the year. Promoted major general in 1944, he commanded the Antwerp base for the British Liberation Army 1944–1945. Major General i/c Administration, Scottish Command, in 1945, he was Chief of Staff, Scottish Command, from 1947 until his retirement from the army in 1948.

Colonel of the Black Watch 1952–1960, in which both his sons served, McMicking was DL for Perthshire in 1961 and was Brigadier in the Royal Company of Archers. He died suddenly of a heart attack in 1963.

MacMILLAN of MacMILLAN, General Sir Gordon Holmes Alexander
(1897–1986), KCB, KCVO, CBE, DSO, MC
The son of the hereditary chief of the Clan MacMillan and educated at St Edmund's, Canterbury and RMC, Sandhurst, MacMillan was commissioned in the Argyll and Sutherland Highlanders in 1915. His First War service was in France, where he was mentioned in despatches and awarded the MC.

Adjutant to his regiment's 2nd Battalion 1917–1920, MacMillan served in the Experimental Brigade 1927–1928 and attended the Staff College, Camberley, 1928–1929. Married in 1929, he served on the staff at the War Office 1930–1934. On the directing staff of the Canadian RMC, Kingston, Ontario, 1935–1937, he was a staff officer at the War Office and with Eastern Command 1937–1940.

In command of 199th Infantry Brigade with Home Forces in 1941, MacMillan was BGS IX Corps in England 1941–1942 and to 1st Army in North Africa in 1943. Commanding first 12th and then 152nd Infantry Brigades in 1943, he was admitted to the DSO during the campaign in Sicily. Appointed to command 15th (Scottish) Division in August 1943, 'Babe' Macmillan led what came to be regarded as 'the most effective and best-led infantry divisions' during the fighting in Normandy (D'Este, 1994, 239). O'Connor, his Corps Commander, regarded him as 'one of the best, if not the best, commanders [he had] ever met' (Baynes, 1989, 221). Wounded in August during Operation BLUECOAT, he assumed command of 49th (West Riding) Division in November, when 'Bubbles' Barker left to command a corps. After the Rhine Crossing, during which Rennie, GOC 51st (Highland) Division, was killed, Horrocks selected Macmillan, 'a most able and popular officer' (Horrocks, 1960, 260), to succeed.

Appointed CB in 1945, MacMillan was Director of Weapons Development at the War Office 1945–1946 and GOC Palestine 1947–1948. Knighted in 1949, he was C-in-C Scottish Command and Governor of Edinburgh Castle 1949–1952 and from then until his retirement in 1955 he was Governor and C-in-C Gibraltar.

With his knighthood enhanced, MacMillan was Chairman of Cumbernauld New Town Corporation 1959–1965 and of Greenock Harbour Trust 1955–1965. Colonel of the Argyll and Sutherland Highlanders 1945–1958, he was Vice-Lieutenant of Renfrewshire 1955–1972. As MacMillan of MacMillan from 1950, he was much honoured in Canada, Holland and Scotland. He died, as the result of a motor accident near his home, in his ninetieth year.

McMULLEN, Major General Sir Donald Jay *(1891–1967), KBE, CB, DSO*
Educated at Bradfield and RMA, Woolwich, and commissioned in the Royal Engineers in 1911, McMullen's First War service was in France and Palestine, where he was mentioned in despatches and admitted to the DSO.

Seconded to the Egyptian government for railway transportation duties 1920–1929, Macmullen married in 1922. A major in 1927 and a lieutenant colonel in 1935, he was Assistant Director of Transportation, Cairo, 1936–1937. Director General of Transportation for the BEF, in France, 1939–1940, he was Inspector and then Director of Transportation at the War Office 1940–1945. He was promoted major general in 1943 and was Deputy Chief of the Transport Division (British zone), Control Commission for Germany, 1945–1948.

Knighted in 1946 and retired from the army in 1948, McMullen lived in Chichester, Sussex.

MacMULLEN, Major General Hugh Tennent *(1892–1946), CB, CBE, MC*
Born in Co. Cork and educated at Clifton and RMC, Sandhurst, MacMullen was commissioned in the East Lancashire Regiment in 1912. A captain in 1915, his First War service was in France, where he was awarded the MC.

An instructor at RMC, Sandhurst, 1923–1927, MacMullen married in 1927 and commanded the 1st Battalion of his regiment 1937–1939. A brigadier in 1940, he was appointed to command an Anti-Aircraft Division in 1941 and was Deputy Assistant Adjutant General at the War Office 1941–1942. Appointed CBE in 1943, and the recipient of an honorary MA from Oxford University, he commanded the South Midland Area from 1943 until his retirement from the army in 1945.

McNEILL, Major General Alister Argyll Campbell *(1884–1971), CB*
Educated at Glasgow High School and Glasgow University, McNeill was gazetted into the Indian Army Medical Service in 1908. Except for service in Palestine in the First War, the whole of his army career was spent in India.

Specializing in surgery, McNeill was a major in 1920, a lieutenant colonel in 1928 and a colonel in 1937. Promoted major general in 1941, he was appointed CB in 1943 and retired from the army the same year.

Retired to Scotland, McNeill was a member of the Royal and Ancient Golf Club at St Andrews.

MACRAE, Major General Albert Edward *(1886–1958), CB, OBE*
Born in Scotland and educated at Dover College and RMC, Kingston, Ontario, Macrae was commissioned in the Royal Artillery in 1906. Married in 1912 and a graduate of the Military College of Science in 1914, he was Assistant Superintendent of the Royal Arsenal 1914–1921.

Assistant Superintendent of Design at Woolwich 1921–1928 and 1929–1934,

Macrae, a colonel in 1935, was Superintendent of Experiments, Shoeburyness, 1934–1937. Chief Superintendent of Design at Woolwich 1937–1939, he was a major general at the outset of war in 1939.

The Ministry of Supply's Representative in Canada 1939–1941, Macrae was the Military Technical Adviser to the Department of Munitions and Supply in Ottawa for the rest of the war. Chief Engineer, Canadian Arsenals Ltd., 1945–1946, he retired from the army in 1946 and, staying on in Canada, was Director of the Gun Division, Canadian Department of Defence in 1951.

MACRAE, Major General Ian Macpherson *(1882–1956), CB, CIE, OBE*

Educated at Edinburgh Academy and completing his medical studies at Edinburgh University in 1903, Macrae was gazetted into the RAMC in 1914. Twice mentioned in despatches and awarded the OBE in 1919, he joined the Indian Army Medical Service that year.

Inspector General of Prisons, Bihar and Orissa, in 1926, Macrae was Governor of the Military Hospital, Peshawar, in 1927. Assistant Director Medical Services, Bombay, 1929–1933, he was Assistant Director of Indian Medical Services 1933–1937. Deputy Director Medical Services Eastern Command, India, 1937–1941, he retired from the army in 1941.

Re-employed as Red Cross Commissioner for Indian troops in Malaya in 1941, Macrae was taken prisoner by the Japanese during the retreat to Singapore. Repatriated in 1945, he retired to his native Scotland.

MACREADY, Lieutenant General Sir Gordon Nevil
2nd Bt (1891–1956), KBE, CB, CMG, DSO, MC

The son of a general and baronet, Macready was educated at Cheltenham and RMA, Woolwich. Commissioned in the Royal Engineers in 1910, his First War service was in France, where he was six times mentioned in despatches, awarded the MC in 1916 and admitted to the DSO in 1918.

Attached to the Supreme War Council, Versailles, 1918–1919, Macready helped organize the Police Force in Poland 1919. Married in 1920, he attended the Staff College, Camberley, 1923–1924 and was Assistant Secretary to the Committee of Imperial Defence, 1926–1932. A student at the Imperial Defence College 1933, he spent the next two years serving on the staff at the War Office. Deputy Director of Staff Duties at the War Office 1936–1937, he was briefly Commandant of the Small Arms School, Hythe, before being appointed Chief of the British Military Mission to the Egyptian Army in 1938.

Assistant CIGS 1940–1942, the 'modest, quick and intelligent' Macready (Young (ed.), 1973, 141) was left in a redundant position at the War Office when Nye, not he, was made Deputy CIGS to Brooke in December 1941. The solution was to send him, along with his former chief, Dill, to Washington. There he was Chief of the British Army Staff until the end of the war.

Knighted in 1945 and retiring from the army in 1946, the same year as he succeeded his father, Macready was Regional Commissioner for Lower Saxony, Control Commission Germany, 1946–1947, and was British Chairman of the

Economic Control Office for 'Bizonia' (the British and American Occupation Zones in Germany) 1947–1949. Economic Adviser to the UK High Commissioner in Germany, 1949–1951, he settled thereafter in Paris. His rather querulous, not to say disagreeable, memoir, *In the Wake of the Great*, was published at his widow's request in 1965.

McCREERY, General Sir Richard Loudon *(1898–1967), GCB, KBE, DSO, MC*
Educated at Eton and RMC, Sandhurst, McCreery was commissioned in the 12th Lancers in 1915. His First War service was in France, where he was severely wounded and awarded the MC in 1918.

Said to be 'one of the greatest horsemen of his generation' (DNB) and the winner of many sporting trophies, McCreery married in 1928, and attended the Staff College, Camberley, 1928–1929. Dubbed 'Dreary McCreery' by Dorman-Smith (Greacan, 1987, 194), though better known to his friends as 'Dick', he was Brigade Major, 2nd Cavalry Brigade, 1930–1933 and commanded the 12th Lancers 1935–1938. Serving on the staff of 1st Division 1938–1939, he was in France with the BEF for the first few months of the phoney war and assumed command of 2nd Armoured Brigade early in 1940.

Admitted to the DSO in June 1940 for his part in operations south of the Somme, McCreery was promoted major general and appointed GOC of the newly-formed 8th Armoured Division that November. Sent to Cairo AHQ by Brooke in March 1941 as adviser on the use of armoured forces, but 'practically ignored . . . and never referred to' (Danchev & Todman, 2001, 235), he was dismissed by Auchinleck in July, but reinstated after the 'Cairo purge' as Alexander's Chief of Staff. Reserved and much imitated for his 'strange hesitant way of speaking' (Richardson, 1985, 160), he also had 'a violent temper' (Roberts, 1987, 134). He saw the campaign in North Africa through, but was deemed by Montgomery to be 'quite out of touch with the practical side of battle fighting' (Alanbrooke, 6/2/22, LHCMA).

Knighted in 1943 and promoted lieutenant general, McCreery commanded X Corps during the Salerno landings and, in September 1944, assumed command of 8th Army in Italy. Present at the surrender of German forces there in 1945, he was GOC-in-C British Occupation forces in Austria and British Representative on the Allied Control Commission for Austria 1945–1946. GOC-in-C BAOR, 1946–1948, he was promoted general in 1948 and after a year as British Army Representative on the Military Staff Committee of the UN, retired from the army in 1949 with his knighthood enhanced.

Colonel Commandant of the RAC 1947–1956, McCreery was Colonel of the 12th Lancers in 1951 and Colonel of the 9th/12th Lancers in 1960. He lived in his retirement in Somerset. Never 'sufficiently recognized' for his achievements, according to Brooke (Bryant, 1965, 411), he stirred controversy in 1959 by publishing an article in the regimental journal criticizing Montgomery for his intolerance and for the over-cautious pursuit of Rommel's *Panzerarmée* after Alamein.

McSHEEHY, Major General Oswald William *(1884–1975), CB, DSO, OBE*
The son of an army surgeon and educated at St Edmund's, Ware, and St Thomas's Hospital, London, McSheehy joined the Royal Army Medical Corps in 1909. Married in 1911 and a captain in 1912, his First War service was in France, where he was twice mentioned in despatches and admitted to the DSO in 1915.

Deputy Assistant Director General of Army Medical Services 1922–1926, McSheehy served in South Africa, India and Malaya before being promoted colonel in 1937 and appointed Deputy Director Army Medical Services at the War Office in 1938. A major general in 1941, he was Deputy Director Medical Services, Southern and Eastern Commands, 1941–1945.

Retired from the army in 1945, McSheehy was Deputy Director of Health, UNRRA, 1945–1946 and Colonel Commandant of the RAMC 1946–1950. Re-married in 1954, he lived in Surrey.

MAJENDIE, Major General Vivian Henry Bruce *(1886–1960), CB, DSO*
The son of a clergyman and educated at Winchester and RMC, Sandhurst, Majendie was commissioned in the Somerset Light Infantry in 1908. He served with the West African Frontier Force in southern Nigeria 1908–1913 and in India 1913–1915 before his battalion was posted to France. Married in 1916 and admitted to the DSO in 1917, he was a brevet major in 1919.

After attending the Staff College, Camberley, 1920–1921, Majendie was Brigade Major with the 14th Infantry Brigade in Ireland. An instructor at Sandhurst 1922–1924 and a keen cricketer, he served on the staff of the West African Frontier Force 1924–1928 and commanded the 2nd Battalion, Somerset Light Infantry, 1929–1933. After attending the Imperial Defence College in 1932, he was on the directing staff of the Staff College, Camberley, 1933–1936. Made Director of Military Training, AHQ India, in 1936, he was 'greatly alarmed', apparently, 'to discover that his son wrote poetry' (Bond, 1980, 69). Promoted major general in 1938, he was appointed GOC 55th (West Lancashire) Division.

Made GOC Northern Ireland District in 1941, Majendie was appointed CB and returned to the War Office in 1943 as President of the Regular Commissions Board. Colonel of the Somerset Light Infantry 1938–1947, he retired from the army in 1946 and was DL for Hertfordshire in 1951.

MALDEN, Major General Clifford Cecil *(1891–1941)*
Of the little that is known about this officer, it appears that after resigning his commission in the Royal Sussex Regiment in 1910, he was re-commissioned in 1911. His First War service was in France. He attended the Staff College, Camberley, 1924–1925, and returned to Camberley as an instructor. A sportsman, he played cricket and hockey for the army. He commanded the 1st Battalion of the Royal Sussex Regiment 1934–1936 and attended the Imperial Defence College that year. A colonel in 1936 and married in 1937, he served on the staff at the War Office 1937–1938.

Director of Military Training at the War Office in 1939, Malden was promoted major general in 1940 and appointed GOC 2nd (London) Division that December. He was killed in a motor accident in March 1941.

MALLABY, Major General Aubertin Walter Sothern
(1899–1945), CIE, OBE
Educated at Brighton College, Mallaby attended the Cambridge young officer's course and was gazetted into the 1st/67th Punjab Regiment (Indian Army) in 1918. He served briefly in Afghanistan, with the Army of the Black Sea 1919–1920 and in India 1920–1929. After attending the Staff College, Camberley, 1930–1931, he spent the next five years on staff employment interspersed with regimental duties. Married in 1935, he served on the staff at the War Office 1938–1941.

Deputy Director of Military Operations 1941–1942, Mallaby was remembered by Kennedy, his chief, as 'a professional of the highest calibre' (Kennedy, 1957, 174).Returning to India, he commanded the 2nd Punjabis in Bengal and later the 19th Hyderabad Regiment in Assam 1942–1943. Director of Military Operations, GHQ India, 1943–1944, he attended the Ottawa QUADRANT conference. Reverting, at his own request, to the substantive rank of brigadier and commanding 49th Indian Infantry Brigade from September 1944, he was murdered in Surabaya by Javanese patriots in October 1945. He left a widow and three children.

MALTBY, Major General Christopher Michael *(1891–1980), CB, MC*
Educated at King's, Canterbury, Bedford School and RMA, Woolwich, Maltby was commissioned on the unattached list in 1910 and was gazetted into the 9th Jat Regiment (Indian Army) the following year. Serving in the Persian Gulf 1913–1914, his First War service was in France, where he was wounded, three times mentioned in despatches and awarded the MC.

A brevet major in 1919, Maltby served on the North-West Frontier 1922–1923 and attended the Staff College, Quetta, 1923–1924. Married in 1927, he attended the RAF Staff College, Andover, 1927–1928 and served on the staff at AHQ India. Senior Staff Officer at Quetta 1932–1934, he commanded the 3rd (Jhelum) Brigade 1935–1937 and the 19th Indian Brigade on the North-West Frontier 1937–1938.

Made commander of British troops in China 1939, Maltby was in command of the Hong Kong garrison in 1941. Deprived of reinforcement and confronting a large and well-informed Japanese invading force, he held on for three weeks before ordering his troops to surrender on Christmas Day.

Released from captivity in 1945, Maltby was repatriated and appointed CB in 1946. He retired from the army that year. DL for Somerset in 1953, he lived the last five years of his life a widower.

MANIFOLD, Major General John Alexander *(1884–1960), CB, DSO*
Educated at Watson's College, Edinburgh, and Edinburgh University,

Manifold was commissioned in the Royal Army Medical Corps in 1909 and married the same year. A captain in 1912, his First War service was in the Mediterranean, Egypt and in German and Portuguese East Africa. Twice mentioned in despatches, he was admitted to the DSO in 1919.

Assistant Professor of Pathology at the Royal Army Medical College 1921–1924, Manifold spent most of the rest of his army career in India. After two years in Poona, he was Assistant Director of Hygiene and Pathology, Western Command, India, 1926–1927, and Assistant Director of Pathology, AHQ India, 1927–1931. After a two-year spell in Calcutta, he was Deputy Director of Hygiene and Pathology, AHQ India, 1936–1939.

A colonel in 1937 and a major general in 1941, Manifold was Director of Hygiene at the War Office 1939–1941 and Deputy Director of Medical Services, Scottish Command, in 1941. He retired in 1944.

MANSERGH, General Sir Edward Robert *(1900–1970), GCB, KBE, MC*
Born and raised in South Africa and educated at RMA, Woolwich, Mansergh was commissioned in the Royal Field Artillery in 1920. Employed on regimental and staff duties at home and abroad for many years, he transferred to the Royal Horse Artillery and was a member of the British Military Mission to Iraq 1931–1935. Awarded the MC in 1932, he was an instructor at RMA, Woolwich, 1936–1937 and was Adjutant there from 1938 to 1939.

A battery commander in Eritrea and Abyssinia 1940–1941, 'Bob' Mansergh was CRA 5th Indian Division in North Africa and Iraq 1941–1943. As an acting major general he was appointed to command the 11th East African Division in the Arakan in January 1945, only to be given command of 5th Indian Division a month later. An 'exceptionally able young officer' (Slim, 1999, 440), he led his command in the re-capture of Rangoon.

Made GOC of XV Corps in 1946, Mansergh was a 'very patient' C-in-C Allied Forces in the Netherlands East Indies before the year was out (Bristow, 1974, 139). Director of the Territorial Army in 1947, he was Military Secretary to the Secretary of State for War 1947–1948. Commander of British Forces in Hong Kong 1949–1951, he was Deputy C-in-C Allied Forces, Northern Europe, 1951–1953 and C-in-C 1953–1956. He was C-in-C United Kingdom Land Forces from 1956 until his retirement from the army in 1959.

Colonel Commandant of the RHA 1957–1970, Mansergh was Chairman of the Westminster Chamber of Commerce 1962–1963.

MARSHALL-CORNWALL, General Sir James Handyside
(1887–1985), KCB, CBE, DSO, MC
Born in India, the son of the Postmaster General of United Provinces and educated at Rugby and RMA, Woolwich, Marshall-Cornwall was commissioned in the Royal Artillery in 1907. A qualified interpreter in several languages before 1914, his First War service was in France, where, working in military intelligence, he was five times mentioned in despatches, awarded the MC in 1916 and admitted to the DSO in 1918.

A member of the British delegation at the Paris Peace conference and appointed CBE in 1919, Marshall-Cornwall was one of the first post-war batch of students attending the Staff College, Camberley. Married in 1921, he served with the Army of the Black Sea 1920–1923, was British delegate to the Thracian Boundary Commission 1924–1925 and was attached to the Shanghai Defence Force in 1927. Military Attaché, Berlin, Stockholm, Oslo and Copenhagen 1928–1932, he was CRA 51st (Highland) Division 1932–1934. Chief of the British Military Mission to the Egyptian Army 1937–1938, he was Director General Air and Coast Defence at the War Office 1939–1940.

Knighted in 1940, after leading the British Military Mission to the French Tenth Army in June 1940, which, effectively, meant arranging the evacuation of British line of communication troops from south of the Somme, 'Jimmy' Marshall-Cornwall was appointed to command III Corps. Head of the British Military Mission to Turkey 1940–1941, he was briefly GOC British troops in Egypt. Judged 'intelligent, but not creatively constructive' (Jones, 1954, 455), and regarded by Auchinleck as 'not always easy to get on with and apt to be tactless' (Dill, 2nd. acc. 6/2/6, LHCMA), he was sent home and appointed GOC Western Command. Leaving that post with 'considerable regret' (Marshall-Cornwall, 1984, 201), he spent a year on War Office duties attempting to harmonize relations between SOE and MI5, and retired from the army in 1943. His only son was killed on active service in Normandy in July 1944.

Active in his retirement, Marshall-Cornwall was attached to the Foreign Office as Editor-in-Chief of captured German Archives 1948–1951. President of the Royal Geographical Society 1954–1958, he dabbled in arms dealing and was the author of numerous military biographies. He wrote his engaging autobiography *Wars and Rumours of War* when well into his nineties. A widower for 18 years, he died on Christmas Day in his ninety-ninth year.

MARTEL, Lieutenant General Sir Giffard Le Quesne
(1889–1958), KCB, KBE, DSO, MC
The son of a general and educated at Wellington and RMA, Woolwich, Martel was commissioned in the Royal Engineers in 1909. His First War service was in France, where, serving with the Royal Tank Corps from 1916, he was five times mentioned in despatches, awarded the MC and admitted to the DSO.

Army and inter-service welterweight boxing champion and acknowledged as a 'brilliant inventive engineer' (Macksey, 1969, 94), Martel was an armoured pioneer with an eye to design. After attending the Staff College, Camberley, 1921–1922, he married, served on the staff of the Directorate of Fortifications and Works at the War Office and was attached to the Experimental Mechanized Force in 1927. A brevet lieutenant colonel in 1928, he was an instructor at the Staff College, Quetta, 1930–1934. After attending the Imperial Defence College in 1935, he was Assistant Director of Mechanization at the War Office 1936–1938. Instrumental in getting the Christie suspension system adopted for Cruiser Tanks, he was Deputy Director of Mechanization at the War Office 1938–1939.

Appointed to command 50th (Northumbrian) Division in 1939, Martel took it to France to form part of III Corps with the BEF. Stationing himself behind troops being 'particularly heavily shelled' during the improvised counter-attack at Arras (Martel, 1949, 160), he, by his own account, rallied stragglers and stabilized the line. However, there was criticism from tank officers who felt 'his powers as a commander and tactician did not match his gifts as a theorist' (DNB).

Made Commander of the Royal Armoured Corps in 1940, Martel had a roving brief to examine tank performance under battlefield conditions. But in his efforts to be constructive he fell-out with colleagues, particularly Hobart, and tended to annoy field commanders. Auchinleck regarded him as 'inclined to be a little bit complacent' (Dill, 2nd. acc. 6/2/12, LHCMA) and Brooke evidently disliked him, to the extent that he abolished the post of Commander RAC.

Knighted in 1943 and made head of the British Military Mission to Moscow, a posting which, as Brooke noted, 'he did not appreciate very much' (Danchev & Todman, 2001, 387), Martel was recalled two years later and, having lost an eye from an injury sustained when his London club was bombed, retired from the army in 1945 with knighthood enhanced. His daughter had been killed in a riding accident in 1941, and with his career 'end[ing] in a series of disappointments' (DNB), he stood unsuccessfully as a Conservative candidate in the 1945 general election.

Colonel Commandant of the Royal Engineers 1944–1945, Martel was Chairman of the Royal Cancer Hospital 1945–1950. Holding a number of directorships with engineering companies, he was, in his retirement, a fairly prolific writer on military subjects.

MARTIN, Lieutenant General Hugh Gray *(1887–1969), CB, DSO, OBE*
Educated at Marlborough and RMA, Woolwich, Martin was commissioned in the Royal Artillery in 1906. Transferring to the Royal Horse Artillery in 1912, his First War service was in France and Mesopotamia. Married in 1915, he was mentioned in despatches and admitted to the DSO in 1918.

Awarded the OBE for his part in operations in Afghanistan, 1919, Martin attended the Staff College, Camberley, 1920–1921. Serving thereafter in India, he was an instructor at the Staff College, Quetta, 1928–1931. Re-married in 1930, he attended the Imperial Defence College in 1936 and, a colonel in 1937, commanded the Mobile Division's Anti-Aircraft artillery. He was, in rapid succession, Senior Staff Officer of 3rd Division in 1938, CRA 4th Division and GOC 3rd Anti-Aircraft Division, before being appointed Major General i/c Anti-Aircraft artillery with the BEF in France 1939–1940. Appointed CB, he was promoted lieutenant general in 1941 and retired from the army the following year.

Military Correspondent for the *Daily Telegraph* 1943–1959, Martin was a frequent contributor to magazines and was author of the *History of the 15th (Scottish) Division.*

MARTIN, Major General John Simson Stuart *(1888–1973), CSI*
The son of a clergymen and educated at Oban High School, in Australia and at Edinburgh University, Martin qualified as a doctor in 1911. Commissioned in the Indian Medical Service the next year and a captain in 1915, his First War service was in Egypt and Mesopotamia, where he was mentioned in despatches and taken prisoner at Kut-al-Amara.

Married in 1924 and a lieutenant colonel in 1931, Martin served the entirety of his career in India. Deputy Director Medical Services, Central Command, 1935–1939, he was a major general in 1943 and retired from the army in 1945.

Having, through marriage, acquired property on the Isle of Skye (about 5,000 acres), Martin lived there for the remainder of his life. As laird of Husabost and Glendale, he became something of a cult figure, wearing the kilt, preaching from the pulpit and, allegedly, glorying in all things Gaelic.

MARTIN, Major General Kevin John *(1890–1958), DSO*
Born in India and educated at Beaumont College and RMA, Woolwich, Martin was commissioned in the Royal Engineers in 1910. His First War service was in France, where he was admitted to the DSO in 1914, was five times mentioned in despatches and, in 1918, served on the general staff of the Allied C-in-C.

Married in 1915, Martin attended the Staff College, Camberley, 1922–1923 and was Assistant Military Attaché in Paris 1927–1928, followed by a two-year spell as Military Attaché in Warsaw. After a further two years serving on the staff in the War Office, he was CRE Baluchistan District 1934–1936.

After attending the Imperial Defence College in 1937 and returning to staff duties at the War Office in 1938, Martin, an acting major general in 1941 and a temporary major general in 1942, was ADC to the King 1942–1945. He retired from the army in 1945. His only son was killed in action in 1941.

MASON-MACFARLANE, Lieutenant General Sir Frank Noel
(1889–1953), KCB, DSO, MC (and bars)
The son of a Scottish doctor-turned soldier and educated at Rugby and RMA, Woolwich, Mason-Macfarlane was commissioned in the Royal Field Artillery in 1909. Postings to South Africa and India were followed by First War service in France and Mesopotamia, where he was awarded the MC.

A games-playing writer of light verse, Mason-Macfarlane married in 1918. After taking part in operations in Afghanistan in 1919 he attended the Staff College, Quetta, in 1920. A staff officer at AHQ, India, 1922–1926, he was Adjutant at the Royal Artillery Training Centre, Muttra, 1926–1928, and served on the staff of Eastern Command, India, 1928–1930. Military Attaché in Vienna 1931–1934, his responsibilities extended to covering Budapest and Berne. After attending the Imperial Defence College in 1935, he was Military Attaché in Berlin, 1937–1939. Having acquired an unrivalled knowledge of the German army, he was briefly Brigadier Royal Artillery at Aldershot in 1939, before being promoted major general and appointed Director of Military Intelligence to the BEF in France.

Underutilized at GHQ, Mason-Macfarlane improvised and commanded a scratch 'Macforce' during the withdrawal to Dunkirk. Though the military value of guarding the line of the River Scarpe was questionable, his 'powerful physique, cool temperament, dynamic energy and, above all . . . his grand sense of humour' (Smyth, 1957, 49), endeared him to his subordinates. Admitted to the DSO and criticized for the tone of his post-Dunkirk BBC broadcast, he was made Deputy Governor of Gibraltar and appointed GOC 44th Division in June 1941. Falling out almost immediately with his corps commander, Montgomery, who claimed he was 'unfit for command', and did 'not understand the handling of a Division' (Dill, 2nd. ac. 4, LHCMA), he was made head of the British Military Mission to Moscow in July 1941.

After a year in Moscow, during which time he fell out with Beaverbrook but formed a working relationship with Cripps, of whom he had 'the happiest recollections' (Butler, 1972, 132), 'Mason-Mac' was made Governor and C-in-C of Gibraltar. Knighted in 1943, he spent several months in southern Italy as head of the Allied Control Commission, negotiating a form of civil government unacceptable to London, but acceptable to the allied commanders and a good majority of the Italian people.

In ill-health, indeed subject to creeping paralysis, Mason-Macfarlane retired from the army in 1945. Moved, apparently, 'by a long-standing lack of sympathy for the ruling party' (DNB), he stood as Labour candidate for North Paddington in the 1945 general election and, to the surprise of many, won the seat from Brendan Bracken. Whether through illness or disillusionment, he applied for the Chiltern Hundreds the next year.

A widower for the last six years of his life, a sad cycle of operations, loneliness and increasing disability made death, when it came, a release. He had not had a particularly good war. Possessing, it is said, all the qualities of a fine fighting soldier, he was, save for the brief life of 'Macforce', never able properly to exhibit them.

MASSY, Lieutenant General Hugh Royos Stokes
(1884–1965), CB, DSO, MC

Born in Pembrokeshire and educated at Bradfield and RMA, Woolwich, Massy was commissioned in the Royal Field Artillery in 1902. He served in West Africa 1907–1911 and, married in 1912, was Adjutant to the 4th East Lancashire Brigade, RFA, 1913–1914. His First War service was in Gallipoli, Egypt and France, where he was awarded the MC and admitted to the DSO.

After attending the Staff College, Camberley, in 1919, Massy spent the next ten years in India. An instructor at the Staff College, Quetta, 1925–1928, he attended the Imperial Defence College in 1930. A colonel in 1932, he returned to India as an instructor at the Senior Officers' School, Belgaum. Brigadier Royal Artillery Southern Command 1934–1938, he was promoted major general and made Director of Military Training at the War Office in 1939.

Deputy CIGS 1939–1940, Massy was, briefly, C-in-C of the North-Western Expeditionary Force in 1940, though he stayed in London for the duration of the Norway campaign. He commanded XI Corps, Home Forces, 1940–1941. Considered by Dill to be 'too old' (Dill 2nd ac. 11, LHCMA), and 'with his increasing deafness a severe handicap' (Tremlett, WSL, 94), though still a year short of retirement age, he eventually retired from the army in 1943,

Colonel Commandant of the Royal Artillery 1945–1951 and High Sheriff of Pembrokeshire in 1946, Massy was Boy Scout Commissioner for the county. A widower for the final five years of his life, he settled in Southern Rhodesia (Zimbabwe).

MAXWELL, Major General Sir Aymer *(1891–1971), Kt, CBE, MC*
Educated at Cheltenham and RMA, Woolwich, Maxwell was commissioned in the Royal Artillery in 1911. Married in 1915, his First War service was in France where he was mentioned in despatches and awarded the MC.

Saying nothing of himself in his *Who's Who* entry, beyond the bald 'War of 1939–1945, Middle East; retired pay 1944', the elements of his wartime soldiering career were made up of him leaving the army in 1919, being re-commissioned in the Scots Guards (supplementary reserve) and serving as Commandant of the Eton OTC. He was CRA 4th Indian Division 1940–1941 and Major General RA, Middle East, 1942–1943.

Chairman of the British Legion, Scotland, 1954–1958, Vice-Lieutenant of the Stewartry of Kirkudbrightshire, Vice-Convener of the County Council 1956–1959 and Convener 1959–1964, Maxwell was knighted in 1957. A member of the Royal Company of Archers, his only son, a captain in the artillery, was killed in action in September 1943.

MAYNE, General Sir Ashton Gerard Oswald Mosley
(1889–1955), GCB, CBE, DSO
Educated at Wellington and RMC, Sandhurst, Mayne was commissioned in 1908 and gazetted into the 13th (Duke of Connaught's) Lancers in 1910. A captain in 1915, his First War service was in Mesopotamia and Palestine. Wounded and thrice mentioned in despatches, he was admitted to the DSO in 1917.

Married in 1916, 'Mo' Mayne was Deputy Adjutant and QMG, AHQ, India, 1919–1920. He attended the Staff College, Camberley, 1920–1921, and returned to India to serve on the staff of AHQ 1922–1923. Chief Instructor at the Equitation School, India, 1922–1923, he served on the staff at the War Office 1927–1931. After attending the Imperial Defence College in 1933, he returned again to India to assume command of the Royal Deccan Horse, and, a brigadier in 1936, he was Director of Military Operations, India, 1938–1939.

Mayne served in the Middle East 1940–1943, first in Eritrea with 9th Indian Brigade, then, promoted major general in 1941, as GOC 5th Indian Division in Syria and Iraq. Appointed CB and promoted lieutenant general in 1942, he was GOC XXI Corps in Iraq before being recalled to India and made GOC Eastern Command in 1943.

Knighted in 1944, Mayne was Principal Staff Officer, India Office, 1945–1946 and retired from the army in 1947. Holding numerous honorary colonelcies in the Indian Army, he was a Fellow of the Royal Society of Arts in 1948. His son, a captain in the artillery, was killed in action in Italy in 1943.

MESSERVY, General Sir Frank Walter *(1893–1974)*, *KCSI, KBE, CB, DSO*
Born in Trinidad, the son of a bank manager, and educated at Eton and RMC, Sandhurst, Messervy, an excellent games-player, was commissioned in the Indian Army in 1913. His First War service was with Hodson's Horse in France, Palestine, Syria and, in 1919, Kurdistan.

A high-spirited polo-playing cavalryman, Messervy spent most of his army career in India. He attended the Staff College, Camberley, 1925–1926, married in 1927 and was a brigade major at Risalpur on the North-West Frontier 1929–1931. An instructor at the Staff College, Quetta, 1934–1937, he commanded the 13th (Duke of Connaught's) Lancers in India, 1938–1939. Upon the declaration of war in 1939 he was sent to the Sudan to serve on the staff of 5th Indian Division.

Made commander of 'Gideon Force', a composite mobile column which harried the Italians in their advance to and retreat from Kassala in Ethiopia, Messervy was in his element urging his men to 'bum on' at all speed (Maule, 1961, 45). Promoted brigadier and given command of 9th Infantry Brigade, he participated in the victorious assault on Keren in Eritrea. Promoted major general and transferred to the western desert, he was appointed to command 4th Indian Division and was admitted to the DSO after distinguishing himself at Sidi Omar during the CRUSADER offensive.

Messervy's cavalry background and striking appearance made him seem the ideal tank commander. A 'great likeable Airedale of a man' (Barnett, 1988, 153), he was appointed GOC 1st Armoured Division in January 1942. Along with the rest of 8th Army he was wrong-footed by Rommel's spoiling attack and, with 1st Armoured Division all but destroyed, he was sent to India only to be immediately recalled and made commander of 7th Armoured Division. Briefly taken prisoner in May (he disguised himself as an officer's batman and, with the nucleus of his staff, escaped), his counter-attack in front of Tobruk achieved no object and cost 7th Armoured Division sixty of its ninety tanks. He was sacked by Ritchie on the grounds that he had 'run out of luck' (Barnett, 1988, 164).

Having 'failed disastrously' as a tank commander (Bidwell & Graham, 1985, 242), Messervy restored his reputation as a fighting commander of infantry in Burma. Made GOC 7th Indian Division in February 1943, he acquired some fame in the Arakan when, with his HQ surprised and overrun by Japanese and wearing pyjamas, he rallied sundry 'clerks, orderlies, signallers and staff officers' in the defence of the 'Admin Box' (Slim, 1999, 207). Awarded a bar to his DSO, he took part in the successful defence of Kohima and, promoted lieutenant general in 1944, replaced Scoones as commander of IV Corps during the campaign to re-conquer Burma.

Having made 'a wonderful recovery from what might have been a blighted career', (Chenevix Trench, 1988, 147), Messervy was knighted in 1945. GOC-in-C Malaya in 1946, and GOC-in-C Northern Command, India, 1946–1947, he was C-in-C of the Pakistan Army, 1947, and retired in 1948. A colourful figure, whose style was 'to lead from the front' while remaining 'not too calculating of the odds' (Slim, 1999, 156), he held numerous honorary colonelcies with the Pakistan Army and was Deputy Chief Boy Scout, 1949–1950. His son was killed in a car accident in 1965.

MICHELMORE, Major General Sir William Godwin
(1894–1982), KBE, CB, DSO, TD
Born in Exeter and educated at Rugby and London University, Michelmore, a member of the London University OTC, was commissioned in the Devonshire Regiment in 1914. First War service was in France, where he was wounded, mentioned in despatches, awarded the MC and, by now a battalion commander, admitted to the DSO in 1919.

Married in 1921, Michelmore pursued his career as a solicitor. As an officer in the Territorial Army he commanded the 43rd (Wessex) Division (TA) 1919–1929 and was Deputy Chief Signal Officer, Southern Command, 1929–1933. A colonel in 1933, he commanded the 4th Battalion of the Devonshire Regiment 1936–1939. He was DL for Devon in 1938.

Made a brigade commander with Home Forces 1939–1941, Michelmore was appointed GOC of the Devon and Cornwall Division in October 1941. Over the remainder of the war he commanded two other lower establishment training formations: the 77th and 45th Divisions, both of which were formed through amalgamation.

Appointed CB in 1945, Michelmore was Chairman of the Devon Territorial and Auxiliary Forces Association 1948–1958. He was Mayor of Exeter 1949–1950 and a JP. He was sometime secretary to the Bishop of Exeter and Deputy Diocesan Registrar. A widower since 1965, he married Montgomery of Alamein's sister, herself a widow, in Exeter Cathedral in 1971.

MILES, Major General Eric Grant (1891–1977), CB, DSO, MC
Educated at Harrow and RMC, Sandhurst, Miles was commissioned in the King's Own Scottish Borderers in 1911. His First War service was in France. Wounded, five times mentioned in despatches, awarded the MC in 1915 and admitted to the DSO in 1917, he was a captain in 1916 and a brevet major by war's end.

After serving on the staff of the Rhine Army in 1920, 'Miles the soldier', as he was sometimes known, attended the Staff College, Camberley, 1921–1922, and served on the staff at the War Office from 1923. Married in 1924 (to the daughter of the Earl of Roden), he was Brigade Major to the Shanghai Defence Force 1927–1928. A major in 1928, he served on the staff at the War Office 1930–1933. After attending the Imperial Defence College in 1934, he commanded the 1st Battalion Royal Berkshire Regiment 1936–1938. On the General Staff in Malaya 1938–1939, he was appointed to command 126th

Infantry Brigade at war's beginning. 'Tall, dark and burly' (Smyth, 1957, 28), he served with the BEF in France with 42nd (East Lancashire) Division.

Promoted major general in 1940, Miles was briefly BGS Home Forces before being appointed GOC 42nd Division in April 1941. He was GOC 56th (London) Division from 1941 to 1943. Moving his division 2,300 miles from Iraq to Tunisia in April 1943, he was wounded in May and invalided home. Appointed CB and made Commander of Kent and South-Eastern District in 1943, he was GOC South-Eastern Command from 1944 to 1946.

Retired from the army in 1946, Miles was Colonel of the KOSB 1944–1954 and a member of the House of Laity, Church Assembly, 1955–1960. He was also Chairman of the Lichfield Diocesan Board of Finance 1960–1971. A widower for the last five years of his life, he lived in Shrewsbury.

MILLER, Major General Austin (1888–1947), CB, MC

Born in Bedford and educated at Bedford School and Cambridge University, Miller was gazetted into the 10th Bengal Lancers (Indian Army) in 1910. Transferring to the Sherwood Foresters in 1914, his First War service was in Egypt and France, where he was awarded the MC.

Married in 1916, Miller attended the Staff College, Camberley, 1921–1922. Spells of regimental soldiering at home, with the Shanghai Defence Force and in Singapore, were interspersed with periods of staff duties. A lieutenant colonel in 1934, he commanded the 1st Battalion Sherwood Foresters 1935–1939 and 164th Infantry Brigade, attached to the 55th (West Lancashire) Division, 1940–1942. Appointed CB in 1942, he was Major General i/c Administration, Scottish Command from 1942 until his retirement from the army in 1945. He died suddenly in Kashmir aged 59.

MILLER, Major General Charles Harvey (1894–1974), CB, CBE, DSO

Educated at Winchester and RMA, Woolwich, Miller was commissioned in the 18th Hussars in 1914. His First War service was in France, where he was twice wounded and mentioned in despatches.

Married in 1923, Miller attended the Staff College Camberley, 1928–1929, and commanded the Trans-Jordan Frontier Force 1932–1936. He commanded the 13th/18th Hussars 1937–1938 and, promoted brigadier, commanded the 5th Cavalry Brigade in Palestine and Trans-Jordan in 1940.

Serving on the staff of 8th Army in North Africa 1941–1942, first as Deputy Adjutant and QMG, then as BGS, Miller saw the campaign through to its successful conclusion in May 1943. Appointed CB, he was appointed Major General i/c Administration, 18th Army Group in Tunisia and MGA 15th Army Group for the campaigns in Sicily and Italy. Admitted to the DSO in 1943, he was heavily criticized by Montgomery for running 'a thoroughly bad administrative set-up' (Hamilton, 1983, 431). Sent home and made MGA Southern Command 1943–1945, he suffered another bout of Montgomery interfering in things that had nothing to do with him and was branded not merely 'a dismal failure' (Hamilton, 1983, 554) but as the officer responsible for the notorious 'mutiny at Salerno'. He retired from the army in 1946.

Chief of Staff to the Duke of Gloucester in Australia 1946–1947, Miller was an elected Fellow of the Royal Commonwealth and Royal Geographical Societies. Retired to Suffolk, he wrote a history of his old regiment and was DL for the county in 1953.

MILLS, Major General Percy Strickland *(1883–1973), CIE*

Educated at Dulwich and Guy's Hospital, Mills qualified as a doctor and entered the Indian Medical Service in 1906. He served in operations on the North-West Frontier and his First War service was in France and Mesopotamia, where he was twice mentioned in despatches.

Married in 1920, a lieutenant colonel in 1925 and a colonel in 1935, Mills was promoted major general in 1937 and was Surgeon General to the Government of Bengal 1937–1941 and an honorary physician to the King over the same period. He retired and went to live in South Africa.

MIRRLEES, Major General William Henry Buchanan
(1892–1964), CB, DSO, MC

Born in Cambridgeshire and educated at Marlborough and RMA, Woolwich, Mirrlees was commissioned in the Royal Field Artillery in 1912. His First War service was in France where he was awarded the MC.

Married in 1922, divorced in 1927 and re-married in 1931, 'Ray' Mirrlees's Second War service began with him commanding 3rd RHA. He was CRA 4th Indian Division 1940–1942. He was admitted to the DSO in 1941, had a bar added in 1942 and, promoted major general, was appointed MGRA, India. He retired from the army in 1946.

Colonel Commandant of the Royal Regiment of Indian Artillery in 1945, Mirrlees seldom set foot in England after the war. He divided his time between his flat in Paris and his home in Geneva.

MITCHINER, Major General Philip Henry *(1888–1952), CB, CBE*

Educated at Reigate Grammar School and St Thomas's Hospital, Mitchiner, a qualified surgeon, joined the Army Medical Services (Territorial Army) in 1914. His First War service was with the Serbian Army at Salonika and he stayed on in that theatre until 1921.

A surgeon at the Royal Northern Hospital 1921–1926, Mitchiner married in 1928. He maintained his connection with the Territorial Army through the London University Officer Training Corps. DL for the County of London in 1939, his Second War Service was mainly at home, but he was a consulting surgeon with the BEF, 1939–1940, and with the Middle East Forces.

Deputy Vice-Chancellor, University of London 1951–1952 and a Fellow of the Royal College of Surgeons, Mitchiner wrote a number of medical books and contributed to medical periodicals.

MOBERLY, Lieutenant General Sir Bertrand Richard
(1877–1963), KCIE, CB, DSO

Educated at Winchester and RMC, Sandhurst, Moberly was commissioned on the unattached list in 1897 and joined the 2nd Punjab Regiment (Indian Army) in 1899. He served on the North-West Frontier and in Somaliland (Somalia) 1903–1904, where he was mentioned in despatches. Married in 1910, his First War service was in Egypt, Gallipoli and the North-West Frontier, where he was wounded, five times mentioned in despatches and admitted to the DSO in 1915.

A brevet lieutenant colonel in 1918, Moberley attended the Staff College, Camberley, 1920–1921. After further service on the North-West Frontier he commanded the Kotal Brigade, was appointed CB in 1929 and promoted major general the next year. After a spell on half-pay, he was Deputy Adjutant and QMG, Northern Command, India in 1932, and Deputy CGS, 1933–1935. Knighted in 1937 and promoted lieutenant general in 1938, he was made QMG, India, and retired from the army in 1940.

A Red Cross Commissioner in India 1940–1943, Moberly lived his last years a widower in Hampshire.

MOLESWORTH, Lieutenant General George Noble
(1890–1968), CSI, CBE

Educated at Bradfield and RMC, Sandhurst, Molesworth was commissioned in the Somerset Light Infantry in 1910. His First War service was in Malta, North China and India, Adjutant to his battalion 1916–1919, he was mentioned in despatches for his part in operations in Afghanistan.

Deputy Assistant Adjutant General, AHQ, India, 1919–1921, Molesworth attended the Staff College, Quetta, 1921–1922, and, staying in India, he later served on the staff of AHQ. He was a brigade major in 1925 and transferred to the 15th Punjab Regiment (Indian Army) in 1928, the year after he married. An instructor at the Staff College, Quetta, 1929–1933, he commanded the 4th/15th Punjab Regiment 1934–1935 and attended the Imperial Defence College in 1935. Deputy Director of Military Operations and Intelligence, AHQ, India, 1936–1938, he was DMI 1938–1941.

Deputy GGS, GHQ India, 1941–1942, Molesworth was directly concerned with the deteriorating internal security situation. Secretary of the Military Department of the India Office 1943–1944, he retired in 1945. The author of several books and a member of the National Savings Committee for the Southern Region 1949–1960, he was also Vice-President of the Hertfordshire Scout Council in 1960.

MONEY, Major General Robert Cotton *(1888–1985), CB, MC*

Of military family and educated at Wellington and RMC, Sandhurst, Money was commissioned in the Cameronians (Scottish Rifles) in 1911. His First War service was in India and France, where he was awarded the MC.

Married in 1917, Money spent most of the inter-war years on regimental duties in India. He attended the Staff College, Camberley, 1922–1923, and was Adjutant to his battalion 1924–1926. Promoted lieutenant colonel, he commanded the 1st Battalion of the Cameronians 1931–1934 and was commander of the Lucknow Brigade 1936–1939.

Commandant of the Senior Officers' School, Sheerness, in 1939, 'Robin' Money was GOC 15th (Scottish) Division from August 1940 to January 1941. Chief of Staff, Northern Command, 1941, he was a District Commander in India from 1942 until his retirement from the army in 1944.

With his only son killed in action in 1940, Money worked for the Ministry of Transport 1944–1952. A widower in 1968, he re-married in 1978 and died in his Hertfordshire home in his ninety-seventh year.

MONRO, Major General David Carmichael *(1886–1960), CB, CBE*

Born and raised in New Zealand, Monro completed his medical studies at Edinburgh University. Temporarily commissioned in the Royal Army Medical Corps in 1914, he received a regular commission in 1917 and went to India the following year

A specialist in surgery, 'Jock' Monro was Personal Surgeon to the C-in-C, India, in 1931. Assistant Professor of Military Surgery at the Royal Army Medical College, London, in 1938, he was a consulting surgeon and Professor of Military Surgery at the RAM College from 1940 to 1945. A major general in 1941, he was Consultant Surgeon to the Middle East Force, Cairo, 1941–1942 and the army representative on the Allied Surgical Mission to Moscow in 1943. In North Africa he developed a system of mobile surgical units, which, in operation helped save many lives

Retired in 1945, Monro was re-employed as a consultant surgeon in Italy and Greece until 1948. A first-class golfer, he married in 1942 and, appointed CB in 1946, he, his wife and their adopted daughter lived in Rochampton.

MONTGOMERY, Field Marshal Sir Bernard Law
Viscount Montgomery of Alamein (1887–1976), KG, GCB, DSO

Of Anglo-Irish stock though born in London, the son of a clergyman, Montgomery spent his early years in Tasmania, where his father was bishop. Educated at St Paul's, where he was quite good at games, and RMC, Sandhurst, he was commissioned in the Royal Warwickshire Regiment in 1908.

Regimental duties on the North-West Frontier and Bombay kept Montgomery in India for four years. He played hockey for the army and his First War service was in France. Badly wounded in 1914, he was invalided home, admitted to the DSO and served out the remainder of the war as a staff officer. Mentioned six times in despatches and an acting lieutenant colonel in 1918, he commanded the 17th Battalion of the Royal Fusiliers with the British Army of the Rhine.

After attending the Staff College, Camberley, in 1920, Montgomery was appointed Brigade Major of the 17th Infantry Brigade in Cork. Brigade Major to the 8th Infantry Brigade in 1922, he served on the staff of the 49th (West

Riding) Division in 1923 and, reverting to the substantive rank of captain, commanded a company of the Royal Warwicks 1924–1925. A major in 1925, he was an instructor at the Staff College, Camberley, 1926–1929. Married in 1927 and made secretary to a War Office committee charged with revising the Infantry Training Manual, he was promoted lieutenant colonel in 1931. Appointed to command the 1st Battalion of the Royal Warwicks in Palestine, he brought it, so it is said, 'to the verge of mutiny by misjudged handling' (Liddell Hart, 1965, 382). In Egypt and India with the battalion over the next three years, he served on the directing staff of the Staff College, Quetta, 1934–1937. By now a widower, he became ever more 'austere, dedicated and eccentric' (Irving, 1981, 162). Commander of 9th Infantry Brigade at Portsmouth 1937–1938, he was promoted major general and appointed to command 8th Division in Palestine 1938–1939.

Appointed GOC 3rd Division at war's outset, Montgomery served in Brooke's II Corps with the BEF in France 1939–1940. On Brooke's recall to England he briefly commanded II Corps during the last stages of the Dunkirk evacuation. Adjudged to have come out 'either a good second or equal first' among the divisional commanders serving in the campaign (Hamilton, 1982, 395), he was appointed CB. Promoted acting lieutenant general, he assumed command of V Corps in July 1940.

Montgomery was to spend the next two years with Home Forces;. He commanded V Corps, then XII Corps, and became GOC-in-C South-Eastern Command in November 1941. Small in stature and often described as 'bird-like' in appearance, he ran his command ('Army' he liked to call it) on a tight rein. A teetotal non-smoker, the fitness regime he imposed on officers and men became legendary. With a reputation for 'having trodden on the corns of the orthodox', his 'ruthless opposition to inefficiency' made him enemies as well as admirers (Clifton James, 1958, 94). To the latter it was 'Monty's' dedication to his profession, coupled with his boundless self-confidence, that made him such a single-minded and successful commander. To those less certain he was destined for greatness, and indeed unconvinced by claims that he ever achieved it, he was 'an able and ruthless soldier and an unspeakable cad' (Harvey, 1978, 148). The second-choice commander-designate for First Army at the beginning of August 1942, he was in Egypt less than a fortnight later; summoned there to command 8th Army after the death of Gott. In this way he contrived to avoid responsibility for the disastrous Dieppe raid and, before the year was out, claimed for himself the credit for the famous victory of El Alamein.

With opinion on Montgomery so divided, it is not surprising that accounts of his post-'Cairo purge' impact on 8th Army vary considerably. To admirers he was the man for the occasion. Brooke, who had worked so hard to promote him, believed 'the hand of God' suddenly appeared 'to set matters right' (Danchev & Todman, 2001, 295). But alongside the post-Alamein 'woe betide the man who tries to belittle the achievements on the battlefield of our Monty' tradition (Pyman, 1971, 68), there emerged a revisionist argument stressing the 'second-hand coat of glory' he wore (Barnett, 1983, 266). Montgomery, and his supporters, made out that the command he inherited from Auchinleck was a 'dog's breakfast' (Montgomery, 1958, 87). Critics maintain that the basis for the Alamein victory was already firmly established.

'Monty', as well as being notoriously mean with money, was incapable of modesty. Selectively generous in his bestowal of patronage, he assembled a stable of loyal young subordinates who, in war and peace, served their master well. But, while they could pander to his self-publicizing egotism and singular inability to say or write anything generous about his predecessors, others found his 'warped and abrasive character' (Marshall-Cornwall, 1984, 167) so repellent that they could find little positive to say about his generalship.

Lacking the intellectual breadth of an original military thinker, Montgomery's vision was uncomplicated. But he was a thorough, tough-minded commander, and, a quality inseparable from his egotism, was adept at registering his personality on subordinates. His confidence spread to those who fought and died for him. His victories, whether in North Africa, Italy or in North-West Europe, were obtained through his ability to deploy numerically preponderant force. His orders were usually clear, he could delegate successfully and his desire to avoid heavy casualties genuine. Quick to criticize others, he never admitted any personal mistakes. Always his plan was the right one. When setbacks occurred, as at Mareth in March 1943, on the Sangro that autumn and in Normandy in 1944, scapegoats were quickly found. Preferring a 'hit 'em for six' approach to battle and laying much emphasis on his own brand of iron control, he ruled out any possibility of attracting praise for subtlety or for improvising solutions to practical problems.

Promoted general and knighted in November 1942, Montgomery remained with 8th Army for another year. He vaunted his own professionalism in the North African, Sicilian and Italian campaigns, yet frequently disobeyed superiors and blackguarded any British or American commander who earned his displeasure. He sneaked on Anderson and had him dismissed, but he was less successful in getting American field commanders to subordinate their egos to him. He clashed severely with Patton during the Sicilian campaign and as severely with Clark in Italy. Conscious that the Mediterranean theatre had become something of a sideshow, he was gratified to be ordered home in December 1943 as commander designate of 21st Army Group and C-in-C Allied Land Forces preparing for the invasion of France.

By now something of a star, Montgomery thoroughly enjoyed receiving the attention of a generally adoring public. Having had the invasion plan thoroughly revised, he made himself visible to as many troops as possible before D-Day. As the joke of the time had it, George VI asked Eisenhower, the Allied Supreme Commander, how he was getting on with 'Monty'. 'Oh, all right sir,' replied Eisenhower, 'though I sometimes think he's after my job.' 'I'm very relieved to hear you say that,' confided the King, 'for you know there are times when I think he's after mine.'

In Normandy Montgomery's response to the sluggishness of his advance was, characteristically, to sack under-performing generals and rationalize failure.

Operation GOODWOOD he claimed, after the bloody repulse of British armour, had not been an intended breakout but a deliberately attritional operation whereby powerful German forces were written down against his anvil upon which the American First Army could hammer. When, in August 1944, Eisenhower took over as C-in-C Allied Land Forces, Montgomery, effectively reduced in status to a mere Army Group Commander, was promoted Field Marshal. With his prestige dented by the failure of the British 1st Airborne Division at Arnhem, he recovered his poise by helping stem the German Christmas offensive in the Ardennes. However, he was nearly dismissed by Eisenhower for stating publicly that it was he who had saved the Americans from defeat. Further disagreements with Eisenhower over the conduct of operations in Germany – whether a 'broad front' or a 'single thrust' – soured relations between the two men for the rest of their lives.

After 'humiliating the German envoys' at the surrender ceremony on Luneberg Heath in May 1945 (Heathcote, 1999, 216), Montgomery became C-in-C British Forces of Occupation, Raised to the peerage in January 1946, he succeeded Brooke as CIGS that June. Over the next two 'uncomfortable years' (DNB) he, allegedly 'stuffed the Army Council with his own stooges' (Young (ed.), 1973, 717), toured considerably, expressed his 'boundless contempt . . . for Attlee and Co,' (Ball, ed., 1999, 630), complained continually about 'belly-achers' and pronounced Africans as being incapable of self-rule. Supporters made allowances for him. Critics deemed him a 'resounding failure' (Morgan, 1961, 200). That he was a homophobe who had, or so it is said, 'homosocial attachments' (Hamilton, 2001, 426), may have had to do with an unhappy and emotionally deprived childhood. Released from the War Office, he was made Chairman of the Western European Union C-in-Cs' Committee in 1948.

Made Deputy Commander of the Supreme Headquarters of the Allied Powers in Europe (SHAPE) in 1951, Montgomery continued in that post until his retirement, aged seventy, in 1958. His *Memoirs*, published that year, caused offence, particularly in America, and a retired Italian general challenged him to a duel. He continued to travel extensively and, having enjoyed a succession of honorary colonelcies, was often in the news. Loaded with honours and honorary degrees, he attracted publicity at the time of Churchill's death when, from South Africa, he announced he could not attend the funeral as the journey would certainly kill him. He did die eleven years later, of heart failure at his home near Alton in Hampshire. Almost to the end he retained the knack of saying the wrong thing.

The controversies Montgomery provoked and, provided he won them, enjoyed in his lifetime, have long since faded away. The 'battle of the memoirs' has, more or less, run its course and the debate on whether his 'single thrust' strategy in Germany would, if implemented, have shortened the war, still less leap-frogged Anglo-American forces to Berlin before the Russians, has lost any of the sting it may once have possessed. Though he is still talked of and written about, the impression of 'Monty' as a quirky, intellectually stunted and basically uninteresting figure is difficult to resist. At one level he resembles the dimly-remembered schoolmaster who, at the time, appeared so strong and dominant, but who, on middle-aged reflection, emerges as a lonely figure of phoney theatricality and empty flamboyance. Yet if this is the view of the post-war generation, there are still old soldiers who, though fully aware of 'Monty's' shortcomings and 'immature, insensitive and ignorant' nature, will still recall echoes of the myth he himself did so much to create – that, in the dark days of 1942, when nothing else mattered except beating Rommel, '[w]e needed him; we needed him very badly' (Fraser, 2002, 177).

MOORE, Major General Francis Malcolm *(1897–1974), CSI, CIE*

The son of a Dublin lawyer and educated at St Columba's College and Trinity College Dublin, Moore, a keen sportsman, was commissioned in the Royal Irish Rifles in 1915. Wounded in 1916, he transferred to the Indian Army in 1917, serving with the 52nd Sikhs in Mesopotamia for the next three years.

Moore's regimental service in India was mainly with the Frontier Force on the North-West Frontier. Married in 1927, he commanded 2nd/16th Punjab Regiment in Malaya in 1940 and raised and commanded the 100th Indian Infantry Brigade in 1941.

Promoted major general in 1943, Moore was appointed to command the newly-formed 34th Indian Division. Briefly made GOC 14th Indian Division in April 1943, he was transferred to a training role with the newly-formed 39th Indian Division. Director of Selection of Personnel at Army HQ, India, 1945–1946, he was Military Adviser-in-Chief to the Indian States Forces from 1946 until his retirement in 1948.

With no children Moore and his wife retired to his native Ireland, settling eventually in Co. Wicklow.

MOORHEAD, Major General Charles Dawson *(1894–1965), CB, DSO, MC*

Few of this officer's personal details are known. Educated at Cheltenham and RMC, Sandhurst, and commissioned in the Manchester Regiment in 1913, Moorheads's First War service was in France, where he was awarded the MC.

Adjutant to his regiment's 2nd battalion in 1921 and married in 1923, Moorhead graduated from the Staff College, Quetta, in 1931 and was an instructor in tactics at the School of Mechanical Engineering, Chatham, 1933–1935. Brigade Major to 8th Infantry Brigade 1933–1937 and a major in 1937, he was a Deputy Assistant Adjutant General at the War Office 1938–1939.

Chief Staff Officer at the BEF's GHQ in France 1939–1940, Moorhead was admitted to the DSO after Dunkirk. He was Deputy Director of Ordnance Services at the War Office 1940–1942, and served in the Middle East 1942–43 as commander of 155th Brigade. He was Deputy Adjutant General, Middle East Command, in 1942, was made CBE in 1943 and retired in 1947.

Moorhead was a Kent County Councillor from 1958, and maintained an active correspondence with *The Times* on the subject of retired officers' pay.

MORGAN, Lieutenant General Sir Frederick Edgworth
(1894–1967), KCB

Born in London, the son of a timber merchant, and educated at Clifton and RMA, Woolwich, Morgan was commissioned in the Royal Artillery in 1913. His First War service was in France, where he was twice mentioned in despatches. A captain in 1916, he married the next year.

Most of Morgan's inter-war soldiering was in India. He attended the Staff College, Quetta, 1927–1928, and, a major in 1932, served on the staff at AHQ, India, 1931–1934. A staff officer at the War Officer 1936–1938, he was promoted colonel and was chief staff officer with 3rd Division 1938–1939.

Put in charge of 1st Armoured Division's support group in 1939, 'Freddie' Morgan served briefly in France in 1940. Operating with 'no teeth at all' (Marshall-Cornwall, 1984, 139) as his infantry had been detached in the vain attempt to garrison Calais, he was evacuated from Brest and made BGS to II Corps. Promoted major general in 1941, he was GOC Devon and Cornwall Division that year and commanded 55th (West Lancashire) Division 1941–1942. Promoted acting lieutenant general in 1942, he was appointed GOC I Corps with Home Forces. In March 1943 he was made Chief of Staff to the Supreme Allied Commander (COSSAC) and charged with planning the opening of the Second Front. Brooke, lukewarm towards the project, apparently told him, 'Well there it is. It won't work but you must bloody well make it' (DNB).

Although Morgan worked hard as COSSAC, even to the extent of sleeping on a camp bed in his office, he was hampered in that there was not, from the beginning, a Supreme Commander to deputize for. Moreover, when the command set-up was put in place, Montgomery, the land forces commander, 'stood up and demolished' the COSSAC plan (Hamilton, 1983, 512). Not all Morgan's work was wasted; the 'Mulberry' artificial harbours were, in part, his idea, but for the rest of the war, and in his memoirs, Montgomery criticized Morgan for 'considering Eisenhower a god' (Montgomery, 1958, 236), for being too pro-American and for leading a campaign, of vendetta proportions, to discredit him.

Deputy Chief of Staff to the Supreme Allied Commander Allied Expeditionary Force (SHAEF) 1944–1945, Morgan was knighted in 1944 and was chief of UNRRA operations in Germany 1945–1946. Dismissed from that post, after claiming that UNRRA was being used by Soviet agents to foment unrest in the western occupation zones, he wrote bitterly of his experiences in post-war Germany in his otherwise good-humoured memoirs *Peace and War: A Soldier's Life* (1961).

Retired from the army in 1946, Morgan was Controller of Atomic Energy 1951–1954 and Controller of Atomic Weapons 1954–1956. He was also Colonel Commandant of the Royal Artillery 1948–1958. Living in Middlesex, he was much honoured in the United States after the war, but received no further British decorations.

MORGAN, Major General Harold de Riemer *(1888–1964), DSO*
Educated at Harrow and Oxford University, Morgan was commissioned in the Buffs in 1910. His First War service was in France where he was admitted to the DSO in 1918 and, in the same year, commanded the 7th Battalion of the Duke of Wellington's Regiment.

Adjutant of the Oxford University OTC 1919–1922, Morgan gained an MA for his services to the University. He graduated, unusually, from the RAF Staff College, Andover, in 1927 and commanded the 5th (Territorial) Battalion of the Royal Northumberland Fusiliers 1936–1939.

Promoted brigadier and made commander of 148th Infantry Brigade in 1939, Morgan was assigned to duties in Norway in April 1940. With his brigade made up of '1,000 ill-armed, under-equipped and untrained men' (Kersaudy, 1990, 114) and named SICKLEFORCE, he landed at Åndalsnes and tried, unsuccessfully, to maintain contact with Norwegian forces and stem the German advance northwards. Promoted major general in 1941, he was GOC 45th Division from April 1941 to January 1943. Brooke pronounced himself 'disappointed' with him and doubted 'very much if he is good enough for the job' (Danchev & Todman, 2001, 156). With his command disbanded, he served on War Office promotion boards until he retired from the army in 1946.

Colonel of the Royal Northumberland Fusiliers 1947–1953, Morgan was DL for Brecknock from 1949. A widower in 1958, he re-married in 1960 and died at his home in Brecon after a short illness.

MORGAN, General Sir William Duthie *(1891–1977), GCB, DSO, MC*
Born in Edinburgh, the son of a doctor, Morgan was educated at George Watson's College and RMA, Woolwich. He was commissioned in the Royal Artillery in 1910. His First War service was in France, where he was four times mentioned in despatches, awarded the MC and admitted to the DSO.

Married in 1921 and mentioned in despatches for his part in operations in Waziristan between 1922 and 1923, 'Monkey' Morgan, a small wiry man, attended the Staff College, Camberley, 1925–1926 and was Military Attaché at the British Embassy in Budapest 1929–1931. Chief Instructor at Woolwich 1934–1938, he served in France with the BEF 1939–1940 as the commander of a regiment of artillery and, latterly, as Chief Staff Officer with Alexander's 1st Division. At his suggestion, apparently, 1st Division was transferred from Barker's I Corp to Brooke's II Corps during the latter stages of the withdrawal to Dunkirk (Nicolson, 1973, 121).

Made BGS 1st Division after Dunkirk, Morgan was promoted major general in 1941 and appointed GOC 55th (West Lancashire) Division. Badly wounded that autumn, when a mortar shell exploded during a demonstration, he was hospitalized for three months before being made CGS Home Forces in 1942. Briefly CGS 21 Army Group, he was edged out by Montgomery on the grounds that 'he had not got the up-to-date operational experience' (Hamilton, 1983, 379), but 'couldn't have been more helpful' when de Guingand replaced him (de

Guingand, 1947, 347). Well-liked by Brooke, he was appointed GOC Southern Command in 1944 and, so as to keep an eye on Alexander, was appointed his Chief of Staff in Italy in 1945.

Knighted in 1945, Morgan was briefly Alexander's successor as Supreme Allied Commander in the Mediterranean. In establishing the 'Morgan Line', separating Italians from Yugoslavs in Friuli, he 'delineated a frontier' (Blaxland, 1979, 282). He commanded the British Army Staff in Washington from 1947 until his retirement from the army in 1950 with knighthood enhanced. Colonel Commandant of the Royal Artillery 1947–1956, he held numerous directorships with engineering companies. Residing in Middlesex, he was DL for the County of London (later Greater London) 1958–1976 and was also Vice-Lieutenant for Greater London 1965–1970.

MORRIS, General Sir Edwin Logie *(1889–1970), KCB, OBE, MC*

The son of a doctor and educated at Wellington and RMA, Woolwich, Morris was commissioned in the Royal Engineers in 1909. His First War service was in France, where he was awarded the MC, and in Italy. Mentioned five times in despatches, he was awarded the OBE in 1919.

A brigade major with the Army of the Black Sea 1919–1921, Morris married in 1921 before attending the Staff College, Camberley. He was an instructor at Camberley 1927–1929 and attended the Imperial Defence College in 1933. Commander RE in India in 1934, he was Deputy Director Military Operations and Intelligence, AHQ, India for the next two years. Deputy Director of Military Operations at the War Office 1936–1938, he was BGS Northern Command 1938–1939.

Promoted major general at war's outset, 'Ted' Morris, a 'shrewd amiable Sapper' (Connell, 1969, 201), was Director of Staff Duties at the War Office 1939–1940. Described as 'an ordinary-looking tall Englishman, [who] is probably a good soldier' (Leutze (ed.), 1972, 389), he was GOC 1st Division in 1941 and commanded II Corps under Home Forces 1941–1942. Considered by Dill to 'have grown rather old for field command' (Dill, 2nd. ac., 9, LHCMA), he was appointed Chief of Staff to the C-in-C, India, in 1942. A lieutenant general in 1943 and knighted upon his return to England in 1944, he was GOC-in-C Northern Command from 1944 until 1946.

British Army Representative on the Military Staff Committee of the UN from 1946 until his retirement in 1948, Morris was Colonel Commandant of the Royal Engineers 1944–1958 and was Chief Royal Engineer 1951–1958. Divorced in 1953 and re-married the same year, he lived in Surrey.

MUNRO, Major General Archibald Campbell *(1886–1961), CB*

The son of a doctor, Munro was educated at Glasgow High School and Glasgow University. Gazetted into the Indian Medical Service in 1908 and a captain in 1911, his First War service was in France and Mesopotamia, where he was mentioned in despatches.

Married in 1925 and Assistant Director of Medical Services, Western District, India, 1937–1940, Munro was Deputy Director of Medical Services, India, 1940–1942 and, appointed CB, was Director of Medical Services, India, from 1942 until his retirement in 1943.

Re-married in 1945, Munro contributed articles to medical journals and the Scottish Geographical Society Journal. He lived in Hampshire.

MURISON, Major General Charles Alexander Phipps
(1894–1981), CB, CBE, MC

Born, raised and educated in Canada, Murison was commissioned in the Royal Field Artillery in 1914. His First War service was in France, where he was wounded, mentioned in despatches and awarded the MC.

Like so many colonials who found soldiering agreeable, Murison stayed in the army. Married in 1920, he spent a dozen years on a captain's pay, serving largely in India. A graduate of the Staff College, Camberley, in 1929, he was a lieutenant colonel in 1939 and, a brigadier in 1940, he was Assistant QMG to the BEF in France 1939–1940.

Murison held a variety of War Office appointments thereafter. Deputy Director of Army Equipment 1942–1943, he was a temporary major general in 1943. He acquired that substantive rank in 1945, after serving two years as Deputy QMG. Chief Administrative Officer, Northern Command, 1945–1948, he retired from the army in 1949.

A contributor of articles to military journals, Murison spent his last years in his native Canada.

MURRAY, General Sir Horatius *(1903–1989), GCB, KBE, DSO*

Educated at Peter Symonds School, Winchester, and RMC, Sandhurst, Murray was commissioned in the Cameronians (Scottish Rifles) in 1923. A keen sportsman, he played football for the army. Transferring to the Cameron Highlanders in 1935, he attended the Staff College, Camberley, 1936–1937, and commanded his regiment's 3rd battalion in 1940.

In North Africa from 1941, 'Nap' Murray (friends likened him to Napoleon in looks and stature) commanded the 1st Gordon Highlanders at Alamein, where he was wounded, and 152nd Brigade with the 51st Highland Division in Tunisia, Sicily and Normandy. A man of 'infectious enthusiasm' (Blaxland, 1979, 190), he was admitted to the DSO in 1943. Appointed GOC 6th Armoured Division in August 1944, he fought the last months of the war in Italy. His bold leadership, apparently, made the forcing of the Argenta Gap a success.

Appointed CB in 1945, Murray was Director of Personal Services at the War Office 1946–1947, GOC 1st Infantry Division 1947–1950, and GOC Northumberland District 1951–1953. Commander of the Commonwealth Division in Korea 1953–1954, he was GOC-in-C Scottish Command and Governor of Edinburgh Castle 1955–1958. He was C-in-C Allied Forces, Northern Europe, from 1958 until his retirement in 1961.

MUSPRATT, General Sir Sydney Frederick *(1878–1972), KCB, CSI, DSO*
The son of an Indian Civil Servant and educated at United Services College and RMC, Sandhurst, Muspratt was commissioned in 1907 and gazetted into the 5th Cavalry Regiment (Probyn's Horse) in the Indian Army in 1908. A captain in 1914, his First War service was in France, where he was mentioned in despatches and admitted to the DSO in 1917.

A brevet lieutenant colonel in 1918, Muspratt attended the Staff College, Camberley, 1923–1924, married in 1925 and commanded the 4th Indian Infantry Brigade at Nowshera 1925–1927. Director of Military Operations, AHQ, India, 1927–1929, he was Deputy Chief of the General Staff, AHQ, India, 1929–1931. Appointed CB, he was Secretary to the Military Department of the India Office 1931–1933. He commanded the Peshawar District, India, from 1933 to 1936, where he took part in operations against the Mohmands, before returning to the India Office in 1937.

A lieutenant general in 1936 and knighted in 1937, Muspratt, apparently, 'fully agreed with [Amery's] policy on India' (Barnes & Nicholson (eds.), 1988, 626). He retired in 1941 and lived out his long autumn years in Hampshire.

N

NALDER, Major General Reginald Francis Heaton *(1895–1978), CB, OBE*
Educated at Dulwich College and London University, Nalder was temporarily commissioned in the Loyal (North Lancashire) Regiment in 1914. Transferring to the East Surrey Regiment in 1915, his First War service was in France and Italy.

Married in 1916, Nalder was seconded to the Royal Engineers Signal Service in 1918 and transferred to the Royal Signals in 1922. In India for most of the 1920s, he attended the Staff College, Camberley, 1926–1927, served on the North-West Frontier 1930–1931 and on the staff at the War Office 1935–1939.

Attached to GHQ of the BEF in France 1939–1940, Nalder was made OBE in 1941 and was CSO, IV Corps, Home Forces, 1940–1941. After serving on special duties in the Middle East, he was Deputy Director of Signals at the War Office 1942–1943. Promoted major general, he was Chief Signal Officer 15th Army Group 1943–1944. He was CSO Allied Armies in Italy 1944–1945 and at Allied Forces HQ 1945–1946.

Appointed CB in 1944 and Director of Signals in India from 1945 until his retirement in 1947, Nalder wrote the official history of British Army Signals in the Second World War (1953). He was Colonel Commandant of the Royal Corps of Signals 1955–1960.

NAPIER, Major General Charles Scott *(1899–1946), CB, CBE*

Educated at Wellington and RMA, Woolwich, Napier was commissioned in the Royal Engineers in 1916. His First War service was in France and in Egypt, where he was mentioned in despatches.

Napier was Adjutant to the Supplementary Reserve 1925–1926. A captain in 1926, he married in 1927 and attended the Staff College, Camberley, 1932–1933. A major in 1935, he served on the staff at the War Office 1935–1937, was Brigade Major, Aldershot Command, 1937–1938, and Brigade Major 1st Anti-Aircraft Brigade in 1939.

A lieutenant colonel in 1939, Napier was briefly Assistant QMG at the War Office, and was attached to the Directorate of Movement, concerned with transporting the BEF to France. A colonel in 1943, he was Chief of Movements and Transportation at SHAEF 1944–1945 and, as such, was in large part responsible for shipping allied forces and their equipment across the Channel from June 1944. A major general in 1944 and made CBE that year, he was appointed CB in 1945. He died after a short illness the following year, leaving a widow and a son.

NAPIER-CLAVERING, Major General Noel Warren
(1888–1964), CB, CBE, DSO

Educated at Clifton and RMA, Woolwich, Napier-Clavering was commissioned in the Royal Engineers in 1908. His First War service was in France, where, a captain in 1915, he was wounded and admitted to the DSO in 1917.

Married in 1921 and a student at the Staff College, Camberley, 1924–1925, Napier-Clavering was a major in 1925 and a lieutenant colonel in 1932. Serving in India, Palestine and in home commands, he shone as a staff officer. Assistant Adjutant and QMG 4th Division 1937–1939, he was Brigadier i/c Administration, British Troops in Egypt 1939–1940.

Promoted major general in 1940, Napier-Clavering was Deputy Adjutant General at GHQ Cairo from 1940–1942. Regarded as 'not a top-notcher' by Auchinleck (Dill 2nd. ac., 6/2/6, LHCMA), he was left behind in Egypt as the campaign moved westwards. Chief of the British Military Mission to the Egyptian Army 1942–1945, he retired from the army in 1945 and settled in Hampshire.

NARES, Major General Eric Paytherus *(1892–1947), CB, CBE, MC*

Educated at Marlborough and RMC, Sandhurst, Nares was commissioned in the Cheshire Regiment in 1911. His First War service was in France, where he was twice wounded, thrice mentioned in despatches and awarded the MC and bar.

A brevet major in 1919, Nares attended the Staff College, Camberley, 1927–1928. Married in 1931 and a lieutenant colonel in 1936, the same year as his wife died, he was appointed to command the 2nd Battalion of the Cheshires, then serving in Palestine, and was Assistant Adjutant and QMG 8th Division 1938–1939.

A temporary brigadier in 1940, Nares spent most of the war years in North Africa and the Mediterranean theatre. Mentioned five times in despatches for his work in distribution and communication, he was appointed CBE in 1941.

Appointed Commander of British troops in Berlin in August 1945 and appointed CB in January 1947, Nares fell ill, was admitted to the Millbank Hospital and died that June.

NAYLOR, Major General Robert Francis Brydges
(1889–1971), CB, CBE, DSO, MC
Educated at Charterhouse and RMC, Sandhurst, Naylor was commissioned in the South Staffordshire Regiment in 1909. Seconded to the Royal Engineers Signal Service in 1912, his First War service was in France, where he was seven times mentioned in despatches and admitted to the DSO.

Transferring to the newly-formed Royal Signals in 1920, 'Frank' Naylor attended the Staff College, Camberley, 1921–1922, and was Brigade Major at the Signal Training Centre 1923–1925. On the brigade staff on Malta 1925–1927, he married the Earl of Strafford's daughter in 1927 and was an instructor at the School of Signals 1927–1928. Employed with the West African Frontier Force 1928–1931, he commanded 3rd Divisional Signals at Bulford 1931–1935. A chief staff officer with Scottish Command 1936–1937, he was Brigadier i/c Administration, Western Command 1938–1939.

Major General i/c Administration at the War Office 1939–1941, Naylor was Deputy QMG 1941–1943 and Vice-QMG in 1943. Commander of L of C, 21st Army Group, North-West Europe, 1944–1945, he was Commander Northumbrian District from 1945 until his retirement from the army in 1946. Colonel of the Royal Corps of Signals 1944–1953, he was twice President of the Royal National Rose Society in the 1960s.

NEAME, Lieutenant General Sir Philip *(1888–1978), VC, KBE, CB, DSO*
Educated at Cheltenham and RMA, Woolwich, Neame was commissioned in the Royal Engineers in 1908. A captain in 1914, his First War service was in France. Awarded the VC in 1914 and admitted to the DSO in 1916, he was five times mentioned in despatches and ended the war a brevet major in the Royal Tank Corps.

On the directing staff of the Staff College, Camberley, 1919–1923, Neame was a member of the gold-medal-winning British Olympic Shooting Team in 1924 and served in India with the Bengal Sappers and Miners 1925–1929. He attended the Imperial Defence College in 1930 and was a staff officer in Waziristan District 1932–1933. BGS, Eastern Command, India, 1934–1938, he was a member of the political-military mission to Tibet in 1936. Described by his obituarist as 'small, wiry and tough', with a countenance 'of almost oriental cast', he was promoted major general in 1937. Commandant of RMA, Woolwich, 1938–1939, he was appointed CB in 1939,

Deputy CGS with the BEF in France 1939–1940, Neame was briefly appointed GOC 4th Indian Division in North Africa in 1940 before being made GOC Palestine, Transjordan and Cyprus. Made Military Governor of Cyrenaica in February 1941, the forces at his disposal were so reduced that he was told by Dill he was 'going to get a bloody nose' (Neame, 1946, 268). He soon received one. Making tactical dispositions that were, according to Wavell, 'crazy' (Pitt, 1986, 250), his forward positions were easily overwhelmed by the Afrika Korps advance. Taken prisoner, along with O'Connor, in April 1941, he spent the next 30 months in Italy, latterly in Campo 12 near Florence where, in addition to attempting escape and drafting his memoirs, 'he did needlework most of the time' (Ranfurly, 1998, 123). Reaching British lines in October 1943 and eager for re-employment, he was upset by the 'lack of jobs for him' (Danchev & Todman, 2001, 532).

Made Lieutenant Governor and C-in-C of Guernsey in 1945 and knighted in 1946, Neame was Colonel Commandant of the Royal Engineers 1945–1955. He retired from the army in 1947. His memoirs, *Playing with Strife* (1946), scarcely dwelt on military matters. Instead he wrote of his pursuit of big game, climaxing with his account of being mauled by a tiger. A keen gardener, a Fellow of the Royal Geographical Society and sometime President of the National Rifle Association, he was DL for Kent in 1955.

NEWTON, Major General Thomas Cochrane *(1885–1976), CB, DSO, OBE*
Educated at Wellington and RMA, Woolwich, Newton was commissioned in the Royal Field Artillery in 1904. Transferring to the Royal Horse Artillery in 1910 and a captain in 1914, his First War service was in India and France, where he was mentioned in despatches and admitted to the DSO.

Awarded the OBE for service in operations in Afghanistan in 1919, Newton married in 1924. A staff officer with the Air Defence Corps 1929–1932, he was chief staff officer with the 2nd (Rawalpindi) Brigade in India 1934–1935 and was Commandant of the School of Anti-Aircraft Defence, Shoeburyness, 1935–1938. He was a major general on the General Staff of Anti-Aircraft Command in 1939.

Retired in 1942, Newton was High Sheriff of Bedfordshire 1945–1946 and was made DL for the county in 1946. He resigned from that position in 1968.

NICHOLLS, Major General Sir Leslie Burtonshaw
(1895–1975), KCMG, CB, CBE
Educated at Cheltenham and London University, and commissioned in the Army Service Corps in 1914, Nicholls's First War service, from 1917, was as an Observer with the RFC. Twice wounded, he was mentioned in despatches.

Married in 1925 and transferring from the RAF to the Royal Signals, Nicholls served with the Shanghai Defence Force 1927–1928 and on the North-West Frontier 1935–1937. Mentioned in despatches for his part in operations in Waziristan, he commanded the 2nd Infantry Divisional Regiment (Royal Signals) with the BEF 1939–1940.

Awarded the OBE, Nicholls served in senior signals appointments in Iran, the Middle East, North Africa, Italy and North-West Europe from 1942–4. He was Deputy CSO with SHAEF 1944–1945. Appointed CB in 1945, he retired from the army in 1946.

Joining the board of Cable and Wireless Ltd., Nicholls was Managing Director in 1950 and Chairman of the Company in 1951. He held numerous other directorships in an active business career and, knighted in 1954, was a part-time member of the Central Electricity Generating Board 1957–1964.

Twice divorced and three times married, a Freeman of the City of London and a keen yachtsman, Nicholls suffered an incapacitating stroke in 1970. He lived in Surrey.

NICHOLS, Major General John Sebastian (1896–1954), DSO, MC

The son of a clergyman and educated at Eton, Nichols was commissioned in the Lincolnshire Regiment in 1915. His First War service was in France, where he was wounded and awarded the MC in 1918.

Awarded a bar to his MC in 1921, while serving with the 21st Punjab Regiment in Waziristan, Nichols attended the Staff College, Camberley, 1930–1931, served as Brigade Major with the Saar International Force and, after a term in the Middle East, was promoted major in 1937. He was attached to the British Military Mission to the Egyptian Army 1938–1939.

Appointed to command the 1st Battalion, the Essex Regiment in Egypt in 1940, 'Crasher' Nichols took command of 151st Infantry Brigade in 1941 and, admitted to the DSO during the CRUSADER battles, was made GOC 50th Division in April 1942. A successful participant in both of the Alamein battles, he suffered at Montgomery's hands in March 1943, when he was made scapegoat for failure in the early phases of the Mareth battle. Described as having made 'a complete mess of it' and 'having no brains' (Hamilton, 1983, 214), he was reduced to the substantive rank of brigadier. Made commander of 182nd Brigade in North-West Europe in 1944, he was put in command of the Special Allied Airborne Reconnaissance Force in 1945.

In command of 114th Infantry Brigade at war's end, Nichols was posted to East Africa to take up command, with the rank of colonel, of the Somaliland (Somalia) Brigade Area. Transferred in 1947 to command the Southern Area of East Africa Command, he retired in 1948.

The rise and fall of 'Crasher' Nichols was due, no doubt, to a variety of factors. But what his wartime trajectory demonstrates was the importance of patronage in making or breaking an officer's career. An 'old desert hand', he had shown himself 'a brave and honourable soldier' (Stewart, 1999, 173). His 'failure' at Mareth may have been due to his own shortcomings, as Montgomery, by this time enraptured by his own 'left hook' success, expressed with such emphatic authority. But the alternative possibility, that too much was demanded of him and his Division and that blame for the failure of the frontal attack lay higher up the chain of command, has scarcely had an airing. Later in the war Leese, Nichols's corps commander at Mareth, had to, as he put it, 'carry the can for Dickie (Mountbatten)'. The possibility remains that Leese withdrew his patronage from Nichols because, embarrassed by his own failure, he needed someone to carry his can.

NICHOLSON, General Sir Cameron Gordon Graham
(1898–1979), GCB, KBE, DSO, MC

Of military family and educated at Wellington and RMA, Woolwich, Nicholson was commissioned in the Royal Artillery in 1915. His First War service was in France, where he was wounded and awarded the MC (and bar).

Transferring to the Royal Horse Artillery in 1917, 'Cam' Nicholson served abroad for most of the 1920s, in India, Iraq, Palestine and Egypt. Married in 1926 and an instructor at Woolwich over the next two years, he attended the Staff College, Camberley, 1931–1932. A cricketer, he was 'a good bat, with beautiful wrists' (Tremlett, WSL, 96). Brigade Major with 2nd Division 1934–1936, he served on the staff at the War Office 1936–1937. From 1938 to 1939 he was an instructor at Camberley.

Appointed to the staff of 45th Division in 1939, the 'tall and quiet-mannered' Nicholson (Blaxland, 1977, 162) was admitted to the DSO in 1940 for his staff work with SICKLEFORCE in Norway. Chief Staff Officer with 18th Division in 1940, he was briefly Deputy CGS Home Forces in 1941, before being appointed to command the Support Group of 42nd Armoured Division. Second in command of 6th Armoured Division in 1942, he was BGS First Army in 1943 and, promoted major general, was made GOC of the newly-formed 44th Indian Armoured Division later that year. Given what he wanted, a field command, he was made GOC 2nd Division in Burma in early 1945. His overcoming of initial setbacks to effect a successful crossing of the Irrawaddy near Mandalay was 'a fine feat of leadership and organization' (Slim, 1999, 433).

Appointed CB in 1945, Nicholson was Director of Artillery at the War Office in 1946 and GOC-in-C West Africa 1948–1951. GOC-in-C Western Command 1951–1953, he was knighted after a short spell as C-in-C Middle East Land Forces. He was Adjutant General to the Forces from 1953 until his retirement in 1956.

Governor of the Royal Hospital, Chelsea, 1956–1961, Master Gunner, St James's Park 1956–1960 and Colonel Commandant, Royal Artillery, 1956–1960, Nicholson retired to Cornwall, bearing with equanimity, it is said, the illness which incapacitated him during his last years.

NICHOLSON, Major General Francis Lothian *(1884–1953), CB, DSO, MC*
The son of a general and educated at Repton and RMC, Sandhurst, Nicholson was commissioned in the Royal West Surrey Regiment in 1903. Transferring to the Indian Army in 1905, he was gazetted into the 37th Dogra Regiment. His First War service was in India and Mesopotamia, where he was twice mentioned in despatches, awarded the MC and admitted to the DSO in 1918.

Mentioned in despatches during operations in Afghanistan in 1919, Nicholson attended the Staff College, Quetta, 1921–1922. Married in 1922, he was a widower the next year. Appointed Brigade Major of the Nasirabad Brigade, he was on the staff of Western Command, India, 1924–1926. Returning to the Dogra Regiment, he re-married in 1927, commanded the 1st Battalion 1926–1930 and commanded the Jhansi Brigade at Quetta 1930–1933. Made Director of Personal Services, AHQ, India, in 1934, he was appointed CB the next year and, promoted major general, was Deputy Adjutant General and QMG, Eastern Command, India, 1937–1938. His last appointment, before retirement in 1941, was as Commander Lucknow District.

NORMAN, Major General Charles Wake *(1891–1974)*, CBE

Educated at Eton and Cambridge University, where he was good at games, Norman was commissioned in the 9th Lancers in 1913. His First War service was short. Wounded in August 1914 and taken prisoner, he spent the next four years in captivity in Krefeld.

Spending the next dozen years on a captain's pay, Norman's regimental duties took him to India and Egypt. Married in 1925, he was an instructor at Sandhurst 1925–1926, attended the Staff College, Camberley, 1927–1928, and assumed the command of his regiment in 1936. He spent the next two years on Salisbury Plain converting to mechanization.

A colonel in 1938, 'Charlie' Norman commanded 1st Armoured Reconnaissance Brigade in France with the BEF 1939–1940. Mentioned in despatches and promoted major general in 1941, he was made GOC 8th Armoured Division. Relinquishing that command when the division reached North Africa in 1942, he was awarded the CBE in 1943 and, returned to England, was GOC Aldershot District 1944–1945.

Retired in 1946, Norman became, as his obituarist put it, 'a much loved squire' in his native Kent. Colonel of the 9th Lancers, 1940–1950, his two sons served with the regiment. A County Councillor 1949–1955, he was also High Sheriff and DL for the county.

NORRIE, Lieutenant General Sir Charles Willoughby Moke *1st Baron (1893–1977)*, GCMG, GCVO, CB, DSO, MC

Of military family and educated at Eton and RMC, Sandhurst, Norrie was commissioned in the 11th Hussars in 1913. His First War service was in France, latterly on the staff of the Tank Corps. Four times wounded, twice mentioned in despatches and awarded the MC and bar, he was admitted to the DSO in 1919.

Reverting to the substantive rank of captain in 1918, Norrie married in 1921, attended the Staff College, Camberley, 1924–1925 and was Brigade Major with the 1st Cavalry Brigade at Aldershot 1926–1930. He commanded the 10th Royal Hussars 1931–1935 and, after attending the Imperial Defence College, commanded the 1st Cavalry Brigade 1937–1938, during which time he supervised the conversion to armour.

Re-married in 1938 and Commander of 1st Armoured Brigade 1938–1940, Norrie was briefly Inspector of the Royal Armoured Corps before being appointed GOC 1st Armoured Division. Arriving in North Africa in November 1941, he was made GOC XXX Corps, 'a role thrust upon him too early as a result of the death of Pope' (Bidwell & Graham, 1985, 242). Known for his personal charm, 'courage, calmness and resolution in adversity' but also for being 'too easy-going with his subordinates' (Carver, 1989, 129) and said to be 'far too nice a country gentleman to be sufficiently ruthless' (Pyman, 1971, 42), he led his corps with distinction in the CRUSADER battles, but to calamitous defeat at 'Knightsbridge' in May 1942. At a time when British armoured formations were being criticized for their 'cavalry ethos', it was perhaps unfair, though understandable, that he should be singled out for attack because of his cavalry background. Having, apparently, 'gripped the situation' (Stewart, 1999, 25) and realized the importance of the Alamein position, he returned to Britain before the battles took place. His last military appointment was as Commander of the Royal Armoured Corps with Home Forces in 1943.

A member of the political-military mission to Algiers in 1944, Norrie was appointed Governor of South Australia in August of that year. He fitted the role sufficiently to have his term of office extended and to be made Governor General and C-in-C of New Zealand in 1952. Retied in 1957 as Baron Norrie, he was Chancellor of the Order of St Michael and St George 1960–1968, held numerous honorary colonelcies, was a member of the National Hunt Committee and, from 1969, the Jockey Club. He lived in Wantage.

NORTON, Lieutenant General Edward Felix *(1884–1954)*, CB, DSO, MC
Educated at Charterhouse and RMA, Woolwich, and commissioned in the Royal Artillery in 1902, Norton served several years in India before the First War. A captain in 1914, his war service was in France, where he was awarded the MC in 1914, was Deputy Assistant Adjutant General at GHQ and admitted to the DSO in 1918.

Attached to the Army of the Black Sea 1922–1923, Norton's duties were light enough for him to be a member of the 1922 Everest expedition and lead the expedition of 1924. Awarded the Founder's Medal of the Royal Geographical Society, he married in 1925 and served on the staff at the War Office 1926–1928, before becoming an instructor at the Staff College, Quetta, in 1929. Commander Royal Artillery 1st Division, Aldershot, 1932–1934, he was BGS Aldershot Command 1934–1938 and Commander, Madras District, 1938–1940.

Appointed CB in 1939, Norton was Acting Governor of Hong Kong 1940–1941 and, promoted lieutenant general, commanded Western (Independent) District, India, for a year before his retirement. Made Colonel Commandant of the Royal Artillery in 1941, he commanded the North Hampshire Home Guard 1942–1944. He was Colonel Commandant of the Royal Horse Artillery 1947–1951.

NOSWORTHY, Lieutenant General Sir Francis Poitiers
(1887–1971), KCB, DSO, MC
Born in Jamaica and educated at Exeter School and RMA, Woolwich,

Nosworthy was commissioned in the Royal Engineers in 1907. A captain in 1914, his First War service was in France, where he was six times mentioned in despatches, awarded the MC and bar and admitted to the DSO (with bar).

A graduate of the Staff College, Quetta, in 1920 and an instructor at the Staff College, Camberley, 1921–1922, Nosworthy was a staff officer at the War Office 1922–1926. Married in 1925, he was, from 1926 to 1930, second in command and Chief Staff Officer of the Sudan Defence Force. After attending the Imperial Defence College in 1931, he was Chief Staff Officer with British troops in China. Commander of 5th Infantry Brigade 1935–1938 and, reported on as being 'unfit for promotion to command a Division' (Marshall-Cornwall, 1984, 100), he was Deputy Chief of Staff, AHQ, India, 1938–1940.

Promoted lieutenant general and appointed GOC IV Corps with Home Forces in July 1940, Nosworthy was seriously injured in November 1941 when a mortar shell exploded during a demonstration. Not re-employed, Brooke had 'some difficulty in making him realize that he had reached his ceiling' (Danchev & Todman, 2001,352). Made C-in-C West Africa in 1943, he returned to England in 1945 and retired from the army the next year.

NOYES, General Sir Cyril Dupré (1885–1946), KCSI, CB, CIE, MC

The son of a clergyman and educated at St Lawrence College, Ramsgate, and RMA, Woolwich, Noyes was commissioned in the Royal Artillery in 1904 Transferring to the 6th Rajput Rifles (Indian Army) in 1907, he served on naval operations in the Persian Gulf 1912–1913 and his First War service was in Egypt and Mesopotamia, where he was mentioned in despatches and awarded the MC.

Married in 1918 and mentioned in despatches for his part in operations in Afghanistan in 1919, Noyes attended the Staff College, Quetta, 1921–1922, and served on the staff of Baluchistan District. An instructor at Quetta 1927–1930, he commanded the 2nd/2nd Punjab Regiment 1930–1930. After attending the Imperial Defence College, he commanded 2nd Indian Infantry Brigade at Rawalpindi 1935–1938. Mentioned in despatches and made CIE for his part in operations in Waziristan in 1937, he was Deputy QMG and Director of Movements and Quartering, AHQ, India, 1939–1940.

Appointed CB in 1939 and a District Commander in India 1940–1941, Noyes was QMG, India, in 1941 and GOC Northern Command, India, in 1942. Promoted general and knighted, he retired from the army in 1943.

NUGENT, Major General John Fagan Henslowe (1889–1975), CB, DSO

The son of an Indian Civil Servant and educated at Downside and RMC, Sandhurst, Nugent was commissioned on the unattached list in 1909 and gazetted into the 28th Punjab Regiment (Indian Army) in 1910. ADC to the Governor of Ceylon 1914–1915, his First War service was in Mesopotamia, where he was wounded, mentioned in despatches and admitted to the DSO.

Married in 1919, Nugent served with his regiment in Afghanistan and on the North- West Frontier. A major in 1925, he attended the Staff College, Quetta, served on the staff of AHQ, India, and commanded the 2nd Battalion 2nd/7th

Rajputs 1934–1935. Assistant Adjutant and QMG Lahore District 1935–1938, he commanded the Bannu brigade in India 1938–1940. Appointed Major General i/c Administration, HQ North-Western Army, in 1941, he retired in 1944.

Settling with his second wife on Jersey, Nugent died after a long illness in a St Helier nursing home.

NYE, Lieutenant General Sir Archibald Edward
(1895–1967), GCSI, GCMG, GCIE, KCB, KBE, MC

The son of a sergeant major and educated at the Duke of York's School, Dover, Nye enlisted in the ranks in 1914. His First War service was in France. Commissioned in the Leinster Regiment in 1915, he was twice wounded and awarded the MC.

Adjutant to his battalion 1919–1922, Nye transferred to the Royal Warwickshire Regiment after the Leinsters were disbanded. A student at the Staff College, Camberley, 1924–1925, he was a staff officer in Air Cooperation 1926–1928 and Brigade Major of 3rd Infantry Brigade 1928–1930. After serving on the staff at the War Office 1931–1932, during which time he qualified as a barrister-at-law, he was on the instructing staff at Camberley 1932–1935. After a further two years of staff duties at the War Office, he married in 1939 and was appointed to command the Nowshera Brigade on the North-West Frontier. A non-drinker, he excelled at billiards.

Made Deputy Director of Staff Duties at the War Office in 1940, Nye became Director the same year. Brooke, surprised by the news that Churchill was seeking a substitute for Dill as CIGS, was positively alarmed to hear rumours that Nye, though 'a quick worker with great vision', was to be the replacement. Dill, apparently, 'had a job to rid [Churchill] of this idea' (Danchev & Todman, 2001, 200). Made Vice-CIGS under Brooke in December 1941, he held that post until June 1946. He was, so it is said, 'loyalty and efficiency personified' (Bryant, 1965, 39).

Knighted in 1944 and tipped as the next Adjutant General, or possibly CIGS, Nye instead retired from the army and became Governor of Madras. He so impressed Nehru, apparently, that he was requested to be made British High Commissioner in India in 1948. In 1952 he became British High Commissioner in Canada. Retired in 1956, he was much honoured with decorations and honorary degrees. He also became a director of the Royal Bank of Canada.

O

O'CONNOR, General Sir Richard Nugent *(1889–1981), KT, GCB, DSO, MC*
Of military family and educated at Wellington and RMC, Sandhurst, O'Connor was commissioned in the Cameronians (Scottish Rifles) in 1910. Signal Officer with the Malta Garrison 1913–1914, his First War service was in France and Italy. His record was outstanding. He was nine times mentioned in despatches, was awarded the MC and admitted to the DSO (with bar).

Adjutant of the 2nd Battalion of the Cameronians in 1919, O'Connor attended the Staff College, Camberley, in 1920 and, after serving briefly on the staff of 3rd Division, was Brigade Major with the Experimental Division, Aldershot, 1921–1924. Adjutant of the 1st Battalion of the Cameronians 1924–1925, he was an instructor at Sandhurst 1925–1927 and at Camberley 1927–1930. He served with his battalion in Egypt 1930–1932 and for the next three years was a staff officer at the War Office. After attending the Imperial Defence College in 1935 he married and was appointed to command the Peshawar Brigade in India. Made Military Governor of Jerusalem and GOC 7th Division in 1938, he was appointed GOC 8th Division in Egypt at war's beginning.

A small man, 'neat as a bird', with the 'shy and gentle air of a scholar' (Barnett, 1983, 22), 'Dick' O'Connor was appointed Commander Western Desert Force in June 1940. That December he began his 'five-day raid' on the fortified camp the invading Italian army had established at Sidi Barrani; so successful was the operation that he carried on harrying the enemy back to and beyond the Libyan border. By February 1941 all of Cyrenaica was in British hands and the Italian Tenth Army had been all but destroyed. His famous 'Fox Killed in the Open' message was sent *en clair* 'for Mussolini's benefit' (Pitt, 1986, 190).

Knighted and made Commander of British troops in Egypt in March 1941, O'Connor was sent by Wavell to assist Neame in stemming Rommel's Afrika Korps advance. As he had 'none of the assertiveness of some small men' (Greacan, 1989, 94), his failure to overrule his friend Neame resulted in both British generals being taken prisoner. Held in Italy, latterly in Campo 12 near Florence, with other captured *prominenti*, he kept himself fit, was always 'a cheerful companion' (Ranfurly, 1998, 123), and 'never for one moment . . . gave up trying to escape' (Baynes, 1989, 146). He made, in all, five unsuccessful attempts at escape before crossing the British lines in December 1943.

That O'Connor was deemed immediately fit for command testifies to his reputation and the fitness regime he maintained in captivity. Montgomery suggested he should be his successor as 8th Army commander (Hamilton, 1983, 476), but in the event he was offered VIII Corps, then preparing for operations in North-West Europe. Described as 'a tower of strength' in welding the various units of his command together (D'Este, 2001, 236) and as successful as any other corps commander in the Normandy breakout, Montgomery had him removed in November 1944 for not being ruthless enough with American subordinates. Promoted general, he was appointed GOC-in-C of Eastern and North-Western Commands, India, and, from 1946 until August 1947, he was Adjutant General to the Forces. He left this office under something of a cloud, always maintaining that he had resigned on principle, whereas Montgomery (then CIGS) put it about that he had not been 'up to the job' (Baynes, 1989, 266) and had been dismissed.

Retired in 1948 and Commandant of the Army Cadet Forces, Scotland, 1948–1959, and Colonel of the Cameronians 1951–1954, O'Connor was a JP for Ross and Cromarty in 1952, as well as being Lord Lieutenant of the county 1955–1964. Re-married in 1963, he was Lord High Commissioner, Church of Scotland General Assembly, in 1964.

OGILVIE, Major General Sir William Heneage (1887–1971), KBE

Born in Chile and educated at Clifton, Oxford University and Guy's Hospital, Ogilvie was married and a qualified surgeon before being commissioned in the Royal Army Medical Corps in 1915. His First War service was in France.

Surgical Registrar at Guy's Hospital in 1920, Ogilvie was re-commissioned in the RAMC in 1939. He was a consulting surgeon with the BEF 1939–1940 and with East African Command 1940–1942. Given the honorary rank of Major General in 1943, he was a consultant surgeon with Middle East Land Forces 1943–1944 and with Eastern Command 1944–1945.

Knighted in 1946, Ogilvie was elected a Fellow of the Royal Society of Medicine and was the recipient of many other awards. A much published author on surgical practice and a keen sailor, he lived in Wimbledon.

OSBORNE, Major General Reverend Coles Alexander (1896–1994), CIE

Educated at Dover County School, Osborne volunteered for service in 1914. His First War service was in France with the Honourable Artillery Company, the Royal West Kent Regiment and with the RFC. Wounded in 1918, he transferred to 15th Sikh Regiment (Indian Army).

Serving on operations in Afghanistan in 1919 and on the North-West Frontier 1920–1922, Osborne attended the Staff College, Quetta, in 1925 and was Tactics Instructor at the Australian Royal Military College, Duntroon, 1928–1930. Married in 1930, he served on the staff at the War Office 1934–1938 and on operations in Palestine in 1938.

Deputy Director of Military Training in India in 1940, Osborne was Commandant of the Staff College, Quetta, 1941–1942. A brigadier in 1941, he was Director of Military Operations, GHQ, India, 1942–1943. Commander of Kohat District 1943–1945, he retired from the army in 1946.

A student at Moore Theological College, Sydney, in 1947, Osborne was ordained that year. Personal Chaplain to the Anglican Archbishop of Sydney 1959–1966, as well as being a director of a television company, he was a Fellow of St Paul's College, Sydney University 1953–1969.

OSBORNE, Lieutenant General Edmund Archibald
(1885–1969), CB, DSO

Educated privately and at RMA, Woolwich, Osborne was commissioned in the Royal Engineers in 1904. A captain in 1914, his First War service was in France. Admitted to the DSO in 1914, he was wounded and mentioned eight times in despatches.

A major in 1921, Osborne attended the Staff College, Camberley, 1921–1922 and married that year. Transferring to the Royal Corps of Signals in 1923, he was o/c School of Signals 1926–1930. On the staff of 3rd Division 1930–1933, he gained a reputation as 'a difficult and unpleasant character' (Cloake, 1985, 51). Appointed to command 157th (Highland Light Infantry) Brigade in 1933, he was posted to Egypt to command the Cairo Brigade the next year. Promoted major general in 1937, he was appointed GOC 44th (Home Counties) Division in 1938 and appointed CB in 1939.

On special duties liaising with Belgian government officials in early 1940, 'Sigs' Osborne took his division over to France to join the BEF in April. He had grown 'very fat', as Brooke noted (Danchev & Todman, 2001, 58). Stationed in Norfolk during the summer of 1940, he was promoted lieutenant general the next year and given command of II Corps.

Retired from the army at the end of 1941, Osborne and his wife settled in Wiltshire. He lived the last five years of his life a widower.

OXLEY, Major General Walter Hayes *(1891–1978), CB, CBE, MC*

Educated at Eastbourne College and RMA, Woolwich, Oxley was commissioned in the Royal Engineers in 1911. His First War service was in Egypt, Palestine and Macedonia. Mentioned in despatches, he was awarded the MC in 1916.

Serving with the Egyptian Army 1918–1919, Oxley married in 1921 and attended the Staff College, Camberley, 1925–1926. Military Attaché to the British Legations in Belgrade and Prague 1929–1931, he was Assistant QMG to the British Military Mission to Egypt 1931–1934, and again, as a 'very efficient senior staff officer'(Marshall-Cornwall, 1984, 107) in 1937. In the immediate pre-war years he was Brigadier i/c Administration, Malta.

Commander of 2nd Infantry Brigade Malta, 1940–1941, 'Oxo' Oxley was awarded the CBE and spent a year with Home Forces commanding 7th Infantry

Brigade before returning to Malta as GOC in 1943. Commissioner of the British Military Mission to Bulgaria 1944–1947, he retired in 1948.

Appointed CB in 1947, Oxley, a keen sportsman and expert shot, settled in Dorset, where he farmed.

OZANNE, Major General William Maingay *(1891–1966)*, *CB, CBE, MC*
Born and educated on Guernsey and at RMC, Sandhurst, Ozanne was commissioned in the Duke of Wellington's Regiment in 1911. His First War service was in France, where he was twice wounded, mentioned in despatches and awarded the MC.

Married in 1920, Ozanne spent the next half-dozen years on a captain's pay. An instructor at the Small Arms School, Netheravon, 1924–1928, he was Chief Instructor there 1933–1936. Commander of 1st Battalion, Duke of Wellington's Regiment, 1936–1939, he was a brigadier at war's outset.

Made GOC of the Norfolk County Division in December 1940, Ozanne found himself re-designated GOC 76th Division in November 1941, when the county divisions were disbanded. He was a trainer of troops until December 1943, when he was transferred to 'special duties' at the War Office. He retired from the army in 1946 and thereafter, from his home in Bury St Edmunds, indulged his passion for golf.

P

PAGE, Major General Sir Charles Max *(1882–1963)*, *KBE, CB, DSO*
Educated at Westminster School and St Thomas's Hospital, Page completed his medical studies in 1908. Serving with the Red Cross in Turkey, 1912–1913, he married in 1913 and joined the RAMC in 1914. His First War service was in France, where he was thrice mentioned in despatches and admitted to the DSO.

A consultant surgeon for most of the inter-war years, and much-published in medical journals, Page was re-commissioned in 1939 and acted as consultant surgeon with the BEF in France, 1939–1940. Granted the rank of major general, he was President of the Association of Surgeons, 1945–1946, and Director of the Accident Service, Radcliffe Infirmary, Oxford, 1943–1946.

Retired to Kent, Page held a number of lecturing posts into old age. He was sometime consulting surgeon to the Metropolitan Police.

PAGET, General Sir Bernard Charles Tolver *(1887–1961)*, *GCB, DSO, MC*
The son of a bishop and educated at Shrewsbury and RMC, Sandhurst, Paget was commissioned in the Oxfordshire and Buckinghamshire Light Infantry in 1907. His First War service was in France, where he was five times mentioned

in despatches, awarded the MC in 1915 and admitted to the DSO in 1917. Twice wounded, he was never fully to recover the use of his left arm.

Married in 1918 and a graduate of the Staff College, Camberley, in 1920, Paget shone as a teacher of officers and trainer of troops. A lieutenant colonel in 1925, he was an instructor at Camberley 1926–1928 and, after attending the Imperial Defence College in 1929, served on the instructing staff at the Staff College, Quetta, 1932–1934, followed by a two-year spell at the War Office. Commander of the Quetta Brigade and Baluchistan District 1936–1937, he was promoted major general and appointed Commandant of the Staff College, Camberley, in 1938.

GOC of 18th Division 1939–1940, Paget was 'summoned at a moment's notice' (DNB) in April 1940 and sent with his divisional staff to Åndalsnes in Norway. There, installed as head of SICKLEFORCE, he supervised the successful withdrawal and evacuation of British troops. It took less than a week, but his 'fine feat of arms' was rewarded with him being appointed CB.

Appointed CGS Home Forces in June 1940, Paget, a 'large-nosed, dark-haired, sharp-tongued' man, who could be 'extremely funny when he chose' (Fraser, 2002, 140), was promoted lieutenant general the following year. Made C-in-C South Eastern Command, his troop-training expertise came to the fore and his hot temper, elephantine memory and capacity to devote 'half and hour's discussion . . . over where a comma should be placed in a sentence' (Pyman, 1971, 61) made him something of a legend. His brusqueness of manner, 'that seemed to combine rudeness and bad temper' (Hamilton, 1982, 516), was put down to the continuous pain he suffered from his war wound. Eager to make training more realistic, he was probably the commander most responsible for instituting battle-drill. Tipped to succeed Dill as CIGS in December 1941, Brooke, ever one to elide his own interests with those of the state, regarded the prospect as 'a tragedy [and] a definite step towards losing the war' (Danchev & Todman, 2001, 198).

Appointed C-in-C Home Forces in December 1941, Paget was knighted the next year. It was probably he who was most responsible for preparing the army for the opening of the second front in Europe. Appropriately appointed C-in-C 21st Army Group in June 1943, he was, just as appropriately, sidelined that December when Montgomery, who described him as having 'very rigid ideas' (Alanbrooke, 6/2/22, LHCMA), was summoned from Italy to assume that command. Always the bridesmaid, and 'bitterly disappointed at not being allowed to use in battle the weapon he had shaped and termpered' (Grigg, 1948), he was appointed C-in-C Middle East Force and divided his time over the rest of the war between Cairo and Baghdad. His younger son was killed in action in Holland in 1945.

Retired from the army in 1946, Paget enjoyed what appears to have been a fantastically busy retirement. Principal of Ashridge College, a Conservative-oriented adult education centre promoting 'good citizenship', he resigned after a row with the governors. He was Colonel Commandant of the Oxfordshire and Buckinghamshire Light Infantry 1946–1955 and Colonel Commandant of the

Reconnaissance and Intelligence Corps 1943–1952. Sometime National Chairman of the Forces Help Society, he was a longstanding Vice-President of the Royal Commonwealth Society for the Blind. Much decorated by foreign governments, he was a Freeman of the City of Cork and DL for Hampshire from 1952. He died at his home in Petersfield at the age of 73.

PAIGE, Major General Douglas (1886–1958), CBE, MC
Born in Totnes and educated at Plymouth College and RMA, Woolwich, Paige was commissioned in the Royal Artillery in 1907. A captain in 1914, his First War service was in France, where he was mentioned in despatches and awarded the MC in 1917.

A major in 1917 and married in 1919, Paige attended the Staff College, Camberley, 1922–1923, and was an instructor at the School of Artillery, Larkhill, 1925–1928. He served for many years on a major's pay in India. A colonel in 1938, he was CRA Malta 1938–1940 and CCRA XI Corps with Home Forces from June until November 1940. A temporary major general in 1941, he was GOC 9th Anti-Aircraft Division from 1941 until his retirement from the army in 1942. Thereafter he was Regional Petroleum Officer for the South Wales Region, 1942–1948.

PAKENHAM-WALSH, Major General Ridley (1888–1966). CB, MC
The son of a bishop and educated at Cheltenham and RMA, Woolwich, Pakenham-Walsh was commissioned in the Royal Engineers in 1908. An instructor at the Australian Royal Military College, Duntroon, 1914–1915, he married in 1915 and his First War service was at Gallipoli and in France, where he was mentioned in despatches and awarded the MC.

British Representative on the International Commission in Teschen 1919–1920, Pakenham-Walsh attended the Staff College, Camberley, 1921–1922 and was an instructor at the School of Military Engineering, Chatham, 1923–1926. On the staff at the War Office 1927–1930, he attended the Imperial Defence College in 1931. Returning to staff duties at the War Office, he collaborated with Winston Churchill in the preparation of his Marlborough biography. Assistant Adjutant General 1934–1935, he was BGS, Eastern Command 1935–1939. Promoted major general and made Commandant of the School of Military Engineering and Inspector Royal Engineers in 1939, he was appointed Engineer-in-Chief to the BEF at war's beginning.

In addition to playing his part in the 'pill-box' affair, which led to Hore-Belisha's removal from office in January 1940, Pakenham-Walsh was wounded during the withdrawal to Dunkirk. Appointed CB, he was made GOC Northern Ireland District and in 1941 was, briefly in command of IX Corps. Brooke, however, found him 'quite incapable of handling the forces under [his] orders' (Danchev & Todman, 2001, 190), and he was made Commander of Salisbury Plain District in 1942. Controller of General Army Provisions at the War Office for Eastern Group, India, 1943–1946, he retired from the army in 1947.

Vice-Chairman of the Development Corporation, Harlow New Town,

1947–1950, Pakenham-Walsh wrote a two-volume history of the Royal Engineers (1959) and was a frequent contributor to military journals. He lived in Haslemere, Surrey.

PARGITER, Major General Robert Beverley *(1889–1984), CB, CBE*
The son of an Indian Civil Servant, Pargiter was educated at Rugby and RMA, Woolwich. Commissioned in the Royal Artillery in 1909, his First War service was on the North-West Frontier and in France. Wounded and mentioned in despatches, he served on the Military Mission to the Baltic States 1919–1921.

Married in 1917, Pargiter attended the Staff College, Camberley, 1923–1924. An instructor at the Staff College, Quetta, 1930–1933, he attended the Imperial Defence College in 1934. Attached to 1st Light Artillery Brigade in Edinburgh 1935–1936 and Deputy Director of Military Operations at the War Office 1936–1938, he was appointed to command 1st Anti-Aircraft Brigade in 1939.

Pargiter's Second War service, after serving in France with the BEF, consisted of successive command of 4th, 7th and 5th Anti-Aircraft Divisions under Home Forces 1940–1943, culminating in his command of 3rd Anti-Aircraft Group in North Africa in 1943. Appointed CB, he was Major General, Anti-Aircraft, with Allied Forces HQ in North Africa and the Mediterranean 1943–1945.

Retired from the army in 1945, Pargiter was Commissioner, British Red Cross and St John War Organization in the Middle East in 1946, and in Malaya (Malaysia) in 1946. He was Colonel Commandant of the Royal Artillery 1951–1954. A widower in 1971 and re-married in 1973, he lived in Kent and died aged 95.

PATON, Major General William Calder *(1886–1979), CIE, MC*
Educated at Glasgow Academy and Edinburgh University, Paton qualified as a doctor in 1910 and joined the Indian Medical Service in 1912. Married in 1915, his First War service was on the North-West Frontier, in Egypt and in Mesopotamia, where he was awarded the MC.

Paton held various appointments on the civil side of the Indian Medical Service. He was Professor of Midwifery at the Medical College, Madras, Civil Surgeon at Delhi and Inspector General of Civil Hospitals, North-West Frontier Province. Surgeon-General, Bengal, 1941–1945, he retired from the army in 1945.

Medical Superintendent, Royal Northern Infirmary, 1945–1948, Paton was also Medical Superintendent, Inverness Hospitals, 1948–1954.

PENNEY, Major General Sir William Ronald Campbell
(1896–1964), KBE, CB, DSO, MC
The son of an Edinburgh accountant, and educated at Wellington and RMA, Woolwich, Penney was commissioned in the Royal Engineers in 1914. His First War service was in France, where he was mentioned in despatches and awarded the MC.

Transferring to the Royal Signals in 1921, Penney, a keen sportsman who played rugby for the army, spent the next five years in India. Married in 1925, he attended the Staff College, Camberley, 1927–1928, and served on the staff at the War Office 1929–1930. Brigade Major with North China Command 1931–1933, he was in India from 1935, where he was admitted to the DSO in 1937 for his part in operations in Waziristan. He attended the Imperial Defence College in 1939, the first Royal Signals Officer ever to do so.

Derided by Dorman-Smith for his 'lack of any sense of humour, combined with religious complacency' (Greacan, 1989, 97), Penney had impressed Auchinleck enough in India for him to request 'Ronny' to be his CSO with 8th Army. A major general in 1941, he served in the North African campaign through to its end with 18th Army Group, and, eager for field command, was appointed GOC 1st Division in October 1943. Involved in the furious fighting on the Anzio beachhead in February 1944, he was 'well regarded' by Truscott (Vaughan-Thomas, 1968, 97), but was described by Clark, the Fifth Army Commander, as 'not too formidable a general but a good telephone operator' (Greacen, 1989, 268). Wounded in the head by a shell splinter, he returned early to his command, but was dogged by ill-health for the rest of the year.

Appointed CB and made Director of Military Intelligence to HQ Supreme Command South-East Asia in November 1944, it fell to Penney to supervise the details of the Japanese surrender in August 1945 and provide emergency supplies for the thousands of liberated prisoners of war. Controller of Munitions at the Ministry of Supply 1946–1949, he retired from the army to be employed by the Foreign Office 1953–1957 as an expert in secure communication systems.

Knighted in 1958 and re-married in 1963, Penney lived in Berwick-on-Tweed.

PERCIVAL, Lieutenant General Arthur Ernest
(1887–1966), CB, DSO and bar, OBE, MC
Born in Hertfordshire and educated at Rugby, Percival was a clerk in a City office before he enlisted in the army in 1914. Temporarily commissioned in the Essex Regiment in 1915, his First War service was in France, where he was wounded, twice mentioned in despatches, awarded the MC and admitted to the DSO in 1918. Commanding the 7th (special) Battalion of the Bedfordshire Regiment in 1919, he had a bar added to his DSO for services in North Russia.

A brevet major in 1919, Percival served in Ireland, 1920–1921 (OBE) and attended the Staff College, Camberley, 1923–1924. Transferring to the Cheshire Regiment, he was a staff officer in Nigeria from 1925 to 1929. Married in 1927, he attended the Royal Naval Staff College, Greenwich, in 1930, was on the instructing staff at Camberley 1932–1932 and commanded the 2nd Battalion of the Cheshire Regiment 1932–1935. He attended the Imperial Defence College in 1935, was a staff officer in Malaya 1936–1938 and BGS Aldershot Command 1938–1939.

Appointed BGS I Corps, under Dill, with the BEF in September 1939, Percival returned to England in February 1940 to assume command of 43rd (Wessex) Division. Briefly Assistant CIGS, again under Dill, in 1940, he was appointed GOC 44th (Home Counties) Division and, promoted lieutenant general and appointed CB, was 'specially selected' by Dill (Kinvig, 1996, 123) in April 1941 as the next GOC Malaya.

In this way Percival's name has become inextricably linked to defeat in Malaya and the loss of Singapore. The extent to which he was responsible for 'the worst disaster and largest capitulation in the history of the Empire' is, however, difficult to assess. The verdict of historians has tended to grow kinder over the years. But just as it was scarcely his fault that his requests for reinforcements were ignored until too late, or that the defence plan he inherited was 'the worst kind of compromise' (Simpson in Keegan (Ed.), 1998, 260), he had plenty of experience of local conditions and must, therefore, bear his share of the blame for neglecting to train troops to fight in jungle conditions. As the retreat down the Malay peninsula developed its own depressing momentum, the inability of the 'over-motorized' British and Commonwealth troops to operate 'off road' proved a fatal drawback.

The greater the frequency with which Percival is described as an able staff officer, the easier it is, by implication, to condemn him as a general temperamentally unsuited for command. This is probably unfair. Though neither a showman nor photogenic, he had energy and the ability to impose his will on subordinates, and none of them, with the possible exception of Heath, at the time or since, made a convincing case for an alternative defence strategy. As it was, 'with his senior commanders showing so little enthusiasm for the fight' (Kinvig, 1996, 213) he may have continued resistance on Singapore for longer than the dictates of honour required. That Brooke, a full two months before the surrender, did 'not feel there is much hope of saving Singapore' (Danchev & Todman. 2001, 212) offers an indication of how gloomily his prospects were regarded in faraway London.

It has been suggested that Percival had 'pathological-achievement motivation' (Dixon, 1976, 247), a condition associated with a weak ego, feelings of dependency, an authoritarian personality and a fear of failure. Such is probably twaddle. Most self-respecting psychologists work directly, only pronouncing after the patient has spent a considerable amount of time 'in the chair'. But even if it is conceded that Percival was, in some way, damaged psychological goods and unfit to serve as GOC-in-C Malaya, we might imagine that someone somewhere along his career-trail would have noticed the symptoms. He was, after all, one of the best-educated and most comprehensively trained soldier the British Army produced in the inter-war years. He may have been flawed, but if so the system of which he was a product, and which had marked him out as 'an officer of exceptional ability and intelligence' (Kinvig, 1996, 92), was also, surely, at fault. The prosaic-sounding alternative, that he was simply unlucky in being required to perform the impossible, is probably closer to the truth.

Comporting himself with great courage and dignity during his years of very uncomfortable captivity and never toadying to his captors, Percival, at the express order of General MacArthur, was present on USS *Missouri* for the signing of the Japanese surrender in Tokyo Bay. Retired from the army in

1946, he was frustrated by the delay in publication of his *War in Malaya*. Ignored in establishment circles, but tireless in his efforts to help other former prisoners of war, he was Colonel of the Cheshire Regiment 1950–1955 and DL for Hertfordshire in 1951. A keen sportsman, and a widower for the last thirteen years of his life, he died at his home aged 78.

PERRY, Major General Henry Marrian Joseph *(1884–1955) CB, OBE*
Educated privately and at Queen's College, Cork, Perry was commissioned in the Army Medical Service in 1907. A captain in 1911, he married the following year. His First War service was in France, where he was a regimental medical officer before commanding a field ambulance unit.

Made OBE in 1919 and a major that year, Perry became an expert on bacteriological and pathological subjects. Much published in medical journals, he was a professor at the Royal Army Medical College 1922–1926 and employed as Director of Medical Scientific Work by the Egyptian Government 1926–1930. A major general in 1935, he was appointed CB in 1937. Honorary Surgeon to the King 1933–1940 and retired in 1941, he was made a Fellow of the Royal College of Physicians the same year.

PETRE, Major General Roderic Loraine *(1887–1971), CB, DSO, MC*
Educated at Downside and RMC, Sandhurst, Petre was commissioned in the South Wales Borderers in 1908. His First War service was in China, at Gallipoli and latterly in the Mesopotamian campaign. Mentioned seven times in despatches, he was awarded the MC in 1916 and admitted to the DSO in 1917.

After serving in Afghanistan in 1919, Petre married in 1922 and attended the Staff College, Camberley, 1923–1924. After three years serving on the staff at the War Office, he transferred to the Dorset Regiment in 1929 and commanded the 2nd Battalion 1932–1935. A staff officer with the Sudan Defence Force 1935–1938, he was Commandant of the Senior Officers' School, Sheerness, 1938–1939.

Appointed GOC 12th Division in October 1939, Petre took it to France in April 1940 where it was assigned to labour duties. The Division was so badly mauled in the defence of Amiens and during the withdrawal to Dunkirk that it was disbanded in June. Meanwhile he was ordered by Gort to collect a scratch collection of units (PETREFORCE) intended to screen the southern flank of the BEF's line of withdrawal. Appointed CB after Dunkirk, Petre was appointed GOC 48th Division. Brooke, observing a divisional exercise in September 1941, noted that it was 'one of the worst' displays he had seen and gave orders that the GOC 'must be removed' (Danchev & Todman, 2001, 182). After briefly serving as commander of IX Corps with Home Forces in 1942, he was made commander of South Midland District. He retired in 1944.

PHILIPPS, Major General Sir Leslie Gordon *(1892–1966), KBE, CB, MC*
Born in Bombay and educated at Bedford School and RMC, Sandhurst,

Philipps was commissioned in the Worcestershire Regiment in 1911. A keen sportsman, he played hockey for the Army and England. Married in 1914, his First War service was in France, where, as a signals officer, he was thrice mentioned in despatches and awarded the MC.

Transferring to the Royal Corps of Signals in 1920, Philipps was Deputy Chief Signal Officer, India, 1932–1935, CSO, Northern Command, India, 1935–1937, and CSO, AHQ, India, 1937–1939. Twice mentioned in despatches for service on operations in Waziristan 1936–1937, he was Commandant of the Signal Training Centre, Jubbulpore, India, in 1940.

Appointed Chief Signal Officer, Eastern Command, in 1940, 'Flipper' Philipps was CSO-in-Chief, Home Forces, 1940–1943. Briefly CSO 21 Army Group in 1943, he was Director of Signals at the War Office from 1943 until his retirement in 1946.

Knighted in 1946, Philipps and his wife lived in Hampshire.

PHILLIPS, Major General Charles George (1889–1982), CB, DSO, MC
Of military family (his father was killed in action in Somaliland in 1902) and educated at Repton and RMC, Sandhurst, Phillips was commissioned in the West Yorkshire Regiment in 1909. Seconded for service with the Somali expedition 1912–1914, his First War service was in German East Africa. A captain in 1914, he was wounded, awarded the MC and commanded 3rd/2nd Battalion King's African Rifles in Portuguese East Africa (Mozambique) 1917–1918.

Admitted to the DSO in 1919, Philipps commanded the 1st Battalion KAR in Nyasaland 1921–1923. Married in 1924 and a lieutenant colonel in 1933, he commanded the 1st Battalion West Yorkshire Regiment 1933–1937 and 146th Infantry Brigade (TA) in 1938.

In April 1940 Philllips took his brigade to Norway. Directed first towards Narvik and then diverted to take part in the threatened seaborne assault on Trondheim, he had a bar added to his DSO for his part in the evacuation from Namsos. A brigade commander in Northern Iceland 1940–1941, he was promoted major general in 1942 and, moving from one climatic extreme to the other, served from then until his retirement in 1944 as GOC British Troops in Gambia and Sierra Leone.

Phillips retired to Nairobi and for many years was a farmer in Kenya.

PHILLIPS, Major General Sir Edward (1889–1973), KBE, CB, DSO, MC
Educated at St Paul's, London Hospital and Durham University, Philipps was commissioned in the Royal Army Medical Corps in July 1914. His First War service was in France, where he was awarded the MC, and Palestine, where he was admitted to the DSO. Four times mentioned in despatches, he was a lieutenant colonel in 1919.

Married in 1921, Phillips, rise in rank and status was regular and steady. A surgeon, much decorated at home and abroad before the Second World War, he was appointed CB in 1945, was Director of Medical Services 21 Army Group 1944–1945, and, knighted in 1946, was Director of Medical Services, British Army of the Rhine, 1946–1948. Re-married in 1947, he retired from the army in 1949.

PIGGOTT, Major General Francis Stewart Gilderoy *(1883–1966), CB, DSO*
Born in London, the son of the one-time Chief Justice of Hong Kong, Piggott was educated at Cheltenham and RMA, Woolwich. Commissioned in the Royal Engineers in 1903 and employed in Tokyo during the Russo-Japanese war, he qualified as a first-class interpreter in Japanese in 1906. Adjutant, RE, in Gibraltar 1906–1910, he was Assistant Military Attaché in Tokyo 1910–1914.

Piggott's First War service was in France. Five times mentioned in despatches, he was admitted to the DSO in 1917. Attending the first post-war course at the Staff College, Camberley, in 1919, he served on the staff at the War Office 1920–1921 and was Military Attaché in Tokyo 1921–1927. Chief Staff Officer (Intelligence) at the War Office 1927–1931, he was Deputy Military Secretary 1931–1935. Promoted major general, he was placed on the half-pay list before returning once again to Tokyo as Military Attaché. Appointed CB in 1937 and brought home in 1939, he retired from the army in 1940. His younger son died on active service in East Africa in 1941.

Senior Lecturer in Japanese at the School of Oriental Studies 1942–1946, Piggott was a member of the MCC and chairman of the Japan Society in London from 1958 to 1961. A widower for the last eleven years of his life, he was a frequent obituarist for *The Times*.

PIGOTT, Major General Alan John Keefe *(1892–1969), CB, CBE*
Of military family and educated at Shrewsbury and Oxford University, Pigott volunteered for service in 1914 and was commissioned in the Royal Irish Rifles that year. Married in 1915, his First War service was in France.

Transferring to the Northumberland Fusiliers in 1922, Pigott transferred to the Royal Berkshire Regiment while attending the Staff College, Camberley, in 1925. A Deputy Assistant Adjutant General at the War Office, 1937–1939, he was a colonel at war's beginning.

Assistant Adjutant General at the War Office 1939–1940, Pigott was appointed Deputy Director of Mobilization after Dunkirk. Made CBE in 1941 and promoted major general in 1943, he was Director of Recruiting and Mobilization from 1943 until his retirement from the army in 1947. Appointed CB in 1946, he lived in Middlesex. His son, a pilot officer in the RAF, was killed in action in 1942.

PILE, General Sir Frederick Alfred, *2nd Bt, (1884–1976), GCB, DSO, MC*
The son of a Lord Mayor of Dublin and educated at 'a rather inadequate mixed school' and RMA, Woolwich (DNB), Pile, a great sportsman though un-

distinguished academically, was commissioned in the Royal Artillery in 1904. After several years in India, he was a captain in 1914. Married in 1915, his First War service was in France, where he was mentioned in despatches, awarded the MC and admitted to the DSO in 1918.

A brevet lieutenant colonel in 1919, Pile transferred to the Royal Tank Corps while attending the Staff College, Camberley, in 1923. Assistant Director of Mechanization at the War Office 1928–1932, he became known as a progressive thinker on mechanization and divorced his wife. Inheriting his father's title in 1931 and re-marrying the next year, he commanded the mechanized Canal Brigade in Egypt 1932–1936. An 'astute and resourceful Irishman' (Marshall-Cornwall, 1984, 127), who was on Liddell Hart's 'select list of commanders of outstanding promise' (Liddell Hart, 1965, 238), he nevertheless lost interest in tanks when, in a move which was to his critics 'blatantly careerist' (Harris, 1995, 201), he sought and obtained the appointment to command the 1st Anti-Aircraft Division in 1937.

Appointed GOC Anti-Aircraft Command at war's beginning, 'Tim' Pile remained in the same post until April 1945. Dalton, who had a low regard for the military mind, regarded him as 'quite one of the most intelligent generals of his kind' (Pimlott (ed.), 1985, 494). Certainly he had a reputation for bold decision-making and encouraging technical innovation in his increasingly feminized command. However, it is doubtful whether Beaverbrook's singing his praises in high places made him many friends in the army. Talked of as a potential successor to Dill as CIGS, Pownall considered him a 'yes-man' (Bond (ed.), 1974, 167), and Brooke, the ever-suspicious inheritor of that mantle, thought him 'a repulsive creature' (Danchev & Todman, 2001, 280).

Made Director General of the Ministry of Works in 1945, Pile enjoyed brief responsibility for the production of prefabricated housing units. Retired from the army, he was Colonel Commandant, Royal Artillery, 1945–1952.

Married for a third time in 1951, Pile held down numerous directorships in concrete and cement companies. He received an honorary doctorate from Leeds University, wrote a book on his years as GOC Anti-Aircraft Command, *Ack Ack* (1949) and was active in charity work. He lived in Hertfordshire.

PILLEAU, Major General Gerald Arthur *(1896–1964), CBE, MC*

Of military family and educated at Wellington and RMC, Sandhurst, Pilleau was commissioned in the Queen's Royal (West Surrey) Regiment in 1914. His First War service was in France, where he was awarded the MC.

Married in 1921 and spending the next thirteen years on a captain's pay, Pilleau was Brigade Major 145th (South Midland) Brigade 1935–1937. A lieutenant colonel in 1939, he commanded 197th Brigade 1941–1942 and, promoted major general in 1944, was Chief of Staff, Middle East Command, 1944–1945.

Acting GOC 9th Army in Iran in 1945 and GOC British troops in the Levant in 1946, Pilleau retired from the army in 1947. Re-married, he lived near Hereford.

PLATT, General Sir William *(1885–1975), GBE, KCB, DSO*
Educated at Marlborough and RMC, Sandhurst, Platt was commissioned in the Northumberland Fusiliers in 1905. Serving on the North-West Frontier of India, he was mentioned in despatches and admitted to the DSO in 1908. A captain in 1914, his First War service was in France, where he was wounded and four times mentioned in despatches.

A brevet lieutenant colonel in 1918, Platt, attended the Staff College, Camberley, 1919–1920, and, married in 1921, served in Ireland 1920–1922. He was a Deputy Assistant Adjutant General at the War Office 1927–1930. Commander of the 2nd Battalion the Wiltshire Regiment 1930–1933, he served on the staff of 3rd Division, Bulford, 1933–1934, and commanded 7th Infantry Brigade 1934–1938. Promoted major general, he commanded British troops in the Sudan 1938–1941 and was Commandant of the Sudan Defence Force.

A 'wiry little terrier of a man', and a 'distinctly crusty martinet' (Mockler, 1984, 195), Platt was promoted lieutenant general and appointed by Wavell to command British troops in Eritrea and conduct the northern thrust into Abyssinia. Exhibiting 'a keen grip on the show' (Dill, 2nd. acc. 11, LHCMA), and, wary enough of the likes of Wingate to pronounce that '[t]he curse of this war is Lawrence in the last' (Bierman & Smith, 2000, 184), he was the acknowledged victor of the six-week-long battle of Keren. He and Cunningham received the surrender of the Duke of Aosta's Italian forces at Amba Alagi in May 1941.

Knighted and appointed GOC-in-C of the newly created East African Command, Platt directed operations to complete the occupation of Madagascar in 1942, though his duties as C-in-C were mainly directed at raising and training formations of African troops destined for the Burma campaign. Promoted general in 1943, and with knighthood enhanced, he retired from the army in 1945.

Colonel Commandant of the Wiltshire Regiment 1942–1954, Platt lived in the Lake District, took a keen interest in the Outward Bound Movement and was, for several years, a member of the Drama Panel of the Arts Council.

PLAYFAIR, Major General Ian Stanley Ord *(1894–1972), CB, DSO, MC*
Of military family and educated at Cheltenham and RMA, Woolwich, Playfair was commissioned in the Royal Engineers in 1913. His First War service was in France, where he was mentioned in despatches, awarded the MC and admitted to the DSO in 1918.

After attending the Staff College, Camberley, 1928–1929, Playfair married in 1930 and served on the directing staff at the Staff College, Quetta. 1934–1937. After attending the Imperial Defence College in 1938, he was appointed Commandant of the Army Gas School.

Director of Plans at the War Office 1940–1941, 'Bungy' Playfair was Chief of Staff, Far East, in 1941, and Chief of Staff, Celyon, in 1942. Appointed CB in 1943, he was made Major General, General Staff 11th Army Group in South-East Asia Command. He retired from the army in 1947.

252

Over a twelve-year period Playfair, along with others, was the author of four volumes of *The War in the Mediterranean and Middle East*, the official history. The father of two sons, he lived in Hythe in Kent.

POLLOCK, Major General Arthur Jocelyn Coleman *(1891–1968), CBE*
The son of an MP and educated at Wellington and RMA, Woolwich, Pollock was commissioned in the Royal Artillery in 1911. His First War service was in France, where he was three times mentioned in despatches and made OBE in 1918.

A staff captain with the Inter-Allied Military Missions in Berlin 1920–1926, Pollock was Chief Instructor at the Anti-Aircraft School, Biggin Hill, 1930–1933. Married in 1936 and a lieutenant colonel in 1937, he commanded 41st Anti-Aircraft Brigade in 1938.

Created CBE in 1941 and promoted major general in 1942, Pollock was GOC Anti-Aircraft Group, Eastern Mediterranean, 1942–1944. Retired from the army that year, he worked with the Ministry of Information 1944–1946 and was head of the Foreign Office's Middle East Information Department 1946–1950.

Living in Sussex, Pollock was a member of the Warningcamp Rural District Council from 1952. He was also the county's Chief Warden for civil defence for a number of years.

POLLOK, Major General Robert Valentine *(1884–1979), CB, CBE, DSO*
Of Anglo-Irish stock and educated at Eton and RMC, Sandhurst, Pollok was commissioned in the 15th Hussars in 1903. ADC to the Lieutenant-Governor, United Provinces, India, 1908–1912, he was ADC to the Governor-General of Australia, 1913–1914. His First War service was at Gallipoli and, after transferring to the Irish Guards, in France. Four times wounded and married in 1916, he was admitted to the DSO in 1917. He commanded the 1st Battalion, Irish Guards, 1917–1918.

A graduate of the Staff College, Camberley, in 1921 'Val' Pollok was Brigade Major, 1st Guards Brigade, 1922–1925. Returning to command his regiment's 1st Battalion 1926–1930, he commanded the Regimental District 1930–1931. Commander of the 1st Guards Brigade at Aldershot 1931–1935, he was Commandant of the Senior Officers' School, Sheerness, 1935–1938.

GOC Northern Ireland District 1938–1940, Pollok was GOC 43rd (Wessex) Division from April 1940 until his retirement in February 1941. Re-employed briefly as a colonel on general staff duties, he reverted to retired pay at the end of the year.

Pollok and his wife retired to live in Limerick. Their only son died on active service in 1945.

POOLE, Major General Leopold Thomas *(1888–1965), CB, DSO, MC*
Educated at Edinburgh Institution and Edinburgh University, Poole was a qualified surgeon before joining the Royal Army Medical Corps in 1912. A captain in 1915, his First War service was in France, where he was three times

mentioned in despatches, awarded the MC in 1917 and admitted to the DSO in 1918.

Serving on operations in Iraq 1919–1920, Poole married in 1922 and became a specialist in the pathology of gas warfare. Mentioned in despatches for his part in operations on the North-West Frontier in 1933, he was Assistant Professor of Pathology 1934–1939 and Director of Pathology at the War Office 1941–1945

Retired in 1946, Poole lived in the Scottish Borders, from where he continued to write articles for medical journals.

POPE, Major General Vyvyan Vavasour (1891–1941), CBE, DSO, MC

Educated at Lancing and RMC, Sandhurst, Pope was commissioned in the North Staffordshire Regiment in 1912. His First War service was in France, where he was twice wounded, five times mentioned in despatches, awarded the MC and admitted to the DSO in 1916. Having had his right forearm amputated, he was a battalion commander at war's end. He was mentioned in despatches for his service with the North Russia Relief Mission in 1919.

Brigade Major to the Curragh Brigade, Ireland, 1920–1922, Pope commanded an Armoured Car Brigade in Egypt 1922–1923. Transferring to the Royal Tank Corp in 1923, he attended the Staff College, Camberley, 1924–1925, and, married in 1926, was Brigade Major at the RTC Centre at Bovington 1926–1927. Serving on the staff with Southern Command 1928–1929, he served on the staff at the War Office 1931–1933 and attended the Imperial Defence College in 1934. Known as one of the 'bright boys' (Lewin, 1976, 61), and effectively in command of the Mobile Force in Egypt in 1936, he was a senior staff officer at the War Office 1936–1937 and was BGS Southern Command in 1938.

Appointed BGS to II Corps in 1939, Brooke was 'very sorry to lose [Pope]' (Danchev & Todman, 2001, 21), when he was made commander of 3rd Armoured Brigade that November. Appointed Inspector of the RAC before Dunkirk, he was assigned to Brooke as adviser on Armoured Fighting Vehicles after the fall of France. Director of AFVs at the War Office 1940–1941 and regarded as 'one of the most able officers of the RTC' (Carver, 1989, 77), he was appointed GOC XXX Corps in August 1941.

Pope was killed, along with most of his staff, in an air crash near Cairo in October 1941. Yet, whereas news of Gott's death a year later, also in an air crash, was regarded as fortunate by the likes of Brooke and Montgomery, Pope's premature end was generally mourned. He was 'approaching the apex of his military career' (Lewin, 1976, 141). Few senior officers, it has been said, 'could have been better qualified for the command' of XXX Corps at that time' (Carver, 2002, 30). He left a widow and a son.

POWNALL, Lieutenant General Sir Henry Royds
(1887–1961), KCB, KBE, DSO, MC

Educated at Rugby and RMA, Woolwich, Pownall was commissioned in the Royal Artillery in 1906. He served in England with the Field Artillery and in

India with the Horse Artillery, his First War service was in France. Mentioned in despatches, he was awarded the MC and admitted to the DSO in 1918.

Married in 1918, Pownall attended the Staff College, Camberley, 1920–1921, and was Brigade Major at the School of Artillery, Larkhill, 1924–1925. On the directing staff at Camberley 1926–1929, a bar was added to his DSO in 1930 after service on operations on the North-West Frontier. A 'first-class horseman' who was 'widely liked but had few intimate friends' (Bond (ed.), 1972, xv), he attended the Imperial Defence College in 1932, and was Military Assistant Secretary to the Committee of Imperial Defence 1933–1935 and Deputy Secretary in 1936. Commandant of the School of Artillery 1936–1938, he was Director of Military Operations at the War Office 1938–1939.

Appointed Chief of General Staff to the BEF in 1939, Pownall was delighted 'to serve under so great a gentleman and so fine a soldier as . . . Gort' (Bond (ed.), 1972, 224). Less than delighted at the outcome of the campaign in France and Flanders and labelled 'completely useless' by Montgomery (Hamilton, 1982, 395), he was knighted and became Inspector-General of the Home Guard in 1940. Commander of British troops in Northern Ireland 1940–1941, he became briefly Vice CIGS and was one of those senior officers tipped to succeed Dill as CIGS (Leutze (ed.),1972, 367). Instead he vacated his post for Nye and was appointed C-in-C, Far East, in December 1941. A lieutenant general in 1942, he was Chief of Staff to the short-lived ABDA Command and was GOC Ceylon 1942–1943. Briefly C-in-C in Persia and Iraq, he was Chief of Staff to Mountbatten, the Supreme Allied Commander, South-East Asia, 1943–1944. With ill-health forcing him to relinquish that appointment, he retired from the army in 1945.

Colonel Commandant of the Royal Artillery 1942–1952 (the year of his wife's death), Pownall, with knighthood enhanced, assisted Churchill in composing his Second World War history, and, after helping in the preparation of a number of the official war histories, relaxed his veto on his own wartime diaries ever being published. When these emerged after his death (two volumes, 1972 and 1974), they were revealing not only on the higher direction of the war but also on Pownall's thoughtful and generally intelligent part in it. No military 'progressive', he nevertheless displayed a good deal of practical common sense. Seeing himself as a privileged member of the nation's warrior caste, he shared its prejudices. But he had the foresight to realize that in the event of war a field force would have to be sent to France and he also foresaw the fall of Singapore months before the Japanese invaded Malaya. Known for being 'a bit idle' (Dill, 2nd. acc. 15, LHCMA), his clear-sightedness and experience made him an outstanding wartime staff officer. Among soldiers he was generally 'charming, considerate, thoughtful and above all loyal' (Bond (ed.), 1974, xvi), though to a non-caste outsider, like the unfortunate 'little yellow Jew' Hore-Belisha, (Kennedy Diary, 4/2/2, LHCMA), he could be a ruthlessly implacable opponent.

On the board of numerous companies, and a keen skier and golfer, Pownall was Chief Commissioner of the St John Ambulance Brigade 1947–1949.

PRATT, Major General Douglas Henry *(1892–1958), CB, DSO, MC*
Educated at Dover College and RMC, Sandhurst, Pratt was commissioned in the Royal Irish Regiment in 1911. After three years in India, his First War service was in France. Married in 1915, he transferred to the Tank Corps in 1916. Three times mentioned in despatches and awarded the MC, he was admitted to the DSO in 1918.

After attending the Staff College, Camberley, 1923–1924, Pratt served on the staff of 42nd (East Lancashire) Division 1926–1928 and was Exchanges Officer at the Australian Royal Military College, Duntroon, 1931–1933. On the staff at the War Office 1934–1935, he commanded the 2nd Battalion of the Royal Tank Corps at Farnborough 1936–1937 and was Assistant Director of Mechanization at the War Office in 1938.

Commander of the tank brigade sent to France with the BEF, Pratt was promoted major general after Dunkirk and sent to Washington as Major General Armoured Fighting Vehicles. It was largely thanks to him that the Sherman Tank, then being developed, was up-gunned to British requirements. Appointed Deputy Director General of the British Supply Mission in Washington in 1943, he retired from the army in 1946.

PRATT, Major General Fendall William Harvey
(1892–1960), CB, CBE, DSO, MC
The son of an Indian Army doctor and educated at Cheltenham and RMA, Woolwich, Pratt was commissioned in the Royal Artillery in 1912. His First War service was at Gallopili, where he was mentioned in despatches, and in France where he was awarded the MC.

Serving with the Army of the Back Sea 1920–1921, Pratt was an instructor at Sandhurst 1922–1925 and at the Artillery Schools at Larkhill and India 1926–1933. He served with the Union Defence Force of South Africa, 1935–1936. A brevet lieutenant colonel in 1936, he married in 1938.

Commander of Medium Artillery with I Corps in France with the BEF 1939–1940, Pratt was CCRA X Corps 1940–1941. Brigadier RA for South Eastern Command 1941–1942, he was CCRA V Corps in Tunisia in 1942–1943 and Brigadier RA 15 Army Group in Sicily and Italy 1943–1944.

Major General RA i/c Training 1944–1945, Pratt was President of the Sandhurst Selection Board from 1946 until his retirement from the army in 1948. He was Colonel Commandant, RA, 1949–1957 and, a keen cricketer (member of MCC, I Zingari, etc.), was President of the RA Cricket Club, 1945–1955. Made DL for Southampton in 1945, he was Mayor of Winchester 1958–1959.

PRICE-WILLIAMS, Major General Harold *(1892- ?), DSO, MC*
Educated at RMA, Woolwich, and commissioned in the Royal Engineers in 1912, Price-Williams's First War service was in France, where he was awarded the MC and admitted to the DSO.

Reverting to the rank of captain at war's end, Price-Williams spent the next ten years on a captain's pay and endured a spell on half-pay upon promotion to major in 1927. A staff officer at the School of Artillery, Larkhill, 1932–1935, he served on the directing staff of the Staff College, Quetta, 1937–1939.

Commander RA, Western (Independent) District, India, at war's beginning Price-Williams was a Brigadier RA and a BGS, before being made Deputy Master General of the Ordnance in India in 1941. He retired from the army in 1943.

PRIEST, Major General Robert Cecil *(1882–1966), CB*

Educated at King Edward's Birmingham, Cambridge University and St Thomas's Hospital, Priest joined the Royal Army Medical Corps in 1909. His First War service was in India and Mesopotamia.

A bacteriologist and something of a specialist in Tropical Medicine, Priest was Examiner in Medicine at Pharmacology at the Egyptian University, Cairo, 1933–1937 and Consulting Physician to British troops in Egypt 1936–1937. Professor of Tropical Medicine at the Royal Army Medical College, he was Consulting Physician to the army 1937–1939 and to the BEF 1939–1940.

A major general in 1937, Priest was Inspector of Army Medical Services from 1940 until his retirement in 1941. He was Consulting Physician, Western Command, 1941–1946 and House Governor, King Edward VII Convalescent Home for Officers, Osborne, 1946–1952. He was also a member of the British Red Cross Society.

PRIESTMAN, Major General John Hedley Thornton
(1885–1964), CB, CBE, DSO, MC

Commissioned in the Manchester Regiment in 1905 and transferring to the Lincolnshire Regiment, Priestman's First War service was in France. Wounded and thrice mentioned in despatches, he was awarded the MC and admitted to the DSO in 1917.

Married in 1915, Priestman attended the Staff College, Camberley, 1921–1922 and was one of a 'very fine team' of instructors at Sandhurst 1923–1924 (Brownrigg, 1942, 52). He served on the staff at the War Office in the later 1920s. After attending the Imperial Defence College in 1929, he commanded 13th Infantry Brigade 1934–1936 in England and in Palestine 1936–1938. In between times he was GOC British troops in the Saar territory during the time of the 1935 plebiscite.

A major general in 1937 and appointed CB in 1939, Priestman was appointed GOC 54th (East Anglian) Division at war's beginning. In February 1941 he switched to command the Essex County Division. When that formation was disbanded in October 1941 he retired.

Colonel of the Royal Lincolnshire Regiment 1938–1948, Priestman's only son was killed in action in 1943. A keen sportsman and member of the MCC, he lived in Hertford.

PURDON, Major General William Brooke *(d. 1950), DSO, OBE, MC*
Educated at Campbell's Academy and Queen's College, Belfast, Purdon was a qualified doctor several years before the outbreak of war in 1914. An Irish rugby international, he joined the Royal Army Medical Corps in 1914 and his war service was in France. Mentioned in despatches, he was awarded the MC and admitted to the DSO in 1917.

Assistant Director of Hygiene at the War Office 1930–1934, Purdon was Director of Hygiene, British troops in India, 1934–1935. Professor of Hygiene at the Royal Army Medical College 1935–1938, he was Commandant and Director of Studies at the Royal Army Medical College 1938–1940. Director of Medical Services with the BEF in France in 1940, he was Deputy Director of Medical Services, Western Command from 1940 until his retirement in 1941.

Medical Superintendent of Queen Mary's Hospital, Roehampton, for the remainder of the war years, Purdon retired to his native Ulster in 1946.

PURSER, Major General Arthur William *(1884–1953), OBE, MC*
Educated at Marlborough and RMA, Woolwich, Purser was commissioned in the Royal Field Artillery in 1903. Married in 1913 and a captain in 1914, his First War service was in France, where, as Adjutant to an RA brigade he was awarded the MC in 1917.

Serving in various staff and instructional posts in the 1920s, Purser spent many years at the School of Artillery, Larkhill. Commander of 1st Heavy Brigade, RA, at Plymouth, 1931–1934, and an instructor at the Senior Officers' School, Sheerness, 1935–1937, he was Brigadier RA, Eastern Command, 1937–1938.

Promoted major general in 1938, and made GOC 66th Division in September 1939, ill-health forced Purser on to the half-pay list and he retired in January 1940 when his command was disbanded.

PYMAN, General Sir Harold English *(1908–1971), GBE, KCB, DSO*
Educated at Fettes and Cambridge University, Pyman was commissioned in the Royal Tank Regiment in 1929. He married in 1933. After serving on the North-West Frontier in 1937, he was promoted captain and assisted the 17th/21st Lancers in their mechanization programme. A student at the Staff College, Quetta, in 1938, he was an instructor there 1939–1941.

Serving with 7th Armoured Division in the western desert from 1941, 'Pete' Pyman was admitted to the DSO in 1942. Commander of 3rd Royal Tank Regiment 1942–1943, a bar was added to his DSO. BGS Home Forces 1943–1944, he was Chief of Staff to Dempsey's Second Army 1944–1945. CGS Allied Land Forces South East Asia 1945–1946, he was promoted Major General in 1945 and appointed CB in 1946.

Chief of Staff, GHQ Middle East Liberation Force, 1946–1949, Pyman was GOC 56th Armoured Division 1949–1951. Director General, Armoured Fighting Vehicles, Ministry of Supply, 1951–1953, he was GOC 11th

Armoured Division, BAOR, 1953–1955. Director of Weapons and Development at the War Office 1955–1956, he was GOC I Corps, BAOR, 1956–1958. Deputy CIGS, 1958–1961, he was C-in-C Allied Forces Northern Europe 1961–1963. He retired in 1964.

Pyman was Colonel Commandant, RTR, 1958–1965 and of the RAC 1963–1966. Incapacitated by a series of strokes, he nevertheless wrote his entertaining memoirs *Call to Arms* (1971), leaving the record of a man who was, as Liddell Hart wrote, 'one of the most brilliant soldiers of the Second World War and the two decades that followed' (Pyman, 1971, vi).

Q

QUINAN, General Sir Edward Pellew *(1885–1960), KCB, KCIE, DSO, OBE*
Commissioned in 1904 and gazetted into the 8th Punjab Regiment (Indian Army) in 1905, Quinan was a captain in 1913. His First War service was in India, where he was wounded, and in Mesopotamia.

Married in 1922, Quinan attended the Staff College, Quetta, in 1922–1923 and served on the staff of Northern Command, India, in the later 1920s. Commander of the 2nd Battalion 8th Punjabis in 1929 and a colonel in 1930, he attended the Imperial Defence College in 1931. An instructor at the Staff College, Quetta, 1933–1934, he commanded 9th (Jhansi) Brigade, India, 1934–1938. Admitted to the DSO in 1938, after service on operations in Waziristan, he commanded Waziristan District 1938–1940.

A major general in 1937 and a lieutenant general in 1941, Quinan was GOC in Iran and Iraq 1941–1942. Promoted general in 1942, he was GOC-in-C Tenth Army 1942–1943. As Auchinleck described him as 'a better administrator than strategist' (Dill, 2nd. ac. 4/7, LHCMA), it was perhaps as well that his command was not an active theatre of operations.

Made Commander of North-Western Army in India in 1943, Quinan, in indifferent health, retired at the end of that year. Colonel of the 8th Punjab Regiment in 1945, he settled near Ilminster in Somerset.

R

RAIKES, Major General Sir Geoffrey Taunton *(1884–1975), Kt, CB, DSO*
Educated at Radley and RMC, Sandhurst, Raikes was commissioned in the South Wales Borderers in 1903. Employed with the Egyptian Army 1913–1915, his First War service was in Egypt and Palestine. Six times mentioned in despatches and admitted to the DSO in 1916, two bars were added by war's end.

Married in 1923 and a student at the Staff College, Camberley, 1924–1925, Raikes was Chief Instructor of Military History and Tactics at Sandhurst 1928–1930. He commanded the 1st Battalion South Wales Borderers 1930–1934 and was an instructor at the Senior Officers' School, Sheerness, 1934–1935. Commander of 9th Infantry Brigade 1935–1937, he was promoted major general in 1937 and, appointed CB, retired the next year,

'Dug out' of retirement at war's beginning, Raikes was appointed GOC 38th (Welsh) Division in September 1939. Retired from the army in 1941 he settled in his native Brecknock and was Lord-Lieutenant for the county 1948–1959.

RAMSDEN, Major General William Havelock
(1888–1969), CB, CBE, DSO, MC
The son of a clergyman and educated at Bath College and RMC, Sandhurst, Ramsden was commissioned in the 'unfashionable but inexpensive' West India Regiment in 1910. His First War service was firstly in German West Africa (Cameroon) and, after transferring to the East Yorkshire Regiment in 1916, in France. There he was awarded the MC in 1918.

Married in 1918, Ramsden spent most of the early 1920s on regimental duties in India and was a weapons training instructor at the Senior Officers' School, Dehra Dun, 1926–1930. With his battalion in India in the early 1930s, he transferred to the Hampshire Regiment in 1936 and commanded the 1st Battalion in Waziristan and Palestine. Mentioned in despatches for his part in operations there, he was admitted to the DSO in 1939.

Commandant of West Lancashire Area in 1939, Ramsden commanded the 25th Infantry Brigade, attached to Martel's 50th (Northumbrian) Division, in France with the BEF, 1939–1940. Promoted major general, he was GOC 50th Division in North Africa 1940–1942 and commanded XXX Corps during the summer months of 1942. Described alternatively as 'a lean Yorkshireman, steady and forceful, . . . who always wore a huge automatic taken from a German officer in the previous war' (Barnett, 1999, 222), or as 'a dull, earnest, pedestrian infantryman, who inspired none of us with enthusiasm and confidence' (Carver, 1989, 128), he was briefly acting commander of 8th Army in North Africa in the wake of the Brooke-Churchill inspired 'Cairo purge'.

Ramsden did not last long in his caretaking capacity. Whether relieved of command because 'in need of a rest and proper nutrition' (Belchem, 1978, 118) or because de Guingand told Montgomery that he was 'bloody useless' (Hamilton. 1982, 604), he was sent back to England to assume command of 3rd Division. Appointed CB in 1943 and made GOC Sudan Defence Force and C-in-C British troops in Sudan and Eritrea, in January 1944, he retired from the army in 1945.

Re-married in 1946, Ramsden settled in Sussex.

RANCE, Major General Sir Hubert Elvin *(1898–1974),GCMG, GBE, CB*
Educated at Wimbledon College and RMC, Sandhurst, Rance was commissioned in the Worcestershire Regiment in 1916. His First War service was in France, where he was wounded three times.

Transferring to the Royal Corps of Signals in 1926 and married the next year, Rance was Adjutant to the 2nd Divisional Signals 1927–1930. After attending the Staff College, Camberley, 1934–1935, he served as a staff officer at the War Office 1936–1938. An instructor at Camberley 1938–1939, he served on the staff at the BEF's GHQ in France 1939–1940.

Appointed to command 4th Divisional Signals in April 1940 and made OBE after Dunkirk, Rance served on the staff at the War Office 1940–1941. Deputy Director, Military Training 1941–1942, he was Director of Technical Training, 1942–1943. BGS Western Command 1943–1945, his attendance on a course at the Civil Affairs Staff College proved an effective means of changing his career. Promoted major general in 1945, he was made Director of Civil Affairs in Burma.

Appointed CB in 1946 and briefly made Deputy Commander of the South-Western District at Taunton, Rance returned to Burma as Governor that year. Regarded by Wavell as 'capable and sensible' (Moon, 1973, 340), he retired from the army in 1947. Burmese independence in 1948 made him temporarily redundant. British co-Chairman of the Caribbean Commission 1948–1950, he was Governor and C-in-C of Trinidad and Tobago, 1950–1955. He was also Colonel Commandant of the Royal Corps of Signals 1953–1962.

RANKIN, Major General Henry Charles Deans *(1888–1965), CIE, OBE*
Educated at Glasgow Academy and Glasgow University, Rankin was a surgeon with a Red Cross Unit serving with the Serbian Army in the Balkan War of 1912–1913. Commissioned in the Royal Army Medical Corps in 1913, Rankin's First War service was in Egypt and Palestine. Three times mentioned in despatches, he was also twice taken prisoner.

Awarded the OBE and married in 1919, Rankin was surgeon to the C-in-C,

India, 1923–1925 and 1927–1931. Physician and Surgeon, Royal Hospital, Chelsea, 1931–1935, he was surgeon to the Governor of Bombay 1936–1937.

Deputy Director Medical Services, GHQ, India, 1941–1943, and DDMS, Southern Army, India, 1943–1945, Rankin was DDMS Eastern Command 1945–1946.

Retired from the army in 1946, Rankin was for many years a member of various Pensions Appeals Tribunals. He lived in Surrey.

RANKING, Major General Robert Philip Lancaster
(1896–1961), CB, CBE, MC
Of military family and educated at Bradfield and the Cadet College, Quetta, Ranking joined the Indian Army in 1915. A cavalryman, gazetted into the 2nd Royal Lancers (Gardner's Horse), his First War service was in France, Palestine and in Syria, where he was awarded the MC.

A captain in 1919, 'Phil' Ranking married in 1928 and attended the Staff College, Quetta, 1929–1930. Brigade Major to the 2nd Sialkot Cavalry Brigade, 1933–1935, he was Assistant Military Secretary, AHQ, India, 1936–1939. He commanded military bases in the Middle East 1940–1941 and served briefly in Greece. Assistant QMG, India, 1941–1942, he was GOC Lines of Communication, Burma, 1942–1943, and GOC 202 Lines of Communication Area, Burma and Assam, 1944–1945. Placed briefly in command of the Kohima-Dimapur area, Slim 'admired the way he and his subordinate commanders faced their peril' (Slim, 1986, 309).

Appointed CB in 1946, Ranking retired in 1948 and settled near Salisbury.

RANSOME, Major General Algernon Lee *(1883–1969),CB, DSO, MC*
American-born, Ransome was educated privately and at RMC, Sandhurst. Commissioned in the Dorset Regiment in 1903, his First War service was in France. Six times mentioned in despatches, he was awarded the MC and, in 1918, was admitted to the DSO (with bar). He commanded the 7th Battalion Royal East Kent Regiment (the Buffs) 1916–1918.

Ransome attended the Staff College, Camberley, in 1919 and served on the staff at Aldershot Command and at the War Office 1920–1925. Married in 1927, he was an instructor at the Australian Royal Military College, Duntroon, 1927–1928 and was Assistant Adjutant General, Aldershot Command, 1931–1933. Commander of the 2nd Indian (Rawalpindi) Infantry Brigade 1933–1935, he was promoted major general, appointed CB in 1937 and retired the following year.

Re-employed in September 1939, Ransome was appointed GOC 46th Division. On retired pay that December, he commanded the 10th (Romsey) Battalion of the Hampshire Home Guard 1942–1944. He lived in Romsey.

RAWSON, Major General Geoffrey Grahame *(1887–1979), CB, OBE, MC*
The son of an Indian Civil Servant and educated at Cheltenham and RMA, Woolwich, Rawson was commissioned in the Royal Engineers in 1908. His First

War service was in France, where he was five times mentioned in despatches and awarded the MC in 1916, and in Salonika, where he was made OBE.

Married in 1919, Rawson transferred to the Royal Corps of Signals in 1920. A Deputy Assistant Adjutant General at the War Office in 1921, he was a lieutenant colonel in 1928. After a spell on half-pay, he was Chief Instructor at the School of Signals 1932–1937 and Deputy Director of Staff Duties at the War Office 1937–1941. Promoted major general in 1941, he was Inspector of Signals with Home Forces from 1941 until 1943 and retired from the army in 1944.

Appointed CB and Colonel Commandant of the Royal Corps of Signals 1944–1950, Rawson lived in London, the last twelve years of his life a widower.

READMAN, Major General Edgar Platt *(1893–1980)*, *CBE*
Educated at Sheffield Central School, Readman volunteered for service in 1914 and, transferring to the Royal Tank Corps in 1917, was commissioned that year.

Married in 1919, Readman transferred to the Royal Army Ordnance Corps in 1923, but left the army two years later. Working in the steel industry, specifically with a machine-tool company, he was a colonel in the Territorial Army in 1934 and commanded 49th (West Riding) Ordnance Company for many years. A brigadier in 1940, his Second World War service was with the RAOC, with a special interest in tank design.

Readman returned to industry in 1945, retiring from the TA in 1951. He held numerous directorships and was Managing Director of the English Steel Corporation Tool Company in 1958.

REDMAN, Lieutenant General Sir Harold *(1899–1986)*, *KCB*, *CBE*
Educated at Farnham Grammar School and RMA, Woolwich, Redman was commissioned in the Royal Artillery in 1917. He served in France and with the British Army of the Rhine.

Still a subaltern, Redman served on the North-West Frontier 1923–1924 and, a captain in 1927, transferred to the King's Own Yorkshire Light Infantry. After attending the Staff College, Camberley, 1929–30, he served on the staff at the War Office 1932–1934. Brigade Major to the 3rd Division 1934–1936, he was on the directing staff at the Senior Officers' School, Sheerness, 1937–1938. On the directing staff at Camberley 1938–1939, he worked with the War Cabinet secretariat 1939–1940.

Commander of the 7th Battalion, KOYLI, 1940–1941 and the 151st Infantry Brigade, in 1941, 'Dixie' Redman was BGS 8th Army 1941–1942. He commanded 10th Indian Motorized Brigade in North Africa 1942–1943, and was Secretary to the Combined Chiefs of Staff 1943–1944. Deputy Commander, French Forces of the Interior in 1944, he headed the SHAEF Mission to the French High Command 1944–1945.

Head of the British Military Mission to France 1945–1946, Redman was Chief of Staff Allied Land Forces, South-East Asia, 1946–1948. Married in 1947, he was Director of Military Operations at the War Office 1948–1951 and Principal Staff Officer to the Deputy Supreme Commander, Europe,

1951–1952. Vice CIGS 1952–1955, he re-married in 1953 and was Governor and C-in-C Gibraltar from 1955 until his retirement from the army in 1958.

Colonel of the KOYLI 1950–1960 and Secretary to the Wolfson Foundation 1958–1967, Redman lived in Dorset.

REES, Major General Thomas Wynford *(1898–1959), CB, CIE, DSO, MC*
The son of a clergyman, Rees was gazetted into the 7th Rajput Regiment, Indian Army, in 1916. His First War service was in India and France, where he was wounded, mentioned in despatches, awarded the MC and admitted to the DSO in 1919.

Mentioned in despatches for his part in operations in Waziristan in 1920 and again in 1924, Rees married in 1926. He was an instructor at Sandhurst 1926–1927 and private secretary to the Governor of Burma 1928–1930. After attending the Staff College, Camberley, 1931–1932, he was Deputy Assistant QMG, AHQ, India, 1935–1937. He served on the staff in Waziristan District 1937–1938 and commanded the 3rd Battalion 6th Rajput Rifles in 1939.

A colonel in 1940, 'Pete' Rees served with 4th Indian Division in North Africa 1940–1941 and commanded 10th Indian Division in Iraq and North Africa in 1942. Despite his reputation for bringing 'to the battlefield that restless energy and impetuous leadership-from-the front that characterized Rommel' (Lewin, 1976, 207), he was dismissed by Gott, his corps commander, in June 1942. Returned to India, he was appointed GOC 19th Indian Division in November 1943. Prominent in the recapture of Mandalay in Burma, his commentary on the assault on Fort Dufferin was broadcast by the BBC. A non-drinking, non-smoking fluent Welsh-speaker, known as 'a devout chapel man, given to community singing . . . [of] the fiery revivalist hymns he loved' (Hickey, 1998, 218), he was a reputedly fearless 'pocket Napoleon' (Slim, 1986, 390). Standing at little more than five feet in height, he was given to wearing bright-coloured scarves when in action.

Made GOC 4th Indian Division in 1945 and appointed CB that year, Rees spent the remaining three years of his military career in India trying to contain pre-independence and partition civil disturbances. Head of the Military Emergency staff in Delhi in 1947, he retired in 1948. Colonel of the Rajputana Rifles in 1946, he was President of the Wales Boys' Brigade 1949–1953 and DL for Monmouthshire in 1955. Honoured by the University of Wales, he was County Commander of the Boy Scouts and Civil Defence Controller of the Cardiff sub-region before his sudden death at the age of 60.

REEVE, Major General John Talbot Wentworth
(1891–1983), CB, CBE, DSO
Educated at Eton and RMC, Sandhurst, Reeve was commissioned in the Rifle Brigade in 1911. A captain in 1914, his First War service was in France. Mentioned in despatches, he was admitted to the DSO in 1919.

Married in 1919 and transferring to the Royal Artillery, Reeve attended the Staff College, Camberley, 1924–1925. Serving on the staff at the War Office

1926–1930, he re-transferred to the Rifle Brigade and commanded the 1st Battalion 1936–1938. Commander of the Hong Kong Infantry Brigade 1938–1941, he was Deputy Adjutant General, Home Forces, 1942–1943. Commander of Sussex District 1943–1944, he was Deputy Adjutant General, Middle East Force, from 1944 until his retirement from the army in 1946.

Reeve was appointed CB in 1946. His only son was killed in action in North Africa in 1942. A widower in 1949, he re-married in 1950 and lived near Bury St Edmunds in Suffolk.

REID, Major General Denys Whitehorn *(1897–1970), CB, CBE, DSO, MC*

Commissioned in the Seaforth Highlanders in 1915, Reid's First War service was in France. Wounded, twice mentioned in despatches and awarded the MC in 1916, he was admitted to the DSO in 1918.

Transferring to the 5th Mahratta Light Infantry (Indian Army), Reid's peacetime soldiering was in India. He attended the Senior Officers' School, Belgaum, in 1938, commanded his regiment's 3rd Battalion 1940–1941 and was 'a tough fearless Scot' (Maule, 1961, 34). Legendarily brave, he fought under Slim at Gallabat and under Heath in Eritrea. Commander of 29th Indian Infantry Brigade in North Africa 1941–1942, he took part in the CRUSADER offensive. As part of Messervy's 7th Armoured Division, his brigade was involved in a number of disastrous actions in and around Tobruk and he was taken prisoner near Fuka in June 1942.

Imprisoned in Italy, Reid, released from captivity in September 1943, crossed American lines that November. Made GOC 10th Indian Division, Leese judged that 'he should be very good in battle, but he is a very slow man' (PRO WO 216/168). However, he served throughout the Italian campaign with distinctive 'verve and enterprise' (Blaxland, 1979, 156). Wounded in late 1944 and earning a bar to his DSO, he was appointed CB in 1945.

Retired from the army in 1947, Reid lived near Wellington in Somerset.

RENNELL of RODD, Major General Lord Francis James
(1895–1978), KBE, CB

Educated at Eton and Oxford University, Rennell volunteered for service with the Royal Field Artillery in 1914. His First War service was in France, and then in Italy, North Africa, Palestine and Syria as an intelligence officer.

Mentioned in despatches, Rennell joined the diplomatic service in 1919. After postings in Rome and Sofia, he resigned in 1924, married in 1928 and worked in the City and for the Bank of England 1929–1932. In between times he was a noted Saharan explorer, receiving the Royal Geographical Society's Founder's Medal.

Recommissioned in 1939, Rennell succeeded his father in 1941. He was Major General, Civil Affairs Administration, in the Middle East, East Africa, Madagascar and Italy. Considered 'awfully good at his job' by Macmillan, despite his 'occasional lapses into a 'prima donna mood' (Macmillan, 1984, 190), he was appointed CB in 1943. Knighted in 1945, he was President of the

RGS 1945–1948. Visiting Fellow, Nuffield College, Oxford, 1947–1959, he was DL for Herefordshire in 1948, and Vice-Lieutenant for the county 1957–1973. With many different interests attracting his 'lively and unusual mind' (DNB), he travelled widely, had a seat on the board of BOAC and was a director of Morgan, Grenfell and Co.

RENNIE, Major General Tom Gordon *(1900–1945), CB, DSO, MBE*
Born in China and educated at Loretto and RMC, Sandhurst, Rennie was commissioned in the Black Watch in 1919. Adjutant to the 2nd Battalion 1930–1932, he married in 1932 and attended the Staff College, Camberley, 1933–1934.

Serving with the 51st (Highland) Division in France with the BEF, Rennie was taken prisoner at St Valery-en-Caux but quickly escaped. Commander of the 5th Battalion, Black Watch, 1941–1942, he commanded 154th Brigade in the reconstituted Highland Division 1942–1943. Admitted to the DSO in 1942 after El Alamein, he served on in Sicily and Italy before being recalled to England in December 1943 and appointed GOC 3rd Division. Subject to some criticism for not pushing his troops more forcefully in the early stages of the campaign in Normandy, he was wounded in June 1944.

Appointed CB, Rennie returned to the fold as GOC 51st (Highland) Division in July 1944. Quickly demonstrating 'that he was the right commander to re-vitalize the Highlanders' (D'Este, 2001, 275) and very much in his element, his 'forebodings' about Operation PLUNDER (Horrocks, 1960, 259), the Rhine crossing of March 1945, proved correct. Killed by a mortar bomb, he left a widow and two children.

RENTON, Major General James Malcolm Leslie
(1898–1972), CB, DSO, OBE
Of military family and educated at Eton and RMC, Sandhurst, Renton was commissioned in the Rifle Brigade in 1916. His First War service was in France where he was severely wounded in 1917.

Deputy Assistant Adjutant General in Iraq 1922–1927, Renton raised and trained native levies. On regimental duties in India for most of the 1930s, he commanded the 2nd Battalion of the Rifle Brigade 1940–1941. As part of O'Connor's Western Desert Force he took part in operations that led to the defeat of the Italian Tenth Army and, admitted to the DSO, was appointed to command 7th Motor Brigade Group in North Africa.

Appointed GOC 7th Armoured Division in June 1942, 'Cal' Renton showed himself a brave and tactically capable commander at Alam Halfa. Too bad-tempered and 'subject to moods' to inspire much affection (Carver, 1989–139) and regarded as 'infuriating', especially when he was right, the word went round that he was a 'black-button' snob' (Roberts, 1987, 92), and 'out of his depth with a divisional command' (Pyman, 1971, 44). He was sent back to England in September, perhaps for no other reason that he had had the temerity to argue with Montgomery, and for causing Horrocks 'all the trouble' (Hamilton, 1982,

644). Commandant of the Senior Officers' School, Sheerness, 1943–1944, he was Head of the British Military Mission to Iraq 1944–1948.

Retired from the army in 1948, Renton was a JP for West Sussex from 1949 and Deputy Commissioner for Sussex St John Ambulance Brigade in 1950. DL for the county in 1956, he was Chairman of the Council of the Anglo-Iraqi Society, 1954–1958.

REVELL-SMITH, Major General William Revell
(1894–1956), CB, CBE, DSO, MC
Born in Melbourne, Australia, and educated at Charterhouse, Revell-Smith joined the Westminster Dragoons in 1914. His First War service was in France, first attached to the Egyptian Expeditionary Force and, from 1916, as a commissioned officer in the Royal Artillery. He was mentioned in despatches and awarded the MC and bar.

A brevet lieutenant colonel in 1918 and married in 1920, it took him 18 years of peacetime soldiering to achieve the equivalent substantive rank. A sportsman and a fine horseman, he was twice winner of the George V Gold Cup in the Olympia Tournament. He commanded 53rd Light Anti-Aircraft Regiment in France with the BEF 1939–1940. Admitted to the DSO after Dunkirk, he commanded 11th Anti-Aircraft Brigade 1940–1942 and, a major general in 1944, was Major General Anti-Aircraft, 21st Army Group, North-West Europe, 1944–1945.

Appointed CB in 1946 and GOC British troops, Malta, from 1948 until his retirement from the army in 1949, Revell-Smith held a number of directorships and was a tobacco farmer in Southern Rhodesia (Zimbabwe).

REYNOLDS, Major General Roger Clayton *(1895–1983), CB, OBE, MC*
Educated at Bradfield and RMA, Woolwich, where he was a keen games player, Reynolds was commissioned in the Royal Artillery in 1914. His First War service was in France, where he was awarded the MC in 1916.

Married in 1918, Reynolds attended the Staff College, Camberley, 1928–1929, and was Staff Captain to the Delhi Independent Brigade in 1931. A Deputy Assistant Adjutant General, AHQ, India, 1932–1936, he served on the staff at the War Office 1939–1940.

Commander of an Anti-Aircraft Brigade, 1941–1942, Reynolds, a 'tower of strength in A.A. Command' (Pile, 1949, 40), was GOC 3rd Anti-Aircraft Group, based in Bristol, 1942–1944. GOC 1st AA Group, London, 1944–1947, he retired from the army in 1948.

Chairman of the West London Group of Hospitals 1949–1951, Reynolds re-married in 1952 and settled in New York State. Among other activities he was sometime Vice Chairman of the United States Pony Club.

RICH, Major General Henry Hampden *(1891–1976), CBE*
Of military family and educated at Aldenham School and RMC, Sandhurst, Rich was commissioned on the unattached list in 1911, and was gazetted into

the 12th Rajputana Infantry Regiment, Indian Army, the following year. His First War service was in India and Mesopotamia, where he was taken prisoner at Kut-al-Amara.

After service on the North-West Frontier, Rich attended the Staff College, Camberley, 1924–1925. Married in 1925, he was a staff captain with the 2nd/6th Rapjputs in 1926 and Brigade Major 11th (Ahmednagar) Brigade, 1926–1928. An instructor at the Staff College, Quetta, 1931–1934, he commanded the 1st Battalion Burma Rifles 1935–1937. Deputy Director, and later Director, of Staff Duties, AHQ, India, 1937–1939, he commanded the Nowshera Brigade 1940–1941.

Promoted major general and appointed GOC of the newly-formed 14th Indian Infantry Division in 1942, Rich was Commander of Assam District 1942–1943. Made CBE in 1943, he was appointed to command the reconstituted Burma Army and, appointed CB, retired in 1944.

Re-employed in 1944 as Head of Indian Prisoners of War Reception in Britain, Rich re-married in 1969. He lived in Essex.

RICHARDS, Major General George Warren
(1898–1978), CB, CBE, DSO, MC
Educated at Oswestry and RMC, Sandhurst, Richards was commissioned in the Royal Welch Fusiliers in 1916. His First War service was in France, where, attached to the Machine Gun Corps, he was awarded the MC in 1918.

Transferring to the Royal Tank Corps in 1920, Richards was Adjutant to the 4th Battalion of the RTC in 1928 and married in 1930. He attended the Staff College, Camberley, 1934–1935. Senior Instructor at the Tank School, Bovington, 1939–1940, he served on the staff of 7th Armoured Division in Egypt 1940–1941.

Commander of 4th Armoured Brigade in North Africa in 1942, 'Rickie' Richards was admitted to the DSO after El Alamein. Commander of 23rd Armoured Brigade Group 1942–1943, he served in Tunisia and Italy and had a bar added to his DSO. Brought home by Montgomery in December 1943, he was appointed Major General RAC 21st Army Group.

Appointed CB in 1945 and Commander of North Midland District in 1947, Richards was GOC 42nd Armoured Division from 1947 until his retirement in 1949.

Settling near Abergavenny, Richards was DL for Monmouthshire in 1965.

RICHARDS, Major General William Watson *(1892–1961), CB, CBE, MC*
Born on Jersey and educated privately, Richards joined the Army Ordnance Corps in 1914. His First War service was in France, where he was awarded the MC.

Employed under the Air Ministry 1924–1927 and married in 1936, Richards was Deputy Director of Ordnance Services with the BEF in France, 1939–1940. Made CBE in 1941, he was Director of Ordnance Services, Middle East Command, 1940–1943 and Director of Clothing and Stores at the War Office

1943–1946. Appointed CB in 1942, he was Director of Ordnance Services at the War Office from 1946 until he retired from the army in 1948.

Colonel Commandant of the Royal Army Ordnance Corps 1947–1957, Richards, a keen sportsman and devout Roman Catholic, lived in Sussex.

RICHARDSON, Major General Alexander Whitmore Colquhoun
(1887–1964), CB, DSO
Educated at Denstone College and joining the 4th (Militia) Battalion of the West Yorkshire Regiment in 1907, Richardson was commissioned in the Bedfordshire Regiment in 1909. A captain in 1913 and married in 1914, his First War service was in France. Admitted to the DSO in 1917, he transferred to the Royal Tank Corps in 1918.

A lieutenant colonel in 1930, Richardson commanded the 4th Battalion of the Royal Tank Corps 1930–1931, but left the army that year to become Operating Manager of the London Omnibus Company. Made Chief Welfare Officer of the London Passenger Transport Board in 1937, he joined the Territorial Army and, as lieutenant colonel, commanded 84th Anti-Aircraft Brigade 1938–1939.

A brigadier in 1940, 'Alec' Richardson commanded 26th Armoured Brigade 1940–1941 and was Director General Armoured Fighting Vehicles at the War Office in 1941. Promoted major general, he was Director of the Royal Armoured Corps 1942–1943, having been sacked by Anderson as his BGS a week into Operation TORCH. Regarded by Penney as 'a bit overwhelmed by it all, and at the same time not fit' (Penney Diary, 3/2, LHCMA), but considered by Montgomery as potentially 'quite good under a skilled or gifted commander' (Hamilton, 1983, 378), he was Chief of Staff 18th Army Group in Tunisia in 1943 and Chief of Staff 15th Army Group in Italy 1943–1944. He retired from the army in 1945. One of his sons was killed in action in 1942.

RICHARDSON, Major General David Turnbull *(1886–1957), CB, MC*
Commissioned in the Royal Army Medical Corps in 1912 and a captain in 1915, Richardson's First War service was in France, where he was awarded the MC.

A major in 1924, Richardson was an assistant professor at the Royal Army Medical College 1928–1932. A lieutenant colonel in 1934, he was Assistant Director of Hygiene at the War Office 1935–1938. Professor of Hygiene at the Royal Army Medical College 1938–1939, he was Deputy Director of Hygiene at the War Office 1939–1940. Assistant Director of Medical Services with the BEF south of the Somme in June 1940, he was Director of Hygiene at the War Office from 1941 until his retirement in 1946

Appointed CB in 1945, Richardson retired to his native Ross-shire.

RICHARDSON, Major General Roland *(1896–1973), CB, MC*
Gazetted into the 13th Frontier Force Rifles (Indian Army) in 1915, Richardson's First War service was in Gallipoli and Egypt, where he was awarded the MC.

A captain in 1918 and a major in 1932, Richardson was Chief Staff Officer,

Lahore Brigade Area, in 1933. After attending the Senior Officers' School, Belgaum, in 1937, he was promoted lieutenant colonel and commanded the 1st Battalion FF Rifles 1937–1938. He was Deputy Director of Staff Duties, AHQ, India, 1939–1941, and commanded a brigade 1940–1941. GOC 7th Indian Division in 1942, he commanded Upper Sind District 1942–1943 and was GOC Trincomalee Forces Area, Ceylon (Sri Lanka), 1943–1945. He retired from the army in 1948 and thereafter lived in Rhodesia (Zimbabwe).

RICHARDSON, Major General Thomas William *(1895–1968), OBE*

The son of a doctor, Richardson was educated at King Edward VI's School, Norwich, and RMC, Sandhurst. Commissioned in the Army Service Corps in 1914 and a captain in 1915, his First War service was in France, where he was twice mentioned in despatches.

Awarded the OBE in 1919, Richardson spent the next 17 years on a captain's pay. He served in Egypt 1919–1924 and was an instructor at the RASC Training Centre 1925–1928. Married in 1921, divorced in 1932 and re-married in 1933, he was Adjutant RASC Rhine Army in 1929 and at RASC, Catterick, 1930–1933. Deputy Assistant Director Supplies and Transport at the War Office 1933–1937, he was Assistant Director Supplies and Transport Hong Kong and China Command 1937–1939.

Officer Commanding No.2 Mobilization Centre 1940–1941, Richardson was Deputy Director Supplies and Transport at the War Office 1941–1943. Promoted major general, he was Inspector of the RASC 1943–1946.

Retired from the army in 1946, Richardson was Regional Food Officer for the Midland Region 1947–1953. Honorary Colonel of 110 Transport Column RASC (TA) 1948–1953, he married for a third time in 1959 and lived in Norwich.

RICKARDS, Major General Gerald Arthur *(1886–1972), DSO, MC*

The son of a judge, Rickards was educated at Eton and RMA, Woolwich. Commissioned in the Royal Field Artillery in 1906, he was a captain in 1914. His First War service was in France, where he was Brigade Major to the Portuguese Division from 1917. Twice mentioned in despatches, he was awarded the MC and admitted to the DSO in 1918.

Brigade Major RA Aldershot 1919–1920 and married in 1920, 'Tex' Rickards served for many years in Egypt and India. A lieutenant colonel in 1935, he commanded 'A' Indian Field Artillery Brigade, Bangalore, 1935–1938, and commanded 44th Anti-Aircraft Brigade, 1938–1940. GOC 12th Anti-Aircraft Division from 1940 until his retirement from the army in 1942, he was 'grieved and disgruntled at having to relinquish the AA defences of London after only six months in command' (Tremlett, WSL, 121).

Chairman of Tetbury Rural District Council 1950–1960, Rickards, a keen sportsman, and member of the MCC, was DL for Gloucestershire in 1953. He was also Branch Visitor for the Soldiers, Sailors and Airmen Families' Association.

RIDDELL-WEBSTER, General Sir Thomas Sheridan
(1886–1974), GCB, DSO
Born in St Andrews and educated at Harrow and RMC, Sandhurst, Riddell-Webster was commissioned in the Cameronians (Scottish Rifles) in 1905. A captain in 1913, his First War service was in France, where he was mentioned in despatches and admitted to the DSO in 1915.

Married in 1920 and a brevet lieutenant colonel in 1923, Riddell-Webster attended the Staff College, Camberley, 1924–1925. After a period serving on the staff at the War Office, he attended the Imperial Defence College in 1929. Commander of the 2nd Battalion the Cameronians 1930–1933, he was an Assistant Adjutant and QMG at the War Office 1933–1934. Commander of Poona (Independent) Brigade Area, India, 1935–1938, he was promoted major general and appointed Director of Movement and Quartering at the War Office 1938–1939.

Deputy QMG 1939–1940, Riddell-Webster was Chief Administrative Officer, Middle East Command, 1940–1941. Regarded as 'able and thorough' (Dill, 2nd. ac., 4, LHCMA), he was appointed GOC-in-C Southern India in 1941. Knighted, he was QMG to the Forces from 1942 until his retirement from the army in 1946.

Colonel of the Cameronians 1946–1951, Riddell-Webster was DL for Angus in 1946. Living in Perthshire, he was President of the British Legion (Scotland) 1949–1965.

RILEY, Major General Sir Henry Guy *(1884–1964), KBE, CB*
Of military family, Riley was educated at Bedford School and was commissioned in the North Staffordshire Regiment, after transfer from the Border Regiment's Militia Battalion, in 1906.

Transferring to the Royal Army Pay Corps in 1910, Riley's First War service was in France, where he was twice mentioned in despatches. Married in 1920, he rose through his corps to become Paymaster-in-Chief and Inspector of Army Pay Offices at the War Office in 1937. Appointed CB in 1938 and retired from the army in 1943, he was knighted the following year.

Colonel Commandant RAPC 1943–1955 and a widower from 1959, Riley lived in Guildford.

RITCHIE, General Sir Neil Methuen *(1897–1983), GBE, KCB, DSO, MC*
Born in British Guiana (Guyana) and educated at Lancing and RMC, Sandhurst, Ritchie was commissioned in the Black Watch in 1914. His First War service was first in France, where he was wounded, and later in Mesopotamia and Palestine, where he was mentioned in despatches, awarded the MC and admitted to the DSO.

On a captain's pay for 14 years, Ritchie served on the staff at the War Office 1923–1927 and attended the Staff College, Camberley, 1929–1930. In India for the next four years, serving as a staff officer with Northern Command, he married in 1937 and commanded the 2nd Battalion King's Own Royal

Regiment in Palestine 1937–1938. Mentioned in despatches and promoted colonel, he was appointed an instructor at the Senior Officers' School, Sheerness, in 1939.

Serving on the staff at the War Office at war's beginning, Ritchie was appointed chief staff officer to Brooke's II Corps with the BEF in France. Having done 'wonderfully well' in the retreat to Dunkirk (Danchev & Todman, 2001, 280), he stayed with Brooke as BGS Southern Command before being appointed GOC of the re-forming 51st (Highland) Division in October 1940. Made Deputy Chief of the General Staff, Middle East Command, in May 1941, he served six months in Cairo. In November the GOC, Auchinleck, who, having sacked Cunningham, 'was looking for a new Army Commander in a hurry' (Kraster, in Keegan (ed.), 1991, 208), appointed him to command 8th Army.

Tall, impressive-looking, with 'a bovine strength about him' (Barnett, 1983, 123) and evidently well-liked by his superiors, Ritchie was kept on after the successful CRUSADER offensive. But, for all that 'you only had to look at him to see that he was a man of strong character and resolute purpose' (Chandos, 1962, 267), he was not a success as 8th Army commander. Whether this was because he lacked 'self-confidence' due to having no previous experience of handling large formations (Dixon, 1976, 128) or because his corps commanders, Norrie and Gott, tended to shut him out of decision-making, or indeed, whether Auchinleck, under 'the sinister influence of Dorman-Smith' (Carver, 2002, 11), kept him on too short a leash, he was responsible for the series of 'defeats in detail' that, via Gazala and the surrender of Tobruk, bundled 8th Army back to the Alamein line in June 1942.

Assuming command of the army himself, Auchinleck sacked Ritchie. By all accounts he took his dismissal well. Yet, in a curious way, and unlike so many other desert generals who had come to grief because their decisions 'were painfully slow' (Bidwell & Graham, 1985, 243), the obscurity he merited eluded him. As curiously, his name is not much mentioned in relation to Auchinleck's notorious reputation as 'a poor picker of men'. Perhaps there is no mystery, for Brooke, Ritchie's friend and patron, was ready to provide rehabilitation and a covering narrative. Having, so the story goes, been pushed on 'much too fast' in North Africa (Danchev & Todman, 2001, 280), a series of mitigating circumstances were paraded which shifted blame for the near destruction of 8th Army away from Ritchie and on to the Auchinleck, Corbett and Dorman-Smith crew.

Ritchie's confidence was restored by having an audience with the King and being made GOC 52nd (Lowland) Division in September 1942. He was appointed to command XII Corps in December 1943. Serving with 21st Army Group in North-West Europe, he committed no crass errors, 'carried out efficiently a series of mechanical operations' (DNB) and was 'his usual straightforward, direct and honest self' (Carver, 1989, 205).

Knighted at war's end and appointed GOC-in-C Scottish Command and Governor of Edinburgh Castle 1945–1947, Ritchie was promoted general and was C-in-C Far East Land Forces 1947–1949. Made commander of the

British Army Staff in Washington and Military Member of the Joint Services Mission in 1949, he retired from the army with knighthood enhanced in 1951.

Colonel of the Black Watch 1950–1952 and appointed to the Royal Company of Archers, Ritchie was much decorated by foreign governments. Settling in Canada, he was a director of the Mercantile & General Re-insurance Co. and held other directorships.

ROBB, Major General William *(1888–1961), CBE, DSO, MC*

A territorial officer with the Northumberland Fusiliers from 1912, Robb's First War service was in France, where he was awarded the MC and rose to command his regiment's 4th battalion.

Transferring to the King's Own Yorkshire Light Infantry in 1919, 'Uncle' Robb served as Adjutant to the 2nd Battalion and served in India on regimental duties 1922–1925 and as a staff officer 1926–1930. A keen sportsman and a brevet lieutenant colonel in 1933, he transferred to the North Staffordshire Regiment and commanded the 1st Battalion in Palestine 1936–1937. He commanded the Portsmouth Garrison 1937–1938.

Appointed to command 9th Infantry Brigade in 1939, Robb served with distinction with the BEF and was admitted to the DSO after Dunkirk. Found to be medically unfit for future active service, he was appointed Commandant of the Senior Officers' School, Sheerness, and in 1941 commanded 73rd Independent Brigade. Promoted major general in 1943, he was GOC Malta 1944–1945.

Retired from the army in 1947, Robb was Colonel of the KOYLI 1947–1950.

ROBERTS. Major General Frank Crowther
(1891–1982), VC, DSO, OBE, MC

The son of a clergyman, Roberts was educated at St Lawrence College, Ramsgate, and RMC, Sandhurst. Commissioned in the Worcestershire Regiment in 1911, his First War service was in France and, by any standard, his record was outstanding. Three times wounded and five times mentioned in despatches, he was awarded the MC, admitted to the DSO and, in 1918, awarded the VC.

A battalion commander at war's end, 'Culley' Roberts was attached to the Egyptian Army in the Sudan 1919–1920. A student at the Staff College, Camberley, 1921–1922, he served again in Egypt 1923–1924 and with the Rhine Army 1925–1926. A staff officer with China Command 1926–1928, he transferred to the Royal Warwickshire Regiment and was attached to the Iraqi Army 1930–1932. Married in 1932, he served on the staff of Northern Ireland District 1935–1936, briefly commanded his regiment's 1st battalion, and was posted to India in 1937. There he commanded the Poona (Independent) Brigade 1938–1939.

Promoted major general in 1939, Roberts was GOC 48th (South Midland) Division from June to October that year. He retired from the army in December

1939 at the very young age of 48. Living into his nineties, he was sometime President of the Gurkha Brigade Association.

ROBERTS, Major General George Philip Bradley
(1906–1997), CB, DSO, MC
Educated at Marlborough and RMC, Sandhurst, 'Pip' Roberts was commissioned in the Royal Tank Corps in 1926. An assistant instructor at the Tank School, Bovington, 1933–1937, he married in 1936 and served with the 6th Battalion RTR in Egypt from 1937 to 1940, latterly as Adjutant.

Deputy QMG 7th Armoured Division in North Africa in 1940, Roberts was Brigade Major 4th Armoured Brigade 1940–1941. He served on the staff of 7th Armoured Division and was Assistant QMG, XXX Corps, 1941–1942. Awarded the MC, he commanded, in the course of 1942, 3rd Battalion RTR and 22nd Armoured Brigade. He was also admitted to the DSO. Acting GOC 7th Armoured Division in January 1943, he commanded 26th Armoured Brigade in Tunisia before returning to England to assume command of 30th Armoured Brigade. Appointed GOC 11th Armoured Division in December 1943, he served in O'Connor's XII Corps in the campaign in North-West Europe and proved himself, so it is said, 'the outstanding British armoured leader of the war' (Baynes, 1989, 185).

GOC 7th Armoured Division 1947–1948 and Commander of Hanover District in 1948, Roberts was Director of the Royal Armoured Corps at the War Office from 1948 until his retirement from the army the next year.

A director of a confectionary company and JP for Kent 1960–1970, Roberts was Honorary Colonel of the Kent and County of London Yeomanry Squadron 1963–1970. He re-married in 1980. His memoirs, *From the Desert to the Baltic* (1987), provide interesting reading.

ROBERTS, General Sir Ouvry Lindfield *(1898–1986), GCB, KBE, DSO*
Educated at Cheltenham, RMA, Woolwich and Cambridge University, Roberts was commissioned in the Royal Engineers in 1917. His First War service was brief, but it was in France.

Married in 1924, Roberts spent a large chunk of the inter-war years in India. A keen sportsman, he played cricket for the army and hockey for the army and Wales. He attended the Staff College, Camberley, 1934–1935 and was Deputy Director of Military Operations and Intelligence, GHQ, India, 1939–1941. He served on the staff of 10th Indian Division in Iraq in 1941 and, flown into the Habbaniyah air base, then besieged by troops loyal to Raschid Ali, demonstrated 'aggressive leadership' (Lewin, 1976, 70) in conducting a successful defence before relief arrived. Admitted to the DSO, he commanded, over the course of 1942, 20th Indian Brigade and 16th Brigade in the Arakan. Appointed BGS, IV Corps, in 1943, he was GOC 23rd Indian Division 1943–1945. Heavily involved in the fighting at Imphal, he was Vice-Adjutant General at the War Office 1945–1947.

Appointed CB in 1946 and GOC Northern Ireland District 1948–1949,

Roberts was knighted in 1950 and appointed GOC-in-C Southern Command in 1949. QMG to the Forces 1952–1955, he retired a general with knighthood enhanced. Thereafter he pursued a successful business career in British Columbia. Colonel Commandant of the Royal Engineers 1952–1962, he was Administrative Officer, University of British Columbia, 1961–1968.

ROBERTSON of OAKRIDGE, General Brian Hubert
(1896–1974), GCB, GBE, KCMG, KCVO, DSO, MC (1st Baron)
Born in Simla, the son of Field Marshal Sir William Robertson, a former CIGS assassinated by the IRA, Robertson was educated at Charterhouse and RMA, Woolwich. Commissioned in the Royal Engineers in 1914, his First War service was in France, where he was thrice mentioned in despatches, awarded the MC and admitted to the DSO in 1919.

Posted to India, Robertson served with the Bengal Sappers and Miners in Peshawar. Mentioned in despatches during operations in Waziristan in 1923, he married in 1926, attended the Staff College, Camberley, 1926–1927, and served on the staff of the disarmament conference at Geneva.

Leaving the army in 1933, the year in which he inherited his father's baronetcy, Robertson became Managing Director of Dunlop, South Africa. Recalled as a reserve officer with South African forces, his work as Assistant QMG in supply and administration during the Abyssinian campaign brought him to the notice of the War Office, and he was appointed Brigadier i/c Administration, 8th Army, in 1941.

Made Commander of Tripoli in 1942, Robertson was Chief Administrative Officer, 15th Army Group in Italy, 1943–1944. At Alexander's Caserta HQ he was 'bluff, tall and old-fashioned' (Ranfurly, 1998, 330) but was recognized as 'an outstanding military administrator' (DNB), and 'a soldier with an intimate knowledge of politics and of strange conjunctures in strange lands' (Chandos, 1962, 379). Knighted and restored to the active list in October 1945, he was Deputy Military Governor, Control Commission, Germany, 1945–1947 and C-in-C and Military Governor of the British Occupation Zone of Germany 1947–1949. British High Commissioner on the Allied High Commission, Germany, 1949–1950, he was C-in-C Middle East Land Forces from 1950 until his retirement from the army in 1953.

Chairman of the British Transport Commission 1953–1961, Robertson was created a life peer in 1961 and returned to the Dunlop company as a director. He held numerous honorary colonelcies, was Vice-President of the Gloucester Association of Boys' Clubs and was DL for the county in 1965. Much decorated by foreign governments, he received an honorary LLD from Cambridge University.

ROBINSON, Major General Alfred Eryk *(1894–1978), CB, DSO*
Educated at Scarborough and RMC, Sandhurst, Robinson was commissioned in the Princess of Wales's own Yorkshire Regiment (Green Howards) in 1914.

Twice wounded and mentioned in despatches, his First War service was in France, where he commanded various entrenching battalions.

A regimental officer during the inter-war years, Robinson attended the Senior Officers' School, Belgaum, in 1937, and, after a spell on half-pay, served on Malta 1938–1939. He commanded the 1st Battalion Green Howards in France, 1939–1940. Admitted to the DSO, he commanded 115th Brigade under Home Forces 1940–1942 and, by now married, was appointed GOC 47th Division in September 1942. When this formation was disbanded in 1944, he was made Director General of Air Defence at the Air Ministry.

Made Commandant-General of the RAF Regiment and Inspector of Ground Combat Training at the Air Ministry in 1945, Robinson retired from the army in 1948. Appointed CB, he was Colonel of the Green Howards 1949–1959, was DL for the North Riding of Yorkshire from 1952 and a JP for the county from 1953.

ROBINSON, Major General Guy St George *(1887–1973), CB, DSO, MC*
Born in Sligo and educated at Malvern and RMC, Sandhurst, Robinson was commissioned in the Northamptonshire Regiment in 1907. Posted to India and Aden as a subaltern, his First War service was in France. Wounded, twice mentioned in despatches, awarded the MC in 1915 and admitted to the DSO in 1917, he ended the war a battalion commander.

Married to the sister of Lord Carson in 1917, Robinson was an instructor at Sandhurst 1919–1923 and attended the Staff College, Camberley, 1924–1925. Commander of the regimental depot in Northampton 1926–1927, he served on the staff at Aldershot Command 1928–1931. A lieutenant colonel in 1933, he commanded the 2nd Battalion Northamptonshire Regiment 1933–1935. Assistant Commandant of the Small Arms School, Hythe, 1935–1937, he commanded the Rangoon Brigade Area 1937–1940.

A brigade commander with Home Forces in 1941, Robinson was promoted major general and appointed to area and northern district commands in successive years. Retired from the army in 1944, he was Colonel Commandant of the Northamptonshire Regiment 1943–1953. A widower for the last 14 years of his life, he lived in Kent.

ROOME, Major General Sir Horace Eckford
(1887–1964), KCIE, CB, CBE, MC
The son of a doctor, Roome passed through RMA, Woolwich, in 1907 and was gazetted into the Bombay Sappers and Miners in 1908. Working for the Survey of India Department in Burma 1910–1914, he was promoted captain. His First War service was in France, where he was awarded the MC in 1916, in Mesopotamia and Persia (Iran).

Married in 1916, Roome served in India with the Survey Department 1918–1926. In England from 1926 he was Deputy CRE, Tidworth, 1928–1931. Returning to India he was Deputy CRE, Poona Brigade Area, 1932–1936 and, after a spell of staff duties at AHQ, India, was Deputy Engineer-in-Chief 1936–1939.

Promoted major general in 1939, Roome was Engineer-in-Chief, Northern Command, India, 1939–1941, and, made CBE, was Deputy Engineer-in-Chief, India, 1941–1943. Engineer-in-Chief, India, 1943–1946, he was appointed CB in 1944, knighted in 1946, and retired in 1947.

Settling on the Isle of Wight, Roome was member of the island's Hospital Management Committee, and Boy Scout Commandant. He was DL for Hampshire in 1951.

ROSS, Major General Robert Knox (1893–1951), CB, DSO, MC

Of military family and educated at Cheltenham and RMC, Sandhurst, Ross was commissioned in the Queen's Royal (West Surrey) Regiment in 1913. His First War service was in France, where he was thrice mentioned in despatches, awarded the MC and admitted to the DSO.

A staff officer with the Egyptian Expeditionary Force 1918–1919, Ross was Adjutant to the Queen's 2nd Battalion in India 1919–1922 and was attached to the Egyptian Army and Sudan Defence Force 1923–1932. Married in 1933, he commanded the 2nd Battalion of the Queen's Regiment 1937–1939.

Mentioned in despatches for service on operations in Palestine in 1939, 'Willie' Ross commanded 160th Brigade with Home Forces 1940–1942. Appointed GOC 53rd Welsh Division in September 1942, he supervised its re-organization as an infantry division and, attached to VIII Corps, led his command in North-West Europe from June 1944 to May 1945. Although he exasperated some subordinates with his 'ponderous methods' (Carver, 1989, 197), he saw the campaign through from beginning to end.

Appointed CB in 1945, Ross commanded Aldershot and Hampshire Districts from 1945 until his retirement from the army in 1946.

ROWCROFT, Major General Sir Eric Bertram (1891–1963), KBE, CB

Educated at Haileybury, Rowcroft spent two years with the Territorial Army before attending RMC, Sandhurst. Commissioned in the Army Service Corps in 1911, his First War service was in France, where he was mentioned in despatches.

A captain in 1917, the same year as his marriage, Rowcroft served on the staff at the War Office 1918–1922. A major in 1930, he was Inspector of Tanks 1932–1936. Mentioned in despatches during operations in Palestine in 1936, he was Deputy Director of Supplies and Transport at the War Office 1939–1942. A key figure in the formation and organization of REME, Rowcroft was appointed CB in 1944 and was Director of Mechanical Engineering at the War Office 1942–1946.

Knighted in 1946 and retired from the Army in 1947, Rowcroft was a director of the Civil Service Supply Association Ltd 1947–1963. He was Colonel Commandant, REME, 1947–1956, and President of the Dorset County British

Legion in 1961. He was also South-West Area President of the 'Old Contemptibles' Association in 1962.

RUSSELL, Lieutenant General Sir Dudley *(1896–1978), KBE, CB, DSO, MC*
Commissioned in the Queen's (Royal West Kent) Regiment in 1916 and gazetted into the 13th Frontier Force Rifles (Indian Army) in 1917, Russell's First War service was brief, but he was awarded the MC during service on operations in Palestine.

Married in 1929, Russell qualified as an interpreter in Pashto in 1936 and attended the Senior Officers' School, Belgaum, in 1938. He commanded the 6th Battalion, Frontier Force Rifles, in 1939. A staff officer with 5th Indian Division in 1940, he served in Eritrea and Abyssinia and helped negotiate the surrender of the Duke of Aosta at Amba Alagi in May 1941. Commander of 5th Indian Infantry Brigade in Cyrenaica in 1942, he was admitted to the DSO before Alamein. Known as 'Pasha', he was 'beefy of build, with a square bristling moustache and a touch of flamboyance' (Blaxland, 1973, 81). Appointed GOC 8th Indian Division in January 1943, he was made CBE and led his command throughout the Italian campaign.

Appointed CB in 1945, Russell was GOC-in-C Delhi and East Punjab Command in 1947, and Chief British Adviser to the Indian Army from 1948 until his retirement in 1954. Knighted in 1950, he and his American-born wife settled in the Bahamas.

RUSSELL, Major General George Neville *(1899–1971), CB, CBE*
Educated at Rugby, RMA, Woolwich, and Cambridge University, Russell was commissioned in the Royal Engineers. Married in 1927, his peacetime soldiering took him to India and Iraq. He was an instructor of engineering at the Canadian Royal Military College, Kingston, Ontario, 1936–1938.

Assistant Director of Transport for the BEF in France 1939–1940, Russell occupied the same role in the War Office after Dunkirk. Assistant Director of Movements and Supply, Middle East Command, 1940–1941, he was briefly a brigade commander in the Middle East before being made Director of Movements in that theatre in 1942. Made CBE in 1943 and Deputy QMG, India, 1944–1945, he retired from the army in 1946.

Appointed CB in 1946, re-married that year, and Transportation Adviser to the Special Commissioner in South-East Asia 1946–1947, Russell was Chairman of British Road Services 1948–1959. A member of the Eastern Area Board, British Transport Commission, 1957–1951, he was a member of the British Railways Board 1962–1964.

S

ST CLAIR, Major General George James Paul *(1885–1955), CB, CBE, DSO*
Educated at Charterhouse and RMA, Woolwich, St Clair was commissioned in the Royal Artillery in 1905. After some years on postings in Ireland, he married in 1911 and his First War service was in France. He was wounded, three times mentioned in despatches and admitted to the DSO in 1917.

Brigade Major with 2nd London Division in 1919, St Clair attended the Staff College, Camberley, 1920–1921 and served on the staff of 42nd (East Lancashire) Division 1931–1933. A lieutenant colonel in 1933, he was an Assistant Adjutant General at the War Office 1937–1939. GOC of the Hampshire County Division in 1941, he faced retirement when his command was disbanded. But his friendship with Brooke extended to frequent lunch engagements and continued employment on War Office duties over the remainder of the war. Made CBE in 1944, his son, an officer in the Cameron Highlanders, was a prisoner of war in Germany from 1942. Appointed CB, he retired from the army in 1945.

Living in Tetbury and DL for Gloucestershire in 1953, St Clair was High Sheriff of the county in 1954.

SAUNDERS, Major General Macan *(1884–1956), CB, DSO*
Of military family and educated at Malvern and RMA, Woolwich, Saunders was commissioned in the Royal Field Artillery in 1903. He was gazetted into the 35th Sikh Regiment (Indian Army) in 1907. A captain in 1914, the year he married, his First War service was with the 2nd Royal Naval Brigade at Antwerp in 1914, in Gallipoli, in Egypt and latterly in Persia (Iran). Wounded and five times mentioned in despatches, he was admitted to the DSO in 1918.

After attending the Staff College, Camberley, in 1920, Saunders was Military Arraché at the British Embassy, Teheran, 1921–1924, and was Deputy Director of Military Intelligence, AHQ India, 1924–1929. Director of Military Intelligence, AHQ India, 1929–1930, he commanded the Wana Brigade in Waziristan 1930–1934. Commander of the Delhi Independent Brigade Area 1934–1936, he was appointed CB. Deputy Adjutant General, AHQ India, 1936–1938, he was commander of Lahore District from 1938 until his retirement in 1940.

Re-employed in 1941 as Chairman of the Central Interview Board for Commissions, Saunders was President of the Services Selection Board 1943–1947. He lived on Jersey, spending his final years in a nursing home.

SAVORY, Lieutenant General Sir Reginald Arthur
(1894–1980), KCIE, CB, DSO, MC
Educated at Uppingham, Hanover, and RMC, Sandhurst, Savory was commissioned in 1915 and gazetted into the 11th Sikh Regiment in 1915. His First War service was at Gallipoli, where he was wounded, mentioned in despatches and awarded the MC, and in Egypt.

Married in 1922, Savory saw regimental service in Siberia, Kurdistan and Iraq, and, after attending the Staff College, Camberley, 1927–1928, was mentioned in despatches during operations on the North-West Frontier in 1930. An instructor at the Indian Military Academy, Dehra Dun, 1932–1934, he received another mention in despatches while serving on operations in Waziristan in 1937.

Assistant QMG, Southern Command, India, 1939–1940, Savory commanded the 11th Indian Infantry Brigade in North Africa and Eritrea 1940–1941. Admitted to the DSO after the battle of Keren, he was made GOC Eritrea before returning to India, via Iran, as GOC 23rd Indian Division. A 'tough, experienced and successful leader . . . who understood the handling of men' (Slim, 1999, 112), he did much to restore troop morale in Assam after the retreat from Burma. Made Director of Infantry in India in 1943, he instituted the jungle-training regime which prepared various formations of XIV Army for the forthcoming campaign to reconquer Burma.

Appointed CB in 1944, Savory was GOC Persia (Iran) and Iraq Command 1945–1946. Adjutant General, India, from 1946 until his retirement in 1948, he was knighted in 1947 and, settling in Somerset, was a county councillor, a JP and, from 1952, DL for the county. Colonel of the Sikh Light Infantry, 1947–1956, he was also Chairman of the Somerset Territorial and Auxiliary Forces Association 1953–1959. He re-married in 1969 and lived the rest of his life in Surrey.

SCARLETT, Major General Hon. Percy Gerald *(1885–1957), CB, MC*
Younger brother of Lord Abinger and educated at Wellington, Scarlett joined the 3rd Battalion Bedfordshire Regiment (Militia) in 1904. Commissioned in 1907, he joined the Buffs (Royal East Kent Regiment), and his First War service was in France, where he was awarded the MC.

After graduating from the Staff College, Camberley, in 1921, Scarlett served on the staff in the War Office 1922–1923. A brigade major at Aldershot 1923–1926, he was a staff officer with the Shanghai Defence Force 1927–1928. Married that year, he returned to staff duties at the War Office before commanding the 2nd Battalion of the Buffs 1932–1934. Chief Staff Officer with Western Command 1934–1936, he commanded 12th Infantry Brigade and was Deputy Constable, Dover Castle, 1936–1938. Commander of the

Deccan District in India in 1938, he was appointed GOC 4th Indian Division in 1939.

In Egypt at war's beginning, Scarlett was appointed Director of Mobilization in 1940. Made Deputy Adjutant General the same year, he retired from the army in 1942. Thereafter he lived in Kent. Colonel of the Buffs 1943–1953, he was DL for the county in 1949.

SCHREIBER, Lieutenant General Sir Edmond Charles Acton
(1890–1972), KCB, DSO

Of military family, 'Teddy' Schreiber was educated at Wellington and commissioned in the Royal Artillery in 1909. His First War service was in France. Admitted to the DSO in 1914, he was a captain in 1915 and, married in 1916, was four times mentioned in despatches.

On a captain's pay for twelve years, Schreiber attended the Staff College, Camberley, 1923–1924, and served on the directing staff at Camberley 1930–1933. A staff officer at the War Office 1934–1937, he was Chief Staff Officer at the Senior Officers' School, Sheerness, in 1938 and Brigadier RA, Southern Command, 1938–1939.

CCRA under Brooke with II Corps in France, with the BEF 1939–1940, Schreiber impressed Brooke enough to be regarded as 'a very great loss' (Danchev & Todman, 2001, 55) when he returned to England to assume command of 61st Division. GOC 45th Division 1940–1941, he was appointed commander of V Corps in April 1941 and reckoned by Dill 'the best potential army commander after Montgomery' (Dill, 2nd. acc. 9, LHCMA), he was duly appointed commander-designate of 1st Army in 1942. Confessing to Paget, the C-in-C Home Forces, that his health would not stand the strain of command in the field (he had a renal condition), he was appointed instead GOC-in-C Western Command. A substantive lieutenant general in 1944, he was briefly GOC-in-C South-Eastern Command, before being knighted and appointed to succeed Gort as Governor and C-in-C, Malta.

Retired in 1947, Schreiber was DL for Devon in 1948 and National President of the 'Old Contemptibles' Association in 1960. He lived in Exmouth.

SCOBELL, Major General Sir Sanford John Paliaret
(1879–1955), KBE, CB, CMG, DSO

Born in Worcestershire of military family and educated at Winchester and RMC, Sandhurst, Scobell was commissioned in the Norfolk Regiment in 1899. Serving in India and in Somaliland, chasing the 'Mad Mullah', he was a captain in 1906, married in 1910 and in August 1914 was attending the Staff College, Camberley. His First War service was in France, where he was admitted to the DSO in 1916.

A staff officer with the Military Mission to the Baltic States in 1919, Scobell served on the staff with the Army of the Black Sea from 1920 to 1923. Returning to England, he was made CMG, commanded the 2nd Battalion of the Norfolk Regiment 1926–1928 and was an Assistant Adjutant General at the War Office

1928–1930. Commandant of the Senior Officers' School, Belgaum, 1930–1932, he commanded the Mhow Brigade Area for the next two year, and in 1934 was promoted major general and appointed to command the Quetta Brigade. Appointed CB in 1935, he commanded Bombay District for the next four years until his retirement in 1939.

Re-employed at war's beginning, Scobell was made GOC Malta in October 1939. Enduring the privations of the siege, he was thought to be the oldest wartime soldier holding an active command. Retired in 1942 he was knighted and was Lieutenant of the Tower of London 1942–1945. He and his wife settled in a village on the Berkshire Downs

SCOBIE, Lieutenant General Sir Ronald MacKenzie
(1893–1969), KBE, CB, MC
The son of an Indian Civil Servant and educated at Cheltenham and RMA, Woolwich, Scobie was commissioned in the Royal Engineers in 1914, the same year as he won three international caps playing rugby for Scotland. His First War service was in France, where he was wounded, twice mentioned in despatches and awarded the MC.

A student at the Staff College, Camberley, 1925–1936, and married in 1927, Scobie was Director of Artillery at the Australian Royal Military College, Duntroon, 1932–1935. He attended the Imperial Defence College in 1937 and was Assistant Adjutant General at the War Office 1938–1939.

Deputy Director of Mobilization at the War Office 1939–1940, Scobie was briefly Deputy Adjutant General at the War Office in 1940 before being posted to the same job with Middle East Command. BGS British troops in the Sudan 1940–1941, he was appointed GOC 6th Division (later 70th Division) in North Africa, which replaced the Australian garrison in Tobruk. Appointed CB and, briefly, Deputy Adjutant General Middle East Command, he was appointed GOC Malta in 1942 and the next year was made Chief of Staff, Middle East Command.

Made GOC British forces in Greece in September 1944, Scobie's duties had less to do with mopping-up pockets of German resistance than with coping with civil war and 'saving the country from Communism'. Though criticized for liking 'to play politics' (Young (ed.), 1973, 616), he negotiated a truce in January 1945. He was knighted, returned to England in 1946 and retired from the army in 1947.

Colonel Commandant of the Royal Engineers 1951–1958 and Lieutenant of the Tower of London 1951–1954, Scobie was a Vice President of the Forces Aid Society and a patron of the Army Rugby Union. He lived in Hampshire.

SCOONES, General Sir Geoffrey Allen Percival
(1893–1975), KCB, KBE, CSI, DSO,MC
Born in Quetta of military family and educated at Wellington and RMC, Sandhurst, Scoones was commissioned in the Royal Fusiliers in 1912 and trans-

ferred to the 6th Gurkha Rifles (Indian Army) the next year. His First War service was in Gallipoli and France, where he was awarded the MC and admitted to the DSO in 1918.

Married in 1918, Scoones graduated from the Staff College, Quetta, in 1923 and, after a series of staff postings, commanded the 2nd Battalion 8th Gurkha Rifles in 1935. He attended the Imperial Defence College in 1938 and was Deputy Director of Military Operations and Intelligence, GHQ India, 1940–1941, and DMO, India, 1941–1942. Promoted major general in 1942, he briefly commanded an Indian infantry division before being appointed to command IV Corps. Responsible for the successful defence of Imphal in 1944, having been caught off-balance by the initial Japanese advance on Kohima, he was criticized for slowness of response. He nevertheless maintained an admirable 'steadiness in crisis' (Evans, 1969, 120). Knighted in the field in 1944 and regarded, perhaps, as 'too steady and not reckless enough' (Malkasian, 2002, 96), he was replaced by Messervy as corps commander and appointed GOC-in-C Southern Command, India.

GOC-in-C Central Command, India, 1945–1946 and promoted general in 1946, Scoones retired from the army in 1947. Said to be 'modest and diffident', the cryptic brevity of his *Who's Who* entry suggests as much. Principal Staff Officer at the Commonwealth Relations Office 1947–1953, he was British High Commissioner in New Zealand, 1953–1957.

SCOTT, Major General James Bruce *(1892–1974)*, CB, DSO, MC

The son of an Indian Civil Servant and educated at Exeter School and RMC, Sandhurst, Scott was commissioned on the unattached list in 1911 and gazetted into the 6th Gurkha Rifles (Indian Army) in 1912. A captain in 1914, his First War service was in France, as part of the Indian Expeditionary Force, and Mesopotamia, where he was awarded the MC in 1918.

Married in 1923 and a major in 1929, Scott served on the staff of AHQ, India, 1931–1935, and commanded the 1st Battalion 8th Gurkha Rifles 1935–1939. Commander of 1st Burma Brigade 1939–1941, it fell to him, as GOC of the hastily-formed BURDIV, to withstand the shock of Japanese invasion.

A 'handsome young-looking man', who 'radiated confidence' (Lunt, 1989, 69), Scott won high acclaim from Slim during the retreat through Burma. Admitted to the DSO and appointed Inspector of Infantry, India, in 1942, he held no further field command, the rest of his army career being devoted to troop training, administration and increasingly onerous internal security duties. Appointed GOC 39th Indian Infantry Division in 1943, he was made District Officer, Peshawar District, the same year. Appointed CB in 1944, he retired from the army in 1947.

SCOTT, Major General John Walter Lennox *(1883–1960)*, CB, DSO

Educated at Dulwich College and Westminster Hospital, Scott joined the Royal Army Medical Corps in 1906. His First War service was in France, where he was thrice mentioned in despatches and admitted to the DSO in 1918. He married in 1916

Deputy Assistant Director General of Medical Services at the War Office 1926–1930, Scott was Assistant Director General 1933–1935. A colonel in 1934, he was Deputy Director Army Medical Services 1935–1937. Promoted major general, he was Director General of Medical Services, Eastern Command, 1937–1939 and Director of Medical Services with the BEF in France 1939–1940. Appointed CB, he retired in 1941.

SCOTT, Major General Thomas *(1897–1968), CB*

Born in Canada and educated there and at Edinburgh University, Scott was commissioned in the Royal Field Artillery in 1915. His First War service was in France, where he was twice wounded and twice mentioned in despatches.

Married in 1922, Scott transferred to the 6th Duke of Connaught's Lancers (Watson's Horse) in India in 1927. Graduating from the Staff College, Quetta, in 1931, he served on the staff of Peshawar District 1933–1936, was mentioned in despatches during operations against the Mohmands in 1935, and, after serving on operations in Waziristan, was a staff officer at AHQ, New Delhi, 1937–1938.

Scott commanded the 1st Cavalry (Skinner's Horse) in the Sudan and Eritrea 1940–1941. Chief Staff Officer for 6th Indian Division in 1941, he served briefly on the staff of Far East Command and was BGS, Central Command, India, 1942–1943. BGS South-East Asia Command 1943–1944, he was briefly Chief of Staff to the C-in-C Ceylon (Sri Lanka), before being appointed Director of Manpower Planning, India, in 1944.

Deputy CGS, GHQ India, 1946–1947, Scott was Major General i/c Administration, Northern Command, India, from 1947 until his retirement in 1948. Appointed CB in 1947, he settled in South Africa.

SELBY, Major General Arthur Roland *(1893–1966), CB, CBE*

Commissioned in the Royal Irish Rifles in 1914 and wounded at Gallipoli in 1915, the remainder of Selby's First War service was as a staff officer in France.

Known everywhere, apparently, as 'Uncle Arthur' (Wilson, 1948, 22), Selby transferred to the Royal Ulster Rifles in 1922. An instructor at the Australian Staff College, Duntroon, 1928–1930, he was an instructor at Quetta in 1931. A staff officer at the War Office 1932–1935, he returned to India after attending the Imperial Defence College in 1937 and, by now a lieutenant colonel, was Chief Staff Officer, Deccan District, 1938–1939.

BGS British troops in Egypt 1939–1940, Selby was Commandant of the Mersa Matruh Garrison 1940–1941 and Commandant of Alexandria Area 1941–1942. Made CBE, he was Deputy Chief of Staff Middle East Command 1942–1943. Appointed CB, he was Chief of Staff, Middle East Command, 1943–1944, and was Chief Administration Officer, Middle East Command from 1944 until his retirement from the army in 1946. Thereafter he lived in South Africa.

SERGISON-BROOKE, see *BROOKE*

SHEARS, Major General Philip James *(1887–1972), CB*
Educated at Oundle and commissioned in the Royal Dublin Fusiliers in 1907, Shears's First War service was in France, where he was twice wounded and mentioned in despatches.

Transferring to the Border Regiment in 1922, Shears was Adjutant to the 1st Battalion 1924–1927. Enduring spells on half-pay before and after being promoted major, he was Commandant of the Army Technical School, Chepstow, 1935–1939, and commanded the Catterick area 1939–1941. GOC Durham and North Riding Division in 1941, he was o/c West Riding District, 1941–1944.

Retired from the army in 1945 and appointed CB, Shears was Colonel of the Border Regiment 1947–1952.

SIMMONS, Major General Frank Keith *(1888–1952), CBE, MVO, MC*
Educated at Cranbrook School, Simmons was commissioned in the Highland Light Infantry in 1907. His First War service was in France, where he was awarded the MVO and MC.

Married in 1922, a student at the Staff College, Camberley, 1922–1923, and a staff officer at the War Office 1923–1927, Simmons divorced and re-married in 1926. Transferring to the Cameron Highlanders in 1928, he was Military Attaché at the Madrid Embassy 1928–1931. Commander of the 2nd Battalion Cameron Highlanders 1932–1936 and Commander of the Southern Brigade in Palestine in 1936, he was Chief Staff Officer with British Forces in Palestine and Transjordan 1937–1939. Commander of Shanghai Area, British troops in China, from 1939 to 1940, he was promoted major general and appointed commander of Singapore Fortress in December 1941. Percival found him 'tactful, courteous and able' (Kinvig, 1996, 128).

Taken prisoner in February 1942, Simmons was released and repatriated in 1945. He retired from the army the following year and settled in Australia.

SIMPSON, General Sir Frank Ernest Wallace *(1899–1986), GBE, KCB, DSO*
Of military family and educated at Bedford School and RMA, Woolwich, Simpson was commissioned in the Royal Engineers in 1916. His First War service was in France, topped off by attending the Officers' School at Cambridge.

Simpson served in Afghanistan and the North-West Frontier 1919–1920. He attended the Staff College, Camberley, 1931–1932 and married in 1934. After serving on the staff at the War Office, he was Brigade Major to 9th Brigade in 1937. A 'tower of strength' to the recently bereaved Brigadier Montgomery (Montgomery, 1958, 33), he was, ever after, one of those young officers 'Monty' wanted close wherever he served.

A lieutenant colonel in 1939 and Assistant Military Secretary at the War Office 1939–1940, 'Simbo' Simpson was admitted to the DSO for his part in organizing the Dunkirk evacuation. BGS V Corps, and later XII Corps, again under Montgomery, 1940–1942, he was destined to follow his patron to Egypt, but remained instead as Deputy Director of Military Operations at the War Office. Regarded by de Guingand as 'a phantom rival' (Richardson, 1987, 79), Simpson was Director of Military Operations 1943–1945 and, supplanting de Guingand, was Vice CIGS to Montgomery 1946–1948. In that capacity he 'tactful[ly] and skilful[ly]' frequently covered for his chief (Richardson, 1985, 214).

Knighted in 1947 and GOC-in-C Western Command 1948–1951, Simpson was Commandant of the Imperial Defence College from 1951 until his retirement from the army with knighthood enhanced in 1954. A member of the Eastern Electricity Board 1954–1963, he was Colonel Commandant of the Royal Pioneer Corps 1950–1961 and the Royal Engineers 1954–1967. A JP for Essex, 1955–1961, he was also DL for the county from 1956.

SINCLAIR, Major General Sir John Alexander
(1897–1977), KCMG, CB, OBE
The son of a clergyman, Sinclair was born in London and educated at West Downs School, Winchester, and the Royal Naval Colleges, Osborne and Dartmouth. A midshipman in the navy 1914–1916, he was invalided out transferred to the Royal Artillery and graduated from RMA, Woolwich, in 1918.

Commissioned in the Royal Field Artillery in 1919, 'Sinbad' Sinclair served with the North Russia Relief Mission in 1919, married in 1927 and was Adjutant to the Honourable Artillery Company 1929–1931. He attended the Staff College, Camberley, 1932–1933. A brevet major in 1936, he was an instructor at the Senior Staff College, Minley, 1938–1939.

Serving as a staff officer at the War Office 1940–1941, Sinclair was briefly Deputy Director of Military Operations before being appointed BGS to South-Eastern Command. CRA 1st Division in 1942, he was Deputy Chief of Staff, Home Forces 1942–1943. Major General, General Staff Home Forces 1943–1944, he was Director of Military Intelligence 1944–1945.

Sinclair's post-war career was with Intelligence. He was Deputy Director of MI6 1945–1950, and Director 1950–1956. Knighted in 1953, the organization received a 'mortal insult' (Wright, 1987, 78) when, in the wake of the Crabb affair in 1956, he was removed from his post by Eden.

SITWELL, Major General Hervey Degge Wilmot
(1896–1973), CB, CVO, MC
Born in Warwickshire and educated at Wellington and RMA, Woolwich, Sitwell was commissioned in the Royal Field Artillery in 1914. His First War service was in France, where he was mentioned in despatches and awarded the MC in 1917.

Married in 1919, Sitwell spent fourteen years on a captain's pay. A graduate of the Staff College, Camberley, in 1932, he was promoted major in 1933 and served on the staff of Western Command 1934–1936. An acting lieutenant colonel in 1939, he served on the staff at the War Office 1939–1941 and commanded 16th Anti-Aircraft Brigade 1941–1942. Sent to Java and, briefly o/c Anti-Aircraft, Dutch East Indies, he was promoted major general and appointed GOC British troops, Java.

A prisoner of war on Formosa and in Manchuria 1942–1945, Sitwell was beaten and subjected to a 'policy of degradation in front of his men'. Warell was impressed by his 'vitality and courage' (Moon, 1973, 172) and he was appointed CB upon his repatriation. Commander of Canal North District, Egypt, 1946–1949, he was Deputy Commander, East Anglia District, from 1949 until his retirement from the army in 1951.

Keeper of the Crown Jewels 1952–1968, Sitwell was made a Fellow of the Society of Antiquaries in 1957. He lived on the Isle of Wight.

SKINNER, Major General Frank Hollamby *(1897–1979), CB, CIE, OBE*
Educated at Kent College, Canterbury, and commissioned from the ranks of the Territorial Army in 1916, Skinner was gazetted into the Indian Army in 1917, joining the 19th Hyderabad Regiment.

Active in operations in Afghanistan and on the North-West Frontier, 'Jerry' Skinner transferred to the 13th Frontier Force Rifles in 1933, He was a Deputy Adjutant and QMG, AHQ India, in 1937 and commanded the 1st Battalion FFR 1938–1940. Assistant Adjutant and QMG to British Forces in Iraq and Persia (Iran) 1941–1942, he was BGS XX Indian Corps 1942–1943. Major General i/c Administration, Eastern Army, India in 1943, he was GOC 39th Indian Division 1944–1945. He commanded Secunderabad District from 1945–1947 and, appointed CB, retired from the army the following year. Thereafter he lived in Sussex.

SLATER, Major General Joseph Nuttal *(1894– ?), CBE, MC*
Commissioned in the Royal Artillery in 1914, Slater's First War service was in France, where he was awarded the MC.

After serving on the North-West Frontier in 1919 and regimental duties in the 1920s, Slater was promoted major in 1931 and was promptly placed on the half-pay list. He was an instructor at the School of Coast Artillery 1932–1935. A lieutenant colonel in 1933, he was Chief Instructor at the Coast Artillery School in 1938.

Commanding the 4th Anti-Aircraft Brigade in North Africa 1939–1941, Slater was made CBE and was Brigadier Royal Artillery with Ninth Army in Iraq and Iran 1941–1942. Brought home, he was appointed GOC 7th Anti-Aircraft Division before passing to the command of 4th Anti-Aircraft Group.

SLIM, Field Marshal William Joseph, 1st Viscount
(1891–1970), KG, GCB, GCMG, GCVO, GBE, DSO, MC
Born in Bristol, the son of a wholesale ironmonger, but brought up in Birmingham in straitened family circumstances, Slim, a pupil-teacher at his

grammar school, and later a clerk in a metal-tube company, saw First War service as an officer courtesy of being a member of Birmingham University OTC. Commissioned in the Royal Warwickshire Regiment in 1914, he was badly wounded at Gallipoli in 1915 and served as a draft-conducting officer in France and, latterly, in Mesopotamia. Re-commissioned in the 'unfashionable but inexpensive' West India Regiment (Heathcote, 1999, 259), he was wounded again, was awarded the MC and, having been invalided to India, was gazetted into the 6th Gurkha Rifles in 1919.

After service on the North-West Frontier 1920–1921, Slim was Adjutant to the 1st/6th Gurkhas for three years. After attending the Staff College, Quetta, in 1926, he married the same year and served on the staff of the Directorate of Military Operations, AHQ, India, 1930–1934. A pulp-fiction writer during this time, 'the prime motive was cash' (Lewin, 1976, 49), his pen-name was Anthony Mills. An instructor at the Staff College, Camberley, 1934–1936, he attended the Imperial Defence College in 1937 and commanded the 7th Gurkha Rifles 1938–1939. That year he was appointed Commandant of the Senior Officers' School, Belgaum.

It was perhaps fortunate for Slim that after such relatively slow career progress, he should spend the first thirty months of the Second World War 'consigned to backwaters' (Anderson in Keegan (ed.). 1991, 304). It meant that he could refine his trade while making mistakes, and suffer the odd spot of bad luck without irretrievably blotting his copybook. His first action, as commander of 10th Indian Infantry Brigade, to retake the Sudanese fort of Gallabat ended in failure. Moreover, he was wounded in the bottom shortly after and sent back to India to recuperate. But in May 1941, thanks to Auchinleck's readiness to send Indian troops to Iraq to quell the Raschid Ali revolt, he found himself promoted major-general and posted to Iraq as GOC 10th Indian Division. Having planned and executed a two-pronged operation against Vichy forces in Syria, he spent the next six months on relatively gentle occupation duties in Iran. Not yet high enough in the Indian Army pecking order for Auchinleck to consider him for a place in Middle East Command, a general who did not know him, Alexander, asked for him to be posted to Burma, there to command the newly-formed 'Burcorps'.

This was an unenviable posting. The retreat through Burma had already cost Hutton his health and his future reputation, and all Slim could achieve after the fall of Rangoon was a scrappy fighting retreat. Made commander of XV Corps in June 1942 and still only an acting lieutenant general, his instinct, to stay on the defensive and improve the equipment, training and, above all, the morale of his troops, was overruled by the aggressively-minded Wavell, the C-in-C, and the no-less belligerent commander of Eastern Army, Irwin.

Thus, though Slim had little to do with the planning or execution of the ill-fated Arakan offensive of 1942–1943, he might easily have been a casualty of failure. Given the brief to guide and effectively spy-on the divisional commanders in the field, his reports on the whole offensive degenerating into desperate attempts to extricate British and Indian troops from exposed positions so exasperated Irwin that, having already removed Lloyd, he took steps to have Slim dismissed, Then came the memorable telegram. 'You're not sacked,' cabled Irwin, 'I am' (Lewin, 1976, 124).

This was a stroke of luck. Commanders more elevated or, at that time, more famous than Slim had paid the price for being unable to 'pull chestnuts out of the fire' (DNB). Dismissal would have been an injustice, but at a level no greater than others had suffered through their own tenuous association with failure. Placed in operational control of Eastern Army, his withdrawal from the Arakan was not masterly. But, as in the retreat from Burma, casualties were minimized and units withdrew more or less intact. He was admitted to the DSO.

Irwin was not the only superior Slim was to see off, but for the next two years he was fortunate in that, for all the organizational changes affecting the campaign in Burma, he saw eye-to-eye with his nominal seniors. With Giffard, GOC-in-C Eastern Command, he struck up an immediate accord. He was also, generally, on good terms with Mountbatten who, from October 1943, was Supreme Commander South-East Asia. In the meantime he made his name as GOC XIV Army – not so much forgotten, as Mountbatten once quipped, as positively never heard of.

Except in one respect Slim was, and certainly strove to make himself, the antithesis of Montgomery. He was modest, he admitted to making mistakes, was earthy and not quirky, and was even-handedly generous in his praise. Yet 'Uncle Bill' courted publicity as assiduously as Montgomery ever did. He may not have worn funny hats or, Father Christmas-like, distributed cigarettes to the troops, but through constant visits and frequent impromptu addresses, he made himself known to his men – in several languages. Montgomery's claim to have restored 8th Army's morale has a shaky, slightly suspect, basis to it. That Slim made XIV Army, and XIV Army made Slim's formidable post-war reputation, is beyond dispute.

Though not devoid of imagination, Slim was a methodical general. Cool towards Wingate and doubtful of the value of long-range penetration tactics, he was sensible enough to appreciate the importance of his troops' morale. He also developed, though more through circumstance than design, a sense that in the climatic and geographic conditions of Burma, the key to operational success, lay in attrition not manoeuvre. He was wrong-footed by the Japanese attack in the Arakan in the spring of 1944, but the 'box' system of defence in depth he had instituted (a distinctly unfashionable doctrine at that time) frustrated the Japanese advance. No less wrong-footed by the Japanese attack towards Imphal later that year, the 'box' system, the imaginative use of air-supply and, bull-headed Japanese insistence on pressing home their assault presented him with the opportunity to 'take advantage of the unexpected . . . and implement his conception of attrition' (Malkasian, 2002,113).

This was victory. With the Japanese XV Army in disarray and retreating beyond the Chindwin, Slim was appointed CB, knighted in the field and found himself, to a degree undreamed of, internationally famous. Unable to trap the enemy between the Chindwin and the Irrawaddy, his own boldness and an ingenious deception plan allowed him to attack Mandalay from the south via Meiktila in early 1945. The manoeuvre 'sealed the fate of the Japanese Burma Army' (DNB), and opened the way to Rangoon, which was captured just as the monsoon broke.

Unassuming, bluff and, despite the determined set of his jaw, decidedly 'common-looking' (Young (ed.), 1973, 542), Slim showed himself a nimble political operator when, immediately after the fall of Rangoon, he dealt Leese, his superior as Allied Land Forces Commander, a career-shattering blow. For reasons which remain obscure, Leese, having decided Slim was tired and should relinquish command of XIV Army, broke the news in high-handed fashion. Putting it about, rather artfully, that he had been sacked and would probably retire, Slim provoked near mutiny among XIV Army staff. The upshot of the affair, both strange and 'unsatisfactory and highly irregular' (Hickey, 1994, 233) was Leese's recall to London and Slim's promotion to general.

Ironically, Slim did relinquish command of XIV Army very soon after. He went on leave to England, met Churchill for the first time and told him his men would not vote Conservative. By the time he returned to Burma as C-in-C Land Forces the war was over. Recalled to England to resuscitate the Imperial Defence College in 1946, he retired from the army in 1948 and joined the Executive of British Railways.

The appointment did not last long. In the early months of 1949 Attlee asked Slim to become CIGS. In all likelihood the request was made because of Montgomery's high-handed insistence that his nominee, Crocker, should succeed him and that Slim, even if dug out of retirement, had neither the knowledge of nor the aptitude for European warfare. In accepting the post, Slim became the first Indian Army CIGS just at the moment when the Indian Army had ceased to exist. Impressive in his 'calm willingness to accept responsibility' (Hamilton, 1986, 727), he was promoted Field Marshal in 1949. He was Colonel of two Gurkha regiments, and of the West Yorkshire Regiment, 1947–1960.

On completing his term as CIGS in 1952, Slim, at the request of the Australian Government, was appointed Governor General and C-in-C. He performed his ceremonial duties, made himself popular by lauding the fighting qualities of Australian troops and wrote his highly regarded and hugely successful memoirs *Defeat into Victory* (1956). His normal five-year tour was extended by two years and when he left Australia in 1960 and was raised to the peerage as Viscount Slim, he took the title of Yarralumla and Bishopston.

Amassing a considerable number of directorships, Slim still found time to receive numerous honorary degrees and attend rallies of the Burma Star Association. Not without his vanities, but always likeable, bluff and common-sensical, Slim, in ill-health towards the end, was justly commemorated in death. The strategic significance of the re-conquest of Burma may have been small, but the campaign so enhanced Slim's reputation that Mountbatten, among others, could say that he was 'the finest general the Second World War produced' (Evans, 1969, 215).

SMALLWOOD, Major General Gerald Russell
(1889–1977), CB, DSO, MC
Commissioned in the East Yorkshire Regiment in 1912, Smallwood's First War service was in France, where he was twice mentioned in despatches and awarded the MC.

After attending the Staff College, Camberley, 1922–1923, Smallwood was, from 1925 to 1926, a staff captain in the Directorate of Organization and Recruiting at the War Office. Brigade Major to 8th Brigade at Devonport 1927–1929, he was an instructor at Sandhurst 1930–1932. After serving on the staff of 47th (2nd London) Division, he commanded the 2nd Battalion of his regiment in England and in Palestine, 1934–1937. A general staff officer with the British Military Mission to Egypt 1937–1939, he commanded a brigade with Home Forces 1939–1941. Admitted to the DSO in 1941, he was GOC British troops in Madagascar in 1942. Appointed CB, he was made head of the training staff of the Greek Army in 1945.

Retired in 1946, Smallwood settled thereafter in Kenya where he farmed for many years.

SMITH, Lieutenant General Sir Arthur Francis
(1890–1977), KCB, KBE, DSO, MC
Of military family and educated at Eton and RMC, Sandhurst, Smith was commissioned in the Coldstream Guards in 1910. His First War service was in France, where he was thrice wounded, five times mentioned in despatches, awarded the MC and admitted to the DSO in 1918.

Married in 1918, Smith, a Christian Scientist, was Adjutant at RMC, Sandhurst, 1921–1924. Commandant of the Guards Depot 1924–1927, he served on the staff of London District 1927–1930. He commanded the 2nd Battalion Coldstream Guards 1930–1934 and the Coldstream Guards Regiment and 4th Guards Brigade 1934–1938.

BGS British Troops in Egypt, 1938–1939, Smith was Chief of Staff, Middle East, in 1940. Respected by Wavell for his courageous outlook and . . . nice sense of humour' (Moon, 1973, 225), but regarded as 'disastrous' by Dorman-Smith (Greacan, 1989, 174), his self-righteousness and tendency to behave 'as if he is a close friend of God' was noted (Ranfurly, 1998, 96). Auchinleck thought him 'rather weary' and sent him home in March 1942 (Dill, 2nd acc. 6/2/12, LHCMA). Knighted and appointed GOC London District and Major General commanding the Brigade of Guards, 1942–1944, he was appointed GOC Persia (Iran) and Iraq Command in 1944. GOC Eastern Command, India, 1945–1946, he was CGS, India, in 1946 and Deputy C-in-C the following year.

With his knighthood enhanced, Smith commanded British forces in India and Pakistan prior to the handover of power in late 1947, and retired from the army the following year. He was Lieutenant of the Tower of London, 1948–1951. His only son died in tragic circumstances in 1953. Having been for years a member of the council of Dr Barnardo's, he was Vice President in 1972.

SMITH, Major General Sir Cecil Miller *(1896–1988), KBE, CB, MC*

Born in Belfast and educated at the Royal Belfast Academical Institution and RMC, Sandhurst, Smith was commissioned in the Royal Inniskilling Fusiliers in 1914. His First War service was in France where, transferring to the Army Service Corps, he was wounded and awarded the MC.

After service at home and in India, 'Smuggins' Smith married in 1930 and, unusually for an RASC man, was a student at the Staff College. Camberley, 1931–1932. His reputation was that of 'a superbly efficient staff officer' (Carver, 1989, 45). He was, it seems, liked and respected in equal measure. An old desert hand before war's beginning, he 'appreciated the problems of supply in the desert . . . and had sensible and practical ideas on how to overcome them' (Roberts, 1987, 1954). Assistant QMG, Middle East Command, 1939–1943, he styled himself Deputy Director of Supplies and Transport and avoided the promotional blind alley of being made Commandant of the Staff College, Haifa. Deputy QMG, Middle East Forces, 1943–1944, he was promoted major general in 1943 and was Deputy Chief of Staff, SHAEF, 1944–1945.

Major General i/c Administration, Northern Command 1945–1947, Smith was appointed CB and was Chief of Staff, Northern Command, 1947–1948. Director of Supplies and Transport at the War Office from 1948 until his retirement in 1951, he was Colonel Comandant of the RASC 1950–1960. Knighted in 1951, he was Chairman of the Ulster Society in London 1964–1973.

SMYTH, Major General Rt Hon. Sir John George
(1893–1983), 1st Bart, VC, MC

The son of an Indian Civil Servant and educated at Repton and RMC, Sandhurst, Smyth was gazetted into the 15th Sikh Regiment (Indian Army) in 1912. His First War service was first in France, where he was awarded the VC in 1915 and later in Western Egypt and the North-West Frontier.

Smyth was mentioned in despatches during operations in Afghanistan in 1919 and, married in 1920, was awarded the MC during operations in Waziristan in 1920. He also saw active service in Mesopotamia. A graduate of the Staff College, Camberley, in 1924 and a brevet major in 1928, he succeeded Slim as the Indian Army instructor at the Staff College, Camberley, 1931–1934. Commandant of the 45th Rattray Sikh Regiment 1936–1939, he was posted home and served on the staff of 2nd London Division 1939–1940. With his first marriage dissolved, he re-married in April 1940.

Commander of 127th Infantry Brigade in France with the BEF in 1940, 'Jacky' Smyth was attached briefly to 'Macforce', was mentioned in despatches and remained in England for a year after the Dunkirk evacuation as commander of 3rd Independent Brigade. Promoted temporary major general in 1941, he returned to India to raise 19th Indian Division, but was soon transferred to command the under-equipped 17th Indian Division in Lower Burma. A 'bright, perky and friendly little man . . . with a wonderful capacity to put young officers at their ease' (Lunt, 1989, 87), he inherited a command with a depleted staff and shorn of two of its brigades. Tasked with delaying the Japanese advance northwards from Tenasserim, he had neither the means, nor perhaps the will, to conduct the kind of fighting retreat envisaged by his superiors. The 'complete cleavage of opinion' between himself and the army commander scarcely heped matters (Smyth, 1957, 153). Concealing his own ill-health as best he could, his notorious order to blow the Sittang Bridge, while thousands of British and Indian troops were left stranded on the far bank, effectively destroyed his Division and hastened the fall of Rangoon. In great pain, dog-tired and famously snubbed by Wavell, he was relieved of his command, hospitalized and, reverting to the substantial rank of brigadier, was invalided out of the army in November 1942.

Banished from India, but well-received on his return to England, Smyth was military correspondent for the *Daily Sketch* and *Sunday Times* 1943–1946. From 1946 to 1951 he was Tennis correspondent for the *Sunday Times* and was also a frequent BBC Wimbledon match commentator. Having stood unsuccessfully for Parliament in the 1945 general election, he was successful in 1950 and represented the Norwood constituency as a Conservative for the next sixteen years. Parliamentary Secretary to the Ministry of Pensions 1951–1953, his backbench duties thereafter did not prevent him being Tennis correspondent for the *News of the World* in the 1950s. Created baronet in 1955, he was a writer of novels, plays and entertainingly self-justifying histories. With one son killed in action at Kohima in 1944 and another pre-deceased him. He was Master of the Farriers Company 1961–1962 and was sworn to the Privy Council in 1962.

SNELLING, Major General Arthur Hugh Jay *(1897–1965)*, CB, CBE

Born in Norwich and educated at Gresham's School, Snelling was gazetted into the 4th Rajput Regiment (Indian Army) in 1915. His First War service was in France and Mesopotamia.

Married in 1919, 'Alf' Snelling took part in operations on the North-West Frontier from 1919 to 1923 and again, with the Royal Indian Army Service Corps, 1932–1933. He attended the Staff College, Camberley, 1930–1931 and, at war's beginning, was Assistant Director of Supplies and Transport, AHQ, India.

Deputy Adjutant and QMG to 10th Indian Division in 1941, Snelling served under Slim's command in the 'minor but active' campaigns in Iraq, Syria and Persia (Iran) in 1941. Brigadier i/c Administration, Ceylon, 1942–1943, he was appointed Major General i/c Administration, XIV Army, in 1943. He encouraged the troops, wherever possible, to grow vegetables and, something of a 'logistic triumph' (Hickey, 1994, 122), arranged for the manufacture of parachutes made of jute. Well thought of by Slim, he was made CBE in 1945 and appointed CB the same year.

Commander of North and Central Burma District in 1945, Snelling was Major General i/c Administration, Southern Command, India, from 1945 to 1947. He retired from the army the following year, but worked for another ten years with the Ministry of Defence. Outlived by his wife, he lived in Camberley.

SNOWDEN-SMITH, Major General Richard Talbot *(1887–1951), CB, CBE*
Born in Tavistock and educated at Kelly College and RMC, Sandhurst, Snowden-Smith was commissioned in the Army Service Corps in 1906. A qualified mechanical engineer, he took up flying in 1910 and bore the Royal Aero Club's pilot certificate number 29. Appointed Inspector of Subsidized Vehicles in 1912, his First War service was in the War Office.

Three times mentioned in despatches, Snowden-Smith was made CBE in 1919 and appointed Director of Mechanical Transport. Deputy Assistant Director of Transport in India in 1925, he was Chief Instructor at the RASC Training College, Aldershot, 1926–1930. Deputy Assistant Director of Supplies and Transport at the War Office 1931–1933, he commanded the RASC Feltham Depot 1933–1934. Assistant Director of Supplies and Transport at the War Office 1934–1937, he was promoted major general and appointed RASC Inspector.

Retired in 1940 but re-employed, Snowden-Smith was made Director of Supplies and Transport at the War Office, and held that post until his retirement from the army in 1943. He was appointed CB in 1942 and was President of the RASC Regimental Association 1943–1946.

SPROULL, Major General Alexander Wallace *(1892–1961), CB, CBE*
Born in Honolulu and educated at St Lawrence College, Ramsgate, and City and Guilds College, Sproull volunteered for service with the Cavalry in 1914. Commissioned later that year in the Royal Engineers (Supplementary Reserve), his war service was in France, where he was wounded.

Married in 1918, Sproull served on the staff at the War Office 1919–1923 and was Assistant Inspector of Engineer Stores 1926–1931. Deputy Assistant Director of Stores at the War Office 1933–1937, he was Inspector of Engineer and Signal Stores in 1937. Deputy Chief Inspector 1937–1940, he was a lieutenant colonel at war's beginning and worked with radar at the Air Ministry in 1940.

Chief Inspector Engineer and Signal Stores 1940–1942, Sproull was Chief Inspector Electrical and Mechanical Equipment from 1942 until 1946. Director General of Armament Production at the Ministry of Supply from 1946 until his retirement from the army in 1947, he was appointed CB that year.

After a year's special appointment at the Ministry of Supply, Sproull was thereafter a successful businessman and company director. A keen sportsman, he had been a member of the army's shooting team during the war years.

SQUIRES, Lieutenant General Ernest Ker *(1882–1940), CB, DSO, MC*
Born in Poona, the son of a clergyman, and educated at Eton and RMA, Woolwich, Squires was commissioned in the Royal Engineers in 1903. Posted to India in 1905, he served with the Bombay Sappers and Miners and married in 1912. His First War service was in France, where he was twice wounded and awarded the MC, and latterly in Mesopotamia, where he was admitted to the DSO.

Mentioned in despatches during operations in Afghanistan in 1919, Squires attended the Staff College, Camberley, 1921–1922, served on the staff of AHQ, India, in the later 1920s, and, returned to England, was BGS Southern Command 1932–1936. Director of Staff Duties at the War Office 1936–1938, he was appointed CB in 1937 and was briefly Commander of Deccan District, India, in 1938. Promoted lieutenant general, he was appointed Chief of the Australian General Staff in 1938. Made Inspector General of Australian Forces in 1939, he died suddenly in March 1940, leaving a widow and three grown-up children.

STABLE, Major General Hugh Huntington (1896–1985), CB, CIE
Educated at Malvern and commissioned from the ranks of the 4th Battalion the Dorset Regiment in 1914, Stable's First War service was in France and Palestine, where he was mentioned in despatches.

Transferring to the Central Indian Horse (Indian Army) in 1919, Stable married in 1923 and attended the Staff College, Camberley, 1929–1930. A staff officer at AHQ, India, in 1932, he was Assistant Military Secretary to the C-in-C, India 1933–1936. Military Secretary to the Viceroy 1936–1938, he was made CIE in 1938 and commanded the 8th King George's Own Cavalry in India 1938–1940.

Assistant Adjutant and QMG, GHQ India, 1940–1941, Stable commanded an armoured brigade in India 1941–1943, before being appointed Deputy QMG at GHQ. Commander of Lucknow Sub-Area 1945–1946, he was Commander of Bihar and Orissa Area in 1947. QMG India in December 1947, he retired from the army in 1950.

Living the rest of his life in South Africa, Stable was a successful businessman and Emeritus Commander of the South African Boy Scouts 1953–1972.

STANHAM, Major General Sir Reginald George (1893–1957), KCB
Educated at Lancing and a territorial before 1914, Stanham was commissioned in the Royal East Kent Regiment (the Buffs) in 1915. His First War service was in France, where he was wounded

Private secretary to the Governor of New South Wales 1918–1919, Stanham married in 1919 and qualified in chartered accountancy the next year. Transferring to the Royal Army Pay Corps in 1920, he was a major in 1930, a lieutenant colonel in 1937 and a colonel in 1940. Deputy Paymaster-in-Chief at the War Office 1941–1942, he was promoted major general and made Paymaster-in-Chief at the War Office in 1943. He was appointed CB in 1946 and knighted in 1948, the year in which he retired from the army.

Settling in South Australia, Stanham maintained a number of consultancies with business concerns before his sudden death at the age of 64.

STAWELL, Major General William Arthur Macdonald
(1895–1987), CB, CBE, MC
Born in India, the son of an Indian Civil Servant, and educated at Clifton and RMA, Woolwich, Stawell was commissioned in the Royal Engineers in 1914.

His First War service was in France, where he was wounded, and latterly in Greece, where he was awarded the MC

Serving with the Army of the Black Sea 1919–1921, Stawell, allegedly, organized a pack of hounds which eliminated the last jackals from Europe. He spent twelve years on a captain's pay. Married in 1926, he attended the Staff College, Camberley, 1928–1929. A major in 1929, he served on the staff at the War Office 1931–1932 and was Brigade Major at Aldershot 1932–1935. Deputy Assistant Adjutant General, AHQ India, 1935–1937, and Deputy Adjutant for Personnel, AHQ India, 1937–1938, he was CRE 4th Division 1938–1940.

Assistant Adjutant and QMG, Southern Command, in 1940, 'Billy' Stawell returned to the War Office, first as a staff officer and then as Deputy Director of Military Intelligence. Commander of 148th Brigade under Home Forces in 1942, he was BGS Home Forces in 1943. From 1943 to 1944 he was head of SOE in the Middle East. Made CBE in 1944, when he returned to England on sick-leave, he was appointed CB in 1945.

Deputy Chief of Operations UNRRA 1945–1946, Stawell was Deputy Chief of the Intelligence Division, Allied Control Commission, Germany, from 1947 until his retirement from the army in 1948.

A keen sailor and golfer, Stawell lived in Southwold in Suffolk, outliving his wife by one year.

STEELE, General Sir James Stuart *(1894–1975), GCB, CB, KBE, DSO, MC*
Born on Co. Antrim and educated at Royal Belfast Academical Institution and Queen's University, Steele had intended to enter the ministry, but was commissioned instead in the Royal Irish Rifles in September 1914. His First War service was in France, where he was mentioned in despatches and awarded the MC in 1917.

After service on the North-West Frontier, Steele transferred to the Ulster Rifles. Married in 1923, he attended the Staff College, Camberley, 1930–1931 and served on the staff of the Canal Brigade, Egypt. Described as 'the most likeable character we had' (Pile, 1949, 35), he transferred to the Sherwood Foresters and commanded the 1st Battalion in Palestine 1937–1939.

Assistant Adjutant General at the War Office in 1939, 'Daddy' Steele was appointed to command 132nd Brigade, then serving with 44th Division with the BEF in France. Admitted to the DSO after Dunkirk, he was appointed GOC 59th (Staffordshire) Division in February 1941. GOC II Corps, under Home Forces, in 1942, he was Deputy Chief of Staff, Middle East Command, 1942–1943. Briefly Deputy Chief of Staff 18th Army Group in Tunisia in 1943, he was Director of Staff Duties at the War Office 1943–1945.

Appointed GOC British troops in Austria in 1946, Steele was knighted and made British High Commissioner in Austria. He was Adjutant General to the Forces from 1947 until his retirement, with knighthood enhanced, in 1950.

Colonel of the Ulster Rifles 1947–1957, Steele was also Colonel Commandant of the Royal Army Education Corps 1950–1959. President of the Army Benevolent Fund 1954–1964, he was sometime President of the Dunkirk

Veterans' Association and organizer of numerous 'pilgrimages' to the Somme battlefields.

STEWART, Major General Hebert William Vansittart
(1886–1975), CBE, DSO
Of military family and commissioned in the Royal Scots Fusiliers in 1906, Stewart, a captain in 1914, served in France in the First War. Admitted to the DSO in 1914, he was also mentioned in despatches.

Married in 1919, Stewart transferred to the Seaforth Highlanders in 1924. Commander of the 1st Battalion 1930–1933, he was an instructor at the Senior Officers' School, Sheerness, 1934–1936. Commander of the 152nd (Seaforth and Cameron) Brigade 1936–1940, he was with 51st Highland Division in the BEF at the time of the fall of France. Wounded and evacuated before the surrender at St Valéry, he was made CBE and appointed to ADC to the King.

Retired in 1944, Stewart was Honorary Sheriff Substitute for Moray and Nairn, Inverness and Ross and Cromarty in 1948. He lived in Nairn.

STEWART, Major General Kenneth Eric Shaw *(1892–1976), MC*
Commissioned in the Prince Of Wales's Own (West Yorkshire) Regiment from the Alderney Artillery (TA) in 1912, Stewart transferred to the Northumberland Fusiliers in 1914. A captain in 1916, his First War service was in Egypt and Gallipoli, and later in France, where he was wounded, mentioned in despatches and awarded the MC.

Transferring to the Royal Tank Regiment, Stewart was an instructor at the RTC School, India, 1928–1931, and was Senior Instructor at the RTC Gunnery School, Lulworth, 1933–1936. Made Commandnat of the RTC School, India, in 1936, he was a colonel in 1937 and was mentioned in despatches during operations in Waziristan. Commandant RTC, India, 1938–1941 and a major general in 1941, he spent the remaining war years in a training role at Bovington.

STOCKWELL, General Sir Hugh Charles
(1903–1986), GCB, KBE, DSO (bar)
The son of a soldier turned policeman, Stockwell was educated at Marlborough and RMC, Sandhurst. Commissioned in the Royal Welch Fusiliers in 1923, he served in West Africa, 1929–1935. Married in 1931, he was an instructor at the Small Arms School, Netheravon, 1935–1938, and Brigade Major Royal Welch Brigade 1938–1940.

Admitted to the DSO after operations in Norway in 1940, Stockwell returned to Africa. After taking part in the invasion of Madagascar, he commanded 30th East African Brigade 1942–1943 and 29th Independent Brigade in Burma 1943–1945. Appointed GOC 82nd West African Division in January 1945, he was made CBE at war's end.

Commander of the Home Counties District 1946–1947, Stockwell was GOC 6th Airborne Division in Palestine 1947–1948. Commandant of the Royal Military Academy, Sandhurst, 1948–1950, he was GOC 3rd Division and

Commander East Anglian District 1951–1952. GOC Malaya 1952–1954, he commanded I Corps BAOR 1954–1956. He had a bar added to his DSO after commanding ground forces at Suez in 1956. A general in 1957, he was Military Secretary to the Secretary of State for War 1957–1959 and Adjutant General to the Forces 1959–1960. From 1960 until his retirement in 1964 he was Deputy Supreme Allied Commander, Europe.

As well as holding down numerous honorary colonelcies, Stockwell was an active chairman of the Kennet and Avon Canal Trust and the Inland Waterways Amenity Advisory Council. A keen cricketer and member of the MCC, he lived near Devizes in Wiltshire.

STONE, Lieutenant General Robert Graham William Hawkins
(1890–1974), CB, DSO, MC
Born in Dover of military family and, because enlisted in his father's yeomanry squadron, decorated with the King's South Africa medal before being educated at Wellington and RMA, Woolwich, Stone was commissioned in the Royal Engineers in 1909. His First War service was at depots in England and in France, where he was five times mentioned in despatches, awarded the MC and admitted to the DSO in 1919.

After attending the Staff College, Camberley, 1923–4, 'Robbie' Stone married in 1928 and served on the staff at the War Office 1930–1933. Commander RE Deccan District, India, 1934–1935, he was 'a delight to serve alongside' as Military Attaché to the Rome Embassy, 1935–1938 (Mott-Radclyffe, 1975, 18) A brigadier in 1938, he was Assistant Commandant and Chief of Staff, Sudan, 1938–1940.

Chief of the British Military Mission to the Egyptian Army 1940–1942, Stone was appointed CB and made GOC British troops in Egypt in 1942. A lieutenant general in 1943, he retired from the army in 1947.

A keen sportsman, Stone was a Fellow of the Royal Geographical Society.

STOPFORD, General Sir Montagu George North
(1892–1971), GCB, KBE, DSO, MC
Of military family and educated at Wellington and RMC, Sandhurst, Stopford was commissioned in the Rifle Brigade in 1911. His First War service was in France, where he was twice mentioned in despatches and awarded the MC in 1917.

Married in 1921 and a student at the Staff College, Camberley, 1923–1924, Stopford was an instructor at Camberley 1938–1939. Appointed to command 17th Infantry Brigade in October 1939, he served under Franklyn in 5th Division in France with the BEF. Admitted to the DSO after Dunkirk, he was GOC 56th (1st London) Division in 1941 before being appointed Commandant of the Staff College, Camberley, in 1942.

Promoted lieutenant general in 1942, Stopford was GOC XII Corps under Home Forces 1942–1943, before being appointed to command XXXIII Corps in Burma. Briefed to train his troops in amphibious operations, he was detailed instead to relieve the pressure on Scoones's IV Corps in the Imphal-Kohima battles of early 1944. Heavily involved in the pursuit of the Japanese across the Chindwin and the Irrawaddy, he was knighted in the field, alongside the other corps commanders of XIV Army in December 1944.

Made GOC XII Army in Burma in 1945, Stopford was C-in-C Allied Land Forces in the Dutch East Indies 1945–1946. C-in-C South East Asia Land Forces 1946–1947, he was GOC-in-C Northern Command from 1947 until, with knighthood enhanced, he retired from the army in 1949.

Colonel Commandant of the Rifle Brigade 1951–1958, Stopford was Chairman of the Army Cadet Force Association 1951–1961 and Vice-President in 1961. He lived in Oxfordshire and was DL for the county in 1962.

STOTT. Major General Hugh *(1884–1966), CIE, OBE*

The son of a doctor and educated at Mercers' School and London University, Stott joined the Indian Medical Service in 1908. Married in 1911 and Surgeon to the Governor of Madras 1913–1914, his First War service was in France and India.

Made OBE in 1918, Stott served in the Afghan War of 1919 and in Persia (Iran) in 1920. Professor of Pathology and Physician at the Medical College, Lucknow, 1922–1937, he was Inspector General of Civil Hospitals, Bihar, 1937–1941. Made CIE and Surgeon General to the government of Madras in 1943, he retired from the army in 1944.

Attached to the Health Branch of the Allied Control Commission in Austria 1945–1946, Stott had a consultancy with the Ministry of Pensions in 1947 and was a councillor in Eastbourne from 1950.

STRETTELL, Major General Sir Chauncy Batho Dashwood
(1881–1958), KCIE, CB

Of military family and educated at Wellington and RMC, Sandhurst, Strettell was gazetted into the 13th Rajput Regiment (Indian Army) in 1901. Transferring to the Punjab Cavalry (Frontier Force) in 1902, his First War service was in France, where he was mentioned in despatches, and in Mesopotamia.

A major in 1919 and Deputy Assistant QMG, Karachi Brigade, the same year, Strettell served in North Palestine in 1921 and married in 1922. Commander of the Cavalry Frontier Force 1924–1928, he was Assistant Adjutant General, Northern Command, India, in 1928. Commander of the Meerut Cavalry Brigade 1929–1932, he was BGS, Southern Command, India, 1932–1934. Deputy QMG, AHQ, India, 1934–1936, he served briefly as QMG and as Deputy Adjutant General at AHQ before being promoted major general and appointed Commander of Peshawar District.

Knighted and retired in 1940, Strettell was re-employed as Group Commandant of Prisoner of War Camps in India. Director of Mobilization and Reconstruction, GHQ, India, 1941–1943, he retired in 1944. Chairman of the Punjab Frontier Force Executive Committee 1954, and Vice-Patron of the

PFF Officers' Association, he was a keen golfer and long-time governor of his old school.

STRONG, Major General Sir Kenneth William Dobson
(1900–1982),KBE, Kt, CB
The son of a university professor and educated at Montrose Academy and RMC, Sandhurst, Strong was commissioned in the Royal Scots Fusiliers in 1920. Married in 1924, he attended the Staff College, Camberley, 1929–1930 and commanded the 4th/5th Battalion of the Royal Scots 1932–1934. A member of the Saar (Plebiscite) Force in 1935, he was defence security officer in Malta and Gibraltar before becoming Assistant Military Attaché at the Berlin Embassy 1938–1939.

A skilled linguist and a lieutenant colonel in 1939, Strong was made head of the German Section of Military Intelligence at the War Office. BGS, Intelligence, with Home Forces 1942–1943, he was appointed Chief of Intelligence to Eisenhower's Supreme Headquarters in the Mediterranean in March 1943. A 'dour and deeply experienced Scot' (Lewin, 1978, 350), indoctrinated in 'Ultra' from the beginning, he was one of those 'outstanding staff officers who served with [Eisenhower] throughout the war' (Eisenhower, 1948,148). He helped in the negotiations leading to the Italian surrender in 1943 and, in common with many other British officers attached to SHAEF, was felt to be 'too closely identified with the Americans for the War Office's liking' (DNB). Having had his advice on a German build-up of forces around Arnhem in September 1944 brushed aside by Montgomery, he was criticized for not forewarning Eisenhower of the Germans' winter offensive in the Ardennes. He did much to stage-manage the surrender of German forces at Rheims in May 1945.

Appointed CB in 1945, Strong was Director General of the Political Intelligence Department of the Foreign Office 1945–1947. Retired from the army that year, he was Director of the Joint Intelligence Bureau, Ministry of Defence, 1948–1964, and Director General of Intelligence, Ministry of Defence, 1964–1966. Knighted that year, he wrote two books on Intelligence in his retirement, married in 1979 and held down a number of directorships with property and insurance companies.

STUART, Major General Douglas *(1894–1955), CB, CIE, OBE*
Of military family, born in Surrey but brought up and educated in Canada, Stuart's First War service was in France, with Canadian forces, from 1916–1918.

Married in 1916, Stuart was wounded and transferred to the 19th Hyderabad Regiment (Indian Army) in 1918. He saw service in Afghanistan and Waziristan 1919–1920 and was mentioned in despatches in both campaigns. After attending the Staff College, Quetta, in 1921, he spent many years as a staff officer at AHQ, India, and at Lucknow. Made OBE in 1933, he was Brigade Major to the Bareilly Infantry Brigade 1934–1936. Appointed to command the 4th Battalion of the 19th Hyderabad Regiment in 1936, he was Deputy Adjutant 7th Division

300

in Palestine in 1937. After attending the Senior Officers' School, Belgaum, in 1938, he was promoted lieutenant colonel and recalled to staff duties at AHQ.

Appointed BGS Eastern Command, India, in 1940, Stuart endured the various command transformations of the war years, ending up as Major General i/c Administration, Eastern Army, in 1945. Made CIE in 1943 and appointed CB in 1946, he was also a Commander of the US Legion of Merit. Retired in 1949, he lived in Oxted, Surrey.

STUDDERT, Major General Robert Hallam *(1890–1968), CB, DSO, MC*

Born in Co. Clare and educated at Clifton and RMA, Woolwich, Studdert was commissioned in the Royal Artillery in 1910. His First War service was in France, where he was three times wounded, five times mentioned in despatches, awarded the MC and admitted to the DSO in 1917.

A brevet major in 1918, Studdert attended the Staff College, Camberley, 1924–1925. He married in 1930 and was Deputy Assistant Director of Mechanization at the War Office 1932–1936. Commander of 4th Field Regiment, Royal Artillery, 1937–1939, he was mentioned in despatches during operations in Waziristan in 1937.

Appointed Commander RA 43rd Division at war's beginning, Studdert moved from his posting in Southern Command after Dunkirk to become CRA IV Corps under Home Forces. Deputy Master General of the Ordnance in India 1942–1945, he was appointed CB in 1946, the year he retired from the army.

Employed in the Board of Trade 1946–1949, Studdert retired to his native Ireland.

SUGDEN, General Sir Cecil Stanway *(1903–1963), GBE, KCB*

Born in Rawalpindi of miitary family and educated at Brighton College and RMA, Woolwich, Sugden was commissioned in the Royal Engineers in 1923. After attending the Staff College, Quetta, 1932–1933, he married in 1934 and served mainly in India in the years before the war. Such were his qualities as a staff officer that he came to Montgomery's attention while serving with South-Eastern Command in 1942.

Summoned to North Africa in October 1942, Sugden was recommended to Eisenhower within a month as a 'pleasant . . . and most loyal and able staff officer' (Kennedy Diary, 4/2/2, LHCMA). He was BGS Operations, Allied Forces HQ, 1942–1943. Director of Plans at the War Office 1943–1945, he was Director of Military Operations 1945–1946.

A member of the British delegations at the Yalta and Potsdam conferences of 1945, Sugden was an instructor at the Imperial Defence College in 1947 and Chief of Staff, HQ, British troops in Egypt 1948–1949. Director of Personnel Administration at the War Office 1949–1951, he was Chief of Staff, BAOR, 1951–1953 and commanded British troops in Hong Kong 1954–1955. Knighted and made C-in-C Allied Forces, Northern Europe in 1956, he was QMG to the Forces 1958–1961.

Retired in 1961, with knighthood enhanced, Sugden was made Master

General of the Ordnance at the War Office. Ill-health forced him to resign his post and he died in a London hospital.

SURTEES, Major General George *(1895–1976), CB, CBE, MC*
Commissioned in the Lancashire Fusiliers in 1914, Surtees' First War service was with the Manchester Regiment in France, where he was wounded, mentioned in despatches five times and awarded the MC.

Returning to his regiment, Surtees was Adjutant at the Lancashire Fusiliers regimental depot 1924–1926 and attended the Staff College, Camberley, 1927–1928. A staff officer with Northern Command 1930–1932, he was Brigade Major 10th Infantry Brigade 1933–1936. He served on the staff at the War Office 1936–1939.

Assistant Adjutant and QMG, British Military Mission to Egypt, 1939–1941, Surtees was Deputy Adjutant and QMG, Sudan, 1941–1942. Deputy QMG Middle East Command 1942 and appointed CB in 1943, he was GOC Lines of Communication, 21st Army Group, North-West Europe, in 1945.

Surtees retired from the army in 1949. He was Colonel of the Lancashire Fusiliers 1945–1955.

SUTTON, Major General Evelyn Alexander *(1891–1964), CB, CBE, MC*
Of military family and educated at Berkhamsted and Charing Cross Hospital, Sutton qualified as a house surgeon in 1914. Commissioned in the RAMC that year and married the next, his First War service was in France and East Africa. There he was twice wounded, mentioned in despatches and awarded the MC.

Director of Medical Services, East Africa Command, 1941–1943, Sutton was Director of Medical Services, 15th Army Group, Italy, 1944–1945. Deputy Chief Surgeon SHAEF 1945–1946, he was Deputy Director of Medical Services, Northern Command, from 1946 until his retirement from the army in 1948.

Appointed CB in 1947, Sutton lived in Hampshire.

SWAYNE, Lieutenant General Sir John George des Réaux
(1890–1964), KCB, CBE
The son of a clergyman, sometime Bishop of Lincoln, Swayne was educated at Charterhouse and Oxford University. Commissioned in the Somerset Light Infantry in 1911, his graduation year, his First War service was short. Taken prisoner at Mons in 1914, he studied languages while in captivity and, married in 1919, was ADC to the Rhine Army Corps Commander the same year.

Adjutant at his regimental depot 1922–1924, Swayne attended the Staff College, Camberley, 1925–1926 and was ADC to the C-in-C Western Command, India, in 1927. A staff officer at the War Office 1927–1929, he was Brigade Major, 7th Infantry Brigade, 1929–1930. Military Assistant to the CIGS 1931–1933, he attended the Imperial Defence College, and was Chief of Staff for the force monitoring the Saar plebiscite 1934–1935. Commander of the 1st Battalion Royal Northumberland Fusiliers 1935–1937, he was an instructor at Camberley 1937–1939.

A brigadier at war's beginning, 'Jack' Swayne was appointed to head the liaison section of the BEF at the French GQC. In France before and after the Dunkirk evacuation, he was made CBE after the campaign. Promoted major general, he was briefly Deputy Chief of the General Staff, Home Forces, before being appointed GOC 4th Division. Chief of the General Staff, Home Forces, in 1942, he succeeded Montgomery as GOC-in-C South-Eastern Command that August. As Montgomery had liked to style himself 'Army Commander' while at South-Eastern Command, it was characteristically ladder-pulling-up of him to deem Swayne's appointment 'amazing' (Hamilton, 1983, 379) and that he was 'not really fit to command Armies because [he] has commanded nothing in battle . . . and lacks experience' (Hamilton, 1982, 773).

Knighted in 1944, Swayne was appointed CGS, India. Though appointed Adjutant General to the Forces in 1946, ill-health forced him to step down before he took up the post, and he retired from the army that year. Colonel of the Somerset Light Infantry 1947–1953, he lived in London.

SYMES, Major General George William (1896–1980), CB, MC

Educated at Bridport Grammar School, Symes was commissioned in the York and Lancaster Regiment in 1915. His First War service was in France with the Machine Gun Corps. He was awarded the MC in 1915 (bar 1917).

On regimental duties for most of the 1920s, Symes attended the Staff College, Camberley, 1930–1931. A brevet major in 1932, he served on the staff in Bombay Brigade area, married in 1939 and was briefly AA and QMG 43rd (Wessex) Division in 1940. Judged by Percival, his divisional commander, as 'not too well in the picture' (PRO WO 282/7), he commanded the 6th Battalion the York and Lancaster Regiment in France, with the BEF as part of 46th Division in 1940. Appointed to command 8th Infantry Brigade after Dunkirk, he was BGS Eastern Command 1941–1942. Made GOC 70th Division in North Africa in February 1942, he presided over the conversion of his command to special duties. On transfer to India in September 1943, Slim thought 70th Division 'one of the finest British formations [he] had ever met', though regarded it as a 'tragedy that it was never allowed to fight in Burma as a division' (Slim, 1999, 141).

Made deputy to Wingate, though frequently snubbed by him, and seeing his Division's units siphoned off to nourish Chindit columns, Symes was 'bitterly disappointed' not to be nominated Wingate's successor (Royle, 1995, 316). Finding himself out of sympathy with Lentaigne, and with little to do in the Burma theatre, he asked to be relieved of his post. Brought home and made Deputy Commander of 21st Army Group's Line of Communication troops in 1944, he was back in India before the year was out, commanding SEAC Line of Communication troops. Commander of South Burma District for the second half of 1945, he was commander of South-West District 1946–1948. GOC 43rd (Wessex) Division 1947–1948 and appointed CB in 1946, he retired from the army in 1949.

Colonel of the York and Lancaster Regiment 1946–1948, Symes settled thereafter in Australia. He was private secretary to the Governor of South Australia 1956–1964 and Honorary Colonel of the 10th Battalion Adelaide Rifles 1958–1960. Re-married in 1967, he was co-founder of the National Trust of South Australia.

SZLUMPER, Gilbert Savil *(1884–1969), CBE, TD*
Educated at King's College School, Wimbledon, and London University, Szlumper followed his father's lead and joined the Engineering Department of the London and South West Railway in 1902. Married in 1913, he was Secretary to the Railway Executive Committee and Senior Railway Transport Officer of the British Army 1914–1919. Commissioned in the Territorial Army in 1916, Szlumper was Docks and Marine Manager L and SW Railway in 1920. Assistant General Manager, Southern Railway, 1925–1937 and General Manager 1937–1942, he was promoted major general in 1939.

The man responsible for transporting the BEF to France and improvising a timetable for the post-Dunkirk 'rush', Szlumper was Director General of Transportation and Movements at the War Office 1939–1940 and Railway Control Officer, Ministry of Transport, 1940–1941. Director-General of Supply Services, Ministry of Supply from 1942, he retired in 1945.

T

TABUTEAU, Major General George Grant *(1881–1940), DSO*
The son of a doctor and educated at Corrig School, Kingstown, and the Royal College of Surgeons, Dublin, Tabuteau qualified in 1903, worked in several Dublin Hospitals and was Surgeon to the Blue Funnel Line before joining the RAMC in 1905. Married in 1910 and a major in 1915, his First War service was in France, where he was thrice mentioned in despatches and admitted to the DSO.

A frequent contributor to the RAMC Journal on such subjects as gunshot wounds to the head, primary excision of wounds and gas gangrene, Tabuteau served in Waziristan in 1923 and was mentioned in despatches during operations in Burma in 1932. Honorary Surgeon to the Viceroy in 1930 and a colonel in 1934, he was Deputy Director of Medical Services, Northern Command, 1934–1937. Promoted major general in 1937 and appointed Director of Medical Services, India, that year. He died suddenly in India in March 1940.

TAYLOR, Major General Sir George Brian Ogilvie *(1887–1973), KBE, CB*
Educated at Cheltenham and RMA, Woolwich, Taylor was commissioned in

the Royal Engineers in 1907. Married in 1915, his First War service was in France and Salonika, where he was Assistant Director of Works to the BEF.

Married in 1919, Taylor attended the Staff College, Camberley, 1920–1921 and served on the Chief Engineer's staff at Aldershot 1922–1924. Deputy Assistant Director of Fortifications and Works at the War Office 1924–1926, he was an instructor at the School of Military Engineering, Chatham, 1926–1929. Chief Engineer to the RAF in Iraq 1929–1931, he was Assistant Director of Works at the War Office 1935–1937.

Chief Engineer, Northern Command, 1937–1939, Taylor was Director of Fortifications and Works at the War Office 1939–1940. Appointed CB in 1940 and placed on the retired list as Inspector General, he was recalled the next year and made Director of Bomb Disposal 1941–1942. Knighted in 1942, he was Engineer-in-Chief, Persia (Iran) and Iraq Command until his final retirement in 1943.

A keen sportsman, Taylor lived in Devon.

TAYLOR, Major General Sir John *(1884–1959), Kt, CIE, DSO*

Educated at Glasgow University and joining the Indian Medical Service in 1906, Taylor's served on the North-West Frontier. His First World War service was in France, where he was twice mentioned in despatches and admitted to the DSO in 1915, and in India.

Married in 1918, Taylor's career alternated between civilian and military appointments. Public Health Commissioner for Assam 1919–1922, Deputy Director of the Pasteur Institute, Rangoon, in 1923, and Director of the Haffkine Institute, Bombay, 1925–1932, he was a lieutenant colonel in 1926. Director of the Central Research Institute, Kasauli, Punjab, 1932–1944, he was a major general in 1941, was knighted in 1942 and retired from the army in 1943.

Editor for many years of the Indian Journal of Medical Research, his only son was killed in the war. Taylor was President of the Flyfishers' Association, 1951–1955, and lived the last five years of his life a widower.

TAYLOR, General Sir Maurice Grove *(1881–1960), KCB, CMG, DSO*

Educated at St Mark's, Windsor, and RMA, Woolwich, Taylor was commissioned in the Royal Engineers in 1900. Married in 1906 and a captain in 1910, he served with Scottish Command and attended the Staff College, Camberley, before service in the First War as a railway transportation officer in France. Seven times mentioned in despatches, he was admitted to the DSO in 1916.

Made CMG in 1919, Taylor was Deputy Director of Movements at the War Office 1919–1921. On the directing staff at Camberley 1921–1925, he was Assistant QMG, Eastern Command, 1925–1927. Commander of 166th South Lancashire and Cheshire Brigade 1927–1931, he was promoted major general in 1930 and was GOC 46th (North Midland) Division 1932–1934. Major General i/c Administration, Aldershot Command, 1934–1937, he was Colonel

Commandant of the Royal Engineers in 1938 and Deputy Master General of the Ordnance 1938–1939.

Made Senior Military Adviser to the Ministry of Supply in September 1939, Taylor was briefly Master General of the Ordnance before he retired from the army in 1941. A keen sportsman and talented musician, he settled in Cornwall and outlived his wife by five years.

TELFER-SMOLLETT, Major General Alexander Patrick Drummond
(1884–1954), CB, CBE, DSO, MC

Of military family, Telfer-Smollett was educated at RMC, Sandhurst, and commissioned in the Highland Light Infantry in 1906. A captain in 1914 and married the same year, his First War service was in France where he was awarded the MC. He was admitted to the DSO in 1919 after service with the North Russia Relief Force.

A brevet lieutenant colonel in 1919, 'Alec' Telfer-Smollett attended the Staff College, Camberley, 1920–1921 and served on the staff at the War Office 1925–1929. Senior Staff Officer to the Inspector General West African Frontier Force 1928–1930, he was Commander of the 1st Battalion Highland Light Infantry 1931–1934 and, after commanding 157th (Highland) Infantry Brigade 1934–1935, commanded British troops in Shanghai 1936–1939. Promoted major general and appointed CB in 1938, he was appointed to what should have been a gentle and dignified end to his career, the Lieutenant Governorship of Guernsey. Evacuated in 1940, the year his wife died, and made Commander of Madras District, he retired from the army in 1942. His elder son was killed in action in 1940.

Commissioner of the British Red Cross, South-East Asia Command, 1944–1946, Telfer-Smollett was Colonel of the Highland Light Infantry 1946–1954, and was made Lord Lieutenant of Dunbartonshire in 1948. Keeper of Dumbarton Castle in 1949, he was also a member of the Royal Company of Archers.

TEMPLER, Field Marshal Sir Gerald Walter Robert
(1898–1979), KG, GCB, GCMG, KBE, DSO

Of military family, Templer was educated at Wellington and RMC, Sandhurst. Commissioned in the Royal Irish Fusiliers in 1916, his First War service was in Ireland and France.

After service in Iraq and Persia (Iran) in 1919, Templer spent many years on regimental duties in Egypt. Married in 1926, he attended the Staff College, Camberley, 1928–1929, and transferred to the Loyal (North Lancashire) Regiment. A staff officer with 3rd Division in 1930, he survived his commanding officer's recommendation that he should be discharged from the army on the grounds of ill-health and inefficiency. A staff officer with Northern Command 1933–1935, he returned to his regiment and served with the 1st Battalion in Palestine, where he was admitted to the DSO. Transferring back to the Irish

Fusiliers in 1937, he served on the staff at the Military Intelligence department of the War Office 1938–1939.

A staff officer at the BEF's GHQ in France 1939–1940, Templer was briefly a member of 'Macforce' and, nearly as briefly, commanded the 9th Battalion Royal Sussex Regiment after Dunkirk, before being appointed to command 210th Infantry Brigade in Dorset. BGS V Corps 1941–1942, he was promoted major general in April 1942 and appointed GOC 47th (London) Division. Already a famous trainer of troops, he allegedly 'inspired the division with enthusiasm, keenness and efficiency' (Cloake, 1985, 94). Wounded when, due to pilot error, a demonstration of the effects of ground attack by aircraft went wrong, he was given the command of II Corps in late 1942, before assuming command of XI Corps in East Anglia early the next year.

Made GOC 1st Division in Tunisia in July 1943, Templer, already known for his 'tremendous energy and uninhibited tongue' (Blaxland, 1979, 35), was sent to Italy in October as a battle replacement commander of 56th (London) Division. Resented in some quarters – Freeman-Attwood, for example, never knew 'why he [was] considered so good' (PRO WO 71/1092) – he was in continuous action on the Volturno and later around Anzio. Appointed GOC 6th Armoured Division in July 1944, he was seriously injured in August during the advance on Florence, when splinters from a lorry blown up by a mine damaged his back. Able to make 'a good story out of his misfortune' (Cloake, 1985, 139), he put it about that he had been hit by fragments from a looted piano.

Attached to HQ, SOE in early 1945, Templer was Director of Civil Affair and Military Government, 21st Army Group, Brussels, and was the executive head of government in the British zone of occupied Germany 1945–1946. Director of Military Intelligence at the War Office 1946–1948, he was Vice CIGS 1948–1950. Knighted in 1949, he was GOC-in-C, Eastern Command, 1950–1952. Made High Commissioner for the Federation of Malaya, he campaigned vigorously against Communist insurgents and, in promoting political reform allegedly coined the phrase 'hearts and minds' (Heathcote, 1999,276). He was at the head of what was, probably, the most successful of the British Army's counter-insurgency campaigns of the post-war years.

Not made C-in-C BAOR in 1954, because his appointment would have offended the West German Chancellor, Adenauer, Templer was CIGS from 1955 until his retirement from the army in 1958. Having derived 'little satisfaction' from his last appointment (Heathcote, 1999, 174), he was, to the end, 'a martinet [whose] appearance – even presence – was intimidating' (DNB). He was much honoured. Colonel of the Royal Irish Fusiliers, 1946–1960, he was Colonel of the Malay Federation Regiment 1954–1959, the 7th Gurkha Rifles 1956–1964 and the Royal Horse Guards 1962–1979. He was also Constable of the Tower of London 1965–1970. Active in charity work and a keen patron of the National Army Museum, he died of lung cancer in London.

THOMAS, General Sir Gwilyn Ivor
(1893–1972), GCB, KBE, DSO, MC (and bar)
The son of the Harpist to Queen Victoria and Edward VII, Thomas was educated at Cheltenham and RMA, Woolwich. Commissioned in the Royal Artillery in 1912, his First War service was in France, where he was twice wounded, awarded the MC (and bar) and admitted to the DSO.

Adjutant to various Territorial Army units during the 1920s, Thomas attended the Staff College, Camberley, 1924–1925 and, married in 1931, attended the Royal Naval College, Greenwich, in 1934. From 1935 to 1936 he was Brigade Major to the 1st Divisional Artillery and in 1938 was seconded to the Home Office staff on ARP duties.

Deputy Director of Recruiting and Organization at the War Office 1939–1940, Thomas was briefly Director of Organization before being appointed CRA 2nd Division. CRA I Corps in 1942, he was appointed GOC 43rd (Wessex) Division that March. Irreverently christened 'von Thoma', he spent two years training his command. Described as 'a small, fiery, very deter-mined and grim gunner . . . without a spark of humour' (Carver, 1989, 116), he led his Division throughout the campaign in North-West Europe.

Commander I Corps District, BAOR, 1945–1947, Thomas was Administrator of Polish Forces under British control in 1947. Knighted in 1947, divorced in 1948 and re-married in 1949, he was GOC-in-C Anti-Aircraft Command 1948–1950 and QMG to the Forces from 1950 until, with knight-hood enhanced, he retired from the army in 1952.

THOMPSON, Major General Sir Treffry Owen
(1888–1979), KCSI, CB, CBE
The son of a clergyman, Thompson was educated at Repton, Oxford University and St George's Hospital, London. A junior houseman in 1912, he joined the RAMC in 1914. A captain in 1915, his First War service was in France and Italy.

Married in 1916, Thompson was Deputy Assistant Director of Hygiene in India 1926–1929 and Assistant Director in Hygiene and Pathology in India 1933–1937. He was Assistant Director of Hygiene at the War Office 1938–1939

A colonel in 1941, Thompson was Deputy Director of Medical Services, Line of Communications, Iraq Forces, in 1941, and Deputy Director of Medical Services in Burma during the retreat. DDMS, Central Command, India, in 1942, he was DDMS, Eastern Army, 1943–1944. A major general in 1944, he was Medical Adviser to the Supreme Commander, South-East Asia, and Director of Medical Services, Allied Land Forces South-East Asia 1944–1945.

DMS in India 1946–1947, Thompson was knighted and retired the next year. He was British Red Cross Commissioner for relief work in India and Pakistan 1947–1949 and Colonel Commandant of the RAMC 1950–1953. A widower in 1958 and re-married in 1959, he lived in North Devon.

THOMSON, Major General James Noel *(1888–1978), CB, DSO, MC*
Educated at Fettes and RMA, Woolwich, and commissioned in the Royal Field

Artillery in 1909, Thomson's First War service was in France. Thrice mentioned in despatches and awarded the MC, he was admitted to the DSO in 1917.

Adjutant at RMC, Sandhurst, 1919–1920, Thomson attended the Staff College, Camberley, 1920–1921. A staff officer at the War Office 1922–1923, he was Brigade Major with 1st Brigade, Rhine Army, 1923–1924. Serving on the staff with the Rhine Army 1924–1926, he was a staff officer to the Major General Royal Artillery, India, 1927–1930. Married in 1929, he attended the Imperial Defence College in 1932, and was Assistant Master General of the Ordnance, India, 1934–1937. A colonel in 1935, he was Brigadier RA, Northern Command, India, 1938–1941.

Appointed GOC 6th Indian Division in 1941, Thomson served for two years on line of communication duties in Iraq and Iran (Persia). Deputy Master General of the Ordnance, India, in 1943, he was appointed CB in 1946 and, retiring that year from the army, stayed on in India after independence.

THORNE, General Sir Augustus Francis Andrew Nicol
(1885–1970), KCB, CMG, DSO
Educated at Eton and RMC, Sandhurst, Thorne was commissioned in the Grenadier Guards in 1904. Married in 1909, his First War service was in France, as commander of his regiment's 3rd Battalion and latterly as commander of a brigade. Seven times mentioned in despatches, he was admitted to the DSO in 1916 (two bars).

Assistant Military Attaché to the Washington Embassy 1919–1920, Thorne was Military Assistant to the CIGS 1925–1926. Commander of 3rd Battalion Grenadier Guards 1927–1931, he was Military Attaché in Berlin 1932–1935. Commander of 1st Guards Brigade 1935–1938, he was GOC London District and Major General commanding the Brigade of Guards 1938–1939.

GOC 48th Division 1939–1940, 'Bulgy' Thorne was mentioned in despatches during the campaign in France and Flanders. A 'fine soldier . . . a fanatic for physical fitness, [and] one of those rare people who could talk to one when young' (Fraser, 2002, 70), he never again held field command. GOC XII Corps 1940–1942, he was charged with defending the Kent and Sussex coast. Knighted and appointed GOC-in-C Scottish Command and Governor of Edinburgh Castle in 1942, he was GOC Allied Land Forces in Norway and head of the SHAEF Mission to Norway in 1945. He retired from the army in 1946, but returned to the active list in 1950 for a year's work with the Norwegian Ministry of Defence.

President of the Old Etonian Association 1949–1950, Thorne was Chairman of the Committee of Visitors to Broadmoor 1949–1964. Well-liked, much honoured by foreign governments, he lived near Reading, kept a house in Lossiemouth and played golf until well into his 80s.

TICKELL, Major General Sir Eustace Francis *(1893–1972), KBE, CB, MC*
The son of an Indian Civil Servant, Tickell was educated at Bedford School and RMA, Woolwich. Commissioned in the Royal Engineers in 1913, his First War

service was in France, where he was awarded the MC, and in Salonika and Palestine.

An instructor at the School of Military Engineering, Chatham, in 1919, Tickell married in 1921 and was an instructor at Woolwich 1924–1927. Posted for service in North China in 1928, he was o/c Royal Engineers officers at Cambridge University 1932–1934. CRE Northern Command 1936–1938, he was CRE 5th Division 1938–1939 and Chief Engineer, British troops in Egypt, at war's beginning.

Appointed Director of Works, Middle East Command, in 1940, Tickell was appointed CB in 1942. Briefly Engineer in Chief, Middle East Command, in 1944, he was Director of Works, 21st Army Group, North-West Europe, 1944–1945. Engineer in Chief, BLA, in 1945, he was knighted and appointed Engineer in Chief at the War Office from 1945 until his retirement from the army in 1949.

President of the Institution of Royal Engineers 1948–1951 and Colonel Commandant of the RE Corps, 1950–1958, Tickell was also Honorary Colonel of the Army Emergency Reserve RE Resource Unit 1953–1959. He lived in Surrey.

TILLY, Major General Justice Crosland (1888–1941), DSO, MC
Born in Bedford of military family, Tilly, commissioned in the Leicestershire Regiment in 1908, served with the King's African Rifles in East Africa 1913–1914. His First War service was in France, where, with the Machine Gun Corps, he was wounded, mentioned in despatches, awarded the MC and admitted to the DSO.

Married in 1919 and transferring to the West Yorkshire Regiment, Tilly served for many years on the North-West Frontier, He transferred again, this time to the Royal Tank Corps, in 1927. He attended the Senior Officers' School, Sheerness, in 1931 and commanded the 5th Battalion RTC in 1934. Chief Instructor at the RTC Central School, Bovington, 1935–1937, and regarded as 'capable' (Lewin, 1976, 87), he was Chief Instructor at the Gunnery Wing of the Army AFV School, Lulworth, 1937–1938.

Commander of 1st Tank Brigade from 1939 to 1940, Tilly was appointed GOC 2nd Armoured Division in May 1940. Posted to North Africa, he was killed in an accident in January 1941. He left a widow and a daughter.

TOLLEMACHE, Major General Edward Devereux Hamilton
(1885–1947), DSO, MC
Educated at Eton and RMC, Sandhurst, and for most of his life heir presumptive to Lord Tollemache, he was commissioned in the Coldstream Guards in 1905. Married in 1909, his First War service was in France, where he was awarded the MC, and in Egypt, where he was admitted to the DSO.

A student at the Staff College, Camberley, in 1920, 'Teddy' Tollemache was Brigade Major to the 2nd Infantry Brigade, Aldershot, in 1923, and commanded the 1st Battalion Coldstream Guards 1925–1928. Assistant Commandant

RMC, Sandhurst 1929–1932, he served on the staff of 1st Division at Aldershot 1932–1936 and commanded 128th (Hampshire) Brigade 1936–1939. Made Commander of Southampton Garrison in 1939, and the Portsmouth Area in 1940, he retired from the army that year.

TOMLINSON, Major General Sir Percy Stanley
(1884–1951), KBE, CB, DSO
The son of an army doctor, Tomlinson was educated at Clifton and University College, Bristol. Qualified in 1908, he joined the Royal Army Medical Corps in 1909. His First War service was in France, where he was three times mentioned in despatches.

In a career that seemed to flit in and out of civilian and military practice, Tomlinson accumulated numerous degrees and fellowships (Royal Society of Medicine, Royal Society of Tropical Medicine and Hygiene, Physician to the King, etc.). He was Deputy Director Medical Services Northern Command, India, in 1934 and Deputy Assistant Director of Medical Organization for War, India, 1935–1936. Director of Medical Services, Middle East Force, 1940–1943, he was Director of Medical Services, 21st Army Group, from September 1943 to November 1944. Knighted, he retired from the army in 1944.

Colonel Commandant of the RAMC 1945–1947, Tomlinson was a member of the BMA Council 1948–1950. His son, a pilot officer with the RAF, was killed in action in 1941.

TOOVEY, Major General Cecil Wotton *(1891–1954), CB, CBE, MC*
Educated at Malvern and gazetted into the 1st Punjab Regiment (Indian Army) in 1911, Toovey's First War service was in India and Mesopotamia. He served in the Afghan and Mahsud campaigns in quick succession and was awarded the MC in 1920 during operations in Waziristan.

Married in 1923 and a student at the Staff College, Quetta, in 1925, Toovey was Deputy Assistant Adjutant General, AHQ India, 1928–1929, and had a bar added to his MC in 1930 after service on the North-West Frontier. After three years on the staff of the War Office he returned to India and received another bar in 1937 after the campaign in Waziristan. He commanded the 3rd Battalion 1st Punjab Regiment 1937–1939 and was Assistant Adjutant General Mobilization and Organization, AHQ India, 1939–1940

A liaison officer in the Middle East 1940–1941, Toovey was Brigadier i/c Lines of Communication in Eritrea in 1941. Deputy Adjutant General, GHQ India, 1941–1943, he was promoted major general and appointed CB. He was commander of Rawalpindi District from 1943 to 1946.

Retired from the army in 1947, Toovey settled in Surrey. He was a member of the governing body of the Docklands Settlements, a governor of his old school and County Commissioner for the St John Ambulance Brigade. He was outlived by his wife and three children.

TOPE, Major General Wilfrid Shakespeare *(1892–1962), CB, CBE*
Educated at Whitgift School, Tope worked in the City and joined the London
Rifle Brigade (TA) in 1909. Commissioned in the Royal Army Service Corps in
1915 and married in 1916, his First War service was in France, where he was
wounded and mentioned in despatches, in Salonika, where he was again
mentioned in despatches, and in the Caucasus.

An instructor at the RASC Training Centre 1925–1927, Tope was a staff
officer at the War Office 1927–1932 and an instructor at RMC, Sandhurst,
1937–1939.

An acting lieutenant colonel in 1939, Tope spent the early war years in the
Middle East. Deputy Director of Supplies and Transport, Middle East Force,
in 1942, he was Deputy Director of Mechanical Engineering, Middle East
Force, 1942–1943. Said to be a 'blunt, direct, no-nonsense engineer', he established the new corps, REME, in that theatre, was made CBE and brought back
to the War Office as Director of Mechanical Engineering. Appointed CB in
1945, he held the same post until he retired from the army in 1950.

Living in Sussex, Tope pursued a successful business career. Re-married in
1954, he was Colonel Commandant of REME 1950–1957.

TREMLETT, Major General Erroll Arthur Edwin *(1893–1982), CB, TD*
Of military family and educated at Christ's Hospital, Tremlett's higher education was spent making his own way in Canada. Volunteering in 1914, he joined
the Royal Artillery, served in France and was commissioned in the field in 1916.

A noted sportsman, Tremlett trained the King's Troop (RA) in equitation for
a number of years, played polo and cricket for the army (and MCC), and was
Chief Gunnery Instructor, Southern Command, 1934–1936. Posted to India, he
left the army in 1938 because of slow promotion and his belief that the Munich
agreement had secured 'peace for our time' (Tremlett, WSL, 121). He was
immediately offered and accepted a lieutenant colonelcy in the Territorial
Army.

Commander of 54th Light AA Regiment with the BEF in France 1939–1940,
Tremlett commanded 44th Light AA Brigade 1940–1942. Promoted major
general, he was appointed GOC 10th AA Division and as such supervised the
anti-aircraft defence of London. Appointed CB, he was Commander of Flying
Bomb Deployment 1945 and commanded 2nd AA Group 1945–1946.

Reverting to the reserve in 1946, Tremlett was chairman of the London
Region RA Association 1945–1946. A Gold Staff Officer at the Coronation of
Elizabeth II and a member of the MCC, he was President of the Devon RA
Association 1957–1967.

TUKER, Lieutenant General Sir Francis Ivan Simms
(1894–1967), KCIE, CB, DSO, OBE
Educated at Brighton College and RMC, Sandhurst, Tuker was commissioned
in the Royal Sussex Regiment, but transferred almost immediately to the

1st/2nd Gurkhas. His First War service was in India and Mesopotamia, where he was wounded.

On active service on the North-West Frontier and in Persia 1919–1921, Tuker married in 1923 and attended the Staff College, Camberley, 1925–1926. Following various junior staff postings in India, he was made OBE and commanded 1st/2nd Gurkhas 1937–1939.

Director of Military Training, GHQ India, 1940–1941, 'Gertie' Tuker was promoted major general in 1941 and appointed GOC of the newly-formed 34th Indian Division. Known for his 'original and independent mind' (Blaxland, 1977, 202) and appointed GOC 4th Indian Division in 1942, he served with 8th Army with such distinction that he was judged 'probably the best tactician in the desert' (Bidwell & Graham, 1985, 242). Admitted to the DSO during operations in Tunisia in 1943, he was appointed CB. Falling ill in early 1944, he was hospitalized and returned to India. Chairman of the Frontier Committee 1944, he was GOC Ceylon (Sri Lanka) in 1945 and, promoted lieutenant general, was GOC Eastern Command, India, 1946–1947. His only failing, according to Auchinleck, was 'of not always keeping his feet on the ground' (Mountbatten 1/D99/2).

Colonel of the 2nd Gurkha Regiment 1946–1948, Tuker retired from the army in 1948. His *While Memory Serves* (1949) was a scathing indictment of British scuttle in the sub-continent, and, settled in Cornwall, he re-married and embarked on an ambitious, though not wholly successful, literary career. His *Approach to Battle* (1963) was well received, though his opera libretti were never transformed into performances. Undaunted by illness and disability, he carried on writing energetically to the end.

U

ULLMAN, Major General Peter Alfred *(1897–1972), CB, OBE*
Born in Surrey and educated at Cheltenham and RMA, Woolwich, Ullman was commissioned in the Royal Engineers in 1915. After attending a young officers' course at Cambridge, his First War service was in East Africa and France, where he was mentioned in despatches.

Spending most of the 1920s on a captain's pay in India, Ullman married in 1929 and served on the staff at the War Office, 1934–1938. Mentioned in despatches during service on operations in Palestine 1938–1939, he was a lieutenant colonel at war's beginning.

With Middle East Forces 1939–1941, Ullman was made OBE in 1940 and served with Home Forces 1942–1943 as Chief Engineer II Corps. Chief Engineer

Iraq and Persia (Iran) Command 1943–1944, he was Chief Engineer 21st Army Group, North-West Europe, 1944–1945.

Deputy Engineer-in-Chief at the War Office in 1945, Ullman was appointed CB and was Chief Engineer, South-East Asia, from 1946 until his retirement from the army in 1948.

URQUHART, Major General Robert Elliott *(1901–1988), CB, DSO (bar)*
Educated at St Paul's and RMC, Sandhurst, Urquhart was commissioned in the Highland Light Infantry in 1920. A 'huge amiable Scot' (Boatner, 1996, 581), he spent more than a dozen years on a captain's pay performing regimental duties at home and in India. After attending the Staff College, Camberley, 1936–1937, he was Deputy Assistant QMG, AHQ India, 1939–1940.

Married in 1939, Urquhart was posted home and was Deputy Assistant Adjutant General 3rd Division in 1940. Assistant Adjutant and QMG 3rd Division 1940–1941, he commanded the 2nd Battalion Duke of Cornwall's Light Infantry 1941–1942. On the staff of 51st (Highland) Division in North Africa 1942–1943, he was admitted to the DSO and commanded 231 (Malta) Brigade in the Sicilian and Italian campaigns. Wounded that September, he had a bar added to his DSO, and was briefly BGS XII Corps before being appointed GOC 1st Airborne Division in December 1943.

Though lacking in airborne experience, Urquhart lost no time in converting himself into a 'Red Devil'. With his command held in readiness for a series of operations that were cancelled at the last minute, he was required to fulfil the most difficult part of MARKET GARDEN that September, taking and holding the bridges at Arnhem. Cut off and effectively lost for much of the ensuing battle, he felt 'idiotic' and 'ridiculous' having to hide from German soldiers in an attic (Ryan, 1999, 247). Unable to influence the outcome of the operation and with his command shattered, he was brought home, appointed CB and, reverting to the substantive rank of colonel, was made Director of the TA and Army Cadet Force at the War Office. He was GOC 16th Division 1947–1948.

Commander of the Lowland District 1948–1950, Urquhart spent the next two years in Malaya as a district commander and as GOC 17th Gurkha Division. He was GOC British troops in Austria from 1952 until his retirement from the army in 1955. A company director in Glasgow for a number of years, his *Arnhem* was published in 1958.

UTTERSON-KELSO, Major General John Edward
(1893–1972),CB, DSO, OBE, MC
Educated at Haileybury and RMC, Sandhurst, Utterson-Kelso was commissioned in the Royal Scots Fusiliers in 1912. Married in 1915, his First War service was in France, where he was five-times wounded, mentioned in despatches, awarded the MC (and bar) and admitted to the DSO (and bar).

An instructor at the Small Arms School, Netheravon, 1928–1932, Utterson-Kelso commanded Line of Communication troops in Palestine and Transjordan

1936–1937. Commander of the 2nd Battalion the Devonshire Regiment 1937–1939, he was an area commander at war's beginning.

Appointed to command 131st Brigade, Utterson-Kelso served under Osborne in 44th (Home Counties) Division, BEF, in 1940. Appointed GOC 47th (London) Division in April 1941, he was the first divisional commander to incorporate battle drill into unit and formation training.

So impressed was Paget, the C-in-C Home Forces, with the value of such training that Utterson-Kelso was made Major General of Infantry and helped develop the GHQ Battle School at Barnard Castle. Appointed CB in 1943 and made GOC 76th Division in March 1944, he reverted to commanding 47th Division that September, just after learning that his son, a lieutenant in the Grenadier Guards, had been killed in France.

Retired from the army in 1946, Utterson-Kelso lived in North Wales.

V

VALON, Major General Alfred Robert (1885–1971), CB, OBE, MC

Educated at London University and commissioned in the Army Ordnance Corps in 1906, Valon married in 1909. His First War service was in France, where he was awarded the MC, and with the North Russian Relief Force in 1919, after which he was awarded the OBE.

Deputy Assistant Director of Ordnance Services at the War Office 1927–1929, Valon was Commandant of the School of Military Engineering 1934–1936. A colonel in 1936, he was Principal Ordnance and Mechanical Engineer at the War Office 1937–1940. Director of Ordnance Services (Engineering) at the War Office in 1940, he was Inspector of Army Ordnance Workshop Services 1940–1942 and was Colonel Commandant, RAOC, over the same period. Retired that year, but recalled to head the newly-formed Royal Electrical and Mechanical Engineers, he was Inspector of REME 1942–1943.

Appointed CB and retired from the army in 1943, Valon worked with the British Council 1945–1949. Colonel Commandant of REME 1942–1951, he re-married in 1951 and was a director of an electrical engineering firm 1955–1963.

VENNING, General Sir Walter King (1882–1964), GCB, CMG, CBE, MC

The son of a Ceylon (Sri Lanka) Civil Servant, Venning was educated at Clifton and RMC, Sandhurst. Commissioned in the Duke of Cornwall's Light Infantry in 1901, he was attached to the West African Frontier Force in 1907. Married in 1909, he was Adjutant to a territorial battalion (12th County of London Rangers) in 1912. His First War service was in France. Thrice mentioned in despatches, he was awarded the MC in 1915 and served thereafter on the staff at GHQ and the War Office.

An instructor at the Staff College, Camberley, 1919–1921, Venning served on the staff at the War Office for the next five years. Assistant Adjutant and QMG to 1st Division at Aldershot 1927–1929, he was Deputy Adjutant and QMG, Eastern Command, India, 1929–1931. Commander of 2nd (Rawalpindi) Infantry Brigade 1931–1934, he was Director of Movements and Quartering at the War Office 1934–1938.

A lieutenant general in 1938, Venning was knighted in 1939 and was QMG to the Forces 1939–1942. Retired that year, with knighthood enhanced, he was made Director General of the British Supply Mission to Washington and held that post until 1946, the year of his wife's death.

Colonel of the Duke of Cornwall's Light Infantry 1935–1947 and Colonel Commandant of the Army Catering Corps 1941–1945, Venning was also Colonel Commandant of REME 1942–1950. Re-married in 1954, he lived in Dorset.

VEREKER, see *GORT.*

VERNEY, Major General Gerald Lloyd *(1900–1957)*, *DSO, MVO*
The son of a knight and educated at Eton and RMC, Sandhurst, Verney was page to George V before being commissioned in the Grenadier Guards in 1919. He served with the Army of the Black Sea 1922–1923, married in 1926 and was ADC to the Governor of South Australia 1928–1929. A captain in 1929, he attended the Staff College, Camberley, 1936–1937 and transferred to the Irish Guards in 1939.

After service in France with the BEF, Verney was an instructor at Camberley in 1940 and commanded the 2nd Battalion Irish Guards 1940–1942. Commander, in turn, of 1st Guards Brigade, 6th Guards Tank Brigade and 32nd Guards Brigade, he fought in Italy in 1943–1944. Appointed GOC 7th Armoured Division in August 1944, as a replacement for Erskine, who his seniors believed had under-performed in Normandy, he was himself replaced as divisional commander in November, having failed 'to cure the division's bad habits well enough to satisfy Montgomery and Dempsey' (D'Este, 2001, 286).

Returning to Italy, Verney commanded the 1st Guards Brigade 1944–1945. Admitted to the DSO, he was appointed Commander of British troops in Vienna 1945–1946 and, after being GOC 56th (London) Division for two years, retired from the army in 1948.

Retired to the family estate in Ireland, Verney shot and fished, and wrote histories of the 7th Armoured and Guards Armoured Divisions. He died suddenly aged 56.

VERSCHOYLE-CAMPBELL, Major General William Henry McNeile
(1884–1964), CIE, OBE, MC
The son of a Church of Ireland clergyman and educated at Marlborough and

RMA, Woolwich, Verschoyle-Campbell was commissioned in the Royal Artillery in 1903. Married in 1910, he joined the Army Ordnance Department in 1912. His First War service was in France, Macedonia, Serbia, Bulgaria and in the Aegean. Mentioned five times in despatches and awarded the MC, he was awarded the OBE in 1919.

A major in 1922, Verschoyle-Campbell attended the Staff College, Camberley, 1923–1924 and was an instructor at the RAOC school 1926–1929. Assistant Deputy of Ordnance Services at the War Office in 1935, he was Director of Ordnance Services, AHQ India, 1936–1940.

A major general in 1938, Verschoyle-Campbell was Deputy Master General of the Ordnance, India, from 1940 until his retirement in 1941. Thereafter he lived in Dublin.

VICKERS, Lieutenant General Wilmot Gordon Hilton
(1890–1987), CB, OBE
Of military family and educated at the United Services College, Westward Ho!, Vickers was commissioned in the Indian Army (unattached list) in 1910. Gazetted into the 13th (Duke of Connaught's Own) Lancers in 1911 and a captain in 1915, his First War service was in France and India.

Made OBE in 1919 and married in 1920, Vickers, a major in 1926, attended the Staff College Quetta, in 1927. Commander of the 13th Lancers 1931–1933, he served on the staff of AHQ, India, 1933–1934. Commandant and Chief Instructor of the Equitation School, Saugar, India, 1934–1935, he was Deputy Director of Staff Duties, AHQ, India, 1935–1937. Commander of Allahabad Brigade area 1939–1940, he was Director of Supplies and Transport, India, 1940–1941.

A major general in 1940, Vickers was Major General i/c Administration, Iraq-Persia (Iran), 1941–1942. Appointed CB and promoted lieutenant general in 1943, he was QMG, India, from 1942 until his retirement in 1944.

Settling in Cheltenham, Vickers was DL for Gloucestershire in 1946 and was Commandant of the Gloucestershire Army Cadet Force 1946–1955. He was the county's Chief Civil Defence Warden 1949–1960 and was for a number of years President of the Haileybury Society. Living well into his nineties he was, as his obituary notice put it, 'the most senior surviving British cavalry officer of the old Indian Army'. His *Practical Polo* was still, apparently, much-thumbed as a coaching manual.

VULLIAMY, Major General Colwyn Henry Hughes *(1894–1972), CB, DSO*
Of military family and educated at Cheltenham and RMA, Woolwich, Vulliamy was commissioned in the Royal Engineers in 1913. His First War service was in France, where he was thrice mentioned in despatches.

A staff officer at Rhine Army HQ in 1919, Vulliamy spent most of the 1920s in India. Transferring to the Royal Signals in 1926, he married and attended the Staff College, Camberley, 1928–1930. Serving on the staff at the War Office

1931–1935, he returned to India, took part in the Mohmand expedition of 1935 and was admitted to the DSO in 1938 after serving on operations in Waziristan.

Chief Signal Officer, Anti-Aircraft Command, 1939–1940, Vulliamy was CSO for the Norwegian Expeditionary Force, April-May 1940. CSO, Home Forces, 1940–1943, he was Signal Officer-in-Chief, Middle East Command, in 1943. Appointed CSO to Eisenhower's Supreme Command HQ in 1943, he remained with SHAEF throughout the campaign in North-West Europe.

Appointed CB in 1945, Vulliamy was CSO, GHQ, India, 1945–1946 and was Director of Signals at the War Office from 1946 until his retirement from the army in 1949. Settling in Hampshire, he was a director of Standard Telephone and Cables Co Ltd. 1949–1967.

VYVYAN, Major General Ralph Ernest *(1891–1971), CBE, MC*
The son of the Chief Constable of Devon and educated at Stubbington School, Exeter, and RMC, Sandhurst, Vyvyan was commissioned in the Worcestershire Regiment in 1910. Married in 1915, his First War service was in France, where he was mentioned in despatches and awarded the MC.

Transferring to the Royal Signals in 1920, Vyvyan obtained a divorce, re-married in 1930 and, a lieutenant colonel in 1931, was Chief Signal Officer, Eastern Command, India, 1932–1935. CSO, Western Command, India, 1935–1939, he was thanked by the Viceroy for his part in recovery operations after the Quetta earthquake.

Chief Signal Officer, Northern Command, India, 1939–1940, Vyvyan was Signal Officer-in-Chief and Director of Signals, GHQ, India, 1941–1945. Made CBE in 1944, he retired in 1946. A member of the MCC and Editor of RUSI Journal 1950–1957, he was also Registrar of the Museum 1948–1958.

W

WADE, Major General Douglas Ashton Lofft *(1898–1996), CB, OBE, MC*
The son of an Essex solicitor and educated at St Lawrence College, Ramsgate, and RMA, Woolwich, Wade was commissioned in the Royal Artillery in 1916 and attended an officer training course at Cambridge. His First War service was in France and Italy, where he was awarded the MC.

Seconded to the Royal Engineers 1919–1921, Wade served in South Russia. Transferring to the Royal Signals in 1921, he was an instructor at the School of Signals 1924–1928. Married in 1926, he attended the Staff College, Camberley, 1933–1934. In India from 1936, he was a staff officer with Baluchistan and Western India Area 1936–1937 and a Deputy Assistant QMG, AHQ India, 1937–1940.

A staff officer at GHQ with the BEF in France 1939–1940, Wade, after serving on the staff of GHQ Home Forces 1940–1941, was made OBE and appointed Assistant Adjutant and QMG 2nd Indian Division in 1941. Deputy Adjutant General, India, 1942–1944, he commanded Madras Area 1944–1947.

Appointed CB in 1946 and GOC Malaya District 1947–1948, Wade returned to England to serve on special duties concerned with war crime sentencing at the War Office until his retirement from the army in 1950. He was Telecommunications Attaché at the British Embassy, Washington, 1951–1954, and Senior Planning Engineer, Independent Television Authority, 1960–1964. Chairman of the Royal Signals Institute 1957–1963, he was also Technical Consultant to the WRVS 1970–1974. Vice Chairman of the Dunkirk Veterans' Association 1962–1967, he was National Chairman 1967–1974.

WAINWRIGHT, Major General Charles Brian *(1893–1968)*, CB
Educated at Wellington and Oxford University, Wainwright volunteered in 1914, was commissioned in the Royal Artillery, but spent his First War service attached to the Royal Flying Corps.

Married in 1917 and an instructor at the School of Artillery, Larkhill, for many years, Wainwright, a major in 1932 and a colonel in 1939, commanded 183rd Brigade on Salisbury Plain from 1939 to 1940 and commanded a corps' medium artillery 1940–1941. CRA 51st Division in North Africa in 1942, he was CRA 79th Division (Hobart's 'Funnies') in 1943. Appointed GOC 54th Division in April 1943, he was transferred in scarcely a month to command 61st Division, a training formation under Home Forces.

Retired from the army in 1948, Wainwright became the Director of the Duck Ringing Research Station at Abberton Reservoir in Essex. A prime mover in the scientific study of migrating wildfowl, he lobbied tirelessly for the Abberton site to be declared a nature reserve and it was said that he individually ringed over 100,000 birds. A member of the council of the Wildfowl Trust, he lived near Colchester.

WAKELY, Major General Arthur Victor Trocke
(1886–1959), CB, DSO, MC
The son of a clergyman and educated at Campbell College, Belfast, and RMA, Woolwich, Wakely (born Robinson) was commissioned in the Royal Engineers in 1906. Married in 1913 and a captain in 1914, his First War service was in France, where he was twice mentioned in despatches and awarded the MC.

A brevet major in 1919 and assuming his wife's family name of Wakely by deed poll, he attended the Staff College, Camberley, 1923–1924 and was a major in 1924. Mentioned in despatches and admitted to the DSO after service in the Mohmand Expedition of 1934, he served on the staff of AHQ, India, 1933–1938 and was BGS Eastern Command, India, 1938–1940.

Promoted major general in October 1940 and appointed GOC 7th Indian Division, Wakely was GOC Lines of Communication, Burma, in 1942. Appointed CB after the retreat, he was GOC 102nd Lines of Communication,

India, 1942–1943 and Director of Movements, Bengal, from 1943 until his retirement from the army in 1945.

Thereafter Wakely and his wife settled in Co. Tipperary.

WALLACE, Major General Charles John *(1890–1943), CB, DSO, OBE, MC*
Of military family and educated at Charterhouse and RMC, Sandhurst, Wallace was commissioned in the Highland Light Infantry in 1910. His First War service was in France, where he was mentioned in despatches, awarded the MC and admitted to the DSO in 1918.

Made OBE after service with the North Russian Relief Force in 1919, Wallace attended the Staff College, Camberley, 1922–1923, was an instructor at Sandhurst 1929–1932, and served on the staff at the War Office 1932–1935. Commander of 3rd (Jhelum) Indian Infantry Brigade, India, in 1939, he was promoted major general in 1940 and appointed Director of Personnel Services at the War Office that year.

In ill-health, Wallace was appointed CB in 1941 and given command of East Central District at Dunstable. He died, presumably of cancer, in Luton hospital in December 1943.

WALSH, Major General George Peregrine *(1899–1972), CB, CBE, DSO*
Educated at Felsted and RMA, Woolwich, Walsh was commissioned in the Royal Artillery in 1918 and served in France that year.

Walsh served in Waziristan 1921–1924 and, after attending the Staff College, Camberley, 1934–1935, was mentioned in despatches while serving in Palestine 1936–1939. Clement Attlee, the leader of the Labour party from 1935, was a cousin.

An instructor at the Senior Officers' School, Sheerness, in 1940, Walsh served on the staff of Southern Command 1940–1941. On special employment in the Middle East in 1941, he served on the staff at GHQ, Cairo, 1941–1942 and was BGS XXX Corps 1942–1943. Leese, his corps commander, described him, at first as 'a very hardworking little man' (Ryder, 1987, 98), but soon came to value him as 'more the agent than the mentor of his chief' (Blaxland, 1979, 21). Known for his 'meticulously efficient' staff work, few beyond Leese took to this 'humourless gunner' (Carver, 1989, 128).

Promoted major general and made Chief of Staff to 8th Army after Montgomery's departure, Walsh campaigned with Leese in Italy and, married while on leave, accompanied his chief to India. There as Chief of Staff to the Allied Land Forces Commander, he became 'renowned for his tactlessness' (Hickey, 1998, 230) and broke the news to Slim that Leese was recommending his removal from command of XIV Army.

In poor health and not lingering long in India after Leese's departure, Walsh was GOC Southern Command 1948–1949 and Director of Weapons and Development at the War Office 1949–1952. Retired from the army in 1954, he was Assistant Controller of Munitions at the Ministry of Supply 1954–1960.

WARD, General Sir Alfred Dudley *(1905–1991)*, *GCB, KBE, DSO*
Educated at Wimborne Grammar School, Ward spent three years in the ranks
before going on to RMC, Sandhurst. Commissioned in the Dorset Regiment in
1929, he married in 1933 and, after attending the Staff College, Camberley,
1934–1935, transferred to the King's Regiment in 1937.

A major in 1939, Ward spent the first three years of the war with Home
Forces. BGS XI Corps in 1942, he commanded 231st Brigade, 1942–1943.
Posted to Italy and made commander of 17th Brigade in October 1943, his 'firm-
jaw[ed], calm and unostentatious manner made such an impression before the
Garigliano crossing and at Anzio' (Blaxland, 1979, 80) that he was made GOC
4th Division in April 1944. Appointed to the DSO that year, he was Chief of
Staff to Scobie, GOC British troops in Greece, 1944–1945, and was made CBE
and appointed CB at war's end.

Director of Military Operations at the War Office 1947–1948, Ward was Commandant of the Staff College, Camberley, 1948–1951. There he was described as
'a strong, gifted and articulate soldier' (Fraser, 2002, 280). GOC I Corps
1951–1952, he was knighted in 1953 and was Deputy CIGS 1953–1956. C-in-C
BAOR 1957–1959, he was C-in-C British Forces in the Near East 1960–1962.
Made Governor and C-in-C of Gibraltar in 1962, he re-married in 1963, helped
introduce Gibraltar's constitution and retired from the army with knighthood
enhanced in 1965.

Colonel of the King's Regiment 1947–1957 and Colonel Commandant of
REME 1958–1963, Ward was DL for Suffolk, 1968–1984.

WARD, Major General Ronald Ogier *(1886–1971)*, *DSO, OBE, MC*
Educated at Magdalen College School, Oxford University, and St
Bartholomew's Hospital, Ward served as a surgeon with the British Red Cross
in the Balkan War 1912–1913. A territorial officer, his First War service was in
France with the Honourable Artillery Company. He was mentioned in
despatches, awarded the MC and admitted to the DSO in 1919.

Married in 1928 and a consultant urological surgeon to a number of London
hospitals, Ward was Officer i/c Surgical Division of the BEF 1939–1940 and of
the Middle East Force 1940–1942. Consultant Surgeon to East Africa
Command 1942–1944, he retired that year.

Alongside his medical honours (FRCS, FRSM, etc.), Ward was sometime
President of the British Association of Urological Surgeons. He received an
honorary doctorate from Leeds University and lived in Sussex.

WARREN, Major General Dermot Frederick William
(1896–1945), *CBE, DSO*
Little is known about this Indian Army officer. Mobilized from the special
reserve in 1917 and gazetted into the 8th Punjab Regiment (Indian Army) that
year, Warren was a captain in 1920.

An instructor at the Army School of Education, India, in 1927 and a staff
officer at AHQ, India, 1927–1931, Warren was a pupil of Slim during his term

as an instructor at Camberley 1933–1934. He was a staff officer with 14th Indian Division in 1942 and commanded 161st Indian Brigade in Burma 1943–1944. Admitted to the DSO after the Kohima battle, Slim, who 'always found it stimulating doing business with him' (Slim, 1999, 439), appointed him GOC 5th Indian Division in September 1944, as a replacement for Evans who was sick.

Successful in maintaining the pursuit of the Japanese towards the Chindwin, Warren was killed in an aircrash in February 1945.

WASON, Lieutenant General Sydney Rigby *(1887–1969), CB, MC*
Born in Scotland and educated at Wellington and RMA, Woolwich, Wason was commissioned in the Royal Artillery in 1907. A captain in 1914, his First War service was in France, Gallipoli, Egypt and in Mesopotamia. Mentioned in despatches, he was awarded the MC (and two bars).

Married in 1920 and an instructor in gunnery at Larkhill 1922–1923, Wason attended the Staff College Camberley, 1924–1925. A staff officer at the School of Artillery 1926–1929, he served on the staff of Western Command 1929–1930. Posted to India in 1933, he served for two years on the staff at AHQ and returned to Western Command as CRA in 1936. Promoted major general, he was Commandant of the School of Artillery 1938–1939.

Appointed Major General Royal Artillery of the BEF at war's outset, Wason was mentioned in despatches during the campaign in France and Flanders. Made commander of 1st Anti-Aircraft Corps after Dunkirk and given to making 'gloomy prophecies' (Seton-Watson, 1993, 44), he retired from the army as a lieutenant general in 1942.

Appointed CB, and employed by the BBC as military correspondent for their European service 1943–1946, Wason lived in Hampshire.

WATERHOUSE, Major General George Guy *(1886–1975), CB, MC*
Educated at Cheltenham and RMA, Woolwich, Waterhouse was commissioned in the Royal Engineers in 1905. Employed on survey work in Nigeria 1910–1913, his First War service was in France, where he was wounded, mentioned in despatches and awarded the MC, and in Salonika.

Graduating from the Staff College, Camberley, in 1920, Waterhouse, whose mother was French, taught English at the Ecole Superiéure de Guerre in Paris 1922–1923. Married, he attended the Royal Naval Staff College, Greenwich, in 1928, and commanded a training battalion RE 1930–1931. Military Attaché at the Paris Embassy 1931–1932, he re-married after the death of his first wife. Inspector of Staff Duties at the British Military Mission in Iraq 1934–1937, he was promoted major general in 1938 and appointed Inspector General of the British Advisory Military Mission to the Iraq Army 1938–1941.

Besieged in the embassy during the Raschid Ali revolt and posted home after, Waterhouse retired from the army. Appointed CB, he was re-employed to command North-West District 1941–1944. He was Deputy Commissioner, British Red Cross, HQ South-East Asia Command in 1945.

WATSON, General Sir Daril Gerard *(1888–1967), GCB, CBE, MC*
Born near Glasgow and educated at the Mercers' School, Watson joined the Royal Mail Steam Packet Company as a clerk accountant. Enlisting with the Royal Fusiliers (10th Battalion) in 1914, he served in France and was commissioned in the Highland Light Infantry in 1915. Married in 1917, he was awarded the MC the same year.

After attending the Staff College, Camberley, 1924–1925, Watson transferred to the Duke of Cornwall's Light Infantry in 1928. A brevet lieutenant colonel in 1931, he commanded the 1st Battalion DCLI 1934–1936 and was Commandant of the Senior Officers' School, Belgaum, India, 1937–1939.

Appointed BGS Eastern Command at war's beginning, Watson was BGS III Corps in France with the BEF in 1940. Promoted major general he was appointed GOC 2nd Division in September 1940. Director of Staff Duties at the War Office 1941–1942, he was appointed CB and made Assistant CIGS in 1942. Ever 'quiet, humorous and extremely efficient' (Smart (ed.), 2001, 112), he was Deputy Adjutant General 1942–1944 and GOC-in-C Western Command 1944–1946.

Knighted in 1945, Watson was Adjutant General to the Forces from 1946 until his retirement from the army in 1947. With knighthood enhanced, he was a member of the Railway Executive 1949–1953 and Chief of General Services, British Transport Commission, 1953–1954. Briefly Secretary General to the BTC in 1955, he retired to live in Sussex.

WATSON, Major General Gilbert France *(1895–1976), CB, DSO, OBE*
Educated at Berkhampstead, Watson was commissioned in the Royal Engineers in 1915. His First War service was in France, where he was twice mentioned in despatches and admitted to the DSO in 1915.

Married in 1917, Watson transferred to the Royal Welch Fusiliers in 1921. He graduated from the Staff College, Quetta, in 1932 and was Brigade Major Canal Brigade, Egypt, 1934–1936. A brevet major in 1936, he was Deputy Assistant Adjutant General at the War Office 1937–1939 and AAG at the War Office 1939–1940.

Awarded the OBE and made commander of 183rd Brigade in 1940, Watson was an Area Commander under Home Forces 1940–1942 and was Deputy Director of Organization at the War Office 1942–1943. Promoted major general, he was Director of Manpower Planning at the War Office from 1943 until his retirement from the army in 1946.

Appointed CB, Watson was Principal Regional Officer, Ministry of Health, for the South-West Region, 1946–1960. A widower in 1962, and re-married in 1964, he lived in Clevedon.

WATSON, Major General Norman Vyvyan *(1898–1974), CB, OBE*
Commissioned in the Royal Artillery in 1915, Watson's First War service was in France, where he was mentioned in despatches.

Watson served in operations in Iraq 1919–1920, married in 1927 and was

Adjutant Auxiliary Services, India, 1928–1931, A student at the Staff College, Quetta, 1933–1934, he served continually on the staff at the War Office for the next five years.

A lieutenant colonel in 1939 and awarded the OBE in 1940, Watson was Deputy Director of Staff Duties at the War Office 1941–1943. Director of Staff Duties, GHQ, India, 1943–1947, he was A/Q Western Command 1947–1949 and Deputy QMG at the War Office from 1949 until his retirement from the army in 1952.

Living in Essex, Watson was General Manager of the Army Kinema Corporation 1952–1957 and Managing Director 1957–1967. He re-married in 1962.

WAVELL, Field Marshal Archibald Percival.
1st Earl, Viscount Wavell of Cyrenaica and Winchester, and Viscount Keren of Eritrea and Winchester (1883–1950), GCB, GCSI, GCIE, CMG, MC
Born in Colchester of military family and educated at Winchester and RMC, Sandhurst, Wavell was commissioned in the Black Watch in 1901, in time to see service in the South African War. In India from 1903, he graduated from the Staff College, Camberley, in 1910, spent a year with the Russian army and, a captain in 1914, was serving on the staff at the War Office when war was declared.

Wavell's First War service was varied. In France in 1915, he lost his left eye, married and was awarded the MC. He later served in South Russia and Palestine. There he came to admire Allenby, the C-in-C of the Egyptian Expeditionary Force, and later wrote his biography, together with several studies of the Palestine campaign. After a short spell with the Supreme Allied War Council at Versailles, he returned to Palestine as Brigadier General, General Staff, XX Corps.

Returning to England in 1920, Wavell commanded a company of the 2nd Battalion, Black Watch, with the British Rhine Army. A colonel in 1921, he was an Assistant Adjutant General at the War Office 1921–1923. A staff officer with the Directorate of Military Operations at the War Office 1923–1926, he spent several months on half-pay 'supplement[ing] his income by writing on military subjects' (Heathcote, 1999, 289). After serving on the staff of 3rd Division on Salisbury Plain, he commanded 6th Infantry Brigade at Aldershot 1930–1934 After a further spell on half-pay, he was promoted major general and appointed to command 2nd Division in 1935.

Stocky, known to be clever, and tough-looking, though already renowned for his taciturnity, Wavell had built up a reputation in the army as 'the most inspiring tactical leader we had' (Marshall-Cornwall, 1984, 100), and was 'recognized as an exceptional trainer of troops' (DNB). Appointed to command British troops in Palestine and Transjordan in 1937, when the Arab rebellion was at its height, he showed some interest in unconventional counter-terrorist measures, in particular Wingate's Special Night Squads, but came to regard peacekeeping between Arabs and Jews as 'a very unsatisfactory and intangible business' (Baynes, 1989–1950). Promoted lieutenant general and made C-in-C Southern Command in April 1938, he delivered the Lees-Knowles lecture on Military History at Cambridge and was sent to Cairo in June 1939 as the newly-installed GOC-in-C Middle East.

With his post up-graded to C-in-C Middle East Command in January 1940, Wavell had a huge area to defend and, when Italy entered the war in June 1940, the forces at his disposal were vastly outnumbered in both East and North Africa. Accepting the loss of British Somaliland with too much equanimity for Churchill's liking, he nevertheless retained an aggressive instinct and proved adept at moving forces from one front to another. Having stalled Italian advances, he went on to win some stunning victories; first in the Western Desert, where O'Connor's 'five day raid' led to the virtual destruction of the Italian Tenth Army in Cyrenaica, and then in Ethiopia and Eritrea, where forces under Cunningham and Platt forced the Italians to capitulate.

Famous throughout the world, Wavell and his 30,000 had little time to rest on their laurels. Moreover, in supporting, however reluctantly, the dispatch to Greece of a large contingent of British and Dominion troops, he neither helped the Greek cause nor insured himself against a German-led counter-attack in North Africa. Indeed, he was never again able to display that sureness of touch he had so ably demonstrated in the winter of 1940–1941. It was as though luck, so fabulously with him before, turned suddenly and irrevocably against him. Said to 'exude serenity' (Ranfurly, 1998, 90), the trouble he knew so well came back to stare him in the face.

With Rommel seizing the initiative in the Western Desert, British forces were bundled back to the Egyptian frontier and three generals went into the bag as prisoners. While evacuation from Greece was carried out successfully, the battle for Crete developed into a costly series of failures and mishap. Meanwhile Wavell, much against his will, was obliged by Churchill to send forces into Iraq and Syria, and, amidst all these distractions, 'too major to be dismissed as mere sideshows' (Fergusson in Carver (ed.), 1976, 222), he had to plan his own offensive in the desert. Badgered by Churchill, and with his Western Desert force substantially reinforced, he launched Operation BATTLEAXE, the object being to relieve Tobruk and destroy Rommel's Afrika Korps. As neither objective was achieved, he was duly sacked in June 1941. Denied the period of leave he asked for and, despite Dill's belief that his 'taciturnity would be a great handicap in India' (Dill, 2nd acc. 11, LHCMA), he swapped places with Auchinleck and travelled by air to sit 'under the pagoda tree' as C-in-C (Beckett, in Keegan (ed.), 1991, 80).

Not having been in India for thirty years, Wavell expressed himself appalled at the state of the sub-continent's preparedness for war. Ever-energetic he travelled throughout South-East Asia on long tours of inspection. The best that can be said of him is that he was not caught by strategic surprise when the Japanese launched their war in December 1941. Like others, though, he was unable to respond tactically to the speed and fury of enemy attacks. Given to underestimate the Japanese soldier and bemoaning his own troops' lack of aggressiveness, his six-week tenure of the American- British -Dutch -Australian (ABDA) supreme command was an irrelevance. Guilty, perhaps, of reinforcing failure, when he despatched the 18th Division to Singapore only days before the surrender, his insistence on defending 'bits of Burma' as far forward as possible led to much subsequent criticism.

Yet to Wavell's admirers, and there were many, the manner in which he greeted every new disaster with the same quiet stoicism was the mark of the man's greatness. Others saw signs of deterioration in his 'increased taciturnity, increased ruggedness, and . . . refusal to admit opinions which did not agree with his own' (Smyth, 1957, 121). Beginning preparations for the ill-fated Arakan counter-offensive as early as September 1942, he also gave Wingate a relatively free hand in forming and training the long-range penetration columns that, better known as the Chindits, were to become famous.

Having recommended himself for promotion to field marshal, Wavell was summoned to London for consultation in April 1943. Accompanying Churchill to Washington on the *Queen Mary*, he was so incensed by Churchill's criticisms of the Burma campaign that he wrote out but did not send a letter of resignation. Returning to London, he was told of his supersession by Mountbatten and, having been considered for the Australian Governor-Generalship, was raised to the peerage and appointed Viceroy and Governor-General of India.

Hanging around London that summer, at times easily bored and socially inept, and on other occasions 'gentle, affectionate and vague' (Rhodes James (ed.), 1984, 439), Wavell was as unaware that he was being fêted by Churchill's critics as he was unconscious that the role marked out for him was to keep India quiet for the duration of the war. He introduced food rationing during the Bengal famine, released Gandhi from prison and tried, 'with limitless patience' (Fergusson in Carver (ed.), 1976, 228), to maintain British authority.

Told by Attlee that he was being replaced by Mountbatten in February 1947, Wavell was granted the customary advancement of one rank in the peerage and returned home. He received honorary degrees from London, Oxford, Cambridge and Aberdeen universities, wrote a number of books and had a success with an anthology the poetry he had memorized. He was High Steward of Colchester and Colonel of the Black Watch. He died of cancer in May 1950 and, though the significance of Churchill not troubling to attend his funeral has often been noted, his own reputation as a 'quiet colossus' of a man, 'uncommunicative, intelligent, imperturbable and full of inward imagination' (Fraser, 1999, 114), probably dates from that moment. He may have been unlucky in that his character was unsuited to the highest level of command as it was exercised in Britain during the war years. But therein, perhaps, lies his enduring attractiveness. He 'never failed to impress and puzzle slightly everyone who met him' (Moorehead, 1940, 132). His famed 'immense capacity to take hard knocks' (Bond (ed.), 1975, 95), coupled with his refusal to pander to his political bosses, represents the historical niche occupied by this singularly enigmatic and yet, for all his gifts, not very successful military commander.

WEEKS, Lieutenant General Ronald Morce,
1st Baron (1890–1960), KCB, CBE, DSO, MC
Born in Durham and educated at Charterhouse and Cambridge University (where he captained the university football XI), Weeks joined Pilkington Brothers in 1912. Volunteering in 1914, he served in France, was commissioned in the Prince of Wales Volunteers and later transferred to the Rifle Brigade. Thrice mentioned in despatches, he was awarded the MC and admitted to the DSO.

A brevet major in 1918, Weeks left the army in 1919 and rejoined Pilkington Brothers. First married in 1922, he was a director of the company in 1926. As a territorial officer, he re-married in 1932 and commanded the 5th Battalion of the Lancashire Regiment (TA) 1934–1938. Chairman of Pilkingtons in 1939, he was also Chief of Staff to 66th Division.

BGS Home Forces in 1940, 'Ronnie' Weeks was promoted major general in 1941 and appointed Director General of Army Equipment. Made Deputy CIGS in 1942, he was 'industrious and decisive' (Danchev & Todman, 2002, xliii). As a member of the Army Council, he reached 'a unique position for a citizen soldier' (DNB). Knighted in 1943, Brooke expressed himself as being 'unbelievably fortunate' in having 'a man of his outstanding ability' beside him (Bryant, 1965, 39). Made Deputy Military Governor and Chief of Staff of the British occupied zone of Germany in 1945, he helped set up the Allied Control Commission but, almost immediately, fell ill and retired from the army.

Returning to the Pilkington Board and Honorary Colonel of 596 Light Anti-Aircraft (South Lancashire) Regiment 1946–1955, Weeks held a number of directorships, including that of the Vickers Group, and was chairman of various public bodies. A Commander of the Legion of Merit (USA), he sought to increase the prestige of technical education and received honorary doctorates from Leeds, Sheffield and Birmingham universities. He was created a baron in 1956.

WEIR, Major General Sir Stephen Cyril Ettrick
(1905–1969), KBE, CB, DSO (and bar)
A New Zealander, educated at Otago Boys' High School, Dunedin, Weir was a trooper with the 6th New Zealand Mounted Rifles 1923–1925. A cadet at RMA, Woolwich, 1926–1927, he was commissioned in the Royal Artillery and served with the British army for the next eight years.

Returning to New Zealand, Weir married in 1936 and commanded 6th New Zealand Field Regiment 1940–1941. He was CRA 2nd New Zealand Division 1941–1944. Admitted to the DSO during operations in Cyrenaica in 1941, a bar was added after El Alamein. Temporary o/c 2nd New Zealand Division in Italy September-October 1944, he was appointed GOC 46th Division in November. As 'General Steve' he held the rare distinction for a New Zealander of commanding an all-British formation during the final phases of the Italian campaign.

Appointed CB in 1945, Weir commanded the Southern Military District of

New Zealand in 1948 and was an instructor at the Imperial Defence College in 1950. QMG for the New Zealand Army 1952–1955, he was CGS New Zealand Army 1955–1960. Knighted, he was New Zealand's ambassador to Thailand 1961–1967.

WELD, Major General Charles Joseph *(1893–1962), CIE, MC*
Educated at RMC, Sandhurst, and commissioned in the Indian Army in 1912, Weld was gazetted into the 13th Frontier Force Rifles in 1913. His First War service was with the Indian Expeditionary Force in France, where he was awarded the MC, and later in India.

A graduate of the Staff College, Quetta, in 1928, Weld married in 1929 and was Deputy Assistant QMG, AHQ India, 1930–1931. Assistant Military Secretary, AHQ India, 1931–1933, he was a lieutenant colonel in 1936. Thrice mentioned in despatches during operations on the North-West Frontier 1936–1938, he was a staff officer in Waziristan 1938–1939.

A brigadier in 1940, Weld commanded a brigade in the Middle East in 1941 and, promoted major general, was GOC Cyprus in 1942. Briefly GOC XXV Corps in Iraq in 1942, he returned to India to command the Meerut District in 1943. Commander of the Rawalpindi area 1943–1945, he was Indian Army Liaison Officer with the India Office in London 1945–1946.

Retired in 1947, Weld settled in his native Hampshire. He commanded a Home Guard Battalion 1952–1957.

WEMYSS, General Sir Henry Colville Barclay
(1891–1959), KCB, KBE, DSO, MC
Educated at Bedford School and RMA, Woolwich, Wemyss was commissioned in the Royal Engineers in 1910. His First War service was in France, Gallipoli, Serbia and Palestine. Wounded, five times mentioned in despatches, admitted to the DSO and awarded the MC, he was Allenby's signals officer in Palestine.

Married in 1919, Wemyss transferred to the Royal Corps of Signals in 1920. He attended the Staff College, Camberley, 1923–1924 and, after three years serving on the staff at the War Office, was an instructor at the School of Signals 1929–1931. A lieutenant colonel in 1933, he was an Assistant Adjutant General at the War Office 1935–1937. After attending the Imperial Defence College in 1938, he was briefly Director of Recruiting and Organization, before being appointed Director of Mobilization at the War Office in 1939.

Adjutant General to the Forces 1940–1941, Wemyss was head of the British Army Mission to Washington until, replaced by Dill in December 1941, he was recalled home. Knighted and promoted lieutenant general, he was Military Secretary to the Secretary of State for War from 1942 until his retirement from the army in 1946.

Colonel Commandant of the Royal Corps of Signals 1944–1948, Wemyss was Director of the Brewers' Society 1947–1957 and was sometime President of the revived Bedford School Holborn Boys' Club.

WEST, Major General Clement Arthur *(1892–1972), CB, DSO, MC*
Born in India, the son of a railway official, West was educated at King's School, Canterbury, and RMA, Woolwich. Commissioned in the Royal Engineers in 1912, his First War service was in France, where he was twice mentioned in despatches and awarded the MC.

A captain in 1917 and an assistant instructor at the School of Military Engineering, Chatham, 1919–1922, West served on the staff at the War Office 1923–1926. After attending the Staff College, Camberley, 1927–1928, he was posted to India as a brigade major in 1930.

Admitted to the DSO in 1932, after service on the North-West Frontier, he served on the staff at AHQ, India, 1932–1934. Deputy Assistant Military Secretary at the War Office 1934–1936, he attended the Imperial Defence College that year and was Deputy Military Secretary and Assistant Secretary to the Selection Board at the War Office 1938–1939.

Military Secretary to the BEF in France in 1939, West was a BGS with Home Forces 1940–1941. BGS to the British Delegation to the New Zealand government 1941–1942, he commanded a district 1942–1943 and was Major General, General Staff, attached to the COSSAC planning team 1943–1944 and SHAEF 1944–1945.

Appointed CB in 1944, despite being labelled 'a dud' by Montgomery (Hamilton, 1986, 364), West was Major General i/c Administration, Southern Command, from 1945 until his retirement from the army in 1947. Thereafter he lived in Sussex, and was General Secretary of the United Kingdom Beneficent Association 1947–1957.

WESTROPP, Major General Victor John Eric *(1897–1974), CB, CBE*
Educated at Bradfield and RMA, Woolwich, Westropp was commissioned in the Royal Engineers in 1916. His First War service was in France.

Transferring to the Royal Corps of Signals in 1921, Westropp married in 1923 and was an instructor at Woolwich 1926–1929. Posted to India in 1930, he served on the North- West Frontier and attended the Staff College, Quetta, 1932–1933. After a further spell of duty on the North-West Frontier, he served in Palestine in 1936 and again from 1938 to 1939, where, as Deputy Assistant QMG to 8th Division, he was mentioned in despatches.

A lieutenant colonel in 1939, Westropp served on the staff at the War Office 1940–1941, latterly as Assistant Adjutant General. Deputy Director of Personnel Services, 1941–1942, he was Deputy Adjutant General to Allied Forces in the Middle East 1942–1943 and Deputy Adjutant General, India, in 1944.

Deputy Chief of Staff to the Allied Control Commission of Germany 1945–1947, Westropp was appointed CB after his term as President of the War Crimes Court at Ravensbruck. Appointed UK Commissioner, Military Security Board, CCG, in 1947, he retired from the army in 1951.

WETHERALL, Lieutenant General Sir Harry Edward de Robillard
(1889–1979), KBE, CB, DSO, MC

Of military family and commissioned in the Gloucester Regiment in 1909, Wetherall's First War service was in France, where he was wounded, mentioned in despatches, awarded the MC and admitted to the DSO.

Married in 1923 and a major in 1927, Wetherall was Chief Staff Officer for weapons training, Scottish Command, 1930–1934. Commander of the 1st Battalion York and Lancaster Regiment 1936–1938, he commanded 19th Infantry Brigade 1938–1940.

GOC 11th African Division in Abyssinia 1940–1941 and GOC East Africa in 1941, Wetherall was GOC Ceylon (Sri Lanka) 1943–1945. He was C-in-C Ceylon from 1945 until his retirement from the army in 1946.

Knighted in 1946 and Colonel of the Gloucestershire Regiment 1947–1954, Wetherall lived in Somerset.

WHISTLER, General Sir Lashmer Gordon
(1898–1963), GCB, KBE, DSO (and 2 bars)

Born in India of military family and educated at Harrow and RMC, Sandhurst, Whistler was commissioned in the Royal Sussex Regiment in 1917. His First War service was in France, where he was wounded and taken prisoner. After serving with the North Russian Relief Force in 1919 he was known thereafter as 'Bolo'.

A regimental officer serving in Germany and India, Whistler was twelve years a lieutenant. Married in 1926, he was Adjutant to the 5th Battalion (TA) of his regiment 1929–1933, and, a captain in 1932, to the 2nd Battalion in India and Palestine 1933–1937. A major in 1938, he commanded the regimental depot at Chichester at war's outbreak.

Commanding the 4th Battalion Royal Sussex Regiment in France with the BEF in 1940, Whistler earned the rare distinction of being twice evacuated from Dunkirk (Smyth, 1967, 80). Admitted to the DSO, he commanded successively 132nd and 131st Brigades in North Africa 1942–1943 and, with a bar added to his DSO, commanded 160th Brigade in Italy. Said to be 'unflappable, very determined, but with a great sense of humour' (Roberts, 1987, 128), and favoured by Montgomery, who regarded him as 'the finest type of British soldier' (Smyth, 1967, 16), he was promoted major general and appointed GOC 3rd Division in June 1944. The second bar to his DSO was added after the campaign in North-West Europe which he saw through to the end.

Appointed CB in 1945 and GOC British troops in Palestine 1946–1947, Whistler served briefly in India, before being made GOC Sudan Defence Corps in 1948. Commander of Northumbria District 1950–1951, he was knighted in 1952 and made GOC West African Command. Appointed GOC-in-C Western Command in 1953, he retired from the army with knighthood enhanced in 1957.

A DL for Sussex in 1957 and Vice-President of the National Small Bore Rifle Association from 1958, 'Bolo' Whistler was Colonel of the Royal Sussex Regiment before dying of cancer aged 67.

WHITAKER, Major General Sir John Albert Charles,
2nd Bt. (1897–1957), CB, CBE
Educated at Eton and RMC, Sandhurst, Whitaker was commissioned in the Coldstream Guards in 1915. His First War service was in France, where he was wounded.

Married in 1923, 'Jack' Whitaker was a staff officer at the Small Arms School, Hythe, 1924–1926, and attended the Staff College, Camberley, 1926–1927. He was Deputy Assistant Adjutant and QMG London District 1932–1933 and served on the staff of Eastern Command 1933–1936. He commanded the 3rd Battalion Coldstream Guards 1936–1938 and was appointed to command the regiment and regimental district in the spring of 1938.

In command of 7th Guards Brigade in France with the BEF 1939–1940, Whitaker was a BGS with Home Forces 1940–1942 and, after a brief period as Chief of Staff, Western Command, was Director of Military Training at the War Office 1942–1945. Ornithologically minded, he often accompanied Brooke on bird-watching trips. He was also, apparently, a 'brilliant shot'.

Appointed CB in 1944, Whitaker succeeded his father in 1945 and retired from the army the following year. Sometime Chairman of the Nottinghamshire TA and AF Association, he farmed land in Nottinghamshire and Perthshire. He was High Sheriff of Nottinghamshire 1950–1951 and Lord High Steward of Retford in 1952.

WHITCOMBE, Major General Philip Sidney *(1893–1989), CB, OBE*
The son of the Bishop of Colchester, Whitcombe was educated at Winchester and was a reserve officer with the Durham Light Infantry in 1914. Transferring to the Army Service Corps, his First War service was in France.

Married in 1919, Whitcombe, a keen games player, played cricket for Essex and the army in the early 1920s. He attended the Staff College, Camberley, 1925–1926, served in India 1928–1929 and was Deputy Assistant Adjutant General, Northern Command, 1934–1936. A staff officer at the War Office 1936–1938, he was a lieutenant colonel in 1939.

Mentioned in despatches after the campaign in France and Flanders, in which he served as Deputy Assistant of Supplies and Transport with the BEF, Whitcombe was Assistant Adjutant and QMG in Gibraltar 1940–1941 and Brigadier i/c Administration 1941–1942. Deputy Adjutant and QMG with British troops in Northern Ireland 1942–1943, he was Major General i/c Administration Eastern Command 1943–1947.

Appointed CB in 1944 and retired from the army in 1947, Whitcombe, a member of the MCC, was a JP in Wiltshire from 1948.

WHITE, Major General Cecil Meadows Frith
(1897–1985), CB, CBE, DSO
Educated at Eton and RMA, Woolwich, White was commissioned in the Royal Field Artillery in 1915. His First War service was in Egypt, Serbia, Greece and in Palestine, where he was mentioned in despatches.

Transferring to the Royal Signals in 1925 and married the same year, 'Slap' White was Brigade Major at the Signals Training Centre 1934–1936. A lieutenant colonel in 1939, he was Chief Signal Officer with 4th Indian Division in the western desert and Abyssinia. Admitted to the DSO in 1940, he was CSO East African Command in 1941 and CSO 8th Army in North Africa and Italy 1941–1944. In that role he was said to be 'efficient, imperturbable and charming' (Richardson, 1985, 130). CSO 21st Army Group, North-West Europe 1944–1945, he 'somehow kept a smiling face' whatever the burdens of his job (de Guingand, 1947, 462).

Appointed CB in 1945, White was CSO Middle East Land Forces 1945–1949 and GOC Catterick District from 1949 until his retirement from the army in 1951. He was Deputy Controller for Civil Defence, Southdown District, in 1958, Civil Defence Officer for Brighton 1960–1965 and finally retired to live in Somerset.

WHITEFOORD, Major General Philip Geoffrey *(1894–1975), OBE, MC*
The son of a clergyman and educated in Stuttgart and at Leatherhead, Whitefoord was a reserve officer with the Lincolnshire Regiment in 1912. Commissioned in the Royal Artillery in 1914, his First War service was in France, where he was twice mentioned in despatches and awarded the MC.

A staff officer at the War Office 1927–1929 and with Southern Command 1929–1931, Whitefoord married in 1930, the same year as he qualified as a barrister-at-law. He attended the Staff College, Camberley, 1934–1935, was a brevet lieutenant colonel in 1935 and, after attending the Imperial Defence College in 1938, served as Chief Staff Officer (Intelligence) at the BEF's GHQ in France 1939–1940.

Awarded the OBE after Dunkirk, 'Jock' Whitefoord served on the staff of 5th Division and was Deputy Director of Military Intelligence at the War Office in 1941. BGS VIII Corps in 1942, he was Major General (Intelligence) with the COSSAC planning staff in 1943. BGS, GHQ, West Africa in 1944, he complained bitterly about his lot, claimed he did 'the minimum of useful work a day' and threatened to appeal to the King to 'get me out of this dreadful place' (Kennedy, 4/3, LHCMA). He was BGS Scottish Command and Chief of Staff, Allied Forces in Norway in 1945.

Retired from the army in 1945, Whitefoord stood unsuccessfully as the Conservative candidate for Lowestoft in 1950 and was a West Suffolk Country Councillor for many years. DL for Suffolk in 1962, he lived the last six years of his life a widower.

WHITELEY, General Sir John Francis Martin *(1896–1970), GBE, KCB, MC*
Educated at Blundell's and RMA, Woolwich, Whiteley was commissioned in the Royal Engineers in 1915. His First War service was in the Balkans and the Middle East, where he was mentioned in despatches and awarded the MC.

After attending the Staff College, Camberley, 1927–1928, 'Jock' Whiteley

332

married in 1929 and was Deputy Assistant Adjutant General, India, 1932–1934. He served on the staff at the War Office 1932–1934.

Made BGS Middle East Command in 1940, Whiteley was Deputy Director of Military Operations under Wavell and Auchinleck, but, after the May 1942 Gazala battles, was criticized by Auchinleck as being 'not cut out for high staff appointments in a field formation'. Pushed aside by the 'dangerous super-numerary' Dorman Smith in July (Richardson, 1985, 103), he was sacked by Montgomery in September on the grounds that he was 'no good' (Dill, 2nd acc. 6/2/13, LHCMA). Transferred to Eisenhower's supreme headquarters in Algiers as Deputy Chief of Staff, he returned with him to Europe and, as Major General, was DCS Intelligence and later DCS Planning and Operations with SHAEF. He became, to Eisenhower, one of his 'constant advisers . . . . in whom [he] reposed his greatest confidence' (Eisenhower, 1948, 259).

After a spell as an instructor at the Imperial Defence College in 1946, Whiteley was Commandant of the National Defence College and Canadian Army Staff College in Canada 1947–1949 and was Deputy CIGS 1949–1953. Knighted in 1950, he was Chairman of the British Joint Services Mission in Washington from 1953 until he retired in 1956.

WHITFIELD, Major General John Yeldham
(1899–1971), CB, DSO (and bar),OBE

The son of a clergyman and educated at Monmouth School and RMC, Sandhurst, Whitfield was commissioned in the Queen's (West Surrey) Regiment in 1918. Employed with the Royal West African Frontier Force 1924–1930, he attended the Staff College, Camberley, 1932–1933.

Married in 1936 and a brigade major with the King's African Rifles 1937–1939, Whitfield commanded the skeleton 40th Division in the Middle East 1942–1943 and, reverting to command 2nd/5th Battalion of his regiment in Tunisia, was admitted to the DSO. Made commander of 15th Infantry Brigade in Italy, he served at Salerno and had a bar added to his DSO after action on the Anzio beachhead. In July 1944 he was appointed GOC 56th Division. Remarkably he had completed the rise from battalion to divisional command within the space of six months. Not given to hide his religious convictions, he 'made impact by his intensity and sincerity' (Blaxland, 1979, 167).

Appointed CB in 1945 and GOC 50th Division and Northumbrian District 1946–1948, Whitfield was Chief of Staff Northern Command 1948–1951 and, from 1952 until his retirement in 1955, was Inspector of Recruiting at the War Office. Colonel of the Queen's Royal Regiment 1954–1959, blindness marred his final years.

WHITTAKER, Major General Robert Frederick Edward
(1894–1967), CB, CBE

Educated at Ardingly College, Whittaker joined the Territorial Army via his school OTC. Commissioned in the Royal Artillery in 1914, his First War service was in France.

Married in 1919, 'Whit' Whittaker, a keen rugby player, served in numerous domestic and overseas postings. A lieutenant colonel in 1938, he left the army to pursue a career with Lloyds Bank that year, but was immediately re-employed as a brigadier with the Territorial Army. Commander of 26th (London) Anti-Aircraft Group 1938–1939 and a Fellow of the Institute of Bankers in 1940, he was GOC 1st Anti-Aircraft Division 1941–1942.

General Manager (Administration), Lloyds Bank 1952–1957, sometime President of the Kent RFU and member of the RFU Committee, Whittaker re-married in 1956 and lived in London. He died after a long illness.

WHITTY, Major General Henry Martin *(1896–1961), CB, OBE*

Of military family and educated at St George's College, Woburn, and RMC, Sandhurst, Whitty was commissioned in the Army Service Corps in 1914. His First War service was in France, where he was mentioned in despatches.

An instructor at the RASC Training Centre 1934–1937 and Deputy Director of Supplies and Transport, Southern Command, 1937–1939, Whitty was ADST at the War Office 1940–1941. He was Deputy Director of Supplies 1941–1942. A major general in 1944, he was Director of Supplies and Transport, Central Mediterranean Force, in 1944 and DST Middle East Land Forces in 1946.

Appointed CB in 1945 and Inspector of the RAOC from 1948 until his retire-ment from the army in 1951, Whitty was briefly Services Adviser to the Ministry of Food. He was Colonel Commandant of the RASC ,1955–1959 and died after a long illness at his home in Sussex.

WILLANS, Major General Harry *(1892–1943), CB, CBE, DSO, MC*

Born in Bedford and educated at Aldenham School, Willans trained as a solicitor before volunteering for service with the Bedfordshire Regiment in 1914. Commissioned in 1915, he served in France, was twice mentioned in despatches, was awarded the MC and admitted to the DSO in 1918.

Married in 1917, Willans left the army in 1919 and was general manager of the Association for Promoting the General Welfare of the Blind. Drawn into the TA, he served again with the Artists Rifles and was re-commissioned in the Bedfordshire Regiment in 1932. Thereafter he commanded a variety of TA units and formations: the Artists Rifles 1933–1938, 2nd (London) Infantry Brigade 1938–1939, and, in June 1940, he was appointed GOC 2nd (London) Division.

The appointment – a rarity for a territorial officer to command a field formation in wartime – was short-lived. In November 1940 Willans was appointed Director General of Army Welfare and Education at the War Office. Under his auspices a system for coping with the welfare and educational needs of a vast conscript army was devised. The Army Bureau of Current Affairs (ABCA) was launched and a series of winter educational programmes inaugurated.

In December 1942 Willans embarked on an extended tour of North Africa. He was killed in February 1943 when the aircraft carrying him from Tobruk crashed on take-off. He left a widow and two daughters.

WILLCOX, Lieutenant General Sir Henry Beresford Dennitts
(1889–1968), KCIE, CB, DSO, MC
Born and brought up in New Zealand, Willcox was commissioned in the Sherwood Foresters in 1912. His First War service was in France and Palestine. Twice wounded, five times mentioned in despatches and awarded the MC, he was admitted to the DSO in 1918.

Married in 1919, Willcox transferred to the East Lancashire Regiment and attended the Staff College, Camberley, 1925–1926. He attended the Imperial Defence College in 1933 and commanded the 1st Battalion East Lancashire Regiment in England and in Palestine 1934–1937. An instructor at the Staff College, Quetta, 1937–1938, he commanded, successively, 15th and 13th Brigades 1938–1939.

Promoted major general at war's beginning, 'Ulysses' Willcox was Inspector of Infantry at the War Office 1939–1940. Appointed GOC 42nd (East Lancashire) Division in June 1941, he was appointed to command I Corps in April 1941. Judged by Brooke to be 'incapable of handling the forces under [his] command' (Danchev & Todman, 2001, 190), he was posted to India and made GOC-in-C of Central Command in 1942. Director of the Indian Army Reorganization Committee in 1944, he was knighted and retired from the army in 1946.

WILLIAMS, Major General Aubrey Ellis
(1888–1977), CBE, DSO (and bar), MC
Educated at Monmouth Grammar School and RMC, Sandhurst, Williams was commissioned in the South Wales Borderers in 1907. A captain in 1914, his First War service was in France, Gallipoli, Egypt and Palestine. He was twice wounded, five times mentioned in despatches, awarded the MC and admitted to the DSO in 1918.

Married in 1922, Williams graduated from the Staff College, Quetta, in 1923 and served on the staff of Western Command, India, 1926–1928. Attached to the staff of the 52nd (Lowland) Division 1929–1931, he was Assistant Military Secretary, India, 1932–1933 and commanded the 1st Battalion South Wales Borderers 1934–1937. A bar was added to his DSO after operations in Waziristan in 1937. Acting commander of 3rd (Jhelum) Infantry Brigade in 1937, he was promoted colonel in 1938.

Commander of 160th Brigade 1939–1940, Williams was promoted major general and appointed GOC 38th (Welsh) Division in May 1940. He was briefly GOC 47th (London) Division in November 1940 before he retired due to illness.

Re-employed for selection board duties in 1941 and retired from the army in 1944, Willaims was made CBE and was Civil Defence Officer for the Isle of Wight 1950–1960.

WILLIAMS, General Sir Guy Charles *(1881–1959), KCB, CMG, DSO*
Born in India of military family Williams was educated at Sherborne. Commissioned in the Royal Engineers in 1900, he served in the South African

War and had postings in Bermuda and East Africa. A captain in 1910, he married in 1912, and his First War service was in France, where he was seven times mentioned in despatches and admitted to the DSO in 1915,

A student at the Staff College, Camberley, in 1919, Williams was a staff officer in the United Provinces District, India, in 1920 and was on the directing staff at the Staff College, Quetta, 1922–1923. Deputy Military Secretary at the War Office 1923–1927, he commanded 8th Bareilly Infantry Brigade in India 1927–1928. An instructor at the Imperial Defence College 1928–1932, he was Chief Engineer, Aldershot Command, 1932–1934. Promoted major general, he was Commandant of the Staff College, Quetta, 1934–1937, and GOC 5th Division 1937–1938.

Appointed C-in-C Eastern Command in 1938 and knighted in 1939, Williams, though respected for his 'administrative and organizing ability', was regarded by Brooke as too devoid of 'strategic and tactical flair' to remain in his command (Danchev & Todman, 2001, 148). Sent, against his will, to New Zealand in May 1941 to advise the government there on defence matters, he retired from the army that November.

Almost at once Williams found work at the BBC. In 1944 he was appointed Resettlement Officer, charged with reinserting returning servicemen and women into the corporation. A widower from 1948, he was Colonel Commandant RE 1940–1951 and Chief Royal Engineer 1946–1951.

WILLIAMS, Major General Sir Leslie Hamlyn *(1892–1965), KBE, CB, MC*
Educated at Dulwich and a territorial soldier with the London Scottish Rifles from 1909, Williams was commissioned in the Suffolk Regiment in 1914. Married in 1915, his First War service was in France and Italy, on attachment to the Army Ordnance Corps from 1915. He was mentioned in despatches and awarded the MC in 1917.

Deputy Director Ordnance Services at the War Office 1939–1940, Williams was Director Ordnance Services in 1940. Director of Warlike Stores at the War Office 1940–1942, he was Controller of Ordnance Services at the War Office until he retired from the army in 1946.

Knighted in 1946, Williams established a new career as a director of the motor manufacturer, Rootes. Re-married in 1948, he broadened his business interests by joining the boards of a number of engineering companies. Master of the Worshipful Company of Carmen 1951–1952, he was Colonel Commandant of the RAOC from 1945.

WILLIAMS, Major General Walter David Abbott *(1897–1973), CB, CBE*
Educated at Brighton College, RMA, Woolwich and, on a young officers' course, at Cambridge University, Williams was commissioned in the Royal Engineers in 1917. His First War service was in France.

A Scholar at Emmanuel College, Cambridge, and a graduate of the university in 1924, Williams married in 1925 and attended the Staff College, Camberley, 1932–1933. An Assistant QMG at the War Office 1939–1940, he was Assistant

Director of Movements 1940–1941 and Deputy Director 1941–1943. Promoted major general, he was Director of Freights in 1943 and Director of Movements from 1945 until his retirement from the army in 1949.

Appointed CB in 1946, Williams was sometime Director of Ports Emergency Planning, Ministry of Transport, and Commissioner for Transport, East Africa High Commission, 1954–1958. He was Principal of the Staff College for Higher Management, Woking, 1958–1965.

WILSON, Major General Bevil Thomson *(1885–1975), CB, DSO*

Born in Canada, the son of a surgeon, Wilson was educated at Clifton and RMA, Woolwich. Commissioned in the Royal Engineers, he served in India and with the Egyptian Army. A captain in 1914, his First War service was in Egypt, Gallipoli, France and Italy. Thrice mentioned in despatches, he was admitted to the DSO in 1918.

Married in 1918, Wilson attended the Staff College, Camberley, 1920–1921, and served on the staff at the War Office 1922–1925. Deputy Assistant Adjutant and QMG, Northern Command, 1927–1929, he was Chief Staff Officer, Sudan Defence Force, 1929–1933. An instructor at the Senior Officers' School, Belgaum, 1933–1935, he was Commander of Lahore Brigade Area, India, 1935–1937 and commanded the Nowshera Brigade on the North-West Frontier, 1937–1939.

Appointed GOC 53rd (Welsh) Division in May 1939, Wilson relinquished his command in July 1941 and retired from the army. Employed with UNRRA and the Control Commission in Germany 1944–1950, he was a member of the Council for the RNIB 1952–1965.

WILSON, Major General Sir Gordon *(1887–1971), KCSI, CB, CBE, MC*

Born in Cheltenham, Wilson studied Medicine at Edinburgh University and joined the RAMC in 1911. His First War service was in France, India and in Mesopotamia, where he was twice mentioned in despatches and awarded the MC.

Married in 1917, Wilson was Deputy Director General Army Medical Services at the War Office 1929–1933 and Deputy Assistant Director of Medical Services in Waziristan 1934–1936. DADMS Northern Command, India, 1936–1938, he was o/c Royal Victoria Hospital, Netley, 1938–1939. Commandant of the Dieppe Sub-Area with the BEF 1939–1940, he was Deputy Director Medical Services, Southern Command, India, 1941–1943 and Director of Medical Services, India, from 1943 until his retirement in 1946.

WILSON, Field Marshal Sir Henry Maitland,
1st Baron (1881–1964), GCB, GBE, DSO

Born in Suffolk of military family and educated at Eton and RMC, Sandhurst, Wilson was commissioned in the Rifle Brigade in 1900. After service in the South African War and postings in Egypt and India, he married in 1915. His

First War service was in France, where he was thrice mentioned in despatches and admitted to the DSO in 1917.

A graduate at the Staff College, Camberley's first post-war course in 1919, Wilson was an instructor at Sandhurst 1921–1923. He commanded his regiment's 1st battalion in India 1927–1930 and was on the directing staff at Camberley 1930–1933. A large man who, inevitably, attracted the nickname 'Jumbo', he enjoyed all field sports, especially riding. He was, however, due to his bulk, a 'difficult man to mount' (DNB). Promoted colonel in 1934, he spent the next nine months on half-pay. Reinstated, he commanded 6th Infantry Brigade at Blackdown in 1935 and, promoted major general, spent a further two years on half-pay before being appointed GOC 2nd Division in August 1937.

Appointed GOC-in-C British troops in Egypt in June 1939, Wilson was made Colonel Commandant of the 2nd Battalion of the Rifle Brigade and had a hand in removing Hobart from command of the putative 7th Armoured Division. Though not directly involved in operations in the Western Desert 1940–1941, he was knighted and in 1941 briefly rejoiced in the title Military Governor of Cyrenaica. Given command of British troops sent to Greece in early April 1941, his 'meticulous if somewhat ponderous mind' (Fraser, 1999, 137) enabled him to supervise their successful evacuation at the end of the month. Almost immediately he was made GOC British Forces in Palestine and Transjordan, and ordered to depose the Raschid Ali regime in Iraq and, with the aid of Free French detachments, mount an invasion of Vichy French Syria.

With these duties discharged, Wilson was not given the desert field command which Churchill, among others, felt he merited. Instead, by now a general, he was pronounced GOC-in-C Ninth Army, with responsibilities in Transjordan and Iraq, which were later extended to the Nile delta. Considered, briefly, as a possible replacement for Auchinleck, Brooke paraded the argument of his age and persuaded Churchill to look elsewhere for a new C-in-C Middle East. In August 1942, after the 'Cairo purge', he was made C-in-C of the newly-created Iraq and Persia (Iran) Command, and GOC-in-C Tenth Army. His task was to defend the region from any German threat emanating from the Caucusus. Still 'immensely fat', and 'looking exactly like . . . an elephant standing on its hind legs' (Ranfurly, 1994, 216), he exuded kindness and wisdom, especially to officers wearing the black buttons of the Rifle Brigade.

Wilson by now had found his niche. He was more of an administrator-cum-diplomat than soldier. He had many varied responsibilities to discharge but scarcely any troops to command. Returning to Egypt from Baghdad in February 1943, he was made C-in-C Middle East, but his task was to support the 8th Army's campaign in Tunisia from his Cairo desk. In addition to sending military missions to Yugoslavia, he was prompted by Churchill that September to be bold and launch the kind of military operation that might bring Turkey into the war on the allied side. The result was the ill-fated invasion of the Dodecanese islands, Cos, Leros and Samos, which, among bitter Anglo-American recriminatory exchanges, resulted in ignominious defeat.

With the great commanders leaving the theatre to prepare for cross-channel operations in North-West Europe, Wilson succeeded Eisenhower as Supreme Commander in the Mediterranean in January 1944. Thoughtfully supportive of operations in Italy, he was powerless to prevent the Americans from launching their landings in the south of France. He did, however, make a point of returning to Athens in December 1944, revisiting the scene of his evacuation more than three years previously. Appointed successor to Dill as head of the British Chiefs of Staff Mission to Washington in December 1944, he was promoted field marshal.

Wilson attended the Yalta and Potsdam conferences, was created a baron in 1946 and remained in Washington until May 1947. Returning to England, he totted up the number of years he had served his King and country abroad and wrote his rather bland memoirs, *Eight Years Overseas* (1949).

In retirement Wilson took an active interest in the affairs of his old school and the Rifle Brigade. Something of a character, he was much admired and respected by those who had served under him. He was Constable of the Tower of London 1955–1960, Though settled in Buckinghamshire, his heart, so it is said, 'remained in Suffolk' (DNB).

WILSON, Major General Nigel Maitland *(1884–1950), CB, DSO, OBE*
Born in Suffolk and, like his more famous elder brother, educated at Eton and RMC, Sandhurst, Wilson was commissioned in the Royal Welch Fusiliers in 1904. Married in 1909, and a captain in 1914, his First War service was in France, where he was mentioned in despatches and awarded the DSO in 1916.

Awarded the OBE after service in Waziristan 1922–1923, Wilson transferred to the 10th Gurkha Rifles (Indian Army). He attended the Staff College, Quetta, 1927–1927 and was Assistant Adjutant and QMG, Rawalpindi District, 1933–1935. Commander of Sind Independent Brigade Area 1935–1936, he was Director of Personnel Services, AHQ India, 1936–1938.

Promoted major general in 1938, a year after his elder brother had acquired that rank, Wilson was Director of Organization, AHQ India, 1938–1940. Retired from the army in 1941, he returned to England, was Colonel of the Royal Welch Fusiliers, 1942–1946 and Secretary to the Lord Great Chamberlain 1945–1948.

WILSON, General Sir Roger Cochrane *(1882–1966), KCB, DSO, MC*
Of military family and educated at Wellington and RMC, Sandhurst, Wilson was commissioned in the Cheshire Regiment in 1901. Serving in India, he transferred to the 5th Mahratta Regiment in 1904 and married the following year. Attending the Staff College, Quetta, when war broke out in 1914, his First War service was in India and Mesopotamia, where he was five times mentioned in despatches, awarded the MC and admitted to the DSO in 1918.

A colonel in 1920, Wilson served with Southern Command, India, and on the staff in Meerut District 1922–1925. Commander of the Manzai Brigade in Waziristan 1926–1930, he endured a year on half-pay before being appointed Commandant of the Staff College, Quetta, in 1931. GOC Rawalpindi

District 1934–1936, he was Secretary to the Military Department at the India Office 1936–1937. Knighted and promoted lieutenant general in 1937, he was Adjutant General, India, until his retirement in 1941.

Promoted General in 1940, Wilson settled in South Africa and served on the staff of the South African Defence Forces 1942–1947. A keen mountaineer and member of the Alpine Club, he lived thereafter in Hampshire.

WILSON, Major General Thomas Arthur Atkinson *(1882–1958), CB*
Educated at Campbell College, Belfast, and RMC, Sandhurst, Wilson was commissioned on the unattached list in 1901 and gazetted into the 2nd Royal Lancers (Gardners's Horse, Indian Army) in 1902. A captain in 1910, his First War service was in France, Egypt and Mesopotamia, where he was mentioned in despatches.

Married in 1918, Wilson attended the Staff College, Quetta, 1919–1920 and commanded Gardner's Horse 1927–1929. An instructor at the Senior Officers' School, Belgaum, 1930–1932, he commanded the 2nd (Sialkot) Cavalry Brigade 1932–1934 and was BGS, Southern Command, India, 1934–1938. Appointed CB in 1938, he was Deputy Adjutant and QMG, Southern Command, India, until his retirement in 1940. Recalled the next year, he was Chief Administration Officer, Southern Command, India, until 1942.

A keen golfer and good shot, Wilson lived in London, outliving his wife by a year.

WILSON, Major General Thomas Needham Furnival
(1896–1961), CB, DSO, MC
Educated at Winchester and RMC, Sandhurst, Wilson was commissioned in the King's Royal Rifle Corps in 1914. His First War service was in France, where he was mentioned in despatches, awarded the MC and admitted to the DSO.

Married in 1922, Wilson attended the Staff College, Camberley, 1928–1929. Deputy Assistant Adjutant General at the War Office 1936–1938, he commanded the 2nd Battalion KRRC 1938–1939.

Commander of 3rd Brigade, part of Alexander's 1st Division, in France with the BEF 1939–1940, Wilson was awarded a bar to the DSO after the Dunkirk evacuation. He was attached to the General Staff, Home Forces, 1940–1942 and was appointed Commandant of the School of Infantry in 1942. Made Director of Infantry in 1943 and a major general in 1944, he retired from the army in 1946.

Re-married in 1946, having divorced his first wife, Wilson, a member of the MCC, was Secretary to the King's Jubilee Trust from 1948 until his death.

WIMBERLEY, Major General Douglas Neil *(1896–1983), CB, DSO, MC*
Born in Inverness and educated at Wellington, RMC, Sandhurst, and Cambridge University (Young Officers' Course), Wimberley was commissioned in the Cameron Highlanders in 1915. His First War service was in France, where he was wounded and awarded the MC.

After serving with the North Russia Relief Force in 1919, Wimberley was Adjutant to the 2nd Battalion Cameron Highlanders in Ireland in 1921. He married in 1925, attended the Staff College, Camberley, 1927–1928 and was Brigade Major with 1st Gurkha Infantry Brigade 1929–1931. A brevet major in 1933, he won the *Army Quarterly* prize essay and served on the staff at the War Office, 1934–1937. He commanded the 1st Battalion Cameron Highlanders in 1939.

In France with his battalion at war's beginning, 'Steve' Wimberley was Chief Instructor at the Senior Officers' School, Sheerness, in 1940, before being appointed to command 13th Brigade and 152nd Seaforth and Cameron Highlanders Brigade 1940–1941. He was GOC 46th Division for less than a month in 1941 before being appointed GOC of the re-forming 51st (Highland) Division that June. Inheriting a formation that was 'sticky and did not move as quickly as it ought' (Danchev & Todman, 2001, 178), he worked hard at infusing it with Highland warrior spirit.

Arriving in North Africa in August 1942, 51st Division fought with distinction at El Alamein, and Wimberley, a flamboyant leader, now dubbed 'Tartan Tam', was admitted to the DSO during the pursuit of Rommel's Panzerarmee. In was due in large part to his panache that the Highland Division, or 'Highway Decorators' as they were known (Latimer, 2002, 127), became the most famous 8th Army formation. Wounded in Sicily, he was brought home and, appointed CB, made Commandant of the Staff College, Camberley, in 1943. Appointed Director of Infantry at the War Office in 1944, he retired from the army in 1946.

Principal of University College, Dundee, 1946–1954, Wimberley was Founder Governor of the Scottish Horticultural Research Institute 1952–1962. A member of the Royal Company of Archers, he was Colonel of the Cameron Highlanders 1951–1961 and Hon. Colonel of the St Andrews University OTC 1951–1963. He received numerous honorary degrees from Scottish universities and was President of the Royal Celtic Society 1971–1974. He lived until well into his 80s in Coupar Angus.

WINGATE, Major General Orde Charles *(1903–1944), DSO*
Of military family, with Plymouth Brethren parents, and educated at Charterhouse and RMA, Woolwich, Wingate, despite being considered 'scruffy, bolshy and unco-operative' (Rooney, 1999, 186), was commissioned in the Royal Artillery in 1923. A well-connected, pronounced individualist who knew how to pull strings, he qualified as an instructor at the Army Equitation School, Weedon, in 1926 and enrolled in a course in Arabic at the School of Oriental Studies.

Attached to the Sudan Defence Force 1928–1933, Wingate travelled widely in East and North Africa. Married in 1935, he served as adjutant in a Territorial Army depot in Sheffield and, with 9th Infantry Brigade on Salisbury Plain, and tried, unsuccessfully, for a place at the Staff College, Camberley. Soon after, he was posted to Palestine as Intelligence Officer to 5th Division. Influenced, perhaps, by family tradition but as likely irritated by the pro-Arab sentiments of his brother officers, Wingate became pro-Jewish – indeed a fervent Zionist. The paramilitary night squads he raised and led on counter-Arab insurgency raids made his name well-known and he was admitted to the DSO in 1938.

Returned to England and swotting for the Staff College entrance examinations, Wingate was Brigade Major to 56th Light Anti-Aircraft Brigade in London at war's beginning. After some string-pulling, he was posted to Khartoum to help organize Abyssinian 'patriots' then gathered around the exiled Emperor, and coordinate guerrilla actions against the Italians. His 'Gideon Force', made up largely of irregulars, contributed significantly to the defeat of the Italians in East Africa, though in his arrogant and rude way he was apt to ride roughshod over those with greater knowledge of local conditions. No respecter of persons, still less rank, his 'unseemly behaviour' extended to 'cool[ing] his bottom in the occasional waterholes, from which others . . . would have to drink' (Thesiger, 1992, 330). Capable of enduring great hardship, tactically imaginative and providing galvanic leadership, he was also a depressive. Having helped restore Haile Selassie to his throne, and having a bar added to his DSO, he tried, within weeks, to kill himself in a Cairo hotel room. Having written adversely on his superiors, he was upset by their adverse reports on him.

Spending his long leave in London 'simmering with resentment' (Rooney, 1999, 191) Wingate still had enough pull with influential contacts to secure a posting to India. Arriving there in March 1943, he pestered Wavell, the C-in-C, with his ideas on 'long-range penetration tactics' and mounting guerrilla-type raids behind Japanese lines in Burma. Given a brigade to train and equip, he launched Operation LONGCLOTH in February 1943, by which his Chindits split into a number of columns operated beyond the Chindwin. The operation was a partial success. The Japanese suffered some destruction and much consternation, though the Chindits were wrecked as a fighting force in the process. Nevertheless, at a time when any good news emanating from Burma was at a premium, Churchill made much of his new jungle hero. Ordering Wingate to attend the Quebec QUADRANT Conference, the Chindits were put on the strategic map. Further operations on a far grander scale were projected.

Wingate is one of those figures about whom opinion is seldom neutral. To his admirers he was the necessary maverick figure who, in his passionate desire to carry the fight to the enemy, shook-up the 'notorious sloth and inertia of . . . GHQ Delhi' (Rooney, 1982, 108). Yet if all blimpish 'curry colonels' were his critics, it has to be admitted that not all his critics were blimps. There was, in India as elsewhere, a natural and not ill-founded distrust of élite forces, the resources they consumed and their morale-sapping impact on the malnourished residual mass. At the time, and since, there was debate over whether, militarily, special forces offered a worthwhile return. What is more, maverick figures are, by definition, not team players, and in this respect Wingate was the quintessential Old Testament-inspired lone wolf. He had vision, he may even have had the stuff of genius, but in his impatient demands and his all too evident disregard for the localized chain of command, he made enemies.

Operation THURSDAY, a much bigger foray behind Japanese lines, was launched in March 1944. Wingate, by now a major general, had the equivalent of a division to deploy. His habit of communicating direct to Churchill persuaded Brooke, in distant London, that 'the strain of operations has sent [him]off his head' (Danchev & Todman, 2001, 534). Supply by air was to be the key, both in terms of landing and in evacuating casualties. It was therefore not inappropriate, and in a way fitting, that less than a month into THURSDAY he was killed when the aircraft carrying him crashed into the Naga Hills in Assam.

The hero was mourned in his death. He left a young widow and infant son. 'Baffy' Dugdale, a fellow gentile-Zionist, who 'never liked him', greeted the news with the thought that 'the hagiography is already far advanced' (Rose, N.(ed.), 1973, 212). She was right. Wingate's feel for irregular warfare was compared with Lawrence of Arabia's. His queer messianic utterances and all-too-evident character flaws were paraded as if to prove his military genius. There were arguments about his status, about the use of the Chindits after his death, and even over the final resting place of his remains. Yet while his admirers never tire of claiming how he was held back by a hidebound reactionary military establishment, what is often overlooked is his instinct for insider methods and how adept he was at manipulating the strings of that same establishment to suit his own purpose.

WINTERTON, Major General Sir Thomas John Willoughby
(1898–1987), KCB, KCMG, CBE

Educated at Oundle and RMA, Woolwich, Winterton was commissioned in the Royal Artillery in 1916 and served in France, 1917–1918.

Transferring to the Oxfordshire and Buckinghamshire Light Infantry in 1918, 'Jack' Winterton married in 1921. Adjutant to a Territorial Army formation 1925–1929, he served in Burma for the next two years. On the staff of the Small Arms School, India, 1933–1935, and a student at the Staff College, Quetta, 1936–1937, he was an instructor at Camberley 1938–1939.

Assistant QMG to the BEF in France 1939–1940, Winterton was Chief Instructor at Camberley 1940–1941. Made BGS to Alexander, then GOC-in-C Southern Command, in 1941, he travelled with Alexander as his Chief of Staff to Burma in 1942. A 'wise, cheerful and fine staff officer . . . and a very agreeable companion' (North (ed.), 1962, 95), he was made CBE and was DCGS, India, 1942–1943.

Reverting to the substantive rank of brigadier, Winterton commanded 123rd Indian Brigade in Burma 1943–1944 and, briefly, a brigade in Italy. Made Deputy Commander of the Allied Commission for Austria in 1945, he was British High Commissioner and C-in-C British Troops in Austria 1950–1951. Knighted in 1950, he was Military Governor of the British and US zone in Trieste 1951–1954, and retired from the army in 1955.

Colonel Commandant of 1st Green Jackets 1955–1960, Winterton was President of the South Berkshire Conservative and Unionist Association 1958–1965 and member of the county St John Ambulance Council. DL for Berkshire in 1966, he spent the last eleven years of his life a widower.

WITTS, Major General Frederick Vavasour Broome
(1889–1969), CB, CBE, DSO, MC
The son of a clergyman, Witts was educated at Radley and RMA, Woolwich, and was commissioned in the Royal Engineers in 1907. Attached to the Bengal Sappers and Miners (Indian Army) in 1913, his First War service was in France and later in Mesopotamia. Thrice mentioned in despatches, he was awarded the MC and admitted to the DSO in 1917.

After service in Iraq in 1920, Witts attended the Staff College, Quetta, 1922–1923. Returning to England, he served on the staff at the War Office 1923–1927 and with the Shanghai Defence Force 1927–1928. Married in 1929, he was on the directing staff at Camberley 1930–1932 and was CRE 5th Division at Catterick 1933–1934 and later in Palestine and Egypt. Commander of 8th Bareilly Brigade in India 1938–1939, he was appointed GOC 45th Division at war's beginning in 1939.

Deputy Chief of the General Staff at the BEF's GHQ in France in 1940, Witts was GOC 59th Division in Scotland 1940–1941. Carrington, then C-in-C Scottish Command, had apparently 'complete confidence in him' (Dill, 2nd acc., 4, LHCMA). Posted to India and made Commander of Bombay District in late 1941, he was GOC-in-C Southern Army, India, from 1942 until his retirement from the army the next year.

Lieutenant Governor and Secretary of the Royal Hospital, Chelsea, 1944–1948, Witts was also an assistant director of the St John Ambulance Brigade over the same period. A Fellow of the Royal Geographical Society and Gloucester County Councillor from 1955 to 1961, he rejoiced in the title of Lord of the Manor and Patron of the Living of Upper Slaughter over the same period. He was DL for the county from 1961.

WOOD, Lieutenant General Sir Ernest *(1894–1971), KBE, CB, CIE, MC*
Gazetted into the Bombay Sappers and Miners (Indian Army) in 1914, Wood's First War service was in India, Mesopotamia and Palestine, where he was awarded the MC in 1917.

Married in 1922, Wood spent almost his entire career in India. Deputy Secretary of the Defence Department, AHQ India, 1936–1938, he was Secretary of the Supply Department 1939–1940. Director General of Supply, India, 1940–1942, he was Administrator General, Eastern Frontier Communications, 1942–1943. Director of the Food Department in 1943, he was Director General of Munitions Production 1943–1945.

Appointed CB,and Deputy Master General of the Ordnance 1945–1946, Wood was QMG, India, 1946–1947. Knighted, he retired from the army in 1948. Controller of Operations for the Colonial Development Corporation

1948–1951, he was Chief of Staff to the Defence Production Board of NATO 1951–1952. Living in Hertfordshire and a keen golfer, he was Director of Civil Defence, Eastern Region, 1955–1960.

WOOD, Major General George Neville *(1898–1982), CB, CBE, DSO, MC*
Educated at Colston's School and RMC, Sandhurst, Wood was commissioned in the Dorset Regiment in 1916. His First War service was in France, Turkey and southern Russia. Wounded and twice mentioned in despatches, he awarded the MC and made OBE.

On regimental duties in the Near East and the Sudan 1921–1925, Wood attended the Staff College, Camberley, 1926–1927. Married in 1928, he served on the staff at the War Office and at Aldershot 1928–1931. In India for the next six years, he commanded the Oxford University OTC 1938–1939 and, as was customary, received an honorary MA.

A staff officer at the War Office 1939–1941, Wood commanded the 12th Battalion West Yorkshire Regiment in 1941 and his regiment's 2nd Battalion 1941–1942. Promoted brigadier, he commanded 4th Infantry Brigade, Home Forces, in 1942 and was BGS Ceylon (Sri Lanka) Army Command in 1943. BGS XXXIII Indian Corps in Assam 1943–1944, he was GOC 25th Indian Division 1944–1946.

Made CBE and admitted to the DSO in 1945, and recommended for a knighthood by Mountbatten, he was appointed CB instead in 1946. GOC Mid-West District and 53rd (Welsh) Division 1947–1950, he was Director of Quartering at the War Office from 1951 until his retirement from the army in 1952. Living in London, he was Colonel of the Dorset Regiment 1952–1962.

WOODS, Major General Edward Ambrose *(1891–1957), CB, CBE, MC*
Educated at Tonbridge and RMA, Woolwich, Woods was commissioned in the Royal Artillery in 1910. His First War service was in France, where he was twice wounded, twice mentioned in despatches and awarded the MC.

Married in 1917, Woods was an instructor at the School of Artillery 1921–1923 and was attached to the Experimental Department at Larkhill, 1927–1929. After a period on half-pay, he was Assistant Superintendent of Works, Woolwich Arsenal, 1931–1933, and an instructor at the Military College of Science 1933–1935. Deputy Inspector of Armaments at the War Office 1936–1940 and Director of Armaments 1940–1943, he was made CBE in 1944. Appointed CB, he retired from the army in 1946.

WOOLNER, Major General Christopher Geoffrey
(1893–1984), CB, MC (and bars)
Educated at Marlborough and RMA, Woolwich, Woolner was commissioned in the Royal Engineers in 1912. His First War service was in France. A captain in 1917, he was wounded, mentioned in despatches and awarded the MC (and two bars).

After service on survey duties in the Gold Coast (Ghana) 1920–1923, 'Kit'

Woolner married and was an instructor at Woolwich, 1924–1927. After attending the Staff College, Camberley, 1927–1928, he served in India for the next four years as a staff officer and in the field. Deputy Inspector and Deputy Commandant of the School of Military Engineering, Chatham in 1939, he was a staff officer at the BEF's GHQ in France in 1939.

Appointed to command 8th Infantry Brigade in February 1940, Woolner appears not to have impressed Montgomery, his divisional commander, enough to gain entry to his 'little black book'. Made GOC Sierra Leone and Gambia in 1941, he was appointed CB in 1942 and made GOC 81st West African Division in Burma 1943–1944. There, in the Arakan, he 'aired some peculiar views on bush fighting' (Hickey, 1998, 110) and was sacked by Christison, his corps commander. Commander of West Midlands District in 1944, he was GOC 53rd (Welsh) Division from 1946 until his retirement from the army in 1947.

WOOTTEN, Major General Richard Montague *(1889–1979), CB, MC*
Born in Oxford and educated at Rugby and RMC, Sandhurst, Wootten was commissioned in the 6th Dragoons in 1909. His First War service was in France, where he was awarded the MC.

Married in 1915, Wootten transferred to the 2nd Dragoon Guards (Queen's Bays) in 1921. He attended the Staff College, Camberley, 1922–1923 and was an instructor there 1928–1931. Commander of the Queen's Bays 1932–1936, he served as Assistant QMG in Palestine and Egypt 1936–1938, before returning to England where, with his wife divorcing him, he served as Assistant then as Deputy Director General of the Territorial Army.

Appointed CB in 1940, Wootten proceeded to have a quiet war. Deputy QMG for UK-based US Forces preparing for operations in North Africa in 1942, he was made a Commander of the Legion of Merit and was District Officer commanding the North Midland District from 1942 until his retirement from the army in 1945.

Re-married, Wootten lived in Buckinghamshire.

WORDSWORTH, Major General Robert Harley *(1894–1984), CB, CBE*
Born and brought up in Australia, Wordsworth, after First War service in Egypt and France with the AIF, transferred to the 6th Lancers (Watson's Horse, Indian Army) in 1918.

A first-class polo player, Wordsworth was mentioned in despatches after operations in Waziristan 1919–1921, married in 1928 and was second in command of his regiment in 1936. Commanding Watson's Horse in 1939, he was GOC 31st Indian Armoured Division in 1941. After commanding 43rd and 44th Indian Armoured Divisions 1941–1944, he was appointed Major General Armoured Fighting Vehicles at GHQ, India, in 1944.

Retired from the army in 1947, Wordswoth returned to Australia and sat as a Senator in the Commonwealth Parliament 1949–1959. He was Administrator of Norfolk Island 1962–1964, before retiring to his home in Tasmania.

WRISBERG, Lieutenant General Sir Frederick George
(1895–1982). KBE, CBE, CB
The son of an artilleryman, Wrisberg was commissioned in the Royal Artillery in 1916. His First War service was in France, where he was wounded.

Married in 1918, Wrisberg was Experimental Officer with the Air Defence Experimental Establishment 1929–1933. He served on the staff at the War Office 1934–1936 and was Assistant Director of Artillery 1936–1938.

Assistant Director of Weapons Production at the War Office 1938–1940, Wrisberg was Director 1940–1943. He was Director General of Weapons and Instrument Production, Ministry of Supply, 1943–1946. Appointed CB in 1945, he was Controller of Supplies, Ministry of Supply, from 1946 until he retired from the army in 1949.

Knighted, Wrisberg was Colonel Commandant of the Royal Artillery 1950–1960 and was Chairman of Linotype and Machinery Ltd. 1960–1966. He lived in Dorset, a widower for the last four years of his life.

Y

YOUNG, Major General Bernard Keith *(1892–1969), CBE, MC*
Born in North Wales and educated at Wellington and RMA, Woolwich, Young was commissioned in the Royal Engineers in 1912. Married in 1916, his First War service was in France, Salonika and Palestine, where he was awarded the MC in 1917.

After service with the Egyptian Army in the Sudan 1918–1919, Young served for many years in India, attached to the Army Service Corps. A major in 1928, he was Deputy Assistant Director of Works at the War Office 1931–1933. Chief Instructor at Woolwich 1936–1938, a colonel in 1937 and a temporary brigadier in 1940, he was an Assistant Adjutant General at the War Office 1938–1939. Commander of an infantry brigade 1940–1941, he was Chief Engineer in the Middle East in 1942. Made CBE in 1943 after the Tunisian campaign, he was Chief Engineer with Home Forces 1943–1944. He retired from the army in 1945.

Settling in Guildford, Surrey, Young was Director General of the Royal Society for the Prevention of Accidents 1951–1959. He died after a long illness.

YOUNGER, Major General John Edward Talbot *(1888–1974), CBE*
Of military family and educated at Wellington and RMA, Woolwich, Younger was commissioned in the Royal Field Artillery in 1919. A captain in 1914, his First War service was in France, where he was mentioned in despatches.

Married in 1919, Younger was an instructor at the School of Artillery, Larkhill, 1919–1923. Instructor in Gunnery with Southern Command 1931–1934, he was Deputy Assistant Director of Artillery at the War Office 1934–1936. A brevet lieutenant colonel in 1936, he was Assistant Director of Artillery at the War Office 1938–1939. At war's outset he was commanding 57th Anti-Artillery Brigade.

Promoted major general, Younger was GOC 4th Anti-Aircraft Division 1939–1940 and GOC 3rd Anti-Aircraft Division 1940–1942. Attached to the British Military Mission in Washington 1942–1943, he retired from the army the next year.

Made CBE in 1945, Younger was a Red Cross Commissioner in the USSR in 1945. A founder member of the Army Ski Association and sometime President of the RA Alpine Club, he lived in Devon, listing his *Who's Who* recreations entry as 'Enjoying old age'.

BIBLIOGRAPHY

Allen, L., *Burma: The Longest War 1941–1945* (Phoenix, 2002)

Avon, Lord, *The Eden Memoirs: The Reckoning* (Cassell, 1965)

Ball, S. (ed)., *The Headlam Diaries, 1935–1951* (CUP, 1999)

Barnes, J. and Nicholson, D. (eds.), *The Empire at Bay: The Leo Amery Diaries 1929–1945* (Weidenfeld & Nicolson, 1983)

Barnett, C., *The Desert Generals* (Cassell, 1960)

Baynes, J., *The Forgotten Victor: General Sir Richard O'Connor* (Brassey's, 1989)

Beauman, Brig. A. B., *Then a Soldier* (Macmillan, 1960)

Beevor, A., *Crete: The Battle and the Resistance* (Penguin, 1991)

Belchem, Maj-Gen. D., *All in a Day's March* (Collins, 1978)

Bidwell, S. and Graham, D., *Firepower: British Army Weapons and Theories of War 1904- 1945* (Allen & Unwin, 1985)

Bierman, J. and Smith, C., *Fire in the Night: Wingate of Burma, Ethiopia and Zion* (Macmillan, 2000)

—— *Alamein: War Without Hate* (Penguin, 2002)

Blaxland, G., *The Plain Cook and the Great Showman: The First and Eighth Armies in North Africa* (William Kimber, 1977)

—— *Alexander's Generals* (Willam Kimber, 1979)

Boatner, M., *The Biographical Dictionary of the Second World War* (Presidio, 1996)

Bond, B. (ed.)., *Chief of Staff: The Diaries of Lt.General Sir Henry Pownall* (London, Leo Cooper, vol. I, 1972, vol. II, 1974)

—— *Liddell Hart: A Study of his Military Thought* (Cassell, 1977)

—— *British Military Policy Between the Wars* (Clarendon, 1980)

Bristow, Brig. R. C. B., *Memoirs of the British Raj: A soldier in India* (Johnson, 1974)

Brownrigg, Lt-Gen. Sir Douglas, *Unexpected* (Hutchinson, 1942)

Bryant, Sir Arthur, *The Turn of the Tide* (Collins, 1957)

—— *Triumph in the West: Alanbrooke War Diaries 1943–1946* (Fontana, 1965)

Butcher, Harry C., *Three Years with Eisenhower* (Heinemann, 1946)

Butler, E., *Mason-Mac: The Life of Lieutenant General Sir Noel Mason-Macfarlane* (Macmillan, 1972)

Carrington, Lord, *Reflect on Things Past* (Collins, 1988)

Carver, M.(ed.)., *The War Lords: Military Commanders of the Twentieth Century* (Weidenfeld & Nicolson, 1976)

—— *Harding of Petherton* (Weidenfeld & Nicolson, 1978)

—— *Dilemmas of the Desert War* (Spellmount, 1986)

—— *Out of Step: Memoirs of a Field Marshal* (Hutchinson, 1989)

—— *Britain's Army in the Twentieth Century* (Pan, 1998)

Chandler, D. and Collins, J (eds.)., *The D-Day Encyclopedia* (Simon & Shuster, 1994)

Chandos, Lord, *Memoirs* (The Bodley Head, 1962)

Chevenix Trench, C., *The Indian Army and the King's Enemies 1900–1947* (Thames & Hudson, 1978)

Churchill, W. S., *The Grand Alliance* (Collins, 1950)

—— *The Hinge of Fate* (Collins, 1951)

Clay, J., *John Masters: A Regulated Life* (Michael Joseph, 1992)

Clayton, T. and Craig, P., *End of the Beginning* (Hodder & Stoughton, 2002)

Clifton James, E., *I was Monty's Double* (Panther, 1958)

Cloake, P., *Templer of Malaya* (Harrap, 1985)

Colville, J., *Man of Valour: The Life of Field Marshal the Vt. Gort* (Collins, 1972)

—— *The Fringes of Power: Downing Street Diaries 1939–1945* (Hodder & Stoughton, 1985)

Coward, N., *Autobiography* (Methuen, 1987)

Cowling, M. *The Impact of Hitler* (CUP, 1975)

Crang, J. A., *The British Army and the People's War* (MUP, 2000)

Danchev, A. and Todman, D. (eds.), *War Diaries, 1939–1945: Field Marshal Lord Alanbrooke* (Weidenfeld & Nicolson, 2001)

de Chair, S., *Morning Glory* (Cassell, 1994)

D'Este, C., *Decision in Normandy* (Penguin, 2001)

de Guingand, Maj. Gen. Sir F., *Operation Victory* (Hodder & Stoughton, 1947)

Dixon, N. *On the Psychology of Military Incompetence* (Cape, 1976)

Eisenhower, D. D., *Crusade in Europe* (Hutchinson, 1948)

Elliot, Maj. Gen. J.G., *The Frontier 1839–1947: The Story of the North-West Frontier* (Cassell, 1968)

Ellis, J., *Cassino: The Hollow Victory* (Aurum Press, 1984)

Evans, G., *Slim as Military Commander* (Batsford, 1969)

Fraser, D., *And We Shall Shock Them: The British Army in the Second World War* (Cassell, 1983)

—— *Wars and Shadows: The Memoirs of Sir David Fraser* (Allen Lane, 2002)

French, D., 'Colonel Blimp and the British Army: Divisional Commanders and the War Against Germany' *English Historical Review, vol. III, 1996*

—— *Raising Churchill's Army: The British Army and the War Against Germany 1919–1945* (OUP, 2000)

Goode, F. D. 'The War Office General Staff 1940 to 1942: A Worm's Eye View' *RUSI Journal*, Jan.-Feb. 1993

Greacan, L. *'Chink': A Biography* (Macmillan 1989)

Grigg, P. J., *Prejudice and Judgment* (Cape, 1948)

Hamilton, N., *Monty: The Making of a General 1887–1942* (Allen Lane, 1982)

—— *Monty: Master of the Battlefield 1942–1944* (Hamish Hamilton, 1983)

—— *Monty: The Field Marshal 1944–1976* (Hamish Hamilton, 1986)

—— *The Full Monty: Montgomery of Alamein* (Allen Lane, 2001)

Harris, J., *Dunkirk: The Storm of War* (David & Charles, 1980)

Harris, J.P., *Men, Ideas and Tanks: British Military Thought and Armoured Forces 1903–1939* (MUP, 1995)

Harvey, A. D., *Collisions of Empire* (Hambledon, 1992)

Harvey, J. (ed.)., *The War Diaries of Oliver Harvey* (London, 1978)

Hastings, M., *Overlord: D-Day and the Battle for Normandy* (Pan, 1984)

Hastings, S., *Evelyn Waugh* (Minerva, 1995)

Heathcote, T. A., *The British Field Marshals: A Biographical Dictionary* (Leo Cooper, 1999)

Hickey, M., *The Unforgettable Army: Slim's XIVth Army in Burma* (Spellmount, 1998)

Hinsley, F. H., *British Intelligence in the Second World War*, vol.I (HMSO, 1979)

Holland, J., *The Aegean Mission: Allied Operations in the Dodecanese 1943* (Greenwood, 1988)

Horrocks, Lt. Gen. Sir B., *A Full Life* (Collins, 1960)

Ismay, Lord, *Memoirs* (Heinemann, 1960)

Irving, D., *The War Between the Generals* (Penguin, 1981)

Jackson, W. G. F., *The Battle for North Africa* (Mason/Charter, 1975)

Jones, T., *A Diary with Letters 1931–1950* (OUP, 1954)

Karslake, B., *The Last Act: The Story of the British Forces in France after Dunkirk* (Leo Cooper, 1979)

Keegan, J., *Six Armies in Normandy* (Penguin 1983)

Keegan, J (ed.)., *Churchill's Generals* (Warner, 1998)

Kennedy, Maj-Gen. Sir John, *The Business of War* (Hutchinson, 1957)

Kersaudy, F., *Norway 1940* (Collins, 1990)

Kinvig, C., *Scapegoat: General Percival and Singapore* (Brassey's, 1996)

Latimer, J., *Alamein* (John Murray, 2002)

Lewin, R., *Man of Armour: A Study of Lieutenant-General Vyvyan Pope* (Leo Cooper, 1976)

—— *Ultra Goes to War* ((Book Club), 1978)

—— *Slim: The Standardbearer* (Wordsworth, 1999)

Liddell-Hart, B., *Memoirs*, vol. II (Cassell, 1965)

Lindsay, D., *Forgotten General: The Life of Andrew Thorne* (Michael Russell, 1987)

Lindsay, O. (ed.)., *A Guards' General: The Memoirs of Sir Allan Adair* (Hamish Hamilton, 1986)

Lunt, J., *The Retreat from Burma* (David & Charles, 1989)

351

Mackenzie, S. P., *Politics and Military Morale: Current Affairs and Citizenship Education in the British Army 1914–1950* (Clarendon, 1992)

—— *The Home Guard* (OUP, 1995)

Macksey, K., *Armoured Crusader: Major-General Sir Percy Hobart* (Hutchinson, 1967)

Macleod, I., *Neville Chamberlain* (Muller, 1961)

Mcleod R. and Kelly, D., *Ironside Diaries* (Constable, 1962)

Macready, Lt-Gen. Sir Gordon, *In the Wake of the Great* (Wm Clowes, 1965)

Malkasian, C., *A History of Modern Wars of Attrition* (Praeger, 2002)

Marshall-Cornwall, J., *Wars and Rumours of War* (Leo Cooper, 1984)

Martel, Lt-Gen Sir Giffard, *An Outspoken Soldier* (Sifton, Praed, 1949)

Mason, D., *Who's Who in World War II* (Weidenfeld & Nicolson, 1978)

Maule, H., *Spearhead General: The Epic Story of General Sir Francis Messervy* (Odhams, 1961)

Minney, R., *The Private Papers of Leslie Hore-Belisha* (Gregg Revivals, 1991)

Mockler, A., *Haile Selassie's War* (OUP, 1984)

Moorehead, A., *Mediterranean Front* (Hamish Hamilton, 1940)

Montgomery of Alamein, *Memoirs* (Book Club, 1958)

Moran, Lord, *Churchill: The Struggle for Survival* (Sphere, 1966)

Morgan, Gen. Sir Frederick *Peace and War: A Soldier's Life* (Hodder & Stoughton, 1961)

Nicolson, N., *Alex: The Life of Field Marshal Earl Alexander of Tunis* (Pan, 1976)

—— *Long Life: Memoirs* (Weidenfeld & Nicolson, 1997)

North, J. (ed.)., *The Memoirs of Field Marshal Earl Alexander of Tunis* (Cassell, 1962)

Pile, Gen. Sir Fredferick, *Ack-Ack:Britain's Defence Against Air Attack During the Second World War* (Harrap, 1949)

Pimlott, B., *Hugh Dalton* (Macmillan, 1985)

—— *The Second World War Diary of Hugh Dalton 1940–1945* (Cape, 1986)

Pitt, B., *The Crucible of War: Wavell's Command* (Cassell, 1988)

Pond, H., *Sicily* (William Kimber, 1962)

Pyman, Gen. Sir Harold, *Call to Arms* (Leo Cooper, 1971)

Ranfurly, Countess *To War with Whitaker: The Wartime Diaries of the Countess of Ranfurly* 1939–1945 (Arrow, 1998)

Rhodes James, R., *'Chips': The Diaries of Sir Henry Channon* (Penguin, 1984)

Richardson, C., *Flashback: A Soldier's Story* (William Kimber, 1985)

Richardson, Gen. Sir Charles, *Send for Freddie: The Story of Montgomery's Chief of Staff, Major General Sir Francis de Guingand* (William Kimber, 1987)

Roberts, Maj-Gen.'Pip', *From the Desert to the Baltic* (William Kimber, 1987)

Rolf, D., *The Bloody Road to Tunis* (Greenhill, 2001)

Rooney, D., *Burma Victory* (Cassell, 1992)

—— *Military Mavericks: Extraordinary Men of Battle* (Cassell, 1999)

Rose, N (ed.)., *'Baffy': The Diaries of Blanche Dugdale 1936–1944* (Valentine Mitchell, 1973)

Royle, T., *Orde Wingate: Irregular Soldier* (Weidenfeld & Nicolson, 1995)

Ryan, C., *A Bridge Too Far* (Wordsworth, 1999)

Ryder, R., *Oliver Leese* (Hamish Hamilton, 1987)

Seton-Watson, C., *Dunkirk-Alamein-Bologna: Letters and Diaries of an Artilleryman* (Buckland, 1993)

Slim, Field Marshal, Vt., *Defeat into Victory* (Pan, 1999)

Smart, N. (ed.)., *Dear Grandmother: The Bickersteth Family Second World War Diaries* vols. I and II (Edwin Mellen, 1999 and 2001)

Smyth, Sir J., *Before the Dawn: A Story of two Historic Retreats* (Cassell, 1957)

Stewart, A., *8th Army's Greatest Victories* (Leo Cooper, 1999)

Strachan, H., *The Politics of the British Army* (Clarendon, 1997)

Swinton, Lord, *I Remember* (Hutchinson, 1958)

Thesiger, W., *The Life of My Choice* (Flamingo, 1992)

Tremlett, E., *Small Fry: The Autobiography of Major-General E.A.E Tremlett* (Unpub. Westcountry Studies Library)

Tuker, Lt-Gen. Sir Francis, *Approach to Battle* (Cassell, 1963)

Vaughan-Thomas, W., *Anzio* (Pan, 1961)

Warner, P., *Auchinleck: The Lonely Soldier* (Sphere, 1982)

—— *Horrocks: The General Who Led From the Front* (Sphere, 1985)

Warren, P., *Singapore 1942: Britain's Greatest Defeat* (Hambledon, 2002)

White, T (ed.)., *The Stilwell Papers* (Sloane, 1948)

Wilson, Field Marshal Lord *Eight Years Overseas, 1939–1947* (Hutchinson, 1948)

Wright, P., *Spycatcher* (Heinemann, 1987)

Young, K. (ed.)., *The Diaries of Sir Robert Bruce Lockhart* (Macmillan, 1973)

Ziegler, P., *Mountbatten* (Collins, 1985)